TIMOTHY BAINBRIDGE

The Penguin Companion to European Union

Third Edition

PENGUIN BOOKS

PENGUIN BOOKS

Published by the Penguin Group
Penguin Books Ltd, 80 Strand, London WC2R ORL, England
Penguin Putnam Inc., 375 Hudson Street, New York, New York 10014, USA
Penguin Books Australia Ltd, 250 Camberwell Road, Camberwell, Victoria 3124, Australia
Penguin Books Canada Ltd, 10 Alcorn Avenue, Toronto, Ontario, Canada M4V 3B2
Penguin Books India (P) Ltd, 11, Community Centre, Panchsheel Park, New Delhi – 110 017, India
Penguin Books (NZ) Ltd, Cnr Rosedale and Airborne Roads, Albany, Auckland, New Zealand
Penguin Books (South Africa) (Pty) Ltd, 24 Sturdee Avenue, Rosebank 2196, South Africa

Penguin Books Ltd, Registered Offices: 80 Strand, London WC2R ORL, England
www.penguin.com

First published 1995
Reprinted with corrections 1996
Reprinted with revisions 1997
Second edition 1998
Reprinted with revisions 2000
Third edition 2002
Reprinted with revisions 2003
4

First edition copyright © Timothy Bainbridge and Anthony Teasdale 1995, 1996, 1997
Second edition copyright © Timothy Bainbridge 1998, 2000
Third edition copyright © Timothy Bainbridge 2002, 2003
All rights reserved

The moral right of the author has been asserted

Typeset in 9/11 pt Minion
Typeset by Mac Style Ltd, Scarborough, N. Yorkshire
Edited and produced by Book Creation Services Ltd, London
Printed in England by Clays Ltd, St Ives plc

À Colombo ou à Nagasaki je lis les Baedekers
De l'Espagne et du Portugal ou de l'Autriche-Hongrie;
Et je contemple les plans de certaines villes de second rang,
Et leur description succincte, je la médite.
Les rues où j'ai habité sont marquées là,
Les hôtels où j'allais dîner, et les petits théâtres.

Ce sont des villes où ne vont jamais les touristes,
Et les choses n'y changent de place pas plus
Que les mots dans les pages d'un livre.

Valéry Larbaud, *Europe* (1913)

Contents

Preface

This book is a Companion rather than a dictionary in that it aims to present not only facts but arguments and analysis too. This is especially true of the longer entries dealing with matters of current controversy (in respect of which it could be said that the arguments are themselves political facts). In some of these entries I have also included a few sentences of speculation: the purpose of these is primarily to point the reader in the direction of what seem to me to be interesting lines of inquiry. To this limited extent the material in this book is projected forward into an uncertain future. I hope that in those entries in which facts, arguments and speculation are combined the distinction between the three elements is sufficiently clear for there to be no confusion between them.

As its title implies, the principal focus of this book is on the institutions, policies and procedures of the European Union. However, to a greater extent than is usually the case, full account has been taken of the large number of other European institutions, many of which predate the Union and overlap with the Union's activities to a confusing extent. Some readers may feel that the book merely mirrors the confusion, but I take the confusion to be part of the picture. There would be something essentially misleading about a book that reduced the European Union to a number of neatly interlocking institutions.

The fact remains that one of the characteristic features of Europe today is the extraordinarily large number of institutions, formal and informal, national, international and supranational, set up for many different purposes at different times on a variety of legal bases, operating in different fields to varying degrees of effectiveness. This *Companion* deals only with the main ones, and seeks to clarify the differences as well as the relations between them without suggesting an orderliness where in fact none exists (indeed, the trend is in the opposite direction). To take a simple example, a comprehensive picture of measures being taken internationally against the drug problem in Europe today would have to take account of the Pompidou Group (the responsibility of the Council of Europe), Interpol, Europol (an aspect of the

Justice and Home Affairs 'pillar' of the Maastricht Treaty, in this field the successor of the Trevi Group), the Schengen Group of countries, the European Parliament's committees of inquiry, the inclusion by the Commission of anti-drug clauses in draft agreements with certain countries, and the European Monitoring Centre for Drugs and Drug Addiction in Lisbon.

Evident in the book as a whole is a historical bias, founded upon the belief that an essential part of understanding the European Union is a knowledge of the course of post-war integration, its failures as well as its successes. The successes are fully dealt with, in the sense that all the steps in the direction of where the Union now finds itself are described. The failures – the wrong turnings along the way – are in some cases as revealing as the successes (for an example, see Fouchet Plan), but considerations of space did not allow them all to be described in detail.

Considerations of space have also made it impossible for entries on individual countries systematically to include basic information on size, population, GNP, form of government, and so on. Instead, these entries concentrate on each country's relations, current and historic, with what is now the European Union, special mention being made of high and low points in the relationship and of characteristic negotiating attitudes and policy priorities considered over time.

Included among the entries are biographies of people who have made notable contributions to European integration. Many of them, of course, had or still have distinguished careers in national politics, but in conformity with the underlying purpose of the book it is primarily their European activities that are described here. Overall, the choice of whom to include may seem somewhat idiosyncratic, but I have given preference to people (such as Aristide Briand and Altiero Spinelli) about whom material is not readily and generally available, at least in English.

With reference to particular areas of policy touched on in this book, my aim has been not so much to give an up-to-the-minute account (almost impossible in any case) of the state of affairs, but to provide the essential historical, political and legal underpinnings of progress to date and currently in prospect. In these entries the focus is almost exclusively upon the actions of the European Union and its institutions, since however valuable the work done by other bodies may be (for example, by the Council of Europe in respect of the protection of the environment), it is the power of the Union to make binding laws that matters in the end. One reason why I have quoted so extensively from the Treaty of Rome and other Treaties (see Note to the Reader) is that few aspects of the Union are so prone to misunderstanding, wilful or otherwise, as the scope and purpose of legislative and other action on the part of its institutions.

Of these institutions, the one described at the greatest length is the European Parliament. There are two reasons for this: it is the most complex of the institutions, and the one that has changed most over the past five decades in terms of its composition and its powers. Even its location is far from straightforward. It also happens to be the most controversial of the institutions.

Another category of entry deals with the technical expressions that constitute so important and characteristic a part of what is sometimes termed 'Eurospeak'. Many of the older expressions date back to the time when French was by far the dominant language in the Six, and, in any case, the institutions and procedures drew heavily on French politico-constitutional models. Some of them have remained French (*acquis communautaire*), some have been at least partially assimilated into English (rapporteur), and some – perhaps the most confusing – have acquired a spurious Englishness in translation in spite of few people being entirely sure of their meaning (comitology, subsidiarity). Irritating though such expressions may be, it must be said that many of them genuinely lack an English equivalent.

Students of language may be familiar with the theory known as the Sapir–Whorf hypothesis. Our apprehensions, so the theory runs, are shaped to a significant degree by the language available to us for the ordering and expression of those apprehensions. This seems to me to explain some of the underlying features of public debate (not solely in the United Kingdom) on European Union. It is not simply the associative power of words like 'sovereignty', 'federalism', 'union', 'intervention' and 'flexibility' which serves to shape attitudes but also the necessarily alien (and sometimes misleading) character of words and expressions it has proved necessary or convenient to invent. Such coinages include 'directive', 'co-decision' and 'variable geometry'. Opinion pollsters know that choice of words is vitally important in the phrasing of a question since it has a decisive bearing on the answer, but the fact that this is generally true of all political discourse needs to be more widely recognized. In making a point about 'long words and exhausted idioms', George Orwell wrote: 'If thought corrupts language, language can also corrupt thought' ('Politics and the English Language', 1946).

The wider problems posed by the multiplicity of official languages in the European Union are well known. Not the least of them is that a controversial idea may become still more controversial in translation, and in unforeseen ways. For example, what is normally referred to in English as the 'hard core' of countries was *feste Kern* in the German original. The word *fest* means 'solid, firm': to translate it as 'hard' introduces associations of exclusiveness and of an unsympathetic attitude to outsiders not present in the original, and it was these associations at least as much as the idea itself that occasioned resentment. In French it was translated as *noyau dur*, the primary meaning of *noyau* being the stone of a fruit, bringing with it associations of durability and germination.

To the outsider, the European Union may be thought to move with glacier-like slowness. This observation will very quickly be found to be false by any-one who seeks to write a book about it that is not already out of date on publication. More than ever, with enlargement to the East in prospect, the integration of Europe is, in the familiar phrase, 'a journey to an unknown des-tination'; and the journey is proceeding with what is on any historical scale quite astonishing speed. When the pace was more leisurely, in the 1960s and 1970s, questions about the ultimate destination were not posed with any great urgency, but now the pace has quickened, the passengers are being thrown about with greater violence, and the demands for clear answers have become more pressing.

It is often remarked that the European Union is *sui generis* in the sense that it fits neatly into no established constitutional model and, moreover, shows no sign of doing so in the future. In the Union's affairs there will continue to be a three-way tension between the supranational, the intergovernmental and the bureaucratic. Some readers will be familiar with the executive toy that consists of a metal ball freely suspended over a triangular base, at each angle of which a magnet is concealed. The ball is set in motion: it wobbles at random, under the influence of each magnet in turn, and finally settles in the magnetic field of one of them. The time taken depends on the vigour with which the initial impulse is given. Something of the same fascination may be felt in observing what hap-pens when a radical new idea is tossed into the Union's institutional system.

So much can be said with some certainty: the European Union will not move into major new areas of policy, with the probable exception of defence and security (the groundwork for which has already been partially laid in the Common Foreign and Security Policy 'pillar' of the Maastricht Treaty). In this sense the move towards a superstate governing every aspect of our lives has been halted. Underpinned by subsidiarity, there will continue to be an uneasy equilibrium between the powers of the Union's own institutions and those of national or regional authorities. Neither the Scandinavians, whose level of contentment with their own institutions is quite high, nor the eastern and central Europeans, who have only recently regained control over their own affairs, seem to me at all likely to be willing to countenance new powers for supranational institutions based in Brussels. At the same time there is a clear majority against the renationalization of areas currently covered by action under the Treaties: hence the equilibrium.

The apogee of legislative action seems to me to have passed. In opting for enlargement, the European Union and its predecessors have moved from a small, relatively homogeneous group of countries to a very much larger, more disparate group. The next wave of enlargement will confirm this trend. Against this background, it is unrealistic to imagine that legislation can play the role it has played so far as the cement of integration. Indeed, the difficulties of drawing up legislation for so disparate a group of countries (unless it is so permeated with opt-outs, derogations and special conditions as to be meaningless) are immense. The future coherence of the Union is likely to depend not on new legislative action but on the enforcement of legislation already in place, and, as things stand at present, enforcement is largely in the hands of member states. The threat of armed conflict has receded with the end of the Cold War, but other less tangible threats have taken its place: rapid economic growth in the Far East, Islamic fundamentalism and poverty on the southern shore of the Mediterranean, and the political uncertainty engendered in the former Soviet Union by the painful transition to a market economy. It remains to be seen whether or not these challenges can act as a motivating force in European integration, and whether or not the Union will show itself capable of rising to them.

Among the few things the Union has in common with other international or supranational bodies is great difficulty in attracting public interest. The debates conducted at Union level, however fascinating to insiders, tend to impinge upon the public consciousness only if they become mixed up with national politics and the mixture normally results in the arguments themselves becoming distorted or confused by virtue of having been articulated in a national context. One day the distinction between European politics and national politics may become clearer, but until then, the curiously hybrid nature of what currently passes for European political debate will continue to stand in the way of a clear understanding of the issues.

Although it is no part of my purpose to attack or defend the European Union in this book, a word about my own position might be useful to readers wanting to make allowances for possible bias. Professionally, I worked in one of the Union's institutions (the European Parliament) for 25 years. I can think of no more severe test of Euro-enthusiasm. However, I still regard European integration as without doubt one of the most worthwhile as well as one of the boldest experiments in the civilized conduct of human affairs ever undertaken, with many remarkable and permanent successes to its credit and with many valuable lessons to be learnt from its less frequent failures. The record deserves to be better known.

Timothy Bainbridge
May 2002

Acknowledgements

In writing this book I have made extensive and I hope accurate use of advice from many friends and colleagues in the European Parliament and elsewhere. In particular, I am grateful to Casilda Grigg for her help when the book was at the formative stage: her confident grasp of the material allied to an unfailing sense of style were invaluable. On the production side, I must express my thanks to Janet Berry, Alison Biesmans, Patricia Halligan, Elspeth Senior, Pat Walsh and Deborah Warren, all of whom devoted their time and technical skills with great good humour to what must have seemed a confusing and disjointed manuscript. At the crucial final stage the work of typing and retyping fell to Lindsay Kirkby: I am especially grateful to her for her patience and help.

Anthony Teasdale made a special contribution to the original edition of this book by providing a number of entries on areas where he has a particular interest or expertise. These included entries on various aspects of the Council of Ministers and on certain important episodes in the European Union's history, such as the Fouchet Plan, the Stuttgart Declaration, and the Werner and Delors reports. The book as a whole benefited greatly from his understanding of the political and economic forces which have shaped the Union.

Dr Paul Beaumont, one of the co-authors of *EU Law*, very kindly read the manuscript in its not-quite final stage. The book owes much to his vigilance, as it does to the copy-editing of Barbara Horn, Helen Williams and Julianne Mulholland.

For help with the second and third editions, I owe a special debt of gratitude to my wife Bettina, my son Alexander, Patricia Halligan, Alastair Graham, Avis Furness, and several correspondents, notably Alan F. Reekie. Antonella Collaro of Book Creation Services oversaw the production of the third edition with great skill and professionalism.

Note to the Third Edition

This fully revised third edition differs from the first (1995) and second (1998) editions in several important respects. I have added about sixty wholly new entries, made some cuts, extended the system of cross-referencing and the synoptic index, and modified some of the tables. Final revisions to the text and to the bibliography were made at the beginning of 2002.

In a book of this kind it is not easy to give the reader an overview of European Union. As it happens, I believe that models and analogies, historical or otherwise, are not of much use in seeking to understand the process of European integration, and that the energy and ingenuity which inform much academic writing about the Union are to a large extent misdirected. Models and analogies seem to me at least as likely to be misleading as to be helpful. Attempts to fit the integration process into a theoretical framework are interesting more for the questions they raise than for the insights they afford. My purpose here is simply to anatomize European Union, to explain something about why it is the way it is, and to describe how it came to be so. General conclusions I leave to the reader.

Timothy Bainbridge
May 2002

A second reprint of this third edition has made it possible to take account of developments since March 2002, notably of course the conclusion of accession negotiations between the European Union and ten of the thirteen applicant countries (see especially **Treaty of Accession**), to correct some figures, and to add a few titles to the Bibliography.

TB
May 2003

Note to the Reader

References to the Treaties

Throughout this *Companion*, references are made to the Treaties on which the European Union is founded. This has been done for two reasons: first, because there is no substitute for knowing what the Treaties actually say; and second, because the relevant Treaty references allow the reader to go into various issues at greater depth with the aid of other books or documents. The great majority of references are to the 1957 Treaty of Rome establishing the European Economic Community (EEC) or to the 1992 Maastricht Treaty, formally the Treaty on European Union (TEU). Specialists will be aware that many of the references to these Treaties could be supplemented by parallel references to other Treaties, such as the 1951 Treaty of Paris establishing the European Coal and Steel Community (ECSC), but in order to prevent the text from becoming overburdened these supplementary references have mostly been omitted.

In conformity with normal academic usage, the different Treaties are referred to by their initials. However, the Maastricht Treaty renamed the European Economic Community as the European Community, and the Treaty of Amsterdam recast and renumbered both the Treaty of Rome and the Maastricht Treaty. In this book, references to the Treaty of Rome before the Maastricht Treaty came into force (using of course the old Article numbers) refer to the Treaty as 'EEC': in all other cases the Treaty is denoted by the initials 'EC'. Elsewhere I have given the old Article numbers (or letters, in the case of the Maastricht Treaty before the Treaty of Amsterdam came into force) only when it has seemed to me useful or necessary for readers to know them. Reference is also made to the Treaty establishing the European Atomic Energy Community (EAEC), to the Single European Act (SEA) and to the 1997 Treaty of Amsterdam (TA, in force since May 1999). In the absence of any indication to the contrary, the year cited is the year in which the Treaty was signed, not the year of entry into force.

European Community or European Union?

Under the Maastricht Treaty 'the European Community' became the official name for the three original Communities, the ECSC, the EEC, and the EAEC (the first of these ceased to exist in July 2002). The European Community is now a component part of the European Union, and legally there remains a difference between the two. In certain contexts the difference is an important one, and wherever necessary the distinction is made clear in this *Companion*. However, for general purposes – and in conformity with the usage adopted by the media – 'the European Union' or 'the Union' is used to refer to what used to be known as the EEC, the European Community, or the Common Market. The only major exceptions to this rule are where reference is being made to the past (it would clearly be nonsensical, for example, to say that the United Kingdom joined the European Union in 1973), in quotations and in compound expressions such as Community law or Community preference.

The ECU and the euro

From 1981 until 1998 the ECU (European Currency Unit) was used in all areas of the Union's finances, including grants to member states under the structural funds, loans from the European Investment Bank, and of course the Budget itself. Conversions from ECUs into sterling or dollars may be made with the following table of average rates:

	£	$
1960s	0.396	1.055
1970s	0.564	1.214
1980s	0.631	1.023
1990	0.714	1.273
1995	0.829	1.308
1998	0.676	1.121

On 1 January 1999, the euro replaced the ECU on a 1:1 basis and fixed exchange rates applied between the euro and the currencies of the member states which were due to substitute the euro for their national currencies in 2002. National currencies in the euro-zone (all member states except Denmark, Sweden and the United Kingdom) have now been phased out. Rates between the euro and all other currencies are determined daily and published in the *Official Journal*, in the financial press, on Ceefax, and on several websites.

The Penguin Companion to European Union

A

Abatement

Under the **Fontainebleau Agreement** the United Kingdom is refunded part of its contribution to the **Budget** of the European Union. The sum, which is calculated annually, is technically known as the abatement, but more commonly as the British Budget rebate or refund (see **British Budget problem, contributions and receipts**).

Accession

The act of joining the European Union is known as 'accession' and the treaties that embody the conclusions of the negotiations between applicant states and the member states of the Union are known as 'Treaties of Accession' (see **enlargement**). Such treaties are complemented by 'Acts of Accession' in which the precise conditions of accession and the adjustments to the founding **Treaties** are specified. The procedures governing accession are set out in Article 49 of the **Maastricht Treaty**. New member states are normally allowed periods of adjustment (known as **transitional periods**) in sectors in which too rapid an adoption of Union rules might cause difficulty; for example, Spain and Portugal had to wait seven years (until 1 January 1993) before **free movement of persons** as provided for under Article 48 (now 39) of the **Treaty of Rome** came into effect.

ACP states

The ACP (African, Caribbean and Pacific) states are the countries originally associated with the member states of the European Union under the 1975 **Lomé Convention** and, since 2000, under the **Cotonou Agreement**. They are associated with each other under an Agreement signed in Georgetown, Guyana, on 6 June 1975. When the Convention was first signed there were 46 ACP states, but the number has since increased to 78 with the admission of Cuba in December 2000. Of the present total, about half are members of the

Commonwealth, and 39 are among the 48 least developed countries (identified by an asterisk in the list below) as officially recognized by the United Nations. The total population of the ACP states is about 650 million people. ACP states may benefit from **European Investment Bank** (EIB) lending as well as from the **European Development Fund**. For further details, see **development policy**. The ACP states are:

Angola*
Antigua and Barbuda
Bahamas
Barbados
Belize
Benin*
Botswana
Burkina Faso*
Burundi*
Cameroon
Cape Verde*
Central African
  Republic*
Chad*
Comoros*
Congo – Brazzaville
Congo – Kinshasa (Zaire)*
Cook Islands
Côte d'Ivoire
Cuba
Djibouti*
Dominica
Dominican Republic
Equatorial Guinea*
Eritrea*
Ethiopia*
Fiji

Gabon
Gambia*
Ghana
Grenada
Guinea*
Guinea Bissau*
Guyana
Haiti*
Jamaica
Kenya
Kiribati*
Lesotho*
Liberia*
Madagascar*
Malawi*
Mali*
Marshall Islands
Mauritania*
Mauritius
Micronesia
Mozambique*
Namibia
Nauru
Niger*
Nigeria
Niue
Palau

Papua New Guinea
Rwanda*
St Kitts and Nevis
St Lucia
St Vincent and the
  Grenadines
Samoa*
Sao Tomé and
  Principe*
Senegal
Seychelles
Sierra Leone*
Solomon Islands*
Somalia*
South Africa
Sudan*
Surinam
Swaziland
Tanzania*
Togo*
Tonga
Trinidad and Tobago
Tuvalu*
Uganda*
Vanuatu*
Zambia*
Zimbabwe

Acquis communautaire

The phrase *acquis communautaire*, sometimes translated as 'the Community patrimony', denotes the whole range of principles, policies, laws, practices, obligations and objectives that have been agreed or that have developed within the European Union. The *acquis communautaire* includes most notably the **Treaties** in their entirety, all legislation enacted to date, the judgments of the **Court of Justice**, and **joint actions** taken in the areas of the **Common Foreign and Security Policy** (CFSP) and **Justice and Home Affairs** (JHA; see also *finalités politiques*).

The significance of the *acquis* is most obvious when new member states join the Union (see **enlargement**). They are legally obliged to accept not only the Treaties, but all previous legal decisions taken by the various Union institutions, all agreements within and between those institutions about their operation, and all international agreements concluded by the Union. Moreover, new member states 'are in the same situation as the present Member States in respect of declarations or resolutions of, or other positions taken up by, the Council ... [or] adopted by common agreement of the Member States'. Accordingly, they are required to 'observe the principles and guidelines deriving from those declarations, resolutions or other positions' and to 'take such measures as may be necessary to ensure their implementation' (Article 4.3 of the Act of Accession relating to Austria, Finland and Sweden).

A good example of this process in practice was the acceptance on accession of the objective of **Economic and Monetary Union** (EMU) by Greece, Spain and Portugal even though they had played no part in shaping that objective, and even though at the time it was embodied only in **Declarations** of the **European Council** rather than in specific Treaty Articles or other legally binding texts.

Although the principle of the *acquis communautaire* is recognized in successive Acts of Accession, it is not referred to explicitly by name, nor does it appear in the Treaties establishing the **European Communities**, the **Merger Treaty** or the **Single European Act** (SEA). However, under the **Maastricht Treaty**, one of the objectives of the European Union is 'to maintain in full the *acquis communautaire* and build on it' in a fashion consistent with 'ensuring the effectiveness of the mechanisms and the institutions of the Community' (Article 2).

The fact that the *acquis communautaire* includes judgments of the Court of Justice is of cardinal importance, since it entails recognition by the member states of the **primacy** of EU law and the principle of **direct effect**. See also **Schengen** *acquis*.

Action Committee for the United States of Europe (ACUSE)

ACUSE was founded by **Jean Monnet** in October 1955, following his resignation as President of the High Authority of the **European Coal and Steel Community** (ECSC) the previous year. Its purpose was to act as a pressure group for closer European integration by bringing together leading personalities of all parties from **the Six**, plus, in later years, the United Kingdom. It played an important part in building momentum towards the **European Economic Community** (EEC) in the mid-1950s, and during the 1960s it acted as an international focus for political opposition to the anti-federalist European policies of President **Charles de Gaulle** of France. ACUSE was dissolved by Monnet himself in 1975. Ten years later a successor body, the Action Committee for Europe, was formed with a similar purpose, but it was far less prominent than Monnet's organization, mainly because it lacked a dominant personality of driving European ambition as its head.

In a famous phrase ACUSE was described by Jean-Jacques Servan-Schreiber as a 'kind of federal authority of the mind'. ACUSE's statements and declarations over its period of greatest influence (1955–67) were published by the Royal Institute of International Affairs (Chatham House) in no. 9 of the European series of booklets, March 1969. An account of ACUSE by Pascal Fontaine may be found in the proceedings of the symposium organized by the Commission to mark the centenary of Monnet's birth (10 November 1988).

Additionality

'Additionality' is a jargon word denoting the principle whereby sums received from the **Budget** of the Union in support of particular projects (most commonly from the **structural funds**) are supposed to be additional to those received from national sources. The great temptation – and few member states have been able always to resist it – is to allow receipts from Brussels to take the place of national aid. A special report by the **Court of Auditors** (*Official Journal*, C68, 9 March 2000) is by far the most detailed study of this problem.

Adenauer, Konrad (1876–1967)

Chancellor of the Federal Republic of Germany from 1949 to 1963, Konrad Adenauer was a key figure in the postwar reconstruction of West Germany and in its reintegration into western Europe and the Atlantic Alliance.

Adenauer entered politics at an early age and by 1917 had been elected Mayor of Cologne. Dismissed by the Nazis in 1933, he went into retirement, but in 1945 re-emerged as Mayor and as a co-founder of the Christian Democratic Union (CDU) in the Rhineland. In October 1945 he was dismissed from the office of mayor by the British Military Governor of the North Rhine province, who accused him of having 'failed in his duty to the people of Cologne', placed restrictions on his movements, and banned him from all political activity. In spite of this the following year he became Chairman of the CDU in the British zone of occupation, and played a central role in the negotiations with the Allies on the Constitution of the new Federal Republic. In

1949, at the age of 73, he was elected to the Bundestag and on 15 September 1949 he was elected (by a one vote margin) as Federal Chancellor.

Adenauer's chancellorship spanned the admission of West Germany into the **Council of Europe** (1950) and the **North Atlantic Treaty Organization** (NATO) (1955). Acting as his own foreign minister from 1951 until 1955, Adenauer ensured West Germany's position as a founder member of the three **European Communities** and resolved the dispute with France over the **Saarland**. At a meeting in Moscow in 1955 he secured the agreement of the Soviet government for the return of German prisoners-of-war still held in the USSR. In 1963 a Franco-German friendship treaty was signed (see **Franco-German cooperation**), an initiative to which Adenauer attached great importance.

In the 1961 Bundestag elections the Christian Democrats lost their overall majority. The coalition with the Free Democrats (Liberals) proved difficult, and in October 1963 Adenauer announced his retirement as Chancellor. He remained a member of the Bundestag and until 1966 continued as chairman of the CDU.

Adenauer took a close and active interest in European unification. In two interviews in an American newspaper in March 1950 he suggested a complete union between France and Germany, but in spite of support from **Charles de Gaulle** this plan came to nothing. In his *Memoirs 1945–1953* (English edn, 1966) he wrote of the **Schuman Plan** of May 1950: 'I was in full agreement with the French Government that the significance of the Schuman proposal was first and foremost political and not economic. This Plan was to be the beginning of a federal structure of Europe.'

By virtue of his dignity, experience, authority and integrity, Adenauer was the ideal embodiment of the 'new Germany' that emerged from the ruins of 1945. Although an enthusiastic supporter of European integration, he was at the same time anxious to establish good relations with the United States. He was on friendly terms both with de Gaulle and with the British. Stephen Spender met him in 1945 when he was again Mayor of Cologne: 'He has an energetic, though somewhat insignificant appearance: a long lean oval face, almost no hair, small blue active eyes, a little button nose and a reddish complexion. He looks remarkably young and he has the quietly confident manner of a successful and attentive young man' (*European Witness*, 1946). He was an extremely astute and determined politician with a European and international reputation that few of his successors as Chancellor have matched.

Advocate-General

The **Court of Justice** of the European Union is composed of 15 judges and 9 advocates-general. The role of the advocate-general, which has no equivalent in English law, is to present, on the basis of the facts and arguments submitted by all the parties, a 'reasoned submission' in open court. This submission, known as the **Opinion**, seeks to identify the points of law at issue, to remind the Court of precedents with a bearing on the case, and to recommend what judgment the Court should reach. The judges then retire to deliberate in camera without the advocate-general being present. The Court usually, but not always, follows the advocate-general's recommendation, which has no legal force but is printed together with the final judgment in *European Court Reports*.

African, Caribbean and Pacific states

See **ACP states**.

Agency

An agency of the European Union is a public authority set up under European law, separate from the Union's institutions and with its own legal personality. There are currently 12 such agencies, the earliest dating from the 1970s. Most have an advisory role of a technical or scientific nature, whilst others administer particular policies. In the interests of decentralization, nearly all the agencies are located away from the Union's main centres of activity. The White Paper on **European governance** published by the **European Commission** in July 2001 envisages more use being made of agencies. A complete list of agencies may be found on the Europa website: most are described individually in this book.

Agenda 2000

Agenda 2000 was the title of a 1,300-page study presented by **Jacques Santer**, then President of the **European Commission**, to the **European Parliament** on 16 July 1997 (*Bulletin of the European Union*, supplement 5/97). Described as a 'detailed strategy for strengthening and widening the Union in the early years of the 21st century', *Agenda 2000* embodied the Commission's assessment of the ten applicant states from central and eastern Europe (see **enlargement**), of the need for further **qualified majority voting** (QMV), of the importance of developing new policies for growth, **employment** and international **competitiveness**, and of reforms to the **structural funds** and the **Common Agricultural Policy** (CAP). The study also proposed in outline a new financial framework (see **future financing**) to cover the years 2000 to 2006. *Agenda 2000* was agreed at a meeting of the **European Council** in Berlin on 24–5 March 1999, although the QMV issue was not settled until the adoption of the **Treaty of Nice** in December 2000.

Airbus

Airbus began in 1965 as an Anglo-French proposal. The West German government expressed a strong interest and a Memorandum of Understanding was signed by the three governments in 1967. Two years later, the British government withdrew, although Hawker-Siddeley (later British Aerospace) remained a partner in its own right. The first Airbus flew in 1972. Six years later, the British government bought its way back into the consortium.

Airbus has about half the market for aircraft seating more than 100 passengers and worldwide its products are flown by 189 operators. The consortium was restructured in 2001 and is now a simplified joint stock company registered under French law. EADS (European Aeronautic Defence and Space Company, composed of Aérospatiale-Matra of France, Daimler Chrysler Aerospace of Germany, and CASA of Spain) owns 80 per cent of the stock, British Aerospace (BAe) the other 20 per cent. The main assembly plant is in Toulouse. Since 2000, the Airbus consortium has been developing the Airbus A380, a superjumbo capable of carrying 555 passengers with a range of 14,800 kilometres.

The Airbus project has given rise to difficulties with the American aircraft industry, especially Boeing, which suspects European governments of subsidizing Airbus in a fashion inconsistent with the rules laid down by the **World Trade Organization** (WTO). The counter to this charge is that Boeing and the rest of the American aircraft industry benefit from enormous *de facto* subsidies by virtue of their close involvement in defence-related research and procurement.

Albania

With the support of Austria–Hungary and against the opposition of Serbia, Albania secured its independence from the Ottoman Empire in 1913. In 1928 it became a monarchy under King Zog. Annexed by Italy in April 1939 Albania fell under Communist rule immediately after the Second World War. Enver Hoxha was in power (first as Prime Minister, later as the leader of the Party of Labour) from 1944 until his death in 1985. The break with Yugoslavia came in 1948, and was followed by a period of closer relations with the USSR and (from 1961 until 1977) with China. During this time Albania became the poorest country in Europe, its isolation underlined by the fact of its being the only European state not to take part in the **Conference on Security and Cooperation in Europe** (CSCE). Albania ceased to be a one-party state in December 1990 and the first free elections were held in March 1991. Albania was admitted to the **Council of Europe** in 1995.

Many Albanians live outside Albania, notably in the Yugoslav province of Kosovo and in Macedonia. Substantial Albanian minorities may be found throughout the Balkans, especially in Montenegro, Croatia, and Greece (which has a long-standing territorial claim to southern Albania, known to the Greeks as Northern Epirus). Their recent history is largely one of oppression abroad – their non-Slav, Muslim identity makes them an obvious target for Serb nationalism – and poverty and corruption at home.

A trade and cooperation agreement between the European Union and Albania was signed in 1992. Since 2000 Albanian products have been allowed duty-free access to the European Union market. In June 2000 the **European Council** meeting in Göteborg authorised the opening of negotiations for a broader agreement with Albania under the **Stabilization and Association Process**. Three months later Albania became a member of the **World Trade Organization** (WTO). The Union gave aid worth more than €1 billion to Albania over the period 1991–2000, much of it under the **PHARE** programme.

Allied Command Europe

Allied Command Europe, one of the key components in the **North Atlantic Treaty Organization** (NATO), covers an area from the north of Norway to Gibraltar and from the Atlantic seaboard to the eastern frontier of Turkey, including the whole of the Mediterranean. Within this area of some 6 million square kilometres live some 400 million people. **Supreme Headquarters Allied Powers Europe** (SHAPE) are at Cateau, near Mons, in Belgium. Allied Command Europe is divided into Allied Forces North (Afnorth, based at Brunssum in The Netherlands), and Allied Forces South (Afsouth), based in Naples.

Allied Command Europe Rapid Reaction Corps (ARRC)

The ARRC was one of many ideas put forward as part of the overall review of the role and structure of the **North Atlantic Treaty Organization** (NATO). With the virtual disappearance of the threat of massive armed attack against any of the NATO states, the Alliance's New Strategic Concept (agreed at the November 1991 NATO summit in Rome) laid emphasis on the need for smaller forces with 'enhanced flexibility, and mobility', among them, in a 'limited but militarily significant proportion, ground, air and sea immediate and rapid reaction elements able to respond to a wide range of eventualities' (point 47). Operational since May 1995, the ARRC includes forces from 14 countries. Its headquarters are in Rheinfelden, Germany. See also **Eurocorps**, **EUROFOR**, **Western European Union**.

Annual work programme (AWP)

The AWP of the **European Commission** is published as a Communication at the end of the year preceding that to which it applies. It is addressed to the

Council of Ministers, the **European Parliament**, the **Committee of the Regions**, and the **Economic and Social Committee**. It assesses progress in the past year, sets out the political and economic context for Commission activity, identifies the current priorities, and lists the legislative and other measures due to be brought forward in the course of the year. The AWP is normally adopted in February of the year to which it applies and is sometimes referred to as the annual policy strategy. The procedure is based on the March 2000 White Paper *Reforming the European Commission* and is designed to improve **transparency**. See also **European governance**.

Antici Group

The Antici Group, composed of the assistants to each of the member states' permanent representatives to the European Union (see **national representations**), is an important body in Brussels decision-making since it prepares the meetings of **COREPER**. It is named after an Italian civil servant, Paolo Massimo Antici, on whose initiative the group was set up in 1975.

Anti-dumping

Dumping, as defined by the **World Trade Organization** (WTO) Agreement, is the placing of goods on an export market at a price that does not reflect the cost of production in the country of origin. A charge of dumping must show evidence of material injury to the domestic industry in the country of importation. Under the European Union's **Common Commercial Policy** (CCP), the **European Commission**, rather than individual member states, is responsible for investigating allegations of dumping and for imposing duties on goods shown to have been dumped (confirmed by the **Council of Ministers** in the form of a Regulation). Anti-dumping decisions may be appealed against in the **Court of Justice** or the **Court of First Instance**. Overzealous use of the Commission's powers in this field may lead to accusations of a **Fortress Europe**.

Approximation

This is the word used in **Articles 94 and 95** of the **Treaty of Rome** to denote what is more commonly known as **harmonization**.

Area of freedom, security and justice

An expression found in Articles 2 and 29 of the Treaty on European Union (the **Maastricht Treaty**) as amended by the **Treaty of Amsterdam**, 'an area of freedom, security and justice' is the principal, all-embracing object of co-operation in the fields of **Justice and Home Affairs** (JHA) between the member states of the European Union. Its origin may be traced back to the 1977 proposal for an *espace judiciaire européen*. The component elements of an area of freedom, security and justice were set out in an Action Plan by the **Council of Ministers** and the **European Commission** on 3 December 1998 (the 'Vienna Action Plan', *Official Journal*, C19, 23 January 1999) and endorsed by the **European Council** at their meeting in Vienna a week later. In October 1999 the European Council held a special meeting in Tampere to discuss how an area of freedom, security and justice could be established.

'Freedom' encompasses **free movement of persons**, human rights (see **Charter of Fundamental Rights**), measures taken against **discrimination** (see also **racism and xenophobia**), and questions with a bearing on **asylum** and immigration. 'Security' covers measures taken against **organized crime** and terrorism (see also **extradition**), **fraud**, and drug-trafficking (see **drugs**). 'Justice' is concerned with equal access to justice, judicial cooperation, the cross-border enforcement of judgments in civil matters, the definition of particular categories of offence and the sentences such offences carry, and **mutual assistance in criminal matters**. A detailed 'scoreboard' covering all these measures was published as a Commission Communication on 24 March 2000: it is brought up to date every six months and may be found on the Europa website.

Arms exports

Although Article 296 of the **Treaty of Rome** largely exempts the **defence industry** in the member states of the European Union from normal **Single Market** rules, it has at various times been suggested that the Union should control member states' arms exports as part of its **Common Foreign and Security Policy** (CFSP). This could only be done on the basis of a code of conduct, limited perhaps in the first instance to a broad definition of 'arms' and a list of regimes (or types of regime) to which arms would not be supplied. Such a code would draw on the experience gained from the Coordinating Committee on Export Controls (COCOM) operating within the **North Atlantic Treaty Organization** (NATO) which from 1949 until 1994 controlled the supply to Communist countries of strategically important goods on the basis of the 'COCOM list'. A code of conduct for arms exports was agreed in June 1998; the aim is to discourage the sale of goods used for 'external aggression or internal repression', initially by means of a fuller exchange of information. In October 1999 it was agreed to strengthen the code by improving the exchange of information between member states and by establishing a common list of equipment covered by the code. See also **European Armaments Agency**.

Articles 94 and 95

These two Articles of the **Treaty of Rome** (formerly Articles 100 and 100a) provide the legal basis for what is commonly known as **harmonization**, i.e., the elimination, by means of the creation of common standards, of barriers to trade that spring from member states' different requirements in respect of health, safety, technical specifications, consumer protection, and product standards generally. The two Articles are accordingly of fundamental importance in the creation of the **Single Market**.

Until the **Single European Act** (SEA) in 1986 progress towards the Single Market had been slow because Article 100 required the **Council of Ministers** to act by **unanimity**. Although Article 100 remained in force, its place as the legal basis for most Single Market measures was taken by Article 100a, which was added to the Treaty by Article 18 of the SEA.

Referring back to Article 14 EC, which underlines the importance of and defined the Single Market, Article 95 allows the Council to act by **qualified majority voting** (QMV) on most Single Market measures. Key exceptions, listed in Article 95.2, are 'fiscal provisions ... the free movement of persons, ... [and] the rights and interests of employed persons', which continue to be dealt with under Article 94.

Under Articles 94 and 95, consultation with the **European Parliament** and the **Economic and Social Committee** is mandatory. In the case of draft legislation brought forward under Article 95, the Parliament plays an influential role under the **co-decision procedure**.

Article 133 Committee

The Article 133 Committee is a committee of national officials meeting regularly in Brussels to prepare the decisions of the **Council of Ministers** in the field of external trade policy. The existence of the Committee is specifically sanctioned by Article 133.3 of the **Treaty of Rome**. This obliges the **European Commission** to secure a negotiating mandate from the Council before opening negotiations with third countries and organizations and to consult the Council continuously during the negotiating process. The Article 133 Committee acts on the Council's behalf and meets at the level of national trade directors or their deputies. Some tasks are delegated to working groups (dealing with such matters as textiles, dumping and steel) or to negotiating groups that convene in international fora, such as the **World Trade Organization** (WTO). The **Maastricht Treaty** extended the Article 133 model to all other international economic agreements with third countries, creating a similar committee or committees for negotiations conducted under Article 300. Notwithstanding the Commission's exclusive right to negotiate on behalf of member states, an **Opinion** of the **Court of Justice** (Opinion 1/94) has reserved to the member states' particular rights with respect to questions of intellectual property, investment and certain services.

Article 308

All three of the founding **Treaties** of the **European Communities** provide a legal basis for action to be taken in furtherance of objectives not covered by specific Treaty Articles. In the **Treaty of Rome** such a basis is to be found in Article 308 (formerly Article 235), which reads:

If action by the Community should prove necessary to attain, in the course of the operation of the common market, one of the objectives of the Community and this Treaty has not provided the necessary powers, the Council shall, acting unanimously on a proposal from the Commission and after consulting the European Parliament, take the appropriate measures.

In a 1971 judgment the **Court of Justice** took a broad view of what 'in the course of the operation of the common market' means, so allowing the **European Commission** to use Article 235 EEC as the basis for its right to negotiate the European Road Transport Agreement (the **ERTA case**, Case 22/70). This was a fundamental decision in defining the Commission's role in external relations.

In general the Commission has been careful not to overuse this Article, but has not always succeeded in avoiding a challenge in the Court. In 1989 the Court ruled in favour of the United Kingdom, which had challenged the enactment on the basis of Article 235 of a vocational training programme for young people (Case 56/88). In spite of occasional controversy, Article 235/308 has proved its usefulness: for example, it is the legal basis for **Cooperation Agreements**, since these are not provided for in the Treaties.

Arusha Convention

The Arusha Convention was a trade and aid agreement between **the Six** and the East African countries of Kenya, Tanzania and Uganda, signed in Arusha, Tanzania, in 1969. It entered into force in January 1971, but was soon superseded by the **Lomé Convention** of 1975.

Asia

In 1980 a **Cooperation Agreement** came into force between the European Community and the Association of South East Asian Nations (ASEAN: Indonesia, Malaysia, the Philippines, Singapore and Thailand). It was later extended as more countries (Brunei, Vietnam, Laos and Cambodia) joined ASEAN, but because of the country's poor human rights record, it has not been extended to Myanmar (Burma), an ASEAN member since 1997. The Agreement is overseen by a Cooperation Committee supplemented by regular meetings of ministers. The European Union also has regular contacts with the less active SAARC (South Asian Association for Regional

Cooperation: Bangladesh, Bhutan, India, the Maldives, Nepal, Pakistan, and Sri Lanka).

Relations with Asia were broadened and intensified in March 1996 as a result of the first Asia–Europe Meeting (ASEM I) in Bangkok. ASEM II, involving the member states of the Union and of ASEAN, China, Japan, and South Korea, was held in London in April 1998. The meeting discussed the promotion of trade and investment, cultural and environmental issues, closer cooperation against drug-trafficking and other forms of international crime, and trade liberalization within the **World Trade Organization** (WTO). A 'Vision Group' was set up to oversee Europe–Asia relations and to prepare for ASEM III in Seoul in 2000, at which the Seoul Declaration on Korea was adopted. ASEM IV was held in Copenhagen in 2002. An Asia–Europe Foundation (ASEF) in Singapore, established in 1997, is responsible for strengthening intellectual and cultural contacts between the two regions.

Assent procedure

The assent procedure was a mechanism introduced by the **Single European Act** (SEA) to give the **European Parliament** the right of **veto** over certain important decisions taken by the **Council of Ministers**. The procedure required the Parliament to give its assent by an absolute majority of its total membership in favour of the act in question before it could be adopted by the Council, and applied to two areas: the conclusion of **Association Agreements** with third states and the **accession** of new member states to the Community. The **Maastricht Treaty** recast both provisions: membership of the Union is subject to approval by an absolute majority of the members of the Parliament (Article 49 TEU), but only an absolute majority of the votes cast is needed for Association Agreements (see Rules 89 and 90 of the Parliament's Rules of Procedure). Under Article 300 of the **Treaty of Rome**, the Parliament's assent must now be given to almost all international agreements, including especially those with budgetary consequences. The assent procedure has also been extended to certain legislative matters, of which the most important are **free movement of persons** and **uniform electoral procedure** (see Weatherill and Beaumont, *EU Law*, 3rd edn, Harmondsworth, 1999).

Assizes

In November 1990, just as the **Intergovernmental Conferences** (IGCs) that led a year later to the **Maastricht Treaty** were getting under way, an all-party conference of about 250 members of the 12 **national parliaments** in the European Community and of the **European Parliament** (MEPs) was held in Rome to discuss **European Union**. This meeting, known as the *assises* (sittings) in French, became known as the 'assizes' in English. The proportion of

MEPs was fixed at one-third of the whole, and the conference was conducted largely on the basis of European Parliament procedures (although there was some argument over whether participants should sit in national delegations, as national parliamentarians preferred, or in **political groups**). A final resolution was adopted that broadly reflected the more 'European' views of the MEPs, as a result of which many national parliamentarians felt that they had been outmanoeuvred; the suggestion that such assizes should be held regularly or even turned into a new Community body (the 'Congress') was rejected.

A 'Declaration on the Conference of the Parliaments' (as the assizes are sometimes known) was appended to the Maastricht Treaty. This simply invites the national parliaments and the European Parliament 'to meet as necessary', and commits the governments to consult such a conference 'on the main features of the European Union'. This **Declaration** was preceded by a general 'Declaration on the role of national parliaments in the European Union', which speaks of the importance of encouraging 'greater involvement' of national parliaments, in the context of which the assizes experiment should be viewed.

In spite of some enthusiasm for the idea within the British **presidency** of the **Council of Ministers** (July–December 1992), no assizes have been held since November 1990. Assizes are not mentioned in the protocol on the role of national parliaments annexed to the **Treaty of Amsterdam**. See also **COSAC**.

Association Agreement

Association Agreements are provided for in the **Treaty of Rome**: 'The Community may conclude with one or more States or international organizations agreements establishing an association involving reciprocal rights and obligations, common action and special procedures' (Article 310). Agreements drawn up under this Article, negotiated by the **European Commission** on a mandate from the **Council of Ministers**, require the assent of the **European Parliament** (see **assent procedure**) and unanimity in the Council.

The Treaty description of Association Agreements is very loose, and such agreements are now conventionally subdivided into four distinct types:

1 **Europe Agreements** (now sometimes known as Pre-Accession Partnership Agreements: see **pre-accession strategy**), with the states of central and eastern Europe: these make explicit provision for eventual full membership of the European Union, but do not guarantee it;

2 Agreements concluded with the countries of the Western Balkans under the **Stabilization and Association Process**;

3 Development Association Agreements, such as those with the **Maghreb** and **Mashreq** states and other Mediterranean countries (see **Mediterranean policy**); the **Cotonou Agreement** is also of this type;

4 The **European Economic Area** (EEA) Agreement with the states of the **European Free Trade Association** (EFTA). Like the Europe Agreements, the EEA Agreement is designed to facilitate full membership of the Union for those states that wish to join.

Although the expression 'Europe Agreement' was not in use at the time it was concluded, the Association Agreement with Turkey (1963) is an agreement of this type, since explicit reference is made to full membership.

It should be noted that association is with the European Community, not with the European Union (see **legal personality**). This means, for example, that associated states are not automatically involved either in the **Common Foreign and Security Policy** (CFSP) or in the cooperation in matters of **Justice and Home Affairs** (JHA), which are activities of the European Union under the **Maastricht Treaty** (see also **structured dialogue**). See David Phinnemore, *Association: Stepping-stone or Alternative to EU Membership?* (Sheffield, 1999).

Association for the Monetary Union of Europe (AMUE)

The AMUE was founded in 1987 as a business pressure group for the adoption of a single currency in Europe. It is supported by a number of leading European multinationals – including Philips, BP Amoco, Volkswagen, Fiat, Alcatel and Solvay – as well as most major European banks. AMUE organizes regular conferences on monetary integration, publishes pamphlets and studies, and adopts policy positions on **Economic and Monetary Union** (EMU). It has national chapters and a small central secretariat based in Paris. Membership is 'open to any business ... provided it shares [AMUE's] vision of Europe as a single currency zone'.

Asylum

The 1948 Universal Declaration of Human Rights states (Article 14) that 'everyone has the right to seek and to enjoy in other countries asylum from persecution'. The definition of a refugee, as set out in the 1951 Geneva Convention (Article 1A), is a person who 'owing to well-founded fear of being persecuted for reasons of race, religion, nationality, membership of a particular social group or political opinion is outside the country of his origin ...'. The Convention was strengthened and brought up to date in a 1967 Protocol on the Status of Refugees. All European Union member states are parties to the Convention and to the Protocol.

Article 33 of the Convention prohibits *refoulement*, the returning of a refugee against his will to a country where 'his life or freedom would be threatened'. This prohibition applies regardless of whether the refugee has yet formally been granted refugee status or asylum. *Refoulement* is also prohibited under Article 3.1 of the United Nations Convention against Torture 'where there are substantial grounds for believing that [the refugee] would be in danger of being subjected to torture'.

The European Union is committed under Article 3.1(c) of the **Treaty of Rome** to affording **free movement of persons** within its territory (i.e. not only for citizens of the Union: see **citizenship**). From this commitment arose the need, in the context of the completion of the **Single Market**, to establish common procedures with respect to the Union's external frontiers. In 1985 some member states signed the **Schengen Agreement**, but the first Union-wide measure specifically to address the problem of asylum was the **Dublin Asylum Convention** of 1990. However, this did not enter into force until 1997, by which time it had been supplemented by various agreements reached at **Council of Ministers** level on particular aspects of asylum policy and the application of the Dublin Convention (see **Eurodac**). The need for such agreements was rendered more urgent by the fact that throughout the 1990s the Union's frontiers, because of economic upheaval in eastern and central Europe, conflict in the Balkans and Afghanistan, and instability in North Africa were under great pressure from would-be immigrants.

The law of asylum is founded upon a number of key concepts, definitions, and distinctions. The way these are applied accounts for most of the variations between member states' asylum policies and procedures. For example, some states do not accept that persecution can emanate from non-state authorities. Others distinguish between persecution in cases where the state is unable or unwilling to afford protection against non-state authorities and persecution in cases where the apparatus of the state has effectively broken down. The great majority of member states – but not all – make use of the 'safe country of origin' concept, under which certain countries are regarded as *prima facie* safe and allegations of persecution in that country as manifestly unfounded. The Dublin Convention allows a refugee's application for asylum to be referred, in the absence of other factors such as family members already legally resident in the country of application, to whichever member state can be shown to be the applicant's point of entry into the European Union. This apparently simple principle is not always easy to apply: refugees may have no idea of the route they took, or may claim to have forgotten, and seldom travel with full documentation. On 23 July 1999 the United Kingdom Court of Appeal decided that a refugee could not be returned to France or Germany under the Convention since in neither country was recognition given to the type of persecution of which the refugee complained, i.e. persecution by a non-state authority. The Dublin Convention also allows, in conformity with normal international practice, a refugee to be returned to any 'safe' country he or she may have passed through en route to the European Union. This principle may also be difficult to apply, for the same reasons: and member states take different views of what constitutes a passage through a safe country. Other variations in member states' asylum policies exist with respect to visas and appeal procedures.

The European Union itself cannot grant or withhold asylum. Applications for asylum must be addressed to the authorities of a particular member state, and it is for that state to decide whether or not grounds exist for asylum to be granted. At their meeting in Tampere in October 1999 the **European Council** agreed that the long-term aim was to establish common procedures for dealing with requests for asylum and eventually to define a uniform status for those given asylum which would be valid throughout the European Union.

A **European Parliament** working paper *Asylum in the EU Member States* (2000) is a useful survey of this rapidly developing area of the law. Guy Goodwin-Gill, *The Refugee in International Law* (2nd edn, Oxford, 1996) puts European Union policy in a wider context. The latest developments may be followed with the aid of the *International Journal of Refugee Law*. Both the United Nations and the **Council of Europe** publish a great deal of material on refugees and asylum. Many of the basic documents may be found in *Human Rights – A Compilation of International Instruments* (Vol. 1, parts 1 and 2, United Nations, New York and Geneva, 1994).

Austria

Like Germany, Austria was occupied by the Allies after the Second World War. The last Soviet troops left Austria in 1955, and the country's present republican constitution dates from that year. A condition of Soviet withdrawal was a constitutional commitment to **neutrality**. For this and for other reasons, Austria has never been a full member of the **North Atlantic Treaty Organization** (NATO). However, Austria did participate in the **Marshall Plan**, was a founder member of the **Organization for European Economic Cooperation** (OEEC) and in 1956 joined the **Council of Europe**. In 1960 Austria became a founder member of the **European Free Trade Association** (EFTA).

Unlike certain other EFTA states, Austria was from the very beginning attracted by the idea of close ties with the European Community. Negotiations (1965–7) for an **Association Agreement** with the Community under Article 238 (now 310) of the **Treaty of Rome** were unsuccessful, but by 1973 Austria, in common with the other EFTA states, had a free trade agreement with the Nine (see **the Six**). By 1977, under the terms of this agreement, most industrial goods were subject to free trade arrangements, and by 1984 these had been extended to all industrial goods. However, the Community's decision the following year to complete the **Single Market** led

Austria, once again, to review the question of accession to the Community. By the end of the 1980s the reduction in East–West tension made it possible for neutral Austria to make explicit its commitment to the West, and on 17 July 1989 a formal application to join the three **European Communities** was submitted.

The application laid emphasis on Austria's commitment to neutrality, and this was dealt with at length in the generally favourable **Opinion** drawn up by the **European Commission** and delivered in August 1991 (*Bulletin of the European Communities*, supplement 4/92). As the Opinion noted, not only did Austria already have free trade with the Twelve, it was already (along with other parties to the **European Economic Area** Agreement) bound to apply most of the Single Market legislation that is a substantial part of the *acquis communautaire*. The problem of neutrality arose primarily because of the **Common Foreign and Security Policy** (CFSP) provisions of the **Maastricht Treaty**. It would clearly be unacceptable if a member state were constitutionally prevented from participating in or carrying out a decision, say, to apply economic sanctions against a third country or to undertake some other action in the foreign policy field agreed by the Union partners. The Commission noted that although Article 299 (formerly Article 224) EC allows member states a **derogation** from Treaty rules in the event of war or where they conflict with 'obligations ... accepted for the purpose of maintaining peace and international security', the application of the latter condition is confined to action agreed by the Security Council of the United Nations.

Negotiations with Austria presented few difficulties and were concluded in March 1994. Austrian accession was approved by the **European Parliament** in May 1994 and by popular referendum on 12 June 1994 (the turnout was 81.3 per cent; 66.4 per cent in favour). Austria became the thirteenth member of the European Union on 1 January 1995. European elections were first held in Austria on 13 October 1996.

In January 2000 a coalition government was in the process of being formed to include, for the first time, the Freedom Party of Austria (FPÖ), then led by the governor of Carinthia, Jörg Haider. The allegedly 'racist' character of the FPÖ, Austria's third largest party in terms of electoral support, led Belgium in a note to the Portuguese **presidency** to demand concerted action by the other member states against Austria. On 31 January 2000 the presidency issued a 'Declaration on behalf of XIV Member States' announcing that diplomatic sanctions would be introduced were a government to be formed in Austria including the FPÖ. A government in which a number of posts (including that of Vice-Chancellor) were held by the FPÖ was formed on 4 February 2000.

The sanctions specified a breaking off of bilateral contacts with the

Austrian government, a withholding of support for Austrian candidates for posts in international organizations, and a downgrading of contacts with Austrian ambassadors to a 'technical level'. Norway and the Czech Republic associated themselves with the sanctions together with several non-European states.

The Austrian government contended that the presidency had no right to issue such a non-unanimous declaration, that the sanctions were contrary to the spirit of solidarity underpinning relations between member states under Articles 2 and 11.2 EC, and that the Austrian government should have been given an opportunity to set out its position. On 14 February 2000 the **General Affairs Council** refused to discuss the matter. In Austria the opposition parties refused to condemn the sanctions, which were proving deeply unpopular with the Austrian people.

On 29 June 2000 the Portuguese government called on the President of the Court of Human Rights (see **human rights**) to nominate three people to report on Austria's observance of human rights (especially with regard to minorities, refugees, and immigrants) and on 'the political nature' of the FPÖ.

On 8 September 2000 the report of the so-called 'Three Wise Men' was delivered to Jacques Chirac as President-in-office of the **European Council**. It recommended lifting the sanctions: this was done four days later. The report also recommended changes to Article 7 TEU under which a member state may face **suspension**, and some of these changes were incorporated as an amendment to Article 7 TEU in the **Treaty of Nice**.

B

Balkans, The

On 29 April 1997, the **Council of Ministers** of the European Union decided on a 'regional approach' to the countries of south-eastern Europe which had not concluded **Europe Agreements** with the Union. The countries concerned are Albania, Bosnia–Herzegovina, Croatia, the Former Yugoslav Republic of Macedonia (FYROM), and the Federal Republic of Yugoslavia (i.e. Serbia and Montenegro, FRY), referred to collectively as the Western Balkans. In accordance with this decision the **European Commission** reports every six months on progress in the region with respect to economic stabilization and structural reform, democracy, the rule of law, respect for human rights, the treatment of minorities, implementation of the Dayton Agreement, and cross-border cooperation. Strengthening the Union's trade and aid relations and political contacts with the region is conditional upon such progress. Since July 1991 a European Community Monitoring Mission (from December 2000 the European Union Monitoring Mission) for the Western Balkans has been based in Sarajevo. Its 75 monitors oversee the implementation of development assistance programmes and compliance with the Dayton Agreement. Their remit covers the whole of ex-Yugoslavia (except Slovenia) and Albania. Since July 1999 a European Union Special Representative has overseen the operation of the Stability Pact for South-Eastern Europe.

At present, only Albania, FYROM and Croatia have agreements with the Union concluded under the **Stabilization and Association Process**. The region receives substantial amounts of humanitarian aid. See also **Mostar**, **PHARE**.

Baltic states

The three Baltic states – Estonia, Latvia and Lithuania – concluded free trade agreements with the European Union in July 1994. All three states are members of the **Council of Europe**. Already linked to the European Union on the basis of **Europe Agreements**, each of the three states has applied for full membership of the Union. Contacts between the Baltic states and Scandinavian countries have also been established within the framework of the **Nordic Council**. A Baltic Council has been formed, composed of a Baltic Council of Ministers and a 60-member Baltic Assembly with a permanent secretariat in Riga (Latvia). Wider cooperation is the aim of the Council of the Baltic Sea States, founded in 1992, with representatives from the Baltic states, Denmark, Finland, Germany, Iceland, Norway, Poland, Russia and Sweden. See also **Kaliningrad, Pact on Stability in Europe**, and the entries on the individual states.

Bank for International Settlements (BIS)

The world's oldest international financial institution, the BIS was founded in 1930, in conjunction with the Young plan to reorder post-First World War reparations and indebtedness. Its role is to promote cooperation between central banks and to facilitate international financial operations. Most European countries' central banks – including the **European Central Bank** – participate in the activities of the BIS, together with the central banks of most of the emerging market economies. Its headquarters are in Basel with a representative office in Hong Kong. About 85 per cent of its total share capital is in the hands of the participating central banks.

Worldwide, about 120 central banks and international institutions place deposits with the BIS. In March 2001 deposits amounted to about $130 billion, or approximately 7 per cent of foreign exchange reserves. Known as the 'central banks' bank', the BIS cooperates closely with the International Monetary Fund and provides a forum for the coordination of international monetary policy.

Barcelona Declaration

See **Mediterranean policy**.

Barents Euro-Arctic Council (BEAC)

Founded in 1993 on the basis of the Kirkenes Declaration, the aim of the BEAC is to foster closer cooperation between the states with an interest in the Barents Sea region (Denmark, Finland, Iceland, Norway, Russia and Sweden), which has 5 million people and an area twice the size of France.

Belgium

See **Belgo-Luxembourg Economic Union, Benelux**.

Belgo-Luxembourg Economic Union (BLEU)

BLEU was set up under a convention signed in 1921, initially for a period of 50 years, Luxembourg having failed to establish a similar arrangement with France. Frontier controls between the two countries were effectively removed on 1 May 1922. From 1971 the Union, which was dissolved in 1940 and reactivated in 1945, was renewed by tacit agreement for 10-year periods. The two countries held their gold and foreign exchange reserves in common, the Belgian and Luxembourg francs were maintained at parity, and each country's currency was legal tender in the other. With the adoption of the **euro** by both countries, the future of BLEU is uncertain. See also **Benelux**.

Benelux

The name Benelux is formed from the first syllables of Belgium, the Netherlands and Luxembourg, and came into general use in the immediate postwar years. The governments-in-exile of the three countries adopted a **customs union** treaty in London in 1944 that led to the establishment of the Benelux Customs Union on 1 January 1948. Ten years later in The Hague a Treaty of Union was signed, which came into force in 1960, by which date the three countries were already linked as members of the three **European Communities**. Article 306 of the **Treaty of Rome** refers to the 'regional unions' between Belgium and Luxembourg (i.e., the **Belgo-Luxembourg Economic Union**, BLEU) and between Belgium, Luxembourg and the Netherlands (i.e., Benelux), and explicitly allows such unions to exist and flourish within the broader Treaty framework. The Benelux arrangement – providing for the free movement of goods, services, capital and labour between the participating countries – was very much seen as a model for the wider economic integration of western Europe. As the **European Economic Community** (EEC) developed, the rationale for Benelux declined, although throughout the integration process it remained significantly in advance of the Community in its chosen fields of activity. The vanguard role once played by Benelux is today performed by the **Schengen Agreement** for complete free movement among its participating states.

The Benelux arrangement is more ambitious than BLEU, with a broader range of goals: common employment and social security policies, close coordination of macro-economic and budgetary policies, and the eventual adoption of a full monetary and fiscal union, with a single currency and harmonized taxes. Although the latter objectives have not been realized, the Benelux countries did succeed in abolishing internal restrictions on trade and adopting a common external tariff some years ahead of the Community as a whole, and in pioneering a passport-free area with common treatment of third-country nationals, something that remains to be achieved throughout the Union several decades later.

Benelux is governed by the Committee of Ministers, assisted by various institutions, including an interparliamentary council, an economic and social council, a court of justice and a secretariat based in Brussels. The secretary-general is always of Dutch nationality. This institutional structure bears a distinct resemblance to that adopted for **the Six** in the 1950s. It reflects the common perceptions of the architects of both systems about the political importance of supranational structures, representational bodies and legal adjudication in economic integration. The costs of Benelux are met by direct contributions from the three countries, Belgium and the Netherlands paying 48.5 per cent each and Luxembourg the remainder.

The word 'Benelux' was invented in 1947 by F. M. Aspelagh, the Belgian correspondent of *The Economist*, to describe the proposed customs union between the three countries. In search of an original and amusing way of popularizing the concept, the author initially lighted on the word 'Nebelux'. 'After some hesitation I changed it to "Benelux". That sounded much better, but I was still not completely satisfied. It sounded more like a brand of vacuum cleaner than a concept of economic geography. Nonetheless I decided to give it a chance, and used it for the first time in *The Economist* on 6 August 1947. The rest is history.'

Benelux is the only survivor of a number of comparable customs unions proposed in the late 1940s and 1950s. France and Italy discussed such a union in 1949, and later considered joining the Benelux arrangement. This was opposed by the Netherlands, on the grounds that it might disrupt the progress then beginning to be made on a broader front (i.e., the **Council of Europe** and the **Organization for European Economic Cooperation**). With exotic names like Fritalux and Finebel (to which must be added the land of Bizonia, an amalgamation of the British and American sectors of occupied Germany), these projects now survive only as fossils in the bedrock of European integration.

The Benelux countries have always been in favour of European integration, which enjoys strong cross-party support. Many Benelux politicians have held high and influential office in European institutions, including **Paul-Henri Spaak** and Sicco Mansholt (see **Mansholt Plan**); Gaston Thorn, **Jacques Santer** (both from Luxembourg) and Jean Rey, who were Presidents of the **European Commission**; and Joseph Luns and Willy Claes, who served as secretaries-general of the **North Atlantic Treaty Organization** (NATO). The policy of Benelux governments within the European Union has been as far as possible to support the Commission as the guardian of the European interest and as a counterbalance to the dominant role inevitably played by the larger states. The fact that **Brussels** and Luxembourg are the headquarters of so many European institutions plays a part in creating a favourable climate of official opinion towards European integration (see **seat of the institutions**). Such integration allows the Benelux countries to play a more influential role as partners than would be allowed them within a conventional power system.

Berlaymont

The 13-storey building in the form of an irregular four-pointed star has become widely known as the headquarters of the **European Commission** in Brussels, and, like 'Whitehall', is used as a symbol of officialdom. Built in the 1960s on the site of a former monastery of the same name, the Berlaymont building was rented by the Commission from the Belgian government. In 1990 it was discovered that the internal walls had a high asbestos content which was potentially injurious to health, and since 1992 the building has been left empty while refurbishment is carried out. The members of the Commission will, in any case, not be returning to the Berlaymont building since they now have their offices with their departments, rather than in close proximity to one another.

Beyen Plan

After the failure to establish the **European Defence Community** (EDC) in 1954, **the Six** decided to seek new areas to which the kind of collaboration set out in the 1951 **European Coal and Steel Community** Treaty could be extended. On 4 April 1955, Johan Willem Beyen, the Foreign Minister of the Netherlands, submitted a memorandum on a **customs union** among the Six. It was this memorandum which led directly via the **Messina Conference** and the **Spaak Committee** to the Treaty establishing the **European Economic Community** (EEC). The Beyen Plan has a strong claim to be a key element in the process which led to the European Union.

Beyen submitted his plan because the Dutch government was not satisfied with the very slow progress being made with the dismantling of restrictions on free trade between the countries of western Europe. He had been alarmed by news of a Franco-German bilateral agreement on trade and investment, and to forestall the possibility of the smaller countries being excluded wanted the matter discussed on a multilateral basis. He had succeeded in making the establishment of 'a common market among the Member States' one of the objectives of the **European Political Community** (EPC), and when plans for an EPC collapsed with the failure of the EDC initiative he revived the proposal in his April 1955 memorandum.

Black Sea Economic Cooperation (BSEC)

The BSEC was set up in 1992 under an agreement signed by Bulgaria, Romania, Turkey and the Soviet Union as a forum for consultation and cooperation on developments affecting the Black Sea area. The membership now also extends to Albania, Armenia, Azerbaijan, Georgia, Greece, Moldova, and Ukraine. BSEC has a Council of Ministers, a Committee of Senior Officials, and a Secretariat. An International Centre for Black Sea Studies was set up in Athens in 1998. A Black Sea Trade and Development Bank became operational in Thessaloniki in 1999.

Bosman case

The Bosman case (*URBSFA* v *Bosman*, Case C415/93) resulted from an action brought by a Belgian footballer, Jean-Marc Bosman. In 1990 Bosman declined to renew his contract with his club, RC Liège, and was accordingly placed on the club's list of players available for transfer. However, in accordance with the rules normally applied between clubs and agreed by football's governing bodies in Belgium (the *Union Royale Belge des Sociétés de Football Association*, URBSFA) and in Europe (UEFA), RC Liège proposed to levy a transfer fee of FB 11,743,000 upon any club which sought to put Bosman under contract. Together with the rules imposing limits on the number of foreign players which clubs were able to field, this provision made it virtually impossible for Bosman to find employment (he also sought employment in France). The case was eventually referred to the **Court of Justice**, which ruled on 15 December 1995 that transfer fees were incompatible with the right of **free movement of persons** guaranteed under Article 48 (now 39) EC and that restrictions on foreign players could not be applied in such a way as to discriminate between citizens of European Union member states (see **discrimination on grounds of nationality**). Professional football organizations are still adjusting to the consequences of the Court's findings.

Bosnia–Herzegovina

In Bosnia–Herzegovina the Muslims were the first to develop a national consciousness, intensified by the anti-Muslim policies pursued by the Serbs both before and after the Second World War. Following the example of Slovenia and Croatia, a referendum on independence was held in February–March 1992. It was boycotted by the Bosnian Serbs, and the result was 99.78 per cent in favour. Independence was declared in April 1992, and immediately led to fierce fighting between Serbs, Croats, Bosnian Muslims, and Bosnian Serbs, widespread destruction of property, and the loss of many lives. International diplomatic efforts secured a peace agreement signed in Dayton, Ohio, in November 1995. Under this agreement Bosnia–Herzegovina is made up of a Serb entity, the Republika Srpska (49 per cent of the territory), and the Federation of Bosnia and Herzegovina (BiH).

The ending of hostilities allowed the European Union's **PHARE** programme to be extended to Bosnia–Herzegovina in 1996. In 2000 under the **Stabilization and Association Process** a 'road map' of legislative and other measures was drawn up as a preliminary to a Stabilization and Association Agreement. Bosnia–Herzegovina became eligible for aid under the **CARDS programme** in 2001. Since 1991 the country has received about €2 billion from the European Union and a further €1.2 billion from the Union's member states. Bosnia–Herzegovina was admitted to the **Council of Europe** in 2002. See also **the Balkans, Yugoslavia.**

Briand, Aristide (1862–1932)

Aristide Briand was a leading Socialist politician of the French Third Republic, several times prime minister and foreign minister from 1925 until his death. He was one of the first advocates of what he called 'a system of European Federal Union', which, as the representative of the French government in Geneva, Briand proposed to the **League of Nations** on 5 September 1929. He drew his inspiration from the Pan-American Union. The 27 European members of the League agreed to discuss the proposal, and on 17 May 1930 the French government circulated a memorandum setting out the proposal in more detail. Briand's memorandum was largely the work of Alexis Léger, a senior official in the Quai d'Orsay, better known as the poet Saint-John Perse who was awarded the Nobel Prize for Literature in 1960.

The memorandum spoke of the need for 'a permanent regime of solidarity based on international agreements for the rational organization of Europe'. Interestingly, Briand cited 'the possibilities of enlarging the economic market' as one of the reasons why such an organization was imperative, and referred to the 20,000 kilometres of new national frontiers within Europe created by the Treaty of Versailles. Throughout the memorandum he stressed that the Federal Union was in no way intended to supplant the League, but instead to work within it as one of the regional organizations specifically sanctioned by the League Covenant. The proposal fell well short of a 'federal' arrangement in the conventional sense: 'It is on the plane of absolute sovereignty and of entire political independence that the understanding between European nations must be brought about ... under a system of federal union fully compatible with respect for traditions and for the characteristics peculiar to each people.' The memorandum was considered in detail by a special study group chaired by Sir Eric Drummond, Secretary-General of the League. There the proposals 'died a lingering death, killed by increasing international friction and mistrust' (A.C. Temperley, *The Whispering Gallery of Europe*, 1938). Jointly with Gustav Stresemann and Austen Chamberlain, Briand was awarded the Nobel Peace Prize in 1926 in recognition of his achievement in negotiating the Locarno Pacts, and is frequently cited, especially by French writers, as one of the founding fathers of the European Community. At the time he made his proposal he was Honorary President of **Pan-Europa**. In *Makers of Modern Europe* (1930) **Carlo Sforza** described Briand's patriotism as 'intense, so deep and so serene that its aggressive side disappears'. Briand's remark – quoted by Sforza – about Joan of Arc is revealing: 'Why did she waste so much energy in expelling the English? In a few generations we should have assimilated all of them; and what a splendid race we might have made'.

British Budget problem

Reduced to its essentials, the British Budget problem – which overshadowed the United Kingdom's relations with the rest of the European Community from 1979 to 1984 – was that although among the poorer member states in terms of per capita gross national product (GNP), the United Kingdom was the second largest net contributor to the **Budget**. Both the pre-1979 Labour government and the post-1979 Conservative government of **Margaret Thatcher** believed this to be inequitable. Various temporary solutions were agreed, but a longer-term settlement was not reached until the Fontainebleau meeting of the **European Council** in June 1984 (see **Fontainebleau Agreement**).

It was realized at the time of the entry negotiations that, because of the way the Community's system of **own resources** worked, the United Kingdom, with its relatively high revenue from tariffs and levies, would be a substantial contributor to the Budget. On the receipts side, the efficiency of British agriculture meant that payments to the United Kingdom under the **Common Agricultural Policy** (CAP) were relatively small. The problem was solved (or rather sidestepped) in three ways: the British were given a seven-year **transitional period**, they were told that new spending policies from which they could expect to benefit were soon to be established and, most importantly, they were assured that if an 'unacceptable situation' were to arise, the Community would find equitable solutions.

Although the **European Regional Development Fund** (ERDF) was established with strong British support in 1973, it was clearly on too small a scale to make a real difference to the overall pattern of the United Kingdom's **contributions and receipts**. Accordingly, the Budget issue featured in the Labour government's **renegotiation** demands of 1974–5. At the Dublin meeting of the European Council in March 1975 a 'corrective mechanism', with which the government expressed itself satisfied, was agreed. However, the mechanism had one fatal flaw: it was triggered only if the member state concerned had an overall deficit on its balance of trade. Thanks to North Sea oil, this was not the case, and nothing was ever paid to the United Kingdom under the Dublin arrangement.

When the Conservatives took office in 1979, the transitional period was over, and the forecasts of British net contributions to the Budget showed all too clearly that the problem was getting worse: from 1980 onwards, Community membership seemed likely to cost the United Kingdom almost £1 billion a year. This was the moment at which, in the view of Christopher Tugendhat, the Commissioner then responsible for the Budget, 'an act of statesmanship' on the part of the French and German leaders, **Valéry Giscard d'Estaing** and Helmut Schmidt, 'could have solved the British budget problem before it got out of hand'. Instead, they chose to turn the issue into 'a trial of strength' (*Making Sense of Europe*, 1986). At the European Council meeting in Dublin in November 1979 Mrs Thatcher was provoked into demanding 'our money back', a phrase that called into question the whole idea of own resources belonging to the Community as of right. It also suggested that the British stance was prompted by the idea of a *juste retour* rather than by a broader notion of equity.

Temporary solutions were found for 1980, 1981, and 1982. By 1983 circumstances had changed in the United Kingdom's favour. The Community was running out of money, and the ceiling on **value-added tax** (VAT) could be raised only with the unanimous agreement of all member states (including ratification by **national parliaments**). At the European Council meeting in Stuttgart in June 1983 Mrs Thatcher made it very clear that her consent was conditional upon a permanent solution to the British Budget problem and upon new measures to enforce budgetary discipline in the Community. A change in French attitudes was perhaps prompted by the realization that in the wake of enlargement to include Portugal and Spain France was also likely to become a net contributor to the Community Budget. A further *ad hoc* arrangement was made for the British net contribution for 1983.

Twelve months of negotiations followed, from which emerged an agreement to calculate the disparity in the British Budget contribution on the basis of the difference between the British share of Community expenditure and the proportion of the Community's VAT-based revenue contributed by the United Kingdom. The **abatement**, as it was known, was to be paid for each year in the form of a reduced VAT-based contribution in the following year, a method that had the advantage (as the Council saw it) of keeping the **European Parliament** out of the picture, the Parliament's budgetary powers being limited to the expenditure side of the Budget. At the Fontainebleau European Council in June 1984 agreement was finally reached, to the effect that the revision of the own resources system, under which the VAT ceiling was finally raised from 1 to 1.4 per cent, would allow the United Kingdom a further *ad hoc* abatement of 1 billion ECUs for 1984 and thereafter a two-thirds reduction in the difference between the British contribution to VAT-based revenue and the amount of Community expenditure in the United Kingdom. As had been the case since 1982, a special arrangement was made that allowed West Germany – by far the biggest net contributor to the Budget – to pay a reduced share of what would otherwise have been a substantial proportion of the British rebate. In its first full year of operation (1985) the rebate amounted to about £1 billion. Since 1984, the rebate has amounted to about £29 billion (pre-1984 refunds to about £3 billion).

Since the Fontainebleau Agreement the rebate has occasionally been called into question, but the arrangement is now certain to last at least until 2006 under an agreement reached at the Berlin meeting of the European Council in March 1999.

In proportion to British GNP or British public sector expenditure the sums at stake were never large. Throughout the negotiations the United Kingdom emphasized that it was prepared to be a modest net contributor to the Budget and that its case rested not on the idea of a *juste retour* but on the assurance given about the resolution of 'unacceptable situations' in the course of the negotiations on British accession to the Community. Although it may be true that the pugnacity of Mrs Thatcher's negotiating style offended and alienated some other member states, it is doubtful if anything less than her tenacity allied to a mastery of complex detail could have yielded, in the end, so satisfactory a result. Nor was it to be expected that a British government firmly committed to constraints on public expenditure could possibly let the issue lie. In retrospect, it reflects little credit on the Community that the problem should have taken so long to resolve and used up so much of the creative energies of ministers, officials and Community institutions.

Bruges speech

On 20 September 1988 **Margaret Thatcher**, then Prime Minister of the United Kingdom, made a speech at the **College of Europe** in Bruges, Belgium, on the future of the European Community. The speech was widely interpreted as a counterblast to the federalist vision of **Jacques Delors**, the President of the **European Commission**, since it reasserted the primacy of the member states within the integration process. The political background, national and European, to the speech is fully described in Hugo Young's biography of Mrs Thatcher, *One of Us* (1989).

The speech did not call into question the United Kingdom's membership of the Community: 'Britain does not dream of some cosy, isolated existence on the fringes of the Community. Britain's destiny is in Europe, as part of the Community.' Nor was Mrs Thatcher opposed to the member states working 'more closely together on the things we can do better together than alone ... whether it be in trade, in defence, or in our relations with the rest of the world'. However, the essence of the speech was the need to maintain the pre-eminence of the member states and to do nothing that might impair that national diversity which was a source of Europe's strength: 'Europe will be stronger precisely because it has France in as France, Spain in as Spain, Britain in as Britain, each with its own customs, traditions and identity.' The speech gave rise to concern not only because of the hostility it showed towards agreed objectives (the abolition of frontier controls, for example) but also because of its essentially intergovernmental vision of the Community's future (see **intergovernmentalism**).

For many commentators the speech was the first unequivocal expression of that distaste for Community institutions which served the Conservatives so badly in the **European elections** held nine months later. Within weeks of its delivery the so-called 'Bruges Group' was founded, formally on a cross-party basis, but in reality mainly composed of Conservatives who shared Mrs Thatcher's (largely illusory) fears of a European superstate in which national identity would be submerged and national **sovereignty** overridden (see '**identikit Europe**').

Brussels

The national capital of Belgium with a population of almost 1 million people, Brussels is also the self-styled 'capital of Europe'. Many European Union institutions and bodies are located there: the **Council of Ministers**, the **European Commission** (see also **Berlaymont**), the **Economic and Social Committee** and the **Committee of the Regions**. The **European Parliament** has many of its staff in Brussels. Most meetings of its committees are held there and, since 1993, a small number of short plenary sessions (see **seat of the institutions**). The **national representations** of the member states are also in Brussels, together with many diplomatic missions accredited to the Union. Most European-wide lobbying organizations have their headquarters in Brussels. Brussels is also the home of the **North Atlantic Treaty Organization** (NATO) (since 1967), the **North Atlantic Assembly** and, since 1990, the **Western European Union** (WEU). Brussels has the second largest press corps in the world, after Washington.

Brussels Treaty

In March 1948, the United Kingdom, France and the **Benelux** countries signed a 'Treaty for collaboration in economic, social and cultural matters and for collective self-defence', commonly known as the Brussels Treaty. It provided for intergovernmental consultations through a ministerial Council and was intended to protect the signatory states against a renewal of German aggression and the increasingly explicit threat from the USSR. The Treaty contained an automatic military assistance provision (Article 5) and called for signatory states to set up a permanent Military Committee. The Treaty was concluded for 50 years and provided the basis both for the **North Atlantic Treaty Organization** (NATO) and for the **Western European Union** (WEU; established by the modified Brussels Treaty of 1954).

Warmly welcomed by President Truman, the Brussels Treaty was largely the initiative of Ernest Bevin, the Foreign Secretary in Britain's postwar Labour government. It built upon the Franco-British **Dunkirk Treaty** signed the previous year, and was a key element in Bevin's policy of what he called 'Western Union'. Introducing the policy in the House of Commons on 22 January 1948, Bevin said: 'The time for consolidation of Western Europe is ripe … The old-fashioned concept of the balance of power should be discontinued.' Britain, he said, was now 'thinking of Western Europe as a unity'. The Brussels Treaty gave rise to great hopes that the United Kingdom was prepared to take the lead in the unification of western Europe. In the event these hopes were disappointed: the economic, social and cultural provisions of the Treaty came to nothing; the defence component was soon rendered more or less irrelevant by the establishment of NATO and it became clear that the United Kingdom was extremely reluctant to take part in the setting up of supranational institutions. The Treaty was, however, of some psychological importance in that it gave encouragement to those in the United States who wanted to see European countries coming together to resolve their postwar problems.

Budget of the European Union

The Budget of the European Union embraces revenue (see **own resources**), expenditure upon common policies, and the running costs of the institutions. The annual procedure for the adoption of the Budget centres upon proposals for expenditure (unlike the budget in the United Kingdom, which is concerned with the raising of revenue). Although the Union engages in borrowing and lending (see below), under Article 268 of the **Treaty of Rome** expenditure must be matched by revenue in each budgetary year. Responsibility for drawing up and implementing the Budget rests with the **European Commission**; the **Council of Ministers** and the **European Parliament** constitute the joint budgetary authority; and the annual audit is carried out by the **Court of Auditors** (see also **discharge procedure**).

The procedure for the adoption of the Budget is an area in which the European Parliament's powers have increased very substantially since 1970. It is set out in Article 272, and each of the main stages has to be completed by a specific deadline in the course of the year preceding that to which the Budget relates.

The first stage is the drawing up of estimates by each institution and the consolidation of these by the Commission into the preliminary draft Budget (PDB). This must be forwarded to the Council by 1 September for adoption as the draft budget (DB)and presented to the European Parliament by 5 October. The Parliament's first reading of the DB is in November, and at this stage it may propose modifications to items of **compulsory expenditure** or adopt amendments to non-compulsory expenditure: the latter are subject to a 'maximum rate of increase', which is calculated by the Commission in the light of growth projections and rates of inflation and which can be changed only by agreement between the Council and the Parliament. Thus amended by the Parliament, the DB is returned to the Council. The Council's second reading takes place with advice from a delegation of the Parliament, and at this stage the amounts of compulsory expenditure – upon which the Council has the last word – are normally fixed. The remaining stage, the Parliament's second reading in December, concentrates upon non-compulsory expenditure (still within the maximum rate). In the negotiations which invariably precede the adoption of the Budget, the Parliament makes frequent use of its power to withhold approval of particular spending proposals by placing sums 'in the reserve' (known as Chapter 100) until the substance and management of the policy are altered in accordance with the Parliament's wishes. If the Parliament is broadly satisfied with the DB overall, it may adopt the Budget by a majority of its total membership and three-fifths of the votes cast; if there are 'important reasons' why it is not satisfied, it may reject the DB as a whole by a majority of its total membership and two-thirds of the votes cast, as it did for the first time in 1979.

If adopted, the Budget can then be implemented. If it is not adopted, a system known as 'provisional twelfths' comes into effect, which requires expenditure in each month to be no more than one-twelfth of the total expenditure in the previous year. This system continues until a new Budget is adopted. The Treaty allows the Commission to submit draft supplementary or amending budgets to take account of unforeseen circumstances.

Although the budgetary procedure and the Budget itself are on an annual basis, multiannual spending programmes involve commitments spread over longer periods. This is done by means of 'differentiated appropriations', in respect of which a distinction is drawn between commitments and payments. Nor is each annual Budget worked out in isolation: all calculations are made within multiannual 'financial perspectives', of which the most recent, covering the period 2000–6, was agreed by the **European Council** in Berlin in March 1999 (see **future financing**).

With successive **enlargements** and the gradual broadening of Community activities, overall expenditure through the Budget has increased very markedly since the 1960s. In 1960, expenditure was about 0.03 per cent of Community gross domestic product (GDP). By the time of the first enlargement in 1973 it had risen to almost 0.53 per cent of GDP and by 1995 to about € 68 billion (1.04 per cent of GDP). But – as the **MacDougall Report** showed long ago – this is well short of the amounts that would be necessary to have a perceptible macro-economic effect on growth patterns, regional development or average levels of prosperity. Nor can it increase much between now and 2006, member states having agreed not to let the Budget exceed 1.27 per cent of GDP. The Budget for 2002 amounted to € 102 billion, broadly equivalent to expenditure in the United Kingdom on the National Health Service (about £65 billion) and in excess of total public expenditure in Denmark. Expenditure was allocated as follows:

price support for agriculture	45.2 per cent
structural funds, including Cohesion Fund	34.5 per cent
internal policies (research, transport, etc.)	6.5 per cent
external policies, including pre-accession aid	8.4 per cent
administration	5.2 per cent

The provisions in the **Maastricht Treaty** on how operational costs arising from the **Common Foreign and Security Policy** (CFSP) or cooperation in the field of **Justice and Home Affairs** (JHA) are met allow member states the choice of charging them to the Budget (in which case the normal procedures apply) or paying for them directly; in both cases administrative costs are borne by the Budget.

Even this summary account of the budgetary procedure is suggestive of the many arguments and finely balanced compromises that have gone into the making of the procedure in its present form. In addition to the Treaty, the procedure is governed by various **interinstitutional agreements**, but these have not always been effective in forestalling or resolving arguments between the Parliament and the Council. For example, in December 1985 the President of the Parliament declared the 1986 Budget adopted, but the Parliament's amendments had exceeded the maximum rate and the Council challenged the Parliament's decision in the **Court of Justice**. The Parliament lost the case, but the 1986 Budget as finally agreed took account of the Parliament's concerns.

The Budget was always intended to be an instrument of policy. However, it is essentially too small to make much difference except in limited areas. This has not prevented the Budget from being a major cause of dispute both between member states (see **British Budget problem**) and between the

European Union expenditure 1970, 1980, 1990, 1995, and 2000 (General Budget,[1] EDF[2] and ECSC[3])

	1970	1980	1990	1995	2000[4]
Total Union expenditure (million €)	3,576	16,455	45,608	68,408	92,254
Per capita expenditure (€)	19	63	139	183	244
Union expenditure as % of public-sector expenditure in member states	2.00	1.70	2.00	2.10	2.40
Annual rate of growth in nominal terms (%)	73.10	11.44	7.90	11.30	8.60
Annual rate of growth in real terms (%)	61.5	1.70	2.60	7.70	8.60
Union expenditure as % of member states' GDP	0.73	0.80	0.94	1.04	1.09

[1] Actual payments from the Budget.
[2] European Development Fund.
[3] European Coal and Steel Community.
[4] As adopted

Source: European Commission, *The Community Budget: The Facts in Figures* (2000), slightly simplified

institutions. The European Parliament – in common with most parliaments at some time in their history – has used its budgetary powers to wrest concessions from the Council and the Commission. The Parliament's powers over non-compulsory expenditure are not limited merely to adjusting (normally increasing) the sums for each item of expenditure, but extend to adjusting the spending priorities overall and securing better oversight of the Commission's management of the Budget by placing sums in the 'reserve'.

In the longer term the Budget can develop only if at least a proportion of the Union's revenue is raised directly from the taxpayer, with the European Parliament having a say in how this is done. At present the Parliament has virtually no responsibility for revenue-raising and this has resulted, understandably, in the Parliament being broadly on the side of increased expenditure. It would be wholly consistent with the practice in other federal or quasi-federal systems if a proportion of an individual taxpayer's taxes went to the central authority directly rather than indirectly through national authorities. Such a system would reflect the extent to which the Budget of the Union bears costs that would otherwise be borne by national budgets, such as agricultural support. If taxation without representation is tyranny, representation without taxation may encourage irresponsibility.

Budgetary discipline

The phrase 'budgetary discipline' denotes the constraints within which the **Budget of the European Union** is drawn up, especially the 'financial perspective' and the limits agreed by member states on **own resources**. Measures to ensure sound financial management are described under **discharge procedure** and **Court of Auditors** (see also **fraud**).

In addition to the requirement in Article 268 of the **Treaty of Rome** that 'revenue and expenditure ... shall be in balance', Article 270 (resulting from the **Maastricht Treaty**) says that 'with a view to maintaining budgetary discipline, the **European Commission** shall not make any proposal for a Community act ... without providing the assurance that [it] is capable of being financed within the limit of the Community's own resources'. This requirement relates only to such costs as may fall upon the Budget; it does not oblige the Commission to assess overall compliance costs. However, under a **Declaration** annexed to the Treaty of Rome, the Commission is required 'to take account in its legislative proposals of costs and benefits to the Member States' public authorities and all the parties concerned'.

The **interinstitutional agreement** reached by the **European Parliament**, the **Council of Ministers**, and the European Commission on 6 May 1999 (*Official Journal*, C172, 18 June 1999) specifies that the 2000–6 financial framework annexed to the agreement is the 'reference framework for interinstitutional budgetary discipline'. The three institutions undertake to regard the amounts set out in the perspective as the 'annual ceiling on Community expenditure'; own resources are allowed to rise to a maximum of 1.27 per cent of overall gross national product (GNP) by 2006. Within these overall ceilings, price support under the **European Agricultural Guidance and Guarantee Fund** (EAGGF) is subject to a particularly tight limit, agreed in 1988, and may not rise by more than 74 per cent of the rise in GNP. See also **future financing**.

Budgetary discipline became linked in the early 1980s with the **British Budget problem** by virtue of **Margaret Thatcher**'s insistence that no new own resources would be forthcoming unless expenditure were made subject to stricter controls than had so far been applied. Two meetings of the **European Council** in Brussels (June 1987 and February 1988) laid the foundations for the present system of budgetary discipline, set out in an October 1993 interinstitutional agreement. This agreement also embodied guidelines for the annual procedure for drawing up the Budget. These were further refined in Annex III of the agreement of 6 May 1999 (see p. 39).

Bulgaria

The first free elections in Bulgaria for more than 40 years were held in June 1990. In 1993 Bulgaria signed a **Europe Agreement** with the European Community, which came into effect on 1 February 1995. At the end of the year, on 14 December 1995, Bulgaria applied for full membership of the European Union.

Bulgaria is one of the poorest of the central and eastern European countries which have applied for membership (see **enlargement**). The currency is the lev. Its industrial output is barely twice that of Luxembourg, although its population is twenty times greater. The **Opinion** of the **European Commission**, published on 15 July 1997 (*Bulletin of the European Union*, supplement 13/97), noted that with respect to the **Copenhagen criteria** Bulgaria could be said only to be 'on its way' to establishing stable democratic institutions. It noted too 'the absence of a commitment to market-oriented economic policies', and estimated that Bulgaria would have real difficulty in adapting to, applying, and enforcing the *acquis communautaire*. Although the Commission did not recommend that bilateral negotiations with Bulgaria should begin in 1998, Bulgaria was included in the 'accession process' outlined by the **European Council** in Luxembourg in December 1997 (see also **European Conference**). Bilateral negotiations with Bulgaria began in 2000.

Bulgaria is a member of the **Council of Europe**, of the **Organization for Security and Cooperation in Europe** (OSCE), and of the **Central European Initiative**. Italy is now Bulgaria's most important trading partner. The target date for Bulgaria's entry into the European Union is 2007.

C

Cabinet

The French word *cabinet* is used to denote the small group of officials who make up the private offices of senior ministers in France and other countries, of members of the **European Commission**, and of other very senior figures in the European Union, such as the President of the **European Parliament**. By virtue of their closeness to persons of political influence, members of *cabinets* can and do play an influential role, which normally extends well beyond the specific responsibilities of the person to whom they are attached.

Capital movements

Article 14 (formerly Article 7a) of the **Treaty of Rome** defines the **Single Market** as one in which all obstacles to the free movement of goods, persons, services and capital have been removed. Article 67 EEC required member states to 'abolish between themselves all restrictions on the movement of capital belonging to persons resident in the member states and any discrimination based on the nationality or on the place of residence of the parties or on the place where such capital is invested'. Articles 68 to 73 EEC set out the means whereby this general principle was to be applied and the exceptions to it. Gradual progress was made in the 1960s and 1970s, leading up to the adoption in 1988 of a general **Directive** requiring capital movements to be entirely freed by July 1990 (Spain, Portugal, Greece and Ireland were allowed to apply restrictions for a little longer). The matter was placed under the general supervisory control of the **Monetary Committee** and the Committee of **Central Bank Governors**. Member states were allowed to take 'protective measures' in the event of 'short-term capital movements of exceptional magnitude' (Article 2 of the Directive).

The **Maastricht Treaty** repealed Articles 67 to 73 EEC with effect from 1 January 1994 and substituted Articles 73a to 73g (now Articles 56 to 60) EC, placing capital movements legislation within the framework of **Economic and Monetary Union** (EMU). Free movement of capital has been assured since that date (except in relation to Greece, which was granted an extension until 1 January 1995), and the **European Central Bank** (ECB) is now the supervisory authority. The legislation applies throughout the **European Economic Area** (EEA). In principle, free movement of capital now extends to transactions involving non-member states.

CARDS programme

The CARDS programme (Community Assistance for Reconstruction, Development and Stabilization) is the main channel for European Union aid to the countries of South-East Europe under the **Stabilization and Association Process**. It was established under Regulation 2666/00 on 5 December 2000 (*Official Journal*, L306, 7 December 2000).

Cassis de Dijon case

The 1979 judgment of the **Court of Justice** in the case known as 'Cassis de Dijon' (*Rewe-Zentrale AG* v *Bundesmonopolverwaltung für Branntwein*, Case 120/78) established that a product lawfully manufactured and on sale in one member state may be imported into another without restriction. This principle, sometimes known as mutual recognition of product standards, is of the greatest importance in facilitating the free circulation of goods within the **Single Market** and obviates the need for detailed **harmonization** of product standards to guarantee such circulation.

Cassis de Dijon is a blackcurrant-based liqueur manufactured in France. The West German spirits monopoly sought to ban its import into the German market on the grounds that its alcoholic content was below the minimum (25 per cent by volume) laid down by German law for liqueurs. The Court did not accept this argument. The case illustrates the role that the Court can play in furthering the objects of the Community, in this case the removal of **nontariff barriers** to trade between the member states.

Cecchini Report

In the **Cockfield White Paper** of June 1985 the **European Commission** identified the legislative measures that would be needed if the **Single Market** were to be created. In 1988 a second report by a committee of experts, chaired by a senior Commission official, Paolo Cecchini, was published under the title *1992: The European Challenge*. This report identified the impediments – such as different national practices, testing standards, and bureaucratic obstruction – that stood in the way of the free flow of goods, services, persons and capital within the Community. The report's calculation that such impediments cost the Community some 5 per cent of its gross domestic product (GDP) annually was widely quoted, as was the assertion that their removal would result in a one-off gain variously calculated at between 4.3 and 6.4 per cent of GDP and deliver non-inflationary growth of 7 per cent in the medium term and 5 million new jobs. The report was based in part on the findings of a survey among 11,000 businessmen, who identified frontier formalities and the failure to agree on Community-wide product standards as the key elements in the problem.

CEDEFOP
See **European Centre for the Development of Vocational Training**.

CEN
See *Comité Européen de Normalisation*.

CENELEC
See *Comité Européen de Normalisation*.

Censure motion
Under Article 201 of the **Treaty of Rome**, the **European Parliament** may dismiss the **European Commission** on the basis of a motion of censure passed by a two-thirds majority of votes cast representing a majority of the Members of Parliament (MEPs). The Commission is required to resign 'as a body' (motions of censure may not be directed against individual Commissioners) but may continue to deal with current business until replaced. The reasons why so few motions of censure have ever been put to the vote are discussed under **European Parliament**.

Central bank governors
The governors of the central banks of the member states of the European Union have gained important new powers since 1980, reflecting the growing importance of coordinated exchange-rate management and monetary discipline. They are closely involved in the operation of the **European Monetary System** (EMS) and in the coordination of monetary policy and, as members of the Governing Board of the **European Central Bank** (ECB), play a very influential role in **Economic and Monetary Union** (EMU).

There is no reference to the central bank governors in the original **Treaty of Rome**. They were first given institutional standing in May 1964, when the Council of Economic and Finance Ministers (**Ecofin Council**) decided to complement the existing **Monetary Committee** by establishing a parallel body to coordinate the activities of the various national central banks at Community level. The resulting organ, known as the Committee of Central Bank Governors, brought together the governors and their senior staff.

The remit of the Committee was to 'hold consultations concerning the general principles and the broad lines of policy of the central banks' and to 'exchange information at regular intervals about the most important measures that fall within the competence of the central banks, and to examine those measures'. In practice, the Committee's work was given real substance only once the promotion of exchange-rate stability had become a major Community objective.

The first attempt to develop EMU, following the **Werner Report** of 1970, led to a major enhancement of the Committee's role. In March 1971 it was entrusted with coordinating intervention on the currency markets to sustain the so-called 'snake'. A decision of the Ecofin Council of the same month strengthened cooperation between central banks in respect of interest rates and money supply. Two years later, in April 1973, the Committee was appointed in its entirety to serve as the board of governors of the new **European Monetary Cooperation Fund** (EMCF).

Although the Werner-inspired EMU project failed, the subsequent development of the EMS in 1978–9 strengthened the position of the central bank governors. When it was decided to relaunch the EMU process at the European Council meeting in Hanover in June 1988 by commissioning the **Delors Report**, the membership of the committee for the new study was composed almost exclusively of the central bank governors.

The organization and remit of the Committee of Central Bank Governors were redefined at the beginning of stage 1 of EMU in July 1990. An 'economic unit' was added to the existing secretariat to provide analytical support to the work of the Committee. The Committee's responsibilities were revised and the right of the Committee's chairman to attend meetings of the Ecofin Council whenever it dealt with matters 'involving the tasks of the Committee' was formalized.

Under the provisions of the **Maastricht Treaty**, the Committee of Central Bank Governors and the EMCF merged in January 1994 to form the **European Monetary Institute** (EMI). In June 1998 the EMI was transformed into the ECB which now controls the operations of a European System of Central Banks.

Central Commission for the Navigation of the Rhine

With its headquarters in Strasbourg, the Commission has a strong claim to be the oldest European organization, having been established by the Congress of Vienna in 1815. It is responsible for all aspects of navigation on the Rhine. The four riparian states (France, Germany, the Netherlands and Switzerland) together with Belgium take part in the work of the Commission. See also **Danube Commission**.

Central European Free Trade Agreement (CEFTA)

CEFTA was signed in Cracow, Poland, in December 1992 by the three **Visegrad States**. The signatories (later joined by Slovenia, Romania and Bulgaria) committed themselves to the progressive establishment of a **free trade area** over the period 1993 to 2001, at the heart of which would be a **common market** in most industrial goods. Except for certain 'sensitive' products, duties on all industrial goods in CEFTA were removed with effect from January 1997. Countries joining the European Union (see **enlargement**) must withdraw from CEFTA.

Central European Initiative (CEI)

The CEI was founded in November 1989 as the Quadrilateral Initiative (Austria, Hungary, Italy and Yugoslavia) on the initiative of the Italian government. The following year it was joined by Czechoslovakia, and was renamed the Pentagonal Initiative. Poland joined in 1991 (Hexagonal Initiative). Its current name was adopted in 1992, with the accession of Croatia, Slovenia and Bosnia–Herzegovina. By 1996 the CEI had been extended to Albania, Belarus, Bulgaria, Macedonia, Moldova, Romania and Ukraine.

The CEI provides a framework for coordination between its member states in the fields of economic recovery, the consolidation of democratic institutions, the environment, transport, energy, and other matters of common interest (including relations with the European Union). The main annual event is the meeting of heads of government, complemented by twice-yearly meetings of foreign ministers and meetings of parliamentarians and national experts. The secretariat is in Trieste and the working language is English.

CEPT

See **European Conference of Postal and Telecommunications Administrations**.

CERN

See **European Organization for Nuclear Research**.

Chamber of States

In a federal state (see **federation**) with a two-chamber parliamentary system, the upper chamber may be composed of representatives of the provinces or regions that make up that state. The lower chamber, by contrast, is composed of directly elected representatives of the people. For example, in Germany the upper chamber (the Bundesrat) is composed of representatives of the *Länder* that make up the Federal Republic. It is sometimes suggested that within the European Union the **Council of Ministers** might develop one day into a Chamber of States, the clear implication being that the real decision-making power would shift to the lower chamber, i.e., the **European Parliament**.

Channel Islands

The Channel Islands and the Isle of Man are not part of the European Union and although free movement of agricultural produce and industrial goods between them and the Union was assured under the United Kingdom's 1972 Accession Treaty, they are not part of the Union's customs territory. They are accordingly exempt from Union rules on the free movement of labour, competition, right of establishment, value-added tax (VAT), and so on, and are not represented in the **European Parliament**.

Channel Tunnel

The idea of a 'fixed link' between England and France was first seriously put forward in the nineteenth century and trial lengths of tunnel were bored on both sides of the Channel in 1882. By the beginning of the 20th century the Channel Tunnel was being proposed as a vital link in a land route from London via Paris, Milan, Belgrade, Constantinople and Aleppo, to Baghdad (and thence to India). However, there was opposition to a tunnel as a potential threat to national security, and – in spite of French support – this opposition was still strong enough to lead the House of Commons to reject a tunnel scheme by 179 votes to 172 in June 1930. The steady postwar growth in cross-Channel passenger and freight traffic led to a tunnel scheme being approved by the British and French Governments in 1966. Nine years later the project was abandoned. In 1982 the Eurotunnel consortium was formed, and their proposal for a rail-only tunnel was accepted. The Anglo-French Channel Tunnel Treaty was signed in Canterbury on 12 February 1986 and ratified the following year. Tunnelling started on the English side in December 1987 and on the French side two months later. The breakthrough was achieved on 1 December 1990, and six months later 150 kilometres of tunnelling (two 50-kilometre railway tunnels and a service tunnel beside them) had been completed. The tunnel was officially opened by the Queen and President Mitterrand in May 1994.

The Channel Tunnel extends between Folkestone and Calais, of which approximately 38 kilometres are under the sea bed. Cars, lorries and coaches are transported on special wagons by frequent shuttle services operating day and night. The tunnel is also used by freight and passenger trains, the latter known as 'Eurostar', on the services between London, Paris and Brussels. In addition to its impact on the ferry services, it is estimated that the Channel Tunnel is saving 20,000 aircraft movements a year. In 2000 the shuttle service carried over 9 million passengers and Eurostar over 7 million.

Built at a cost of over £9 billion by a consortium of ten French and British companies, the Channel Tunnel is the most ambitious of several major European transport infrastructure projects (see **trans-European networks**). These include a bridge across the Straits of Messina, a bridge-and-tunnel scheme across the Great Belt (the sea channel between Sealand and Jutland in Denmark), and a bridge between Denmark and Sweden. The Channel Tunnel is the world's second longest railway tunnel, after the 53.85-kilometre Seikan tunnel between the islands of Honshu and Hokkaido in Japan, bored through solid rock at a depth twice as great.

Charlemagne Prize

The Charlemagne Prize (Karlspreis), awarded annually by an independent committee composed of citizens of Aachen, is intended to honour those who have made an outstanding contribution to European unification. First awarded in 1950 to **Richard Coudenhove-Kalergi**, the prize has since been awarded to **Alcide de Gasperi** (1952), **Jean Monnet** (1953), **Konrad Adenauer** (1954), **Winston Churchill** (1955), **Paul-Henri Spaak** (1957), **Robert Schuman** (1958), General George Marshall (1959; see **Marshall Plan**), **Walter Hallstein** (1961), **Edward Heath** (1963), the **European Commission** (1969), **Roy Jenkins** (1972), Leo Tindemans (1976; see **Tindemans Report**), King Juan Carlos of Spain (1982), Henry Kissinger (1987), **François Mitterrand** and **Helmut Kohl** (jointly in 1988), **Jacques Delors** (1992), Tony Blair (1999), and many others. The prizewinner's medal shows Charlemagne (crowned in Aachen in 800) seated on his throne.

Charter of Fundamental Rights

At the meeting of the **European Council** in Cologne in June 1999 it was decided that 'at the present stage of development of the European Union, the fundamental rights applicable at Union level should be consolidated in a Charter and thereby made more evident'. The scope of the Charter was set out in more detail in a supplementary decision: 'this Charter should contain the fundamental rights and freedoms as well as basic procedural rights guaranteed by the European Convention for the Protection of Human Rights and Fundamental Freedoms (the **European Convention on Human Rights** (ECHR); see also **human rights**) and derived from the constitutional traditions common to the Member States, as general principles of Community law. The Charter should also include the fundamental rights that pertain only to the Union's citizens. In drawing up such a Charter account should furthermore be taken of economic and social rights as contained in the **European Social Charter** and the Community Charter on the Fundamental Social Rights of Workers'. The exact status of the Charter was left undecided, the European Council adding only that at some future date consideration would be given to 'whether, and, if so, how the Charter should be integrated into the treaties'. The background to this proposal was the strong feeling that if the European Union was to progress beyond being merely an essentially economic construct with political aspirations it was in need of a moral base. The possibility of becoming a signatory to the ECHR – and thereby incorporating its provisions into the *acquis communautaire* – had been ruled out by the **Court of Justice** (Opinion 2/94). Accordingly, the only alternative was for the Union to draw up a Charter of its own.

At its meeting in Tampere in October 1999 the European Council entrusted the drafting of the Charter to a Convention composed of:

- 15 representatives of the members of the European Council;
- 16 members of the **European Parliament** (MEPs);
- 30 members of **national parliaments**;
- a member of the **European Commission** representing the President of the Commission.

The Convention met for the first time in December 1999. The chairman was Roman Herzog, the former President of Germany. A small drafting committee composed of representatives of the constituent elements of the Convention (MEPs, national parliamentarians, the Council, the Commission) prepared texts for submission to the Convention. The Charter was completed in draft in September 2000, adopted at the meeting of the European Council in Nice in December 2000 and thereafter proclaimed by the European Parliament, the Commission, and the **Council of Ministers**. In a 'Declaration on the Future of the Union' annexed to the **Treaty of Nice** the member states committed themselves to considering the status of the Charter in the course of the **Intergovernmental Conference** (IGC) due to begin in 2004.

The Charter contains 54 Articles divided into seven chapters: Dignity, Freedoms, Equality, Solidarity, Citizens' Rights, Justice, and General Provisions. The rights contained in the Charter fall into three broad categories. First are the basic universal rights, such as the right to life, freedom from arbitrary detention, and so on, as set out in the ECHR and in the constitutions of most member states. Second are the civil and political rights associated with **citizenship** of the European Union. Third, and most controversial as far as differences between member states are concerned, are the economic and social rights pertaining to employment, health care, living standards, working conditions and other areas covered by the European Social Charter and the Charter on the Fundamental Social Rights of Workers. On the one hand, there are member states – such as the United Kingdom – in which there is little or no formal recognition of such rights and, on the other, member states in which such rights are not only recognized but guaranteed.

Apart from disagreements, major or minor, within the Convention on the substance or formulation of particular rights, certain differences of approach became evident in the Convention's proceedings. First, there were those who interpreted the Convention's mandate as exclusively one of consolidation, i.e. the Charter was not to break new ground but assemble and codify existing rights. Others regarded the drawing up of the Charter as an opportunity to move the European Union forward in an area not systematically touched on in the Treaties of Rome, Maastricht, Amsterdam and the Charter itself as an essential component of a 'European Constitution'. Second, there was the question of whether the Charter should be declaratory only or whether it should possess the force of law. Third, should it be agreed to make the rights contained in the Charter enforceable at law, what should be the machinery for enforcement? Should it be through national courts, with or without an ultimate right of appeal to the European Court of Justice in Luxembourg? Or should enforcement – on the model of the ECHR – ultimately be entrusted to a body specially set up for the purpose? Fourth, what should be the relation between the Charter and the Treaties? Should it eventually be incorporated into the Treaties, or should it remain separate, even though this would mean that certain rights were in the Treaties (such as the right of free movement) and others – perhaps more fundamental – were not? Fifth, exactly who is bound to respect the rights in the Charter? The Union itself cannot be bound, since unlike the European Community, it does not possess **legal personality**; and even if a way were found of binding the Union's institutions, this might still not cover areas in which decision-making is largely intergovernmental, such as the **Common Foreign and Security Policy** and cooperation in the field of **Justice and Home Affairs**. Finally, given that all the Union's member states and all the applicant states are signatories to the ECHR, there was thought by some to be a risk of confusion, duplication of effort, and conflicting jurisdiction arising from the existence of a Charter.

Some of these arguments remained unresolved, as is evident from the final text of the Charter (published as a brochure by the European Parliament in October 2000). The Charter goes beyond the ECHR, not least because it addresses problems which have only arisen relatively recently (human cloning, for example (Article 3.2) or data protection (Article 8)). However, in some of these areas the absoluteness of the right in question is qualified by the addition of the phrase 'in accordance with the national laws governing the exercise of this right' (for an example, see Article 10.2 on conscientious objection). In other cases, the right is not proclaimed but merely 'recognized' (see Article 25 on the rights of the elderly). It may be questioned whether some of the rights are really fundamental, such as 'the right of access to a free placement service' (Article 29), and there are other inclusions of questionable relevance to a Charter of Fundamental Rights, such as the observation that 'political parties at Union level contribute to expressing the political will of the citizens of the Union' (Article 12.2).

At present, the Charter does not possess the force of law. However, as solemnly proclaimed by the institutions of the Union, it is of political significance, and is already a point of reference for legislative action and for decisions of the Court of Justice. Clearly, the Charter will assume the role currently played by the ECHR in Article 6 of the Maastricht Treaty, which obliges the Union to respect fundamental rights. Formally, the Charter is addressed 'to the institutions and bodies of the Union ... and to the Member States only when they are implementing Union law' (Article 51). The same Article asserts that the Charter 'does not establish any new power or task for the Community or the Union, or modify powers and tasks defined by the Treaties'.

Unlike the ECHR, the Charter establishes no machinery for enforcement. Chapter VI, 'Justice', contains only generalities about the legal process (presumption of innocence, the right to a fair trial, and so on). Some of the Charter's provisions would be certain to give rise to disputes were they ever to be given the force of law (such as the unqualified right to Council, Commission, and European Parliament documents (Article 42); see **transparency**) or the right not to be 'removed, expelled or extradited to a State where there is a serious risk [of facing] the death penalty, torture or other inhuman or degrading treatment or punishment' (Article 19.2)). The legal uncertainty to which the existence of a legally binding Charter would give rise is minimized by Article 52, which says that where rights in the Charter correspond to those in the ECHR the two should be regarded as identical in meaning and scope. However, the vagueness with which some of the Articles are worded must vitiate their usefulness in legal proceedings.

Charter of Paris

The signing of the Charter of Paris for a New Europe on 21 November 1990 by the states participating in the **Conference on Security and Cooperation in Europe** (CSCE) was widely regarded as the end of the Cold War. Made possible by the collapse of Soviet hegemony in central and eastern Europe, the Charter reiterated the ideas and principles set out in the **Helsinki Final Act** and marked the transition of the CSCE from a negotiating process to a permanent institution. The signatory states declared that 'henceforth our relations will be founded on respect and cooperation'.

In the section headed 'New structures and institutions of the CSCE process', the Charter noted the need for 'a new quality of political dialogue and cooperation and thus development of the structures of the CSCE'. The structures, set out in detail in a supplementary document, included a Council composed of Foreign Ministers, a Committee of Senior Officials, a small permanent secretariat based in Prague, an Office for Free Elections (since renamed) in Warsaw, a Conflict Prevention Centre in Vienna, and a CSCE parliamentary assembly. The CSCE Assembly met for the first time in

Budapest in July 1992 and has a small secretariat in Copenhagen. See **Organization for Security and Cooperation in Europe** (OSCE).

Christian Democracy

Christian Democracy, the largest and most successful family of centre and centre-right political parties in postwar Europe, can trace its intellectual antecedents back to the nineteenth century. Today's Christian Democrat (CD) parties are descended from those which sided with the Church in the disputes between Church and State, and which took the lead in opposing the essentially secular Socialist parties based upon universal suffrage.

By far the most influential CD parties are the Christian Democratic Union (CDU) of Germany and its Bavarian sister-party, the Christian Social Union, but CD parties are also well established in the **Benelux** countries. Until its recent collapse, the Italian CD party was the second largest in Europe, and had been in power, alone or in various coalitions, since the war. By contrast, CD parties have always been weak in Scandinavia. In France, the *Mouvement Républicain Populaire* (of which **Robert Schuman** was a prominent member) was overshadowed by parties made up of followers of **Charles de Gaulle**. In Spain and Portugal the legacy of the Franco and Salazar dictatorships was to secularize politics, thus ruling out explicitly confessional parties, although in both countries the CD have close allies. In Ireland the CDs are represented by Fine Gael, in Greece by New Democracy, and in Austria by the Austrian People's Party.

In the **European Parliament** the CDs and their allies form the Group of the European People's Party (EPP; see **transnational political parties**), since 1999 the largest of the **political groups**. From 1953 until 1975 the CDs had been by far the largest group in the Parliament, but the arrival of British Labour parliamentarians finally gave the advantage to the Socialists. Many newly emergent parties in central and eastern Europe claim a kinship with the EPP. The Christian Democratic International links European CD parties with CD parties in other countries, mainly in Central and South America.

Christian Democrats, including **Konrad Adenauer** and **Alcide de Gasperi** as well as Schuman, were among the most active early supporters of European integration. Unlike the Socialists, the CD parties voted solidly in favour of the **Treaty of Paris** and the **Treaty of Rome** when they were submitted to **national parliaments** in the 1950s. The first president of the **European Commission** was a German CD, **Walter Hallstein**. Other prominent CDs include former Italian Foreign Minister, Prime Minister and President of the European Parliament, Emilio Colombo (see **Genscher–Colombo Plan**), Leo Tindemans (see **Tindemans Report**), and the former President of the Commission **Jacques Santer**.

All CD parties lay emphasis in their policy pronouncements on the role of people in society, and on the need for the free market to be tempered by social justice. Many have strong links with Christian trade unions and the Roman Catholic Church. On institutional questions CDs are federalists almost without exception. They are supporters of the Atlantic Alliance. Some CD parties take their confessional basis very seriously, and this leads them for example to condemn abortion and to oppose most forms of genetic engineering.

The problem for the CDs in recent years has been the fact that although CD parties are well established in most member states of the Union, the Union was set to expand northwards and eastwards into countries lacking any CD tradition – a problem that the Socialists did not have to face. This meant either a compromise with orthodox CD principles in the search for new allies or a diminished standing in an enlarged Union. The prospect of an alliance with the British and Danish Conservatives in the European Parliament brought the issue to a head: and with some misgivings the CDs opted for compromise. Within a few years, the EPP will have a majority of parties that are not, strictly speaking, CD parties in terms of their origin, history or source of inspiration. The success in recent years of right-wing parties has allowed the CDs to retain their self-image as the parties of the centre, but once they no longer have opponents on their right they may find it increasingly difficult to find a position to occupy that distinguishes them from moderate Socialists.

Although there is a very small CD party in the United Kingdom, it is not affiliated to the EPP. Some commentators have suggested that had Christian Democracy ever taken root in the United Kingdom, it would have been among moderate members of the Labour Party. It was Labour's postwar Chancellor, Sir Stafford Cripps, who wrote *Towards Christian Democracy* (1945).

R.E.M. Irving, *The Christian Democratic Parties of Western Europe* (Edinburgh, 1979), is useful as background. Michael Burgess, 'Political Catholicism, European unity and the rise of Christian Democracy' is a revealing essay (see M. L. Smith and P.M.R. Stirk, *Making the New Europe*, 1990). Two very valuable recent studies are David Hanley, *Christian Democracy in Europe: a Comparative Perspective* (1994) and Emiel Lamberts (ed.), *Christian Democracy in the European Union* (Leuven, 1997).

Churchill, Winston (1874–1965)

Winston Churchill's reputation as one of the pioneers of postwar European integration rests primarily on his **Zürich speech** of 1946 (see also **United States of Europe**), but Churchill's belief that the future of western Europe was bound up with closer integration had been expressed three years earlier in his 'morning thoughts' (Michael Charlton, *The Price of Victory*, 1983). Churchill was one of the first political figures to express support for what he called 'the United States of Europe', in an article in the New York *Saturday Evening Post* of 15 February 1930, since in his view the **League of Nations** needed the support of large regional groupings. After the war Churchill devoted several major speeches to the theme of a united Europe, of which one of the best-known was delivered at the 1948 **Congress of Europe** in The Hague and in which he called for a 'European Assembly' as 'the voice of United Europe' (see also **European Army**). However, on being returned to power as Prime Minister in 1951 Churchill did not materially alter the European policies of the previous Labour government, notably their rejection of the **Schuman Plan**.

This apparent contradiction may be explained by Churchill's ambivalent attitude to British participation in moves towards European unity and his belief that the United Kingdom's first responsibility was to the British Empire. In his *Saturday Evening Post* article Churchill said:

The attitude of Great Britain toward unification or 'federal links' would, in the first instance, be determined by her dominant conception of a United British Empire. Every step that tends to make Europe more prosperous and more peaceful is conducive to British interests ... We have our own dream and our own task. We are with Europe but not of it. We are linked, but not comprised. We are interested and associated, but not absorbed.

In Zürich 16 years later he referred to Great Britain only as 'the friend and sponsor of the new Europe', but in a speech in the Albert Hall on 14 May 1948 (a week after the Congress in The Hague) he said that 'if Europe united is to be a living force, Britain will have to play her full part as a member of the European family'. Earlier that year he had said that 'this European policy of unity can perfectly well be reconciled with and adjusted to our obligations to the Commonwealth and Empire of which we are the heart and centre' (House of Commons, 23 January 1948). However, as presented in Martin Gilbert's biography, the balance of the evidence seems to be that towards the end of his life Churchill did not favour British membership of the **European Economic Community** (EEC) when the question arose in the 1960s.

Churchill's view of the United Kingdom's world role was at the point of overlap between three interlocking circles: the Commonwealth, the Atlantic Alliance and Europe. What he would have thought of the supranational institutions on which the European Union is founded must remain a matter for speculation (although some idea may be gained from his view of the Schuman Plan; see **European Coal and Steel Community**). With regard to **sovereignty**, he admitted in The Hague that European unity required 'some sacrifice or merger of national sovereignty', but he added that 'it is also possible ... to regard it as the gradual assumption by all the nations concerned of that larger sovereignty which can alone protect their diverse and distinctive customs and characteristics and their national traditions'.

Churchill's active career was exceptionally long and eventful. His views certainly changed over time (as indeed did the United Kingdom's circumstances) and perhaps at no point were fully thought through, but the fact that he lent his enormous prestige to the cause of European unity in the decade after the war was of cardinal importance.

Churchill's 1930 article 'The United States of Europe' is in his *Collected Essays* (ed. Michael Wolff, 1986). His speeches are in his *Collected Speeches* (ed. Robert Rhodes James, 1981). For a contrary view of Churchill as a European prophet, see Lord Beloff, 'Churchill and Europe', in Robert Blake and William Roger Louis, *Churchill* (Oxford, 1993).

Citizens' Europe
See **People's Europe**.

Citizenship

The **Maastricht Treaty** amended the **Treaty of Rome** to create citizenship of the European Union. Under Article 17 EC, 'every person holding the nationality of a Member State shall be a citizen of the Union' (the **Treaty of Amsterdam** added 'Citizenship of the Union shall complement and not replace national citizenship'). Succeeding Articles set out the rights appertaining to citizenship: 'to move and reside freely within the territory of the Member States' (Article 18); to vote and stand for election in municipal and European elections in the member state in which he or she resides (Article 19); to receive protection from diplomatic and consular authorities of any member state in any country in which the member state of which he or she is a national is not represented (Article 20); to petition the **European Parliament** and refer matters to the **Ombudsman** (Article 21). Under Article 22 these rights, now also contained in the **Charter of Fundamental Rights**, may be strengthened or supplemented by the **Council of Ministers**, acting unanimously on a proposal from the **European Commission** and after consulting the European Parliament under the **co-decision procedure**, although the Council is still required to act by unanimity.

In a **Declaration** annexed to the Treaty it is specified that 'the question whether an individual possesses the nationality of a Member State shall be settled solely by reference to the national law of the Member State concerned'. States may forward to the Council **presidency** details of those who are to be considered their nationals for the purpose of establishing their claim to citizenship of the Union. This is particularly important for the United Kingdom, which in the British Nationality Act 1981 has defined several distinct categories of British national; of these, only British citizens, British subjects with the right of abode and those who are British Dependent Territories citizens by virtue of a connection with Gibraltar are entitled to citizenship of the Union.

Many opponents of the Maastricht Treaty suggested that the creation of Union citizenship, an initiative of the Spanish government, was one more move in the direction of a European superstate. Although it is true that the idea of citizenship is normally associated with a state (but not exclusively: we may speak of 'Commonwealth citizens'), the Declaration noted above specifically leaves entitlement to citizenship in the hands of member states. In fact, citizenship of the Union is no more than a very modest enhancement of the rights nationals of member states already enjoy, and the most important of them, the right to move and reside freely anywhere in the Union, is quite significantly restricted by various provisions designed to prevent people of inadequate means becoming a 'burden' on the social security system of the member state where they choose to reside. It will be noted too that voting in national elections anywhere in the Union is not a generalized right. All proposals to this effect meet with objections from member states with large numbers of potential voters possessing the nationality of another member state (for example, Luxembourg has many Portuguese). Citizenship is to be distinguished from the measures taken in connection with a **People's Europe**, although several of these, such as the **European passport**, are intended to give citizens of the member states a livelier sense of their new status as citizens of the Union. See K. Edes and B. Giesen (eds), *European Citizenship between National Legacies and Postnational Projects* (Oxford, 2001).

Cockfield White Paper

In March 1985 the **European Council** decided to give priority to the creation of 'a single large market by 1992', and called upon the **European Commission** to draw up 'a detailed programme with a specific timetable before its next meeting'. The task fell to Lord Cockfield, the newly appointed Commissioner responsible for trade matters within the Community (the so-called '**internal market**'). The White Paper he produced for the June 1985 meeting of the European Council in Milan identified some 300 legislative measures that would be needed to establish the **Single Market**. These measures were concerned with three kinds of barrier to trade: physical barriers (frontier controls), technical barriers (such as different product standards) and fiscal barriers (different rates of excise duty and value-added tax). The list of measures was accompanied by a timetable specifying deadlines both for Commission draft proposals and for the Council's final decisions. The Milan meeting of the European Council endorsed the White Paper, the ambitiousness of which was a powerful influence on the negotiations that led to the **Single European Act** (SEA; see also **Cecchini Report, non-Europe**).

Lord Cockfield was never in any doubt about the political importance of the Single Market. In the conclusion of his White Paper he wrote:

Europe stands at the crossroads. We either go ahead – with resolution and determination – or we drop back into mediocrity. We can now either resolve to complete the integration of the economies of Europe; or, through a lack of political will to face the immense problems involved, we can simply allow Europe to develop into no more than a free trade area.

His own account of the Single Market programme is to be found in his essay 'The real significance of 1992' in Colin Crouch and David Marquand (eds), *The Politics of 1992* (1990) and in Cockfield, *The European Union: Creating the Single Market* (Oxford, 1994).

Co-decision procedure

'Co-decision' is a procedure introduced by the **Maastricht Treaty** to reinforce the role of the **European Parliament** in the legislative process. It is set out in Article 251 of the **Treaty of Rome**. The main difference between the co-decision procedure and the **cooperation procedure** is that the former allows the Parliament to veto by an absolute majority of its total membership a legislative measure upon which agreement cannot be reached with the **Council of Ministers**.

The co-decision procedure was modelled on a procedure that already existed in relation to the **Budget** of the European Union, under which the Parliament and the Council, as the 'joint budgetary authority', endeavour to reach agreement in a **conciliation** committee. In the absence of such an agreement the Parliament can, as a last resort and by an absolute majority, reject the Budget.

One important side-effect of the co-decision procedure is that it weakens the power of the **European Commission**. By negotiating in the conciliation committee, the Council and the European Parliament can largely exclude the Commission.

The key areas in the Treaty of Rome to which the co-decision procedure was first applied were the free movement of workers (Article 40 EC), **freedom of establishment** (Article 44), **Single Market** measures (Articles 94 and 95), education (Article 149), culture (Article 151), health and consumer protection (Articles 152 and 153), **trans-European networks** (Article 156) and the environmental action programmes (Article 175.3).

The **Treaty of Amsterdam** extended co-decision so that it is now the normal mode of Council–Parliament collaboration in the legislative field. The cooperation procedure has been retained only in respect of **Economic and Monetary Union** (EMU). The co-decision procedure has been simplified. If the Parliament does not amend the Commission's proposal, or if the Council accepts the Parliament's amendments, the measure can be adopted without the need for a second reading. If neither is the case, the Council draws up a common position, which the Parliament can approve, reject by an absolute majority of its members, or amend by the same majority. In the event of the Council not accepting the Parliament's amendments, the conciliation committee is convened to resolve the differences, but the measure can only be adopted with the agreement of both sides. The Council may on the other hand accept the amendments, by **qualified majority voting** (QMV) in the event of a positive opinion from the Commission or by unanimity if the Commission is opposed. The key areas to which the co-decision procedure has been extended since the Treaty of Amsterdam entered into force are:

- rules to prohibit **discrimination on grounds of nationality** (Article 12);
- **social policy** measures formerly contained in the Social Protocol, except those subject to unanimity in the Council (Article 137);
- most of the measures taken under the **environment policy** (Article 175).

Co-decision is also used with respect to the following provisions newly added by the Treaty of Amsterdam:

- incentive measures for **employment** (Article 129);
- **equal treatment** measures (Article 141);
- various **public health** measures (Article 152);
- general principles of **transparency** (Article 255);
- combating **fraud** (Article 280);
- statistics (see **Eurostat**: Article 285);
- establishment of an independent advisory authority on data protection (Article 286).

The provisions of the Treaty of Amsterdam, supplemented by those in the **Treaty of Nice**, were generally reckoned to be a substantial reinforcement of the Parliament's powers. There is much recondite information in Roger M. Scully, 'The European Parliament and the co-decision procedure: a reassessment', *Journal of Legislative Studies*, Vol. 3, no. 3, Autumn 1997 (see also in the same issue an opposing view by George Tsebelis and Geoffrey Garrett).

Cohesion

The word 'cohesion' was introduced into the **Treaty of Rome** by the 1986 **Single European Act** (SEA), which added a new Title V on 'economic and social cohesion' (now Articles 158 to 162). This was done on the insistence of the poorer member states, which feared that the completion of the **Single Market** would further strengthen the position of the more prosperous states. 'Cohesion' was the term used to encompass the notions of solidarity and harmonious economic development. The basic text was agreed at a meeting of the **European Council** in Luxembourg in December 1985. See Liesbet Hooghe (ed.), *Cohesion Policy and European Integration* (Oxford, 1996).

Cohesion Fund

The original text on **cohesion** in the **Treaty of Rome** did little more than reiterate the role of the **structural funds** and provide for better coordination between them. This did not satisfy the poorer states, because although by 1986 several of them were benefiting from the **Integrated Mediterranean Programmes** (IMPs), these programmes were due to end in 1992. In Maastricht in December 1991, agreement was reached on a further change to the Treaty requiring the **Council of Ministers** to establish a Cohesion Fund by December 1993. The purpose of the Fund is 'to provide a financial contribution to projects in the fields of environment and **trans-European networks** in the area of transport infrastructure' (Article 161 EC). A protocol on economic and social cohesion annexed to the **Maastricht Treaty** restricted access to the Cohesion Fund to member states with a per capita gross domestic product (GDP) of less than 90 per cent of the Union average (i.e., to Greece, Ireland, Portugal and Spain) and obliged them to pursue economic policies tending towards **convergence**. These conditions were further refined at the Edinburgh meeting of the European Council in December 1992 (see **Edinburgh Growth Initiative**). Expenditure from the Cohesion Fund amounted to €16.7 billion over the period 1993–99. Appropriations from the **Budget** for the Fund amount to €18 billion over the period 2000–6. A Cohesion Report is published annually. A review of beneficiaries' eligibility was undertaken in 2003.

College of Europe

Founded in 1949 in Bruges, Belgium, on the basis of a resolution adopted by the European Cultural Conference (see **European Cultural Centre**), the College of Europe offers postgraduate courses in various disciplines relevant to European integration. It has about 375 students of about 40 nationalities; the languages of instruction are English and French. It has an additional site at Natolin, near Warsaw. The lecture to mark the opening of the College's academic year is normally delivered by a well-known European figure, the most celebrated recent example being Margaret Thatcher's **Bruges speech** of September 1988. Although the College is in part financed by a contribution from the **Budget** of the European Union, it is not a Union body (see also

European Institute of Public Administration, European University Institute).

COMECON

COMECON, or CMEA (the Council for Mutual Economic Assistance), was established in January 1949 to promote and facilitate all forms of economic cooperation between the Communist states of central and eastern Europe. Founder members were the USSR, Bulgaria, Czechoslovakia, Hungary, Poland and Romania, countries that had been prevented by Stalin from taking part in the **Marshall Plan** and from joining the **Organization for European Economic Cooperation** (OEEC). Membership was later extended to Albania (1949–61) and the German Democratic Republic (1950), and to non-European Communist states: Mongolia (1962), Cuba (1972) and Vietnam (1978). Under Article 4 of the COMECON Charter adopted in 1959, all decisions had to be unanimous, but in fact the organization was overwhelmingly dominated by the USSR. The headquarters of COMECON were in Moscow.

The first formal contacts between COMECON and the European Community took place in 1976, at a time when the USSR was still barely prepared to recognize the Community and when the Community disputed COMECON's right to negotiate on behalf of its member states. Unsurprisingly, these contacts led to no concrete result and were broken off after the USSR's invasion of Afghanistan in 1980. Resumed six years later, the negotiations resulted in a mutual recognition agreement in 1988, by which time the Community had concluded commercial agreements (in most cases limited to specific sectors) with Bulgaria, Czechoslovakia, Hungary, Poland and Romania. Within a year or so of the 1988 agreements the Community had wide-ranging commercial agreements with all European COMECON states except the German Democratic Republic (whose trade with the Community was covered by special arrangements: see **German reunification**), including the USSR.

The collapse of the Soviet empire in central and eastern Europe in 1989–90 completely transformed trading patterns between COMECON states and led to the strongest of the COMECON economies, that of the German Democratic Republic, becoming part of the European Community. In June 1991 the remaining members of COMECON resolved to wind up the organization; this was formally accomplished in September 1991. Since then, almost all the European states formerly belonging to COMECON have applied to join the European Union and **Europe Agreements** have been concluded with Hungary, Poland, the Czech Republic, Slovakia, Bulgaria, Romania and the Baltic states.

Comité Européen de Normalisation (CEN)

Set up in 1961, CEN is a body concerned with laying down technical specifications for goods and services in all fields except electrical goods (for which the equivalent body is CENELEC, set up in 1973). Nineteen countries and fourteen affiliates take part in CEN and CENELEC, which are financed by membership fees and grants from the **European Commission** and the **European Free Trade Association**. CEN and CENELEC have taken over much of the detailed work of **harmonization** since the adoption in 1985 of the 'new approach'. CEN is known in English as the European Committee for Standardization.

Comitology

The word 'comitology' is used to denote the complex of issues that centre upon the various types of committee which oversee the implementation of **EU law**. The role of these committees has given rise to disputes with a direct bearing on the balance of power between national authorities and institutions of the European Union, notably the **European Commission** and the **European Parliament**. Not yet fully assimilated into English, 'comitology' is a translation of the French *comitologie*. It was first used in C. Northcote Parkinson's *Parkinson's Law* (1958) and defined in his *In-laws and Outlaws* (1962) as the study of committees and how they operate ('the latest of the biological sciences').

Article 211 of the **Treaty of Rome** states that, in addition to the powers of decision it enjoys as of right, the European Commission exercises 'the powers conferred on it by the **Council [of Ministers]** for the implementation of the rules laid down by the latter' (i.e., Community law). Both types of Commission power are subject to the supervision of various committees (see below), all of them composed of national experts with a Commission official in the chair. Their subject matter is for the most part highly technical: for example, seed types, food additives, the thickness of safety glass. However, many committees deliberate on matters of very great concern to the interested parties as well as to national governments, and their essentially secretive mode of operation has prompted fears about the extent to which they are subject to adequate democratic control.

It was recognized at the time of the negotiations that led to the **Single European Act** (SEA) that the abundance of technical legislation made necessary by the **Single Market** programme would in turn lead to a further proliferation of committees. Accordingly, the opportunity was taken to clear the undergrowth by classifying the various types of committee and codifying their powers. The Commission produced a proposal that the Council adopted in 1987 in a radically modified form, against the wishes of the Commission and the European Parliament, in a fashion inconsistent (so it was alleged) with member states' undertakings at the time of the SEA. The Parliament sought to have the Council's decision annulled by the **Court of Justice**, but the action was rejected as inadmissible.

In the 1987 decision the three basic types of committee were laid down as follows:

1 An advisory committee, which is empowered to deliver **Opinions** on Commission proposals; the Commission is required only to 'take utmost account' of such Opinions (Procedure I).
2 A management committee, which similarly delivers Opinions on Commission proposals; in this case the Commission can be forced to incorporate the committee's Opinion by the Council acting by **qualified majority**. If the Committee fails to deliver an Opinion, the Commission proposal takes immediate effect (Procedure II). Management committees are most commonly used in connection with the detailed implementation of the **Common Agricultural Policy** (CAP).
3 A regulatory committee is similar to a management committee, except that in the event of the rejection of a Commission proposal or the failure to deliver an Opinion the matter is referred to the Council. Under this procedure (III), the Council may reject the proposal by simple majority within three months.

The choice of which type of committee is responsible for overseeing the implementation of a piece of legislation is specified in the legislation itself, to which the Parliament may propose amendments. In a report to the European Parliament in 1989 the Commission professed itself to be content with the system, on the grounds that it was normally able to enlist the support of the national experts who sit on the various committees and in the light of the fact that reference to Council (with the possibility of a veto) under Procedure III above was very rare indeed.

The European Parliament is less content, regarding the committee system as part of the **democratic deficit**. Without necessarily challenging the need for such committees or altering the basic typology, the Parliament has tended to favour opening up committee proceedings or laying upon committees the obligation to keep the Parliament's own committees in touch with their deliberations and decisions. The Commission is understandably ambivalent about these ideas, since it could not necessarily count upon the Parliament as an ally.

There is a wealth of descriptive and statistical detail in Rhys Dogan, 'Comitology: little procedures with big implications', *West European Politics*, Vol. 20, no. 3, July 1997.

Commission
See **European Commission**.

Committee of Inquiry

The right to set up temporary Committees of Inquiry was given to the **European Parliament** in the **Maastricht Treaty** and is set out in Article 193 of the **Treaty of Rome**. Although the Parliament was already making use of such committees, before this new provision came into effect (November 1993) their authority derived solely from Rule 136 (now 151) of the Parliament's internal rules of procedure. A Committee of Inquiry may be set up at the request of one-quarter of the Parliament's total membership 'to investigate, without prejudice to the powers conferred by this Treaty on other institutions or bodies, alleged contraventions or maladministration in the implementation of Community law' (compare the powers of the **Ombudsman**). It may not investigate matters which are *sub judice*. The sensitive question of the Committee's access to documents and to testimony from officials was settled in an **interinstitutional agreement** of 19 April 1995 (*Official Journal*, L113). A Committee of Inquiry is entitled to receive from the authorities of the member states and from European Union institutions 'the documents necessary for the performance of its duties', except for those withheld 'by reasons of secrecy or public or national security'. On a 'reasoned request', national authorities and European Union institutions 'shall designate the official or servant whom they authorize to appear' before the committee: these witnesses 'shall speak on behalf of and as instructed by their governments or institutions', and are bound by considerations of secrecy and public or national security. Normally a Committee of Inquiry must meet in public and complete its work within a year (although extensions up to a maximum of six months are allowed) by submitting a report to a full session of Parliament.

It will be noted that a Committee of Inquiry does not have the power to subpoena *particular* witnesses. Great offence was caused in September 1996 when the British Minister of Agriculture refused to appear before the committee examining the BSE affair. See Michael Shackleton, 'The European Parliament's new committees of inquiry: tiger or paper tiger?', *Journal of Common Market Studies*, Vol. 36, no. 1, March 1998.

Committee of the Regions

The **Maastricht Treaty** established a new European Union body, the Committee of the Regions (Article 263 EC). This was done at the instigation of Germany and Spain, both countries with a strong regional element in their constitutional arrangements. The Committee, composed of 222 'representatives of regional and local bodies', has 'advisory status'. Since July 1994 it has had its own secretary-general and now has its own secretariat. Members of the Committee of the Regions and their substitutes are appointed for a four-year term by the **Council of Ministers** on proposals from the member states. Although this is not required by the Treaty, nearly all members of the Committee hold elective office at regional or local level in their countries of origin (see also **regionalism**). Members sit in alphabetical order but have formed **political groups**. Much of the work is done in the six committees.

Consultation of the Committee of the Regions is specifically required by the Treaty only in respect of economic and social **cohesion, Trans-European Networks** (TENs), telecommunications, energy policy, education, culture, employment, the environment, vocational training, and transport. However, under Article 265 EC, the Council, the **European Commission**, or the **European Parliament** may consult the Committee, and the Committee itself may on its own initiative submit **Opinions** on matters affecting regional interests.

Common Agricultural Policy (CAP)

The CAP has been for many years the most important European policy in terms of the number of people directly affected, its share of the **Budget** and the extent of the powers transferred from national to European level. Its origins may be traced back to the original compact between France and West Germany when the **Treaty of Rome** was first being drafted by **the Six**: guaranteed markets for French agricultural products in exchange for wider markets for German manufactured goods.

The objectives of the CAP are set out in Article 33 EC: an increase in agricultural productivity by means of 'technical progress and ... the rational development of agricultural production', 'a fair standard of living for the agricultural community', stable markets, the 'availability of supplies', and 'reasonable prices' for consumers. Underpinning these objectives are three essential principles: the free movement of agricultural products within the member states, **Community preference** and financial solidarity in the sense that all member states must share in the costs arising from the CAP.

That agriculture should be subsidized was not in doubt, since in common with all other European countries the Six already supported their agricultural sectors in various ways. In seeking to establish the basis for a common system, the Six opted for support by means of price mechanisms rather than direct income support (a decision taken at the **Stresa Conference**), operated with the aid of European market organizations (usually known as regimes) for the various products (Article 34 EC). The first of such organizations, for cereals, pork, eggs and poultry meat, came into effect in 1962, several others following over the next four years.

Initially, the **European Commission** sought only to coordinate national agricultural policies. The first attempt at reform came with the **Mansholt Plan**, first published in 1968. The Plan sought to reduce the number of people employed in agriculture and to encourage the formation of larger, more efficient units of agricultural production. These reforms were to be effected through the 'guidance' section of the **European Agricultural Guidance and Guarantee Fund** (EAGGF, more commonly known by its French acronym, FEOGA) set up in 1962 and divided into two sections in 1964. Although eventually adopted in a less ambitious form, the Mansholt Plan set the pattern for the development of the CAP.

It is easy to understand why in the Treaty objectives of the CAP, drawn up at a time when food shortages in western Europe were still a vivid memory, such emphasis was laid on increases in agricultural productivity. However, by the early 1980s greater efficiency, backed by technical progress, was resulting in huge, unsaleable surpluses of certain products, at an enormous cost to the Budget. The taxpayer, it was said, was paying twice over, first through higher prices and second through subsidized storage or disposal of unwanted produce. Subsidized exports were doing damage to other countries' export markets, and notorious episodes like the sale of cut-price butter to the USSR further damaged the credibility of the CAP with the public.

In 1983 the Commission published proposals for fundamental reform, which were followed up two years later by a Green Paper. Basically, the Commission sought to bring supply and demand into balance, cut back on open-ended price support, compensate farmers for loss of income and introduce new ways ('stabilizers') of reducing production still further in certain problem sectors. However, it was not until February 1988 that the **European Council** was able to agree on a comprehensive package of reform measures, including an 'agricultural guideline' limiting the growth of CAP expenditure to 74 per cent of the growth in the Budget overall (see **future financing**).

The 1988 decisions were followed up by further measures affecting the CAP, such as the reform of the **structural funds**, the extension of **quotas**, the introduction of **set-aside**, measures to encourage early retirement from agriculture, and schemes to encourage farmers to use less intensive production techniques and to diversify away from products already in surplus. The needs of the rural economy are met by the LEADER + ('Liaison entre actions de développement de l'économie rurale', *Official Journal*, C180, 1 July 1994) and LEADER II programmes.

The reform process was taken a stage further with the publication of additional Commission papers in February 1991 and July 1991. These papers, put forward by Ray MacSharry, the Irish Commissioner responsible for the CAP, were the basis for another reform package agreed by the **Council of Ministers** at a 50-hour meeting in May 1992. The centrepiece was a move away from near-total reliance on price support towards direct income aids over the period 1993–6. This was accompanied by substantial reductions in guaranteed prices and the introduction of extremely complicated schemes to compensate farmers in the short term for loss of income.

The reforms have not altered the procedures under which the CAP is managed. The special Committee on Agriculture, an offshoot of COREPER (see also **national representations**), prepares meetings of the Council of Agriculture Ministers, with the aid of several other specialized committees. Each product covered by the CAP has its own **management committee**. The system of price support has many variations, but basically it requires the Commission to present annually a set of price proposals for the following marketing year. These proposals are discussed with the **European Parliament** (although expenditure in this sector is classified as **compulsory expenditure** under Article 272.9 EC) and eventually agreed by the Council of Ministers. If the price that can be obtained for a product within the Union falls below the agreed price, unsold produce may be purchased and taken into **intervention** and stored for future sale or disposal. If the produce can be sold outside the Union but only at a price below the agreed price, then the producer becomes entitled to an export refund to cover the difference. Intervention buying is by far the largest single item in the whole Budget. A further measure of protection is provided by levies on imported produce so that it enjoys no price advantage over what is produced within the Union. Alternatively, domestic producers may receive some form of production subsidy. Not all the products covered by CAP regimes benefit from both intervention and external protection. Overall, such regimes cover some 90 per cent of total agricultural production within the Union.

Within this very broad overall picture, all kinds of special schemes – for particular products, for particular types of farming, for particular regions, for small farms, etc. – have been introduced, some only of short duration, many of them prompted less by strictly agricultural considerations than by the requirements of social, regional or environmental policy or by those emanating from international pressure.

The CAP was further complicated by the agrimonetary system, the so-called 'green currencies'. The breakdown in 1969 of the Bretton Woods international monetary system resulted in a degree of price instability that was in conflict with the requirement in Article 39 EC for stable markets (see above). Accordingly, a method for converting CAP prices into the national currencies in which farmers are actually paid ('green rates') was introduced, together with monetary compensatory amounts (MCAs) to be paid or levied on member states' trade in agricultural products to prevent any exploitation of the difference between market rates and green rates. Initially introduced on a temporary basis, the agrimonetary system was a central feature of the CAP for over 20 years, and was eventually radically modified as part of the 1992 reforms. The new system, which applied to the bulk of CAP expenditure (including the **Common Fisheries Policy**), eliminated MCAs as incompatible with the **Single Market** and brought green rates and market rates more closely into line pending the accomplishment of **Economic and Monetary Union** (EMU) and payments to farmers in **euros**.

This outline of the mechanisms that govern the CAP illustrates the extent to which, since its inception, it has allowed ample scope for **fraud**. The system is so complex that fair and equal enforcement of the rules governing payments from the CAP – a matter largely in the hands of member states' authorities – is extremely difficult. Efforts to make the system simpler have met with only limited success.

The CAP has long been an irritant in international trade relations. First, Commonwealth countries such as Australia and New Zealand resented the loss of British markets as a consequence of the United Kingdom's accession to the Community in 1973, a loss only partially compensated for by special arrangements for butter and lamb. More recently, Australia and New Zealand became leading members of the Cairns Group of countries fiercely critical of the Community's stance on agricultural matters in GATT. The United States too had some well-publicized arguments with the Community over such matters as subsidies for oilseed production, and these were not resolved until the so-called 'Washington Accord' of November 1992 (almost two years after the Uruguay Round of international trade negotiations had been due to end). More generally, the CAP and the possibility that its principles and mechanisms might be extended to other sectors have contributed to the fear of a **Fortress Europe**. The fact remains that in spite of the protection afforded under the CAP and the degree of self-sufficiency, the Union is by far the world's largest importer of agricultural products.

Throughout its 30-year history the CAP has attracted criticism not only as the cuckoo in the budgetary nest but also as a uniquely wasteful, bureaucratic way of supporting agriculture, managed on the basis of marathon negotiating sessions in Brussels among ministers over whom agricultural lobbies exercise an unhealthy sway. The CAP, it is said, shields farmers from market disciplines, prevents food from being bought on the 'world market' and cuts across other policies. This is particularly true in the United Kingdom, with its small and relatively efficient agricultural sector (the result of an agricultural revolution two centuries ago) and a public used to 'cheap food' for several generations by virtue of the Empire and Commonwealth connection. The

United Kingdom has a particular grievance in that low receipts from agricultural spending were one of the causes of the **British Budget problem**. The CAP's defenders point to it as the 'cornerstone' of European integration and as the policy by which the member states have achieved self-sufficiency in most temperate products, relatively stable prices and a growth in farm incomes at a time when expenditure on food (as a percentage of consumer expenditure overall) is steadily falling throughout the industrialized world. Food prices have risen more slowly than prices generally and, in any case, decisions on prices taken under the CAP directly affect only the price paid to the producer: prices in the shops reflect other costs, such as processing, packaging, transport and retail margins. Some of the most dramatic rises have been in relation to products not covered by the CAP, such as coffee and tea. Moreover, the CAP has promoted and facilitated a shift away from employment on the land, which at any other period of European history would have been accompanied by extreme hardship and possibly violent revolution. In 1958 employment in agriculture within the Six was some 20 per cent of total employment. By 1990 it had fallen to 5.5 per cent (the average for the European Union overall is now 4.5 per cent, with a high of 17 per cent in Greece and a low of 1.6 per cent in the United Kingdom). The number of agricultural holdings is slowly falling (it was just under 7 million in 1997) and the number of large holdings is slowly increasing as a percentage of the total (8.6 per cent in 1997). There remain great differences between member states.

Together with agriculture itself, the CAP is going through a time of great uncertainty. Budgetary pressures will remain acute; there are new member states to accommodate, with heavily subsidized agricultural sectors and many mountainous or sub-arctic regions to consider; and there is the need to open up the Union to agricultural exports from central and eastern Europe. There is a growing world demand for food and a more liberal international trading environment. Within the Union, there is public concern about food quality, **food safety**, and animal welfare and a demand for simple, more transparent legislation. The **Treaty of Amsterdam** requires the impact on the environment to be taken account of in all Union policies. In several member states agricultural lobbies remain powerful, backed by a significant rural vote, and in the European Parliament the Committee on Agriculture has often shown itself to be ambivalent about reform proposals involving hardship for farmers. And there are obvious injustices in a system that tends to reward large, efficient farmers in prosperous countries with relatively small agricultural sectors such as Denmark and the Netherlands. For these and for other reasons, the CAP will remain a sensitive area (proof of this is the fact that the agricultural portfolio in the Commission is never given to someone from one of the large member states). The resolution of the problems affecting the CAP is made no easier by the fact that the definition of 'efficiency' in agriculture is no longer clear-cut and the Treaty objectives are no longer self-evidently right. Wyn Grant, *The Common Agricultural Policy* (Basingstoke, 1997) is a comprehensive but readable treatment of the subject.

Common Commercial Policy (CCP)

The CCP is named in Article 3 of the **Treaty of Rome** as one of the activities of the **European Economic Community**, and its main elements are set out in Articles 131 to 134 EC. Linked as they were in a **customs union**, it was obviously essential for the member states to draw up common policies with respect to their trading relations with the rest of the world. Article 112 (now 132) EEC required them to harmonize their systems of export aids, and Article 113 (now 133) EEC identified the need for 'uniform principles' to underpin the CCP with regard to tariff rates (see **Common External Tariff**), the conclusion of trade agreements, liberalization measures, the promotion of exports, and instruments of commercial defence against dumping and subsidies (see **anti-dumping**). The role of the **European Commission** as negotiator on behalf of the member states (see also **Article 133 Committee**) is laid down in this Article, under which the **Council of Ministers** is empowered to act by **qualified majority voting** (QMV). The powers of the **European Parliament** in this field are described under **assent procedure**.

The European Union is by far the biggest trading bloc in the world. If trade between member states is excluded, the Union has a 19.2 per cent share of world trade, outstripping both the North American Free Trade Area (NAFTA) with 18.1 per cent and Japan with 9.6 per cent. Both the Union and the **European Economic Area** (EEA) have a favourable trade balance in both goods and services with the rest of the world. Member states have substantial investments in very many countries. The Union itself has trade or **Cooperation Agreements** with some 120 countries worldwide (see also **Association Agreements, Europe Agreements**). Trade represents some 18 per cent of the Union's GDP.

Historically, the European Union has been in favour of free trade, calling for the 'progressive abolition of restrictions on international trade and the lowering of customs barriers' (Article 131 EC). The Commission represents the member states in the trade talks conducted in the **World Trade Organization** (WTO) and in other bodies such as the **Organization for Economic Cooperation and Development** (OECD) and the United Nations Conference on Trade and Development (UNCTAD). Once the effects of the **Generalized System of Preferences** (GSP) are taken into account, the Union has one of the lowest average levels of industrial tariff in the world (although this low average conceals high tariffs in certain 'sensitive' sectors such as textiles and consumer electronics).

The sectoral breakdown of the Union's visible trade has changed little in the past few years. Surpluses in chemicals, machinery and transport equipment compensate for deficits in raw materials and energy. Other sectors are broadly in balance. Geographically, the outstanding change has been the steady growth since 1980 in the proportion of overall trade taken up by industrialized countries at the expense of developing countries (although the latter still represent about a third of the total). The United States is by far the Union's most important trading partner, followed by Japan (for imports) and Switzerland (for exports). The states of south-east Asia (Hong Kong, Singapore, South Korea and Taiwan) are among the fastest-growing markets. However, partly as a consequence of the **Single Market** programme, trade between member states is growing more quickly than trade between the Union and the rest of the world (see **intra-Community trade**).

In spite of substantial national and political differences between member states in trade policy, the Union has, on the whole, achieved a high degree of coherence and consistency in trade matters. This is not to say that it has always acted wisely or even in good time (such are the difficulties in arriving at common positions), but in most areas member states have accepted the need to act as one. Notorious exceptions to this include the French and Italian restrictions on imports of Japanese cars, the unilateral embargo introduced by Greece on trade with the former Yugoslav republic of Macedonia, and the last-minute bargaining instigated by France over the GATT Agreement. The Union has also largely succeeded in dispelling the fears of a **Fortress Europe** prompted by the Single Market programme, in spite of the recession still affecting the economies of many member states.

In the institutional field, problems may arise over the relation between the CCP and the **Common Foreign and Security Policy** (CFSP) since a trade embargo may be used as a political weapon. A new Article 301 was added to the Treaty of Rome by the **Maastricht Treaty**, empowering the Council in the event of a CFSP decision 'to interrupt or to reduce, in part or completely, economic relations with one or more third countries', to take 'the necessary urgent measures ... by a qualified majority on a proposal from the Commission'. In such circumstances it is probable that the trade of some member states will be worse affected than that of others, and the use of the qualified majority could hardly fail to be controversial.

Common Customs Tariff
See **Common External Tariff**.

Common European Security and Defence Policy (CESDP)
The CESDP is part of the **Common Foreign and Security Policy** (CFSP), one of the two so-called '**pillars**' erected by the **Maastricht Treaty**. Until the

Helsinki meeting of the **European Council** in December 1999 it was known as the European Security and Defence Policy, but the initials ESDP were thought to be too similar to ESDI, the European Security and Defence Identity (i.e. the strengthening of the European component of the **North Atlantic Treaty Organization** (NATO)). Article 17.1 TEU, as revised by the **Treaty of Amsterdam**, specifies that the CFSP 'shall include all questions relating to the security of the Union, including the framing of a common defence policy ... which might lead to a common defence, should the European Council so decide'. In the same Article the **Western European Union** (WEU) is described as 'an integral part of the development of the Union providing the Union with access to an operational capability' and provision is made for the gradual integration of the WEU into the Union (a process more or less completed by the revised version of Article 17 contained in the **Treaty of Nice**). Article 17.3 says 'the Union will avail itself of the WEU to elaborate and implement decisions and actions of the Union which have defence implications' and makes it clear that the European Council 'guidelines' drawn up in the CFSP context also govern WEU actions undertaken on the Union's behalf. The special position of member states which also belong to NATO is acknowledged and the ESDP is required to be compatible with that of NATO. The scope of the CESDP includes 'cooperation ... in the field of armaments' (see **defence industry, European Armaments Agency**) and the Petersberg tasks (see **Petersberg Declaration**).

At meetings in Cologne (June 1999) and Helsinki (December 1999) the European Council discussed the CESDP. In Cologne it was decided to appoint Javier Solana, formerly secretary-general of NATO, as **High Representative** for the CFSP; five months later in November 1999 he was also appointed as secretary-general of the WEU. In Helsinki it was agreed that 'cooperating voluntarily in EU-led operations, Member States must be able, by 2003, to deploy within 60 days and sustain for at least 1 year military forces of up to 50,000–60,000 persons capable of the full range of Petersberg tasks'. The **Political Committee** has been superseded by the **Political and Security Committee**, and is backed up by a Military Committee composed of the national Chiefs of Defence and a military staff composed of officials from the member states on secondment to the secretariat of the Council of Ministers. Their role is to provide expertise on military questions, to draw up situation reports, to operate an early warning system and to monitor security-related aspects of the CFSP. Member states' commitment of military assets is to be 'based on their sovereign decision'. Special arrangements are being put in place for liaison with NATO, with candidate states, and with 'other European states engaged in political dialogue with the Union' such as Russia and Ukraine. Day-to-day conduct of CESDP operations is left to a 'committee of contributors', which all European Union member states, whether contributing or not, have the right to attend (for further details, see Annex IV of the Presidency Conclusions). For a helpful survey of these developments, see Simon Duke, *The Elusive Quest for European Security* (Basingstoke, 2000) and 'CESDP: Nice's overtrumped success', *European Foreign Affairs Review*, Vol. 6, no. 2, Summer 2001.

The European Council meeting in Laeken (December 2001) adopted a Declaration on the operational capability of the CESDP. Noting that 'the development of military capabilities does not imply the creation of a **European army**', the Declaration said that 'the European Union has established crisis-management structures and procedures which enable it to analyse and plan, to take decisions and, where NATO as such is not involved, to launch and carry out military crisis-management operations'.

Common External Tariff (CET)

The Common External Tariff CET, also known as the Common Customs Tariff (CCT), is the means whereby duties are imposed on goods entering the Union. A necessary feature of a **customs union**, the CET is managed by the **European Commission** under the **Common Commercial Policy** (CCP). Revenues from the imposition of the CET form part of the Union's **own resources**.

Common Fisheries Policy (CFP)

Article 32 of the **Treaty of Rome** makes it clear that fish and fish products are to be considered as agricultural products, and in consequence the CFP is based on the same principles as the **Common Agricultural Policy** (CAP). The first CFP was drawn up by **the Six** in the early 1970s with a view to presenting the applicant states – Denmark, Ireland, Norway and the United Kingdom, all of them with important fishing interests – with a *fait accompli*. It was partly the unacceptability of this CFP that caused Norway to vote against membership in the 1972 referendum. The major concession secured by the three new member states was an extension of coastal fishing rights from 6 to 12 miles (9.6 to 19.3 kilometres), a significant move away from the principle of free access enshrined in the Treaty.

The situation was radically transformed in 1975 by the unilateral declaration by several Atlantic states of 200-mile (322-kilometre) exclusive economic zones (EEZs). These EEZs, confirmed in 1982 in the Convention on the Law of the Sea, had the effect of denying access to many fishing grounds traditionally fished by fleets from the member states. The following year a revised CFP was agreed for a 10-year period, to be followed by a review and an extension for a further 10 years. This review was completed by the **Council of Ministers** in December 1992 and a new Regulation adopted.

The CFP recognizes the 12-mile coastal exclusion zones (see above) as long as 'traditional rights' are respected and operates a system of total allowable catches (TACs)) and quotas. The most controversial aspect of the CFP is the decommissioning of vessels and the payment of compensation to owners and fishermen. Technological advances, which make fishing more efficient, together with the need to conserve fish stocks, have resulted in the total fleet (some 80,000 vessels) being greatly in excess of actual requirements. The **European Commission** proposed very drastic cuts and the creation of a new Objective 6 under the **structural funds** Regulation, which would have allowed fishing communities affected by the cuts to receive assistance. In the event the cuts were made less drastic and the Objective 6 proposal was turned down, but the need for a licensing system for fishing boats was accepted. Objective 2 in the 1999 revision of the structural funds Regulation provides for assistance towards modernization from the Fisheries Guidance Instrument (FGI).

The Union is the world's third largest fishing power (after China and Peru) and a net importer of fish products. Fishing is an important industry in many peripheral regions where there are few alternative forms of employment. Overall, fisheries employ more than 260,000 people in the member states. Aquaculture employs a further 85,000. The scientific evidence points to the need to conserve fish stocks more prudently, such stocks having been badly affected by over-fishing and marine pollution.

Some of the pressure on the fish stocks in the European Union's waters is relieved by agreements that allow access to the EEZs of other countries. There are now 26 agreements on fisheries, some of them allowing reciprocal access, and approximately a fifth of the total catch of the Union's fleet is in the waters of non-member countries. Many of these agreements, such as those with developing countries in the Indian Ocean and the South Atlantic, involve the payment of financial compensation.

Enforcing CFP rules remains a problem. Quotas and TACs, allocated among member states, are drawn up annually with reference to particular species. In some fishing grounds this may require fishermen to discard by-catches of species for which the quota has already been met. Enforcement is still largely the responsibility of member states' own inspectorates, although since 1983 there has been a small inspectorate attached to the Commission whose job it is to ensure that enforcement is even-handed (see Regulation 2847/93, *Official Journal*, L261, 20 October 1993). Measures have been agreed to regulate mesh sizes and to address the problem of '**quota-hopping**' (see also **Factortame case**). The Commission published a Green Paper, *The CFP after 2002* (COM (2001) 135) in March 2001.

Common Foreign and Security Policy (CFSP)

One of the two intergovernmental '**pillars**' of the **Maastricht Treaty**, the CFSP embraces all those means by which the European Union seeks to exercise influence in foreign affairs (setting aside exclusively economic or commercial aspects of external relations) and to develop a **Common European Security and Defence Policy**. Articles 11 to 28 of the Maastricht Treaty are concerned not so much with the substance of the policy (although a set of broad and uncontroversial objectives is laid down in Article 11) but with the machinery for consultation between member states and Union institutions on CFSP matters and for 'concerted and convergent action'.

The CFSP, which developed out of and replaced the system known as **European Political Cooperation** (EPC), does not make use of the **legal instruments** specified in Article 249 of the **Treaty of Rome**. Instead, it is based on 'principles ... and general guidelines' supplemented by 'common strategies ... in areas where the Member States have important interests in common' (Article 13 TEU), laid down by the **European Council**. The **Council of Ministers** is empowered to make recommendations for common strategies and subsequently to translate them into joint actions or common positions, both of them agreed by unanimity (Article 23). If unanimity cannot be reached, the Council may, by **qualified majority voting** (QMV), refer the matter to the European Council for a unanimous decision. To date, there have been four common strategies: on Russia, Ukraine, the Mediterranean, and the Middle East. The adoption of joint actions and common positions on the basis of a common strategy which has already been agreed, together with implementing decisions, may be by QMV (62 votes in favour cast by at least 10 member states), except for those with military or defence implications where unanimity applies (see also **constructive abstention**). The Council may also issue **Declarations**. The Council is assisted by the High Representative for the CFSP and by the **Political and Security Committee** (see also **policy planning and early warning unit**). It may also appoint special representatives in particular geographical areas where the Union is heavily involved (Article 18.5). The **European Commission** is 'fully associated' with the CFSP (Article 27), but does not enjoy an exclusive **right of initiative**. The **European Parliament** has the right to be consulted and to be 'kept regularly informed' on all aspects of the CFSP (Article 21).

The cost of any CFSP actions is borne either by the **Budget** or by the member states 'in accordance with a scale to be decided'. The Political and Security Committee is instructed to work alongside COREPER (see **national representations**) in monitoring the international situation, contributing to Council meetings and following up CFSP decisions.

Article 19 makes particular reference to the obligation laid upon member states belonging to the Security Council of the **United Nations** to 'consult and keep the other Member States fully informed'. Permanent members (i.e.,

France and the United Kingdom) are required to 'ensure the defence of the positions and the interests of the Union'.

Although the CFSP provisions in the Maastricht Treaty were a substantial advance on EPC they did not significantly enhance the role of the European Parliament. Under Article 21 the presidency is invited merely to 'consult the European Parliament on the main aspects and the basic choices' of the CFSP and to ensure that the Parliament's views 'are duly taken into consideration'. The presidency and the Commission are instructed to keep the Parliament informed of CFSP developments, and, because CFSP matters are now dealt with by the Foreign Affairs Council, the Parliament's normal rights with respect to oral and written questions and the submission of recommendations apply in full to the CFSP.

The alleged inadequacy of democratic control, at the national or European level, is an argument that was raised when EPC was first established and is still being raised in respect of the CFSP. The counter-arguments are based on the self-evident need for speed and confidentiality in this field, and on the fact that whether or not the procedures are strictly within the ambit of the Community institutions, ministers in any case remain responsible to their **national parliaments**. This is of particular importance when CFSP decisions have to be taken by unanimity (see above), including the CFSP 'guidelines' set by the European Council. The arguments as far as national parliaments are concerned are very fully set out in a House of Lords' report entitled *Scrutiny of the Intergovernmental Pillars of the European Union* (November 1993).

Another argument heard since the origins of EPC is that the procedures allow only for a 'lowest common denominator' approach with the result that the European Union has all too often failed to exercise an influence commensurate with its political and economic weight. While admitting that EPC procedures allowed individual member states to hold the others to ransom (as Greece attempted to do over Macedonia), the fact is that there is always a balance to be struck between national sovereignty – of which foreign policy is a key expression – and the common interest. Whether the same happens under CFSP procedures remains to be seen. What might be for some critics a lack of cohesion is for others a welcome flexibility. Within international institutions like the United Nations or multilateral negotiating fora like the **Conference on Security and Cooperation in Europe** the member states have held together reasonably well. The CFSP procedures allow individual member states to continue to deal with essentially bilateral foreign policy problems with only minimum reference to other member states, but if there exists a general political will to deal with an issue on a cooperative basis, the CFSP procedures will enable this to be done. However, as in other areas, procedures can of themselves neither engender such a will nor substitute for it.

Common Market

The 'Common Market' was the name by which what later became the European Community was generally known, although, strictly speaking, it referred only to the **European Economic Community** established under the **Treaty of Rome**. As a technical expression to denote the commercial relations between member states of the European Union, its place has been taken by **Single Market**.

Common position

The end of the first stage of the two-reading **cooperation procedure** and **co-decision procedure** is reached when the **Council of Ministers** agrees on a 'common position'. This common position will often take account of amendments put forward by the **European Parliament** at first reading (see below) and may also be influenced by the opinions of the **Economic and Social Committee** and the **Committee of the Regions**. The common position is sent back to the European Parliament for the second reading.

The two-reading procedure was introduced by the 1986 **Single European Act** (SEA) which came into effect in July 1987. Studies have shown that more than 40 per cent of the Parliament's first-reading amendments are accepted in the Council's common position. This estimate should be treated with some caution, since no distinction is drawn between technical or linguistic amendments and those that substantially alter the proposal.

The expression 'common position' is also found in the **Maastricht Treaty** provisions on the **Common Foreign and Security Policy** (CFSP). Article 15 TEU enjoins the Council of Ministers to 'adopt common positions [which] shall define the approach of the Union to a particular matter of a geographical or thematic nature', and member states are instructed to 'ensure that their national policies conform to the common positions'. A similar provision may be found in Article 34.2 TEU, with reference to **Justice and Home Affairs** (JHA).

Common transport policy

Although Article 3 of the **Treaty of Rome** called for 'a common policy in the sphere of transport' (see also Article 70 EC), few specific requirements were laid down. Article 71 EC refers only to the need for 'common rules applicable to international transport', rules governing the provision of transport services by non-residents in each member state, 'measures to improve transport safety' and 'any other appropriate provisions'. In its original form Article 84 (now 80) EEC specified that the common transport policy applied only to rail, road and inland waterways, but this was amended by a provision in the 1986 **Single European Act** (SEA) that allowed the **Council of Ministers** to decide whether and how to extend it to sea and air transport.

In spite of the experience gained from the removal of subsidies and discriminatory price-fixing under the earlier **European Coal and Steel Community** (ECSC) Treaty, progress towards even the basic aims of a common transport policy was extremely slow. In 1982 the **European Parliament** brought a case under Article 175 (now 232) EEC against the Council of Ministers for **failure to act**: in 1985 the **Court of Justice** ruled partially in the Parliament's favour and since then progress has been a little faster.

The central problem has been to combine liberalization with **harmonization** of the conditions of competition. Substantial state involvement in transport is at least as old as the building of the **railways**, and vested interests, public and private, are numerous, powerful and well entrenched in the transport sector. At the same time transport costs have a significant impact on economic activity and competitiveness, especially in the peripheral regions, and on individual travellers and taxpayers. Finally, the interaction between transport, energy use and the environment is now widely accepted, as is the contribution that an efficient transport system can make to the success of the **Single Market** and of **enlargement**. In terms both of its contribution to the Union's gross national product (GNP) and the number of people directly or indirectly employed, the transport sector has a claim to be among the very largest industries in Europe.

In May 1965 the Council of Ministers adopted a framework decision on the harmonization of provisions affecting competition in rail, road and inland waterway transport. However, it was not until 1968 that the normal Treaty rules on **competition policy** were applied to this sector (although in a way that allowed many exemptions and **derogations** to be granted). The following year agreement was reached in the form of two Regulations governing drivers' hours and the installation of recording equipment (the tachograph) in certain vehicles in commercial use. Both Regulations have since been revised.

Another difficult area was that of technical specifications for road vehicles. Most controversial of all were those for heavy lorries. Maximum width, height, total weight and weight per axle were laid down in 1984 (revised 1986), but at first only for international traffic between member states. Further work was done in connection with the need to facilitate the free flow of goods under the Single Market programme.

Article 73 EC allows **state aids** to be maintained 'if they represent reimbursement for the discharge of certain obligations inherent in the concept of a public service' (see **services of general economic interest**). This provision, of great importance to the railways, obviously required a common definition of a 'public service' and accounting systems that would allow revenues from state aids to be clearly identified. Both these aims were achieved in a series of Regulations over the period 1969 to 1991.

With respect to roads, the most significant recent achievement has been the introduction, with effect from 1 January 1993, of a system of Community licences governing access to the market for commercial road transport. This system replaced the restrictive and protectionist system of quotas in force until that date. Progress has also been made on the liberalization of cabotage regulations for goods and passenger transport. Of the various cost factors affecting road transport, the ones that have proved most difficult to deal with are taxes on fuel and on heavy goods vehicles and the issue of road tolls.

Notwithstanding the provisions of Article 84 (now 80) EEC, the **Court of Justice** ruled in 1974 that Treaty rules on competition applied to air transport (see also **Nouvelles Frontières case**). The first substantial package of measures was agreed in December 1987 in the form of two Regulations (since revised) covering air transport between member states and the nature of the exemptions from competition rules that the Council was able to grant. The **European Commission** was given supervisory and investigative powers similar to those it already possessed in other areas of competition policy. As a result of these Regulations and the subsequent revisions competition rules now broadly apply to the air transport sector, domestic and international, within the member states. Restrictions, however, remain on the access of new airlines to established routes, on the development of new routes and on cabotage. Some of these problems were partially resolved in a second package of measures adopted in June 1992. Included in this package was a new Regulation on air fares, under which an airline may be granted approval for a new fare between two member states as long as neither government raises an objection (previously, both governments had to give their consent). The Commission has a right of final decision in the event of a dispute. This is intended to facilitate and encourage competition between airlines (see also **Eurocontrol, single European sky**).

The main aim of policy in the sea transport sector has been to open up competition within the member states and to allow European fleets to meet competition from low-cost third countries. Two packages of measures have been adopted, the first in December 1986 on the application of competition rules and the second in June 1992 on cabotage. The Commission has proposed the creation of a European shipping register (EUROS) and more stringent rules on the carriage of dangerous goods, including those capable of causing serious pollution.

Progress towards a common transport policy is being carried forward under a Commission study entitled *Sustainable Mobility*, which sets out longer-term transport objectives in relation to other policy areas such as energy and the environment. The Commission has identified 58,000 kilometres of roads, 23,000 kilometres of high-speed railway lines, and 250 airports as the essential basis of the Union's transport infrastructure. Also of relevance to transport policy is the programme of **trans-European networks** (TENs) introduced into the Treaty of Rome (Articles 154 to 156) by the **Maastricht Treaty**. TENs are intended to help create a cost-effective transport system, planned on a European basis, with special attention to the development of the high-speed rail network. 'Sustainable surface transport' features prominently in the sixth framework programme (2002–6) of **research** undertaken by the European Union. The Commission's current priorities for transport were set out in September 2001 in *European Transport Policy for 2010: Time to Decide* (COM (2001) 370). They include the revitalization of the railways, measures to improve safety and to relieve congestion, projects to develop the infrastructure especially in relation to eastern Europe, and the application of the Galileo (satellite navigation) technology.

Transport is widely recognized as an area of growing importance for the Union. This is due not only to the impact of the Single Market but also to the need to establish better links with central and eastern Europe. This is in marked contrast to the very slow progress made in the 1960s and 1970s. A European Transport Community was an idea considered by **the Six** in the 1950s, based on the model of the ECSC, and eventually rejected in favour of the **European Economic Community** and the **European Atomic Energy Community** (Euratom). Experience to date with the common transport policy suggests that the decision was a judicious one.

Communism

The Communist parties of western Europe were at the apogee of their influence during the immediate postwar years, helped by their links with resistance movements in continental Europe and by the fact that the Soviet Union had been an ally of the West. Since then they have been (with some exceptions) in long and probably terminal decline, a process accelerated by the Soviet interventions in Hungary (1956) and Czechoslovakia (1968) and the break-up of the Soviet empire in central and eastern Europe. The rise of so-called 'Eurocommunism' (that is, Communist policies tempered by a willingness to work through democratic institutions and without subservience to Moscow) may be seen in retrospect to have slowed but not halted this progressive decline.

Communist parties were unremittingly hostile to the first moves towards European integration. Taking their cue from Moscow, they interpreted the **Marshall Plan** as American imperialism backed by military–industrial interests and the **North Atlantic Treaty Organization** (NATO) as an instrument of American domination. Communist parties voted against the **Treaty of Paris** and the **Treaty of Rome** in the **national parliaments** of **the Six**. Until the Eurocommunism of the 1970s Communists remained almost wholly uninvolved in European integration, the only notable exception being **Altiero**

Spinelli (who later left the party). Soviet support for Communist parties in the West is vividly documented in C. Andrew and V. Mitrokhin, *The Mitrokhin Archive* (Harmondsworth, 1999).

Eurocommunism was mainly an Italian phenomenon, and the fact of its being pro-European was one of its principal distinguishing features. However, the other well-established western European Communist party, the French, remained loyal to Moscow. The division ran through other Communist parties, such as the Greek Communists (who developed both pro- and anti-European wings) and through the Communist group in the **European Parliament** (see **political groups**), although it was not until 1989 that it finally split apart. In policy terms Eurocommunism was indistinguishable from moderate Socialism, and in the 1984 European elections in Italy the Communists secured a larger share of the votes than the Christian Democrats. The triumph was short-lived, and by 1990 the party was split, the majority of its Members of the European Parliament (MEPs) joining the Socialists two years later. The Communists are the fifth largest group in the Parliament. They have chosen the name United European Left, although, in fact, they remain divided into old-style Communists and Eurocommunists, and can normally be relied upon to vote with the Socialists.

Communitization

An area of policy is said to have been 'communitized' when it is brought within the ambit of the institutions and decision-making procedures set out in the **Treaty of Rome**. It is used especially of policies developed initially in the second or the third of the '**pillars**' set up by the **Maastricht Treaty** and then wholly or partially transferred to the first 'pillar', that is, to the European Community itself. For example, the **Treaty of Amsterdam** 'communitizes' that portion of the **Justice and Home Affairs** (JHA) policy which is concerned with freedom of movement across frontiers. Since such communitization normally entails changing the Treaties it can only be done on the basis of unanimous agreement. A similarly ugly neologism, 'budgetization', is used to denote items of expenditure which are incorporated into the **Budget** of the European Union, as distinct from those which remain the direct responsibility of member states. For example, the salaries of Members of the European Parliament (MEPs), which are paid by national exchequers, are not 'budgetized'.

Community Plant Variety Office (CPVO)

An **agency** of the European Union, operational since April 1995 and based in Angers (France), the CPVO administers the system of intellectual property rights applicable to plant varieties set out in Regulation 2100/94 (*Official Journal*, L227, 1 September 1994).

Community preference

'Community preference' is a well-established feature of the **Common Agricultural Policy** (CAP) under which, by a system of import levies and export refunds, member states are expected and encouraged to give preference to agricultural goods from within the Union over those from outside. Such practices run obviously counter to the doctrine of free trade and tend to maintain prices of products covered by CAP rules at relatively high levels.

Community preference gave rise to difficulties at the time of British accession to the European Community, since the British government did not want to place imports from Commonwealth countries (such as butter from New Zealand) at a disadvantage. More recently, Community preference created problems in the negotiations on the **General Agreement on Tariffs and Trade** (GATT) and in respect of agricultural imports from central and eastern Europe. Community preference also imposes constraints on imports of agricultural products from developing countries that compete with those covered by the CAP.

Community preference is vigorously supported by member states (such as France, Denmark and Ireland) with large agricultural sectors and substantial exporting capacity. This support could at one time be based on the **Treaty of Rome**: Article 44.2 referred to the system of minimum prices under the CAP and added that they 'shall not be applied so as to form an obstacle to the development of a natural preference between Member States'. In a 1994 ruling, the Court of Justice confirmed that Community preference was not a principle of Community law (Case C 353/92, *Greece* v *Council*) and Article 44 was repealed by the **Treaty of Amsterdam**.

Community trade mark

Under Regulation 40/94 (*Official Journal*, L11, 14 January 1994) businesses may protect a trade mark throughout the **European Economic Area** (EEA) by registering it with the Office for Harmonization in the Internal Market (OHIM), an **agency** of the European Union based in Alicante, Spain. Previously, full protection could be guaranteed only under separate procedures in each member state. A similar Regulation (Regulation 6/02, *Official Journal*, L3, 5 January 2002) applies to designs. The OHIM publishes an *Official Journal*, a *Community Trade Mark Bulletin* and a *Community Designs Bulletin*.

Competition policy

The operation of 'a system ensuring that competition in the internal market is not distorted' is one of the activities of the European Community under Article 3.1(g) of the **Treaty of Rome**. Article 81 prohibits undertakings from entering into 'agreements ... and concerted practices which may affect trade between

Member States and which have as their object or effect the prevention, restriction, or distortion of competition within the common market'. Included under this heading are price-fixing and market-sharing arrangements, production controls, and discriminatory contracts intended to place particular trading parties at a disadvantage. However, exempted from this general prohibition are agreements or practices that contribute to 'improving the production or distribution of goods or to promoting technical or economic progress, while allowing consumers a fair share of the resulting benefit' (Article 81.3).

Article 82 prohibits 'any abuse by one or more undertakings of a dominant position within the common market or in a substantial part of it ... in so far as it may affect trade between Member States'. Articles 81 and 82 apply to all economic sectors except the **Common Agricultural Policy** (CAP) and the **common transport policy**, which have their own competition rules. The coal and steel industries were covered by Articles 65 and 66 of the **Treaty of Paris** until the expiry of the latter in 2002.

Under Article 86 publicly owned undertakings (including monopolies of a commercial character) are bound by the rules of competition 'in so far as the application of such rules does not obstruct the performance ... of the particular tasks assigned to them. The development of trade must not be affected to such an extent as would be contrary to the interests of the Community.'

Article 85 gives the **European Commission** a general responsibility to enforce Articles 81 and 82 in cooperation with the authorities of member states and the right to conduct investigations either at their request or on its own initiative. The means whereby the Commission may discharge this responsibility were defined in Regulation 17/62 (*Official Journal*, 13, 21 February 1962). Under this Regulation the Commission is empowered to request information from undertakings suspected of practices prohibited under Articles 81 and 82. The Commission may carry out 'all necessary investigations', including examination and copying of business records, 'ask for oral explanations on the spot' and 'enter any premises, land and means of transport' owned by the undertakings under investigation. The Commission may impose fines on undertakings found to have supplied 'incorrect or misleading information' or to have failed to supply information on request. The Commission may also 'by decision' impose fines ranging from €1,000 to €1 million 'or a sum in excess thereof but not exceeding 10 per cent of turnover in the preceding business year' on undertakings found to have infringed Articles 81 and 82, assessed with regard 'to the gravity and to the duration of the infringement' (for example, in 1998 the Commission fined Volkswagen €102 million for trying to prevent its Austrian and German customers from taking advantage of lower car prices in Italy). Failure to supply information, submit to an investigation or abandon a prohibited practice may incur a 'periodic penalty payment' imposed by the Commission at rates ranging between €50 and €1,000 a day. The Commission is under an obligation to keep the relevant national authorities informed of an investigation and its decisions may be reviewed in the **Court of First Instance** in the event of a fine being imposed. Subject to these provisos, its powers in respect of suspected infringements of competition rules are absolute.

The Commission is required to draw up an annual report on its activities in respect of competition policy. This report is debated by the **European Parliament**. The competition rules apply to any enterprise doing business within the Union even if it has neither branches nor subsidiaries on Union territory (this was established by the Court of Justice in a 1988 ruling concerned with woodpulp).

Competition policy (which also covers **state aids** and **merger controls**) is one of the areas in which the Commission is most powerful, and the decisions that the Commission is required to take are sometimes very sensitive politically. In recent years four very active Commissioners, Peter Sutherland, Sir Leon Brittan, Karel Van Miert and Mario Monti, have been instrumental in making competition policy much more effective. It was obvious that if the **Single Market** programme was to bring benefits to consumers, the removal of trade barriers would have to be accompanied by a vigorous competition policy. Among the most controversial issues are the block exemptions from competition rules granted, for example, to exclusive distribution agreements – such as those in the motor industry – and franchise agreements. Some of the more bureaucratic requirements have been eased: there is no longer any obligation to inform the Commission of an agreement between undertakings that together have less than a 5 per cent share of the market within the Union for the products affected by the agreement.

Doubts remain as to whether the Commission has adequate resources, in staff numbers and expertise, to enforce the competition policy. Even with the cooperation of national authorities (whose own standards of enforcement are uneven), Commission investigations continue to give rise to complaints about delays and unnecessary secrecy. Complaints against the Commission in this field may be brought in the Court of First Instance. It has also been suggested that a new European agency, independent of the Commission, should be set up to enforce competition rules, but this has been resisted by the Commission on the grounds that essentially political judgments are often involved in competition cases. This and other related issues are very fully discussed in a report by the House of Lords Select Committee on the European Union, *Reforming EC Competition Procedures* (February 2000). See also Michelle Cini and Lee McGowan, *Competition Policy in the European Union* (Basingstoke, 1998) and Robert Lane, *EC Competition Law* (Harlow, 2000).

Competitiveness

The need for European industry to remain competitive in the global economy was one of the reasons for the adoption of the **Single Market** programme. Competitiveness is a theme which is also relevant to several other areas of European Union activity, such as **research** or **social policy** (i.e., measures relating to employment). The **Treaty of Amsterdam** amended Article 2 of the **Treaty of Rome** to put 'a high degree of competitiveness' on a par with other economic and social objectives such as sustainable growth, a high level of employment and the raising of the standard of living.

In 1993 the **European Commission** published a White Paper entitled *Growth, Competitiveness and Employment: The Challenges and Ways Forward into the 21st Century*. This was discussed by the **European Council** at its meetings in Brussels (December 1993), Essen (December 1994) and Amsterdam (June 1997). 'Improving European competitiveness' is referred to in the **Resolution** on Growth and Employment adopted in Amsterdam.

In 1995, **Jacques Santer** as President of the Commission appointed a 'Competitiveness Advisory Group'. The Group attempted to define a specifically 'European' notion of competitiveness and to draw up a typology of competitiveness capable of being translated into instruments for the systematic evaluation of economic performance. The Group's report has been published in Alexis Jacquemin and Lucio R. Pench (eds), *Europe Competing in the Global Economy* (Cheltenham, 1997). A new Advisory Group has been appointed. See also **Molitor Group**.

Compulsory expenditure

Compulsory expenditure (sometimes known as obligatory expenditure) is a technical term used in relation to the **Budget**. The definition, which is not set out very clearly in the Treaties, is 'such expenditure as the budgetary authority is obliged to enter in the budget by virtue of a legal undertaking entered into under the Treaty or an act adopted by virtue of this Treaty' (**Interinstitutional Agreement** of 6 May 1999). The difference between compulsory and non-compulsory expenditure is essentially political, since it has a bearing on which arm of the joint budgetary authority, the **Council of Ministers** or the **European Parliament**, has the last word on the various items in the Budget: the Parliament has the last word only on non-compulsory expenditure. Easily the most important element within compulsory expenditure is price support under the **Common Agricultural Policy** (CAP). Arguments over the classification of expenditure have occasionally arisen between the Council and the Parliament. About 45 per cent of the total Budget is compulsory expenditure: in 1980 it was over 80 per cent.

Concentric circles

The idea of concentric circles is used most commonly as a model of how Europe as a whole might develop. Typically, the member states of the European Union occupy the central core; members of the **European Economic Area** occupy a second circle; European states with **Association Agreements** make up a third circle; and in some models a fourth circle is composed of other former Eastern bloc countries. All versions of this model allow for movement from one circle to another, the assumption being that countries will gravitate towards the central core.

The model is also sometimes used to describe how the Union itself should operate. A central core is composed of activities in which all member states participate, surrounded by a second circle of activities in which member states may choose to be involved. In some models a third circle of activities offers a further choice of options, in which non-member states may also become engaged. Decision making in the second and third circles is carried out not under **Treaty of Rome** procedures – the scope of which is limited to activities in the central core – but by means of intergovernmental procedures. This model, of which there are many variants, is sometimes referred to as the **variable geometry** Europe.

There are several examples of a Europe of concentric circles, although there is no authority for such a model in the founding Treaties. The **Exchange-Rate Mechanism** (ERM) of the **European Monetary System** (EMS), as set up in 1979, was outside the central core by virtue of the fact that sterling was not involved and the Italian lira was in a broader band. Similarly, only 13 of the 15 member states participate in the **European Space Agency**, plus Norway and Switzerland. And the development model set out in the **Maastricht Treaty** – a 'Union' based upon three '**pillars**' – could also be expressed as an inner and an outer circle, since the provisions for cooperation in justice, home affairs, security and foreign policy lie outside the central core by virtue of their essentially intergovernmental character and the possibility that non-member states may become involved (see also **flexibility**).

Conciliation

'Conciliation' is the word used to describe the procedure whereby the **European Parliament** and the **Council of Ministers** seek to resolve their differences over the substance or wording of a legislative text. Introduced in 1975 as part of the procedure for reaching agreement on the **Budget**, conciliation has since become an important feature of the **co-decision procedure**. Conciliation takes place in a conciliation committee composed of Members of the European Parliament (MEPs) and the Council. Agreement requires the support of a majority among the MEPs and a **qualified majority** in the Council.

Confederation

The main difference between a confederation and a **federation** is that the former lays more emphasis on the independence of the constituent parts, the corollary of which is a weaker central authority. The longest-established confederation in Europe is Switzerland, with its unique mixture of central institutions and a vigorous tradition of local decision-making at the level of the cantons. The distinction is neatly caught in two German expressions: *Staatenbund* (a confederation of states) and *Bundesstaat* (a federal state).

Conference on Security and Cooperation in Europe (CSCE)

The CSCE, the first stage of which was concluded by the signing of a 'Final Act' in Helsinki on 1 August 1975, was an attempt to reconcile the conflicting interests of the Atlantic Alliance and the countries of the **Warsaw Pact**. All European countries (except Albania, which did not join the CSCE until June 1991) took part in the negotiations that resulted in the Final Act together with the United States and Canada, a total of 35 states. Broadly, the countries of the Eastern bloc were interested in military security and in extending economic and technological cooperation with the West, while the countries of the West were interested in promoting human rights in the East.

These different priorities were reflected in the four 'baskets' into which the Final Act was divided. Basket I was concerned with security and disarmament. It laid down certain principles for the conduct of relations between states: respect for sovereignty, non-interference in internal affairs, inviolability of frontiers, renunciation of force as a means of settling disputes, and respect for human rights. Basket II dealt with economic, scientific and technological cooperation and the protection of the environment. Basket III was entitled 'Cooperation in Humanitarian and Other Fields'. The fourth Basket was concerned with following up the commitments entered into by the signatory states. The Helsinki Final Act prompted the formation of many human rights monitoring groups in the countries of the Eastern bloc.

The Helsinki meeting was succeeded by CSCE follow-up meetings in Belgrade (1977–8), Madrid (1980–3), Vienna (1986–9) and Helsinki (1992). In between such meetings, expert groups discussed particular aspects of the subjects covered by the Final Act, such as human rights, cultural and human conflicts, and the peaceful settlement of disputes. Linked to the CSCE were the conferences on confidence and security-building measures (CSBM: Stockholm, 1984–6) and on conventional forces in Europe (CFE: 1989–92). Of the follow-up meetings, the one that yielded the most substantial results was the meeting concluded in Vienna in January 1989. For the first time a permanent mechanism for monitoring human rights was agreed by all 35 countries.

The following year, heads of government met in Paris for the first time since the 1975 meeting in Helsinki. The first CFE Treaty was signed on 19 November 1990 and the **Charter of Paris** for a New Europe two days later. The Paris summit, originally proposed by Mikhail Gorbachev, was a forum for reviewing the changes taking place in central and eastern Europe and for finding ways of overcoming the remaining divisions. Also signed in Paris was the so-called 'Vienna Document', a new package of CBMs agreed in Vienna just before the summit. The CSCE Paris summit marked the end of the Cold War.

Congress of Europe

Held in The Hague in May 1948, the Congress of Europe was attended by more than 800 politicians, lawyers, academics, economists, etc., from almost every country in Europe. Its President-of-Honour was **Winston Churchill**. It was organized by the International Committee of the Movements for European Unity and led directly to the foundation in October 1948 of the **European Movement**.

The Congress adopted a 'Message to Europeans', which called for 'a united Europe, throughout whose area the free movement of persons, ideas and goods is restored'. This would be underpinned by a 'Charter of Human Rights', a Court of Justice to guarantee those rights, and a 'European Assembly where the live forces of all our nations shall be represented'. These ideas were worked out in more detail in a political report considered by the Congress, which prompted a number of specific resolutions adopted by unanimity.

John Masefield, the Poet Laureate, addressed the Congress and wrote a poem about it afterwards:

> This is the light that has been kindled here,
> A hope to man through half a hemisphere.
> Hope that is brightness in Earth's darkest day
> A glorious gift for guests to take away.
>   (quoted in Anthony Sampson, *The New Europeans*, 1968)

The Congress, the name of which was a deliberate echo of the 1815 Congress of Vienna attended by the victorious powers at the end of the Napoleonic wars, represents the high-water mark of enthusiasm for European integration in the immediate postwar period. It sought, on an all-party basis, to bring pressure to bear upon governments and to enlist popular support for integrationist ideas. Although it had substantial impact at the time, the Congress may be seen in retrospect to have been not wholly successful. The main ideas put forward were embodied the following year in the statute of the **Council of Europe**. The European Movement organized in May 1998 a Congress of Europe in The Hague to mark the fiftieth anniversary of the first

Congress and published a facsimile edition in English, French and German of the three original 1948 resolutions together with the 'Message to Europeans'.

Conservatism

Although the Conservatives have a claim to be the longest-established political family in Europe, there were no Conservative parties of any importance in **the Six**. Consequently, it was not until the **accession** of Denmark and the United Kingdom to the European Community in 1973 that a Conservative Group was formed as one of the **political groups** in the **European Parliament** and Conservatives participated in both the **European Commission** and the **Council of Ministers**. However, the Christian Democrats (see **Christian Democracy**) retained their position as by far the strongest political force among the parties of the centre and the centre-right. In May 1992 the British and Danish Conservative Members of the European Parliament (MEPs) joined the Christian Democrats as allied members in the Group of the European People's Party (the Conservatives do not sit with the Christian Democrats in the Parliamentary Assembly of the **Council of Europe**).

Although in recent years the Labour Party has become identified as 'the Party of Europe' in the British political context, it was in fact the Conservative government of Harold Macmillan that in 1961 first sought British membership of the European Community, thereby abandoning the reservations of **Winston Churchill** and Anthony Eden; the Party has maintained its pro-European stance (with varying degrees of enthusiasm) ever since. The Danish Conservative Party (founded as the Party of the Right, Høyre, in the nineteenth century, and refounded as the Conservative Party in 1915) has also been consistently pro-European, as has its Norwegian counterpart (which retains the name Høyre).

In most European languages 'conservative' means 'reactionary', and only in Denmark, Latvia, Lithuania, Poland and the United Kingdom are there parties with the word 'Conservative' in their name. The Conservatives' image as a party lacking a confessional basis, hostile to federalism (see **federation**), strongly committed to free market economics and uninterested in social questions (an image powerfully reinforced by **Margaret Thatcher**) makes them an object of suspicion to Christian Democrats, who pride themselves on their position as parties of the centre. One of the aims of the **European Democrat Union**, founded in 1978, was to overcome this Conservative–Christian Democrat divide, but it was only partially successful.

Some of the newly formed parties in central and eastern Europe have drawn inspiration from, for example, the privatization programme carried out by Conservative governments in the United Kingdom, but in the longer term they are not likely to develop into authentic Conservative parties. In the

European Union, Conservatism will probably remain an Anglo-Scandinavian phenomenon, while maintaining good bilateral relations with parties such as the Christian Democrats in Germany, the Moderates in Sweden, the Partido Popular in Spain, and elements within the centre-right in France. The fullest and fairest account of the merger between the Conservative MEPs and the Christian Democrats is Karl Magnus Johansson, *Transnational Party Alliances* (Lund, 1997).

Constituent assembly

Historically, a constituent assembly is a body of elected parliamentarians that is set (or sets itself) the task of drawing up and enacting a constitution, often against a background of revolution. Within the first directly elected **European Parliament** (1979–84) there were many Members who saw this as the Parliament's historic role. Before the elections of June 1979 a poll was taken among 742 candidates (62 per cent of whom were elected) to establish what proportion of them saw the Parliament as a constituent assembly. The results showed very wide variations between the nationalities: over 88 per cent of Belgian, German, Italian and Luxemburgish candidates supported the idea, by comparison with 29 per cent of British candidates, 11 per cent of Danish candidates, and only 3 per cent of French candidates.

In the Parliament **Altiero Spinelli** soon established himself as the leader of those demanding a new constitution for the Community. He was responsible for the creation of the **Crocodile Club** and later (January 1982) for the setting up of the Committee on Institutional Affairs. Briefly, his aim was for the Parliament to adopt a constitution and then, with the aid of **national parliaments** and national governments, to set in train the process of **ratification**. The draft constitution would be the main issue in the second European elections of 1984: public debate would centre upon its provisions and (if all went well) the parties supporting the constitution would be swept to power. Soon after, the constitution would enter into force.

For a number of reasons, this did not happen. The **Draft Treaty establishing the European Union** (DTEU), as the constitution was called, was not adopted in its final form until February 1984, too late for it to be included in party manifestos, and by a majority, which, although comfortable, was hardly overwhelming (237 votes to 31 with 43 abstentions, in a Parliament of 434 members).

Since 1984 the European Parliament has on several occasions returned to the idea of being a constituent assembly. In 1989, a referendum was held in Italy inviting the electorate to endorse (which they did) the proposal that the 1989–94 European Parliament should be a constituent assembly. The Parliament's most recent attempt to draw up a new constitution (the Herman Report, adopted in February 1994 with 154 votes in favour, 84 against and 46 abstentions) called for a 'constitutional convention' to be held bringing together MEPs and members of national parliaments. Working on the basis of the Herman Report, this convention would prepare 'guidelines for the constitution of the European Union, and ... assign to the European Parliament the task of preparing a final draft'. See **Laeken Declaration**.

Constitution for Europe

At present, the **Treaties** serve as the Constitution of the European Union. The suggestion that the specifically constitutional elements – whether or not in a modified form – of the Treaties should be abstracted from the other provisions and embodied in a separate document has been made with increasing frequency since the process of Treaty revision was first undertaken in the mid-1980s (see **Intergovernmental Conference** (IGC)). It has also been suggested that the **Charter of Fundamental Rights** adopted in December 2000 should be incorporated into such a Constitution.

The argument for a Constitution rests on the need for greater clarity (see also **simplification, transparency**). The constitutional elements in the Treaties are widely scattered and would, it is alleged, benefit from being brought together into a coherent, intelligible whole with the repetitions excised, the language brought up to date, and the substance made consistent with the jurisprudence of the **Court of Justice**. This might diminish the alienation and bewilderment thought to be characteristic of public attitudes to the Union. In particular, it might serve to provide clear-cut answers to questions about the division of responsibility between the Union and national, regional, or local authorities and thereby help to safeguard the principle of **subsidiarity**.

An adjunct to this argument is the suggestion that in future only the Constitution of the Union should be subject to the very strict rules for Treaty amendment set out in Article 48 of the **Maastricht Treaty** (i.e. unanimity among all the governments and **ratification** in all the national parliaments of the member states). Non-constitutional provisions in the Treaties could be amended under a simpler procedure. This would, it is suggested, circumvent the problem after enlargement of amending the Treaties in a Union of 25 or more members.

Those who oppose the idea of a Constitution claim that it would be a decisive step in the direction of transforming the Union into a state. They point to the practical difficulty of distinguishing between the constitutional and non-constitutional elements in the Treaties, to the problems such a distinction might pose for the homogeneity of the law contained in or flowing from the Treaties, and to the possibility that the fragile consensus upon which some provisions are based might fall apart if the text were to be disassembled. And could the provisions of a Constitution expressed in simple, accessible language be at the same time sufficiently precise to serve as the legal base for legislation?

Both the **European Commission** and the **European Parliament** favour the drawing up of a Constitution. At the Commission's request the **European University Institute** (EUI) has already prepared a model Basic Treaty of only 95 Articles (the four Treaties currently in force contain over 700 Articles). Both Jacques Chirac, the President of France (speech to the Bundestag, June 2000), and Johannes Rau, the President of Germany (speech to the European Parliament, April 2001), have expressed support for a Constitution. In December 2001 the **Laeken Declaration** adopted by the **European Council** concluded that 'If we are to have greater transparency, simplification is essential' and directed the Convention which is preparing the 2003 IGC to examine the question.

The EUI's Basic Treaty is available on the Europa website or (with commentaries) in Kim Feus (ed.), *A Simplified Treaty for the EU* (2001). See also the Commission's *A Basic Treaty for the European Union* (COM (2000) 434, 12 July 2000).

Constructive abstention

Sometimes referred to as 'positive abstention', constructive abstention is a procedure which has been introduced into the European Union's **Common Foreign and Security Policy** (CFSP) by the **Treaty of Amsterdam** (Title V, Article 23 TEU). Constructive abstention allows a member state to abstain in a vote in the **Council of Ministers** without blocking an otherwise unanimous decision. The abstaining state is absolved from taking any part in the implementation of the decision, yet remains bound not to impede any action flowing from it. The abstaining state must bear its share of any costs arising from the decision, except in the case of 'operations having military or defence implications' (Article 28 TEU). Constructive abstention is designed to give member states in real difficulties over a particular proposal an alternative to using the **veto**. Member states remain free to abstain in the normal way without their abstentions being construed as 'constructive' within the meaning of Article 23 TEU. If under the **qualified majority voting** (QMV) system the votes of the member states opting for constructive abstention amount to more than one-third of the total, the decision in question is not adopted. *Mutatis mutandis*, this procedure could be extended to other policy areas in which the veto applies.

Consultation procedure

The **Treaty of Rome** provides for consultation with many different institutions and bodies under various decision-making procedures, but the expression 'consultation procedure' is normally reserved for the simplest form of one-stage consultation between the **Council of Ministers** and the **European Parliament**. This is to distinguish it from other procedures under which the

Parliament has more power to enforce its views (see **assent procedure, cooperation procedure, co-decision procedure**; see also **reconsultation**).

Originally, virtually all the Parliament's powers were exercised under a simple consultation procedure, and neither the Council nor the **European Commission** was obliged to take much account of the Parliament's views. In the 1970s the Parliament acquired additional powers over the **Budget**. The indispensability of consultation with respect to legislation was first underlined in the 1979 **isoglucose case**, and the other procedures have been developed since that date. However, there are several important areas of decision making – such as the **Common Foreign and Security Policy** (CFSP) and **Economic and Monetary Union** (EMU) – in which the European Parliament's involvement remains limited to simple consultation.

Consumer policy

The original **Treaty of Rome** made no provision for consumer policy, but **Article 95**, added by the **Single European Act** (SEA), refers to the need for 'a high level of protection' for consumers in the **Single Market**. Not until the **Maastricht Treaty** added a new Article 129a (now 153) was there a legal base for 'specific action which supports and supplements the policy pursued by the Member States to protect the health, safety and economic interests of consumers and to provide adequate information to consumers'. Article 153.5 allows member states to maintain or introduce 'more stringent protective measures', in line with a principle laid down by the **Court of Justice** in the 1986 Danish beer-can case (*Commission* v *Denmark*, Case 302/86: see **environment policy**). Article 3.1(t) EC specifies that 'a contribution to the strengthening of consumer protection' is one of the 'activities of the Community'.

In spite of the frailty of the legal base in the original Treaty, an outline programme for consumer policy was adopted by the **European Council** in 1972. However, except for the setting up of the Consumers' Consultative Committee the following year, little was achieved. The first Consumer Action Programme was adopted in 1975 (*Official Journal*, C92, 25 April 1975). As in other areas, the drive to complete the Single Market led to more rapid progress, since it was evident that opening markets would meet with fierce consumer resistance unless high standards of consumer protection were maintained. Broadly, the aim was to enable consumers to make informed choices between competing products, to make use of goods or services safely, to be in a position to claim redress in the event of not being satisfied, and to make the range of goods available to consumers as wide as possible by establishing common product standards (see **harmonization**).

The first of these aims led to measures on unit pricing, on standard quantities for prepackaged products, on labelling and on misleading advertising. The second aim has resulted in legislation on the use of additives in foodstuffs, on dangerous substances and on general product safety. The third aim gave rise to the controversial Product Liability Directive of 1985, which entitles the consumer to bring proceedings against the producer of a product that has caused damage without having to prove negligence on the part of the producer. Other related measures include legislation on door-to-door sales, on common rules for all forms of credit, on package holidays and timeshare sales, on toy safety, on unfair terms in contracts and on cosmetic products.

In 1990 the Consumers' Consultative Committee became the Consumers' Consultative Council, and at about the same time the Consumer Policy Service was set up in the **European Commission**. In order to monitor the application of consumer policy measures the Commission has sought to assist national consumer bodies (virtually non-existent in many member states) and in particular to promote more cooperation between them. The main Brussels-based consumers' lobby is the European Bureau of Consumers' Unions, known by its French acronym BEUC. Information to consumers is made available through a network of European Consumer Information Centres ('euroguichets'). (See also **Europe Direct**.)

In the light of the limited legal base for consumer policy and the application of **subsidiarity** it is clear that there is little scope for a substantial extension of consumer protection measures. It is more likely to be a question of refining existing measures, for example, in the light of new scientific evidence. The interests of consumers are, however, a key factor in **competition policy** and in moves to reform the **Common Agricultural Policy** (CAP). The BSE crisis prompted the European Council at its meeting in Luxembourg in December 1997 to discuss **food safety**. A Declaration on the subject was adopted and annexed to the presidency conclusions. The current Consumer Action Programme, covering the period up to 2003, was adopted in 1999 (*Official Journal*, L34, 9 February 1999). See also **European Food Safety Authority**, **precautionary principle**. Geraint Howells and Thomas Wilhelmsson, *EC Consumer Law* (Aldershot, 1997) is a lucid general survey.

Contributions and receipts

The overall pattern of member states' contributions to and receipts from the Union's **Budget** is difficult to calculate, since the **European Commission**, the only institution in possession of all the figures, is wary of providing information that in its view tends to encourage a narrow 'profit and loss' approach to membership of the Union. The economic costs of membership, it may be argued, can be expressed in cash terms, whereas many of the economic benefits, some of them long-term, cannot be so expressed. The Union's revenue under the system of **own resources**, although it is broken down into 'contributions' from each member state, is in fact composed of monies to which the Union is entitled as of right, not of subscriptions analogous to those paid to other international organizations. Agricultural levies and customs duties under the **Common External Tariff**, which form part of the Union's own resources, are collected by member states on the Union's behalf and paid over, the member states retaining 25 per cent of the proceeds to cover their collection costs. One side-effect of this system is that tariffs and levies payable on goods imported through Rotterdam will appear as part of the Netherlands' 'contribution', whatever the final destination of the goods.

Detailed calculations of contributions and receipts were first made in the late 1970s when the argument over the British contribution (see **British Budget problem**) first arose. More recently, they have entered into the discussions on **future financing**, the prospect of a fifth own resource, and **enlargement**, since, inevitably, applicant states want to know how much membership will cost (see also *juste retour*).

The fullest and clearest official tables showing contributions and receipts may be found in the Commission's annual reports entitled *Allocation of EU Operating Expenditure by Member State*. The table below uses the figures given in tables 2b, 3f, and 6 from the report for 2000.

By far the biggest contributor is Germany. The biggest beneficiaries in GNP terms are Greece, Ireland and Portugal. Spain has the highest gross receipts.

Calculations of future contributions and receipts are very hazardous. Some member states, notably France, receive substantial sums in agricultural price

Payments and receipts by member state 2000

	Payments as % of total	Receipts as % of total	Balance (€ million)	Balance as % of GNP
Austria	1.8	1.7	−543.5	−0.27
Belgium	8.0	5.2	−327.3	−0.13
Denmark	2.1	2.0	169.1	0.10
Finland	0.8	1.7	216.9	0.17
France	10.8	14.9	−1415.3	−0.10
Germany	22.0	12.5	−9273.2	−0.47
Greece	1.3	6.7	4373.9	3.61
Ireland	1.3	3.2	1674.6	1.83
Italy	9.7	13.1	713.4	0.06
Luxembourg	0.2	1.1	−65.1	−0.35
The Netherlands	11.4	2.7	−1737.7	−0.44
Portugal	1.2	3.9	2112.0	1.93
Spain	6.0	13.1	5055.9	0.86
Sweden	2.6	1.5	−1177.4	−0.50
United Kingdom	20.9	9.5	−3774.7	−0.25

Source: European Commission, *Allocation of EU Operating Expenditure by Member State*, Tables 2b, 3f, and 6.

support from the **European Agricultural Guidance and Guarantee Fund** (EAGGF), but the actual level of such receipts is dependent upon movements in world prices and other factors. Similarly, projections of member states' contributions to the VAT-based and GNP-related own resources contain assumptions about economic performance.

Convention
See **Laeken Declaration**.

Convergence
Convergence is a term used to denote the coming together of the economies of the member states of the European Union. It may relate to their performance, to the policies which direct them, (rarely) to their essential structures, or to all of these. The expression was first widely used in the early 1970s (see **Werner report**). It is now most commonly heard in relation to the criteria used to judge member states' eligibility for stage 3 of **Economic and Monetary Union** (EMU): see **convergence criteria**.

Convergence criteria
The timetable for **Economic and Monetary Union** (EMU) laid down in the **Maastricht Treaty** as an addition to Article 109 of the **Treaty of Rome** (now Article 116) makes EMU conditional upon the 'sustainable convergence' of the economies of member states (Article 121.1). The first of the four convergence criteria is 'a high degree of price stability ... apparent from a rate of inflation which is close to that of, at most, the three best performing Member States'. The second is the elimination of public sector deficits defined as 'excessive' in accordance with criteria laid down in Article 104 and in a protocol on the **excessive deficit procedure**. The third is observance of the 'normal fluctuation margins' provided for in the **Exchange-Rate Mechanism** (ERM) for at least two years, with no devaluation against the currency of any other member state. The fourth criterion, which relates to the sustainability of the convergence, is the level of long-term interest rates, which must not exceed by more than 2 per cent the average of interest rates in the three best-performing member states, assessed in terms of price stability. It will be noted that the criteria are purely 'nominal' and relate to the performance of the national economies and not to their structure.

Under the same Article the **European Commission** and the **European Monetary Institute** (EMI) are required to make regular reports to the **Ecofin Council** on the economic performance of member states with reference to these four criteria. Together with other economic indicators, these reports enabled the Council (meeting as the **European Council**) to decide on 2 May

Application of the convergence criteria

	Rate of inflation (%)[1]	Long-term interest rates (%)[1]	Annual deficit/surplus (% of GDP)[2]	Gross deficit (% of GDP)[2]
Reference value	2.7	7.8	≤3	≤60
Austria	**1.1**	5.6	−2.3	64.7
Belgium	1.4	5.7	−1.7	118.1
Denmark[3]	1.9	6.2	1.1	59.5
Finland	1.3	5.9	0.3	53.6
France	**1.2**	5.5	−2.9	58.1
Germany	1.4	5.6	−2.5	61.2
Greece	5.2	9.8	−2.2	107.7
Ireland	**1.2**	6.2	1.1	59.5
Italy	1.8	6.7	−2.5	118.1
Luxembourg	1.4	5.6	1.0	7.1
The Netherlands	1.8	5.5	−1.6	70.0
Portugal	1.8	6.2	−2.2	60.0
Spain	1.8	6.3	−2.2	67.4
Sweden[4]	1.9	6.5	0.5	74.1
United Kingdom[3]	1.8	7.0	−0.6	52.3
EU	1.6	6.1	−1.9	70.5

[1] The figures in columns 1 and 2 are based on an average of monthly figures during the period February 1997–January 1998. The 'reference values' are derived from an average of the figures pertaining to the three best performing member states with respect to price stability (in bold) plus 1.5 percentage points for rates of inflation and 2 percentage points for interest rates.

[2] For more details, see **excessive deficit procedure**.

[3] Not participating in stage 3 of EMU, and not assessed in the Ecofin Council's Recommendation of 1 May 1998.

[4] Although without a formal opt-out, Sweden gave notice of not wishing to participate in stage 3 of EMU. The Council's assessment disqualified Sweden from stage 3 on the grounds that the krona had failed to respect the 'normal fluctuation margins' within the ERM.

Source: European Commission, EMI, Council Recommendation of 1 May 1998.

1998 that 11 member states (Greece did not meet the criteria, and Denmark, Sweden and the United Kingdom did not wish to proceed) would take part in the third stage of EMU, which began on 1 January 1999. The Council's findings are set out in the table above. Greece was subsequently admitted, and adopted the **euro** on 1 January 2002.

Cooperation Agreement

Article 133 of the **Treaty of Rome** specifies that the **Common Commercial Policy** (CCP) should be based on 'uniform principles', one of which is the conclusion of tariff and trade agreements. These are negotiated by the **European Commission** on the basis of a mandate laid down by the **Council of Ministers** and under the general oversight of the **Article 133 Committee**. Consultation of the **European Parliament** is not, strictly speaking, required for agreements concluded under Article 133 (see **Article 308**), although Parliament is closely involved in the negotiations (see **Luns–Westerterp procedure**).

The simplest form of trade agreement, normally concluded for a period of five years and often restricted to a particular product, is now known as a 'first generation' agreement. This is because in the 1980s it was found necessary to conclude more elaborate and ambitious agreements providing for economic and other forms of cooperation over a wider field. Article 113 (now 133) was not thought to be an adequate legal base for such 'second generation' Cooperation Agreements, and so Article 235 (now 308) was used in addition. Consultation with the European Parliament is mandatory under this Article. Cooperation Agreements of this type, which are each managed by a joint committee, normally allow for financial assistance from the Union and are open-ended in the sense that they contain a *clause évolutive*, which provides for cooperation to be extended into new fields. Agreements of this type have been concluded with India, China, Pakistan and several countries in Latin America.

A still more ambitious 'third generation' of Cooperation Agreements has since been developed. These are similar to the 'second generation' agreements, but contain extra elements such as human rights clauses, joint undertakings in the fight against drug-trafficking, and regular political contacts. Such agreements have been concluded with certain countries in Latin America and the Mediterranean and are a model for future relations with many countries in south-east Asia. The human rights clauses in particular have proved controversial, since some countries regard them as a form of interference in their internal affairs. Agreements involving institutionalized political contacts and those with 'important budgetary implications' require Parliament's approval under the **assent procedure**.

Cooperation procedure

The cooperation procedure, which is set out in Article 252 of the **Treaty of Rome,** was introduced by the 1986 **Single European Act** (SEA) as a means of strengthening the role of the **European Parliament** in the legislative process, thus going some way towards correcting the **democratic deficit**. This, it was feared, had been opened still wider by the extension under the SEA of **qualified majority voting** (QMV) in the **Council of Ministers**. It allows for the Parliament to be consulted twice before a legislative measure is enacted (see below). The cooperation procedure was further developed by the **Maastricht Treaty** as the **co-decision procedure** (Article 251 EC).

Under the cooperation procedure the **European Commission** forwards a draft proposal to the Council of Ministers. At the same time the European Parliament (and frequently the **Economic and Social Committee** and the **Committee of the Regions**) begins its examination of the proposal; when completed, this is forwarded to the Council as the Parliament's **Opinion**. The Council's conclusion, adopted by QMV, is reached in the form of a **common position**, and this is sent back to the Parliament accompanied by an explanation of the views of the Council and the Commission. The Parliament may then, by simple majority, adopt the common position or fail to take action: in either case, the Council may then proceed to formal enactment of the proposal as embodied in its common position. However, by absolute majority, the Parliament may seek to amend the common position or reject it altogether.

If the Parliament votes to reject a common position, the Council must act unanimously to have it reinstated. If (as is more usual) the Parliament has adopted amendments to the common position, the Commission then has an opportunity to re-examine its original proposal in the light of these amendments, and to forward the results of the re-examination to the Council with all the Parliament's amendments. The Council may adopt by unanimity amendments that the Commission has not incorporated in its revised proposal. Also by unanimity, it may amend the revised proposal. It may adopt and enact the revised proposal by QMV. If it fails to take a decision within a deadline, the proposal falls.

The introduction of the cooperation procedure (the SEA came into force in July 1987) not only gave the Parliament a second opportunity to influence the substance of legislation but also changed the balance of power between the institutions of the Union to the Parliament's advantage. By using the threat of outright rejection, the Parliament was in a stronger position to enforce its views upon the Commission and the Council. The procedure also required the Parliament to exercise greater discipline as a consequence of the need to muster an absolute majority to reject or amend the Council's common position (this in turn has had an effect on relations between the **political groups** in the Parliament).

The cooperation procedure has been criticized for being too complicated. At one stage in the negotiations that led to the SEA a much simpler solution was proposed: the Council of Ministers should deliberate on a legislative proposal as amended by the Parliament. This was not acceptable to certain member states, which took the view that this procedure would make the Parliament too powerful, nor to the Commission, which feared the virtual elimination of the 'brokerage' role from which much of its power derives. The procedure that finally emerged was a compromise. Under the **Treaty of Amsterdam** the cooperation procedure has been largely superseded by the co-decision procedure. See David Earnshaw and David Judge, 'The life and times of the European Union's cooperation procedure', *Journal of Common Market Studies*, Vol. 35, no. 4, December 1997.

Copenhagen criteria

At its meeting in Copenhagen in June 1993, the **European Council** agreed that all the central and eastern European countries with **Europe Agreements** 'that so desire shall become members of the [European] Union'. The conditions were listed as:

stability of institutions guaranteeing democracy, the rule of law, human rights and respect for and protection of minorities; ... a functioning market economy, as well as the capacity to cope with competitive pressure and market forces within the Union; [and] the ability to take on the obligations of membership, including adherence to the aims of political, economic and monetary union.

The **Opinions** drawn up by the **European Commission** on the applicant states (see **enlargement**) assessed each state's eligibility for membership of the Union in the light of these criteria.

In 1995 the Commission published a White Paper entitled *Preparation of the Associated Countries of Central and Eastern Europe for Integration into the Internal Market of the Union*. It lists 899 measures in 23 sectors as a means of helping applicants prepare for the **Single Market**. Each applicant's 'score' on this so-called 'Harmonogramme' is an index of the extent to which domestic legislation has been adapted to meet Single Market requirements.

COREPER

'COREPER' is derived from *Comité des représentants permanents* (Committee of Permanent Representatives), a body provided for in Article 207 of the **Treaty of Rome**. The Permanent Representatives are the Brussels-based ambassadors of the member states of the European Union (see **national representations**). COREPER's most important task is the preparation of meetings of the **Council of Ministers** (see also **political directors**, **UKREP**). COREPER is descended from the coordinating committee, known as COCOR, which prepared ministerial meetings in the **European Coal and Steel Community** (ECSC) and which was established in February 1953. The fullest description of COREPER is Jaap W. de Zwaan, *The Permanent Representatives Committee* (Amsterdam, 1995).

COREU

COREU is the system by which the foreign offices of the member states of the European Union exchange information in the form of circulated telegrams, telex messages and faxes, under the overall supervision of the **political directors** and their assistants (the 'European correspondents'). First devised as an essential tool of **European Political Cooperation**, the COREU network, involving many thousands of communications every year, has been maintained as part of the **Common Foreign and Security Policy** (CFSP). The COREU network is also used when member states give their consent to a measure under a written procedure.

Corpus Juris

The *Corpus Juris* (literally, 'body of law') was drawn up by a group of eight academic lawyers at the behest of the **European Commission** and published in April 1997. Its status is that of an independent report. Composed of 35 Articles, the *Corpus Juris* is intended to help the fight against fraud affecting the Union's financial interests by providing a uniform code of law defining fraudulent or corrupt practices and setting out the ground-rules for legal action (evidence, rights of appeal, etc.). The intention is to overcome the obstacles to an effective anti-fraud policy which spring from the diversity of national laws and procedures. Within its field the *Corpus Juris*, if adopted, would take precedence over national law, and would be the first instance of an autonomous body of European Community criminal law. For this reason, and also because it would lead to the creation of a European Public Prosecutor, the *Corpus Juris* has caused concern among some civil liberties experts and others opposed to the idea of an *espace judiciaire européen*. The report by the House of Lords Select Committee on the European Communities, *Prosecuting Fraud on the Communities' Finances – the Corpus Juris* (May 1999) is a conspicuously full and clear treatment of the issue.

COSAC

COSAC (*Conférence des Organes Spécialisées dans les Affaires Communautaires*) is composed of representatives from the various committees specializing in European affairs in the **national parliaments** of the member states of the European Union and from the **European Parliament**. It was established in Paris in November 1989, and stems from an initiative on the part of the French National Assembly in May 1989 which was subsequently taken up at the Madrid Conference of Presidents of national parliaments and of the European Parliament. COSAC meets every six months. The **Treaty of Amsterdam** includes a **protocol** on the role of national parliaments in the European Union in which COSAC is for the first time given treaty status.

Under this protocol, COSAC 'may make any contribution it deems appropriate ... in particular on the basis of draft legal texts which ... the Member States may decide by common accord to forward to it'. However, 'contributions made by COSAC shall in no way bind national parliaments or prejudice their position'. This protocol does little more than formalize the current state of affairs.

COST

The scheme known as COST (European Cooperation in the Field of Scientific and Technical Research) was set up in 1971 to promote cross-frontier collaboration between 19 European countries in such fields as information technology, environmental protection, meteorology, health care and transport. Thirty-three countries now participate in COST.

Cotonou Agreement

The Cotonou Agreement, signed in Cotonou (Benin) on 20 June 2000 by representatives of the European Union's member states and 77 African, Caribbean and Pacific countries (the **ACP states**), succeeded and replaced the **Lomé Convention** as the principal instrument of the Union's **development policy**. The 92 signatories, about half the total membership of the United Nations, have a total population of over 1 billion people (639 million ACP, 376 million EU), roughly one-sixth of the population of the world.

The 100 Articles of the Agreement, concluded for 20 years, have as their main purpose 'to promote and expedite the economic, cultural and social development of the ACP States' (Article 1) on the basis of a partnership. The Agreement makes provision for regular and wide-ranging political dialogue (Article 8), specifying that 'the Partnership shall actively support the promotion of human rights, processes of democratization, consolidation of the rule of law, and good governance' (Article 9.4). Throughout, emphasis is placed on the eradication of poverty, on the role of the private sector, non-governmental organizations (NGOs), and civil society generally, and on coordination with the Union's other policies. In spite of opposition from some ACP states, Article 13 requires all signatory states to accept without question the return of any of their own nationals found to be illegally on the territory of another signatory state.

The Agreement provides for institutions identical to those in the Lomé Convention: an ACP–EU Council of Ministers, meeting at least once a year and taking decisions 'by common agreement' (Article 15); a Committee of Ambassadors in Brussels (Article 16); and an ACP–EU Joint Parliamentary Assembly meeting twice a year and composed of 77 Members of the **European Parliament** and a representative from (or appointed by) the Parliament of each of the ACP states (Article 17).

Articles 19 to 33 set out the 'development strategies', including 'institutional development and capacity building'. Economic and trade cooperation is dealt with in Articles 34 to 54. Of those, the most important is Article 36, which provides for the negotiation of Economic Partnership Agreements over the period 2002–7 between the Union and individual ACP states (or groups of states), tailored to their specific needs and priorities. These Agreements are to be compatible with **World Trade Organization** (WTO) rules and will enter into force in 2008.

The financial provisions of the Agreement are contained in Articles 55 to 83. These cover specific points such as debt relief (Article 66), structural adjustment (Article 67), measures to mitigate the effect of short-term fluctuations in ACP states' export earnings (Article 68), and guarantees for private sector investment (Article 77). In conformity with the practice established under the Lomé Convention, the Cotonou Agreement has annexed to it a Financial Protocol, valid for a period of 5 years. The bulk of the funding will come from the **European Development Fund** (EDF), worth €13.5 billion over the period 2001–5, to which must be added €1.7 billion from the **European Investment Bank** (EIB). This EDF, the ninth in the series, was criticized for being smaller than its immediate predecessor. However, of the 8th EDF, €9.9 billion remained unspent at the time the Cotonou Agreement was negotiated, and this sum, taken in conjunction with the 9th EDF and EIB resources, means that some €25 billion is available to ACP states.

The special problems of 'least developed, landlocked, and island' countries (LDLICs) are recognized and addressed in Articles 84 to 90 of the Agreement (the LDLICs are listed in Annex VI). The remaining Articles deal with the formal arrangements for the entry into force and implementation of the Agreement. It should be noted that although South Africa is a signatory to the Agreement and a full participant in its political dimension, it is excluded from some of its trade and development provisions. Relations between the Union and South Africa are governed by a Trade, Development and Cooperation Agreement signed in Pretoria in October 1999.

The Cotonou Agreement has gone some way towards assuaging the fears of those who thought that the European Union, as a result of **enlargement** and a new interest in developing a comprehensive **Mediterranean policy**, might be turning away from the ACP states. To a substantial extent the Agreement builds on 25 years of experience of the Lomé Convention whilst recognizing its shortcomings (strikingly illustrated by the fact that ACP countries' share of the European market has fallen from 6.7 per cent in 1976 to 2.8 per cent in 1999). The more explicit emphasis on good governance, the wider use of decentralized cooperation, and greater recognition of the role of NGOs should all contribute towards greater political maturity in relations between the Union and the ACP states. Other areas in which the Cotonou Agreement represents an advance on the Lomé Convention include simpler, more transparent procedures for the disbursement of development aid, tighter financial controls, and a more differentiated approach to ACP states' particular problems. The Agreement also takes full account of the WTO-inspired moves towards liberalization in trade relations.

A great deal of background information on the Cotonou Agreement may be found in issue 181 (June–July 2000) of *The Courier*, published by the Directorate-General for Development of the **European Commission**. A special issue of *The Courier* (September 2000) reproduces the text of the Agreement, accompanied by many explanatory articles.

Coudenhove-Kalergi, Count Richard (1894–1972)

Born in Tokyo, the son of a diplomat in the Austro-Hungarian Embassy and a Japanese mother, Coudenhove-Kalergi was the best-known pioneer of the idea of a united Europe throughout the second quarter of this century. In Berlin and Vienna in the 1920s Coudenhove-Kalergi began his campaign for what he called **Pan-Europa** in a long series of books and articles. In 1922 he founded his 'Pan-European Union' and in October 1926 he convened a 'European Congress' in Vienna. This was followed by further congresses in Berlin (1930), Basel (1932), Vienna (1935) and New York (1943). He received the support and sympathy of many of the leading statesmen of the day (such as Walter Rathenau, **Aristide Briand**, **Winston Churchill** and Thomas Masaryk) and of other figures in public life (such as the violinist Bronislaw Hubermann). Thomas Mann, for example, agreed to join the Committee of the Pan-European Union and wrote to Coudenhove-Kalergi (17 September 1926) describing it as an 'idea that the world so stands in need of' (*Letters*, trans. R. and C. Winston, Harmondsworth, 1975). In 1943 he drew up a constitution for a **United States of Europe** and submitted it for approval to all the foreign ministers of European states opposed to the Axis powers. After the war, at a meeting in Gstaad on 5 July 1947, he founded a 'European Parliamentary Union' with himself as Secretary-General. In 1952 he refounded his Pan-European Union, which became a member organization of the **European Movement** (although it later broke away). Coudenhove-Kalergi's approach to European integration was essentially political, as opposed to the more technocratic, economically oriented approach of **Jean Monnet** and his supporters. This led him to sympathize very strongly with **Charles de Gaulle**, who, from a different standpoint, also viewed European integration in political terms and whose principled opposition to the division of Europe brought about by the Yalta Agreement Coudenhove-Kalergi much admired ('he draws no dividing line between politics and history'). Although Coudenhove-Kalergi's ideas met with a sympathetic response among many politicians and intellectuals of all parties and nationalities, he was never successful in attracting mass support. An account of his activities and ideas may be found in his *An Idea Conquers the World* (1953), and an assessment of his importance in an essay by Ralph White in P.M.R. Stirk (ed.), *European Unity in Context* (1989).

Council for Mutual Economic Assistance
See COMECON.

Council of Economic and Finance Ministers
See Ecofin Council.

Council of Europe
Founded in 1949, the Council of Europe is an intergovernmental consultative organization with a current membership of 45 countries representing about 780 million people. Four countries have 'special guest status' (see below). It was set up in response to a resolution adopted by the 1948 **Congress of Europe**, with its seat (at the suggestion of Ernest Bevin) in **Strasbourg**, and is not an institution of the European Union. Much of its work is concerned with human rights, education, culture and cooperation in such fields as the protection of the environment, medical ethics and the fight against drugs. More recently, the Council of Europe has been very active in respect of constitutional and legislative reform in the countries of central and eastern Europe.

The founder members of the Council of Europe were Denmark, Sweden, the United Kingdom, Norway, Ireland, Italy, Luxembourg, France, the Netherlands and Belgium. In 1949 they were joined by Greece and Turkey, in 1950 by Iceland, and (in an act of reconciliation first suggested by **Winston Churchill**) by the Federal Republic of Germany in 1951. Austria joined in 1956 once Russian forces had withdrawn from Austrian territory. Cyprus, Switzerland and Malta joined in the 1960s, Portugal, Spain and Liechtenstein in the 1970s, San Marino and Finland in the 1980s. The first of the former Communist countries to join were Hungary (1990) and Czechoslovakia (1991). They have since been followed in rapid succession by Albania, Andorra, Armenia, Azerbaijan, Bosnia-Herzegovina, Bulgaria, Croatia, Estonia, Georgia, Latvia, Lithuania, Macedonia, Moldova, Poland, Romania, Russia, Slovenia and Ukraine. In 2003 Serbia and Montenegro became the forty-fifth member state. The United States, Canada, Japan, the Holy See, and Mexico have observer status.

The three main institutions of the Council of Europe are the Committee of Ministers (foreign ministers or their deputies), the Parliamentary Assembly (formerly the Consultative Assembly, composed of 291 members and 291 substitutes appointed from and by **national parliaments** and divided into five **political groups**), and the Congress of Local and Regional Authorities of Europe. The Council of Europe has its own secretariat of approximately 1,300 officials, headed by a secretary-general elected by the Assembly. Meeting in plenary session four times a year, the Parliamentary Assembly adopts **Resolutions** addressed to the Committee of Ministers, which takes decisions by consensus, addressed to member states in the form of Recommendations. The Congress (which is bicameral, with one chamber for local authorities and another for regional authorities) may also adopt Resolutions. The official languages of the Council of Europe are French and English, but interpretation from and into German, Italian and Russian is also provided at meetings of the Parliamentary Assembly and the Congress. The Assembly's 14 committees meet in Paris or Strasbourg. The Court of Human Rights, also in Strasbourg, is an organ of the Council of Europe (for further details, see **human rights**).

Unlike the institutions of the European Union, the institutions of the Council of Europe have no power to make laws. Instead, a consensus reached at the level of the Committee of Ministers may be embodied in a convention, which is then open for signature by individual states. Less formally, the consensus may be drawn up as a charter or code. There are now some 150 conventions, charters or codes: among the best known are the 1950 **European Convention on Human Rights**, the 1954 European Cultural Convention, the 1979 Berne Convention on the protection of rare and endangered animals and plants, the 1981 Convention on data protection and the 1990 Convention on measures to locate, freeze and confiscate assets associated with organized crime.

The Council of Europe has an annual budget made up largely of contributions from member states. It operates certain specialized loan facilities: for example, under its 'Eurimages' programme, European film companies can borrow against estimated revenues from co-productions.

In its historical context the Council of Europe was a compromise between those who advocated European integration along supranational lines and those who, although in favour of a wide measure of cooperation, wanted national governments to retain firm control over the process. In its very early years the Council of Europe was indeed the main forum for debate over the future of Europe: it was where, for example, Churchill first called for the creation of a **European Army**. However, like many compromises, it satisfied nobody. Governments largely ignored the Council's Recommendations and by 1951 **the Six** had with the signing of the **European Coal and Steel Community** (ECSC) Treaty embarked upon a more ambitious project. The first blow to the Council of Europe's prestige came in 1952 when the ECSC Common Assembly, not the Council of Europe Assembly, was chosen to draw up the treaty for a **European Political Community** (although a compromise solution was later found in the form of an *ad hoc* assembly). By the end of the 1950s the focus of attention had shifted decisively away from the Council of Europe and towards what was to become the European Community and, later, the European Union.

Until the end of the 1980s the importance of the Council of Europe was limited to three main areas. First, it was a forum in which countries not belonging to the European Community could remain in touch with the integration process. Second, membership of the Council of Europe was an indispensable proof of democratic credentials for countries (like Portugal and Spain in the mid-1970s) wanting to regain their international respectability after periods of dictatorship. This aspect of the Council's role was reinforced by the decision to suspend the membership of Greece and Turkey during periods of military rule, and played an important part in the Council's re-emergence after the collapse of Communism. Third, the Council made steady and substantial progress in the field of human rights, an area largely excluded from the European Community Treaties.

Since 1989 the Council of Europe has acted as an antechamber for countries of central and eastern Europe, the majority of which are, in the longer term, interested in membership of the European Union. In response to their demands the Council has set up a European Commission for Democracy through Law, based in Venice, to advise on questions of legal and constitutional reform and the operation of democratic institutions. The Council has also inaugurated a series of summit meetings for heads of government, the first of which was held in Vienna in October 1993 and a second in Strasbourg in October 1997. In November 1998 a committee chaired by Mario Soares, former President of Portugal, presented its proposals on the Council's future development.

Council of Ministers

The Council of Ministers is the principal decision-making body within the European Union. It has both executive and legislative powers, the former delegated in many areas to the **European Commission** and the latter in some cases exercised jointly with the **European Parliament** (see **co-decision procedure**). The Parliament and the Council form the joint budgetary authority (see **Budget**). The Council is responsible for authorizing, overseeing and concluding negotiations with non-member countries. Under the **Common Foreign and Security Policy** (CFSP) and **Justice and Home Affairs** (JHA) provisions of the **Maastricht Treaty**, the Council may adopt **common positions** or take **joint actions**. Overall, the Council acts within guidelines laid down by the **European Council** of heads of state or of government. The **presidency** of the Council changes every six months. Formerly entitled the Council of Ministers of the European Communities, since the entry into force of the Maastricht Treaty (November 1993) the Council has styled itself the Council of the European Union.

Articles 202 to 210 of the **Treaty of Rome** set out the powers, composition and procedures of the Council. Article 202 gives the Council the power to coordinate the economic policies of member states, to take decisions and to confer implementing powers on the Commission. Article 203 requires the Council to be composed 'of a representative of each Member State at ministerial level, authorized to commit the government of that Member State' (this wording, introduced by the Maastricht Treaty, allows federal states such as Belgium or Germany to be represented if necessary by a minister from a provincial or *Land* government). Article 205 specifies that decisions should normally be taken by majority and lists the weightings for the vote of each member state under the **qualified majority voting** system (see below). The same Article says that abstentions do not count in decisions requiring unanimity. The Council's Rules of Procedure were published in the *Official Journal* on 28 August 2002 (L230). Article 9 of these Rules specifies that when the Council acts 'in its legislative capacity . . . the results of votes . . . shall be made public', together with explanations of votes and formal statements. This also applies to the adoption of common positions in the course of the **co-operation procedure** or the **co-decision procedure**, but not to CFSP or JHA matters except by unanimous agreement. The Helsinki meeting of the European Council (December 1999) adopted a large number of practical reforms to the Council's working methods (see Annex III of the Presidency Conclusions) including better forward planning, the stricter application of deadlines, more thorough preparation at official level, and an enhanced role for the incoming presidency.

The Council of Ministers may convene in any configuration it chooses. In practice, it divides its work into several distinct subject-based councils that operate in parallel. The senior council within this structure is the Council of Foreign Ministers (officially called the **General Affairs Council**), and the Foreign Minister of each member state is its lead representative on the Council. Exceptionally, the European Council may meet as the Council of Ministers, for example, when the decision was taken on stage 3 of **Economic and Monetary Union** (EMU; Article 121 EC).

The Foreign Affairs Council normally meets monthly, as do the Councils of Agriculture Ministers and of Economics and Finance Ministers (see **Ecofin Council**). There are regular, but less frequent, meetings of the Industry, Environment, Research, Transport, Social Affairs, Fisheries and Budget Councils. Less frequent still are meetings of ministers of development, energy, justice, consumer affairs, regional affairs, culture, education and health. From time to time joint or 'jumbo' Councils may be arranged to discuss issues that cross the boundaries of any one Council's responsibilities. In all, the Council has in recent years met on average about 80 times a year.

Although the Council of Ministers is the chief forum for the representation of national interests in the decision-making process, the Council's acts are those of a fully-fledged Union institution, made on behalf of and in the name of the Union as a whole. In its capacity as the legislature, the Council can adopt any of the types of **legal instrument** provided for in the Treaties. It can also issue non-binding recommendations to member states or adopt **Resolutions**. Its other non-legislative activities usually take the form of 'conclusions' – issued by the presidency, with or without the unanimous approval of the whole Council – which represent the emerging lines of an agreement that may subsequently be converted into legislative action.

The Council can take decisions by **unanimity**, QMV or simple majority voting. The Treaties provide that, except where otherwise prescribed, simple majority voting will be the norm. However, in nearly all areas the Treaties require either QMV or unanimity. For the greater part of the Community's history, unanimity was the operating principle of the Council, even where theoretically a decision could be taken by qualified or simple majority. The extension of majority voting in 1966, when the third stage of the 'transitional' phase of the Community's development came into effect, was overshadowed by an informal agreement, concluded in January of that year, known as the **Luxembourg Compromise**. This in practice gave any member state a right of **veto** on a matter that it considered to touch on a 'very important' national interest. This meant that votes were rarely, if ever, taken, except sometimes on detailed agricultural or budgetary issues, and an objection from any member state – whether or not a 'very important' interest was really at stake – was enough to kill a proposal.

The member state holding the presidency is responsible for organizing the business of the Council, assisted by a permanent general secretariat of 2,500 officials based entirely in Brussels and grouped into six policy-related directorates-general. They draw up the minutes, suggest compromise texts to the presidency and ensure that the acts of the Council are properly transposed into legal form and duly published in the *Official Journal*. The Council's legal service, which advises on the form and Treaty basis of any proposal, carries considerable authority. However, the Council secretariat's influence on the content of decision making is often inversely proportional to the size of the member state holding the presidency. The five largest member states tend to find that their own **national representations** in Brussels are so large that they can free themselves of reliance on the technical expertise and institutional memory of the Council secretariat. Smaller member states are much more reliant.

Officials from the national representations meet together regularly to prepare the various decisions to be taken by the Council. There are two tiers, **COREPER** (see also **national representations**) and working groups. COREPER brings together the ambassadors of member states, their deputies and relevant colleagues, to discuss the agenda of forthcoming meetings of the Council. COREPER's influence is often greater than that of the

Council. In the foreign policy field a **Political and Security Committee** performs many of the same functions as COREPER and in the justice and home affairs field a coordinating committee does the same.

Working groups, made up of mid-rank civil servants from the national representations and (where necessary) domestic ministries, prepare the ground before items are taken to COREPER and then the full Council. The purpose of discussion in both tiers is to identify in precise detail the points of agreement and discord on any proposal, and to try to resolve remaining disagreements so that the higher body (COREPER or the full Council) can focus on major points of dispute. Once a point has been settled at a lower level, the presidency will try to avoid its being reopened at a higher level. The power of mid-rank civil servants in this system is thus significant. Council agendas are divided into A and B points, the former being issues that have already been satisfactorily concluded at an official level.

COREPER and the working groups are also serviced by the Council secretariat and chaired by the country holding the presidency. As in the full Council, the Commission is normally present at, and participates in, all their meetings.

The Council normally meets in Brussels, but three times a year (April, June and October) it meets in Luxembourg, as part of the 1965 arrangement on the provisional location of various institutions (see **seat of the institutions**). In addition, the presidency normally convenes one 'informal' weekend meeting of each Council in its own country (see **Gymnich meetings**). These are, by definition, not formal or official meetings of the Council, and have no legal status. Usually they are devoted to open-ended discussion of large and difficult problems on the Council's agenda, in the hope of finding new common ground. Informals do not reach conclusions as such, and normally issue no communiqués. They can, however, be the scene for important political breakthroughs, although their rather cloudy and often unverifiable outcomes can render them easy prey to sensationalist media reporting.

Similar to full Council meetings but distinct from them in law are the gatherings of 'Representatives of the Governments of Member States meeting in Council'. These take certain decisions which the Treaties specify as being for the member states acting collectively by 'common accord' rather than for the Council as an institution of the Union. Sometimes these decisions are taken in practice by the European Council and then formalized as having been taken by representatives 'meeting in Council' later, and include matters such as appointments to the Commission or the **Court of Justice** and the location of the institutions. The right of Members of the European Parliament to put questions to the Council does not extend to matters decided on the basis of agreement between the governments of member states.

In spite of hesitant moves in the direction of greater openness (see **transparency**), the Council remains the most secretive as well as the most powerful of the institutions of the Union. The **Treaty of Amsterdam**, in an amendment to Article 151 (now 207) E C, required the Council to adopt rules governing the public's access to Council documents within two years of the Treaty's entry into force (i.e. by May 2001). A decision of December 1999 (*Official Journal*, L9, 13 January 2000) specifies that agendas of the Council and its preparatory bodies, when the Council is acting 'in its legislative capacity' together with a list of the relevant Council documents, should be made available to the public.

What is unlikely to happen even in the longer term is that the Council will become a **Chamber of States** in a bicameral system, in which the Commission would be the real European government and the European Parliament the principal legislative body. This, in simple terms, is what some of the enthusiasts for European integration in the 1950s thought would happen. One of the central features of the institutional development of the Union is the permanence and vitality of national interests as represented in the Council, which celebrated its 2,000th meeting (since 1967) on 21 April 1997. Meetings of the Council take place in the Justus Lipsius building in Brussels, named after a sixteenth-century Flemish humanist and scholar. The Council publishes an annual review of its work in the form of a report by the secretary-general.

Court of Auditors

Expenditure by institutions of the European Union is subject to both internal and external controls. Internal controls are the responsibility of the Directorate-General for Financial Control and the Internal Audit Service in the **European Commission** and of similar bodies in other institutions. External controls have since 1977 been the responsibility of the Court of Auditors, a separate institution composed of one appointee (or 'Member') from each member state and a staff of about 550 people. It is based in Luxembourg.

External financial controls, of which the Court is the principal symbol, have been very substantially strengthened since the establishment of the European Communities. Initially, responsibility for financial control was vested with a small Audit Board composed for the most part of officials from the national audit offices or Ministries of Finance of the member states. Under a Council Decision of 15 May 1959 the Audit Board – the members of which were appointed for a five-year period by the **Council of Ministers** – was required 'to exercise its functions in the general interest of the Communities'. Its main task was to draw up a report on the Communities' annual income and expenditure, a report that was forwarded to the Council and (from 1970) the **European Parliament** with the annual accounts prepared by the Commission as part of the **discharge procedure**.

The first **enlargement** of the Community (1973), several well-publicized instances of fraud in the **Common Agricultural Policy** (CAP), and the growth in the size of the **Budget** reinforced a feeling, especially among Members of the European Parliament, that the Audit Board lacked the resources, independence and authority to do its job effectively. The Parliament was also interested in strengthening its own powers of democratic control over Community expenditure, and the new Audit Office for which the Parliament pressed was expected to work very closely with the Parliament's Budgets Committee. A report entitled *The Case for a European Audit Office* was published in September 1973.

In July 1975 the representatives of the member states signed a treaty on budgetary and financial provisions, which, *inter alia*, enhanced the budgetary powers of the European Parliament. Under this treaty, which came into effect in 1977, important changes were made to external financial controls. The Audit Board was replaced by a Court of Auditors. The term of office of the Members of the Court was extended from five to six years, and they were given the right to elect from among their own number a president for a renewable three-year term. The Council is required to consult the European Parliament on appointments to the Court.

The Court's composition and powers are set out in Articles 246 to 248 of the **Treaty of Rome**. Its remit covers not only all the Union institutions but all national, regional and local bodies that receive or handle Union funds both in the member states and elsewhere (for example, in developing countries). Since the definition of Union funds includes not only those entered in the annual Budget but also borrowing and lending through the **European Investment Bank** (EIB), the total volume of expenditure for which the Court is responsible is very large.

The Court's findings are contained in a report adopted by simple majority of its Members in November every year. The Court is required to draw up a 'statement of assurance' that all revenue and expenditure is consistent with the relevant legal provisions, that good accounting practice has been followed, that financial management has been sound and that financial objectives have been met (Article 248). This is done on the basis of documentary or on-the-spot audits. The Court also produces special reports on particular subjects, and is required to give its opinion on any changes proposed by the Commission to the financial regulations or to the system of **own resources**.

The title 'Court' is a misnomer. It was chosen because several member states have similar bodies known as 'courts', but in fact the Court has no power to pass sentence, insist on repayment of misappropriated funds or impose any kind of sanction. The Court's powers are confined to drawing irregularities and shortcomings to the attention of the responsible authorities in the institution concerned, which may or may not act upon the Court's advice. If no action is taken, all the Court can do is to draw attention to the fact in a subsequent report and withhold its approval of the institution's accounts for the financial year in question. The Court has persistently drawn attention to the Council's failure adequately to consider the Court's reports, a criticism endorsed by the House of Lords Select Committee on the European Communities (*Fraud against the Community*, February 1989; *Financial Control and Fraud in the Community*, July 1994). The **Maastricht Treaty** gave the Court the full status of an institution, which allows the Court to bring actions in its own right in the **Court of Justice** against other Union institutions in order to protect its prerogatives.

There is some evidence that the effectiveness of the Court of Auditors has been diminished by the fact that there is no consensus within the Community or even among the Members of the Court on the proper role of an auditor. The narrow definition of auditing is concerned solely with the correspondence between the allocation of funds, the disbursement of those funds and the propriety of the accounting procedures. A broader definition would give the Court autonomous investigative powers and allow it to undertake 'value for money' auditing, but so far there has been great reluctance to allow the Court a more political role, and the Court has not pressed for it.

Court of First Instance (CFI)

Article 11 of the **Single European Act** (SEA) authorized the **Council of Ministers** to 'attach to the **Court of Justice** a court with jurisdiction to hear and determine at first instance … certain classes of action or proceeding brought by natural or legal persons'. This provision was added to the **Treaty of Rome** as Article 168a (now 225). Briefly, its purpose was to relieve the overburdened Court of Justice of certain categories of action (see below) that were already taking up a disproportionate amount of the Court's time. The CFI, composed of a judge from each member state appointed for six years (the judges elect their own president for a three-year term), became operational on 1 November 1989. Cases are normally heard by a panel of three or five judges.

The jurisdiction of the CFI at first extended to disputes between the Community institutions and their employees (staff cases); actions brought against the **European Commission** under the **Treaty of Paris** in respect of levies, production quotas, prices, restrictive agreements and concentrations; and actions brought against the Commission for wrongful application or failure to apply the competition provisions of the Treaty of Rome. In 1993 the CFI's jurisdiction was extended to include actions (other than those brought by Community institutions or member states) to annul Community legislation, for failure to enact such legislation and certain other types of action.

Actions relating to anti-dumping measures and to intellectual property, except those brought by the Community or member states, were transferred from the Court of Justice to the CFI in 1994. Decisions of the CFI may be appealed against in the Court of Justice within a two-month deadline, but only with respect to points of law. The CFI is not empowered to give **preliminary rulings**.

Court of Justice

The Court of Justice, which is based in Luxembourg, is the final arbiter in disputes arising from the Community **Treaties** or the legislation based upon them. It was one of the four Community institutions established in 1951 under Article 7 of the **European Coal and Steel Community** Treaty. It has a general responsibility under Article 220 of the **Treaty of Rome** establishing the **European Economic Community** (EEC) and Article 136 of the Euratom Treaty (see **European Atomic Energy Community**) 'to ensure that in the interpretation and application [of these Treaties], the law is observed'.

The structure, jurisdiction and powers of the Court are laid down in the Treaties; the references that follow are to the Treaty of Rome. The organization and procedures of the Court are set out in the Statute of the Court, annexed as a protocol to each of the three Treaties. The Court consists of 15 judges (Article 221), one from each member state. The judges are assisted by nine **advocates-general** (Article 222). The task of the advocates-general is to make 'reasoned submissions' in open court on the cases upon which the Court is required to adjudicate. Both the judges and the advocates-general are appointed by the governments of the member states for a six-year term (Article 223), but to ensure continuity, a system of partial replacement is applied every three years, with the possibility of reappointment. The President of the Court is elected by the judges from among their number for a three-year term, and may be re-elected. The judges and advocates-general are required to be 'persons whose independence is beyond doubt and who possess the qualifications required for appointment to the highest judicial offices in their respective countries or who are jurisconsults of recognized competence'. The Court normally sits as a panel of three or five judges, and less frequently in plenary session, for which a quorum of seven is sufficient. The senior official of the Court is the Registrar.

The Court's main areas of jurisdiction are as follows:

1 Failure on the part of a member state to fulfil a Treaty obligation (Articles 226 to 228)
   Such an action may be brought either by the **European Commission** or by another member state. In both cases the Commission is required to deliver a 'reasoned opinion', having given the state or states concerned an opportunity to submit observations. If the Court finds that a member state has

failed to fulfil a Treaty obligation, the state is required 'to take the necessary measures' or pay 'a lump sum or penalty payment' (Article 228.2).

2 Judicial review (Articles 230, 231 and 233)

The Court is empowered to 'review the legality' of **legal instruments** adopted by the **Council of Ministers** or the Commission, and certain acts of the **European Parliament**. Actions under this provision may be brought by the Council, the Commission, or by a member state, or by the European Parliament (but only to protect its own prerogatives). Individuals or entities possessing legal personality may also bring such actions in respect of Regulations or Decisions directly concerning them, but these actions are heard in the **Court of First Instance** (CFI). The Court may declare void the legal act which is the subject of the complaint, and require the offending institution to take the 'necessary measures'. The most common grounds for bringing an Article 230 action is the inadequacy of the legal base.

3 Failure to act (Articles 232 and 233)

If the Council, the Commission or (since the **Maastricht Treaty**) the European Parliament fails to act and in so doing infringes a requirement laid down in the Treaties, a member state or any Community institution (Commission, Council or Parliament, and, since the Maastricht Treaty, the **Court of Auditors**) may bring an action before the Court 'to have the infringement established'. Individuals may bring such actions on the same basis as in 2 above. Once again, the Court may require the offending institution to take the 'necessary measures'.

4 Preliminary rulings (Article 234)

In the event of a question of Treaty interpretation or the validity or interpretation of acts of the Community institutions being raised before a national court, that court may request the Court of Justice to give a **preliminary ruling**. The Court's ruling *must* be sought when such a question is raised before a national court against whose decisions there is no final appeal. The Article 234 procedure is used to resolve any question of incompatibility between Community law and national law.

The Court also has jurisdiction in cases brought by Community officials against the Community institutions and disputes involving the Community's **competition** rules, but in such cases the Court's jurisdiction is now exercised by the CFI, introduced under the **Single European Act** and established under a Council Decision of 24 October 1988.

The number of cases brought before the Court has increased spectacularly since 1970. In that year 79 cases were brought, but by 1985 the number had increased to 433 and is now running at an annual average of well over 400 (of which over half are requests for preliminary rulings). Even though many cases are disposed of in groups, and although some do not result in the Court having to give a final judgment, the backlog of cases pending has inexorably increased (and it was this that led to the decision to establish a Court of First Instance). A preliminary ruling usually takes more than 18 months to be delivered, and a direct action is rarely resolved in less than two years.

The Maastricht Treaty introduced several changes to the Treaty of Rome provisions concerning the Court of Justice. The Court was given the power to impose 'a lump sum or penalty payment' on a member state found to have failed to fulfil a treaty obligation (now Article 228.2). Legal acts of the European Parliament could be challenged under the judicial review procedure, and failure to act on the part of the Parliament could also be subject to an action before the Court if the Treaty was thereby infringed. The **European Central Bank** was also brought within the Court's jurisdiction.

The Court's procedures are based almost wholly on written submissions from the contending parties. One of the Union's official **languages** is chosen as the procedural language, but otherwise the normal Community rules on the use of official languages apply. French and English are the working languages. The governments of member states and Union institutions may choose to intervene in actions in which they are not directly involved. There is no appeal against the Court's judgments, which are published periodically in *European Court Reports*. They are binding with effect from the date of delivery. Judgments are delivered in the name of the Court as a whole, i.e., dissenting opinions (if any) are not recorded.

Under Articles 105 to 107 of the 1992 Agreement establishing the **European Economic Area** (EEA) the Court (together with the CFI, the **European Free Trade Area** (EFTA) Court and the courts of final appeal in the EFTA countries) is required to transmit its judgments on matters covered by the EEA Agreement to the EEA Joint Committee, which is responsible for the 'homogeneous interpretation of the Agreement'.

The Court has played a discreet but substantial role in furthering the objectives laid down in the Treaties, a role similar to that played by the United States Supreme Court with respect to the US Constitution. The Court has done this by working within a tradition of interpretation that allows the 'ultimate purpose' of a piece of legislation to be taken into consideration. This means that it is entirely legitimate, with respect to a particular text, to take not only the exact purport of the words into account, but also anything that may usefully and convincingly be adduced about the intention behind the words. This has resulted in the Court tending to give a 'dynamic' rather than a strictly literal interpretation of Treaty provisions, and this has proved a key element in some of the Court's most noteworthy judgments (see also **EU law**). The classic account of this aspect of the Court's work is Hjerte Rasmussen, *On Law and Policy in the European Court of Justice* (Dordrecht, 1986). Also of great interest is Lord Slynn of Hadley, 'What is a European Community law judge?', *Cambridge Law Journal*, Vol. 52, no. 2, July 1993, and Karen J. Alter, 'The European Court's political power', *West European Politics*, Vol. 19, no. 3, July 1996.

Croatia

Croat enthusiasm for the creation of the Kingdom of Serbs, Croats and Slovenes (later **Yugoslavia**) in 1918 soon waned when they found themselves treated as a subject people within Greater Serbia. During the Second World War the German forces of occupation allowed a puppet state in Croatia a brief and inglorious independence, for which the Croats paid dearly in the period of Communist rule after 1945 (although Marshal Tito was himself a Croat). Amidst international misgivings, Croatia declared itself a sovereign state in June 1991, thereby prompting an armed conflict with Serbia which ended with a cease-fire in January 1992.

Croatia has received assistance from the European Union since 1991, most of it in the form of relief aid for housing, utilities, health care, refugees, and so on. An agreement between the Union and Croatia under the **Stabilization and Association Process** was signed in July 2001. Croatia was admitted to the **Council of Europe** in 1996. See also **the Balkans**.

Crocodile Club

Founded in Strasbourg in 1980 and named after the restaurant in which its members met, the all-party Crocodile Club was the creation of **Altiero Spinelli** and other Members of the **European Parliament** (MEPs) who shared his enthusiasm for institutional reform. The Club acquired more official status as the Federalist Intergroup for European Union and continues to produce a bilingual newsletter (*Crocodile*) on institutional matters.

Cultural policy

Cultural policy is primarily the responsibility of the **Council of Europe**. Since the early 1950s the Council of Europe has been very active in respect of the documenting and conservation of historic buildings, the mounting of major exhibitions, the safeguarding of minority cultures, the role of culture in education and the promotion of cross-frontier cooperation in various fields of creative activity (for example, through the 'Eurimages' programme). To this end, as in other areas of the Council of Europe's work, various conventions have been drawn up. Since 1987 the Council of Europe has established a number of 'European Cultural Routes' centred upon themes such as the pilgrimage to Santiago de Compostela, the Vikings, the silk trade, etc. At the level of symbolism, the Council of Europe was also responsible for the **European anthem** and the **European flag**.

A new Article 128 (now 151) was added to the **Treaty of Rome** by the **Maastricht Treaty**. This Article refers to the contribution to be made 'to the flowering of the cultures of the Member States, while respecting their national and regional diversity and at the same time bringing the common cultural heritage to the fore', but does not allow 'any harmonization of the laws and regulations of the Member States'.

Earlier references to cultural policy may be found in such documents as the 1973 declaration on **European identity**, the 1975 **Tindemans Report** on European Union, the 1983 **Stuttgart Declaration**, and the 1985 report of the **People's Europe** Committee. From the mid-1980s a series of agreements was reached, although because there was no legal base many of them lacked legislative force. They included measures to combat audio-visual piracy, the introduction of a **European City of Culture** scheme, the encouragement of commercial sponsorship for cultural activities, the provision of money in the **Budget** to contribute towards the translation and publication of 'important works of European culture', various measures on copyright and a common system of export licences for goods of cultural value. Certain **Single Market** measures also have a cultural dimension: for example, the tax treatment of secondhand goods and of auction houses. The European Community Youth Orchestra was founded in 1985 to mark European Music Year.

In November 1992 the **Council of Ministers** drew up guidelines for Community cultural action which emphasized that such action 'should not supplant or compete with activities organized at national or regional level, but provide added value and promote interchange between them'. A cultural action programme, known as Culture 2000, with a budget of €167 million over the period 2000–4, was agreed in December 1999 (Decision 508/00, *Official Journal*, L63, 10 March 2000). See also **European Cultural Foundation**, **European University Institute**. Matthias Niedobitek, *The Cultural Dimension in EC Law* (1997) is a useful survey.

Customs union

A customs union is a territory within which there are no internal barriers to the free movement of goods and in respect of which a single set of rules, tariffs, quotas, etc., is applied to goods entering the territory from outside. The expression is normally used to denote a territory within which two or more contiguous states have agreed to form such a union. A customs union is recognized as a 'regional trading arrangement' under the **World Trade Organization** (WTO) Agreement, and the members of a customs union are exempt from the requirement to accord 'most favoured nation' treatment to non-members.

A customs union may be either an end in itself or a means towards a political end. In the 19th century the best-known examples of customs unions were the Prussian-dominated *Zollverein* and the abolition of the restrictions on trade applied by the city-states of pre-unification Italy: before 1848, for example, there were no fewer than eight tolls payable at frontiers on goods being transported over the 240 kilometres from Milan to Florence. Both these examples are customs unions that were quite clearly an economic means to a political end. The **Belgo-Luxembourg Economic Union** (BLEU) and the Switzerland–Liechtenstein customs union are examples of arrangements with an exclusively economic purpose.

The **League of Nations**, through its Committee for European Union, attempted to foster the establishment of customs unions. But in 1933 G. D. H. and Margaret Cole, in a section headed 'The strangling of European trade' in *The Intelligent Man's Review of Europe Today*, commented: 'The moral is that if Europe is to be lifted out of the present depression … this cannot possibly be accomplished by a direct attack on tariffs, embargoes, exchange restrictions and the other secondary phenomena of national distress, but only by a courageous attempt to remove the underlying economic causes of the trouble.' Six years later such very modest progress as had been made was halted by the outbreak of war. However, the period immediately after the war gave rise to several proposals for new customs unions in western Europe. The French expressed an interest – partly as a means of containing Germany – in a customs union with Italy and the **Benelux** countries. Other combinations, with ingenious names like Fritalux or Finebel, were suggested. The Scandinavian countries too were discussing a customs union among themselves, although both Sweden and Denmark were more interested in establishing themselves in continental markets. The Americans, both bilaterally and through the Organization for European Economic Cooperation (see **Organization for Economic Cooperation and Development**), did their best to encourage the removal of barriers to trade within western Europe. The British, on the other hand, adopted a more cautious attitude, because they were suspicious of the federalist ambitions held all too clearly by many of the advocates of closer integration and because they believed the United Kingdom's involvement in a European customs union to be incompatible with the system of Commonwealth preference and the sterling area upon which their trading arrangements were still largely based. The political and economic background to those discussions is set out in Chapter VII of Alan Milward, *The Reconstruction of Western Europe 1945–1952* (1984).

The failure of the **European Defence Community** in 1954 prompted the pioneers of European integration to try economic means to secure their objective (see **Beyen Plan**). With the success of the **European Coal and Steel Community** (ECSC) behind them, it was obviously the time to attempt something similar on a more ambitious scale. The **Treaty of Rome** lays down as one of the foundations of the **European Economic Community** (EEC) 'a customs union which shall cover all trade in goods and which shall involve the prohibition between Member States of customs duties on imports and exports and of all charges having equivalent effect, and the adoption of a common customs tariff in their relations with third countries' (Article 23 EC). Ambitious deadlines were set for the progressive elimination of customs duties and quantitative restrictions (i.e., quotas) on trade between member states. A general exemption (Article 30) was granted to allow restrictions to be maintained 'on grounds of public morality, public policy or public security; the protection of health and life of humans, animals or plants; the protection of national treasures ... [and] of industrial and commercial property'.

Eighteen months ahead of schedule, the customs union among **the Six** was completed. In a declaration to mark the occasion on 1 July 1968 the **European Commission** announced: 'By beginning the unification of the European territory in this first form, the Six are taking a decisive step in the economic history of the continent.' But, the Commission said, the customs union must lead on to economic union, which in turn would lead on to 'a political Europe ... [with] genuine federal institutions'.

As with all customs unions, economists are divided in their assessment of what impact the removal of tariffs and quotas had on trade among the Six, and on the balance between 'trade creation' and 'trade diversion' effects (see Dennis Swann, *The Economics of Europe*, 9th edn, 2000). What is undeniable is that over the first 10 years of the EEC's existence (1958–68) trade between the member states grew by an annual average of 28.4 per cent. In spite of this, progress towards economic union proved much more difficult. The removal of tariffs and quotas left **non-tariff barriers** intact. The service sector was assuming greater importance in the economy as a whole, and **freedom of establishment** and the harmonization of national legislation regulating, for example, banking and insurance were far from being achieved. Fiscal harmonization was proving a sensitive subject for certain member states. And by the early 1970s, with the first of the oil crises, it was clear that the years of postwar growth in the 1950s and 1960s were at least temporarily at an end. The EEC's political energies were directed towards other areas, such as **enlargement** and institutional reform. Nevertheless, the customs union achieved on 1 July 1968 was an essential first step and was recognized internationally as a substantial triumph for the EEC. Not until 1 January 1993, with the establishment of the **Single Market**, was a step of such significance taken towards one of the key objectives of the Treaty.

Cyprus

Cyprus became a British protectorate in 1878, but by the 1920s there was widespread support among Greek Cypriots for union (*enosis*) with Greece.

The island became independent in 1960. In 1974, the last year of military rule in Greece, Turkish forces invaded Cyprus to protect the Turkish minority population, and since that date the northern third of the island has been under Turkish control. In 1983 the 'Turkish Republic of Northern Cyprus' (TRNC) proclaimed its independence. The TRNC is not recognized internationally, and successive United Nations (UN) Resolutions have condemned the partition of the island.

The year before the Turkish invasion Cyprus concluded an **Association Agreement** with the Community. The Agreement was intended to lead in two stages to a **customs union**. The first stage was not completed until 1987, and the second stage is due for completion in 2002. In line with UN Resolutions, the Community recognizes the government of the Republic of Cyprus as the only duly constituted authority entitled to speak on behalf of the island's population (some 800,000 people, of whom about 18 per cent are Turkish Cypriots living in the TRNC). Accordingly, protests from the TRNC side were ignored when on 3 July 1990 the Cypriot government applied for full membership of the Community on behalf of the whole island. Both the leader and the parliament of the TRNC have refused to be in any way associated with negotiations between Cyprus and the European Union.

The **Opinion** of the **European Commission** was generally favourable (*Bulletin of the European Communities*, supplement 5/93). Cyprus was shown to have adapted very well to Community policies under the Association Agreement. It now has a per capita gross domestic product (GDP) substantially higher than that of Greece or Portugal. The Commission noted that both the communities on the island supported Cypriot membership of the Union in the belief that it would help to resolve internal tensions. However, the Commission also drew attention to the problem that would arise if there were no internal constitutional settlement before accession negotiations began, and in general terms to the need to address the issue of **micro-states** being admitted to the Union. The member states broadly endorsed the Commission's conclusions, and at the Corfu meeting of the **European Council** in June 1994 they agreed that in the next round of **enlargement** negotiations Cyprus and Malta would be given priority. The Luxembourg meeting of the European Council (December 1997) agreed that the negotiations with Cyprus would begin in 1998. In Helsinki (December 1999) the European Council said that a political settlement of the Cyprus dispute was not a precondition of the country's admission into the Union. Negotiations were concluded in 2002 and Cyprus signed the **Treaty of Accession** in Athens in April 2003 with no solution to the Cyprus dispute in prospect.

Cyprus is a member of the **Council of Europe** and the **Organization for Security and Cooperation in Europe**. The Cyprus dispute was referred to among the Commission's reservations in its 1989 Opinion on possible Turkish accession to the Community (see **Turkey**). Since February 1994 there has been an official European Union observer at talks between the Cypriot government and the TRNC.

Czech Republic

Czechoslovakia was re-established as a free and independent country with the election of Václav Havel (a leading member of the Charter 77 reform movement) as President in December 1989. However, less than three years later, the Czech and Slovak parliaments passed a resolution in October 1992 creating two separate countries with effect from 1 January 1993 (they remain linked in a **customs union**). The **Europe Agreement** between Czechoslovakia and the European Union, signed in December 1991, had to be renegotiated. The Agreement with the Czech Republic came into effect on 1 February 1995.

The Czech Republic applied for membership of the European Union on 23 January 1996. The **Opinion** of the **European Commission**, published on 15 July 1997 (*Bulletin of the European Union*, supplement 14/97), found that the Czech Republic satisfied the **Copenhagen criteria**. The Commission concluded that there were no substantial problems in the way of Czech membership (60 per cent of Czech trade was already with the Union), and recommended that negotiations with the Czech Republic should begin in 1998. At its meeting in Luxembourg in December 1997 the **European Council** endorsed this recommendation. Negotiations were concluded in 2002 and in April 2003 the Czech Republic signed the **Treaty of Accession**. On 13–14 June 2003 the Czech people voted in favour of Union membership by 77.3 per cent to 22.67 per cent.

The Czech Republic is a member of the **Council of Europe**, the **Organization for Security and Cooperation in Europe**, the **Central European Initiative**, the **Central European Free Trade Agreement**, and (since 1999) the **North Atlantic Treaty Organization**. An exceptionally interesting essay on Czechoslovakia is Eric Stein, 'Musings at the grave of a federation' in Deirdre Curtin and Ton Heukels (eds), *Institutional Dynamics of European Integration* (Volume II of *Essays in Honour of Henry G. Schermers*, Dordrecht, 1994).

D

Danube Commission

With its headquarters in Budapest, the Commission, founded under a Convention in 1948, is responsible for all matters relating to navigation on the Danube, including pollution controls, safety, and the registration of vessels. Austria, Bulgaria, Croatia, Germany, Hungary, Moldova, Romania, Russia, Slovakia, Ukraine, and the Federal Republic of Yugoslavia take part in the work of the Commission, which is modelled on the **Central Commission for the Navigation of the Rhine**.

Declaration

The results of discussions at meetings of the **European Council** are expressed in the form of 'conclusions of the Presidency'. Latterly, these have been supplemented by Declarations embodying more detailed agreements on points of substance. These Declarations have no legal force, but can be of great political importance as pointers to future legislative action. For example, the Dublin meeting of the European Council in June 1990 agreed a long Declaration on the environment. Declarations are also made in the context of the **Common Foreign and Security Policy**, normally by the **presidency** of the **Council of Ministers**. When the Council has formally agreed a Declaration, it is issued as a Declaration by the European Union. When the Council has not had an opportunity to meet, the presidency may, after consulting the member states, issue a Declaration on behalf of the European Union.

Most Treaties have annexed to them Declarations and **protocols**. A Declaration, unlike a protocol, has no legal force, but is intended to have political force, and may touch on matters not dealt with or imperfectly resolved in the main body of the Treaty. Declarations may also take the form of an undertaking to examine or re-examine an issue at some future date, or of an agreed interpretation of some provision in the Treaty. Some Declarations may be made in the name of only certain parties to the Treaty, and often result from the desire of individual governments to make formal statements for particular domestic reasons.

Defence industry

In January 1996 the **European Commission** published a study which identified the special problems faced by European defence-related industry since the end of the Cold War and called for a restructuring of the industry and an opening up of defence procurement within the European Union. It is estimated that there has been a 37 per cent fall in employment in the industry since 1984. Moreover, the balance of trade with the United States in defence-related equipment has shown a marked deterioration: European exports to the United States, which in 1985 stood at one-quarter of the value of imports from the United States, had fallen to one-sixth by 1995. The European market is fragmented: intra-Community trade is a tiny proportion of total trade, since Article 296.1(b) of the **Treaty of Rome** effectively exempts member states' defence industries and defence procurement from normal **Single Market** disciplines. There remains a high level of state involvement in the industry, 90 per cent of which is concentrated in five states: France, Germany, Italy, Sweden, and the United Kingdom. The end of the Cold War has resulted in much fiercer competition with American suppliers in export markets, competition which European suppliers are ill equipped to meet.

No action having resulted from the Commission's 1996 study, a second communication was published in November 1997 as *Implementing European Union strategy on defence-related industries* (COM(97) 583). This suggested a number of concrete actions, some based on a **common position** under the **Common Foreign and Security Policy** (CFSP) and others on the relevant articles of the Treaty of Rome. They included a simplified licensing system for technology transfer between member states, application to the defence sector of the rules on **public purchasing**, a further attempt to introduce the **European Company Statute** to provide a suitable framework for Union-wide collaboration between defence suppliers, and a review of the defence industries' special needs in the context of **research** and the reform of the **structural funds**. As far as procurement and the standardization of equipment are concerned, it was proposed that the Union should work in very close collaboration with the **Western European Union** (WEU: see also **European Armaments Agency**). The Commission wants action along these lines to be taken using Article 17.1 of the **Maastricht Treaty** as the legal base. This article, as amended by the **Treaty of Amsterdam**, says that 'the progressive framing of a common defence policy will be supported, as Member States consider appropriate, by cooperation between them in the field of armaments' (see also **arms exports**).

de Gasperi, Alcide (1881–1954)

Born in the Trentino (north-east Italy, then belonging to Austro-Hungary), de Gasperi's political career began as a member of the Imperial Parliament in Vienna. In 1918 he took Italian citizenship and became active as a journalist. A devout Catholic, he was one of the founders of the Partito Popolare Italiano (a forerunner of **Christian Democracy**). He was arrested and imprisoned in 1927 for his opposition to Fascism, but was released as a result of the intercession of Pope Pius IX, who secured for him a minor post in the Vatican library. De Gasperi continued his political work both as a Christian Democrat and as a member of the Resistance. During the Second World War he drew up the political programme of a new, specifically Catholic, political party and in 1943 outlined in *Idee recostruttive della Democrazia Cristiana* the structure of the post-Fascist Italian state. He guided Democrazia Cristiana during the delicate period between the armistice and the constitution of the new state. In December 1944 he became Foreign Minister, and Prime Minister a year later. His position was confirmed when Democrazia Cristiana emerged as the largest party, with 35 per cent of the vote, in the elections for the constituent assembly held in June 1946. He was Prime Minister in the eight coalition governments that ruled Italy in the period up to 1953. He was active both in the postwar reconstruction of Italy (he was a strong advocate of regional autonomy) and in ensuring that Italy played a full part in the Atlantic Alliance and in the movement towards European integration led by **Robert Schuman** and **Jean Monnet**. In 1954 he was elected President of the Common Assembly of the **European Coal and Steel Community**, the forerunner of the **European Parliament**. He died in August 1954, a few days before the collapse of the **European Defence Community**. Alcide de Gasperi is regarded, particularly by Italian Christian Democrats, as one of the founding fathers of the European Community.

de Gaulle, Charles (1890–1970)

The wartime leader of the Free French, Charles de Gaulle withdrew from politics in 1946. He returned to power in 1958 (the year in which the **European Economic Community** came into operation), and was elected President the following year.

The Constitution of the Fifth Republic, largely designed by de Gaulle, gave the president substantial powers and (in its revised form, adopted by referendum in 1962) an independent political mandate of seven years. Among de Gaulle's highest priorities were the re-establishment of French pre-eminence in world affairs, most especially in Europe, and reconciliation with Germany (see **Franco-German cooperation**). De Gaulle's concern with French prestige and with national **sovereignty** led him to take a largely unsympathetic view of a Community built upon and administered by supranational institutions. However, he remained a strong supporter of European integration as a counterpoise to American dominance. That such integration should be along French lines became very clear in the abortive negotiations on the **Fouchet Plan** in 1961.

In 1963 and again in 1967 de Gaulle vetoed the United Kingdom's applications to join the European Community. De Gaulle saw the United Kingdom as a rival to French influence in Europe, and mistrusted the British attachment to free trade and the close British association with the Americans. His decision in 1966 to withdraw from the integrated military command structure of the **North Atlantic Treaty Organization** (NATO) was also prompted by a mistrust of American involvement (see also **Soames affair**).

In the early 1960s de Gaulle quarrelled with the **European Commission**, then led by its first president, **Walter Hallstein**. This quarrel was one of the causes of the 'empty chair crisis' of 1965 and the so-called **Luxembourg Compromise** reached the following year. Underlying these disputes was de Gaulle's vision of a *Europe des patries* in which the nation-states should remain pre-eminent.

De Gaulle was largely successful in restoring French self-esteem in the wake of the conflicts in Indo-China and Algeria and the chronic political instability that characterized the Fourth Republic. The political party that he founded (originally the *Union pour la Nouvelle République*) is still a powerful force in French politics as the *Rassemblement pour la République* (RPR). Many of de Gaulle's ideas about the way in which Europe should be integrated were taken up by his successors: for example, the creation of the **European Council** by **Valéry Giscard d'Estaing** was intended to strengthen the role of the states in Community decision-making.

De Gaulle retired in 1969 and died the following year. His autobiography remained unfinished. The standard biography of de Gaulle is by Jean Lacouture, *De Gaulle* (3 vols, Paris, 1984–6).

Delors, Jacques (b. 1925)

Jacques Delors entered politics through the civil service and the trade union movement. A Socialist, he was elected to the **European Parliament** in 1979, and returned to national politics in 1981 on his appointment as Economics and Finance Minister. Four years later, in 1985, he became President of the **European Commission**, serving until January 1995.

Delors was by far the most influential President of the Commission since **Walter Hallstein**. His presidency was marked by the **Single Market** programme, the accession of Portugal, Spain, Austria, Finland and Sweden (see **enlargement**), **German reunification**, the **Single European Act** (SEA) and the **Maastricht Treaty** (the latter containing the timetable for **Economic and Monetary Union** (EMU; see also **Delors Report**), the agreement on **future financing**, and the **European Economic Area** (EEA). In all these developments Delors was personally and deeply involved.

On the debit side of his presidency was the mood of crisis and uncertainty in 1992–3, triggered by the rejection of the Maastricht Treaty in the first Danish referendum of June 1992 and its near-rejection in the French referendum three months later. This was accompanied by the shocks to the **Exchange-Rate Mechanism** (ERM) in September 1992 and August 1993. Delors brought to the presidency a broad strategic vision, a clear model of the society and of the Union he wanted to create, and an inexhaustible appetite for detail. At the same time his management style within the Commission itself was criticized for a certain aloofness. He established good working relations with the principal European leaders of his day (with the partial exception of **Margaret Thatcher**) and with the European Parliament. Delors is now president of Notre Europe, a research and policy group (or *laboratoire des idées*) founded in 1996.There is an astute, comprehensive and sympathetic portrait of Delors in Charles Grant's *Delors: The House that Jacques Built* (1994). Also of interest is Helen Drake, 'Political leadership and European integration: the case of Jacques Delors', *Western European Politics*, Vol. 18, no. 1, January 1995.

Delors Report

The Delors Report of April 1989 made recommendations on **Economic and Monetary Union** (EMU) that led directly to the **Intergovernmental Conference** (IGC) on EMU and to the EMU provisions of the **Maastricht Treaty**. The Hanover meeting of the **European Council** in June 1988 invited a committee composed of the **central bank governors** of the member states and three independent economists under the chairmanship of **Jacques Delors** to study and bring forward proposals for 'concrete stages' leading to EMU. The Committee's unanimously agreed report was discussed by the European Council in Madrid in June 1989.

The first chapter of the report made the case for EMU as an essential complement to the **Single Market**. The second chapter set out the key components of EMU, including a **European Monetary Institute** (EMI) and a **European Central Bank** (ECB), and the need for 'irrevocably fixed exchange rates between national currencies and, finally, a single currency'. National economic policies, it was proposed, would have to be 'placed in an agreed macroeconomic framework and be subject to binding procedures and rules'. The report recognized that a greater degree of **convergence** in respect of the economic performance of member states would have to be achieved if EMU were to work successfully. The third and final chapter set out the three stages ('discrete but evolutionary steps') in which EMU would be created. Crucially, the report observed that for the whole enterprise to secure the necessary credibility 'the decision to enter upon the first stage should be a decision to embark on the entire process'. The report reached the inevitable conclusion that proposals of this importance would, if agreed, have to be embodied in changes to the **Treaty of Rome,** and so it recommended the convening of an IGC under Article 236 EEC (since replaced by Article 48 TEU).

In Madrid the main obstacle was the position of the British government of **Margaret Thatcher.** Most other countries were prepared to accept the report's proposals, but Mrs Thatcher was unwilling to let sterling enter the **Exchange-Rate Mechanism** (ERM) under stage 1 of EMU, very unwilling to allow embarking upon stage 1 to be construed as a commitment to the whole EMU process and very unenthusiastic about the idea of an IGC on EMU. Under strong pressure from her Chancellor of the Exchequer, Nigel Lawson, and her Foreign Secretary, Sir Geoffrey Howe – both of whom had threatened to resign – Mrs Thatcher announced her acceptance of stage 1 on condition that stages 2 and 3 be left open and no IGC convened. The Delors Report, the European Council concluded, was 'a good basis for further work'. This compromise, unsatisfactory to most member states, lasted throughout the autumn, but at the Strasbourg meeting of the European Council in December 1989 it was agreed, on a proposal from President Mitterrand and against a lone British objection, to convene an IGC on EMU the following year.

Democratic deficit

The phrase 'democratic deficit' is loosely used to characterize decision-making procedures in which insufficient provision is made for democratic control. In fact, the expression refers specifically to powers transferred under the Treaties from the national level to the Community or Union level, and to the extent to which powers formerly subject to a satisfactory degree of democratic control at the national level cease to be subject to the same degree of control once so transferred. The expression is most commonly used to support arguments for increasing the powers of the **European Parliament,** but those opposed to such an increase point to the greater role that **national parliaments** might also play in ensuring that decisions are arrived at in a democratic fashion. This latter argument was given new force by the fact that since the **Single European Act** (SEA) decisions in the **Council of Ministers** have normally been taken on the basis of **qualified majority voting** (QMV), thus depriving national parliaments of the power of veto they enjoyed by virtue of the *de facto* unanimity required by the **Luxembourg Compromise.** The **Maastricht Treaty** sought to reduce the democratic deficit by granting the European Parliament a right of co-decision (see **co-decision procedure**) in certain areas. However, it also established important new areas of Union activity – the **Common Foreign** and Security Policy (CFSP) and Justice and Home Affairs (JHA) – with only very modest provision for parliamentary involvement, national or European. See Giandomenico Maiore, 'Europe's "democracy deficit": the question of standards', *European Law Journal*, Vol. 4, no. 1, March 1998.

Demography

Of a world population now exceeding 6 billion people, about 13 per cent live in Europe (785 million in the member states of the **Council of Europe** and a further 24 million in European states not belonging to the Council). With an average annual growth rate of 1.75 per cent, the population of the world is on course to double in 40 years. In the Council of Europe member states the growth rate is falling: it was only 0.1 per cent in 2000. Only two countries (Iceland and Turkey) have a total fertility rate roughly equal to or exceeding the 'replacement' rate of 2.1 children per woman. United Nations projections suggest a 4 per cent decline in Europe's population by 2025.

Not only are Europeans declining as a percentage of the total world population (they were 18 per cent of the population in 1970), they are also significantly older on average. This has resulted in unusually high dependency ratios: the number of people not of working age expressed as a percentage of the number of people of working age. For the member states of the European Union, the figure is 48.4 per cent, but in Sweden, with its significantly higher proportion of old people in the population as a whole, the figure is 55.3 per cent.

These broad averages conceal wide variations. In northern Europe (Scandinavia and the British Isles) life expectancy is longer and the proportion of the population over 65 correspondingly higher. In central and eastern Europe the proportion of the population under 15 tends to be well above the European average, but this is as much a consequence of lower life expectancy as of higher birth rates.

Population density also varies widely within Europe. With 1239 people per square kilometre, Malta is one of the most densely populated countries in the world; with only 3 people per square kilometre, Iceland is one of the emptiest. Within the European Union the extremes are the Netherlands (385 people per square kilometre) and Finland (15 people per square kilometre).

In all European Union member states except Ireland the number of immigrants exceeds the number of emigrants. By far the highest percentage of inhabitants of foreign citizenship is to be found in Luxembourg (37.3 per cent), followed by Austria (9.4 per cent), Germany (8.9 per cent), and Belgium (8.4 per cent). For most other member states, including the United Kingdom, the figure is below 5 per cent.

The Council of Europe publishes a comprehensive annual report entitled *Recent demographic developments in Europe*, from which the above information is taken (2001 edition). The **European Commission** publishes a similar but less detailed annual report on the demographic situation in the European Union. See also David Coleman (ed.), *Europe's Population in the 1990s* (Oxford, 1996).

Denmark

In the 1960s Denmark followed the United Kingdom, a fellow member of the **European Free Trade Association** (EFTA), in applying to join the Six. The vetoes twice exercised by **Charles de Gaulle** on British entry had as a side-effect the blocking of Danish entry too. Like the United Kingdom, Denmark joined the Community on 1 January 1973, after an October 1972 **referendum** in which 63.3 per cent of the votes were cast in favour of membership. The key argument was economic: a substantial proportion of Danish trade was with the United Kingdom, and it was felt that Denmark could not afford to see the British market disappear behind the **Common External Tariff** (CET).

For the remainder of the 1970s and the first half of the 1980s Denmark played its full part as a responsible, law-abiding, but not especially enthusiastic member of the Community. The relationship was neatly symbolized by the Market Committee, the Danish parliament's instrument for controlling Danish ministers in the **Council of Ministers** (see **national parliaments**), which served to reassure public opinion that moves towards closer integration could not be made without national parliamentary authority.

In 1988 Denmark gained an important victory in the so-called 'Danish beer-can case' (*Commission* v *Denmark*, Case 302/86; see **environment policy**), which established the principle that member states were free to impose more stringent requirements in pursuit of Treaty objectives than those agreed at Community level. As one of the richest member states with an efficient and profitable agricultural sector, Denmark was reticent about attempts to reform the Community's finances and the **Common Agricultural Policy** (CAP), and took only a negative interest in institutional reform.

From the mid-1980s a mood of growing hostility to European Union and the threat it allegedly posed to traditional Danish liberties coincided with a period of unstable minority government. In February 1986 a referendum was needed to ratify the **Single European Act** (SEA) – 56.2 per cent voted in favour – since the previous month the Danish parliament had voted to reject it on the grounds that it gave more powers to the **European Parliament**. Matters were finally brought to a head by a referendum on 2 June 1992, when by a majority of less than 2 per cent (45,000 votes) the Danish people voted against the **Maastricht Treaty** in spite of the fact that the Danish parliament had approved it.

In October of that year the Danish government published a paper entitled *Denmark in Europe*. In essence, this laid down conditions – mainly in the form of exemptions and **opt-outs** from what had been agreed at Maastricht – for the holding of a second referendum. The Edinburgh meeting of the **European Council** in December 1992 reached agreement on the Danish demands, which reflected the preoccupations that had led to the 'No' vote in June. The Maastricht Treaty provisions on **citizenship** were clarified; Denmark's decision not to participate in stage 3 of **Economic and Monetary Union** (EMU) was recognized, as was its refusal to become involved in 'decisions and actions of the Union which have defence implications' (which would include ceding the **presidency** of the Council as necessary); and the right of a member state to introduce or maintain more stringent provisions was reiterated with respect to working conditions, social policy, consumer protection and the environment. A second referendum was held on this basis in May 1993 and, with 56.8 per cent of the vote in favour, the Danish electorate approved the Maastricht Treaty. In the June 1994 European elections anti-Maastricht candidates secured 4 of the 16 Danish seats in the European Parliament. On 24 May 1998 the **Treaty of Amsterdam** was approved in a referendum with 55.1 per cent of the votes cast in favour. On 28 September 2000 the Danes, against the advice of their government, voted by 53.1 per cent to 46.9 per cent against adopting the **euro** (to which the krone is nevertheless linked).

As the United Kingdom has the Commonwealth and the 'special relationship' with the United States, so Denmark has Nordic cooperation (see **Nordic Council**) as an alternative focus of loyalty to the European Community. For 21 years Denmark was the only Scandinavian member of the Community, and thought of itself as a bridge between the two while enjoying a unique status in each. As a small country with an economy closely linked to Germany's, Denmark's future within the Union will depend in part on the success or failure of EMU. Meanwhile, Denmark can be relied upon to resist any large-scale moves towards closer integration. There is an analysis of the politico-legal consequences of the special arrangements made for Denmark in relation to the Maastricht Treaty in David Howarth, 'The compromise on Denmark and the Treaty on European Union', *Common Market Law Review*, Vol. 31, no. 4, August 1994.

Derogation

A derogation is a temporary waiver from a Regulation or a Directive (see **legal instruments**). Derogations are normally granted only by unanimous agreement of the Council of Ministers (see **EU law**). Under Article 122.1 of the **Treaty of Rome** member states that do not meet the **convergence criteria** are automatically entitled to a derogation from the arrangements to adopt the **euro** as part of the third stage of **Economic and Monetary Union** (EMU).

Development policy

Development policy was at first limited, in the words of Article 131 (now 182) of the **Treaty of Rome**, to the 'non-European countries and territories' that had 'special relations' with one or other of the member states and which were listed in Annex IV of the Treaty. The purpose of associating these **overseas countries and territories** (OCTs) with the Community was 'to promote [their] economic and social development ... and to establish close economic relations between them and the Community as a whole'. As a first step, member states undertook to apply the same rules to trade with the OCTs as they applied to trade with each other, and each OCT would in return accord to all member states and to other OCTs the same treatment in matters of trade as was applied to the member state with which it had 'special relations'. At the time of **the Six** the OCTs were all Dutch or French overseas possessions, but as the process of decolonization got under way in the 1960s it became obvious that something more ambitious was called for. This led to the conclusion of the **Yaoundé** and **Arusha Conventions** in 1963 and 1969 with 21 newly independent African states. British accession to the Community in 1973 meant that similar arrangements had to be made with a large number of former British possessions. The European Union now has **Association Agreements** with some 120 developing countries worldwide.

The **Maastricht Treaty** added a section on development cooperation to the Treaty of Rome (Articles 177 to 181). It underlines the fact that 'Community policy ... shall be complementary to the policies pursued by the Member States', and requires Community action to 'contribute to the general objective of developing and consolidating democracy and the rule of law, and to that of respecting human rights and fundamental freedoms'.

The centrepiece of this policy is the **Cotonou Agreement**, signed in Cotonou, the capital of Benin, in 2000. The Agreement governs trade and aid arrangements with the **ACP states**, allowing all ACP industrial products and most ACP agricultural products free access to the Community market. The Agreement makes available €13.5 billion (approximately £9 billion) under the **European Development Fund** over the period 2001–5.

The European Union and its member states are by far the biggest donors of development assistance worldwide, their contribution representing more than half of total official development aid, and more than that of the United States and Japan combined. In particular, they are the biggest aid donors in sub-Saharan Africa, South America and southern Asia (India, Pakistan, Nepal, Bangladesh and Sri Lanka). Aid represents about 0.55 per cent of total gross national product (GNP): short of the United Nations target of 0.7 per cent, but steadily growing. All member states except Greece are members of the Development Assistance Committee (DAC) of the **Organization for Economic Cooperation and Development** (OECD).

The Union's development policy has certain special characteristics that set it apart from the policies of other major aid donors. First, aid is distributed more evenly across the range of recipient countries. The six largest beneficiaries of aid receive only about 20 per cent of total Union aid, by comparison with 44 per cent of US aid and 50 per cent of Japanese aid. This underlines the fact that aid from the Union is disbursed with less regard for strategic or commercial factors. However, particularly under Article 9 of the Cotonou Agreement, more emphasis is now being laid on observance of human rights and 'good government' in recipient countries. Another distinctive feature is the fact that the Union gives more aid than other donors to agricultural and rural development projects, which represent some 50 per cent of total expenditure.

The Union and its member states are also the most important trading partners of the developing countries, taking over 20 per cent of Third World exports. Under the Union's **Generalized System of Preferences** (GSP) many Third World products enjoy privileged access. The concerns of developing countries that the European Union was becoming protectionist as a consequence of the **Single Market** programme (see **Fortress Europe**) and was turning its attention to central and eastern Europe have not been borne out by the Union's current policies.

Only a small proportion of the total aid budgets of member states is spent through the Union. The overall figure is about 17.5 per cent, but this conceals wide differences: barely 7 per cent of Denmark's aid budget is disbursed through the Union, while the equivalent figure for Greece is 87 per cent. Both the Union and the individual member states make contributions to the various United Nations specialized aid agencies (such as the High Commission for Refugees and the World Food Programme), and the member states also make independent contributions to other multilateral aid agencies, most notably the International Bank for Reconstruction and Development and the International Development Agency. Another important feature of the Union's aid policy is that the main instrument, the European Development Fund, is made up of direct contributions from member states and is not part of the **Budget** (and is for this reason not subject to the **European Parliament**'s powers of decision and control over budgetary matters). Other forms of development expenditure are, however, 'budgetized'. European Development Fund expenditure is about 45 per cent of total development expenditure.

Development policy with respect to non-ACP countries outside Europe and the Mediterranean basin is best considered area by area.

Africa

All African states south of the Sahara are signatories to the Cotonou Agreement, although South Africa, which was admitted to membership in April 1997, does not benefit from the trade provisions of the Agreement. South African trade with the European Union is governed by a trade agreement finalized in March 1999. Development aid to South Africa is given under the European Recovery and Development Programme for South Africa, which had a budget of 500 million ECUs (approximately £350 million) over the period 1996 to 1999). For North Africa, see **Maghreb** and **Mashreq**.

Central America and the Caribbean

All the independent states in the Caribbean (but not yet Cuba) are signatories to the Cotonou Agreement. Aid is also given to the countries of the Central American Common Market: Costa Rica, El Salvador, Guatemala, Honduras and Nicaragua.

South America

Development policy in South America is founded upon relations with regional groupings:

- the Andean Community, established in May 1969 as the Andean Pact (Bolivia, Ecuador, Colombia, Peru and Venezuela);
- the Latin American Integration Association, established in 1980, replacing the Latin American Free Trade Association (Argentina, Bolivia, Brazil, Chile, Colombia, Ecuador, Mexico, Paraguay, Peru, Uruguay and Venezuela);
- the Mercosur Council, which manages the **customs union** established in 1991 between Argentina, Brazil, Paraguay and Uruguay.

These bodies form part of the Latin American Economic System, set up in 1975, which also includes the countries of the Central American Common Market (see above) and a number of countries in the Caribbean.

The Middle East

The oil-rich Arab countries and the United States are the largest aid donors in this region (a very high proportion of US aid is concentrated upon Israel). Aid of various types has been given to all countries in the region: Israel, Jordan, the Lebanon, Syria, the Yemen Arab Republic. Iran and Iraq have received only food or emergency aid (see also **Mashreq**).

Southern Asia

The European Union is the largest (and Japan the next largest) aid donor in the region, which includes India, Pakistan, Sri Lanka, Bangladesh, Afghanistan and a number of small states bordering on northern India. Although it is outside the Cotonou Agreement, India receives more Union aid than any other country in the world.

Far East

Japan is the largest aid donor in the region, but aid from the European Union – especially to China – has shown a marked increase over the past decade. Other major beneficiaries include Thailand, Indonesia and the Philippines.

There is a very full and critical account of the neo-colonial character of the European Union's development policy in Enzo R. Grilli, *The European Community and the Developing Countries* (Cambridge, 1993).

D'Hondt system

Named after a Belgian political scientist, the d'Hondt system is widely used in continental Europe as a feature of various forms of proportional representation. It is also used within the institutions of the European Union (especially the **European Parliament**) as a formula for distributing a fixed number of positions (such as committee chairs) among groups of different numerical strengths or among various nationalities.

The following example illustrates how the d'Hondt system works. Seven posts have to be distributed among five political parties as follows:

	A	B	C	D	E
Number of members	110	80	42	30	16

The d'Hondt system requires these numbers to be divided first by 1, then by 2, then by 3, and so on as necessary. The resulting quotients are then ranked by size, the seven highest establishing the entitlement to the seven posts available:

	A	B	C	D	E
$\div 1$	110.0	80.0	42.0	30.0	16.0
$\div 2$	55.0	40.0	21.0	15.0	8.0
$\div 3$	36.7	26.7	14.0	10.0	5.3
$\div 4$	27.5	20.0	10.5	7.5	4.0

The d'Hondt system favours large parties but also protects the position of other parties. If the allocation were simply put to the vote, Party A could combine with Party B, C or D to deny posts to other parties. Several variants exist that correct the bias in favour of large parties. For the purpose of the calculation parties can choose temporarily to pool their numbers. From the example given above it will be seen that the d'Hondt system can be used to establish not only entitlement to posts but also the order of bids: Party A has first, third and sixth choice, Party B second and fifth, and so on. A fuller description of the d'Hondt system may be found in any handbook of electoral systems.

Victor d'Hondt published his *Système pratique et raisonné de la représentation proportionnelle* in 1882. The system was originally devised to ensure an equitable distribution of parliamentary seats among Catholics and Liberals and between the different language communities in Belgium (see A.M. Carstairs, *A Short History of Electoral Systems in Western Europe*, 1980).

Differentiated Integration
See flexibility.

Direct effect
Together with **primacy**, direct effect is one of the fundamental principles of **EU law**. In its judgment in the Van Gend en Loos case (Case 26/62), the **Court of Justice** said:

Independently of the legislation of Member States, Community law ... not only imposes obligations on individuals but is also intended to confer upon them rights which become part of their legal heritage. These rights arise not only where they are expressly granted by the Treaty but also by reason of obligations which the Treaty imposes in a clearly defined way upon individuals as well as upon the Member States and upon the institutions of the Community.

In other words, the **Treaties** are not merely a compact between states entailing rights and obligations for those states and for the institutions established by those Treaties, but are the foundations of a distinct legal order entailing rights and obligations for individuals (see Weatherill and Beaumont, *EU Law*, 3rd edn, Harmondsworth, 1999; see also **Francovich case**, **Van Duyn case**). Two provocative and informative articles are Ilan Sebba, 'The doctrine of "direct effect": a malignant disease of Community law', *Legal Issues of European Integration*, 1995/2 and Sacha Prechal, 'Does direct effect still matter?', *Common Market Law Review*, Vol. 37, no. 5, October 2000.

Directive
A Directive, under Article 249 of the **Treaty of Rome**, is 'binding, as to the result to be achieved, upon each Member State to which it is addressed', but leaves 'to the national authorities the choice of form and methods'. Normally, a Directive will set a deadline for the necessary measures to be taken at the national level. For a description of a framework Directive and the difference between a Directive and a **Regulation**, see **legal instruments**. See also **co-decision procedure**, **EU law**, **direct effect**, **Francovich case**. Sacha Prechal, *Directives in European Community Law* (Oxford, 1995) is a lucid and magisterial treatment of the subject.

Directorate-general (DG)
A (DG) is the main administrative unit within the **European Commission**. Each Commissioner is responsible for one or more DGs, of which there are at present 23 (see below). The DGs, which vary in size, are each headed by a director-general and are dedicated to particular areas of policy. Most are located in Brussels. In addition to the DGs, there are a number of other

services, such as the Legal Service, the Translation Service, the Statistical Office (see **Eurostat**), and the **European Community Humanitarian Office** (ECHO). See also **agency**.

Directorates-General
Agriculture (AGRI)
Budget (BUDG)
Competition (COMP)
Development (DEV)
Economic and Financial Affairs
  (ECFIN)
Education and Culture (EAC)
Employment and Social Affairs
  (EMPL)
Energy and Transport (TREN)
Enterprise (ENTR)
Environment (ENV)
External Relations (RELEX)
Financial Control (FC)
Fisheries (FISH)
Health and Consumer Protection
  (SANCO)
Information Society (INFSO)
Internal Market (MARKT)
Justice and Home Affairs (JAI)
Personnel and Administration
  (ADMIN)
Press and Communication (PRESS)
Regional Policy (REGIO)
Research (RTD)
Taxation and Customs Union
  (TAXUD)
Trade (TRADE)

Services
Enlargement (ELARG)
EuropeAid Cooperation Office
  (AIDCO)
European Anti-Fraud Office
  (OLAF)
Eurostat (ESTAT)
Group of Policy Advisors (GOPA)
Humanitarian Aid Office (ECHO)
Internal Audit Service (IAS)
Joint Conference and Interpretation
  Service (SCIC)
Joint Research Centre (JRC)
Legal Service (SJ)
Publications Office (OPOCE)
Secretary-General (SG)
Translation Service (SDT)

The acronyms are used to identify the directorates-general and services in electronic communications, directories, etc.

Discharge procedure

Under Article 275 of the **Treaty of Rome** the **European Commission** is required to submit annually to the **European Parliament** and the **Council of Ministers** 'the accounts of the preceding financial year relating to the implementation of the budget ... [and] a financial statement of the assets and liabilities of the Community'. The responsibility for approving these accounts (known as 'granting the discharge') rests with the Parliament under Article 276, acting with the aid of a recommendation from the Council and the annual report of the **Court of Auditors**. The discharge procedure is an important element both in **budgetary discipline** and in the Parliament's powers with respect to the **Budget**. It was the Parliament's refusal in March 1998 to grant discharge on the 1996 accounts which led to the tabling of a **censure motion** in January 1999 and the resignation of the Commission two months later.

Discrimination

Two Articles of the **Treaty of Rome** prohibit specific types of discrimination. Article 12 prohibits **discrimination on grounds of nationality**. Article 141 prohibits sex discrimination with respect to pay and employment (see **equal treatment**). Under the **Treaty of Amsterdam**, a new Article 13 EC significantly widens the scope of European Union action against discrimination by empowering the **Council of Ministers** 'to take appropriate action to combat discrimination based on sex, racial or ethnic origin, religion or belief, disability, age or sexual orientation'. Enjoyment without discrimination of the rights set out in the **European Convention on Human Rights** is itself a right, and as such is guaranteed under the 1977 Joint Declaration on Human Rights, under Article 6 of the **Maastricht Treaty** and under the **Charter of Fundamental Rights** of the European Union. It is important to note that all these provisions apply only in areas covered by the Treaties, although most commentators have concluded from the fact that Articles 12 and 13 EC are in the section of the Treaty of Rome entitled 'Principles' and from the case-law of the **Court of Justice** that non-discrimination is in fact a general principle of Community law. 'New means of combating all forms of discrimination and inequalities in connection with the labour market' are supported by the European Social Fund under an initiative known as EQUAL (see *Official Journal*, C127, 5 May 2000) over the period 2000–6. See also **human rights**.

Discrimination on grounds of nationality

Discrimination on grounds of nationality between nationals of the member states is prohibited under Article 12 of the **Treaty of Rome** in all areas covered by the Treaty. Article 39.2 EC prohibits discrimination specifically in respect of employment, pay and working conditions.

'Employment in the public service' is an important exception to this provision, under Article 39.4 EC. Different countries have different definitions of what constitutes 'public service', and in response to a case involving Belgian railways the **Court of Justice** laid down its own definition: employment 'connected with the specific activities of the public service in so far as it is entrusted with the exercise of powers conferred by public law and with responsibility for safeguarding the general interests of the State, to which the specific interests of local authorities ... must be assimilated' (*Commission* v *Belgium*, Case 149/79). This definition would clearly include national and local civil servants, the armed forces and the police as part of the public service, but exclude many public-sector employees. For example, in recent years the **European Commission**, prompted by questions in the **European Parliament**, has taken action against rules requiring tour guides attached to tourist offices in Italian cities to be Italian. The Commission has also brought pressure to bear upon educational establishments to allow all nationals of the member states to enjoy the same treatment with regard to tuition fees as nationals of the home state.

The Treaty provisions prohibiting discrimination on grounds of nationality are of great importance in relation to **free movement of persons** and **freedom of establishment**, especially in frontier areas, and in connection with travel and tourism. Also of interest is the case of Mr Cowan, a British tourist mugged on the Paris Metro, who was denied the compensation for victims of criminal violence to which he would have been entitled had he been French. The Court of Justice ruled that as a tourist he was a recipient of services, a sector covered by the Treaty, and was therefore entitled to the same protection and compensation as a French citizen (Case 186/87).

Dooge Committee

Otherwise known as the Ad Hoc Committee for Institutional Affairs, the Dooge Committee (chaired by James Dooge, an Irish Senator) was set up at the **European Council** meeting in Fontainebleau in June 1984. Its task was 'to make suggestions for the improvement of the operation of European cooperation in both the Community field and that of political, or any other, cooperation'. The Committee was deliberately modelled on the **Spaak Committee** in the sense that its members were personal representatives of the members of the European Council and of the President of the **European Commission**. The Committee presented an interim report in November 1984 and a final report in March 1985.

The Committee called for a 'qualitative leap ... demonstrating the common political will of the Member States', and the eventual formulation of 'a genuine political entity ... i.e. a European Union'. Foreshadowing the **Maastricht Treaty**, this Union would act 'according to procedures which could vary depending whether the framework is that of intergovernmental cooperation, the Community Treaties, or new instruments yet to be agreed'. Among the 'priority objectives' the Committee endorsed the idea of a

single market created 'on the basis of a precise timetable' (an idea then being worked out in what was published three months later as the **Cockfield White Paper**) and a strengthening of the **European Monetary System** (EMS). Under 'Promotion of the common values of civilization' the Committee supported measures to protect the environment, the introduction of a 'European social area, as the logical follow-on from an economically integrated, dynamic and competitive Community', and the promotion of common cultural values.

The section on 'the search for an external identity' was more cautious. The recommendations amounted to a few practical measures for improving **European Political Cooperation** (EPC), including the creation of an EPC secretariat, the gradual incorporation of security issues into EPC and greater efforts 'to draw up and adopt common standards for weapons systems and equipment'.

The final section on changes to the institutions and procedures was the most radical. A majority of the Committee supported more frequent use of **majority voting** in the **Council of Ministers**, with the requirement for unanimity being applied only 'in certain exceptional cases'. The **presidency** would be obliged to put a matter to the vote within 30 days at the request of three member states or the Commission. The British, Danish and Greek representatives also accepted that more use would have to be made of majority voting, but wanted to grant the presidency more discretion and to retain the practice laid down in the **Luxembourg Compromise** of allowing discussion to continue until unanimity was reached whenever a member state considered that 'very important interests' were at stake.

The Committee proposed to reduce the number of Commissioners to one for each member state. The president should be appointed by the European Council, and he or she should then propose to the governments the names of the other Commissioners. At the beginning of its term of office, the Commission 'should receive a vote of investiture on the basis of its programme' from the **European Parliament**.

The Committee proposed that the Parliament should enjoy a right of co-decision with the Council, although in a way different from that eventually adopted in the Maastricht Treaty (see **co-decision procedure**). The Parliament should also have the right to give its approval to all accession and **Association Agreements** (see **assent procedure**) and should have 'responsibility in decisions on revenue' as part of the **Budget** procedure. The Committee pointed to the 'increased representativeness' that would flow from the 'standardization of voting procedures' for European elections (see **uniform electoral procedure**).

In conclusion, the Committee recommended the calling of an **Intergovernmental Conference** (IGC) 'to negotiate a draft European Union

Treaty'. When their report was considered at the Milan meeting of the European Council in June 1985, the proposal to convene an IGC was carried by majority vote, the British, Danish and Greek representatives voting against. This was the IGC that negotiated the **Single European Act** (SEA).

The vote in the European Council was the final proof of what had become evident in the Dooge Committee's discussions and in their final report: a fundamental division between a minority who favoured only a minimalist approach to institutional reform and a majority prepared to go much further. Almost every page of the report contained footnotes and reservations, and the Danish and Greek representatives entered general reservations at the end. As an exercise in moving the Community forward, the Dooge Committee was only partially successful and cannot compare with the Spaak Committee. Nevertheless, many of its proposals were taken up either in the SEA or later in the Maastricht Treaty.

Double majority

The idea of a 'double majority' has been widely canvassed in the current review of the **qualified majority voting** (QMV) system used in the **Council of Ministers**. A double majority would be attained if a proposal commanded the support of a majority of member states representing more than half the population and casting enough weighted votes *either* for the QMV threshold to be reached *or* for more than half the weighted votes to be in favour. Some have

The member states: population and weightings

	Population (millions)	% of total	Votes	% of total
Germany	81.6	21.9	10	11.5
United Kingdom	58.3	15.7	10	11.5
France	58	15.6	10	11.5
Italy	57.2	15.4	10	11.5
Spain	39.6	10.6	8	9.2
The Netherlands	15.5	4.2	5	5.7
Greece	10.5	2.8	5	5.7
Belgium	10.1	2.7	5	5.7
Portugal	9.8	2.6	5	5.7
Sweden	8.8	2.4	4	4.6
Austria	8.0	2.2	4	4.6
Denmark	5.2	1.4	3	3.4
Finland	5.1	1.4	3	3.4
Ireland	3.6	1.0	3	3.4
Luxembourg	0.4	0.1	2	2.3
Total	**372**	**100**	**87**	**100**

seen the double majority as a substitute for unanimity (see **veto**), others as a means of forestalling the possibility of member states representing a majority of the population being outvoted. The table on p. 137 shows the weightings currently attached to member states' votes in the Council and the population of each state. To take a hypothetical example, under the present system seven states with a combined population of 45.9 million people (12.3 per cent of the Union's total) could block a proposal supported by all other states.

The **Treaty of Nice**, although it does not introduce a double majority system, does allow any member state to request verification that a measure adopted by QMV has the support of at least 62 per cent of the Union's population.

Draft Treaty establishing the European Union (DTEU)

The DTEU, adopted by the **European Parliament** in February 1984 by 237 votes to 31 with 43 abstentions, was largely the work of **Altiero Spinelli**. It was the Parliament's principal contribution to the negotiations that led to the 1986 **Single European Act** (SEA).

Spinelli believed that the 1979–84 Parliament, the first to be directly elected, had a historic right and moral duty to act as a **constituent assembly**. Working initially with friends and associates in the **Crocodile Club**, Spinelli was instrumental in setting up the Institutional Affairs Committee of the Parliament in January 1982. As the Committee's principal **rapporteur**, Spinelli drew up a draft treaty, which was approved in outline on 14 September 1983. This was then submitted to constitutional experts and presented to the Parliament for final adoption the following February.

Article 1 DTEU proclaimed the establishment of a European Union. The institutions of the Union followed the familiar pattern of Parliament, **Council of Ministers, European Commission, Court of Justice** and **European Council,** but with some differences. For example, the Council of the Union (Article 20 DTEU) was to be made up of 'representations' of the member states 'led by a minister who is permanently and specifically responsible for Union affairs'. More original was the distinction in Article 10 DTEU between 'common action' and 'cooperation', the latter being essentially intergovernmental in character (in this area the DTEU anticipated the 'pillar' structure of the **Maastricht Treaty**). Provision was made for activities to be transferred from the sphere of cooperation to common action, but not vice versa. In parallel with this was a distinction between exclusive competence for the Union and concurrent competence – that is, competence exercised jointly with member states (Article 12 (DTEU)). The same Article contains a definition of **subsidiarity**, referred to in general terms in the Preamble: 'The Union shall only act to carry out those tasks which may be undertaken more effectively in common than by the Member States acting separately.'

The most controversial of the 87 Articles was Article 82 DTEU. This allowed for the Treaty to enter into force once it had been ratified 'by a majority of the Member States of the Communities whose population represents two-thirds of the total population of the Communities'. By this provision Spinelli sought to circumvent the procedure for treaty revision then contained in Article 236 of the **Treaty of Rome**, which required unanimous agreement (Spinelli in any case always underlined the fact that the]s[dteu]/s[was an entirely new treaty, not an amendment to an existing one). However, the way Article 82 DTEU was worded prompted opposition from those who feared it would lead to a **two-speed Europe**.

In the event, only the Belgian and Italian parliaments adopted resolutions calling for the DTEU to be ratified. More cautious expressions of support were received from other parliaments. However, in June 1984 at the Fontainebleau European Council the heads of government set up what became known as the **Dooge Committee** to prepare proposals on institutional reform. The Committee endorsed the idea of a new treaty, and proposed that it be guided, among other suggestions, 'by the spirit and method of the draft treaty voted by the European Parliament'.

When the DTEU was adopted in outline by the Parliament in a form some way removed from his original intentions, Spinelli had the perfect simile. He compared himself to the fisherman in Hemingway's *The Old Man and the Sea*, who catches his huge fish after a long struggle, only to find on reaching the shore that, lashed to the side of his boat, his catch has been largely eaten away during the voyage home.

Drugs
See **European Monitoring Centre for Drugs and Drug Addiction**, **Europol**, **Pompidou Group**.

Dual mandate
In the European Union someone who is a member both of a national parliament and of the **European Parliament** is said to hold a 'dual mandate'. Although the dual mandate is not prohibited under the **European Elections Act** of 1976, it is contrary to national electoral law in several member states. It is also prohibited by many political parties under their own internal rules.

Until the first European elections in 1979 all Members of the European Parliament (MEPs) held a dual mandate since all were appointed by and from **national parliaments**. By the 1970s the growth in the Parliament's activities was already making the dual mandate very demanding, and although there were still many dual mandate MEPs in the 1979–84 Parliament, within a few years the number was negligible.

A dual mandate MEP does not draw two full salaries. In the United Kingdom he or she is entitled to one-third of the House of Commons salary (as in all member states except the Netherlands, the two salaries are the same).

There are those who advocate the dual mandate on the grounds that it promotes and facilitates contact between the European Parliament and national parliaments, and so helps to keep any sense of rivalry to a minimum. It also allows prominent figures in national politics to become involved (however superficially) in European politics, which may, in turn, raise the level of public interest in the European Parliament. On the other hand the steady increase in the degree of expertise and commitment required to be an effective MEP makes the dual mandate practically impossible in all but exceptional cases.

Dublin Asylum Convention

The Convention, signed in 1990 but in force only since 1997 (*Official Journal*, C254, 19 August 1997), provides for applications for **asylum** to be examined by whichever member state of the European Union first receives the asylum-seeker (not always easy to establish in the case of illegal entrants without papers), unless there are good reasons why the case should be handled by another member state. It is designed to forestall the possibility of asylum-seekers trying one member state after another (or several member states simultaneously) in order to gain entry into the Union, and is a logical extension of the commitment under Article 14.2 of the **Treaty of Rome** to create 'an area without internal frontiers in which the free movement of … persons … is ensured' (see **free movement of persons**). The Convention also allows the authorities of member states to exchange information on asylum-seekers (including finger-prints under a system known as **Eurodac**). It does not affect the eligibility for asylum or the procedures for examining applications for asylum, both of which are laid down in the 1951 United Nations Convention on Refugees. Under the **Maastricht Treaty** asylum questions are now handled within the framework of cooperation in the fields of **Justice and Home Affairs** (JHA; see also **External Frontiers Convention**). An Action Plan on asylum was adopted by the European Council in Vienna (December 1998) on the basis of proposals by a High Level Working Group on Asylum and Immigration. The aim is to establish a Common European Asylum System.

Dunkirk Treaty

Signed in March 1947, the Treaty of Dunkirk between the United Kingdom and France was the first postwar European security pact. Composed of only six Articles, of which the second required the signatory states to provide each other with 'military and other support and assistance' in the event of an attack, the Treaty was concluded for an initial period of 50 years, after which it was to remain in force unless either party gave a year's notice of withdrawal.

The Treaty was a 'regional arrangement' of the type encouraged by Article 52 of the United Nations Charter. As the preamble makes clear, it was directed against the possibility of 'a renewal of German aggression', and was prompted by the French government's sense of France's vulnerability (the only other security pact France had at the time was with the USSR). The Treaty led directly to the more ambitious **Brussels Treaty** of 1948.

Duty-free goods

It was originally supposed that with the establishment of the **Single Market** on 1 January 1993 the sale of duty-free goods to passengers travelling within the European Union would cease. Not only would such sales mean the maintenance of frontier controls, based as they were on the idea that the goods were being 'exported' they were incompatible with the logic of a Single Market, and gave rise to distortions in the conditions of competition between different modes of transport. However, as the deadline approached, the **Ecofin Council** of 11 November 1991 agreed that since **value-added tax** (VAT) had not yet been harmonized, duty-free goods for travel within the Union would be phased out over a period ending on 30 June 1999. On 14 December 1992, the Council adopted 'Guidelines for the control of tax-free sales in the Community' under which a system of vendor control was introduced. The 1991 decision to end duty-free sales in 1999 was confirmed by the Ecofin Council in May 1998.

The first duty-free sales were on board ships at sea. The principle was extended to air travel: the first duty-free shop was opened at Shannon airport in Ireland in 1947. Since then, the industry has grown enormously, to the point at which many ferry operators and airports are heavily dependent on the revenue from duty-free sales. Ending such sales for travel within the Union would, they argued, not only put many small operators out of business, it would involve very significant job losses and a substantial increase in ticket prices. It was estimated that of duty-free sales in the member states in 1996, 71 per cent were generated by goods purchased by those travelling within the Union. On the other hand, duty-free sales meant that travellers were benefiting from a subsidy, worth some £1.6 billion per annum, at the expense of the taxpayers in general; they subsidized airlines and ferries at the expense of the railways (this problem is particularly acute in respect of the **Channel Tunnel**); and they encouraged the consumption of cigarettes and alcohol, which together represented half of total sales and two-thirds of total profits.

E

Ecofin Council

The Council of Economics and Finance Ministers of the European Union, widely known as Ecofin, is the second most important division of the **Council of Ministers** after the **General Affairs Council**. It meets on average once a month, usually on a Monday, to discuss the macro-economic situation in the member states, coordinate the Union's position in international financial institutions (such as the International Monetary Fund), and adopt legislation in respect of tax harmonization, financial liberalization and the financing of the Union. The Ecofin Council is also responsible for the application of **budgetary discipline** and the coordination of export credit policy among the member states. (The annual **Budget** is discussed in the Budget Council – often the same ministers – rather than by Ecofin.) The finance ministers meet informally at least once every six months in the country holding the **presidency** of the Council. In preparing major decisions the Ecofin Council is assisted by the **Economic and Financial Committee**, a high-level group of national officials. The Ecofin Council's responsibilities were formally extended by the **Maastricht Treaty** to include overall supervision, in collaboration with the **European Monetary Institute** (EMI), of the progress of member states towards **Economic and Monetary Union** (EMU) with particular reference to the **convergence criteria** and the **excessive deficit procedure**. The Ecofin Council retained its general responsibility for EMU after stage 3 began in January 1999, although ministerial representatives of the 12 states that introduced the **euro** as the single currency in January 2002 also meet separately in a grouping known as 'euro-12'. See also **Exchange-Rate Mechanism**.

Economic and Financial Committee

Composed of 34 members (two representatives from each member state, two from the **European Commission** and two from the **European Central Bank**), the Committee took over the functions of the **Monetary Committee** from the beginning of the third stage of **Economic and Monetary Union** in January 1999 (Article 114 EC).

Economic and Monetary Union (EMU)

The provisions governing EMU, which has a strong claim to be the boldest economic experiment of all time, were added to the **Treaty of Rome** by the **Maastricht Treaty**. They set up a number of new institutions and specified the stages by which EMU was to be achieved, by 1999 at the latest (see below).

Although the most ambitious of the European Union's objectives, EMU was not mentioned in any of the **Treaties** until the 1986 **Single European Act** (SEA). The goal of EMU was first set at a meeting of the heads of government of **the Six** in The Hague in 1969, with 1980 as the target date. This decision led to the 1970 **Werner Report** and was repeated at the Paris **summit** of October 1972, but the adverse economic circumstances of the early 1970s resulted in little being achieved. The idea of EMU was relaunched by **Roy Jenkins** as president of the **European Commission** in 1977, and with strong support from Helmut Schmidt and **Valéry Giscard d'Estaing** this led to the **European Monetary System** (EMS). EMU was taken up again by **Jacques Delors** in 1985, and was mentioned both in the Preamble and in an amendment to the Treaty of Rome contained in the SEA. In 1988 work began on what became known as the **Delors Report**, which in turn led to the decision to convene an **Intergovernmental Conference** (IGC) on EMU. The conclusions of this IGC were a key component of the Maastricht Treaty.

The Maastricht Treaty mentions EMU in the Preamble, and refers to it together with the **Single Market** in Article 2 as one of the means by which the Union will 'promote economic and social progress which is balanced and sustainable'. A reference to EMU was added to Article 2 EC by the Maastricht Treaty, and Article 32 EEC (since repealed) referred to 'the irrevocable fixing of exchange rates leading to the introduction of a single currency, the ECU, and … a single monetary policy and exchange-rate policy', but the main elements of the institutions managing EMU and the stages by which it was to be achieved are set out in Articles 98 to 124.

The first stage, by a decision of the Madrid **European Council** in June 1989, began on 1 July 1990, with the removal of exchange controls in 8 of the 12 member states (with the others to follow), the inclusion in principle of all currencies in the narrow band of the **Exchange-Rate Mechanism** (ERM), and measures to encourage convergence (see **convergence criteria**). No new institutions were required. The second stage began on 1 January 1994, with the newly created **European Monetary Institute** (EMI), based in Frankfurt, gradually assuming a coordinating role. During this stage member states except Denmark and the United Kingdom were expected to take steps, if necessary, to make their central banks independent of government. Before the end of 1996 the **Council of Ministers** at the level of heads of government was to decide, by qualified majority, whether a majority of countries (not including Denmark: see below) satisfied the convergence criteria, so that the transition could be made to the third stage by those that qualified. The Council was also supposed to decide whether it was appropriate to begin the third stage and, if so, when (the **European Parliament** had to be consulted). In the event, at its meeting in Madrid (December 1995) the European Council abandoned the option of starting the third stage in 1997 and adopted 1 January 1999 as the definitive starting-date for all participating countries. On 2 May 1998 the European Council (meeting as the Council of Ministers) decided on the basis of reports from the Commission and the EMI that all member states except Denmark, Sweden and the United Kingdom (which did not wish to proceed) and Greece (which did not qualify) would take part in stage 3 of EMU. They also appointed the president and other board members of the **European Central Bank** (ECB). The 12 participants (Greece was subsequently allowed to join) represent some 20 per cent of the world economy.

The single currency was originally specified as the ECU, but in Madrid in December 1995 the European Council decided to call it the **euro**. At the beginning of stage 3 the participating states adopted the 'irrevocably fixed' rates at which the euro was to be substituted for national currencies and took 'the other measures for the rapid introduction of the ECU [the euro] as the single currency' (Article 123 EEC). The ECB is the sole issuing authority for euro banknotes.

As well as a single currency the third stage entailed the creation of a **European System of Central Banks** (ESCB), composed of the ECB (replacing the EMI) and representatives of the national central banks. Member states that did not proceed to the third stage are in effect excluded from these institutions (see **derogation**) but at least every two years or at the request of a member state its qualifications for entry are re-examined by the Council after consultation with the European Parliament and with advice from the Commission and the ECB. See also **Stability and Growth Pact**.

Protocols annexed to the Treaty of Rome contain the statutes of the EMI, the ESCB and the ECB. Another commits all signatory states, 'whether they fulfil the necessary conditions for the adoption of a single currency or not, [to] respect the will for the Community to enter swiftly into the third stage'. The protocol on the British **opt-out** recognizes that 'the United Kingdom shall not be obliged or committed to move to the third stage ... without a separate decision to do so by its government and parliament'. Denmark was granted a similar opt-out, but a year later at the Edinburgh European Council in December 1992 Denmark's definitive decision not to participate in the third stage was recognized. When ratifying the Maastricht Treaty both the German Bundestag and the Netherlands parliament secured a say in the decision to move to stage 3 (for the German position, see **Karlsruhe judgment**).

Since the Maastricht Treaty was signed, economic recession and instability in the currency markets (arising partly from Germany's high interest rates, maintained as a consequence of **German reunification**) cast doubt on whether or not EMU was attainable and on how strictly the **convergence criteria** would be applied. EMU raises, in the most acute form, the question of a **two-speed Europe** (see also **variable geometry**), since it prefigures the emergence of a **hard core** of member states, including France and Germany, sharing a common currency. It also raises, in the perspective of longer-term **enlargement**, the question of **wider versus deeper**, since EMU constitutes a deepening well beyond anything the applicant states from central and eastern Europe could hope to take part in for at least a generation.

Most important of all, EMU raises issues of **sovereignty**. EMU entails the transfer of powers hitherto exercised exclusively by governments to an independent ECB, including the right to authorize issues of currency, which, together with the associated right of seigniorage, has been the exclusive prerogative of monarchs for literally thousands of years. But it also invites governments to reflect on the limitations of sovereignty, since without EMU the Union's economic future would have been dominated by the Deutsche Mark, with the German economy further strengthened by its privileged access to the new markets of central and eastern Europe. EMU was seen by many as the only means of containing German economic hegemony in the longer term.

The Maastricht Treaty and the Treaty of Rome do not describe EMU as an end in itself but as one contributing to 'economic and social progress' (Article 2 TEU) and 'price stability' (Article 4.2 EC). The underlying contention is that the efficiency and therefore the benefits of the Single Market can be maximized only if consumers, manufacturers, traders and investors are spared the costs and risks involved in currency exchanges. Competition will be made keener if prices can be compared more clearly across borders. It is also argued that the Union will be better able to advance its interests in international economic fora with a common currency and be less vulnerable to large-scale currency speculation. Nowhere is any explicit connection made between EMU and political union.

EMU places monetary powers in the hands of the ECB, but leaves fiscal powers with member states. The **Budget** of the European Union is too small to be an effective instrument of macro-economic policy, and likely to remain so. In any case, the Treaty provisions make no mention of any role the ESCB and ECB might play in decisions on the Budget. The German government insisted that the ECB, modelled on the Bundesbank, should be wholly independent of national governments and Union institutions; it remains to be seen whether a controversial new body that is not allowed to take instructions itself will have the authority and the political acumen to play an effective role in the continuous negotiations that underpin Union decision-making.

Economic and Social Committee (ESC)

The ESC of the European Union is an unelected tripartite representative body, established by the **Treaty of Rome** (Articles 257 to 262 EC), which advises the **Council of Ministers** on draft legislation in certain subject areas. The ESC – frequently known as 'EcoSoc' – is not one of the five institutions of the Union: the Council, the **European Commission**, the **European Parliament**, the **Court of Justice** and the **Court of Auditors**. Instead, it 'assists' the Council and Commission. It has few formal powers, no budget of its own, and a failure on its part to deliver an Opinion can only delay the Council from adopting the legislative act in question for one month. Under the **Treaty of Amsterdam** it may be consulted by the European Parliament.

The ESC consists of 222 members and an equal number of substitutes nominated by member states for a renewable four-year term. Those chosen are 'representatives of the various categories of economic and social activity, in particular, representatives of producers, farmers, carriers, workers, dealers, craftsmen, professional occupations and representatives of the general public' (Article 257 EC). In practice each member state, whose delegations range in size from 6 to 24, nominates individuals drawn from three categories: employers, trade unionists and 'other interests'. Three groups corresponding to these categories are established through the ESC's rules of procedure. Most governments nominate equal numbers to each category even though it is not strictly necessary for them to do so. Members of the ESC are paid no salary, but receive travel and accommodation expenses.

The ESC's two-year presidency rotates between the three groups, and the Committee is managed by a bureau also composed on a tripartite basis. The ESC conducts its advisory work by means of nine 'sections' covering different areas of Union activity. When a legislative proposal is received, the relevant section will nominate a small 'working group' from among its members to prepare a draft report, including suggested amendments to the Commission's text. The report of the working group, which acts by consensus and does not vote, is normally accepted by the section meeting more or less intact. The section then communicates the opinion so agreed to the monthly plenary session of the ESC. Amendments to the draft report are admissible from any member at either section or plenary stage.

Members vote in a personal capacity, and sit alphabetically rather than by group. In practice, however, the employers (Group One) and trade unionists

(Group Two) each tend to vote as a bloc, giving the representatives of 'other interests' (Group Three) the decisive votes. Members from the latter category, who are often self-employed, tend to represent the prevailing ideological assumptions of the ruling parties in the countries that nominate them. Members from Groups One and Two, by contrast, are often appointed by national governments on the basis of recommendations by employers' organizations and trade unions.

The ESC has frequently been criticized as a throw-back to the corporatist assumptions of the 1950s and 1960s in continental Europe with their emphasis on the role of the '**social partners**'. Its conception owes much to the French *Conseil Économique et Social*, which featured in the constitutional design of both the Fourth and Fifth Republics. There has been frequent talk of abolishing the ESC. For a long time after the first direct elections in 1979 the European Parliament was particularly critical of the ESC's continued existence, especially after the latter started to publicize itself, rather maladroitly, as 'the other European Assembly'. However, in the **Maastricht Treaty**, the ESC was in effect strengthened by being linked to a new advisory body, the **Committee of the Regions**.

Economic Commission for Europe (ECE)

A regional commission of the **United Nations**, the ECE was established in 1947 with its headquarters in Geneva. The governments of every European country together with Israel, Canada and the United States participate in the ECE, which is intended to promote cooperation between participating states over a wide range of technical, industrial and economic issues. The ECE holds an annual plenary session but most of the work is done in committees, working parties and meetings of experts. The working languages are English, French and Russian. The 1975 Final Act of the **Conference on Security and Cooperation in Europe** sought to encourage signatory states to use the ECE to implement the Act's provisions in the economic, technical and environmental fields. The ECE cooperates as necessary with many intergovernmental and non-governmental organizations of a very specialized character (such as the European Flexible Bulk Container Association or the International Federation of Pedestrians) and has done useful work on technical specifications and statistical information.

ECU

See **European Currency Unit**.

Edinburgh Growth Initiative

Agreed at the Edinburgh meeting of the **European Council** in December 1992, the Edinburgh Growth Initiative was a multiannual programme of coordinated measures undertaken at both Community and national level to counteract recession. The emphasis was on capital investment and investment in a more highly skilled, more flexible workforce.

At the Community level the Edinburgh Growth Initiative included a temporary loan facility of about £4 billion within the **European Investment Bank** (EIB) to help finance infrastructure projects (especially **trans-European networks**) and a new **European Investment Fund** with a capital of about £1.6 billion intended in particular to benefit small and medium-sized enterprises (SMEs). The **structural funds** were to be doubled over the six-year period 1994–9 and a **Cohesion Fund** worth almost £11 billion was set up over the same period. The EIB loan facility was increased in 1993. The **European Commission** estimated that the Edinburgh Growth Initiative was responsible for an extra 0.6 per cent of real gross domestic product in 1994.

Education policy

Article 149 of the **Treaty of Rome** added by the **Maastricht Treaty** allows the Community to 'contribute to the development of quality education by encouraging cooperation between Member States and, if necessary, by supporting and supplementing their action, while fully respecting the responsibility of the Member States for the content of teaching and the organization of education systems and their cultural and linguistic diversity'. The Article specifies that action is to be aimed at 'developing the European dimension in education', especially the teaching of languages, encouraging student and teacher exchanges and fostering cooperation with non-member countries and international organizations such as the **Council of Europe**. Article 150 EC deals with vocational training. In both these areas, the **Council of Ministers** is empowered to adopt 'incentive measures' or Recommendations (see **soft law**); 'harmonization of the laws and regulations of the Member States' is specifically excluded, as it is in **cultural policy**. The **Treaty of Amsterdam** brought vocational training within the scope of the **co-decision procedure**. Policy-making is assisted by the Eurydice network, operational since 1980, which monitors education systems in 30 European countries. The European Commission published *Towards a Europe of Knowledge* (COM(97) 563) in 1997, setting out priorities for action over the period 2000–6.

This new legal base for education policy reflected but did not extend the scope of measures already taken in this field, many of them based on a first action programme of 1976 (see **European Centre for the Development of Vocational Training, European Training Foundation, European University Institute, Socrates, Leonardo, mutual recognition of qualifications**). Both the Council of Europe and the **Organization for Economic Cooperation and Development** publish a wide range of material on education.

Elysée, Treaty of the

See **Franco-German cooperation**.

Employment

The **Treaty of Rome** was drafted at a time of high employment in western Europe. Treaty provisions on employment were few, and limited to relatively minor aspects of employment such as vocational training. Only recently has employment become a major area of policy, the legal basis of which has been greatly expanded by the **Treaty of Amsterdam** (see **social policy**).

Until the mid-1980s, almost the only **European Community** involvement in measures to promote employment was through the **structural funds**. With the campaign to create the **Single Market** came the idea that the Community needed a 'social dimension', in order to ensure that the more competitive economic environment would not lead to higher unemployment and a diminution of hard-won rights at the workplace. At a meeting in Strasbourg in December 1989, the **European Council** (with the exception of **Margaret Thatcher**) adopted the so-called 'Social Charter' (see **European Social Charter**). Unemployment remained worryingly high.

In 1993 the **European Commission** drew up a White Paper entitled *Growth, Competitiveness and Employment: the challenges and ways forward into the 21st century*. This was discussed at the Brussels meeting of the European Council on 10–11 December 1993 and accepted as 'a reference point for future work'. The White Paper showed how unemployment in the Union had risen during the late 1980s, and that by comparison with the United States and Japan, the Union had a far higher proportion of long-term unemployment (more than 40 per cent of the total had been unemployed for over a year) and a preponderance of young people. Unemployment might be cyclical in that it was related directly to changes in the level of economic activity, structural in so far as it related to underlying changes in the factors of production, or technological in the sense that it might originate from a failure to keep pace with technological advances. The Commission set a target of 15 million new jobs by the year 2000, an ambitious total given the failure of member states to create more than about 3 million jobs since 1974 (compared with almost 30 million in the United States). The Commission identified the main causes of unemployment as low rates of growth and of investment, declining international **competitiveness**, relatively high labour costs (wage and non-wage), failure to take advantage of new technology, 'inflexible' labour markets in the sense of low geographical and sectoral mobility, and an ageing population. The European Council accepted this analysis. On 22 December 1993 the **Council of Ministers** adopted a 'Recommendation on the broad guidelines of the economic policies of the Member States and of the

Community', including exploiting the full potential of the **Single Market**, speeding up the completion of **trans-European networks** (TENs), reducing the indirect cost of labour, increasing expenditure on **research** and, most of all, securing 'non-inflationary, strong and employment-creating growth, lasting over many years and respecting the environment'. The Council also made some suggestions to member states on how access to training and the mobility of labour might be improved.

The Commission followed up this Recommendation in a July 1994 White Paper on *European Social Policy: a way forward for the Union*. This referred to 'the **European social model**', defined as a 'unique blend of economic wellbeing, social cohesiveness and high overall quality of life'. At the same time it accepted the importance of maintaining Europe's international competitiveness as the key to job creation, which is identified as the main priority against a background of high unemployment. The White Paper recognized the absence of consensus among member states on the role of European legislation in creating high labour standards and on the balance to be struck between such standards and a flexible, competitive labour market. Partly for this reason, the White Paper did not lay the groundwork for major new initiatives in social policy, preferring instead to consolidate progress so far achieved and to continue to press for solutions to problems already raised (such as the treatment of immigrant workers, improvements to the quality and availability of vocational training, and the need for further action on the **free movement of persons**). It pointed out that 52 million people in the Union live below the 'poverty line', i.e., in households in which the expenditure is less than half the national average, and that demographic changes are steadily reducing the number of persons of working age as a proportion of the population as a whole (see **demography**).

A discussion on employment was the main item on the agenda of the Essen meeting of the European Council in December 1994. 'The fight against unemployment and equality of opportunity for men and women' were described as 'the paramount tasks of the European Union and its Member States'. However, no further action on the part of the Union – except for an annual Joint Report on employment by the Commission and the Council of Ministers – was called for: instead, the European Council enjoined member states to promote investment in vocational training, to reduce non-wage labour costs, to encourage more flexible ways of working, and to give special help to the young and long-term unemployed. One year later in Madrid, the European Council noted 'generally positive results'.

In 1996 the Commission published a report entitled *Action on Employment: a confidence pact*. Together with a memorandum from President Chirac of France on the 'European Social Model' this provided the basis for the

European Council's 'The Jobs Challenge: The Dublin Declaration on Employment' (December 1996). Except for a stronger emphasis on competitiveness and references to the need for complementary employment initiatives at the local level, the Dublin Declaration added little to the Essen strategy.

The summation of this activity was a meeting of the European Council in Luxembourg on 20–1 November 1997 which was devoted to the question of employment (the 'Jobs Summit'). The European Council agreed to apply in advance of their being ratified the new provisions on employment in the Treaty of Amsterdam (see also **Employment and Labour Market Committee**), especially those with a bearing on the coordination of member states' employment policies (Article 128 EC). The aim was 'to create for employment, as for economic policy, the same resolve to converge towards jointly set, verifiable, regularly updated targets'. The European Council welcomed the establishment by the **European Investment Bank** (EIB) of an 'Amsterdam Special Action Programme' (given extra urgency by its acronym ASAP) with help from the **European Investment Fund**, worth some 10 billion ECUs (£6.7 billion) over three years and entailing the setting up of a European Technology Facility to provide venture capital to small and medium-sized enterprises (SMEs) in the high-technology sector. The guidelines for member states' employment policies in 1998 are: improving employability (training, retraining, vocational guidance), developing entrepreneurship (including the reduction of non-wage costs, now averaging some 42 per cent of total employment-related costs), encouraging adaptability, and strengthening equal opportunities (see **equal treatment**). In all these matters the **social partners** are to play a leading role. Of a total workforce of some 155 million, the service sector accounts for 66.3 per cent of employment, industry for 29.3 per cent and agriculture for 4.5 per cent.

Employment and Labour Market Committee

Set up by the **Council of Ministers** in December 1996, the Committee is composed of two representatives from each member state and two representatives of the **European Commission**. Its role is to advise the Council and to promote the exchange of information and experience between member states on all matters pertaining to employment. The **Treaty of Amsterdam** added a new Article to the **Treaty of Rome** (Article 130) in which the committee is given Treaty status as an advisory body 'to formulate opinions at the request of either the Council or the Commission or on its own initiative'. Under a new Article 128.4 EC, also added by the Treaty of Amsterdam, the Employment Committee takes part in the Council's annual review of member states' employment policies.

Empty chair crisis

The 'empty chair' (or *chaise vide*) crisis took place in the period July–December 1965, when French ministers, on the instructions of President **Charles de Gaulle**, refused to take part in meetings of the **Council of Ministers** and the French permanent representative (see **national representations**) was withdrawn from Brussels. On 18 October 1965 this manoeuvre was reflected in the **European Parliament** by a refusal on the part of Gaullist members to take part in votes on matters with a bearing on the Community's future. The empty chair crisis was and remains the most serious breakdown in the Community's operation.

The empty chair crisis was part of President de Gaulle's long dispute with the Community and its institutions (particularly the **European Commission** under the presidency of **Walter Hallstein**), which resulted eventually in the **Luxembourg Compromise** of January 1966. France was opposed to the Commission's proposals for financing the **Common Agricultural Policy** (CAP), to the introduction of **own resources**, to the granting of more extensive budgetary powers to the European Parliament and, in particular, to the prospect of **majority voting** being introduced into the deliberations of the Council of Ministers. In more general terms France was also opposed to what it saw as the supranational pretensions of the Community institutions (see also **Fouchet Plan**).

None of France's partners among **the Six** shared these objections to developments in the Community, many of which had been specifically provided for in the **Treaty of Rome**. The empty chair crisis resulted in a victory for France in the sense that the practice followed in the Council after the Luxembourg Compromise embodied the French view of how the Council should operate. The introduction of own resources was postponed until 1970. Whether or not it was a tactic intended primarily to secure de Gaulle's re-election to the presidency of France in December 1965 is open to dispute.

Energy policy

Since the coal industry was covered by the **European Coal and Steel Community** (ESC) Treaty and nuclear energy by the **European Atomic Energy Community** (EAEC or Euratom) Treaty, the **Treaty of Rome** in its original form contained no reference to energy policy. A new energy chapter was proposed in the negotiations that led up to the **Maastricht Treaty**, but it was decided to come back to this question in the 1996 **Intergovernmental Conference** (IGC). However, three incidental references were added to the Treaty of Rome: Article 31 (since repealed) listing 'measures in the spheres of energy, civil protection and tourism' among the 'activities' of the Community, Article 154 on **trans-European networks** (TENs) and Article 175.2 on environmental measures 'significantly affecting' the energy options of a member state. The energy industries are covered by the normal Treaty rules on **competition**, state aids, etc., and indigenous energy supplies are treated as 'natural resources' within the meaning of Article 174.1 EC, which requires their 'prudent and rational utilization'.

The first attempt at a comprehensive energy policy was made in a Decision of the **Council of Ministers** in April 1974, prompted by the unedifying and ill-coordinated scramble for energy supplies that followed the first oil crisis. A more considered statement on long-term (to 1995) energy objectives was drawn up in September 1986. It was decided that the Community should seek to reduce its dependence on imported energy, that member states should encourage energy-saving schemes, that minimum stocks should be maintained against emergencies and that encouragement should be given to research into alternative sources of energy. In line with the first objective, coal was to be made more competitive.

In fact, progress has been made in respect of most of these objectives. Energy consumption per capita has fallen by about 30 per cent since 1975, and energy dependence from 60 to 48 per cent. However, formidable obstacles remain in the way of an energy policy, of which the most striking is the continuing controversy over nuclear energy. Although nuclear energy represents about 15 per cent of the Union's total energy production, this figure conceals very wide disparities between member states. Many produce no nuclear energy at all, whereas in France nuclear energy accounts for almost 40 per cent of total production. These figures underline the enormous differences between the overall pattern of energy production in member states, differences that may also be found in respect of coal and natural gas.

The main difficulty in the way of ensuring that in the European Union coal (hard coal and lignite) retains its present share (about 14.5 per cent) of the energy market is that imported coal is now cheaper than coal mined in the member states. Only the United Kingdom, Germany, Spain and France are coal producers, and understandably the idea that coal production in these countries should be subsidized meets with resistance from other member states and other energy suppliers.

At present the emphasis is on opening up the energy market by encouraging cross-border trade in energy and more competitive pricing policies. Commitments entered into at the United Nations Conference on Environment and Development (Rio de Janeiro, 1992) and elsewhere on the environmental aspects of energy policy are also being reflected in proposals for new legislation. Energy-related projects (including the **Joint European Torus**) are the second largest element in the current framework programme for **research**. Finally, the **European Energy Charter** is designed to promote cooperation and reciprocal market access with the countries of central and eastern Europe and the former Soviet Union.

Engrenage

Literally 'meshing in' (as of cog-wheels), *engrenage* is a term used to describe the practice of involving national civil servants with the work of the Union institutions, notably the **European Commission**. This involvement was of particular importance in the early development of the Community, not only because the Commission was then much smaller and less influential but also because it furnished a means whereby national bureaucracies could be encouraged to approach problems (especially those of a technical nature) from a European standpoint and acquire the habit of working together, which was essential to the functionalist theory of integration (see **functionalism**). For this reason, *engrenage* became and remains an established feature of Brussels decision making. The present scale of *engrenage* is best demonstrated by the large number of Brussels-based committees staffed jointly by Commission officials and national civil servants (see **comitology**) and of 'national experts' working in Brussels on short-term contracts.

Enhanced cooperation

See **flexibility**.

Enlargement

Enlargement is the process by which countries join the European Union. Article 49 of the **Maastricht Treaty** specifies that 'any European State … may apply to become a member of the Union. It shall address its application to the Council, which shall act unanimously after consulting the Commission and after receiving the assent of the European Parliament, which shall act by an absolute majority of its component members' (see also **Association Agreements**).

In practice, the procedure is as follows:

1 application by the candidate state to the **Council of Ministers**;
2 delivery of formal **Opinion** by the **European Commission** (this can take up to three years) and consultation with the **European Parliament**;
3 if the Council, acting unanimously, decides to go ahead, negotiations then begin between the applicant state and the **presidency** of the Council (representing the member states) and the Commission;
4 a draft **accession** treaty is initialled by the applicant state and by representatives of the member states;
5 approval by an absolute majority of the total membership of the European Parliament under the **assent procedure**;

6 **ratification** by all signatory states 'in accordance with their respective constitutional requirements' (Article 49 TEU; this may involve a referendum, especially if amendments to the applicant country's constitution are involved);

7 formal signature of accession treaty;

8 entry into force on an agreed date (although there will normally be **transitional periods** in certain sectors, e.g., **free movement of persons**).

The basic qualifications for full membership of the Union are that the applicant is a European state (see **Morocco**), that it is able and willing to assume the political and economic obligations of membership, that it is ready to accept the *acquis communautaire* (including the *finalités politiques*), and that it is a democracy in which **human rights** are respected and guaranteed (see **Copenhagen criteria, European Conference**).

Of the current applicants two (Turkey and Cyprus) have long-standing Association Agreements, and the remainder have **Europe Agreements**. A very substantial proportion of every applicant's trade is already with the Union and several applicants already participate very actively in the **structured dialogue**.

It was the end of the Cold War which removed the inhibition that neutral countries such as Austria, Finland, Malta, Sweden and Switzerland had previously felt about becoming too explicitly aligned with the West (see **neutrality**). It also led to applications for membership from Hungary, Poland and other former Communist countries. The European Council meeting in Copenhagen in June 1993 agreed that the associated countries in central and

Table 1   New member states, 1973 to 1995

Country	Applied	Joined
Ireland	July 1961	January 1973
United Kingdom	August 1961	January 1973
Denmark	August 1961	January 1973
Greece	June 1975	January 1981
Portugal	March 1977	January 1986
Spain	July 1977	January 1986
East Germany	–	October 1990, as a consequence of **German reunification**
Austria	July 1989	January 1995
Sweden	July 1991	January 1995
Finland	March 1992	January 1995

The impact of enlargement is summarized in the following table:

Table 2   Impact of enlargement (1995 data)

Number of member states	Increase in area (%)	Increase in population (%)	Increase in total GDP (%)[1]	Change in per capita GDP (%)	Average per capita GDP (EUR 6 = 100)
From 6 to 9	31	32	29	−3	97
From 9 to 12	48	22	15	−6	91
From 12 to 15[2]	43	11	8	−3	89
From 15 to 26[3]	34	29	9	−16	75

[1] Adjusted for purchasing power standards
[2] Including former East Germany
[3] I.e. the Union plus all applicants except Malta and Turkey.

Source: European Commission

eastern Europe 'that so desire shall become members of the Union'. At its meeting in Essen the following year (December 1994) it defined a '**pre-accession strategy**' based on the Europe Agreements, the structured dialogue, and the **PHARE** programme.

Inevitably, enlargement became entangled with other priorities. The European Council meeting in Maastricht in December 1991 agreed that negotiations with applicant states could begin 'as soon as the Community has terminated its negotiations on **own resources** and related issues in 1992', and invited the Commission to submit a paper on enlargement to the next meeting of the European Council in Lisbon (published as 'Europe and the challenge of enlargement', *Bulletin of the European Communities*, supplement 3/92). However, by the time of the Lisbon meeting the Danish referendum result on the Maastricht Treaty had introduced a further element of uncertainty with respect to the future shape and character of the Community, and the discussion on enlargement was necessarily only tentative. The heads of government were able merely to reaffirm their determination that the Community should remain open to duly qualified applicants and that negotiations should proceed from the beginning of 1993. Allowing time for ratification, this meant that no enlargement could take place before 1995 at the earliest.

In the event, the Danish problem was resolved and the negotiations with Austria, Finland, and Sweden were completed in time for them to join the Union in January 1995. By then, Hungary and Poland had applied for membership, and it was certain that others would follow. However, the imminence of the 1996 **Intergovernmental Conference** (IGC) led the European Council to decide in December 1994 that no decisions would be taken until the IGC

Other applications for membership have been as follows:

Table 3   Applications for membership, 1962 to 1996

Country	Applied	Joined
Norway	April 1962	Draft accession treaty rejected by referendum, September 1972.
Turkey	April 1987	Unfavourable Commission Opinion, December 1989 but accepted as applicant by Helsinki European Council, December 1999.
Morocco	July 1987	Rejected by the Council as a non-European state.
Cyprus	July 1990	Favourable Commission Opinions, June 1993. Negotiations concluded in 2002 (see **Treaty of Accession**).
Malta	July 1990 (withdrawn October 1996 but later renewed)	
Switzerland	June 1992	Inactive, but remains 'on the table'
Norway	December 1992 (second application)	Draft accession treaty rejected by referendum, November 1994.
Hungary	March 1994	In June 1993 the European Council recognized membership as a long-term goal for all former Eastern bloc countries willing and able to join the European Union. The Commission's Opinions were published in July 1997. Negotiations concluded with all countries except Bulgaria and Romania in 2002 (see **Treaty of Accession**).
Poland	April 1994	
Romania	June 1995	
Slovakia	June 1995	
Latvia	October 1995	
Estonia	December 1995	
Bulgaria	December 1995	
Lithuania	December 1995	
Czech Rep.	January 1996	
Slovenia	June 1996	

was completed. The outcome of the IGC, the **Treaty of Amsterdam**, was agreed in June 1997. The following month the Commission published *Agenda 2000* to accompany the Opinions on the central and eastern European applicants and recommended that negotiations should begin in 1998 with the Czech Republic, Estonia, Hungary, Poland and Slovenia, as well as with Cyprus.

This was a controversial recommendation. Under pressure from several member states the European Council at its meeting in December 1997 agreed instead that in March 1998 a 'European Conference' should be held which would 'bring together the Member States of the European Union and the European States aspiring to accede to it and sharing its values and internal and external objectives'. Later in the same month, the 'accession process' would be set in train for all applicants 'on the basis of the same criteria and ... on an equal footing ... evolutive and inclusive ... [within] a single framework'. Subsequent to this, bilateral negotiations would begin with Cyprus and the five states identified in the Commission's *Agenda 2000* study. The pre-accession strategy would be intensified and 'pre-accession partnerships' established with all applicant states, with an annual review which would allow bilateral negotiations to begin with any one of the applicant states not included in the first wave. In December 1999 the European Council meeting in Helsinki gave full recognition to Turkey as an applicant state and called for bilateral negotiations to begin with Romania, Slovakia, Latvia, Lithuania, Bulgaria and Malta. It was agreed that 'the Union should be in a position to welcome new Member States from the end of 2002' (i.e. after ratification of the outcome of the 2000 Intergovernmental Conference, the **Treaty of Nice**).

No official definition exists of what is meant in the Treaty by a 'European State'. Membership of the **Council of Europe** extends to countries, such as Turkey and Cyprus, whose claims to being European on geographic grounds are slight, although Turkey has long been accepted as a European member of the **North Atlantic Treaty Organization** (NATO). To require applicant countries to be Christian would exclude Turkey, the Muslim republics emerging from the break-up of Yugoslavia and those once part of the USSR. Neither geographically nor culturally has there ever been a clearly defined eastern frontier of Europe.

The requirement that applicant states be democratic and respect human rights is more clear-cut. The Preamble to the Maastricht Treaty refers to the member states' 'attachment to the principles of liberty, democracy and respect for human rights and fundamental freedoms and of the rule of law', and Article 6 TEU commits the Union to respect fundamental rights. By virtue of accepting the *acquis communautaire* applicant states become party to the tripartite Council–Commission–European Parliament declaration of 1977 on human rights and the **Charter of Fundamental Rights**. Applicant states are in effect required to be parties to the Council of Europe's European Convention on Human Rights and to accept the right of individual petition under the Convention. It was on the issues of democracy and human rights that the Community refused to conclude Association Agreements with the Spain of General Franco and the Portugal of Salazar (both countries applied as long ago as 1962) and 'froze' the Association Agreement with Greece during the seven-year dictatorship of the Colonels (1967–74). For many years doubts persisted about Turkey's human rights record, and these were often raised as arguments against Turkish accession. The Treaty of Amsterdam contains new provisions for the **suspension** of member states found guilty of a 'serious and persistent' breach of human rights, later revised in the Treaty of Nice.

The problems presented by continuing enlargement are primarily institutional, political and economic. Although there has recently been a move in the direction of more decisions being taken in the Council by **qualified majority voting** (QMV), many of the most important can still be taken only by unanimity (changes to the **Treaties**, for example, or to the system of own resources). Similarly, the kind of consensus that is the foundation of the Union's **Common Foreign and Security Policy** (CFP) is already difficult to attain, and can only become more difficult as the number of member states increases and their interests become more diverse. The Treaty of Amsterdam, although it failed to resolve either the question of QMV or the number of Commissioners in an enlarged Community, placed an upper limit of 700 on the number of Members of the European Parliament MEPs. Although the limit is now 732, it will entail some reduction in member states' current entitlement to seats in the Parliament. The Treaty also introduced **constructive abstention**.

Small states present a particular problem: it would clearly not be reasonable to allow Cyprus, for example, to block a decision acceptable to all the other member states. The system for rotating the **presidency** may have to be reviewed again, since the task of occupying the presidency is an increasingly complex one likely to impose intolerable strains on smaller states. Even larger states, which could expect to hold the presidency every 10 years or so, would find it more difficult by virtue of having fewer officials with experience of previous presidencies. **Languages** also present a problem. The 11 official languages currently in use give rise to 110 language combinations, but with 20 languages the number of combinations would rise to 380, with enormous consequences in cost and potential inefficiency.

The central political problem springs from the inevitably more heterogeneous nature of an enlarged Union. Across the whole range of issues agreement becomes more difficult to reach, unless it is achieved with the aid of so many derogations and special protocols as to render it more or less meaningless. Equal implementation and enforcement of Union legislation at the national level also become much more difficult, especially for countries in central and eastern Europe; the example of the concessions that had to be made to the former East Germany is instructive. Acceptance of the *acquis communautaire* (some 12,000 pages of rules and regulations) poses great difficulties both for countries that have been suffering from gross over-regulation for almost two generations and for those that have not yet allowed regulation so broad a scope within national (especially economic) life.

The differences in prosperity between the Union and the applicants are very striking. The poorest of them is Bulgaria with a per capita gross domestic product (GDP) around 23 per cent of the European Union average. The most prosperous, Cyprus, has a per capita GDP almost four times greater. Disparities on this scale suggest that the countries of central and eastern Europe will require enormous transfers of resources from the **structural funds** and that it will be a long time before they are ready for the full range of **Single Market** disciplines and those implicit in a single currency (see Table 4). The difficulty of negotiating with so heterogeneous a group of countries is compounded by the fact that each country, perfectly properly, wants its claim to membership to be considered on its individual merits, while demanding, in the name of equal justice, that any agreement reached with one applicant should be extended to all.

Table 4 The applicant states in order of prosperity (GDP per head as a percentage of the European Union average, adjusted for purchasing power standards)

	Population (millions)[1]	GDP per head (% of EU average)[2]	Contribution of agriculture to gross value added (%)[2]
Cyprus	0.75	82	4.2
Slovenia	1.99	71	3.6
Czech Rep.	10.28	60	3.9
Malta	0.39	52	2.5
Hungary	10.04	51	4.8
Slovakia	5.40	48	4.5
Poland	38.65	39	4.0
Estonia	1.44	37	6.7
Lithuania	3.70	29	8.4
Turkey	64.82	29	15.0
Latvia	2.42	28	4.5
Romania	22.45	27	14.8
Bulgaria	8.19	23	17.3

[1] 2000
[2] 1999

Source: Eurostat, Statistical Yearbook on Candidate and South-East European Countries (2001 edn)

Estimates of the cost of enlargement vary widely. The Commission's estimate in *Agenda 2000* is that the overall cost can be contained within the budgetary ceiling of 1.27 per cent of the Union's GDP. At the Berlin meeting of the
European Council in March 1999 it was agreed in the discussion on **future
financing** that the costs arising from enlargement (i.e. pre-accession aid and
increased expenditure on agriculture and the structural funds) would be
allowed to rise to 18.6 per cent of the Budget by 2006, by which time it was
assumed that six new member states would have joined the Union. PHARE
would remain constant at €1.56 billion annually until then. On the other
hand, enlargement is a long-term investment in Europe's stability and prosperity: the value of the European Union's trade with the 166 million relatively
poor consumers in the applicant states is already greater than that of trade
with the United States. There is a great deal of information on this subject in
a House of Lords report entitled *The Financial Consequences of Enlargement*
(November 1997).

Behind these arguments lies the question of **wider versus deeper**.
Widening makes deepening more difficult; deepening, in turn, makes widening more difficult, since it makes the criteria for entry into the Union more
demanding. Even if it can be shown that successive enlargements have on the
whole quickened the pace of integration, the Union is now faced with
enlargement on an unprecedented scale. This fact alone is a token of the
Union's success and at the same time the greatest single challenge it has to
face. The hard fact remains that the Treaties are so framed and the *acquis
communautaire* so developed that only advanced, industrialized democracies
with stable institutions can meet the obligations they entail without difficulty.
This is especially true of several of the Union's key objectives, such as
Economic and Monetary Union (EMU), even if the political issues are set
aside. However, if the Union were to ease the requirements implicit in the
Treaties and in the *acquis communautaire* and to lose sight, however temporarily, of its objectives, it could lose a momentum that it might never
recover. Alan Mayhew, *Recreating Europe* (Cambridge, 1998) is a comprehensive and authoritative study of all the issues.

Environment policy

Not referred to in the original **Treaty of Rome**, environment policy became
an area for Community action on the basis of a decision at the October 1972
meeting of the **European Council**. Articles dealing with the environment
(Articles 174 to 176 EC) were added to the Treaty by the 1986 **Single
European Act** (SEA); in their original form, they contained the first Treaty
reference to **subsidiarity**. Environmental protection is referred to in the
preamble to the **Maastricht Treaty**, which added 'a policy in the sphere of

the environment' to the list of Community activities contained in Article 3 EC. Most environmental legislation, together with decisions on which areas are to be the subject of legislative action, is now covered by the **co-decision procedure**.

Article 176 EC allows member states to maintain or introduce 'more stringent protective measures'. This provision arose from a judgment of the **Court of Justice** in the Danish beer-can case (*Commission* v *Denmark*, Case 302/86). The Court ruled that a Danish law to the effect that beer and soft drinks could be marketed only in reusable containers was justified in terms of the protection of the environment, which was to be regarded as taking precedence over the obligation on member states under Article 30 (now 28) EEC not to enact measures restricting imports from other member states. The incorporation of this ruling into the Treaty is of great importance to other member states with high standards of environmental protection.

Environment policy has always been based on successive 'action programmes': the current programme, the fifth, was agreed in December 1992. These programmes are underpinned by a series of principles set out in Article 174.2, those of preventive action, of rectification at source wherever possible and of polluter responsibility (the 'polluter pays principle'). Emphasis is also laid on the importance of other policies being assessed in terms of their impact on the environment. In 1990 it was decided to establish a **European Environment Agency** to help monitor the state of the environment and in 1992 an eco-labelling scheme was agreed for products recognized as 'environmentally friendly' in accordance with Union-wide criteria.

The principle of preventive action was reinforced by the requirement laid down in a 1985 Directive that all projects, public or private, above a certain cost should be the subject of an Environmental Impact Assessment. The extent to which this was controversial with member states may be illustrated by the fact that it was the twenty-third draft that was eventually agreed; the Directive came into force in 1988.

Legislation at Union level applies to air pollution (pollutants from motor vehicles, greenhouse gases, sulphur dioxide), water pollution (both bathing water and drinking water), waste disposal, the transport of dangerous substances and noise. Much of this legislation sprang from the need to prevent member states' different standards in these matters acting as a barrier to the **free movement of goods** or to fair and equal competition within the **Single Market**. Within the Union, access to information held by public authorities on the state of the environment is guaranteed under a Directive adopted in June 1990 (Directive 90/313, *Official Journal*, L158, 23 June 1990). The right to a remedy in the case of environmental damage is more problematic, since most legal systems require there to be a direct link between the alleged damage and the personal or economic interests of the complainant.

For the protection of the natural environment, the Union works very closely with international bodies and within guidelines laid down by international conventions. It has used its position as a major trading power to stamp out the trade in products derived from seal pups and is being pressed to take similar action with respect to exotic birds and tropical hardwoods. The Union is a party to many international conventions on areas particularly at risk, such as the Mediterranean (Barcelona Convention, 1976) and the Antarctic (Canberra Convention, 1980), and was represented at the United Nations conferences on Environment and Development (Rio de Janeiro, 1992) and on Climate Change (Kyoto, 1997).

Environmental protection has been identified through opinion polls as an area in which there is a consistently high level of public support for action at Union level. This is reflected in the many resolutions on environmental matters adopted by the **European Parliament**. It is also an area in which various collaborative projects are being undertaken with the countries of central and eastern Europe, such as those under the **PHARE** programme. The **enlargement** of the Union has increased the number of member states with a strong interest in environment policy. For these reasons, it is an area in which Union involvement is certain to increase.

Equal treatment

Equal pay for men and women is guaranteed under Article 141 (formerly 119) of the **Treaty of Rome**. 'Pay' is defined as 'the ordinary basic or minimum wage or salary and any other consideration … which the worker receives … in respect of his employment from his employer'. This principle was enshrined in a Directive adopted by the **Council of Ministers** on 10 February 1975 and further enforced by a ruling from the **Court of Justice** (*Gabrielle Defrenne* v *Sabena*, Case 43/75) stating that Article 119 EEC was of **direct effect** in cases of 'direct and overt discrimination'. The Court's 1995 ruling in the Kalanke case (*Kalanke* v *Freie Hansestadt Bremen*, C450/93) placed limits on positive action going beyond the removal of the disadvantages experienced by the 'under-represented sex'. However, in the 1997 Marschall judgment (Case C409/95) the Court allowed, in the event of a male and female candidate possessing identical qualifications, priority to be given to the woman.

In a 1990 judgment of the Court the phrase 'and any other consideration' in Article 119 EEC (see above) was held to include redundancy payments and payments under an occupational pension scheme (*Barber* v *Guardian Royal*

Exchange Assurance Group, commonly referred to as 'the Barber judgment', Case C262/88). As with the Defrenne case, the Court ruled that its judgment was not of retroactive effect (except in respect of claims already submitted), but in view of the enormous implications of the ruling for employers and pension schemes throughout the member states, the governments added a **protocol** to the **Maastricht Treaty** stating that claims could not be made under the Barber judgment for periods of employment prior to 17 May 1990. (See also judgments of September 1994, especially the 'Coloroll' case, Case C200/91.)

Since equal pay was the only aspect of equal treatment specifically covered by the Treaty, Directive 76/207 (*Official Journal*, L39, 14 February 1976) on access to employment, training, promotion and working conditions was enacted under Article 235 EEC (see **Article 308**). Article 5.1 made it clear that 'working conditions' included dismissal, and in a 1986 judgment the Court ruled that compulsory retirement was a form of dismissal and thus covered by the requirements of equal treatment (*Marshall* v *Southampton and South-West Hampshire Area Health Authority*, Case 152/84). In Case C177/88 the Court ruled that refusal to employ someone on grounds of pregnancy constituted **discrimination** and in a second case, *Webb* v *EMO Air Cargo* (Case C32/93), that pregnancy was inadequate as grounds for dismissal.

Finally, in 1978 the Council adopted Directive 79/7 (*Official Journal*, L6, 10 January 1979) on equal treatment in respect of social security schemes, including those for the self-employed. However, it was not possible to reach agreement on the equalization of pensionable ages for men and women, and Article 7 allows member states to continue applying their own rules to this and other sensitive matters.

Equal treatment was also addressed in the Social Protocol (see **Social Chapter**) annexed to the Maastricht Treaty, and basically the key legislation is now in place. Changes to the Treaties allowed policies on equal treatment to move beyond matters related to pay and unemployment. Under Article 2 of the Treaty of Rome 'promotion of equality between men and women' is a 'task' of the European Community. Article 3.2 EC, added by the Treaty of Amsterdam, says that 'in all the activities referred to in this Article, the Community shall aim to eliminate inequalities, and to promote equality between men and women'. An Advisory Committee on Equal Opportunities was established in 1981. Equal treatment is a good example of how over a 20-year period legislation may be underpinned, reinforced and occasionally advanced by rulings of the Court of Justice. However, as a **Eurostat** study of May 2001 on equal pay for work of equal value makes clear, there are still serious discrepancies: only in four member states do women's earnings in industry and services exceed 85 per cent of men's, and in no state do they reach 90 per cent.

There is a helpful study of equal treatment in Evelyn Ellis, 'Recent developments in European Community sex equality law', *Common Market Law Review*, Vol. 35, no. 2, April 1998. Equal treatment is given high priority in the European Union's overall **employment** strategy.

ERASMUS

See **Socrates**.

ERTA case

On 20 March 1970 the **Council of Ministers** discussed the position to be taken by the member states of the European Community in relation to the European Road Traffic Agreement, then being negotiated under the auspices of the United Nations **Economic Commission for Europe**. The **European Commission** challenged the Council's conclusions in the **Court of Justice** (Case 22/70) on the grounds that since road transport was a Community matter the **Treaty of Rome** (Article 228 (now 300) EEC) gave the Commission an **implied competence** in the negotiating procedure that the Council had ignored. The Court decided in the Commission's favour with respect to the admissibility of the Commission's complaint, thus confirming the principle that one Community institution may challenge an act of another, but rejected the substance. The ERTA case was of great importance in that it served to establish the role of the Commission in external relations.

Espace judiciaire européen

Variously translated as 'European legal area' and 'European judicial area', the *espace judiciaire européen* was a proposal put forward by **Valéry Giscard d'Estaing** as President of France in 1977. The idea behind the proposal was to establish a common framework in respect of all those legal matters with a Community dimension (for example, member states' policies on **extradition**, visas, **asylum**, police procedures), since the absence of such a framework might impede cooperation between police forces, immigration officers and judicial authorities. At a more abstract level the *espace judiciaire européen* was regarded as a contribution to a sense of **European identity** by virtue of its guaranteeing citizens of the member states a common corpus of basic legal rights. As might have been expected, progress towards what is now called the area of **freedom, security and justice** has been slow in the face of legal, constitutional, political and practical difficulties, but the easing of frontier controls under the **Single Market** programme has made the need for cooperation in the field of law and order more urgent. Concrete results were achieved at the practical level (see **Europol, Schengen Agreement, Trevi Group**), much of it outside the framework of the Community institutions. The **Council of Europe**, for example, has long been active in this field: the European conventions on extradition (1957), mutual assistance in criminal matters (1959), and the suppression of terrorism (1977) were all drawn up by the Council. The procedures laid down in the **Justice and Home Affairs** (JHA) '**pillar**' of the **Maastricht Treaty** initially meant that work in this area was essentially intergovernmental in character (see **intergovernmentalism**), but under the **Treaty of Amsterdam** and the **Treaty of Nice** decisions can be taken in conformity with normal European Community procedures (see also **Schengen** *acquis*).

Estonia

In common with the other **Baltic states**, Estonia was annexed by the Soviet Union in 1940 and occupied by Germany from 1941 until 1944. Independence was fully restored in August 1991. Estonia has concluded a **Europe Agreement** with the European Union which came into force in February 1998 (a Free Trade Agreement came into effect in January 1995). Estonia's application for full membership of the European Union was made on 24 November 1995 (see **enlargement**).

The **Opinion** of the European Commission, published on 15 July 1997 (*Bulletin of the European Union*, supplement 11/97), concluded that Estonia satisfied all the **Copenhagen criteria** and recommended that negotiations with Estonia should begin in 1998. This was endorsed at the **European Council** meeting in Luxembourg in December 1997. Negotiations were concluded in 2002, and in April 2003 Estonia signed the **Treaty of Accession**.

Estonia is a member of the **Council of Europe** and of the **Organization for Security and Cooperation in Europe** (OSCE). See also **Nordic Council**.

EU law

Until the European Union came into existence with the entry into force of the **Maastricht Treaty** in 1993 and the **Common Foreign and Security Policy** (CFSP) and **Justice and Home Affairs** (JHA) **pillars** started to make laws, what is now called EU (European Union) law was, strictly speaking, Community law, since only the three European Communities had the power to make law. The expression 'EU law' encompasses both Comminuty law and the law emanating from the institutions and procedures, still largely intergovernmental (see **intergovernmentalism**), set out in the Maastricht Treaty.

EU law is of three basic types: the **Treaties** and related instruments; legislation, mainly in the form of Regulations, Directives, Joint Actions, Decisions and Resolutions; and the case-law embodied in rulings of the **Court of Justice**. Together these constitute the major part of the *acquis communautaire*, to which may be added international agreements to which the Union (or rather, strictly speaking, the European Community: see **legal personality**) is a party.

Sometimes referred to as primary legislation, the Treaties are the basis of the European Union's legal order. As amended by the Acts of Accession consequent upon successive **enlargements**, by the **Single European Act** (SEA) by the Maastricht Treaty, and by the **Treaty of Amsterdam**, they serve as the Union's constitution and as the legal basis for all legislation. They are dynamic in that they not only establish a particular set of relations between signatory states but also set out a programme of action for the future. They lay down a pattern of rights and obligations not so much between the signatory states as between the states and the Communities thereby established. They enjoy **primacy** in that they and the legislation based upon them take precedence over national law (see below). They are self-contained in that they contain provisions (i.e., procedures and institutions) for enforcement, interpretation and the settlement of disputes without recourse to outside bodies. These characteristics combine to make the Treaties profoundly different from other international treaties.

Although the Treaties have the force of law, not all their provisions are of **direct effect**. Some Treaty Articles confer specific rights upon individuals (direct effect), while others confer rights only by virtue of the obligations they impose upon member states. In both cases such rights are enforceable at law. However, there are also Articles that embody general principles that must first be translated into specific legislation before they can have legal effect. Many cases before the Court of Justice have centred upon the distinction that must be drawn between these different types of Treaty commitment.

The Treaties apply throughout the territory of the member states, with the exception of the **Faeroes** and the British Sovereign Base Areas in Cyprus, and the partial exception of the Finnish Åland Islands, the **Channel Islands** and the Isle of Man (Article 299 EC). Special arrangements, differing from case to case, apply to all these territories and to **Gibraltar**. **Greenland** is now listed among the **overseas countries and territories** (OCTs). The Treaties also apply extra-territorially in the case of firms operating inside the member states but whose headquarters are outside (a principle established in Case 48/69, *ICI* v *Commission*, and of great importance in **competition policy**).

The power conferred by treaty upon the Union institutions to make laws distinguishes the Union from essentially intergovernmental organizations such as the **Council of Europe**. Founded upon the doctrine of the separation of powers, the legislative procedures set out in the Treaties give each of the four main institutions a specific role: the **European Commission** proposes new laws; the **European Parliament** examines and may amend them; the **Council of Ministers** adopts the legislation in its final form, sometimes jointly with the Parliament; and the Court of Justice adjudicates on disputes arising from the interpretation and application of Community law. This basic model is subject to many variants: the **Budget** procedure is significantly different, and both the SEA and the Maastricht Treaty introduced new procedures that affect the balance and distribution of powers between the institutions (see also **Treaty of Amsterdam** and especially **co-decision procedure**).

Secondary legislation (sometimes referred to as derived legislation) is made up of the legislative acts of the Union institutions, primarily Regulations, Directives and Decisions. Article 249 EC defines these three types of legal instrument. A Regulation 'shall have general application. It shall be binding in its entirety and directly applicable in all Member States' (i.e., without the need for national implementing legislation: see below). Regulations are published in the Official Journal and enter into force either on the date specified in the text or on the twentieth day after publication (Article 254 EC). Much of the day-to-day management of the **Common Agricultural Policy** (CAP) is carried out by means of Regulations, with the Commission acting on the basis of powers granted to it by the Council of Ministers. The Commission may also make Regulations in its capacity as the institution responsible for implementing Council Decisions (Article 202 EC), and the Council too may make Regulations in order to discharge its responsibilities under the Treaties. A Regulation can be used only in cases provided for by treaty and must be based on a specific Article or Articles of one or more of the Treaties. A general reference to a Treaty or to **Article 308** EC is not sufficient.

A Directive is 'binding, as to the result to be achieved, upon each Member State to which it is addressed, but shall leave to the national authorities the choice of form and methods'. Directives, which must be based on a specific Treaty Article, have to be implemented in national law by governments of member states acting in accordance with their normal constitutional procedures, and most Directives are sufficiently loosely worded to allow member states a degree of flexibility in the details.

A Decision, which may be issued either by the Council or the Commission, is 'binding in its entirety upon those to whom it is addressed'. Like a Regulation, it must be based on a specific Treaty Article and needs no national implementing legislation. It may be addressed to a member state, a corporation or an individual. 'Administrative Decisions' are for the most part either internal acts of the institutions (e.g., on staff matters) or Decisions by the Commission on the allocation of funds or the execution of policies such as those concerned with dumping or **state aids**.

Article 249 EC also allows the Council and the Commission to deliver Recommendations and **Opinions**, but since these have 'no binding force' they are not regarded by all authorities as part of EU law in the strict sense. Their purpose is primarily to persuade or to assist in the interpretation or application of other legal acts.

In the CFSP and JHA pillars Article 249 EC does not apply and a different set of legal instruments is used (described under **joint action**). The procedures are also different and there is only very little scope for recourse to the Court of Justice in the event of a dispute.

The deliberations of the Union institutions may also be published in the form of **Declarations, Resolutions**, Communications, Action Programmes, Guidelines, and so on. As a general rule, these are not of binding effect and many fall into the category of 'framework legislation'; that is, a comprehensive statement of aims and principles in a particular policy area, which is then followed up by detailed legislative proposals (see also **soft law**). For such acts to have juridical force, they must be consistent with procedural requirements, confer rights or impose obligations on persons, Union institutions or member states, and be subject to judicial review in the Court of Justice. Access to all legislation, both in draft and enacted, is currently being made easier in the name of **transparency** (see also **simplification**).

Some idea of the volume of legislation currently in force may be gained from the fact that the 1992 Agreement on the **European Economic Area** (EEA) lists some 1,700 items of legislation in 22 annexes. Legislation is stored in the CELEX database within 17 subject areas. An annual directory is published, giving the reference numbers of all legislative acts currently in force (the earliest dates from 1952), with the exception of acts of very limited scope and duration relevant to the day-to-day management of the CAP or the **customs union**. A Commission press release of 6 December 2001 estimated the total volume of Community law as equivalent to about 80,000 pages of the *Official Journal*, or about 10 per cent of the law currently in force in the member states. The Commission aims to reduce this by 25 per cent by January 2005, and to this end withdrew 100 proposals no longer regarded as necessary or relevant.

If a member state has difficulty in applying a Regulation or implementing a Directive, it may seek a temporary waiver, known as a **derogation**. The Regulation or Directive may make specific provision for such derogations, which are normally granted only with the unanimous consent of the Council and only for a limited period. If a derogation is granted, national law (if any) continues to apply to the matter covered by the Regulation or Directive in question. Exceptionally, a member state may apply national legislation that is stricter than the relevant EU legislation, in order, for example, to protect the environment (this was the subject of a Court ruling in 1988 in the case of *Commission* v *Denmark, Re Disposable Beer Cans*, Case 302/86: see **environment policy**).

Article 10 EC enjoins the member states to 'take all appropriate measures, whether general or particular, to ensure fulfilment of the obligations arising out of this Treaty or resulting from action taken by the institutions of the Community'. The responsibility for ensuring that member states do this falls to the Commission under Article 226 EC:

If the Commission considers that a Member State has failed to fulfil an obligation under this Treaty, it shall deliver a reasoned opinion on the matter after giving the State concerned the opportunity to submit its observations. If the State concerned does not comply with the opinion within the period laid down by the Commission, the latter may bring the matter before the Court of Justice.

As noted above, one of the criteria for establishing whether or not a legislative act has juridical force is the extent to which it confers rights or imposes obligations on persons, institutions or member states. The situation with regard to Regulations and Decisions is relatively straightforward, but several cases have been brought in the Court of Justice to establish whether or not a Directive, adopted but not yet implemented in national law, confers rights. Broadly speaking, if the wording of a Directive is sufficiently precise and unambiguous and the time limit for its implementation in national law has expired, that Directive may be said to confer rights on individuals in their dealings with the state and to take precedence over national law (see **Francovich case**).

The Treaties and the legislation based upon them are neither sufficiently precise nor sufficiently comprehensive to cover all legal eventualities. This fact has provided scope for the Court of Justice, as the interpreter of EU law and as the arbiter of disputes, to contribute very fundamentally to the corpus of EU law.

The Court's prime function is to 'ensure that in the interpretation and application [of the Treaties] the law is observed' (Article 220 EC). The Court's position is an exceptionally powerful one, in that there is no appeal from its rulings, it can strike down as illegal the legislative acts of member states or Union institutions, and it is a source of law in its own right. Nevertheless, springing as it does from a variety of legal traditions, it has had to bring about a synthesis of these traditions with respect both to its mode of operation and the substance of its judgments. Its power to interpret EU law is exercised in the light of the fundamental purposes of the Treaties and the internal logic of particular policies, and this has led the Court (as is the case with the United States Supreme Court) to play an important 'integrationist' role. This role is wholly consistent with Articles 31 and 32 of the 1969 Vienna Convention on the Law of International Treaties: 'A treaty shall be interpreted ... in the light of its object and purpose'. Interpretations may be incidental to a judgment or embodied in a **preliminary ruling**.

As a supreme court, the Court of Justice is not formally bound by precedent. However, the self-evident need for consistency, coherence and equality of treatment ensures that precedents are taken into account, although no point of law is ever settled by reference to precedent alone. The precedents that have guided the Court in a given judgment are cited in the reasoning (see below).

Judgments of the Court are published periodically in *European Court Reports*. The only authentic text of a judgment is the one in the language of the case. A judgment is composed of two parts: the reasoning (which will normally draw upon the submission of the **advocate-general**); and the judgment itself. Underpinning the Court's judgments and EU law as a whole are certain fundamental doctrines, some of them familiar in national law and others arising from the unique nature of the Union. Among them are the autonomy of EU law – its separateness from national law and the independence of the law-making and law-enforcing Union institutions – and the functional and programmatic unity of the **European Economic Community** and the **European Atomic Energy Community** (Euratom) as participants in a joint endeavour within the framework of the Union. These two doctrines are complemented by a third, that of the primacy of EU law. This was expressed in the Court judgment in the *Van Gend en Loos* case in 1963 (Case 26/62): 'The Community constitutes a new legal order of international law, in favour of which the States within certain areas have limited their sovereign rights.' The duties of national courts to apply EU law were spelt out the following year in *Costa* v *ENEL* (Case 6/64). In its judgment the Court emphasized that EU law cannot be overridden by 'domestic legal provisions ... without being deprived of its character as Community law and without the legal basis of the Community itself being called into question'. In recent years both **subsidiarity** and **proportionality** have become concepts essential to an understanding of the legal framework.

In a famous 1974 judgment Lord Denning, then Master of the Rolls, described the impact of EU law upon English law as a 'rising tide', which, inexorably, makes its way up the broad estuaries into the very smallest creeks and inlets of national life (*Bulmer* v *Bollinger* [1974]). Based upon a continental tradition of civil law, EU law is indeed substantially different from English law, but this should not obscure the fact that it is also different from any other comparable body of law. It has some of the characteristics of international law, but of municipal law too; it is both public and private; and it relies on both enactment and precedent. It draws, however, upon a common heritage of principles – due process, equality before the law, *non bis in idem*, the right to be heard – which serve to mitigate the unfamiliarity of its procedures. EU law has served both to advance the process of integration along the paths set out in the Treaties and to consolidate such progress as has been made. Whether or not the law can continue to play so central a role in a more heterogeneous Union in which attitudes to law widely differ is open to question.

There are several excellent general introductions to EU law (see section 5 of the Bibliography). A revealing and informative article is Trevor C. Hartley, 'Five forms of uncertainty in European Community law', *Cambridge Law Journal*, Vol. 55, no. 2, July 1996.

EUREKA

The European Research Cooperation Agency, known as EUREKA, was established in 1985 to encourage cross-border research projects in advanced technology. A French initiative, it was intended to reduce the fragmentation from which European high-technology industries suffered by comparison with their American and Japanese competitors. EUREKA participants include almost all European countries.

EURES

Operational since 1993, EURES is a database linking the national employment services in the 15 member states of the European Union, Norway, and Iceland, together with 18 cross-border services active in the same field. In addition to notices of vacancies, EURES offers analyses of the various labour markets and details of living and working conditions.

Euro

At its meeting of December 1995 in Madrid, the **European Council** decided to name the single currency the euro – in spite of the reference in the **Treaty of Rome** (Article 32(a) (formerly 4.2)), as amended by the **Maastricht Treaty**, to the **ECU** as the single currency to be introduced in stage 3 of **Economic and Monetary Union** (EMU). At the same meeting the timetable for the introduction of the euro was agreed, on the basis of the outline in Articles 3(a).2, 109 (g) and 109 (l) (now 4.2, 118, and 122) EEC. The legal status of the euro was fixed a year later at the European Council in Dublin. These technical and legal arrangements were set out in two Regulations adopted in Amsterdam in

June 1997. The euro was introduced on 1 January 1999 in all participating states (see **convergence criteria**), its value in the national currencies of these states having been irrevocably fixed. As a currency in its own right, the euro is now used for all transactions by the **European Central Bank** (ECB), and for all new issues of government bonds. From 1 January 1999 the euro replaced the ECU on a 1:1 basis in all areas of the Union's finances.

The symbol for the euro is €, which the **European Commission** has been using since December 1996. It was endorsed by the **European Monetary Institute** (EMI) on 15 July 1997. Euro banknotes (issued by the ECB) and euro coins (issued by national authorities in accordance with a standard design but with different national motifs on the reverse) were introduced on 1 January 2002. Euro banknotes have been issued in denominations of 5, 10, 20, 50, 100, 200, and 500 euros, euro coins (1 euro is made up of 100 cents) in denominations of 1, 2, 5, 10, 20 and 50 cents and 1 and 2 euros. The stability of the system of which the euro is the centrepiece is reinforced by the **Stability and Growth Pact** and a new **Exchange-Rate Mechanism** ('ERM 2').

There are innumerable articles, pamphlets, booklets and books on the single currency. Two very thorough studies, written from opposing points of view as far as British participation is concerned, are Christopher Johnson, *In with the Euro, Out with the Pound* (Harmondsworth, 1996) and John Redwood, *Our Currency, Our Country* (Harmondsworth, 1997).

Euro-Atlantic Partnership Council (EAPC)
See **North Atlantic Cooperation Council**

Eurobarometer

Eurobarometer is the name given to the twice-yearly surveys of public opinion in the member states of the European Union carried out by polling organizations on behalf of the **European Commission**. Such surveys have been conducted and published regularly since 1973, and are composed of both 'tracking' questions, used to establish overall trends, and questions that relate to current issues. A standard sample of 1,000 people is used in each member state, except for Luxembourg (500 people), the United Kingdom (1,000 in Great Britain, 300 in Northern Ireland), and Germany (1,000 in the former West Germany, 1,000 in the former East Germany). The regular surveys are supplemented by *ad hoc* surveys on particular issues, such as drug abuse, German reunification or biotechnology, or among particular sectors of society, such as the young or the self-employed. Of particular interest is the twenty-fifth anniversary edition of *Eurobarometer* (Autumn 1998), which summarizes trends over the period since 1973. This under-explored aspect of European integration is well surveyed in William Wallace and Julie Smith, 'Democracy or technocracy? European integration and the problem of popular consent,' in Jack Hayward (ed.), *The Crisis of Representation in Europe* (1995).

Eurocontrol

The European Organization for the Safety of Air Navigation was founded in 1960 to promote and facilitate cooperation among participating states in all aspects of air safety. Its headquarters are in Brussels, and it also operates the Upper Area Control Centre at Maastricht in the Netherlands.

All member states of the European Union participate in Eurocontrol, together with Cyprus, Malta, Turkey, Norway, Hungary, Switzerland, Slovenia, the Czech Republic, Slovakia, Romania, Croatia, Bulgaria, Macedonia, Monaco and Moldova. Eurocontrol has not developed as intended into an international agency responsible for air traffic control in western Europe as a consequence of the reluctance of countries, for political and sometimes military reasons, to surrender national control of their airspace or even to press ahead with the technical coordination of different systems. However, attempts to wind up Eurocontrol altogether have so far been resisted, although western European airspace remains subject to several autonomous administrations operating from various centres. The report published in January 1994 by the Comité des Sages for Air Transport and entitled *Expanding Horizons* called for a renewed effort to harmonize and integrate air traffic control systems in Europe and for Eurocontrol procedures to be reformed to allow decisions to be taken by majority vote. A revised Eurocontrol Convention of June 1997 introduced a number of institutional changes.

Eurocorps

On 14 October 1991 President **François Mitterrand** of France and Chancellor **Helmut Kohl** of Germany informed the President-in-Office of the **European Council** that they proposed to form a Franco-German corps in which the armed forces of other **Western European Union** (WEU) states could participate. At a meeting in La Rochelle on 22 May 1992 a timetable for the setting up of a corps of 35,000 troops was agreed. The headquarters would be in Strasbourg, France, and the corps, initially under the command of a German general, would be fully operational by October 1995. A joint committee would oversee relations between participating countries and other organizations concerned with security. Since the La Rochelle agreement Belgium, Luxembourg and Spain have all joined Eurocorps which has a complement of almost 50,000 troops.

The idea of a Eurocorps is consistent with the provisions in Articles 11 to 28 of the **Maastricht Treaty** on the **Common Foreign and Security Policy** (CFSP) and with the decision to strengthen the WEU as the European element within the **North Atlantic Treaty Organization** (NATO). Coordination of the Eurocorps with NATO was the subject of an agreement reached on 21 January 1993 by the North Atlantic Council, SACEUR (Supreme Allied Commander Europe) and the Chiefs-of-Staff of the states participating in the Eurocorps. Under this agreement Eurocorps forces are 'double-hatted'; that is, they may be assigned either to NATO or to national authorities within the WEU framework. For the foreseeable future the Eurocorps is likely to be dependent upon the United States in respect of satellite intelligence and rapid deployment by air or by sea.

The Eurocorps, which builds upon the experience gained from the Franco-German brigade (see **Franco-German cooperation**), is still some way short of the '**European Army**' envisaged as a key component of the **European Defence Community**. Its role, reflecting the new security situation in Europe brought about by the ending of the Cold War, will be centred upon crisis management, peace-keeping and humanitarian action rather than straightforward deterrence. The crisis in Yugoslavia and the general sense of European helplessness that it engendered created the climate of opinion from which grew the idea of the Eurocorps, together with the realization that the United States was neither willing nor able to go on playing the role of global policeman (see 'The European Corps', Document 1400, WEU Assembly, 23 November 1993). At the Franco-German summit in Toulouse in May 1999 it was agreed that the Eurocorps might become a European Rapid Reaction Corps. See also **Allied Command Europe Rapid Reaction Corps, EUROFOR**.

Eurocrats

'Eurocrat' is a mildly pejorative term, modelled on the word 'bureaucrat', to denote an official of one of the institutions or bodies of the European Union. The total number of such officials is about 32,000, of whom about 21,000 work for the largest of the institutions, the **European Commission**. Between a quarter and a third of these officials are employed in connection with interpretation and translation.

With a few exceptions at very senior level, recruitment is done on the basis of publicly advertised competitions organized by language, on the basis of which 'reserve lists' are drawn up of eligible people who may subsequently (sometimes months or years later) be offered specific posts as they become available. For many years, the normal age limit for recruitment was 35, but with a view to the eventual abolition of the limit it was raised to 45, both for the Commission and for the **European Parliament**.

Posts within each institution are divided into four grades: A-grade posts (LA for translators and interpreters), for which a university degree is necessary; B-grade posts, e.g., archivists, senior secretaries and office managers; C-grade posts, most of them secretaries; and D-grade posts, e.g., ushers, drivers and security staff. Proficiency in at least two official **languages** is required for all grades. Within each grade are numerical rankings, from 1 (the most senior) down to 8 in the case of A grades, to 3 (B grades), to 5 (C grades), and to 4 (D grades). A director-general, for example, is an A1, a director an A2, a head of division an A3, and so on. Each of these numerical rankings contains a number of 'steps', which are largely indicative of length of service. Only nationals of the member states may be employed in the institutions, and informal quotas are established to ensure an appropriate distribution of A-grade posts among the various nationalities.

Promotion within the institutions is based upon internal competitions judged by 'juries' upon which the staff unions are represented. However, senior posts (A3 and above) are not infrequently filled by *parachutage*; that is, by someone brought in from outside (usually from a national civil service) or someone who has entered the institution by some unorthodox means, for example, via the cabinet of a Commissioner or one of the **political groups** in the European Parliament.

Under a **protocol** to the **Treaty of Rome** employees of the institutions of the European Union – as is normally the case with employees of international organizations – are exempt from national income tax on their salary and expenses wherever they work, but not from most other forms of tax. Instead, they pay income tax to the Union itself at rates of up to 40 per cent. An independent report prepared by a Danish firm of consultants, published in June 2000, shows that overall net remuneration in the Commission and the other institutions of the Union is lower than in comparable multinationals, lower than in member states' permanent representations (although pay for non-expatriates is higher than that of national civil servants), and broadly similar to that in other international organizations.

The compulsory retirement age is 65, but officials can retire earlier with a reduced pension. When a new member state joins the Union, posts have to be found at every level within the institutions for nationals of that member state. For long-serving officials, their retirement may be brought forward by 'golden handshakes' or occasionally by means of what is known as *pantouflage* (from *pantoufles*, French for slippers), the creation of agreeable sinecures.

In general, the institutions of the Union are not overstaffed. Many posts in the Commission remain unfilled because of budgetary constraints, and there is more recourse than in the past to short-term contracts. The number of posts has not kept pace with the widening of the Union's responsibilities, although this problem could be partially solved by more flexible procedures for transfers from one field of activity to another within the same institution.

There are very few general studies of Eurocracy. **Altiero Spinelli**'s *The Eurocrats*, David Coombes's *Politics and Bureaucracy in the European Community: A Portrait of the Commission of the EEC* and Anthony Sampson's *The New Europeans* are all more than 30 years old. Slightly more recent is the 1979 Spierenburg Report, which contains an analysis as true now as it was then of certain structural shortcomings in the Commission. Some entertaining glimpses of the upper reaches of the Commission may be found in **Roy Jenkins**'s 1989 *European Diary* covering his period as President (1977–81) and in Charles Grant's biography of **Jacques Delors**, *Delors: The House that Jacques Built* (1994). A comprehensive study is Geoffrey Edwards and David Spence, *The European Commission* (Harlow, 1995). Also of great interest is Edward C. Page, *People who Run Europe* (Oxford, 1997).

Eurodac

Agreement on the need for a European Union system to allow the fingerprints of asylum-seekers and illegal immigrants to be taken and stored to facilitate the application of the **Dublin Asylum Convention** was reached in 1991. However, because the **Treaty of Amsterdam** altered the legal base upon which the necessary legislative action could be taken, the present system, known as Eurodac, was not in place until Regulation 2725/00 was adopted on 11 December 2000 (*Official Journal*, L316, 15 December 2000). The Regulation allows basic data, including fingerprints, to be taken from all asylum applicants and illegal immigrants over the age of 14. The data are stored centrally by the **European Commission**. Relevant data may be exchanged, with appropriate safeguards for confidentiality, with member states' authorities. The data may be kept for a maximum of 10 years in the case of asylum-seekers, but must be deleted if the subject is granted citizenship by a member state. Data on illegal immigrants may be kept for two years or until the subject is given a residence permit or leaves the territory of the Union. See also **asylum, free movement of persons.**

Eurofighter

An agreement between the British, German, Italian and Spanish governments to develop the so-called Eurofighter, a high-performance European fighter aircraft, was signed in December 1997. A production contract for 620 aircraft was signed the following year. The costs will be shared as follows: United Kingdom 37.5 per cent, Germany 30 per cent, Italy 19.5 per cent, Spain 14 per cent. Greece has also undertaken to buy the Eurofighter, which is due to enter service in 2002. The French aerospace industry is developing a rival aircraft, the Rafale.

EUROFOR

EUROFOR is an international rapid reaction force consisting of land forces from France, Italy, Portugal and Spain. Announced at the Lisbon meeting of the **Western European Union** (WEU) in May 1995 and established in November 1996, its headquarters are in Florence. EUROFOR can call upon a maximum of 20,000 troops, but its basic complement is about 5,000 troops. A EURO-FOR battalion can be mobilized in three to five days. A ministerial committee composed of the defence ministers of the participating states is responsible for all aspects of EUROFOR's operations. By a decision of this committee, EUROFOR may be placed at the disposal of the WEU, the **North Atlantic Treaty Organization** or the **United Nations** for what are now known as Petersberg tasks (see **Petersberg Declaration**). EUROFOR's working language is English.

A similar force, EUROMARFOR, has been created for naval operations. Both EUROFOR and EUROMARFOR remain open to other states willing and able to participate. See also **Allied Command Europe Rapid Reaction Corps, Eurocorps**.

Eurogroup

In 1968 the defence ministers of the European countries belonging to the **North Atlantic Treaty Organization** (NATO), with the exception of France and Iceland, decided to set up an informal twice-yearly meeting in order to coordinate their positions more closely on security issues and thus to strengthen Europe's contribution to the Atlantic Alliance. Known as the 'Eurogroup', these meetings provided a forum in which member states of the European Community could discuss specifically European security questions without infringing Ireland's neutrality or compromising France's status as a member of the Alliance outside NATO's integrated military command. In 1986 the **Single European Act** (SEA) made it possible for member states of the Community to discuss 'political and economic aspects of security' (Article 30.6 SEA) and five years later this provision was further developed in the **Maastricht Treaty** (see **Common Foreign and Security Policy**). The **Western European Union** (WEU) has now taken the place of the Eurogroup as the main European component of the Atlantic Alliance (see also **Independent European Programme Group**).

Eurojust

Eurojust (more formally, the European Judicial Cooperation Unit) is the name given to a body 'composed of national prosecutors, magistrates, or police officers of equivalent competence, detached from each Member State' to be set up in accordance with a decision reached at the Tampere meeting of the **European Council** (October 1999). The **Treaty of Nice** provided the legal base for this in amendments to Articles 29 and 31 of the **Treaty of Rome**. Eurojust's role is 'facilitating the proper coordination of national prosecution authorities and ... supporting criminal investigations in organized crime cases ... as well as ... cooperating closely with the **European Judicial Network**' (Presidency conclusions, point 46).

Euromyths

'Euromyths' is the general term given to the stories about the 'barmy Brussels bureaucrats' that regularly feature in the British press. The great majority of them have no basis in fact. Most take the form of some threat to the British way of life. In November 1992 the Foreign Office attempted to refute some of the most frequently repeated Euromyths. Three distinct types of story were identified: 'Euromyths', which have no basis in fact; 'Euroscares', largely founded upon misapprehensions as to the impact or purpose of some agreed measure; and 'Eurolunacies', defined as 'genuine examples of unnecessary or intrusive Community rules'. This typology was repeated in *Facts and Fairytales*, a 1993 booklet, and in two brochures published by the London office of the **European Commission**. The Commission identified a very important fourth category of story, those in which the outrage or absurdity springs from the overzealous implementation or enforcement by national authorities of a measure agreed in Brussels or which may be traced back to regulations of purely national origin.

As a form of subversive, anti-bureaucratic humour, Euromyths have extraordinary resilience and vitality. Unfortunately, the refutation is almost always less arresting than the original story. Although not exclusively a British phenomenon, Euromyths in the United Kingdom, in terms of abundance and variety, exceed those to be found in other member states. They are both a symptom and a cause of the low esteem in which the institutions of the European Union, especially the Commission, are generally held.

Europa

In ancient times 'Europa' was both a person and a geographical expression. The myth of Europa is well known: the daughter of Agenor, King of Tyre, she attracted the attentions of Zeus. In order to seduce her, he transformed himself into a bull and, having enticed her on to his back, carried her away to Crete. There she eventually married the King of Crete and bore several sons, one of whom was King Minos, the builder of the labyrinth.

Geographically, Europa originally denoted the mainland of Greece, as opposed to the islands. As Greek colonization extended north and west, so the territory known as Europa was similarly extended, in contradistinction to Asia and Libya (North Africa). This tripartite division of the known world was the one adopted by Herodotus and later by the Romans. The growth of the Roman Empire brought with it a further extension of Europa as far as the Rhine to the north, the Straits of Gibraltar to the south and the British Isles to the west.

Europe's eastern frontier was always more problematic, as indeed it has remained. In the absence of an obvious geophysical feature most ancient geographers settled on the River Don as the frontier. Only centuries later did the Ural Mountains become the accepted eastward limit of Europe.

Neither myth nor geography can shed much light on the origin of the word 'Europa'. Some etymologists have traced it back to a Semitic word, *Erib*, meaning darkness (i.e., the direction in which the sun set). But if the word is of Greek origin, it means 'broad-faced' (possibly an attribute of the moon goddess), and there the trail goes cold.

The origin of the 'idea of Europe', the growth of a sense of European identity and the connection between Europe and Christendom are discussed in Denys Hay, *Europe: The Emergence of an Idea* (1957; rev. edn Edinburgh, 1968). See also Chapter 1, 'The problem of definition', in Max Beloff, *Europe and the Europeans* (1957); and Chapter 1, 'The discovery of Europe', in J. R. Hale, *The Civilization of Europe in the Renaissance* (1993).

Europe à la carte

Similar to '**variable geometry**' and open to the same objections, 'Europe *à la carte*' is a model of European integration in which individual member states decide whether or not to participate in a particular activity on a case-by-case basis. It is the opposite to the holistic approach to integration, and if widely adopted would result in the undermining of the notion of an *acquis communautaire*. The expression 'Europe *à la carte*' was first used by the German sociologist (and later Commissioner) Ralf Dahrendorf, writing as 'Wieland Europa' in *Die Zeit*, July 1971. See also **flexibility**.

Europe Agreements

A new type of **Association Agreement** under Article 310 (formerly 238) of the **Treaty of Rome**, Europe Agreements were devised to allow central and eastern European countries to strengthen their commercial and political ties with the European Union. The first Europe Agreements were signed in 1991 with Czechoslovakia, Hungary and Poland. An important feature of Europe Agreements is the emphasis laid on institutions and procedures allowing for political dialogue. All the Agreements provide for the progressive removal of barriers to free trade, for economic and technical cooperation and for financial assistance.

Article 1 of each of the Europe Agreements says that the aim of the Agreement is 'to provide an appropriate framework for [the associated state's] gradual integration into the Community'. No deadline is set. The associated state is required to ensure that future legislation is compatible with Community legislation as the major condition for integration into the Community. Complete free trade is to be established over a 10-year period.

Political dialogue is conducted at several levels, including that of heads of state with the **presidency** of the Council and the president of the **European Commission**, an Association Council at ministerial level, parliamentary contacts with the **European Parliament**, and regular consultation between foreign offices and embassies.

The Europe Agreements with Hungary and Poland came into force in February 1994, and those with Bulgaria and Romania in February 1995. The dissolution of Czechoslovakia on 1 January 1993 made it necessary to modify the 1991 Agreement in negotiations with the two successor states, the Czech Republic and Slovakia, and for temporary Agreements to remain in force. Europe Agreements have since been extended to the Baltic states and Slovenia. The overall condition is that these countries operate a market economy based upon free elections, the rule of law and respect for human rights.

By way of complement to the Europe Agreements, provision has been made for '**structured dialogue**' between the European Union and the countries of central and eastern Europe. This dialogue is based upon their participation three times a year in meetings of the **Council of Ministers** (see also **European Conference, pre-accession strategy**).

There is a great deal of useful background material on Western Europe's postwar relations with central and eastern Europe in Peter van Ham, *The EC, Eastern Europe and European Unity* (1993).

Europe des patries

Literally a 'Europe of nation-states' (*l'Europe des nations*), *Europe des patries* is a phrase associated with **Charles de Gaulle**. It encapsulates a model of European integration in which the states are the essential building blocks, and in which the decision-making procedures reflect the pre-eminence of the states within the system (see **intergovernmentalism**).

Europe Direct

Launched in June 1998, Europe Direct is a campaign mounted by the **European Commission** to make citizens of the European Union more aware of their rights (see p. 574 for details of the Europe Direct website). The campaign has four main themes: the **euro**, **equal treatment** for men and women; living, working and travelling in the European Union; and consumer protection in the **Single Market** (see **consumer policy**). The campaign is complemented by a jobs database (see **EURES**) and a Dialogue with Business.

Europe 2000

Europe 2000: the development of the Community's territory was the name of a study published by the **European Commission** in 1991. It sought to combine data on economic activity, land use, population movements, telecommunications and transport links to give a composite picture of the member states as a basis for action in particular sectors (such as **trans-European networks**). Among the study's findings was the emergence of a southern 'arc of prosperity' stretching from Catalonia through Mediterranean France into northern Italy, to which Austria and Bavaria may now be added, complementing the well-established London–Amsterdam–Ruhr–Paris quadrilateral in the north. The study drew attention to the problems likely to arise as a result of rapid population growth on the Community's southern frontier and the difficulties still faced by peripheral regions in seeking to attract investment, a much higher proportion of which is now flexible with respect to the choice of location.

EuropeAid Cooperation Office

Operational since 1 January 2001, the office is responsible for the overall coordination of about 80 per cent of the European Union's development assistance budget (approaching €10 billion per annum), including **TACIS**, **MEDA**, and the **European Development Fund** (EDF) in some 150 countries. It is not concerned with humanitarian aid, pre-accession aid (see **enlargement**), or aid given under schemes elaborated as part of the **Common Foreign and Security Policy**. See **Humanitarian Aid Office**.

European Agency for the Evaluation of Medicinal Products

Set up under Regulation 2309/93 (*Official Journal*, L214, 24 August 1993) and operational from 1995, the Agency offers a centralized Union-wide registration procedure for new medicinal products, for both human and veterinary use. The Agency also coordinates the work of analogous national agencies, which continue to certify, on the basis of mutual recognition, products not intended for circulation throughout all member states. To this end the Agency, which is based in London, operates a network linking the 3,000 national officials and experts in the field. Financed from the **Budget** and from fees paid by the pharmaceutical industry, the Agency allows registration procedures to be speeded up and minimizes duplication of effort among national agencies.

European Agency for Reconstruction (EAR)

Established in February 2000 and based in Thessaloniki, the EAR manages the European Union assistance programmes in Kosovo, Serbia and Montenegro. It is an **agency** of the Union, responsible to the **Council of Ministers** and to the **European Parliament**, and is overseen by a Governing Board composed of representatives of the **European Commission** and of the Union's member states. The EAR's budget exceeds €500 million per annum. Its priorities are the rebuilding of the physical infrastructure (housing, transport, utilities), the development of a market-based economy, and the establishment of free democratic institutions under the rule of law. For more information, see Regulation 2667/00 of 5 December 2000 (*Official Journal*, L306, 7 December 2000). See also **CARDS programme, Stabilization and Association Process**.

European Agency for Safety and Health at Work

An advisory committee on safety, hygiene and health protection at work was set up in 1974 to assist the **European Commission** with the drafting of legislation in these areas. In 1990 the Commission proposed the establishment of an **agency**, and in October 1993 it was agreed that this Agency should be located in Spain (see **seat of the institutions**). Bilbao was the city chosen by the Spanish government. The role of the Agency, set up under Regulation 2062/94 (*Official Journal*, L216, 20 August 1994), is to gather and disseminate information on health and safety at work, coordinate national actions and research programmes, and provide technical support for the Commission in these areas.

European Agricultural Guidance and Guarantee Fund (EAGGF)

As its name implies, the EAGGF (sometimes known by its more pronounceable French acronym FEOGA, *Fonds européen pour l'orientation et la garantie agricole*) is concerned with two quite distinct purposes. The 'guidance' part of the Fund is one of the **structural funds** and gives assistance to help reform farm structures and to develop rural areas. The 'guarantee' section, much the larger, is responsible for the price support that is a key feature of the **Common Agricultural Policy** (CAP; see **intervention**). The EAGGF was set up under Article 40.4 of the **Treaty of Rome** and came into operation in 1962.

The guidance section of the EAGGF is directed towards objectives laid down in the 1999 reforms of the structural funds. Objective 1 is to support 'the development and structural adjustment of regions whose development is lagging behind', i.e. those with a per capita GDP less than 75 per cent of the European Union average. Special attention is paid to the most remote regions, such as the French overseas departments and the Azores, Madeira, and the Canary Islands, and to the sub-arctic agricultural regions of Finland and Sweden. Objective 2 is concerned with 'the economic and social conversion of … declining rural areas … and depressed areas dependent on fisheries', – which also get assistance from the Fisheries Guidance Instrument (FGI: see **Common Fisheries Policy**).

Action under the EAGGF, to which the **European Investment Bank** (EIB) may also contribute, is taken in conformity with development plans drawn up by member states and agreed with the Commission as Community Support Frameworks. All EAGGF support is given in the form of grants. The LEADER programme for rural development supplements the projects brought forward by member states.

The guarantee section of the EAGGF pays for the intervention buying of produce when prices fall below the minimum guaranteed prices fixed annually for each product. Only certain products are covered by a common organization of the market (sometimes known as a 'regime') involving intervention; those that are represent about 70 per cent of total agricultural production. Such products also benefit from export refunds, paid from the guarantee section of the EAGGF, when prices on world markets fall below those within the member states. A further 25 per cent of agricultural production is covered only by external protection and not by intervention. The remaining 5 per cent of agricultural production may also be a charge upon the EAGGF in the form of other types of price support or direct aids to producers.

About 95 per cent of EAGGF expenditure is in the guarantee section, which is classified as **compulsory expenditure** within the **Budget**. The EAGGF overall is almost half of the Budget.

European anthem

An orchestral arrangement by Herbert von Karajan of the main theme of the last movement of Beethoven's *Ninth Symphony* (his setting of Schiller's 'Ode to Joy' for choir, soloists and orchestra) was adopted in 1962 by the **Council of Europe** as the European anthem.

European Armaments Agency

A European Armaments Agency was identified in paragraph 5 of the first of the two **Declarations** on **Western European Union** (WEU) annexed to the **Maastricht Treaty** as a 'proposal [to] be examined further'. The Franco-German summit of May 1994 called for the creation of such an agency, open to all WEU states, as a further development of the already extensive bilateral cooperation between the two countries on arms-related issues. Progress to date has centred upon the Western European Armaments group (WEAG), an ancillary body of the WEU. The WEAG, originally involving all European members of the **North Atlantic Treaty Organization** (NATO) except Iceland, now has 19 participating states and is supplemented by a Eurpean Defence Industries Group (EDIG). The aim of WEAG is to promote harmonization of weapons and equipment, to introduce more competition into the market, to monitor technical developments relevant to the supply of military goods, and to encourage more cooperation among European manufacturers. In November 1996 WEU ministers established a Western European Armaments Organization (WEAO) to explore common procurement. Under a 'master-plan' agreed in Rome two years later, the WEAO may prove to be the proto-type of a European Armaments Agency. For the background to this proposal, see **Independent European Programme Group**. See also **defence industry**.

European Army

On 11 August 1950 **Winston Churchill** moved a resolution in the Consultative Assembly of the **Council of Europe** that called for 'the immediate creation of a unified European Army subject to proper European democratic control and acting in full cooperation with the United States and Canada'. Although the resolution was passed, it was not acted upon by the Committee of Ministers, but Churchill's speech made a great impact and was part of the current of ideas that flowed into the **Pleven Plan** of September 1950, which, in turn, pro-vided the basis for the 1952 agreement on a **European Defence Community** among **the Six.**

The background to Churchill's proposal was the outbreak of the Korean War on 25 July 1950 and the worsening situation in central and eastern Europe as the Communist parties strengthened their hold. The proposal was controversial not least because it implied that the Germans should be allowed to rearm. The following month the United States suggested that German divisions should be allowed to serve within the **North Atlantic Treaty Organization** (NATO), which had been founded the previous year; however, West Germany did not become a member until 1955. Churchill's reference to 'proper European democratic control' clearly meant that he saw this as a task for the Council of Europe, but in fact the Council has never become involved in security matters. More than 40 years later, the proposal for a European Army was partially realized in the 1991 decision to establish the **Eurocorps.**

European Arrest Warrant
See **extradition**.

European Atomic Energy Community (EAEC)
Commonly known as Euratom, the European Atomic Energy Community was established by **the Six** under a treaty signed in Rome on 25 March 1957, the same day as the better-known **Treaty of Rome** establishing the **European Economic Community**. The object of Euratom, in the words of Article 1 EAEC, was to create 'the conditions necessary for the speedy establishment and growth of nuclear industries'.

After the failure of the **European Defence Community** it was clear that if the impetus of European integration was to be maintained, progress would have to be made on some less controversial front. The **Spaak Committee** had been invited to consider the areas of agreement identified by the 1955 **Messina Conference** and these, it was thought, could be subdivided into a proposal for a **customs union** (see **Beyen Plan**) and another for an atomic energy community along the lines of the **European Coal and Steel Community** (ECSC). Accordingly, two treaties were drafted (see **Pierre Uri**), of which the one on atomic energy was thought at the time to be the more important.

The enormous potential of atomic energy was fully realized in the early 1950s, as was the damage that could be done if fissile materials were to fall into the wrong hands. It was also realized that, like coal and steel in an earlier generation, the possession of nuclear weapons could be decisive in the event of war and the French were nervous about the possibility of nuclear weapons being in German hands. Western Europe's reliance on the Middle East for its energy needs was underlined in the most dramatic way possible when as a result of President Gamal Abdel Nasser of the United Arab Republic seizing control of the Suez Canal on 26 July 1956 petrol rationing had to be introduced. All these factors pointed in the direction of a common effort on the part of the Six to develop atomic energy.

The institutions of Euratom were set up on the same quadripartite model that had served for the ECSC: an Assembly, a **Council of Ministers**, a Commission (see **European Commission**) and a **Court of Justice**, advised by an **Economic and Social Committee** (Article 2 EAEC). The Assembly, the Court, and the Economic and Social Committee were, from the beginning, institutions common to all three Communities, but until the 1965 **Merger Treaty** came into force in July 1967 Euratom had its own Brussels-based Commission and its own Council of Ministers. As was the case with the Commission provided for under the Treaty of Rome, the powers of the Euratom Commission were more limited than those of the ECSC's High Authority. The first President of the five-member Euratom Commission was a Frenchman, Louis Armand. A Scientific and Technical Committee of national experts was attached to the Commission in an advisory capacity.

The procedures and the **legal instruments** used by Euratom are the same as those used by the European Economic Community. The chapter headings of the Euratom Treaty indicate the range of activities pursued under the Treaty: promotion of research; dissemination of information; health and safety; investment; supplies of 'ores, source materials and special fissile materials' (the responsibility of the Euratom Supply Agency); safeguards; and external relations.

Of particular interest is the **Joint Research Centre** (JRC) established under Article 8 EAEC. Managed by the Commission, the JRC is in fact composed of eight separate institutes spread over five sites: Ispra (Italy), Petten (the Netherlands), Karlsruhe (Germany), Geel (Belgium) and Seville (Spain). The **European University Institute** (EUI) was also founded under the Euratom Treaty.

From 1957 until 1967 Euratom had its own budget, divided into two parts, one for administration and another for research and investment. In 1967 the administrative budget was incorporated into the European Economic Community's general **Budget** and three years later the research and investment budget was also merged with the general Budget.

European Bank for Reconstruction and Development (EBRD)

The EBRD, based in London, is devoted to promoting structural reform and the transition to a market economy in the countries of central and eastern Europe and the former Soviet Union. It is not to be confused with the **European Investment Bank** (EIB) or the **European Central Bank** (ECB). The EBRD has a membership of 33 lender and 27 borrower countries, the latter known as 'countries of operation'.

The EBRD was created as a response to the collapse of Communism in central and eastern Europe. In 1989 President **François Mitterrand** of France proposed the creation of a specialized development bank to promote economic restructuring and the liberalization of markets in the region, which would in turn help to underpin the transition to democracy. Less explicitly, the French government perhaps hoped to create a 'European' body that would counterbalance American economic and political influence. Many Western governments were initially sceptical, arguing that assistance could as effectively be directed to the region through bilateral channels or through established international agencies such as the International Monetary Fund (IMF), the World Bank or the EIB. However, with strong German support the proposal was endorsed by the **European Council** at Strasbourg in December 1989. It was agreed that membership of the EBRD would be open to non-European countries, but the member states of the Community, the Community itself and the EIB would together have a majority shareholding (51 per cent). The United States is the largest single shareholder (10 per cent), followed by France, Germany, Italy, Japan, and the United Kingdom (8.5 per cent each).

The Strasbourg decision resulted in the EBRD being given a mandate 'to foster the transition towards open market-oriented economies and to promote private and entrepreneurial initiative in the central and eastern European countries committed to and applying the principles of multi-party democracy, pluralism and market economics'. In April 1990 Jacques Attali, special adviser to President Mitterrand, and widely credited as the originator of the idea, was appointed as President of the EBRD (against opposition from Japan and the United States, but with British support in exchange for French support for London as the EBRD's headquarters).

The EBRD began operations a year later. The 'countries of operation' are Albania, Bulgaria, the Czech Republic, Hungary, Poland, Romania, Slovakia, the former Soviet Union (including the Baltic states) and the former Yugoslavia. The EBRD operates according to sound banking principles and promotes good business practices. It seeks to complement the private sector, not compete with other sources of finance.

The EBRD's subscribed capital was doubled in April 1997 to 20 billion ECUs (about £16 billion), and lending may not exceed this amount. At least 60 per cent of its lending in each country must be to private-sector projects, although this gives rise to problems of definition in respect of projects in countries in which the boundaries of the public and private sectors are difficult to draw. The EBRD deals directly with project sponsors as well as with governments, and offers loans at near-market rates. It may also take an equity stake or offer loan guarantees. It is both a merchant bank, dealing with commercially competitive borrowers, and a development bank, promoting the development of infra-structure in recipient countries, with a commitment to respect the environment. The EBRD plays an important part in improving nuclear safety.

The collapse of the Soviet Union and of Yugoslavia not only greatly increased the number of countries of operation but also made the problem of reconstruction more complex, and on a scale beyond what the EBRD's founders originally envisaged. The EBRD publishes an annual *Transition Report*, which gives a unique overview of the process of economic reform.

European Broadcasting Union (EBU)

Founded in Torquay in 1950 and based in Geneva, the EBU enables broadcasting companies in almost every European country, together with those in North Africa and the Middle East, to consult each other on legal, technical, legislative and commercial aspects of cross-frontier broadcasting. Through Eurovision and Euroradio the EBU also promotes international collaboration in programme production and transmission. EBU, which works in English and French, is involved with the European Union's MEDIA **programme,** has official relations with the **Council of Europe** and collaborates with similar regional broadcasting unions worldwide.

European Central Bank (ECB)

Article 4a (now 8) of the **Treaty of Rome**, added by the **Maastricht Treaty**, established both a European System of Central Banks (ESCB) and a

European Central Bank (ECB), to be set up as soon as the decision was taken to proceed to stage 3 of **Economic and Monetary Union** (EMU). The precursor of both bodies was the **European Monetary Institute** (EMI) in Frankfurt, which came into operation in January 1994. A statute covering the ESCB and the ECB is annexed as a **protocol** to the Treaty of Rome. Only those member states that participate in stage 3 are represented in the ESCB and the ECB, which came into operation on 1 June 1998.

The ESCB is the means whereby the governors of the participating states' central banks (which, under Articles 108 and 109 EC, must be independent of national governments) play a role alongside the ECB in the overall direction of EMU. In line with Article 4.2 EEC, its 'primary objective [is] to maintain price stability' and its basic tasks are to 'define and implement' monetary policy, to conduct foreign exchange operations, 'to hold and manage the official foreign reserves of the [participating] Member States', and 'to promote the smooth operation of payment systems'. Article 30 of the ESCB statute requires participating states to provide the ECB with foreign reserve assets up to €50 billion, each state being compensated by an equivalent claim on the ECB. The ESCB is also responsible for 'the smooth conduct of policies pursued by the competent authorities relating to the prudential supervision of credit institutions and the stability of the financial system' (Article 105.5 EC).

The ECB, which is part of the ESCB, is like its precursor the EMI based in Frankfurt and managed by a Governing Council composed of central bank governors and an Executive Board (the president, the vice-president, and four other members, appointed by the participating member states after consultation with the **European Parliament** and the Governing Council). The president-in-office of the **Ecofin Council** and a member of the **European Commission** are able to participate in meetings of the Governing Council, but without the right to vote. The ECB is required to draw up an annual report on the activities of the ESCB and on monetary policy, for presentation to the **European Council**, the **Council of Ministers**, the European Parliament and the Commission (Article 113.3 EC). It has a general right of consultation on all legislation, European or national, in its areas of competence (Article 105.4 EC).

The ECB has the 'exclusive right' to authorize the issue of **euro** banknotes. The ECB also has the power to authorize member states' issues of euro coins, the specifications of which have been laid down by the Ecofin Council under the **cooperation procedure**.

The decision-making bodies of the ECB are the Governing Council and the Executive Board. The Council, composed of the Board and the governors of national central banks, takes decisions by simple majority, each member having one vote, the quorum being two-thirds. Certain decisions allow votes to be weighted in accordance with participating states' share of the ECB's capital. In such cases a majority is at least half the shareholders and two-thirds of the subscribed capital. The Council is required to meet at least 10 times a year (Statute, Article 10).

The Board is composed of the president, the vice-president and four other members. All are full-time employees with a non-renewable term of office of up to eight years. Each has one vote, and decisions are taken by simple majority (Statute, Article 11). The 'political agreement' of 2 May 1998 which resulted in the first ECB president, Wim Duisenberg, being appointed on the understanding that he would 'not want' to serve the full eight-year term was widely criticized as casting doubt on the ECB's independence.

The ECB's decisions are in the form of Regulations and Decisions (see **legal instruments**). Both must be published in the *Official Journal*. The ECB may also make recommendations and deliver **Opinions**. In certain circumstances it may impose fines on undertakings that do not comply with its Regulations and Decisions.

European Centre for the Development of Vocational Training

Sometimes known by its French acronym CEDEFOP (*Centre européen pour la développement de la formation professionelle*), the Centre is an **agency** established in 1975 as a body to advise the **European Commission** on various aspects of **social policy** concerned with training: vocational training, comparability of training qualifications, the retraining of women wishing to go back to work, etc. Initially based in Berlin, the Centre has been moved to Thessaloniki. Persons appointed by national governments, employers' organizations and trade unions as well as the Commission participate in the work of the Centre. Under a Regulation of 1990, a new body, the **European Training Foundation**, was set up to encourage and assist vocational training schemes in the countries of central and eastern Europe.

European City of Culture

Since 1985 the Council of Ministers of Culture in the European Union has chosen a 'European City (from 1999 "Capital") of Culture'. The city so designated benefits from support from the **Budget**. To date, the title has been bestowed on the following cities:

1985 Athens	1992 Madrid	1999 Weimar
1986 Florence	1993 Antwerp	2001 Rotterdam, Oporto
1987 Amsterdam	1994 Lisbon	2002 Bruges, Salamanca
1988 Berlin	1995 Luxembourg	2003 Graz
1989 Paris	1996 Copenhagen	2004 Genoa, Lille
1990 Glasgow	1997 Thessaloniki	
1991 Dublin	1998 Stockholm	

Exceptionally, in view of the symbolic importance of the new millennium, nine cities were named for the year 2000: Avignon, Bergen, Bologna, Brussels, Cracow, Helsinki, Prague, Reykjavik and Santiago de Compostela.

A parallel scheme for a 'European Cultural Month', involving cities outside the Union was established in 1992. Budapest, Cracow, Graz, Nicosia, Ljubljana, Riga, Basel, Valletta, Linz, Plovdiv and St Petersburg have been named as participants in this new project, which, like the 'Cultural Capital' scheme, entails a very full programme of concerts, exhibitions, film festivals and other cultural events. With effect from 2004, a new procedure for choosing a European Capital of Culture has been introduced (Decision 1419/99, *Official Journal*, L166, 1 July 1999).

European Coal and Steel Community (ECSC)

The ECSC was established by the Treaty of Paris in 1951. The first of the three European Communities (the others being the **European Economic Community** and the **European Atomic Energy Community**), the ECSC was based upon the **Schuman Plan** of 1950. On 9 May 1950 **Robert Schuman**, the French Foreign Minister, proposed that French and German coal and steel production should be 'pooled' and placed under a common supranational authority, an initiative that owed its origin to **Jean Monnet**. In the event not only France and West Germany but also Belgium, Italy, Luxembourg and the Netherlands decided to take part, thus forming **the Six**. The ECSC Treaty was concluded for a period of 50 years (Article 97), whereas the EEC Treaty (the **Treaty of Rome**) and the Euratom Treaty are of indefinite duration. The ECSC Treaty expired on 23 July 2002.

The coal and steel industries were chosen as the two industries essential to the waging of war. If they were placed under a common supranational authority, war between the signatory states would be, in Schuman's words, 'not only unthinkable, but materially impossible'. Coal and steel were also essential to economic recovery, and the experience already gained from the economic cooperation that was a condition of the economic aid received under the **Marshall Plan** suggested that recovery would be more rapid if European countries abandoned the elaborate prewar system of tariffs and quotas. The elimination of such restrictions on trade in coal and steel products among the Six was a prime objective of the ECSC Treaty, together with common prices, a common policy on imports, measures to enforce competition and the harmonization of state aids.

The ECSC Treaty, which after ratification came into effect in July 1952, provided for four main institutions: a Special Council of Ministers; a High Authority (of which Monnet was the first president); a Common Assembly composed of 78 members nominated from among Members of Parliament in the signatory states; and a Court of Justice for the settlement of disputes. The Treaty thereby established the institutional framework that was later used for the more ambitious European Economic Community: the ECSC's High Authority was the prototype of the **European Commission**, and the Common Assembly developed into the **European Parliament**. Although by 1958 the two other Communities had been created, the institutions of the ECSC remained legally separate until the **Merger Treaty** of 1965. All were based in Luxembourg, a 'provisional' arrangement that was to have lasting consequences for the **seat of the institutions**. A **protocol** on relations with the **Council of Europe** was annexed to the ECSC Treaty. It called upon governments to recommend to **national parliaments** that the members appointed to sit in the ECSC Common Assembly 'should preferably be chosen from among the representatives to the Consultative Assembly of the Council of Europe' (Article 1). Both the Common Assembly and the High Authority of the ECSC were required to forward annual reports on their activities to the Council of Europe (Articles 2 and 3). The motive behind these provisions seems to have been to answer the criticism that the ECSC and the Council of Europe, in spite of their very different structures and areas of responsibility, might develop on the basis of mutual jealousy. The protocol makes it clear that at the time the Council of Europe was regarded as the senior partner.

The ECSC remains the best example of **functionalism**: that is, integration centred upon a strictly limited field with common institutions possessing only the powers required to discharge their responsibilities effectively. Trade in coal and steel products between the Six rose very rapidly throughout the 1950s, while the extensive use of the High Authority's powers to break up cartels and monopolies kept price rises to a minimum.

However, both the structure of the ECSC and the range of powers exercised by its institutions embodied many compromises and ambiguities. Monnet's original preference was for a sovereign 'High Authority', but the **Benelux** countries – drawing on their experience of a **customs union** – insisted that the High Authority should be overseen by governments acting through a Council of Ministers. The Common Assembly's powers of control were to be exercised over the High Authority, not over the Council. While the objectives of the ECSC were consistent with free market philosophy (price transparency, competition, limits on state aids), the institutions were also given powers of a more *dirigiste* character: to control imports, for example, or to set prices and place limits on production in the event of a crisis in the coal or steel industries. The hybrid nature of the ECSC's institutions and the tension between the different economic philosophies underpinning the ECSC's powers set a pattern for the European Economic Community.

The British attitude to the Schuman Plan and to the establishment of the ECSC was ambivalent. On the one hand, there was enthusiasm for the prospect of a lasting reconciliation between France and Germany; on the other, there was opposition to the idea of a 'High Authority' and to the loss of sovereignty that the existence of such an authority might entail. The discussion exposed the fault-lines running through the political parties, which, over 50 years later, are still evident. The first point to be settled was whether to take part in the negotiations on the Schuman Plan. **Winston Churchill**'s speech in the House of Commons on 27 June 1950 neatly expressed the dilemma:

If he [Sir Stafford Cripps, the Labour Chancellor] asked me, 'Would you agree to a supranational authority which has the power to tell Great Britain not to cut any more coal or make any more steel, but to grow tomatoes instead?' I should say, without hesitation, the answer is 'No'. But why not be there to give the answer?

The French government had (perhaps wisely) made acceptance in principle of a High Authority a condition of taking part in the discussions on the plan. In the Consultative Assembly of the Council of Europe, Conservatives, led by Harold Macmillan, put forward an alternative proposal that would have brought the institutions of what became the ECSC under the auspices of the Council and greatly reduced their supranational character. This proposal attracted little support, and the Six signed the Treaty of Paris on 18 April 1951. Although the Treaty made no provision for associate membership of the ECSC, the United Kingdom concluded an **Association Agreement** with the Six in December 1954.

The supranational institutions provided for, however modestly, under the ECSC Treaty marked a decisive break with the intergovernmental model of integration (see **intergovernmentalism**) typified by such bodies as the Council of Europe and the **Organization for Economic Cooperation and Development** (OECD). The significance of this was not lost upon **Konrad Adenauer**, who in a speech to the Bundestag in 1952 spoke of the 'political meaning' of the ECSC being 'infinitely larger than its economic purpose ... For the first time in history, countries want to renounce part of their sovereignty, voluntarily and without compulsion, in order to transfer it to a supranational structure'. For the United States, John Foster Dulles, the acting Secretary of State, welcomed the Schuman initiative as 'brilliantly creative', adding that it could 'go far to solve the most dangerous problem of our time, namely the relationship of Germany's industrial power to France and the West'. The ECSC and its supranational apparatus were also a decisive step beyond the postwar proposals for the internationalization of the Ruhr and the **Saarland**, although these helped to create the climate of opinion in which the Schuman Plan could find acceptance. The economic and political background to the Schuman Plan and the ECSC is set out in Alan Milward, *The Reconstruction of Western Europe 1945–51* (1984).

The ECSC was soon overshadowed by the European Economic Community. In March 1959 the High Authority sought to use its emergency powers in the coal industry, but failed to persuade the Council of Ministers to declare the 'state of manifest crisis' which was a necessary preliminary to the use of emergency powers. In the 1970s the Commission (as the successor to the High Authority) used its powers under the ECSC Treaty to restructure the Community's steel industry (the so-called Davignon Plan); these powers were used again to effect further restructuring in the wake of recession and stiffer competition from central and eastern Europe. The ECSC Treaty's provisions for aids to miners' housing and retraining helped mining communities adjust to the decline of the coal industry. However, nothing was done under the ECSC Treaty that could not, with modest adjustments, be brought within the ambit of the Treaty of Rome when the ECSC Treaty expired in July 2002.

European Commission

Sometimes referred to as the 'civil service' of the European Union, the European Commission is unique among international bureaucracies by virtue of its combination of administrative, executive, legislative and judicial activities and responsibilities. In a strict sense the Commission is the 'college' of 20 Commissioners (see below), but the term is also used to denote all the European civil servants (*fonctionnaires*) who work for the institution. Of some 21,000 Commission employees, approximately 18,000 work in Brussels, the official 'seat' of the Commission (see **Berlaymont, Eurocrats**).

Under Article 213 of the **Treaty of Rome** the Commissioners are 'chosen on the grounds of their general competence'. The **Maastricht Treaty** extended their term of office from four to five years in order to align it with that of the **European Parliament** (Article 214 EC), which now plays a decisive role in the appointment of Commissioners. Governments of member states acting 'by common accord' nominate 'after consulting the European Parliament' the president-designate in the year preceding that in which the new Commission is due to take office. They then choose, in consultation with the president-designate, their nominees as the other members of the Commission. Once chosen, the nominees are 'subject as a body to a vote of approval by the European Parliament', and if such approval is granted the governments may then proceed to formal appointment. Vacancies among the Commissioners caused by death or retirement are filled by agreement among the member states; only in the case of appointing a new president is there an obligation to secure the approval of the European Parliament. The Treaty of Rome requires the governments' nominee as president-designate to be 'approved' by the Parliament. Once so approved, the president-designate consults with the governments on the appointment of the other Commissioners. The Treaty also specifies (Article 219) that 'the Commission shall work under the political guidance of its President'.

Article 213 specifies that there shall be 20 Commissioners, and that this may be changed only by unanimous agreement. In effect, this means two Commissioners from each of the five largest states, and one from each of the rest. The number of Commissioners has increased with each **enlargement** of the Union, since Article 213 also says that the Commission 'must include at least one national of each of the Member States'. Initially, there were 9 Commissioners. For a brief period after the entry into force of the **Merger Treaty** in 1967 there were 14, but this was reduced to 9 in 1969 and then raised to 13 in 1973 with the first enlargement. Since then, the total has increased to 20 with the **accession** of Greece, Portugal, Spain (two Commissioners), Austria, Finland and Sweden. After extensive 'hearings' in the European Parliament's committees, the Commission for 1999–2005 was approved by the Parliament on 15 September 1999 by 414 votes to 142 with 35 abstentions. A list of these Commissioners will be found at the end of this entry.

Much stress is laid on the independence of Commissioners. Article 213 requires them to be 'completely independent in the performance of their duties ... [and] neither seek nor take instructions from any government or from any other body'. They are prohibited from engaging 'in any other occupation, whether gainful or not'. On appointment, Commissioners commit themselves to remain independent in an oath sworn before the **Court of Justice** in Luxembourg. Individual Commissioners may be dismissed only by the Court on application from the **Council of Ministers** or the Commission itself. Collectively, the Commissioners may be dismissed by the European Parliament (see **censure motion**).

The Commission may appoint one or two vice-presidents. The allocation of portfolios is also decided (not always entirely amicably) by the Commissioners themselves on a proposal from the president. Each Commissioner takes responsibility for one or more of the 36 **directorates-general** and other ancillary services (such as the Legal Service or **Eurostat**) into which the Commission is divided. The Commissioners meet regularly, normally on Wednesdays, and although Article 219 allows decisions to be taken by simple majority, in practice all major decisions are taken by consensus and the Commission operates on the basis of collective responsibility. Each Commissioner is assisted by a small cabinet. The most senior official in the administration is the secretary-general.

The powers of the Commission are set out in Article 211. First, the Commission must 'ensure that the provisions of this Treaty and the measures taken by the institutions pursuant thereto are applied'. This function, with reference to which the Commission is sometimes referred to as the 'guardian of the Treaties', empowers the Commission to take action – ultimately, by referring the matter to the Court of Justice – if an institution or, under Article 226, a member state is in default of its Treaty obligations (see **reasoned opinion**). Second, the Commission may make Recommendations (see **legal instruments**) or deliver **Opinions** on matters covered by the Treaty. Third, the Commission has 'its own power of decision and [may] participate in the shaping of measures taken by the Council and by the European Parliament in the manner provided for in this Treaty'. This general formulation embodies two quite distinct powers: first, the Commission's autonomous role in such areas as **competition policy**; and, second, its **right of initiative** in the legislative procedure and its involvement at every stage of the legislative process. Finally, the Commission is required 'to exercise the powers conferred on it by the Council for the implementation of the rules laid down by the latter'. Sometimes known as the Commission's 'management role', this is especially important in relation to the day-to-day operation of the **Common Agricultural Policy** (CAP), the **Common Commercial Policy** (CCP) and other areas in which under the **Treaties** action at the Union level has largely replaced that at the national level (but see also **management committee**, **comitology**).

In addition to the powers laid down in Article 211 the Commission is responsible for negotiating on behalf of member states all bilateral and multilateral agreements to which the Union is a party (Articles 133 and 300 EC). Under Article 302 the Commission has a general responsibility for 'the maintenance of all appropriate relations' with the United Nations, its specialized agencies, and other international bodies. The Commission has information offices in all member states and delegations in many other countries, including nearly all the countries associated with the Union through the **Cotonou Agreement**.

The Commission's role in the **Budget** procedure is to draw up the preliminary draft budget with the help of estimates prepared by the other institutions. Under Article 274 the Commission is responsible for implementing the Budget and submitting accounts at the end of each financial year as part of the **discharge procedure**. The Commission is also responsible for the management of the **structural funds**.

Underpinning all these powers is what Article 211 refers to as the Commission's 'own power of decision', that is, the right to decide for itself on the substance and timing of a particular proposal or other action. For example, throughout the legislative procedure, the Commission has the right to withdraw or amend its proposal; it may decide whether or not to accept amendments put forward by the European Parliament; and it can choose if, when and upon what grounds to bring an action before the Court of Justice. It is the exercise of this power of decision that qualifies the Commission as an autonomous political institution rather than a simple bureaucracy (see also **annual work programme**).

In their original form, the **Common Foreign and Security Policy** (CFSP) and **Justice and Home Affairs** (JHA) provisions of the Maastricht Treaty restricted the role of the Commission. Although in both areas the Commission was to be 'fully associated' (Articles 18.4 and 36 TEU) with developments, it had no exclusive right of initiative and in general terms was less strongly placed to influence the decisions taken by virtue of the essentially intergovernmental nature of the procedures (see **intergovernmentalism**). This situation began to change with the entry into force of the **Treaty of Amsterdam** (see also **Schengen** *acquis*).

Although extensive, the Commission's powers within the decision-making process are less than those of the **High Authority** of the 1951 **European Coal and Steel Community** (ECSC), upon which the Commission is modelled. This is apparent not least in the choice of name: 'Commission' – the ordinary French word for a committee – has none of the grandeur of 'High Authority', and was accordingly chosen by the drafters of the Treaties of Rome establishing the **European Economic Community** (EEC) and the **European Atomic Energy Community** (Euratom) as less provocative. From 1958 until 1967 the ECSC's High Authority and the EEC and Euratom Commissions led separate lives, but from July 1967 they were brought together as the Commission of the European Communities under the 1965 Merger Treaty.

By the time the Merger Treaty was being negotiated, the EEC Commission under its first President, **Walter Hallstein**, had aroused the opposition of French President **Charles de Gaulle**. De Gaulle took exception to what he saw as the Commission's pretensions (such as Hallstein's insistence on receiving the credentials of foreign diplomats accredited to the Communities). De Gaulle used the Commission as the target for his dislike of supranational institutions in general and denounced it in a number of well-publicized press conferences (especially that of 15 May 1962). His dislike of the Commission was partially responsible for the **'empty chair crisis'** of 1965 and so for the **Luxembourg Compromise** of January 1966.

Whatever hostility the Commission may have aroused on the part of the larger member states, the smaller states have always attached great importance to the Commission's role as the guardian of a broader European interest. The involvement of the Commission in all areas and at every level of Union activity is seen as a safeguard against a directorate of large states. This is why, for example, in the **qualified majority voting** (QMV) procedure a distinction is drawn between the majority necessary to adopt a Commission proposal and the majority needed when there is no proposal. It also explains why the smaller states strongly supported **Roy Jenkins** when as Commission President he sought to ensure (against French opposition) that he and his successors had the right to attend international economic summits on behalf of the Community as a whole.

One of the central facts about the Commission is that it has not developed into a European government. The Council of Ministers has shown little inclination to become a **Chamber of States** and the European Parliament has succeeded in exercising greater political authority over the Commission's legislative activities.

On the whole, the Commission has been the loser in the shifting balance of power between the institutions. It has, however, maintained – with some difficulty – its independence of action. What difference the Parliament's recently acquired powers over the appointment of Commissioners (see above) will make remains to be seen.

The fact that the Commission is not elected gives rise to criticism. However, it is precisely the fact of the Commission's *not* being elected that allows the present institutional balance to be maintained, a balance broadly satisfactory to the governments of member states. The procedure under which an incoming Commission must secure the approval of the European Parliament is thought to give the Commission greater democratic legitimacy while falling well short of conferring an independent political mandate.

The 'Brussels bureaucrats' are held in generally low public esteem in the member states, particularly in those with a vigorous popular press. Although in recent years there has been a marked improvement in the quality of publicly available materials on Commission activities and a greater awareness of the need to counter **Euromyths**, the Commission is still very poor at explaining the background to its legislative initiatives. However, the Commission has a good reputation as a relatively open bureaucracy by comparison with most national civil services, and has been active in encouraging greater **transparency** within the Union's institutions.

The Commission has a poor record in respect of its own internal organization. As long ago as 1979, the Spierenburg Report identified the main failings: low motivation among Commission officials, over-elaborate hierarchies of authority, inflexible responses to changing priorities, all compounded by the usual rivalry and intrigue inevitable in international bureaucracies in relation to appointments and promotions (see **Eurocrats**). Very little action followed from this report.

Much more serious was the crisis which resulted in the resignation of the whole Commission in March 1999. In March 1998 the European Parliament refused to approve the accounts for 1996 because of its dissatisfaction with the general standard of management in the Commission and the lack of democratic accountability in the fight against **fraud**. In December 1998 approval was again refused because of the failure of Commission President **Jacques Santer** to convince the Parliament that action was being taken in response to the Parliament's demands. A censure motion was tabled against the Commission and debated the following month. By this time serious criticisms were appearing in the press and elsewhere of the performance of individual Commissioners (especially Edith Cresson) but none of them showed any willingness to resign. In spite of this, the censure motion was not adopted. Instead a 'Committee of Independent Experts' (CIE) was set up 'to examine the way in which the Commission detects and deals with fraud, mismanagement and nepotism [and to review] Commission practices in the awarding of all financial contracts'. The first part of the CIE's report (15 March 1999) was thought to be so damning that the Commissioners resigned as a body within hours of it becoming available. Had they not done so, they would have been dismissed by a censure motion adopted at the next plenary session of the Parliament. However, in accordance with Article 201 of the Treaty of Rome they continued to deal with current business until the Parliament formally endorsed the appointment of their successors in September 1999.

The resignation of the Santer Commission was the culmination of growing dissatisfaction with the Commission's performance over a whole decade. The oldest of the dossiers examined by the CIE was concerned with the 1989 Year of Tourism. The Commission had been conspicuously slow to address the allegations of corruption in the allocation of external contracts (although by 1999 no fewer than 76 organizations or individuals were the subject of criminal proceedings or internal inquiries). Irregularities were also at the heart of the second and third dossiers investigated by the CIE, the **MEDA programme** and the **European Community Humanitarian Office** (ECHO). The investigation of the **Leonardo** programme showed how the Commission had subcontracted the management of the programme to a French firm acting as a Technical Assistance Office without adequate supervision, and had failed to take decisive action on the allegations of fraud and mismanagement which began to emerge in 1996. The CIE also examined the irregularities in the awarding of contracts in the field of nuclear safety and in the Commission's own security services.

Overall, the CIE's report revealed a pattern. An understaffed Commission was constantly being invited to take on new responsibilities, resulting in excessive use of, and reliance on, external contractors. Ignorance of the details of how programmes were being managed was evident at the highest levels. Internal procedures for investigating irregularities were opaque and cumbersome. Financial controls were inadequate. Most serious of all, responsibility was so widely diffused as to be extremely hard to attribute: as the Committee remarked, 'it is becoming difficult to find anyone who has even the slightest sense of responsibility'.

The CIE published a second report on the reform of the Commission on 10 September 1999. Some of the recommendations have already been enacted by **Romano Prodi**, who was chosen at the Berlin meeting of the **European Council** in March 1999 to succeed Jacques Santer.

Among the reforms most regularly suggested was a reduction in the number of Commissioners, initially by allowing only one from each state, since there are not enough jobs of broadly equivalent weight to provide work for 20 Commissioners. The matter was provisionally resolved in a 'Protocol on the enlargement of the European Union' annexed to the **Treaty of Nice**, but this was repealed in the **Treaty of Accession** which the ten new member states signed in Athens in April 2003. As each new member state joins the Union, it will be entitled to nominate a Commissioner. These Commissioners together with the existing Commission will hold office until 31 October 2004, by which time a new Commission, 'composed of one national of each Member State', will have been chosen to hold office until 31 October 2009.

Proposals for reform not requiring Treaty changes were brought forward in a White Paper, *Reforming the Commission* (COM(2000) 200) on 1 March 2000. The priorities are to make responsibilities clearer, to increase accountability, to improve transparency and efficiency (partly by means of decentralization), to avoid overload and to improve staff training and management. A new Internal Audit Service has been created and a Code of Good Administrative Behaviour drawn up. More radical changes require amendment of the Financial Regulation and of the Staff Regulations, and this could only be done in agreement with the other Union institutions (see also **European governance**).

Of the 140 or so Commissioners (including Members of the High Authority) there have been since 1951, about one third had experience of middle-ranking or high ministerial office in their country of origin before going to Brussels. Christian Democrats, Conservatives and Socialists have held 70 per cent of the positions, their shares roughly equal: a further 11 per cent have been Liberals. The remainder have had non-party backgrounds as senior diplomats or international civil servants. Until 1994 there had been only two women. There are few examples of Commissioners returning to national political life at a high level. Of the 20 Commissioners who took office in September 1999, 16, including the President, are new. Ten have held major political office (three as prime minister, finance minister or foreign minister) in their country of origin. All but four have been members of their national parliaments and two have also been MEPs. Individually, they have all agreed to resign if requested to do so by the President. See Andrew MacMullen, 'European Commissioners 1952–1995: national routes to a European elite' in Neill Nugent (ed.), *At the Heart of the Union* (Basingstoke, 1997).

Commissioners are paid an annual salary (with pensions) of approximately €17,000 a month, vice-presidents and the president slightly more. Their salaries and pensions are paid from the Budget of the European Union; classified as **compulsory expenditure**, they are fixed in relation to the pay of the most senior rank within the Commission's services, that of director-general.

The case for the Commission – the boldest of all the institutional experiments embodied in the Treaties – must ultimately rest on whether it works, and whether the Union would work better if radical changes were made to the Commission's role. On the whole, the Commission does work. The very rapid progress made since the 1950s could not have been achieved without the Commission acting as motivator, monitor and proposer of compromises, nor without the longer-term view of the integration process that the Commission provides. For books on the Commission, see **Eurocrat**.

The following table lists the Presidents of the Commission (the Commission of the European Economic Community, 1958–67, and the Commission of all three Communities since the Merger Treaty came into force in 1967):

Presidents of the Commission

Period of office.	President	Country of origin	Party
1958–67	Walter Hallstein	West Germany	Christian Democrat
1967–70	Jean Rey	Belgium	Liberal
1970–2	Franco Maria Malfatti	Italy	Christian Democrat
1972–3	Sicco Mansholt	The Netherlands	Socialist
1973–7	François-Xavier Ortoli	France	UDR (Gaullist)
1977–81	Roy Jenkins	United Kingdom	Labour
1981–5	Gaston Thorn	Luxembourg	Liberal
1985–95	Jacques Delors	France	Socialist
1995–9	Jacques Santer	Luxembourg	Christian Democrat
1999–	Romano Prodi	Italy	Centre-left

Commissioners and their portfolios, 2000–5

President Romano Prodi (Italy)	• Secretariat-General, Legal Service, Press and Communications
Vice-president Neil Kinnock (United Kingdom)	• Personnel and Administration, with special responsibility for reform
Vice-president Loyola de Palacio (Spain)	• Transport, Energy
Mario Monti (Italy)	• Competition
Franz Fischler (Austria)	• Agriculture, Rural Development, Fisheries
Erkki Liikanen (Finland)	• Industrial Enterprise, Information Society, Tourism
Frederik Bolkestein (The Netherlands)	• Internal Market, Taxation, Customs Union
Philippe Busquin (Belgium)	• Research, Joint Research Centre
Pedro Solbes Mira (Spain)	• Economic and Monetary Affairs, Eurostat
Poul Nielson (Denmark)	• Development, Humanitarian Aid
Günter Verheugen (Germany)	• Enlargement
Christopher Patten (United Kingdom)	• External Relations
Pascal Lamy (France)	• External Trade
David Byrne (Ireland)	• Health, Consumer Protection
Michel Barnier (France)	• Regional Policy, Intergovernmental Conference
Viviane Reding (Luxembourg)	• Education, Culture, Publications
Michaele Schreyer (Germany)	• Budget, Financial Control, Anti-Fraud Office
Margot Wallström (Sweden)	• Environment
Antonio Vitorino (Portugal)	• Justice and Home Affairs
Anna Diamantopoulou (Greece)	• Employment and Social Affairs

European Communities

The phrase 'European Communities' is used to denote the **European Coal and Steel Community** (ECSC; **Treaty of Paris**, 1951), the **European Economic Community** (the EEC or 'Common Market'; **Treaty of Rome**, 1957), and the **European Atomic Energy Community** (Treaty of Rome, known as the Euratom or EAEC Treaty, 1957). Since the 1965 **Merger Treaty** the three Communities have shared the same institutions while remaining legally distinct, and have always had the same membership (**the Six**, 1951–72; the Nine, 1973–80; the Ten, 1981–5; the Twelve, 1986–94; the Fifteen, 1995–). In the **Maastricht Treaty** the European Economic Community was officially renamed 'the European Community', and this remains a separate entity within the European Union established by that Treaty (see also **legal personality**).

Since the Maastricht Treaty came into effect, the **Council of Ministers** of the European Communities has called itself the Council of the European Union. The **European Commission** is still formally the Commission of the European Communities or, for most purposes, simply the Commission.

European Community Humanitarian Office (ECHO)

ECHO was set up within the **European Commission** in 1991 to make the provision of humanitarian aid more efficient, especially by improving coordination with relief agencies and by enabling the European Union to respond more promptly to calls for emergency aid. ECHO became fully operational in 1993, in which year aid was given to some 50 countries on the basis of over 700 project contracts. Its place has now been taken by the **Humanitarian Aid Office**. Overall, more than 90 per cent of humanitarian aid was given in response to man-made emergencies, such as wars and other regional conflicts. Aid is drawn both from the **Budget** of the European Union and from the **European Development Fund**. The Union works very closely with non-governmental organizations (NGOs), for the allocation and distribution of humanitarian aid. Overall, NGOs handle about half of the aid granted by the Union. The United Nations and its specialized agencies (the High Commission for Refugees, the World Food Programme and the World Health Organization) are also important partners in the aid effort. The United Nations has set up a coordinating body (the Department for Humanitarian Affairs) in collaboration with which the Union is seeking to improve the international community's preparedness to respond to calls for emergency aid.

The self-evident need for decisions on humanitarian aid to be taken promptly has given rise to special procedures. Within the relevant allocations in the Budget, the Commission can make many of the decisions on its own authority, subject to the overall supervision of the **Council of Ministers** and the **European Parliament**, to which an annual report is submitted.

European Company Statute

The original proposal for a European Company Statute dates back to 1975, as an attempt by the **European Commission** to facilitate the creation of new multinational companies. The most controversial feature of the proposal was the requirement that workers' rights should be protected by the introduction of a two-tier board, structured along German lines. This met with strong resistance from many employers and several governments, and was eventually dropped. A second proposal was brought forward in 1989 in the form of a statute that companies could choose to adopt (and secure certain tax advantages by so doing). As a **Single Market** measure, it might have benefited from the **qualified majority voting** (QMV) provisions introduced by the **Single European Act** (SEA), but, in fact, since it dealt with 'the rights and interests of employed persons' (Article 95.2 of the **Treaty of Rome**), the requirement that the **Council of Ministers** must be unanimous continued to apply. Political agreement having finally been reached in the Council of Ministers in December 2000, a Regulation on the European company ('Societas Europaea') and a separate Directive on employee involvement in the European company were adopted on 8 October 2001 (Regulation 2157/01 and Directive 01/86, *Official Journal*, L294, 10 November 2001). See also **European Economic Interest Grouping, European Social Charter**.

European Conference

At its meeting in Luxembourg in December 1997, the **European Council** decided to establish an annual European Conference as a 'multilateral forum for political consultation' between the member states of the European Union and 'the European States aspiring to accede to it and sharing its values and internal and external objectives'. The conditions for attending the Conference were listed as:

a commitment to peace, security and good neighbourliness, respect for other countries' sovereignty, the principles upon which the European Union is founded, the integrity and inviolability of external borders and the principles of international law and a commitment to the settlement of territorial disputes by peaceful means, in particular through the jurisdiction of the International Court of Justice.

The first Conference was held in London in March 1998. The Conferences are chaired by the country holding the **presidency** of the European Union.

The Conference was devised at least in part as a means of reassuring those applicant countries not involved in the first round of bilateral accession negotiations (see **enlargement**) that their aspirations were being taken seriously and within the 'single framework' of which the European Conference is the principal symbol. It was also hoped that attendance at the Conference would be a consolation for Turkey, but in the event the Turkish government rejected the invitation. At its meeting in Helsinki in December 1999 the European Council agreed to 'review' the future of the European Conference.

European Conference of Ministers of Transport

Set up in 1953 on the initiative of the OEEC (see **Organization for Economic Cooperation and Development**), the European Conference of Ministers of Transport meets once a year with participants from 49 countries (including associates and observers). Concerned primarily with road transport, railways and inland waterways, it is a forum in which governments can discuss technical, administrative and economic aspects of transport policy, on the basis of detailed work at official level. The Conference's main conclusions may be adopted in the form of Conventions, more usually as Resolutions. The Conference is an important source of statistics on transport use, accidents, investment, traffic forecasts and related issues.

European Conference of Postal and Telecommunications Administrations (CEPT)

Known by its French acronym, CEPT was founded in 1959 within the Universal Postal Union (founded 1874). CEPT links the administrations of 44 countries. It provides a forum in which all aspects of posts and telecommunications can be discussed, including tariffs and the standardization of equipment. CEPT is also involved in the technical, legal and commercial aspects of electronic and satellite communications.

European Convention on Human Rights (ECHR)

Formally the Convention for the Protection of Human Rights and Fundamental Freedoms, the ECHR was drawn up under the auspices of the **Council of Europe** and signed in Rome on 4 November 1950. It came into effect on 3 September 1953. For further details, see **human rights**.

European Council

The European Council (not to be confused with the **Council of Ministers** or the **Council of Europe**) is the name given to the regular meetings – sometimes known as 'summits' – of the heads of state or of government of the Council of Ministers of the European Union and the president of the **European Commission**. This cumbersome formula stems from the fact that the presidents of France and sometimes of Finland (the heads of state) attend the European Council together with their prime ministers (the heads of government). Since 1986 the foreign ministers of the member states and one additional Commissioner have also attended neetings of the European Council, which are held either in the country holding the **presidency** of the Council of Ministers or in Brussels. In Nice (December 2000) it was agreed from 2002 to hold one meeting in Brussels during each six-month presidency and to hold all such meetings in Brussels once the number of member states has grown to 18 or more. In Seville (June 2002) it was agreed to meet four times a year.

The **Treaties** establishing the **European Communities** make no mention of the European Council. The first meeting of heads of state or of government was held in Paris in February 1961, and further meetings followed in Bonn (July 1961), Rome (May 1967), The Hague (December 1969), Paris (October 1972) and Copenhagen (December 1973). At a meeting in Paris in December 1974 **Valéry Giscard d'Estaing** suggested that a European Council should be established that would meet three times a year with the possibility of additional special meetings. This was agreed, and the first formal meeting of the new body was held in Dublin in March 1975, the main item for discussion being the conclusion of the British **renegotiation**.

A regular rhythm of three meetings a year was maintained until 1985, by which time the role of the European Council had been more fully set out in the **Stuttgart Declaration**. In 1986 Article 2 of the **Single European Act** (SEA) gave the European Council official recognition as a Community body. The frequency of its meetings was laid down as 'at least twice a year' and the list of those entitled to attend was extended to include the foreign ministers and the additional Commissioner. Since June 1987 the president of the **European Parliament** has been invited to address the meeting but not to take part in the main proceedings. A Declaration annexed to the **Maastricht Treaty** confirms the practice of inviting economic and finance ministers to meetings of the European Council at which matters relating to **Economic and Monetary Union** (EMU) are discussed. A list of the more important meetings of the European Council since 1969 is to be found at the end of this entry.

The Maastricht Treaty (Article 4) describes the European Council's role as being to 'provide the Union with the necessary impetus for its development and … define the general political guidelines thereof'. The same Article obliges the European Council to submit to the European Parliament a report after each of its meetings and an annual report 'on the progress achieved by the Union'. The role of the European Council is therefore essentially twofold: first, to provide overall political direction to the Union; and second, to resolve problems that have proved intractable at Council of Ministers level. A typical European Council agenda will reflect both elements, encompassing a wide-ranging review of some important issue, domestic or foreign, often on the basis of a Commission paper, and then a more narrowly focused discussion of some internal problem. The Treaty also requires the European Council to 'define the principles of and general guidelines for the **Common Foreign and Security Policy**' (CFSP: Article 13.1 TEU).

Decisions of the European Council, which are only very rarely put to the vote, are embodied in statements of the president-in-office ('conclusions of the Presidency'; see also **Declaration**). However, to become law they must follow the normal decision-making route, starting with a Commission draft.

European Council meetings afford opportunities for bilateral discussions between leaders. They provide a forum in which political leaders may appear in splendid surroundings, engage in personal diplomacy and take dramatic initiatives; more importantly, these leaders are obliged to invest personal and political capital in the Union's development. They are structured to allow meetings (including lunches and dinners) of varying degrees of intimacy, and because the apparatus of officials, interpreters, security and so on is reduced to a minimum, at least some of the original informal character of European Council meetings is preserved. Inevitably, however, they attract the press and media, representatives of which may easily exceed 1,000 at the average meeting.

Initially opposed by devout Europeans on the grounds that it strengthened the intergovernmental character of the Community (see **intergovernmentalism**), the European Council is now accepted as a necessary part of the Community system (a view shared by **Jean Monnet**, who in a letter to President Giscard d'Estaing described the creation of the European Council as 'the most important decision for Europe since the **Treaty of Rome**'). Recognition came most slowly in the European Parliament, which felt that it lacked any means of influencing or scrutinizing European Council decisions: not until December 1981 were European Council meetings reported to the Parliament by the head of state or of government holding the presidency, a practice begun by **Margaret Thatcher**, continued by all her successors, confirmed in the Stuttgart Declaration and formalized in the Maastricht Treaty.

As some commentators have pointed out, the impulse-giving role of the European Council can very easily be overshadowed by the need to solve problems. If a problem is referred to the European Council, it can only be because neither at official level nor at Council of Ministers level has it been possible to find agreement. Such problems are usually both intrinsically complex and politically sensitive; and by the time they reach the European Council they may well be urgent too. So it can easily happen that a meeting is dominated by a single issue, and less urgent matters (which may well be more important in the longer term) remain unresolved. The problem-solving function places temptation in the way of the Council of Ministers, since a minister in real political difficulty may wish to transfer the risk of domestic odium to his or her prime minister.

The same problem was touched on in the 1985 report by the **Dooge Committee** on institutional questions: 'The trend towards the European Council's becoming simply another body dealing with the day-to-day business of the Community must be reversed. [It] should play a strategic role and give direction and political impetus to the Community.' In the period since 1985 the trend has been checked if not wholly reversed; and although the European Council is far from being the 'Provisional European Government' that Jean Monnet intended it to be (see Chapter 21 of his *Memoirs*), it is certainly true that all major initiatives in the Union, even if they do not originate in the European Council, must be endorsed by it.

The following is a list of the most important meetings in the period 1969–2003.

The Hague, 1–2 December 1969
President Georges Pompidou of France lifts the French veto on British accession to the European Community.

Paris, 19–20 October 1972
The Prime Ministers of Denmark, Ireland and the United Kingdom attended this summit, although the accession of these three countries did not formally take place until January 1973. The member states commit themselves to **Economic and Monetary Union** (EMU) and to converting 'their entire relationship into a European Union' by the end of the decade.

Paris, 9–10 December 1974
Decision to establish the European Council. Leo Tindemans, Foreign Minister of Belgium, requested to draw up a report on European Union (see **Tindemans Report**).

Dublin, 10–11 March 1975
Settlement on British **renegotiation**.

Rome, 1–2 December 1975
Agreement on the **European passport** and on **European elections** (planned for 1978).

Brussels, 12–13 July 1976
Agreement on the total number of seats in the **European Parliament**, and on the allocation of seats to each member state.

Brussels, 5–6 December 1977
Agreement on the introduction of the European Unit of Account (see **European Currency Unit**) from 1 January 1978.

Bremen, 6–7 July 1977
Decision to create the **European Monetary System** (EMS).

Brussels, 4–5 December 1978
Resolution on the EMS. '**Three Wise Men**' commissioned to draw up a report on the Community institutions.

Dublin, 29–30 November 1979
British Budget problem first raised.

Venice, 12–13 June 1980
Venice Declaration on the situation in the Middle East.

London, 26–27 November 1981
Discussion of the **Genscher–Colombo** proposals on European Union. New impulse given to the accession negotiations with Portugal and Spain.

Stuttgart, 17–19 June 1983
Adoption of the Solemn Declaration on European Union (see **Stuttgart Declaration**).

Fontainebleau, 25–26 June 1984
Final settlement of the British Budget problem, accompanied by agreement on new **own resources** and on **budgetary discipline**. Establishment of the **People's Europe** committee and the **Dooge Committee**.

Brussels, 29–30 March 1985
Agreement on **Integrated Mediterranean Programmes**.

Milan, 28–29 June 1985
Agreement (by qualified majority) to convene an **Intergovernmental Conference** (IGC) to discuss institutional reform. Endorsement of the **Cockfield White Paper**.

Luxembourg, 2–3 December 1985
Agreement in principle to extend **qualified majority voting** (QMV) in order to complete the **Single Market** programme by the end of 1992, to increase the powers of the European Parliament, to give **European Political Cooperation** a sounder legal base, and to extend Community competences (all set out in the Single European Act, agreed by the Foreign Affairs Council on 16–17 December 1985).

Brussels, 11–13 February 1988
Agreement on measures to complete the Single Market, on budgetary and agricultural questions (including 'set-aside') and on the **structural funds**.

Hanover, 27–28 June 1988
Committee invited to draw up a report on EMU (see **Delors Report**).

Madrid, 26–27 June 1989
Agreement on the various stages leading to EMU.

Strasbourg, 8–9 December 1989
Adoption of the **Social Charter**. Decision to convene an IGC (see **Maastricht Treaty**) and on the **European Bank for Reconstruction and Development**.

Dublin, 25–26 June 1990
Identification of the main issues for the IGCs on political union and EMU.

There were two extra meetings in 1990, on **German reunification** (Dublin, 28 April) and on the Gulf crisis and EMU (Rome, 27–28 October).

Maastricht, 9–10 December 1991
Agreement on the Maastricht Treaty.

Lisbon, 26–27 June 1992
Agreement on guidelines for the **enlargement** of the Community.

Birmingham, 16 October 1992
Declaration on 'a Community close to its citizens' (see **subsidiarity**).

Edinburgh, 11–12 December 1992
Agreement on special arrangements for Denmark to allow a second referendum on the Maastricht Treaty. Agreement on **future financing**. Decision to allow enlargement negotiations to begin with Austria, Finland and Sweden. Adoption of the **Edinburgh Growth Initiative**. Definitive decision on seat of the European Parliament (see **seat of the institutions**).

Copenhagen, 21–22 June 1993
Discussion of Commission White Paper *Growth, Competitiveness and Employment*. Decision that central and eastern European countries with **Europe Agreements** which 'so desire shall become members of the European Union' (see **Copenhagen criteria**). Discussion of openness (see **transparency**) and **fraud**.

Brussels, 29 October 1993
(This extraordinary meeting took place three days before the entry into force of the Maastricht Treaty.) Decision on stage 2 of EMU (to begin 1 January 1994). Establishment of priority topics for the **Common Foreign and Security Policy** (CFSP) and **Justice and Home Affairs** (JHA) cooperation.

Brussels, 10–11 November 1993
Adoption of action plan on **employment** on basis of Commission White Paper (see above, June 1993). Agreement on **Pact on Stability in Europe**.

Agreement on representation in Commission, European Parliament, etc., of applicant states.

Corfu, 24–25 June 1994
Identification of projects for **trans-European networks**. Commitment to include Cyprus and Malta in next round of enlargement. Establishment of **Reflection Group** to prepare 1996 IGC.

Essen, 9–10 December 1994
Further discussion of employment, financing of trans-European networks, strategy for central and eastern Europe, **Mediterranean policy**, and fraud.

Cannes, 26–27 June 1995
Agreement on **Europol** convention. Report on **racism and xenophobia**.

Madrid, 15–16 December 1995
Full discussion on EMU and decision on the **euro**. Final preparations for the 1996 IGC (launched in Turin on 29 March 1996).

Florence, 21–22 June 1996
Further discussion on employment. Review of action against drugs. Decisions on elimination of BSE.

Dublin, 13–14 December 1996
Further discussion on EMU and the new **exchange-rate mechanism** (ERM 2). Review of progress in the IGC and of action against international crime.

Amsterdam, 16–17 June 1997
Conclusion of the IGC (**Treaty of Amsterdam**). Discussion on EMU. Resolutions on stability, growth and employment (see **Stability Pact**) and on ERM 2.

Luxembourg, 20–21 November 1997
Special meeting on employment ('jobs summit').

Luxembourg, 12–13 December 1997
Final decision on enlargement. *Agenda 2000* discussion.

London, 2–3 May 1998
Decision on stage 3 of EMU.

Cardiff, 15–16 June 1998
Further discussion on employment. March 1999 deadline set for *Agenda 2000* decisions. Discussion on institutional and budgetary questions and 'bringing the EU closer to people'. Informal European Council meeting planned for October 1998.

Vienna, 11–12 December 1998
Final preparations for stage 3 of EMU. Progress reports on *Agenda 2000* and enlargement. Adoption of 'Vienna Strategy for Europe'.

Berlin, 24–25 March 1999
Agreement on *Agenda 2000*. Appointment of **Romano Prodi** as President-designate of the Commission.

Cologne, 3–4 June 1999
Appointment of Javier Solana as Secretary-General of the Council and **High Representative** for the CFSP. Confirmation that an IGC will be convened 'early in 2000' on institutional reform. Review of Stability Pact for **the Balkans**.

Tampere, 16–17 October 1999
Discussion on 'a Union of freedom, security and justice' (asylum and immigration, racism and xenophobia, police and judicial cooperation, money laundering). Agreement on a committee to draft a **Charter of Fundamental Rights**.

Helsinki, 10–11 December 1999
Agreement on enlargement, institutional reform, and defence and security aspects of the CFSP. Adoption of 'guidelines for reform' of the working methods of the **Council of Ministers**. Acceptance of Turkey as an applicant state.

Lisbon, 23–24 March 2000
Agreement that the Union should become 'the most competitive and dynamic knowledge-based economy in the world': progress to be reviewed every spring. Commitment to 'a European Area of Research and Innovation' (see **research**).

Santa Maria de Feira, 19–20 June 2000
Review of the **Common European Security and Defence Policy** (CESDP). Endorsement of the eEurope 2002 Action Plan (the 'dot.com summit'). Partial agreement on further **tax harmonization**. Adoption of a common strategy on **Mediterranean policy**.

Nice, 7–9 December 2000
Adoption of the **Treaty of Nice**. Endorsement of the Charter of Fundamental Rights and of the **European Social Agenda**.

Stockholm, 23–24 March 2001
Definition and discussion of the 'Stockholm priorities' (full employment, fostering entrepreneurship, improving mobility, harnessing new technologies, etc.). Review of relations with Russia.

Göteborg, 15–16 June 2001
Review of enlargement and the CESDP.

Laeken, 14–15 December 2001
The **Laeken Declaration**. Review of the **area of freedom, security and justice**.

Barcelona, 15–16 March 2002
Review of Lisbon agenda, foreign affairs.

Seville, 21–22 June 2002
Review of CESDP, enlargement, asylum and immigration. Reform of European Council.

Brussels, 22–25 October 2002
Enlargement, relations with NATO, institutional reforms.

Copenhagen, 12–13 December 2002
Conclusion of enlargement negotiations (see **Treaty of Accession**).

Brussels, 21 March 2003
Review of Lisbon agenda.

European Court

'European Court' may refer either to the **Court of Justice** of the European Communities in Luxembourg or the Court of Human Rights in Strasbourg (see **human rights**). The former, an institution of the European Union, adjudicates on disputes arising from the interpretation or application of the **Treaties** or the legislation based upon them; the latter, an institution of the **Council of Europe**, is concerned solely with cases brought under the **European Convention on Human Rights**.

European Cultural Centre

Established in Geneva in 1950 on the basis of a resolution adopted at the 1948 **Congress of Europe**, the Centre's main activities were directed towards a better and wider understanding of European culture. Latterly, the Centre took an interest in **regionalism**. The Centre was involved in the creation of the **College of Europe**, the **European Organization for Nuclear Research** and the **European Cultural Foundation**. The Centre was wound up in 2001.

European Cultural Foundation (ECF)

Established in Geneva in 1954 as an offshoot of the **European Cultural Centre**, the ECF moved to Amsterdam in 1957. Active in 23 countries, the ECF – with the aid of many specialized bodies – works through schools, colleges, universities, the media and cultural organizations to promote cross-frontier cooperation in the social, cultural, educational and environmental fields, linked to European integration. The ECF was the model for a similar European Foundation proposed in the 1976 **Tindemans Report** (see also

European Union), but no progress was made with this proposal because of objections from the Dutch government.

European Currency Unit (ECU)

The original European Unit of Account (EUA) was introduced simply as a means of facilitating the European Communities' bookkeeping and as such was used in connection with the **Budget**. When the **European Monetary System** (EMS) was established in 1979, the ECU was brought into service and in 1981 it replaced the EUA.

Like its predecessor, the ECU was a 'basket' of national currencies, each currency's weighting within the basket being fixed as a percentage in line with each country's share of the Union's gross national product (GNP) and of internal trade. The composition of the ECU was frozen on 1 November 1993 in connection with the beginning of stage 2 of **Economic and Monetary Union** (EMU). Currency movements against the dollar were reflected in the central rate of the ECU, which in turn could be used to give cross-rates for or between the national currencies of the member states.

The ECU established itself in international money markets as a stable alternative to the dollar, the Deutsche Mark and the pound sterling. It was also used as a denomination for bank deposits and travellers' cheques, and for bookkeeping in respect of transactions involving several currencies; for example, European railways used the ECU when each company's share of revenue from the sale of international tickets was being calculated. The ECU was backed by the **European Monetary Institute** (EMI; the successor to the **European Monetary Cooperation Fund**), to which countries participating in the EMS made available 20 per cent of their gold and dollar reserves. With the exception of some 5 and 50 ECU gold and silver coins minted in Belgium in 1987 to commemorate the thirtieth anniversary of the **Treaty of Rome**, the ECU was not legal tender in any part of the Union.

The proposal for a 'hard ECU' as a common European currency was put forward by the British government in 1990 in the course of the **Intergovernmental Conference** (IGC) on EMU. The idea was that the ECU should circulate alongside national currencies and would float against them in the EMS. It would be 'hard' in the sense that it could not be devalued. If it found sufficient support it might evolve over time into a single currency. The idea was not adopted.

The **Maastricht Treaty** gave the ECU a central role in the third and final stage of the process leading to EMU. Articles 3(a).2, 109(g), and 109(l) (now 4.2, 118 and 123) EEC required the 'irrevocable fixing' of exchange rates between national currencies and the ECU, which was specified as the single currency. At this point the ECU would have ceased to be a basket currency and would have become a currency in its own right, with the **European Central Bank**

(ECB) as the issuing authority. In spite of the Treaty references to the ECU as the single currency, the Madrid meeting of the European Council in December 1995 agreed to rename the single currency the **euro**. From 1 January 1999 the euro replaced the ECU on a 1:1 basis in all areas of the Union's finances.

By coincidence, the *écu* was a medieval French coin, so called because it bore a shield on one face (the Portuguese escudo is of the same origin).

European Defence Community

With the outbreak of the Korean War in 1950 British and American demands for German rearmament became more insistent. In August 1950 **Winston Churchill** put forward a resolution in the Consultative Assembly of the **Council of Europe** that called for the creation of a **European Army** under the authority of a European defence minister and subject to democratic control by the Assembly. The resolution was passed by 89 votes to 5 with 29 abstentions. In this European Army, Churchill said in his speech, 'we would all play an honourable and active part'.

On 24 October 1950 the French government put forward a proposal to create among **the Six** a European Defence Community (EDC) within which a re-armed West Germany could be contained. The proposal, known as the **Pleven Plan**, was for a European Army under a single commander to which member states would second units. The institutional structure was to be the same as that for the **European Coal and Steel Community**: a Council of national ministers, a nine-member Commission, a parliamentary assembly and a Court of Justice. Of the 40 divisions, 14 would be French, 12 German, 11 Italian and 3 from the **Benelux** countries, and mixed so that no corps would consist of troops solely of one nationality. There was to be one uniform and one flag, and senior officers would be drawn from all nationalities and be responsible to the institutions of the EDC. The EDC would have its own budget, and make provision both for common procurement and joint training. The EDC Treaty was signed in Paris on 27 May 1952.

At the suggestion of **Alcide de Gasperi**, the Italian Prime Minister, the Treaty also contained provisions in Article 38 for a common external policy and a customs union, but it was left to the newly established ECSC parliamentary assembly (the forerunner of the **European Parliament**) in collaboration with the Consultative Assembly of the Council of Europe to fill in the details. This they did in the form of an ambitious complementary draft Treaty for a **European Political Community** on the grounds that a federal army would need to be made responsible to federal institutions.

In the Benelux countries, West Germany and Italy ratification of the EDC Treaty was accomplished without any serious difficulties. However, in France fear of German domination and loss of national sovereignty gave rise to many misgivings among parties of the extreme left and the nationalist right (notably the supporters of **Charles de Gaulle**), and the French government put forward a number of additional **protocols** to the draft Treaty to safeguard French interests. These were discussed inconclusively at a conference in Rome in February 1953. Both the United Kingdom and the United States were asked to support the EDC, but this – for different reasons – they declined to do. As Theodore H. White wrote, 'The United States Army wanted German troops, flesh and blood soldiers, quickly, not a long philosophical discussion about the creation of a new super-state' (*Fire in the Ashes*, 1954).

At a conference in Brussels in August 1954 a final attempt was made to salvage the EDC on the basis of a revised Treaty, but this failed to resolve the difficulties. On 30 August 1954 the French National Assembly voted by 319 votes to 264, with 43 abstentions, to postpone discussion of the Treaty *sine die*, thus effectively killing it. Its victorious opponents sang 'The Marseillaise'.

The failure of the EDC was the first serious setback for the proponents of European unification, but less than a year later, in June 1955, the Six met at the **Messina Conference** to explore whether progress could be made instead on the economic front (see **Beyen Plan**). And a month after the National Assembly's vote, the British government convened a meeting in London of representatives of the six EDC signatory states, the United Kingdom, the United States and Canada to discuss defence cooperation, a meeting that led to the establishment of the **Western European Union**.

European Democrat Union (EDU)

The EDU was founded in Schloss Klessheim near Salzburg in 1978 as an association of Conservative and Christian Democratic political parties, partly in response to the closer links that Socialist parties were then forming in the years immediately preceding the first **European elections** in 1979 (see **transnational political parties**). Replacing an informal system of annual interparty meetings, the EDU aimed to promote the exchange of ideas and the pooling of experience among like-minded parties with the aid of standing committees and working groups. Then, as now, its membership was drawn from parties inside and outside the European Community. The EDU was for Scandinavian parties in particular an important means of keeping in touch with Community developments and for many years was virtually the only forum in which Conservatives and French Gaullists cooperated with Christian Democrats. The EDU now has 43 members or permanent observers, including many from central and eastern Europe. For many years, it was chaired by the Austrian People's Party. In the 1980s the EDU became a component part of a wider organization along the same lines, the International Democrat Union, which includes among others the

Republican Party in the United States and centre-right parties in Australia and Japan. At its 20th anniversary meeting in April 1998, the EDU resolved 'to unite the Christian Democrat, Conservative and like-minded centrist parties, and to merge the existing organizations in one new European party organization' (i.e. the European People's Party (EPP): see **transnational political parties**). The EPP and the EDU adopted a joint working programme in Berlin in 2001 and the process of unification was virtually complete by the end of 2002.

European Development Fund (EDF)

The EDF is the means whereby financial aid is granted to 78 developing countries under the **Cotonou Agreement**. It is governed by a **protocol** annexed to the Agreement: the current EDF (2001–5), the ninth in the series since the **Lomé Convention** was first signed in 1975, makes available €13.5 billion and a further €1.7 billion from the **European Investment Bank** (EIB).

The EDF is not part of the **Budget** of the EU, being financed by direct contributions from member states. This has given rise to disagreement with the **European Parliament** and an action in the **Court of Justice** (which the Parliament lost: Case C316/91). There is a very detailed description of the sixth, seventh and eighth EDFs in the annual report of the **Court of Auditors** for 2000.

European Economic Area (EEA)

Established by a treaty signed in Oporto on 2 May 1992, the EEA is a **free trade area** of 18 countries and about 380 million people. It is responsible for about 40 per cent of world trade. The member states are the 15 member states of the **European Union** and Iceland, Liechtenstein and Norway. Switzerland signed the EEA Treaty but rejected it by referendum in December 1992 (a week later Liechtenstein accepted the Treaty by referendum; this decision was reaffirmed in April 1995). A **protocol** making the necessary adjustments to the Treaty was signed on 17 March 1993 and the Treaty came into effect on 1 January 1994.

The EEA Treaty is an **Association Agreement** under Article 310 of the **Treaty of Rome**. It consists of 129 Articles of general provisions, 50 protocols covering specific issues, and 22 annexes listing those portions of the *acquis communautaire* that under the Treaty apply throughout the EEA. With very few exceptions, the EEA Treaty takes precedence over other bilateral or multilateral agreements to which the signatory states are party. Article 121 EEA specifies that the Treaty should not affect other regional cooperation arrangements such as the **Nordic Council**, the customs union between Switzerland and Liechtenstein, and the cross-border agreements between Austria and Italy.

The EEA Treaty owed its origin to the mutual desire on the part of the member states of the **European Free Trade Association** (EFTA) and the

Community to have closer links. Although each of the EFTA states had a bilateral free trade agreement with the Community (the last barriers to trade in industrial goods were removed on 1 January 1984), all parties agreed in the 1984 Luxembourg Declaration to extend their cooperation still further (the expression *espace économique européen* was used for the first time in this Declaration). This was given greater urgency by the Community's decision to undertake the **Single Market** programme. The first steps were to simplify the formalities governing trade, and in 1986 negotiations began to extend the use of the Single Administrative Document to the EFTA states (see **free movement of goods**). The accession of Spain and Portugal to the Community in the same year was used as a pretext to adjust and extend the free trade agreements into new areas, such as scientific and technological cooperation. In 1987 the Community laid down the so-called 'Interlaken Principles', which made it clear that the Single Market programme enjoyed absolute priority and that the EFTA states could not expect indefinitely to enjoy the economic benefits of free trade with the Community yet choose to stay outside.

In a speech to the **European Parliament** on 17 January 1989 **Jacques Delors**, the President of the **European Commission**, expressed the Community's willingness to move towards 'a new, more structured partnership with common decision-making and administrative institutions'. Eighteen months later (20 June 1990) negotiations began for the EEA Treaty.

The institutions of the EEA are as follows:

- The EEA Council meets at least twice a year at ministerial level. It is composed of representatives of the governments of the signatory states and of the Commission (Articles 89 to 91 EEA).
- The EEA Joint Committee meets at least once a month. It is composed of senior officials of the signatory states and takes decisions by consensus, the EFTA states speaking with one voice (Articles 92 to 94 EEA). The EEA Joint Parliamentary Committee, composed of Members of the European Parliament (MEPs) and parliamentarians from the EFTA states, is required to hold at least two general sessions a year. It has no specific decision-making role but instead may adopt non-binding reports or Resolutions on matters covered by the EEA Treaty (Article 95 EEA).
- The EEA Consultative Committee plays a similar role. It is composed of members of the **Economic and Social Committee** and the EFTA Consultative Committee (Article 96 EEA).

Monitoring the EEA Treaty is carried out by the Commission in the Union and by the EFTA Surveillance Authority in the EFTA states. An EFTA Court is established to work in cooperation with the **Court of Justice** (the original proposal, for a common EEA Court, was ruled unlawful in an **Opinion** of 14 December 1991 by the Court of Justice as inconsistent with the

Court's prerogatives as laid down in the EEC Treaty and with the autonomy of the Community's legal order).

The institutions of the EEA have no sovereign authority. The EEA Treaty requires them to work in parallel with the Union institutions on the basis of consultations and the exchange of information. Legal acts of the Union on matters covered by the EEA Treaty are followed up in an annex to the Treaty agreed in the Joint Committee, with a view to ensuring both legal homogeneity and uniformity of application. Article 107 EEA allows national courts and tribunals in EFTA states to seek rulings in the Court of Justice on the interpretation of EEA rules; such rulings are binding.

The fundamental purpose of the Treaty is to allow the free movement of goods, persons, services and capital throughout the EEA. **Free movement of goods** (Articles 8 to 27 and 53 to 65 EEA) applies to nearly all industrial goods and some agricultural products. Approximately 800 items of Union legislation on the free movement of goods have been integrated into the Treaty. **Free movement of persons** (Articles 28 to 35 EEA) covers all employed and self-employed persons, with the exception of those in the public service. The entire *acquis communautaire* in this field is integrated into the Treaty. Similarly, **freedom to provide services** (Articles 36 to 39 EEA) is extended throughout the EEA, as are (with only minor, mostly temporary, exceptions) **capital movements** (Articles 40 to 45 EEA).

By way of complement to the four freedoms the EFTA states are enabled under the EEA Treaty to take part in Union **research** programmes. Cooperation in the field of **environment policy** and consumer protection is strengthened. In a Declaration annexed to the Treaty the EFTA states express their support for the 1989 **Social Charter**. The EFTA states also undertake to contribute to social and economic **cohesion**; this is of direct benefit to the Union's poorer regions. The financial aid is administered by the **European Investment Bank** (EIB). State monopolies of a commercial character are to be adjusted or progressively eliminated, with some exceptions for those maintained by the Nordic countries on the sale of alcohol. Union rules on competition and state aids are the model for similar rules applying throughout the EEA.

The EEA Treaty was the most ambitious and comprehensive treaty ever concluded by the Twelve. It remains open to new members (countries acceding to the Union have to join the EEA since the Treaty is part of the *acquis communautaire*; countries joining EFTA may choose whether or not to join the EEA). The major areas of Union policy remaining outside the EEA are relations with third countries (both trading relations and development policy), fiscal policy, the **European Monetary System** (EMS) and **Economic and Monetary Union** (EMU), the **Common Agricultural Policy** (CAP), and the **Common Fisheries Policy** (CFP). Nor does the EEA Treaty cover the **Justice** and Home Affairs (JHA) and **Common Foreign and Security Policy** (CFSP) '**pillars**' of the **Maastricht Treaty**. The future of the EEA is uncertain, since three of the original six EFTA signatories (Austria, Finland and Sweden) have joined the European Union, and Switzerland shows no sign of reversing its referendum decision.

For a commentary on the EEA Treaty by three lawyers from the EFTA Surveillance Authority, see Thérèse Blanchet, Risto Piipponen and Maria Clément, *The Agreement on the EEA* (Oxford, 1994).

European Economic Community (EEC)

The EEC was established by **the Six** under the 1957 **Treaty of Rome**. Since the entry into force of the **Maastricht Treaty** in November 1993 it has been officially renamed the European Community (see **European Communities**). The main institutions of the EEC are described under **Council of Ministers, Court of Justice, European Commission** and **European Parliament**; see also especially **EU law, customs union** and **Single Market**. For the origins of the EEC, see **Beyen Plan, Messina Conference**, and **Spaak Committee**.

European Economic Interest Grouping (EEIG)

Substantial differences between member states in the field of company law are thought to inhibit cross-frontier economic activity. The **freedom of establishment** provisions of the **Treaty of Rome** provide for certain basic features of company law to be harmonized under Article 44.2 (g). In the absence of any progress with the long-projected **European Company Statute** a further measure was taken in 1985 under **Article 308** (formerly 235) to allow small and medium-sized companies (SMEs) to cooperate within the framework of an EEIG that would be recognized throughout the member states.

European Economic Space

The original translation into English of *espace économique européen*, used for the first time in 1984, and since October 1990 officially known in English as the **European Economic Area** (EEA).

European elections

Elections to the **European Parliament**, known as European elections, are held every five years under Article 190 of the **Treaty of Rome**. The first European elections took place in 1979; before that date the Parliament was composed of Members (MEPs) appointed by and from **national parliaments**. The Treaty originally envisaged that elections would be held on the basis of a **uniform electoral procedure**, but the **Treaty of Amsterdam** modified this to allow elections 'in accordance with principles common to all Member States'. The

Table 1 Electoral systems used in European elections (1999)

Proportional representation, national lists

with preferential voting:

- Austria (4% threshold)
- Denmark
- Finland
- Luxembourg
- The Netherlands
- Sweden (4% threshold)

closed list:

- France (5% threshold)
- Germany[1] (5% threshold)
- Greece (3% threshold)
- Portugal
- Spain

Proportional representation, regional lists

with preferential voting:

- Belgium (4 regions)
- Italy (5 regions)

closed list:

- Great Britain (11 regions)

Multi-member constituencies, single transferable vote

- Ireland (4 constituencies)
- Northern Ireland (1 constituency)

[1] Parties may choose to present lists on a national or a *Länder* basis, but there is only one national constituency.

Parliament adopted a set of such principles (the Anastassopoulos report) in July 1998.

Because of different national traditions on voting, European elections take place over an agreed four-day period around the second weekend in June, allowing some member states to vote on a Thursday (as in the United Kingdom) and others on a Sunday. No results are announced until all polling stations are closed.

Figure 1 shows the results of the five European elections held to date, in terms of the relative strengths of the **political groups** in the European Parliament, together with the overall turnout. More detailed country-by-country results may be found in a number of sources. Table 2 shows the results of the June 1999 European elections by country and political group affiliation. Table 3 shows the UK results for each of the five European elections by seats won and percentage share of the vote. From these tables, it may be seen that overall turnout is slowly declining. The UK turnout has been consistently well below the average, although it should be noted that voting is notionally compulsory in Belgium, Greece and Luxembourg, and is regarded as a 'civic duty' in Italy. The turnout figures are also affected by the fact that national or local elections are sometimes held at the same time as European elections, making overall comparisons more difficult. The timing of the next enlargement (May 2004; see **Treaty of Accession**) allows newly acceding states to take part in the June 2004 European elections.

European elections are often described as 'second order' elections, in the

Figure 1   Percentage of seats held by main political groups, 1979–99

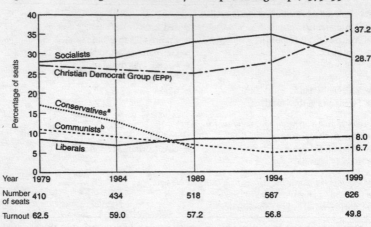

Year	1979	1984	1989	1994	1999
Number of seats	410	434	518	567	626
Turnout	62.5	59.0	57.2	56.8	49.8

[a] In May 1992 the British and Danish Conservatives joined the EPP as allied members.
[b] After the 1989 European elections, the Communists formed two separate groups, one pro-Europe (28 MEPs) and one anti (14 MEPs). Most of the pro-Europeans joined the Socialist Group in January 1993, the remainder forming the core of the United European Left (see Table 2).

sense that voter interest and voter behaviour are closer to those observed in local elections and by-elections than in general elections. Broadly speaking, parties that do well in a national contest may expect to do well in European elections held either at the same time or a few months afterwards. This phenomenon helped the British Conservatives in 1979 and the Forza Italia Party in 1994. Governing parties may expect to do badly if European elections fall within the period of mid-term unpopularity. Before 1999 the swings that resulted from this were particularly marked in the United Kingdom because of the simple majority voting system in single-member constituencies.

It cannot be said that European elections are decided on European issues. Most parties make only half-hearted attempts to focus the electorate's attention on such issues, and then (unsurprisingly) only if the polls indicate that this might be advantageous to them. Nor do they get much help from the media, most of which prefer the much more familiar parameters of domestic political debate, such as party splits, clashes of personality and governmental discomfiture. Still less do the campaigns focus upon the European Parliament itself. The hard fact remains that many of the issues in which the average elector is interested – for example, housing, local transport, education, law and order – are never or only very indirectly dealt with in the Parliament, the

Table 2   Composition of the European Parliament in July 1999 by member state and political group

Member state	Political group								Total	Turnout
	EPP	PES	ELDR	Green	UEL	EN	EDD	IND		
Austria	7	7		2				5	21	49.4
Belgium	6	5	5	7				2	25	91.0
Denmark	1	3	6		1	1	4		16	50.4
Finland	5	3	5	2	1				16	30.1
France	21	22		9	11	13	6	5	87	46.8
Germany	53	33		7	6				99	45.2
Greece	9	9			7				25	75.3
Ireland	5	1	1	2		6			15	50.2
Italy	34	17	7	2	6	9		12	87	70.8
Luxembourg	2	2	1	1					6	87.3
The Netherlands	9	6	8	4	1		3		31	30.0
Portugal	9	12			2	2			25	40.0
Spain	28	24	3	4	4			1	64	63.0
Sweden	7	6	4	2	3				22	38.8
United Kingdom	37	30	10	6			3	1	87	24.0
Total	**233**	**180**	**50**	**48**	**42**	**31**	**16**	**26**	**626**	**49.8**

Key: EPP = European People's Party (Christian Democrats, Conservatives, Gaullists, Forza Italia); PES = Socialists; ELDR = Liberals; Green = Greens and Regionalists; UEL = United European Left/Nordic Green Left (including Communists); EN = Europe of Nations (French and Italian nationalists, Fianna Fail); EDD = Europe of Democracies and Diversities (anti-EU Danes, UK Independence Party, French defenders of rural traditions); IND = Independents.

agenda of which broadly reflects the way in which the Treaties are framed. Summaries of the campaigns may be found in the *Times Guides* and in Martin Westlake, *A Modern Guide to the European Parliament* (1994).

The European elections are the world's first and only international elections. In 1999 they involved an electorate of about 290 million people (of whom about 144 million voted), an electorate larger than any except that of India. However, as the results indicate, the campaign was, as before, made up largely of 15 national campaigns with local variants in particular regions. Nor do the results provide much hard evidence of Europe-wide political trends, since losses for one party in one country are often compensated for by gains for a related party in another. The role of **transnational political parties** remains extremely limited and the level of media interest low. In spite of determined efforts in some member states, the number of voters who chose to use their new right to vote in their country of residence within the Union rather than in their country of origin (see **citizenship**) was very small. The 1999 European elections were a disappointment to those who believed that the prominent role played by the Parliament in forcing the resignation of the **European Commission** in March 1999 would raise the level of voter interest and mark a stage in the

Table 3   Results of the European elections in the United Kingdom[a] by seats held and percentage of vote in Great Britain[b]

Party	Seats % of vote				
	1979	1984	1989	1994	1999
Conservatives	60[c]/50.6	45/40.8	32/34.7	18/27.6	36/35.8
Labour	17/33	32/36.5	45/40.1	62/44	29/28
Liberal Democrats/Alliance	–/13.1	–/19.5[d]	–/6.7[e]	2/16.6	10/12.7
Scottish Nationalist Party	1/1.9	1/1.7	1/2.7	2/3.2	2/2.7
Plaid Cymru	–/0.6	–/0.8	–/0.8	–/1	2/1.8
Other	–/0.8	–/0.7	–/15.2[f]	–/7.6[g]	5/19[h]
Total number of seats	**78**	**78**	**78**	**84**	**84**

[a] In the three-seat multi-member constituency of Northern Ireland each of the three main parties (Democratic Unionist Party, Ulster Unionist Party, Social Democratic and Labour Party) secured one seat in each of the five elections.

[b] Turnout (UK) was 32.3% in 1979, rose very slightly to 32.6% in 1984, 36.3% in 1989, and 3634% in 1994, then fell to 24% in 1999.

[c] Including 1 in a September 1979 by-election.

[d] Alliance composed of Liberal Democrats and SDP.

[e] 6.2% for Liberal Democrats (SLD), 0.5% for SDP.

[f] Of which 14.9% for the Greens.

[g] Of which 3.2% for the Greens.

development of transnational democracy. There is a comprehensive survey of European elections in Cees van der Eijk, Mark Franklin and Michael Marsh, 'What voters teach us about Europe-wide elections: what Europe-wide elections teach us about voters', *Electoral Studies*, Vol. 15, no. 2, May 1996 (reprinted in Pippa Norris, ed., *Elections and Voting Behaviour*, Aldershot, 1998).

European Elections Act

The European Elections Act, adopted by the **Council of Ministers** in September 1976, is the basis on which **European elections** were first held in 1979. The Act, the result of a decision taken at a meeting of the **European Council** in Paris in December 1974, allowed each member state (within certain broad parameters) to choose its own electoral system for European elections, pending the introduction of a **uniform electoral procedure**, and laid down the number of seats per member state. For further details, see **European Parliament**.

European Energy Charter

Proposed by Dutch Prime Minister Ruud Lubbers in 1990, the European Energy Charter was agreed in principle by 48 signatory states in December 1991 at a conference in The Hague. The Charter is intended to open up cross-frontier competition in the energy market, particularly between eastern and western Europe, by the creation of a legal framework and guidelines for market access. Such competition will help to stimulate economic recovery in the countries once part of the Soviet bloc. The Charter was followed by a binding European Energy Charter Treaty, signed in December 1994 by all European countries, including the republics of the former Soviet Union. The Treaty, which recognizes the rights of signatory states over their energy resources, entered into force in April 1998.

European Environment Agency (EEA)

Established on the basis of Regulation 1210/90 of 7 May 1990 (*Official Journal*, L120, 11 May 1990), the EEA is an **agency** of the European Union responsible for the collection and dissemination of data on the state of the environment. Such data, gathered by means of a 'European environment information and observation network', is an essential adjunct to the Union's **environment policy**, not least in respect of the fair and equal Union-wide enforcement of environmental legislation. The Agency did not come into operation for several years, because agreement could not be reached on where it should be located. By a **European Council** Decision of 29 October 1993 the Agency is sited in Copenhagen (see **seat of the institutions**). Iceland, Liechtenstein, and Norway are also members of the Agency.

European flag

The European flag – a circle of 12 five-pointed gold stars on a dark blue background – was devised originally by the **Council of Europe** for its own use. Adopted by the Parliamentary Assembly in October 1955 and by the Committee of Ministers two months later, the flag was adopted by the **European Commission** in 1985 for general use by the Community institutions.

Correctly described in heraldic terminology as 'on a field azure, a circle of twelve mullets or, their points not touching', the European flag triumphed over two alternative designs. The first was the very colourful flag of Count Richard Coudenhove-Kalergi's **Pan-Europa**, a golden disc representing the sun of Apollo on a blue background with a red cross superimposed, emblematic of Europe's Graeco-Christian heritage. The second was the flag of the **European Movement**, a large green E on a white background. A variant of this flag was used by the European Commission until 1985.

The present design was largely the work of Paul Levy, the Council of Europe's Director of Information in the early 1950s. The Turks, then as now members of the Council of Europe, objected on principle to any design incorporating a cross, but did not realize that a circle of 12 gold stars is also a Christian symbol: the Virgin Mary's halo (Revelation 12:1). The fact of there having been 12 stars and 12 member states of the European Community in 1985 (accession treaties having been concluded with Spain and Portugal) was coincidental; it was never proposed to follow the example of the Stars and Stripes in the United States and add a star for each new accession.

In line with the recommendations of the Adonnino Committee on a **People's Europe** the European flag is now very widely used. It may be seen on car numberplates, umbrellas and the vehicles of European Union observers and aid workers, as well as on Commission publications. Fliers of the flag and users of the symbol should note that the gold stars must have their single points uppermost.

European Food Safety Authority (EFSA)

First proposed by the **European Commission** in November 2000 on the basis of a December 1999 report by three independent experts, agreement on the EFSA (but not on its final location) was reached in the **Council of Ministers** in January 2002 (Regulation 178/02, *Official Journal*, L31, 1 February 2002). The role of the EFSA is to give independent scientific advice on all aspects of **food safety**, to maintain contact with the relevant national and international authorities, to operate an early warning system of developments likely to compromise food safety, and to provide information to the general public. The same Regulation sets out the general principles and requirements of food safety law.

Although in part modelled on the Food and Drug Administration (FDA) in the United States, the EFSA does not have the same wide-ranging legal powers as the FDA nor the same level of resources (the FDA has a staff of over 9,000 people and can call upon the services of 2,000 scientists). However, by acting as a focus for public concerns, the EFSA is intended to increase the public's confidence in the Union's ability to handle public health issues.

European Foundation for the Improvement of Living and Working Conditions

The Foundation, a European Union **agency**, was set up under Regulation 1365/75 of 26 May 1975 (*Official Journal*, L139, 30 May 1975). Located in Dublin, its task is to gather and disseminate information on living and working conditions, promote and coordinate research, and to furnish technical support to the institutions of the European Union in these areas.

European Free Trade Association (EFTA)

EFTA was established by the Stockholm Convention of 1960 in order, in the words of Article 2, 'to promote ... a sustained expansion of economic activity, full employment, increased productivity and the rational use of resources, financial stability and continuous improvement of living standards' underpinned by 'fair competition' and with a view to contributing to 'the harmonious development and expansion of world trade' (the phrase used in the **General Agreement on Tariffs and Trade** (GATT)). The original signatory states were Austria, Denmark, Norway, Portugal, Sweden, Switzerland and the United Kingdom (known as the Seven, to distinguish them from **the Six**: see below). Iceland acceded to the Convention in March 1970 and Finland in January 1986, having been an Associate member since 1961. Denmark and the United Kingdom withdrew from the Convention on joining the **European Economic Community** in January 1973, as did Portugal in January 1986. Liechtenstein became a member in 1991. Austria, Finland and Sweden left EFTA on joining the European Union in January 1995, leaving only Iceland, Norway, Switzerland and Liechtenstein as EFTA states. EFTA was initiated as a reaction to the setting up of the European Economic Community under the **Treaty of Rome** among the Six in 1957 (see **Maudling Committee**). It had not proved possible to establish a **free trade area** among all members of the Organization for European Economic Cooperation (see **Organization for Economic Cooperation and Development**) to which both the Six and the Seven belonged, mainly because the Six were anxious to move towards a more ambitious form of association with political goals and supranational institutions. The Six were intent in the first instance upon forming a customs union, and, fearing that this would restrict access to the markets of these countries, the Seven decided to set up a looser free trade area (for industrial products only) of an essentially intergovernmental character (see **intergovernmentalism**). Relations between EFTA and the European Union are described under **European Economic Area** (EEA).

The Stockholm Convention formally established only one institution, the EFTA Council. The Council is composed of one representative of each member state and meets twice a month at official level and twice a year at ministerial level. Decisions, each member state having one vote, are normally reached by consensus, but limited scope exists for majority - voting too. This structure is reflected in the specialist Standing Committees composed of officials, which advise the Council. Parliamentarians from EFTA states meet regularly with Members of the **European Parliament** (MEPs). EFTA's headquarters in Geneva deals mainly with relations with non-member states, the EFTA secretariat in Brussels covers EEA affairs, and the Luxembourg office coordinates statistical cooperation with **Eurostat**.

European governance

The White Paper on European governance (COM(2001)428), launched by **Romano Prodi**, the President of the **European Commission**, on 25 July 2001, was drawn up in response to the perception that 'people are losing confidence in a poorly understood and complex system … The Union is often seen as remote and at the same time too intrusive'. The White Paper is a contribution to the re-examination of the European Union's working methods being undertaken in the light of **enlargement**, the **Intergovernmental Conference** due to be convened in 2004, and the political pressure for reform prompted by the enforced resignation of the Commission in 1999.

The notion of 'governance' is defined as embracing 'rules, processes and behaviour that affect the way in which powers are exercised at European level, particularly as regards openness, participation, accountability, effectiveness and coherence': in other words, 'governance' is concerned more with the style than with the substance of European decision-making. The analysis and recommendations in the White Paper are set out under four main headings, the first of which is 'Better involvement and more openness'. The Commission proposes to make more use of advice from regional and local bodies (with the assistance of member states and the **Committee of the Regions**) and from the trade unions, non-governmental organizations, and professional bodies which make up 'civil society'. In parallel with this aim is the need to step up efforts to keep the public informed about European Union activities with the help of the media, databases such as EUR-Lex, and the Commission's Europa website (see also **open method of coordination, transparency,**).

The second heading is 'Better policies, regulation and delivery'. Here the first essential is more rigorous examination of any call for legislative action, and in particular the application of the principles of **subsidiarity** and **proportionality**. The White Paper proposes that fuller, more discriminating use should be made of the wide range of **legal instruments** available to the Union and that the possibility of 'co-regulation' should be explored ('co-regulation combines binding legislation and regulatory action with actions taken by the actors most concerned' (see **soft law**). The Commission intends to draw up guidelines on the use of expert advice. Monitoring compliance will to a greater extent be the responsibility of regulatory **agencies**, and compliance will be made easier by continuing efforts towards the **simplification** of European Union law.

The third heading, 'Global governance', puts the White Paper's proposals into a broader international context. The Commission intends to examine more systematically the impact of European Union policies, current or proposed, on non-member countries and to review all aspects of the Union's external representation with a view to securing greater coherence. The final heading, 'Refocused institutions', deals with what individual institutions can do to contribute to the achievement of the White Paper's objectives.

In conformity with those objectives the White Paper was drawn up as a document for discussion. The Commission will appraise and reflect upon the comments it receives and publish its findings by the end of 2002. As the White Paper says, 'the linear model of dispensing policies from above must be replaced by a virtuous circle, based on feedback, networks and involvement from policy creation to implementation at all levels ... It is time to recognize that the Union has moved from a diplomatic to a democratic process'.

European identity

In December 1973 at the Copenhagen **summit** the member states of the European Community adopted a '**Declaration** on the European identity'. The Declaration was in three sections: the first dealt with 'the unity of the nine Member States of the Community' and concluded with the reaffirmation of their intention to transform 'the whole complex of their relations into a **European Union** before the end of the present decade'. This section reviewed progress by the Nine (see **the Six**) towards the establishment of a common market, common institutions and **European Political Cooperation** (then in its infancy), all founded upon 'the cherished values of their legal, political and moral order ... [and] the rich variety of their national cultures'. The Nine emphasized that 'the construction of a united Europe ... is open to other

European nations who share the same ideals and objectives'. The second section dealt with 'the European identity in relation to the world'. It set out basic guidelines for 'a common policy in relation to third countries', and in its review of the Community's external relations emphasized that 'European unification is not directed against anyone, nor is it inspired by a desire for power'. The very brief concluding section underlined 'the dynamic nature of the construction of a United Europe' and reiterated the commitment to European union.

Coming so soon after the first **enlargement** of the Community (which had caused Denmark and the United Kingdom to leave the **European Free Trade Association** (EFTA) and Norway to hold a referendum, which rejected Community membership), the Declaration was an important affirmation of the Community's internal solidarity and openness to the outside world. Both in language and in content it foreshadowed some of the themes and policies that were to preoccupy the Community throughout the 1970s and 1980s, such as 'speaking with one voice' in foreign affairs, development policy and detente. However, subsequent events showed the timetable for European union to be over-optimistic and confidence in the Nine's solidarity exaggerated: within a year of the Declaration the Community's coherence had been seriously damaged by the oil crisis and the British demand for a **renegotiation**.

The phrase 'European identity' reappeared in the ninth preamble of the **Treaty of Rome**, as amended by the **Maastricht Treaty**, in which the **Common Foreign and Security Policy** (CFSP) is said to 'reinforce the European identity'. 'To assert its identity on the international scene' is one of the objectives of the European Union under Article 2 TEU. Paradoxically perhaps, the **Treaty of Amsterdam** amends Article 6 TEU by enjoining the Union to 'respect the national identities of its Member States'.

European Initiative for Democracy and Human Rights (EIDHR)

The EIDHR, launched by the **European Parliament** in 1994, groups together those elements in the **Budget** of the European Union which give financial support to projects designed to help stabilize democracy in central and eastern Europe, ex-Yugoslavia, Albania, the Newly Independent States, Mongolia, the **ACP states** and several countries in Asia.

European Institute of Public Administration (EIPA)

Based in Maastricht in The Netherlands with antennae in Barcelona, Luxembourg and Milan, the Institute was founded in 1981 as a study centre for lawyers, academics and administrators concerned with European integration, especially those aspects with a direct bearing on the quality of management in the public service. The working languages are English and French. Representatives of the governments of the member states of the Union and of the **European Commission** make up the Board of Governors, but the Institute is not a European Union body (see also **College of Europe, European University Institute**). The EIPA has established links with Norway, Switzerland and the countries which have applied to join the Union.

European Investment Bank (EIB)

Set up under Articles 129 and 130 of the **Treaty of Rome** (now Articles 266 and 267), the EIB has as its main role the financing of capital investment in the member states and in certain non-member countries, especially those in central and eastern Europe, the Mediterranean and developing countries associated with the Union under the **Cotonou Agreement**. The Treaty requires the EIB to operate on a non-profit-making basis and 'to contribute ... to the balanced and steady development of the common market in the interest of the Community'. The EIB's capital, raised to €100 billion with effect from January 1999, is subscribed by member states, and the ministers of finance act as its Board of Governors. The headquarters of the EIB are in Luxembourg. Its management structure is set out in a statute annexed as a **protocol** to the Treaty of Rome. In February 2002 it was proposed that a Euro-Mediterranean Bank should be established as a subsidiary of the EIB.

Working in collaboration with the **structural funds**, the EIB offers loans at rates of interest that reflect market rates to public authorities or private enterprises. The sectors in which the EIB is active are transport, telecommunications, the environment, energy, industry, agriculture and services, with particular emphasis on cross-frontier projects. Loans do not normally exceed 50 per cent of total investment costs, except for projects covered by the **Edinburgh Growth Initiative**. The EIB has its own project appraisal staff. The EIB's lending is now over €30 billion (about £18.75 billion) a year. Further details may be found in the EIB's annual report.

European Investment Fund (EIF)

The **European Council** meeting in Edinburgh in December 1992 agreed on the establishment of an EIF, involving both the **European Investment Bank** (EIB) and privately owned banks in investments in **trans-European networks** and in the encouragement of small and medium-sized enterprises (SMEs). The EIF was set up under Article 30 of the EIB's statute in March 1994: more than 50 banks in the then 12 member states agreed to become founder members of the EIF.

European Judicial Network

The European Judicial Network was set up in June 1998 as a **joint action** under Article K3 (now Article 34) of the **Maastricht Treaty** (*Official Journal*, L191, 7 July 1998). It is a 'network of judicial contact points ... between the Member States'. These contact points are 'active intermediaries with the task of facilitating judicial cooperation ... particularly in action to combat forms of serious crime' (Article 4.1 of the Joint Action). The Network, which is serviced by the secretariat of the **Council of Ministers**, meets occasionally in Brussels.

European League for Economic Cooperation (ELEC)

Founded in March 1947 as the *Ligue Indépendante de Coopération Européenne*, ELEC adopted its present name a year later. In the words of one authority, it was set up as 'an élite group, more particularly of acknowledged economic experts ... to prepare the way for economic cooperation by international committee work' (Walter Lipgens, *A History of European Integration*, Vol. 1, 1982). Many of its most prominent members had been members of governments-in-exile in London during the Second World War. ELEC was organized on a national basis, with sections in the United Kingdom, France, Belgium and Luxembourg. It now has 19 national sections. Throughout its history ELEC – which still exists – has laid emphasis on voluntary cooperation as a means to integration, and has thus set itself apart from the common institutions that underpin the European Union.

European Monetary Cooperation Fund (EMCF)

The EMCF was set up in 1973 as part of the Community's first attempt to achieve **Economic and Monetary Union** (EMU; see **Werner Report**). By the mid-1970s it was clear that the attempt had failed, and the EMCF had fallen into disuse. However, it was revived when the ECU was introduced in 1979 as part of the **European Monetary System** (EMS). Participating member states agreed to deposit 20 per cent of their gold and dollar reserves with the EMCF, which issued ECUs in exchange. Interventions by central banks on the exchange markets as part of the **Exchange-Rate Mechanism** (ERM) were regulated by the EMCF, which was also able to offer short-term credits to help member states' balance of payments. At the beginning of stage 2 of EMU on 1 January 1994 the EMCF was wound up and its functions were taken over by the **European Monetary Institute** (EMI).

European Monetary Institute (EMI)

Under Article 109(f) (now 117) of the **Treaty of Rome**, as amended by the **Maastricht Treaty**, the EMI was set up in Frankfurt at the beginning of stage

2 of **Economic and Monetary Union** (EMU) on 1 January 1994. The EMI was intended to be the precursor of the **European Central Bank** (ECB), the central institutional feature of stage 3 which came into operation on 1 June 1998. The Governing Council was made up of the **central bank governors**.

The EMI's role (Article 117.2) was to strengthen both cooperation between central banks and the coordination of the monetary policies of member states, to 'monitor the functioning of the **European Monetary System**' (EMS), take over the tasks of the **European Monetary Cooperation Fund**, and to 'facilitate the use of the ECU [now the **euro**] and oversee its development'. In addition, the EMI had a general responsibility to make preparations for stage 3 of EMU. The EMI, acting by a two-thirds majority of its Council, was empowered to draw up **Opinions** or Recommendations 'on the overall orientation of monetary policy and exchange-rate policy' and on 'policies which might affect the internal or external monetary situation', in particular the functioning of the EMS. It could also make Recommendations to member states 'concerning the conduct of their monetary policy'. It had a general right of consultation with respect to legislation in its areas of competence. The statute of the EMI was annexed as a **protocol** to the Treaty of Rome.

European Monetary System (EMS)

The EMS, which came into operation in March 1979, was intended to create 'a zone of monetary stability in Europe' and to strengthen cooperation between member states with respect to monetary policy. Its central features were the **European Currency Unit** (ECU) and the **Exchange-Rate Mechanism** (ERM).

The EMS was launched by **Roy Jenkins** in his first year (1977) as President of the **European Commission**, after the failure of the first attempt to achieve **Economic and Monetary Union** (EMU; see **Werner Report**). With strong support from Chancellor Helmut Schmidt and President **Valéry Giscard d'Estaing**, the EMS was established in a Resolution adopted by the **European Council** in Brussels in December 1978. Described as 'a fundamental component of a more comprehensive strategy aimed at lasting growth with stability, a progressive return to full employment, the harmonization of living standards and the lessening of regional disparities', the EMS was accompanied by measures to help the economic development of less prosperous member states, including a new subsidized loan facility from the **European Investment Bank** (EIB). Technical and administrative improvements to the EMS were made by the **Ecofin Council** in 1987 (the 'Basle–Nyborg Agreements').

Although all member states participated in the EMS, they were not thereby required to join it. The pound sterling did not join the EMS until

October 1990 and left in September 1992. The Greek drachma did not join the EMS until March 1998, and the Swedish krona has never joined. Membership of the EMS entailed being part of the 'basket' of currencies that determined the value of the ECU and depositing 20 per cent of gold and dollar reserves with the **European Monetary Institute** (EMI).

The EMS was never explicitly and formally described as a step towards EMU but as a system with merits of its own. However, if EMU is successfully attained, there is little doubt that it will have been built to a substantial extent on the experience gained from the EMS.

European Monitoring Centre for Drugs and Drug Addiction (EMCDDA)

A European Union **agency** based in Lisbon, the EMCDDA was set up under Regulation 302/93 of 8 February 1993 (*Official Journal*, L36, 12 February 1993). It became operational in 1995. Its main task is to supply member states and European institutions with objective and comparable information on drugs and drug addiction throughout Europe. The EMCDDA publishes a bi-monthly newsletter, *Drug Net Europe*, an annual *Report on the state of the drugs problem in the European Union*, and other material.

European Monitoring Centre on Racism and Xenophobia.
See **racism and xenophobia**.

European Movement

Founded in 1948, the European Movement is the principal all-party pressure-group on behalf of European integration. It brought together a very large number of postwar groups in western Europe active in the European cause. Its first presidents-of-honour were the French Socialist leader Léon Blum, **Winston Churchill**, **Alcide de Gasperi** and **Paul-Henri Spaak**. The most notable event in the Movement's history was the **Congress of Europe** held in The Hague in 1948. The Movement played an influential part in the establishment of the **Council of Europe**, the **College of Europe**, the **European Cultural Centre**, and in early attempts to design a **European flag**. It has national branches in 32 countries, in some of which the movement is subsidized from public funds.

European Organization for Nuclear Research (CERN)

Normally known by its French acronym, CERN (*Conseil Européen pour la Recherche Nucléaire*) dates from a July 1953 convention drawn up under the auspices of the United Nations and is not formally associated with the European Union. CERN has 19 member countries and is dedicated to 'subnuclear research of a pure scientific and fundamental character'. Based in Geneva, it has experimental facilities for particle physics that are among the most advanced in the world of which the centrepiece is an underground circular tunnel, the Large Electron Positron (LEP) storage ring, 27 kilometers in circumference. A Large Hadron Collider (LHC), the most powerful in the world, is due for completion in 2005. CERN is supported financially by direct contributions from participating states with an annual budget of 875 million Swiss francs and a staff of about 2,900 people. In *The New Europeans* (1968) Anthony Sampson recalls asking a scientist at CERN how many people in Europe really understood the research being carried out there. The answer was 'about 12'; it is doubtful if the situation is very different today.

European Parliament

The European Parliament is composed of 626 Members (MEPs) elected in Union-wide **European elections** held every five years. It has its official 'seat' in Strasbourg (see **seat of the institutions**), but its committees meet in Brussels and its secretariat is divided between Brussels and Luxembourg. Now possessing legislative, supervisory and budgetary powers, the Parliament had only modest beginnings as the Common Assembly of the **European Coal and Steel Community** (ECSC) in 1952.

History, composition and procedure

One of the four main institutions of the European Union, the European Parliament is primarily responsible for exercising democratic scrutiny and control over the Union's decision-making process.

Article 7 of the 1951 Treaty of Paris establishing the **European Coal and Steel Community** (ECSC) made provision for four institutions: a High Authority (later the **European Commission**), a Special **Council of Ministers**, a **Court of Justice** and a Common Assembly. The Assembly, described in more detail in Articles 20 to 25 of the Treaty, was to 'consist of representatives of the peoples of the States brought together in the Community' and to exercise 'supervisory' powers. Its 78 MEPs were to be nominated by the **national parliaments** of the Six from among their own members in accordance with procedures laid down by each member state. The seats were allocated as follows:

Belgium	10
France	18
Italy	18
Luxembourg	4
The Netherlands	10
West Germany	18

However, even at this early date it was foreseen that the MEPs would one day be directly elected rather than nominated, and under Article 21.3 of the Treaty the Assembly was empowered to draw up 'proposals for elections by direct universal suffrage in accordance with a uniform procedure in all Member States' (see **uniform electoral procedure**).

In common with the other institutions of the ECSC the Assembly's headquarters and its secretariat (originally 37 people) were established in Luxembourg. Luxembourg could not, however, offer the necessary facilities for plenary sessions of the Assembly, which was required to work in the four official languages used among the Six: French, German, Italian and Dutch. In July 1952 the ECSC foreign ministers decided that plenary sessions of the Assembly should be held in Strasbourg. **Jean Monnet** relates in his *Memoirs* how the secretary-general of the **Council of Europe** offered to organize the first session of the Assembly, as part of an attempt, Monnet suspected, to 'take over our parliamentary and ministerial institutions'. In the event, the session was organized by the secretaries-general of the six national parliaments, and opened on 5 September 1952. To underline its separate identity, the Assembly met not on the premises of the Council of Europe but in the Strasbourg Chamber of Commerce. **Paul-Henri Spaak** was elected president by 38 votes to 30, the MEPs voting on party lines although **political groups** had not yet been formed.

The first important change in the status and composition of the Assembly was brought about by the entry into force on 1 January 1958 of the **Treaties** establishing the **European Economic Community** (EEC) and the **European Atomic Energy Community** (Euratom). These two Treaties also provided for each Community to have an Assembly, and – as was done with the Court of Justice and the **Economic and Social Committee** – the remit of the already existing ECSC Assembly was expanded to cover all three Communities under the 'Convention on certain institutions common to the European Communities' signed in Rome at the same time as the EEC and Euratom Treaties. The number of MEPs was almost doubled, to 142, but since no progress had been made with direct elections they were still nominated by their national parliaments:

Belgium	14
France	36
Italy	36
Luxembourg	6
The Netherlands	14
West Germany	36

The first plenary session of the enlarged Common Assembly was held in March 1958. **Robert Schuman** was elected its first president. The powers of the

Assembly as set out in the EEC and Euratom Treaties were broadly similar to those laid down in the ECSC Treaty, except that they were now described as 'advisory' as well as 'supervisory' (Article 137 EEC, since revised).

At the first session the new Assembly adopted the name 'European Parliamentary Assembly' in place of the old 'Common Assembly'. Four years later, in March 1962, it changed its name in French and Italian to 'European Parliament' ('Parliament' was already used in the Dutch and German versions of the Treaties). 'Assembly' continued to be used in English for official purposes (often with dismissive intent) until the change to 'Parliament' was formalized in Article 3 of the **Single European Act** (SEA) of 1986.

With the **accession** of Denmark, Ireland and the United Kingdom in 1973, the number of MEPs was further increased from 142 to 198 (Denmark 10, Ireland 10, the United Kingdom 36) and Danish and English were added as official languages. The British and Danish Conservative MEPs formed a new political group, bringing the total to six. In line with the practice followed in other member states, British MEPs were appointed to reflect the strength of the political parties in the lower House, although the MEPs could be drawn from either House of Parliament. This gave the Conservatives 18 of the United Kingdom's entitlement of 36 seats, the Liberals 1 and the Labour Party 17. However, the Labour Party's official policy was in favour of renegotiating the terms of British entry into the Community and, pending the results of such a **renegotiation**, against participating in the Community institutions. Accordingly, the Party did not take up the seats allocated to it. This allowed the Liberals to take an extra seat, and an independent peer took another. Not until after the **referendum of June 1975** did the Labour Party take up the 18 seats to which they were by then entitled, having secured a 42-seat majority over the Conservatives in the October 1974 General Election.

The shifts within the British delegation served to emphasize the extent to which the European Parliament at this stage in its development was merely an outgrowth of national politics in the member states. The practice of nominating MEPs from national parliaments meant that the composition of all delegations was constantly changing to take account of national election results. During the period of the 'nominated' European Parliament, 1952–79, about 750 MEPs served in the Parliament, some for a few months, others for many years. All were required, by Treaty, to exercise a '**dual mandate**': to be members both of their national parliaments and of the European Parliament. Meanwhile, the powers and responsibilities of the latter were steadily increasing, and it was becoming more and more evident that substance would soon have to be given to the Treaty commitment on direct elections.

In December 1974 the **European Council**, meeting in Paris, decided that direct elections to the European Parliament should be held 'as soon as possible'. The European Council called upon the Council of Ministers to take a decision on the matter in 1976, with a view to direct elections being held 'at any time in or after 1978'. The Paris communiqué added 'the competence of the European Assembly will be extended, in particular by granting it certain powers in the Communities' legislative process'. Both the British and the Danish governments declined to commit themselves on the introduction of direct elections.

In January 1975, after two years of discussions, the European Parliament adopted the Patijn Report on direct elections, the one subject in relation to which the Parliament, rather than the Commission, enjoys a **right of initiative** (Article 190). The Report proposed that the number of MEPs be increased to 355, that each member state's allocation of seats be strictly related to its population (although Luxembourg, as a special case, was left with the 6 seats it had had ever since 1958) and that the elections should be held on the same day throughout the Community. In the **European Elections Act**, adopted by the Council of Ministers in September 1976, the Parliament's recommendations on these points were largely ignored: the total number of MEPs was fixed at 410; the four large member states (France, Italy, the United Kingdom and West Germany) would – in spite of population variations amounting to several million people – each have the same number of MEPs (81); and because of different national traditions with regard to the day of the week upon which voting normally takes place, member states were left free to choose any date within a four-day period. The Act laid down the allocation of seats as follows (Article 2):

Belgium	24
Denmark	16
France	81
Ireland	15
Italy	81
Luxembourg	6
The Netherlands	25
United Kingdom	81
West Germany	81
Total	**410**

Both the total number of seats and the allocation of seats to member states had already been fixed at the Luxembourg meeting of the European Council in July 1976.

The parliamentary term was fixed at five years (Article 3). MEPs could be members of their national parliaments, but could not be government ministers, Commissioners, European civil servants, judges in the Court of Justice or members of the **Court of Auditors**, of the Economic and Social Committee or of the Board of Directors of the **European Investment Bank** (EIB; Article 6). Membership of the **Committee of the Regions** is also incompatible with membership of the Parliament. The right of the Parliament to draw up proposals for a uniform electoral procedure was reiterated (Article 7), but, as in the Patijn Report, the choice of electoral system and the arrangements for by-elections were left to the discretion of individual member states, pending the introduction of a uniform electoral procedure (for which neither the Patijn Report nor the Act set a deadline).

At the Rome meeting of the European Council in December 1975 the date for direct elections was fixed as May or June 1978. However, difficulties with the enabling legislation in the House of Commons (the terms of the Lib–Lab pact required the Labour government to attempt to introduce a regional list system, which was rejected by the House) meant that the Copenhagen meeting of the European Council in April 1978 decided to postpone the elections for one year until 7–10 June 1979.

The 1979 direct elections, the first international elections in history and involving an electorate of more than 190 million people (exceeded only by that of India), attracted a Community-wide turnout of 62.5 per cent. This overall figure concealed substantial differences: turnout ranged from 91.4 per cent in Belgium, where voting is notionally compulsory, to 32.3 per cent in the United Kingdom. (For detailed results, see **European elections**.) At its first session in July 1979 the European Parliament elected the French Liberal Simone Veil as its president. Five months later, for the first time in its history, the Parliament used its power under Article 203 (now 272) to reject the Community **Budget** for the following year.

The first directly elected Parliament, 1979 to 1984, set the pattern for subsequent Parliaments in several ways. It showed a real determination not only to use its powers to the full and to increase them wherever possible but also radically to reform the Community's whole institutional structure. This resulted in the Parliament's **Draft Treaty establishing the European Union** (DTEU; the Spinelli Treaty) of February 1984 and a host of resolutions on institutional questions. It sought, with only very partial success, to resolve the practical difficulties arising out of having three places of work, and decided in July 1981 no longer to hold plenary sessions in Luxembourg. Its growing importance internationally was marked by the address given to the Parliament by President Anwar Sadat of Egypt in February 1981, the first of many such addresses by heads of state. It resolved in September 1982 to bring an action in the Court of Justice under Article 175 (now 232) against the Council of Ministers for the Council's '**failure to act**' in the matter of a **common transport policy**. For the first time, a report at the end of a presidency was given to the Parliament by the president-in-office of the European Council (**Margaret Thatcher** in December 1981). In April 1982 the Parliament tightened its control over Community spending by deferring its grant of **discharge** to the Commission for 1980. The interest and excitement of the directly elected Parliament's first term were not matched in subsequent years.

The accession of Greece in 1981 and of Portugal and Spain in 1986 brought the total number of MEPs to 518. In July 1990 it was decided to admit 18 'observers' from the former East Germany, initially to be appointed by the East German Volkskammer and later by the Bundestag. These observers had speaking rights in committees and political groups but not in plenary sessions, and could neither vote nor hold office. This was obviously only a temporary solution. **German reunification** meant that Germany had a population some 20 million people greater than that of the next largest member state, and clearly this had to be reflected in the number of German MEPs in the Parliament. The suggestion that they be increased by 18 aroused strong opposition from the French, and the matter was not resolved until the Edinburgh meeting of the European Council in December 1992. At the same time, the opportunity was taken to adjust the overall allocation of seats, with effect from the June 1994 European elections. Since the accession of Austria, Finland and Sweden in January 1995 the situation has been as follows (pre-1994 numbers in brackets):

Austria	21		Italy	87	(81)
Belgium	25	(24)	Luxembourg	6	(6)
Denmark	16	(16)	The Netherlands	31	(25)
Finland	16		Portugal	25	(24)
France	87	(81)	Spain	64	(60)
Germany	99	(81)	Sweden	22	
Greece	25	(24)	United Kingdom	87	(81)
Ireland	15	(15)			

The organizational structure of the Parliament is laid down in its Rules of Procedure, with respect to which the Parliament is sovereign under Article 199 EC. A president is elected for two and a half years at the beginning and at the mid-point of every five-year term. Since July 1979 the presidents have been as follows:

1979–82	Simone Veil (France, Liberal)
1982–4	Pieter Dankert (The Netherlands, Socialist)
1984–7	Pierre Pflimlin (France, Christian Democrat)
1987–9	Lord Plumb (United Kingdom, Conservative)
1989–92	Enrique Baron (Spain, Socialist)
1992–4	Egon Klepsch (Germany, Christian Democrat)
1994–7	Klaus Hänsch (Germany, Socialist)
1997–9	José-Maria Gil-Robles (Spain, Christian Democrat)
1999–2002	Nicole Fontaine (France, Christian Democrat)
2002–	Pat Cox (Ireland, Liberal)

The president is required under Rule 19 to 'direct all the activities of Parliament and of its bodies', as well as 'to open, suspend and close sittings ..., maintain order ..., [and] put matters to the vote'. The president represents the Parliament 'in international relations, on ceremonial occasions and in administrative, legal or financial matters'. The president's powers may be delegated, normally to one of the vice-presidents (see below). The president may lead delegations from the Parliament taking part in the **conciliation** procedure with the Council (Rule 82). It is the president's responsibility formally to request **reconsultation** of the Parliament in the event of the Council or the Commission failing to abide by the Parliament's **Opinion** on a legislative proposal or if the 'nature of the problem with which the proposal is concerned substantially changes' (Rule 71). The president is also responsible (Annex IV, Rules 4 and 5; Article 272.7 EC) for declaring the Union's Budget adopted. Since June 1987 the president of the Parliament has been able to address meetings of the European Council.

Vice-presidents of the Parliament are elected every two and a half years at the same time as the president, but the political groups normally agree upon the list of candidates. Together with the president and (in an advisory capacity) the quaestors (see below), the vice-presidents make up the Bureau of the Parliament. The principal task of the Bureau is to take 'financial, organizational and administrative decisions' (Rule 22). Vice-presidents share with the president the task of presiding over plenary sessions of the Parliament. The body known as the Conference of Presidents (Rules 23 and 24) is composed of the president and the leaders of the political groups. It is responsible for 'decisions on the organization of Parliament's work and ... legislative planning', including the drawing up of the Parliament's agenda. It is enjoined under the Rules to 'endeavour to reach a consensus on matters referred to it', but, if necessary, it may take votes with each leader's vote being weighted to reflect the size of his or her political group.

The Parliament has 17 standing committees. Each committee has its own officers elected every two and a half years, but in practice the candidates for these posts and the number of places in each committee allocated to each of the political groups are decided by agreement among the groups on the basis of the **d'Hondt system**. The Committees are as follows:

1 Foreign Affairs, Human Rights, Common Security and Defence Policy
2 Budgets
3 Budgetary Control
4 Citizens' Freedoms and Rights, Justice and Home Affairs
5 Economic and Monetary Affairs
6 Legal Affairs and the Internal Market
7 Industry, External Trade, Research and Energy

8 Employment and Social Affairs
9 Environment, Public Health and Consumer Policy
10 Agriculture and Rural Development
11 Fisheries
12 Regional Policy, Transport and Tourism
13 Culture, Youth, Education, the Media and Sport
14 Development and Cooperation
15 Constitutional Affairs
16 Women's Rights and Equal Opportunities
17 Petitions

Under Rules 150 and 151, the Parliament may also set up temporary committees or **Committees of Inquiry** 'to investigate alleged contraventions of Community law or instances of maladministration in the implementation of Community law'. The right to set up such Committees of Inquiry was one of the powers granted to the Parliament in the **Maastricht Treaty** (Article 193 EC).

The Parliament's standing committees meet at least once a month in Brussels for two days. As far as possible, committee meetings are not held at the same time as plenary sessions in Strasbourg. Occasionally committees hold meetings elsewhere in the Union, but committees do not have their own budgets and any expenditure (such as that involved in the organization of 'hearings' with expert witnesses) must be approved by the Bureau. Most committee meetings are held in public, but committees are free to decide to hold them in private. Commission representatives attend and often take part in committee meetings, and at least once in each **presidency** the president of the relevant Council will attend a meeting of the appropriate parliamentary committee. At all meetings full interpretation is provided, documents are available in all official languages, and full minutes are kept. Contacts with other parliaments outside the Union are maintained through a system of delegations, each with its own officers. In the case of countries with which the Union has **Europe Agreements** or is negotiating treaties of **accession**, these delegations are known as joint parliamentary committees. Few of these delegations follow a regular pattern of meetings, but in most cases meetings are held alternately in the Union and in the country or countries concerned.

In addition to these delegations and joint parliamentary committees, there is the ACP–EU Joint Assembly, an organ of the **Cotonou Agreement**. Composed of a representative of each of the **ACP states** and an equal number of MEPs, the Joint Assembly has a general responsibility for overseeing the implementation of the Convention. It meets for a week-long session twice a year, once in the Union and once in one of the ACP states.

For most of the year the Parliament works in a monthly cycle: two weeks during which the committee meetings take place, one week kept as far as possible free of committee meetings so that the political groups can meet; and a fourth week spent in Strasbourg. This cycle is suspended in August for the summer holiday and interrupted in autumn because there is usually a second part-session in October devoted to the Budget. Other meetings – of the Bureau, the Conference of Presidents, delegations, etc. – have to be fitted into this cycle, together with additional two-day plenary sessions held five or six times a year in Brussels. The need to secure premises and interpretation normally means that all meetings are fixed well in advance.

The Treaty of Rome (Article 196) requires the Parliament to hold an annual session, which begins on the second Tuesday in March. In a year in which European elections are held, the European Elections Act of 1976 (Article 10) specifies that the newly elected Parliament shall meet on the first Tuesday after one month has elapsed since the last day of polling (a Sunday). A Court of Justice ruling of 1964 established that the Parliament, whether or not it is actually sitting, is in continuous session: this ruling allows the regulation governing MEPs' immunities to apply throughout the year. Technically, therefore, the plenary sessions in Strasbourg and Brussels are part-sessions of an annual session, although they are normally referred to simply as plenary sessions.

The business of a plenary session consists for the most part of debates on reports adopted in committee and brought forward for consideration by the Parliament as a whole. The report is presented by the committee's **rapporteur**; the representatives of each of the political groups are given precedence in the debate that follows; the responsible Commissioner may intervene, especially if the Commission wants to comment on the proposals for amendment contained in the report; other MEPs may take part in the debate, within the limit of the speaking-time allocated to their political groups for the day; and once the debate is completed, the time at which the report is to be voted upon is announced from the chair. Provision exists for reports to be taken without debate. Other regular items on the plenary session agenda include question time to the Commission and the Council; statements by the Commission and/or the Council on major issues (sometimes followed by a debate); three hours set aside for debates on 'topical and urgent subjects of major importance' (up to a maximum of five), which enable the Parliament to discuss crises, disasters and infringements of human rights; a report by the Commission on action taken in response to the Parliament's Opinions and **Resolutions**; and at the beginning and end of every presidency, a report by the president-in-office of the Council or the European Council on the presidency's programme of work. Special events in the Parliament's annual calendar are the presentation by the president of the Commission of the Annual

General Report; the presentation, also by the president, of the Commission's **annual work programme**; the presentations by the president of the Court of Auditors of the Court's annual report; the adoption by the Parliament of the report on the Commission's farm price proposals; and the first and second readings of the Budget.

The Parliament's views on legislation are expressed in the form of reports embodying Opinions. Under Rule 159 these reports are composed of draft amendments (if any) to the proposal, a draft legislative resolution and an explanatory statement. A report may also contain Opinions drawn up by committees other than the one primarily responsible. Non-legislative reports contain only a draft resolution, an explanatory statement and the motion or motions to which the report refers. In neither case does the explanatory statement have any legal force. In line with Articles 21 and 39 of the Maastricht Treaty the Parliament may also address Recommendations to the Council on the **Common Foreign and Security Policy** (CFSP) and in the field of **Justice and Home Affairs** (JHA).

Voting in plenary sessions is normally by show of hands, but the numbers can be checked electronically by a system requiring MEPs to use voting cards. Exceptionally, and only by request, votes can be taken by electronic roll-call, and only in these cases will the record attached to the daily minutes show how individual MEPs voted. The quorum is a third of the Parliament's total membership, but votes are valid and voting may continue however few MEPs are present until the president, on request, formally establishes that the meeting is inquorate. A verbatim record (known as 'the Rainbow', from the variously coloured sheets upon which it was once typed) of speeches in the original language of delivery is published daily and in its final form translated into the official languages and annexed to the *Official Journal*.

Of all the institutions of the European Union, the Parliament is the one that has changed the most in point of its status, powers and composition. However, in respect of its internal organization, it has changed very little, except that the political groups now dominate the system even more than before. All major decisions are arrived at on the basis of deals between the leaders of the groups: for example, over the period 1987–99 the two largest groups, the Socialists and the European People's Party, did not contest the presidency. This is in contrast with the United States Congress, in which the committees play a much more influential role. The Parliament's efficiency is handicapped by not having a single place of work, but only a small minority of MEPs is seriously committed to resolving the problem.

The Parliament is very slowly securing more coverage (not all of it sympathetic) in the media. Again, some of the difficulties spring from not having a single place of work and from the fact that newspapers and broadcasting organizations find it troublesome and expensive to cover the proceedings of a Parliament that works in many languages, is seldom in one place for more than a few days, deals with some very abstruse subjects, has a power of final decision only in a few cases and is largely composed of people of whom the electorate has never heard. The Parliament does not make the job of the media any easier by voting at fixed times (sometimes the following day) to suit MEPs' convenience rather than at the end of each debate. This arrangement helps to address the problem of absenteeism, the subject of much media criticism of the Parliament (not wholly unjustified: 199 MEPs were absent from the vote on the Maastricht Treaty, 7 April 1992; 143 MEPs were absent from the vote on the **Treaty of Amsterdam**, 19 November 1997; 70 MEPs were absent from the vote on stage 3 of **Economic and Monetary Union**, 2 May 1998). The Parliament is also widely criticized for voting itself substantial annual increases in its budget, which has doubled since 1979 to reach € 974 million in 2002 (this figure does not include MEPs' basic salaries, which are paid from national exchequers: see below).

The Treaty of Amsterdam placed an upper limit of 700 on the number of MEPs, but the **Treaty of Nice** raised this to 732. In the **Treaty of Accession** which the new member states signed in Athens in April 2003, a new allocation of seats was decided with effect from July 2004. Until that date newly acceding states may appoint members of their national parliaments to serve as MEPs, initially as observers.

Members

The Treaty of Rome originally envisaged that MEPs would be elected on the basis of a uniform electoral procedure. No progress was made with this. Instead, the Parliament used the modified version of the relevant Treaty Article 190 to adopt, in July 1998, a procedure based upon 'principles common to all Member States', but the Council has not acted on the matter. Elections continue to be held in accordance with national electoral laws, all of them – since the abandonment of 'first-past-the-post' in Great Britain – using proportional representation. The number of seats for each member state was laid down in the European Elections Act 1976, since modified by successive accession treaties, by the decision taken by the European Council in December 1992 and by the Treaties of Amsterdam and Nice. It can be altered only by unanimous agreement.

The Act specifies that MEPs 'shall vote on an individual and personal basis. They shall not be bound by any instructions and shall not receive a binding mandate' (Article 4). Under the terms of an agreement reached between member states in 1978, MEPs' basic salaries are paid from national exchequers and are subject to national tax at rates equivalent to those applied to national

MPs. This means that there are wide discrepancies (British MPs' and MEPs' pay is about average at £55,118 per annum). However, there is a common system for expenses and allowances, which are paid from the European Parliament's budget, indexed for inflation and calculated in euros. Within the Union MEPs are entitled to claim an economy-class air fare (plus the journey to and from the airport, plus a variable distance allowance) or car or train travel at about €0.66 per kilometre for the first 500 kilometres, and about €0.27 per kilometre thereafter (plus the distance allowance) for any official meeting. Outside the Union, travel expenses are normally paid on a 'costs incurred' basis. For all official meetings within the Union MEPs are paid an attendance allowance, worth about €257 a day, as long as he or she has 'signed in' for the day in question. MEPs are also entitled to an office allowance, paid automatically, of about €3,620 a month, and a further €12,305 a month for the employment of staff, paid on the presentation of contracts of employment. MEPs can also claim travel costs, up to a maximum of about €3,574 a year, for attendance in an official capacity (i.e., on the basis of an official invitation) at meetings, conferences and so on anywhere in the world. MEPs have free office accommodation on the European Parliament's premises in Brussels and in the Palais de l'Europe in Strasbourg.

An MEP is normally a full member of one of the Parliament's 17 specialized committees and a substitute member of another. He or she may also be a full member of one of the Parliament's interparliamentary delegations. In an average month an MEP will spend three nights in Strasbourg at one of the Parliament's plenary sessions, and six or seven nights in Brussels at committee meetings, additional plenary sessions, delegation meetings, or meetings of his or her political group. Persistent absentees (assessed on the basis of participation in roll-call votes) are liable to have their daily allowances cut by half.

MEPs' immunities are set out in Articles 8 to 10 of the **protocol** on the privileges and immunities of the European Communities annexed to the Treaty of Rome. MEPs 'shall not be subject to any form of inquiry, detention or legal proceedings in respect of opinions expressed or votes cast by them in the performance of their duties' (Article 9). Within their own member states MEPs enjoy immunities from arrest and legal proceedings similar to those extended to national MPs; elsewhere in the Union, they enjoy 'immunity from any measure of detention and from legal proceedings' except when found *in flagrante delicto* (Article 10). Only the Parliament itself can waive the immunity of an MEP. The **Treaty of Amsterdam** amends Article 138 EC to require the Parliament, having sought the opinion of the Commission and 'with the approval of the Council acting unanimously, [to] lay down the regulations and general conditions governing the performance of the duties of its Members' (Article 190 EC), but in 1999 the Council and Parliament found it impossible to reach agreement on the so-called 'Members' Statute'.

MEPs are obliged to record their financial interests in a register kept for this purpose, and to declare such interests when taking part in a debate on a matter connected with them.

The European Parliament has an unusually high proportion of women MEPs (almost a third of the total) compared with most national parliaments. The turnover of MEPs at European elections is also unusually high: of the 626 MEPs elected, less than half had sat in the previous parliament. However, there are substantial variations between national delegations, with the Irish and German delegations having the highest average length of service.

The background of MEPs also varies considerably from one country to another. About a quarter of MEPs have been, or are, members of their national parliaments, of whom 40 currently exercise a dual mandate. About 10 per cent of MEPs have held ministerial office in their home countries, and many have held office at local or regional level as mayors or presidents of regional assemblies. The list of well-known people who have been elected as MEPs since 1979 (including Willy Brandt, Jacques Chirac, Giulio Andreotti, Valéry Giscard d'Estaing, Jacques Delors, Lord Plumb, Jacques Santer, Georges Marchais, Leo Tindemans, Wilfried Martens, and Poul Schlüter) can be misleading. Many of them have simply headed their party lists for the elections and resigned from the Parliament at the earliest opportunity, or taken little part in its activities.

This cursory study of the background of MEPs (set out in much greater detail in Francis Jacobs, Richard Corbett and Michael Shackleton, *The European Parliament*, 4th edn, 2000) illustrates the fact that in most countries there is a much less sharp distinction than there is in the United Kingdom between a national or local political career and a career in the European Parliament. The use of national or regional lists as the basis for European elections enables the transition from one sphere of political activity to another to be made much more easily. Although some British former MEPs have become MPs and gone on to be ministers, to date no British Commissioner has been an MEP: all have come from the House of Commons or, in one case, the House of Lords.

Powers

The powers of the European Parliament fall under four main headings: powers relating to legislation, to the Budget, to the conclusion of international agreements, and general supervisory powers. The Parliament can scrutinize and amend all proposals for legislation under a variety of procedures (see

assent procedure, co-decision procedure, consultation procedure, cooperation procedure), and in many areas has a right of veto over such proposals if agreement cannot be reached with the Council. It can, within a maximum rate of increase, make modifications to the proposals for expenditure in the Budget and, in certain circumstances, reject the Budget outright. The Parliament's assent must be obtained before agreements can be concluded with non-member countries or international organizations. The Parliament is consulted on appointments to the European Commission, which it can dismiss and whose activities are subject to the Parliament's overall supervision.

Since it was founded in 1952 the powers of the European Parliament have grown very substantially. The growth has occurred in four ways: as European integration has been extended into new areas (so-called 'horizontal' growth); as a result of formal agreements arrived at between the member states and normally embodied in changes to the Treaties; on the basis of judgments of the Court of Justice (see **isoglucose case**); and in the form of **interinstitutional agreements**. Over this period the Parliament itself has consistently pressed for more powers, usually in the name of redressing the so-called **democratic deficit**, but to date there are no instances of the Parliament seizing power, as most national parliaments have done at some time in their history.

The basic outline of the Parliament's powers was discernible in the ECSC Treaty. The Common Assembly was entitled to discuss the annual report that the High Authority – the forerunner of the Commission – was required to lay before it by February at the latest of each year; by a two-thirds majority it could pass a motion of censure on the High Authority, thus forcing its members to resign 'as a body'; the High Authority was required to answer oral or written questions put to it by Members of the Assembly; and the Assembly was able to put forward proposals for amendments to the ECSC's budget. However, in spite of the 'supervisory' role that the Assembly was required by treaty to play, it was not the Assembly but the Consultative Committee attached to the High Authority – composed of between 30 and 51 people involved in the coal and steel industries and appointed by the member states – which the High Authority was required to consult. Inevitably, the substance of the Assembly's work was technical rather than political (the only major exception being the Assembly's involvement in the debates on a **European Political Community** and a **European Defence Community** in the early 1950s).

With the establishment of the EEC and Euratom in 1958, the Assembly (known as the European Parliament from 1962) was given new powers. Its size was increased from 78 to 142 MEPs. However, its role in legislation remained marginal: until the coming into force of the SEA in July 1987 the Parliament's powers were limited to the giving of Opinions and the submission of amendments on draft legislation, which the Council was obliged to refer to it.

However, neither the Commission nor the Council was formally obliged to incorporate the Parliament's views and amendments in the legislation finally adopted. The Parliament's assent was required before the conclusion of new **Association Agreements** under Article 238 (now 310) EC but, curiously, not for new Accession Treaties under Article 237 (now Article 49 TEU).

As far as the Parliament's supervisory powers are concerned, the power to dismiss the Commission on the basis of a **censure motion** carried by a two-thirds majority of votes cast representing more than half the total number of MEPs (Article 201; Rule 34 of the Parliament's Rules of Procedure) has never been used. It was attempted for the first time in June 1976, but the motion – tabled by Conservative MEPs on the Commission's chronic failure to deal with dairy surpluses – was overwhelmingly defeated. Since June 1976 motions of censure have been put to the vote on only five occasions, most recently in January 1999. All were defeated. However, it is clear that if the Commission had not resigned in March 1999 on the publication of a very critical report by the Committee of Independent Experts a censure motion would have been carried at the following plenary session.

There are several reasons why the Parliament has never used the most dramatic of its powers. In most areas the Parliament tends to regard the Commission as an ally, not an adversary, and there is little point in sacking Commissioners if the Parliament has no say (as was the case until recently) in who might replace them. Most Commissioners have sufficiently good party links to be able to appeal in the name of party loyalty to enough MEPs to make the two-thirds majority difficult to attain, and there are only very few issues for which enough cross-party support could be obtained to secure the majority necessary to pass a censure motion. The Treaty requires a minimum of three days to elapse between the President's announcement of the receipt of a motion of censure and the vote, thus making it almost inevitable that a motion tabled during one part-session will not be voted on until the next, allowing ample time for MEPs to have second thoughts.

Under Article 232 EC the Parliament is empowered, like other institutions of the Union and the governments of member states, to bring an action in the Court of Justice against the Commission or the Council for 'failure to act'. In September 1982 the Parliament decided to bring such an action for the first time against the Council, for the latter's persistent failure to adopt a **common transport policy** within the meaning of Article 74 (now 70). Nearly three years later, after legal arguments on both the substance and admissibility of the Parliament's action, the Court delivered a judgment in the Parliament's favour (22 May 1985, Case 13/83).

As noted above, the ECSC Treaty (Article 23) required the High Authority to answer oral or written questions from Members of the Common Assembly.

A similar provision was included with respect to the Commission in the EEC Treaty (Article 197), but it was not until 1973 that the Parliament made provision in its part-session agendas for a regular question time to the Commission. The Council, which is not under a similar Treaty obligation to answer MEPs' questions, agreed of its own volition in 1960 to reply to questions on matters that the Council had already considered, but again no regular question time was instituted until 1973. In 1975 it became possible to put questions to the foreign ministers meeting in **European Political Cooperation**. In 1983 the Council confirmed its willingness to answer written and oral questions in the **Stuttgart Declaration**.

No limit is placed upon the number of written questions that an MEP may ask (Rule 44). The questions are forwarded to the Commission or the Council through the president of the Parliament, and are supposed to be answered within six weeks and published in the *Official Journal*. 'Priority questions', limited to one per MEP per month, are defined as those requiring immediate answer but 'no detailed research'; for these the deadline is three weeks.

Oral questions for question time are limited to one per MEP to each of the institutions (Commission and Council; Rule 43). They are submitted through the president's office. Although guidelines annexed to the Rules of Procedure require questions and answers to be brief and question time to be briskly conducted, lacklustre chairing, long-winded participants and procedural disputes usually ensure that very few questions are fully dealt with. Question time, which since 1973 has been dominated by British MEPs, takes place with barely a handful of MEPs present and neither press nor public. A representative of the presidency answers on behalf of the Council; members of the Commission are normally expected to answer questions in their own areas of responsibility, although technically answers are given on behalf of the Commission as a whole. A procedure was introduced in 1994 whereby questions can be put to the President of the Commission.

In addition to written questions and oral questions for question time, the Parliament may address to the Commission or the Council questions for oral answer in response to which a Resolution may be tabled and voted upon (Rule 42). Such questions may be tabled by a committee, a political group or a minimum of 32 MEPs. The decision whether or not to place such a question on the agenda rests with the Conference of Presidents, which may decide to use a different procedure. This procedure allows the Parliament to explore issues in more depth than is possible in question time.

Although it was not recognized in the founding Treaties, every citizen of the Union has 'the right to address, individually or in association with other citizens or persons, a petition to Parliament' (Rule 174 of the Parliament's Rules of Procedure). This right, which dates from 1953, was given formal recognition in a 1989 Council–Commission–Parliament Joint Declaration and in the Maastricht Treaty (Article 194 EC). Since 1979 the number of petitions has risen from 57 to over 800, many of them mass petitions (of which one, on testing cosmetics on animals, was signed by more than 2.5 million people). Petitions have to relate to a matter in which there is some Union competence and which affects the petitioner directly. They are considered in the first instance by the Parliament's Petitions Committee. Once found admissible and duly considered, a petition may give rise to various forms of action: it may be referred to the appropriate parliamentary committee; it may be drawn to the attention of the Commission or the authorities in a member state; or the petitioner may draw upon the Parliament's support in resolving the problem at issue. The Petitions Committee submits an annual report to the Parliament.

In the period leading up to the SEA (1987), the most significant increase in the Parliament's powers was in relation to the Budget. The switch from a system of contributions by member states to one that gave the Community its **own resources** under the Treaty of Luxembourg of 22 April 1970 was accompanied by measures to increase the Parliament's say in the allocation of expenditure (although not in revenue-raising). These measures were further strengthened in a second Treaty signed in Brussels on 22 July 1975 (effective from 1 June 1977) based upon the proposals in the **Vedel Report** of 1972. The effect of these two Treaties was to make the Parliament and the Council the joint budgetary authority. Basically, the Parliament was given the last word on non-compulsory expenditure, although its scope for increasing expenditure was limited by the maximum rate of increase fixed annually. This is calculated by the Commission, on the basis of economic growth, rates of inflation and levels of public expenditure in the member states. The Council retained the last word on **compulsory expenditure**, including, most notably, price support under the **Common Agricultural Policy** (CAP), which represents almost half the overall Budget. The 1975 Treaty (Article 12, amending Article 203 (now 272) EEC) allows the Parliament to reject the Budget as a whole 'if there are important reasons', and ask for a new draft to be submitted to it. The Parliament rejected the Budget for the first time in 1979 and again in 1984. The president of the Parliament is responsible for declaring the Budget adopted; his decision in December 1985 to declare the 1986 Budget adopted led to an action by the Council in the Court of Justice on the grounds that the maximum rate of increase had been exceeded. The Court found in favour of the Council (Case 34/86), but the new Budget agreed in July 1986 was broadly consistent with the Parliament's wishes.

The 1975 Treaty was supplemented by a Council–Commission–Parliament Joint Declaration of 4 March 1975 establishing a **conciliation** procedure.

This was designed to forestall the possibility of the Parliament using its budgetary powers to impede legislation with 'appreciable financial implications' already agreed by the Council. The procedure may be triggered by either the Council or the Parliament, and allows representatives of the Parliament to meet face-to-face with the Council in order to reconcile differences. Seldom used at first, the conciliation procedure is now an established feature of the annual Council–Parliament discussions on the Budget, and – informally at least – its scope has been gradually widened.

Although the Parliament's powers with respect to the Budget are substantial, they are circumscribed in several ways, and relations with the Council have often been bad as a consequence of disputes in the course of the budgetary procedure. First, because the Parliament has almost no say in revenue-raising, it is denied those opportunities (of which most national parliaments have at some time in their history taken advantage) of gaining power by withholding supply. Second, the classification of expenditure into compulsory and non-compulsory and the exclusion of certain types of expenditure (such as the **European Development Fund**) from the Budget have denied the Parliament an opportunity to examine and amend the Budget as a whole. Arguments over the classification of particular items in the Budget have frequently given rise to disputes between the Parliament and the Council. Third, as noted above, the rate of increase laid down by the Commission limits the scope for increasing non-compulsory expenditure: the rate can be changed only by agreement between the Council, acting by qualified majority (see **qualified majority voting**), and the Parliament, with the support of a majority of MEPs and three-fifths of the votes cast. On the other hand, the Parliament's position as part of the joint budgetary authority has been strengthened by its participation in the Council–Commission–Parliament 'interinstitutional agreement on budgetary discipline and the improvement of the budgetary procedure', first concluded in 1988. This agreement represented a move away from budgeting on a strictly annual basis and set a framework for Community expenditure over a four-year period.

In line with the Parliament's increased budgetary powers were extensions in its powers of budgetary control. Under the Treaty of 22 July 1975 the Parliament was given an exclusive right of **discharge**.

As noted above, the original Treaties made only very modest provision for involving the Parliament in the negotiation and conclusion of international agreements. Negotiations are conducted by the Commission on the basis of a mandate laid down by the Council. In 1964 the Dutch Foreign Minister, Joseph Luns, then President-in-Office of the Council, wrote to the Parliament to express the Council's willingness to involve the Parliament in the discussions preceding the opening of negotiations for new Association Agreements and to keep Parliament informed of the progress of negotiations. This was known as the Luns Procedure. Nine years later, with the support of the Commission, this procedure was extended to all trade and commercial agreements under a procedure known as the **Luns–Westerterp procedure**. **Cooperation Agreements**, since they were not provided for in the Treaty, were concluded on the basis of Article 235 EEC (see **Article 308**), under which consultation of the Parliament was anyway mandatory.

The communiqué issued after the meeting of the European Council in December 1974 said not only that direct elections to the European Parliament should be held as soon as possible, but that 'the competence of the European Assembly will be extended, in particular by granting it certain powers in the Communities' legislative process'. However, the first directly elected Parliament saw no immediate increase in its formal powers when it met for the first time in July 1979. Direct elections gave the Parliament greater legitimacy and hence more authority; more importantly, the elections created a Parliament largely composed of full-time MEPs, as opposed to the part-time MEPs in the Parliament that preceded it. It would clearly be more difficult for the Council and the Commission to ignore the Parliament's views, and MEPs would have the time, the tenacity and the expertise to enforce those views. The importance of the Parliament was dramatically underlined in the Court of Justice's 'isoglucose' ruling of 1980, which confirmed that a Council decision was void unless the Opinion of Parliament had been not merely sought but actually obtained.

High on the new Parliament's list of priorities was the desire for greater formal powers in decision making. The most ambitious of the Parliament's initiatives in this field was the Draft Treaty establishing the European Union (DTEU) adopted in February 1984. In 1980, **Altiero Spinelli** and others set up the **Crocodile Club** of Federalists and other enthusiasts for institutional reform. Two years later, in January 1982, the Parliament created a new Committee on Institutional Affairs whose central task would be the drawing up of a wholly new treaty. The theory was that the first directly elected Parliament would play the role of **constituent assembly**. The new treaty would be adopted and the Parliament would then – through the media, through political parties, through national parliaments and through direct appeals to the public – set about securing support for its provisions. The DTEU would be the centrepiece of the 1984 European elections campaign: political parties would express support for it in their manifestos, and the election results would constitute a massive public endorsement of European union.

In the event, because of internal difficulties, the DTEU was not finally adopted until February 1984 by 237 votes to 31 with 43 abstentions (in a Parliament that by then contained 434 members). This meant that the DTEU was obviously too late to be included in party manifestos and that the process of winning support in national parliaments had to be abandoned. In no country except Italy did the DTEU feature prominently in the 1984 European elections campaign.

The DTEU did, however, win general support from the governments of Italy, the Netherlands, Belgium, West Germany and, most significantly (although somewhat ambiguously), France. In a speech to the European Parliament as President-in-Office of the European Council on 24 May 1984, President **François Mitterrand** said that France was willing 'to examine and defend your project, the inspiration behind which [France] approves. I therefore suggest that preparatory consultations leading up to a conference of the Member States concerned be started up.'

Such a conference – an **Intergovernmental Conference** (IGC) under Article 236 EEC (now Article 48 TEU) – was precisely what Spinelli and his colleagues had hoped to avoid, since the treaty amendments that a conference would bring forward were subject to ratification (and, therefore, the possibility of a veto) in each member state. The Parliament under Spinelli's guidance had sought to get round this provision by claiming that the DTEU was not an amendment to the existing Treaties but a wholly new treaty, which would come into force *automatically* once a majority of member states, representing two-thirds of the Community's population, had ratified it. President Mitterrand's decision to press for an IGC meant that the governments had regained the initiative.

The Parliament was not the only institution concerned with institutional reform. At the governmental level the **Genscher–Colombo Plan** of November 1981 proposed that a 'European Act' should be adopted by the member states 'as a further contribution to the establishment of the European Union'. In emasculated form the European Act was eventually promulgated as the Solemn Declaration on European Union made at the Stuttgart meeting of the European Council in June 1983 (see **Stuttgart Declaration**). As far as the Parliament was concerned, the Declaration provided for closer involvement in decision making (including the conclusion of agreements with non-member countries) and a more substantial say in appointments to the Commission, but no new powers.

At the Fontainebleau meeting of the European Council in June 1984, the heads of government decided to set up a committee (variously known as the Ad Hoc Committee or the **Dooge Committee**, after its Irish chairman) composed of their personal representatives, some of whom were MEPs or former MEPs. The task of the Committee – modelled on the **Spaak Committee**, which had done much of the preliminary work on the Treaty of Rome – was to bring forward recommendations on institutional reform. In its report, submitted to the Milan meeting of the European Council in June 1985, the Committee recommended a new treaty, based on the *acquis communautaire* and the Stuttgart Declaration and 'guided by the spirit and the method' of the Parliament's DTEU. Three representatives – from Denmark, Greece and the United Kingdom – dissented from this view, in the belief that changes could simply be made to the existing Treaties. By a majority vote the Milan European Council decided to convene an IGC under Article 236 EEC.

The result of the IGC (the first of its kind in the history of the Community) was the Single European Act (SEA), which was signed in February 1986 and which came into force in July 1987. It introduced two new procedures, both of which significantly strengthened the Parliament's legislative role. Henceforth the normal procedure – under which the Parliament scrutinizes a proposal for legislation and adopts in plenary session an Opinion, which may embody amendments to the Commission's text – was to be known as the consultation procedure. The first new procedure, known as the cooperation procedure, allows the Parliament two readings, the second of them on the basis of the Council's preliminary conclusions, known as the **common position** (Article 252). The second innovation in the SEA was the **assent procedure**, which gave the Parliament a right of assent over Association Agreements and Accession Treaties (including supplementary protocols to existing agreements).

Substantial additions to the Parliament's powers were contained in the Maastricht Treaty, many of them as amendments or additions to the Treaty of Rome. Of these, the most important was the co-decision procedure (Article 251), which extended the cooperation procedure to allow the Parliament an opportunity to negotiate directly with the Council in a conciliation committee and a right of veto at the final stage if agreement could not be reached. Also of importance were the Parliament's new powers with respect to the appointment of members of the European Commission (Article 214), the use of which in July 1994 almost resulted in the Parliament rejecting **Jacques Santer** as the successor to **Jacques Delors**. The Maastricht Treaty also gave the Parliament the right to be consulted on appointments to the Court of Auditors and to the presidency of the **European Central Bank** (ECB), formalized the Parliament's right to set up committees of inquiry (Article 193), empowered the Parliament to appoint an **Ombudsman** (Article 195) and came close to granting the Parliament a **right of initiative** (Article 192).

Less satisfactory to the Parliament was its only marginal involvement in the new 'pillars' of the Maastricht Treaty, the **Common Foreign and Security Policy** (CFSP) and **Justice and Home Affairs** (JHA). The Parliament has the right to be consulted and kept informed in both areas and may make recommendations, ask questions and hold annual debates, but it has no right to examine and amend proposals in either field, still less to exercise a right of veto. With the incorporation of the **Schengen** *acquis* into the Treaty of Rome, this state of affairs is gradually changing.

The Treaty of Amsterdam increased the Parliament's powers by giving it the right to approve the member states' nominee as president of the Commission (Article 214.2 EC). More importantly, it extended the co-decision procedure into almost all areas in which the cooperation procedure currently applies. In fact, the cooperation procedure is now limited almost exclusively to issues relating to **Economic and Monetary Union** (EMU), and the procedures for involving the Parliament in legislation in all other areas have been reduced to three: assent, co-decision, and simple consultation. The most recent changes to the Parliament's powers may be found under **Treaty of Nice**. Richard Corbett, *The European Parliament's Role in Closer EU Integration* (Basingstoke, 1998) is an authoritative account of the Parliament's involvement in institutional reform.

The powers of the European Parliament as laid down in the Treaties were directed primarily against the Commission, because it was assumed that the Commission would develop into a European government. The central fact with which the Parliament has had to come to terms is that the governments, through the Council and later the European Council and most recently the essentially intergovernmental 'pillars' of the Maastricht Treaty have remained the key element in the decision-making process. The principal tension within the system has not been between the Parliament and the Commission but between the Parliament and the Council. Indeed, the Parliament and the Commission are often on broadly the same side of the argument, but the Parliament has to vent its frustration against the Commission because its opportunities for doing so against the Council are so much more limited.

Some governments have more or less consistently supported the Parliament's ambitions for more powers. Italy, Germany and the **Benelux** countries have usually been on the Parliament's side, whereas France, the UK and Denmark have been ambivalent or openly hostile. As *Eurobarometer* has shown, a similar divergence of view is evident among the national electorates.

The most difficult area for the Parliament – because it led to direct rivalry with the Council – has been securing an increase in its legislative powers, but it may be asked whether legislation (in the sense of new legislative proposals) will ever again be as important in the life of the Union. In a larger, more heterogeneous Union the emphasis will be less on new legislation and more on enforcement. The Parliament's record on following up its own decisions is poor. This relates not so much to its formal powers but to its internal organization and the inclinations of its members, most of whom prefer the sensation and the glamour of being involved in great decisions to the more painstaking labour involved in ensuring that they are followed up, the law properly applied and money from the Budget spent effectively.

Within a national parliament a broad consensus exists on the role of a parliament and, by extension, on the role of an individual parliamentarian. Such a consensus is much less evident in the case of the European Parliament, which draws on two quite different traditions: the Latin tradition, in which parliament's role is to legitimize decisions of the executive; and the more adversarial Anglo-Saxon tradition, in which parliaments are deliberately set apart from executives (and their supporting bureaucracies) so that they may criticize them more effectively. The difference between the two traditions may be illustrated by MEPs' attitudes to question time, which is almost wholly dominated by those coming from the latter tradition.

In common with most continental parliaments, the European Parliament is oriented towards consensus. This is made easier by the fact that it does not sustain a government and by the fact that a high proportion of its work is of a technical nature that does not lend itself to political divisions. Still in evidence too is the feeling, dating back to the Parliament's uncertain beginnings, that to have any influence within the system the Parliament's opinions have to command unanimous or near-unanimous support. The rapporteur system upon which the work of the committees is based is also oriented towards consensus. This feature of the Parliament's operational style was powerfully enhanced when the SEA came into effect in July 1987, since under the cooperation procedure the Parliament was required to act by an absolute majority of its members. The effect of this on the behaviour of the political groups is noted elsewhere. Cross-party consensus may indeed have served its principal purpose of getting **Single Market** legislation on to the statute-book in good time, but it lessened still further the scope for party-political debate and created habits of mind that serve to render issues over a wider field less clear-cut and therefore less arresting to the public. The price paid for this is the indifference of the media and a low turn-out in European elections. Unless the Parliament can establish itself as the forum in which competing views on the big issues affecting Europe's future are addressed and debated, rather than merely homogenized, it will fail to live up to its supporters' expectations. As **Winston Churchill** remarked, 'Building up a European Parliament must be gradual ... It should roll forward on a tide of facts, events and impulses rather than by elaborate constitution-making' (speech in the Consultative Assembly of the Council of Europe, 11 August 1950).

European passport

The European passport was first discussed at the Paris **summit** of December 1974 and again in Rome the following year. The **Council of Ministers** adopted two **Resolutions** in June 1981 and June 1982 to settle the details, and the passport was gradually introduced from 1 January 1985. The long period of gestation was caused by disagreements between member states over the colour and format; the issue was further complicated by the wish on the part of some governments to introduce machine-readable pages, which in turn prompted arguments over what data should be included.

The European passport is in fact not a European passport at all, but a passport produced in a uniform format agreed among member states: smaller than the old British passport, with a semi-soft red cover (variously described as 'Bordeaux' or 'Burgundy') bearing the words 'European Community' in the appropriate language as well as the name of the country of issue. The member states remain the issuing authorities.

The idea of a European passport is intended to have both symbolic and practical importance. The fact that all citizens of what is now the **European Union** have passports in a common format is meant to reinforce the notion of a **People's Europe** and to underline the idea of a common **citizenship**. At the practical level, a common-format European passport helps to ensure that all citizens of the European Union can instantly be recognized as such at the Union's internal and external frontiers and receive equal treatment at the hands of national authorities.

European Patent Convention

Signed in 1973 by the **Benelux** countries, France, Germany, Switzerland and the United Kingdom, the European Patent Convention created the European Patent Organization (EPO) and offers patent protection throughout the signatory states. It is the largest regional patent system in the world, and now covers all 15 member states of the European Union, Liechtenstein, Monaco, Switzerland, Cyprus and Turkey. The EPO's executive body, the European Patent Office in Munich, operational since 1977, is also important as a supplier of technical information, and is active internationally in the World Intellectual Property Organization and through bilateral contacts with national patent offices in central and eastern Europe. Agreement on a patent which would be valid for the whole of the European Community has for many years been blocked by disagreement over which language regime should apply, not solely for patent applications and the patent itself but for legal proceedings for opposition, revocation or invalidity. The most likely solution seems to be that applications could be made in any of the recognized official languages, but that a more limited number of languages would be available for proceedings. It is proposed that the European Community should become a member of the EPO in its own right. See Vincenzo Di Cataldo, 'From the European patent to a Community patent', *Columbia Journal of European Law*, Vol. 8, no. 1, Winter 2002.

European People's Party (EPP)

Founded in 1976, the EPP is the Union-wide organization of Christian Democrat parties and their allies. See **Christian Democracy, transnational political parties**.

European Police College (CEPOL)

At the meeting of the **European Council** in Tampere (Finland) in October 1999 it was decided to set up a European police college to train senior police officers. The formal decision was taken on 22 December 2000 (*Official Journal*, L336, 30 December 2000). The aim of the European Police College (known as CEPOL) was set out in Article 6 of the Decision: 'to help train the senior police officers of the Member States by optimizing cooperation between CEPOL's various component institutes. It shall support and develop a European approach to the main problems facing Member States in the fight against crime, crime prevention, and the maintenance of law and order and public security, in particular the cross-border dimensions of those problems'. CEPOL is managed by a governing board and has its own secretariat. It is financed by GNP-related contributions from member states. An annual report is presented to the **Council of Ministers**, the **European Commission** and the **European Parliament**.

European Political Community

In 1950 the proposal for a **European Defence Community** (EDC: see also **Pleven Plan**) gave rise to the suggestion that the federal army provided for in the EDC Treaty should be under the control of an elected supranational authority to be known as the EDC Assembly. Under Article 38 of the Treaty this proposal was to be worked out in detail by the Assembly of the **European Coal and Steel Community** (ECSC). On 10 September 1952 the foreign ministers of **the Six** set this work in hand: the ECSC Assembly (the forerunner of the **European Parliament**) was invited 'to draft a Treaty constituting a European Political Authority'. The proposals contained in this Treaty became known as the European Political Community (EPC).

That this task should be entrusted to the ECSC Assembly aroused the jealousy of the Consultative Assembly of the **Council of Europe**. This problem was solved by requiring the ECSC Assembly to be temporarily enlarged, drawing on members of the Consultative Assembly from the national parliaments of the Six. This enlarged ECSC Assembly, known as the Ad Hoc Assembly, met in **Strasbourg** under the presidency of **Paul-Henri Spaak**.

The draft Treaty was adopted by the Assembly on 10 March 1953. Under Article 1 it established 'a European Community of a supranational character ... founded upon a union of peoples and States, upon respect for their personality and upon equal rights and duties for all'. The Community was to be equipped with a two-chamber Parliament, the first ('the People's Chamber') made up of 'deputies representing the peoples united in the Community', the second (the Senate) made up of 'senators representing the people of each State'. The former were to be directly elected every five years, the latter were to be elected by **national parliaments**. In principle, France, Germany and Italy each had 63 deputies and 21 senators; the first chamber had 268 members, the Senate 87. France was given seven extra deputies 'in order to take into account its overseas departments and territories'. The Parliament held two sessions every year.

The administration of the Community was in the hands of a European Executive Council. The president, elected by the Senate, appointed the other Council members, of whom not more than two could be of the same nationality. They were to be known as 'Ministers of the European Community'. The Council as a whole had to receive a vote of confidence from both chambers of the Parliament, either of which had the power to dismiss it. However, if the People's Chamber voted by a majority of less than three-fifths to dismiss the Council, the Council could then choose either to resign voluntarily or to dissolve the Chamber; the latter option could be overruled only by a vote of the Senate to dismiss the Council.

A Council of National Ministers was responsible for 'harmonizing the action of the European Executive Council with that of the Governments of Member States'. It was composed of one member from each government, with a rotating presidency.

The Court of Justice of the ECSC would act as the Court for the Community, which was also to be equipped with an Economic and Social Council 'in an advisory capacity'. Laws required the assent of both chambers. The Senate was empowered to request a second reading. The president of the European Executive Council was responsible for promulgating laws duly adopted, and the Council had the power to issue 'regulations to ensure the implementation of the laws of the Community'.

The Community would take over the powers and functions of the ECSC and the EDC, as well as pursue its own specific objectives. Prominent among these was the establishment of 'a common market among the Member States, based on the free movement of goods, capital and persons' (see **Beyen Plan**). The Budget of the Community was made up of what would now be called **own resources** (which included taxes levied by the Community) and contributions from member states fixed by unanimous agreement in the Council of National Ministers.

Never formally rejected, the EPC Treaty was abandoned when on 30 August 1954 the French National Assembly voted against the EDC Treaty. As a project it was extremely ambitious, for although the basic institutional structure of the EPC reflected the quadripartite scheme already in place under the ECSC Treaty, there were many very striking differences in terms of the balance of power between the institutions. The extensive powers of the 'Ministers' in the European Executive Council were a substantial advance on those of the ECSC High Authority, and completely overshadowed those of the Council of National Ministers. The relation between the two bodies affords a very instructive comparison with the powers of the **European Commission** and the **Council of Ministers** as set out in the **Treaty of Rome** four years later. Similarly, to take only one example, the right of the European Executive Council to dissolve the Parliament was far in excess of anything contemplated before (or since) in the Commission–Parliament relationship. Overall, much of the language of the EPC Treaty would be echoed in the Treaty of Rome. As **Jean Monnet** remarked of the EPC Treaty:

Nothing that has been conscientiously made in this way is ever useless: for, by working together, everyone acquires a better knowledge of his partners and their problems, and he passes it on to others in his turn ... The constitution-makers were ... insufficiently [cautious] when they imagined that European unity would *begin* with the establishment of a federal political system ... It was a step in the right direction; but it proposed to go too fast, without waiting for the force of necessity to make it seem natural in the eyes of Europeans (*Memoirs*, English edn, 1978).

See R.T. Griffiths, *Europe's First Constitution* (2000).

European Political Cooperation (EPC)

EPC refers to the procedures used from 1970 to allow member states of the European Community to discuss and coordinate their positions on foreign affairs and, where appropriate, act in concert. The principal decision-making body was the Conference of Foreign Ministers meeting in Political Cooperation. EPC procedures were replaced from November 1993 by those laid down in the **Common Foreign and Security Policy** (CFSP) provisions of the **Maastricht Treaty** (see also **COREU, political directors**).

From the 1960s onwards it was evident, most notably in the foreign affairs field, that there were areas in which, although they were not formally within the competence of the European Economic Community, governments of member states could usefully act in consultation and in concert with one another. At a **summit** meeting in The Hague in December 1969 **the Six** invited their foreign ministers to make proposals for political unification. This was done in a report drafted by a committee of senior officials chaired by Vicomte Étienne Davignon of the Belgian foreign ministry (and later a long-serving member of the **European Commission**) and known as the first Davignon Report. The Report was submitted to the governments of the Six and to those of the four applicant states (Denmark, Ireland, Norway and the United Kingdom), debated in the **European Parliament** and adopted in its final form by the foreign ministers on 27 October 1970.

The Report made four basic recommendations. Foreign ministers should meet every six months in what was known as the Conference of Foreign Ministers meeting in Political Cooperation, to distinguish it from the **General Affairs Council**; the heads of foreign ministries should form a Political Committee (see **Political and Security Committee**); six-monthly meetings known as 'colloquies' should be held with the Political Affairs Committee of the European Parliament; and the president-in-office of the **Council of Ministers** should submit an annual report on political cooperation to the Parliament. In addition, a regular exchange of telegrams, coordinated by the **presidency**, would ensure a copious flow of information between foreign ministries (see COREU). These proposals were described in the Report as 'the first practical endeavours to demonstrate to all that Europe has a political vocation'. A second Davignon Report, requested at the Paris summit in October 1972, increased the frequency of ministers' meetings to four times a year and strengthened the involvement of embassies of member states, including those accredited to international organizations.

The main feature of EPC was its intergovernmental character. It took place largely outside the Community framework: the Commission had no right of initiative, the foreign ministers were not subject to the procedures laid down in the Treaty for decision making in the Council, recourse could not be had to the **Court of Justice**, and not until 1976 was the Conference of Foreign Ministers meeting in Political Cooperation prepared to answer questions from the European Parliament. The range of subjects included 'all important foreign policy questions [which] concern European interests whether in Europe itself or elsewhere where the adoption of a common position is necessary or desirable' (second Davignon Report, paragraph 11), but, although part of the *acquis communautaire*, EPC remained outside the Treaty.

The so-called London Report on EPC, adopted in October 1981, made some important improvements to the procedures, including a swifter response to crises, fuller involvement on the part of the Commission, the creation of the **troika** and the addition of a small EPC secretariat based in Brussels. More importantly, the London Report mentioned 'security' for the first time in the context of EPC, in line with an agreement reached at an informal meeting of foreign ministers in Venlo, the Netherlands, earlier in the year.

When EPC was finally given Treaty status in Title III of the 1986 **Single European Act** (SEA) the provisions did little more than codify the procedures already established. The drafting made it clear that EPC remained outside the normal ambit of the Community institutions (although the Commission was to be 'fully associated' and the European Parliament 'closely associated' with it). The signatory states expressed their readiness 'to coordinate their positions more closely on the political and economic aspects of security' (Article 30.6 SEA).

The story of EPC is well told in Simon Nuttall, *European Political Cooperation* (1992).

European Refugee Fund

On 28 September 2000 the **Council of Ministers** agreed to bring together into a single legal and budgetary instrument various measures taken with respect to refugees in the European Union (*Official Journal*, L252, 6 October 2000). The European Refugee Fund, with a budget of € 216 million over the period 2000–4, can contribute towards member states' costs relating to reception facilities, measures to promote repatriation and reintegration, studies, pilot projects, and exchanges of personnel.

European Regional Development Fund (ERDF)

Although the Preamble to the **Treaty of Rome** contains a commitment to 'reducing the differences between the various regions and the backwardness of the less-favoured regions', agreement was not reached on the establishment of the ERDF until 1972; it came into operation three years later. The creation of the ERDF was largely a British initiative, in the belief that receipts from the Fund would help compensate for the bias in the **Budget** towards agriculture. In the event, the ERDF began on a very small scale indeed and was initially shared between member states on the basis of fixed quotas.

The role of the ERDF was defined by the **Maastricht Treaty** in an amendment to the Treaty of Rome (Article 160) as being 'to help to redress the main regional imbalances in the Community through participation in the development and structural adjustment of regions whose development is lagging behind and in the conversion of declining industrial regions'. In common with the other **structural funds** the ERDF is directed towards particular objectives, first drawn up in 1988 and revised in 1999. The ERDF is concerned mainly with Objectives 1 and 2: underdeveloped regions and those particularly affected by the decline of traditional industries such as coal, steel, shipbuilding and textiles (underdeveloped regions are those with a per capita GDP less than 75 per cent of the European average). The problems of inner cities are also addressed. Only projects in regions defined by the **European Commission** as qualifying for assistance may receive ERDF aid. The ERDF also contributes to the development of rural areas (see **European Agricultural Guidance and Guarantee Fund**).

Assistance from the ERDF is given in the form of grants within 'Community Support Frameworks' agreed with member states on the basis of development plans. Such assistance must complement, not substitute for, assistance from national sources (see **additionality**). In the Objective 1 regions ERDF assistance may not exceed 75 per cent of the total cost of a project and may not be less than 50 per cent of the total cost met from public funds. In Objective 2 regions these figures are reduced to 50 and 25 per cent respectively.

More than 80 per cent of the structural funds, which amounted to almost €30 billion in 2000, is allocated to Objectives 1 and 2. This and the establishment of the **Committee of the Regions** further encourage the trend for local and regional authorities to establish their own direct links with the Commission instead of being obliged to operate through national government departments (see also **regionalism**).

European Social Agenda

In March 2000 the **European Council** meeting in Lisbon set the strategic goal of transforming the European Union into 'the most competitive and dynamic knowledge-based economy in the world, capable of sustained economic growth with more and better jobs and greater social cohesion'. By 2010 it is hoped to raise the employment rate from 61 to 70 per cent of the active population and to raise the proportion of working women from 51 to 60 per cent of women of working age. On 28 June 2000 the **European Commission** published its report *The Social Policy Agenda* (COM(2000)379). The Agenda was discussed and adopted at the European Council meeting in Nice in December 2000: the text is annexed to the Presidency Conclusions. It lays down the priorities and the measures to be taken in the field of **social policy** over the period 2001 to 2005.

The Agenda is set out under six headings: more and better jobs (see **employment**); anticipating and capitalizing on change in the working environment; fighting poverty and all forms of exclusion and **discrimination**; modernizing social protection; promoting gender equality (see **equal treatment**); and strengthening the social policy aspects of **enlargement** and the European Union's external relations. The Agenda provides for regular monitoring of progress towards these goals, on the basis of the **open method of coordination**, and reiterates the commitment made in Lisbon to an annual review by the European Council every spring. A full mid-term review will take place in 2003. See also **European social model**.

The Commission publishes a 'scoreboard' on implementing the Agenda (COM(2001)104) and has drawn up an *Action plan for skills and mobility* (COM(2002)72).

European Social Charter

The original European Social Charter (not to be confused with the **Social Chapter** or with the European Community's 1989 Charter on the Fundamental Social Rights of Workers: see below) is the counterpart in respect of economic and social rights of the **European Convention on Human Rights** of 1950. Agreed in Turin in 1961 by the **Council of Europe**, the European Social Charter entered into force in 1965.

The Charter, composed of 38 Articles, an appendix, and 2 additional **protocols**, binds signatory states to accept at least 5 of a 'compulsory nucleus' of 7 basic rights, each in a separate Article. Overall, a signatory state must accept at least 10 of the Articles of the Convention. The basic rights are: the right to work (under which governments accept as 'one of their primary aims and responsibilities the achievement and maintenance of as high and stable a level of employment as possible, with a view to the attainment of full employment'), the right to organize, the right of collective bargaining, the right to social security, the right to social and medical assistance, the right to family benefits, and the right of migrant workers and their families to protection and assistance. Other rights are concerned with issues such as working conditions, special protection for young workers and vocational training – a total of 19 rights in all. Four further rights were set out in a 1988 protocol: equal opportunities and equal treatment, information and consultation, workers' involvement in questions of health and safety at the workplace, and special care for the elderly. Signatories to the protocol must agree to be bound by at least one of these.

Unlike the European Convention, the Charter is not backed up by judicial machinery for enforcement. Instead, observance is monitored by a Committee of Experts of not more than seven members appointed for a six-year term by the Committee of Ministers. It is the job of this Committee to examine the biennial reports submitted by the signatory states. Its conclusions and the reports are then forwarded to a subcommittee of the Council of Europe's Governmental Social Committee, which in turn forwards them to the Committee of Ministers. The Parliamentary Assembly may also submit its views on the conclusions of the Committee of Experts. In extreme cases the Committee of Ministers may decide, by a two-thirds majority, to make 'necessary recommendations' to a signatory state in default of its obligations under the Charter. The ambitious scope of the Charter is thus vitiated by the feebleness of the enforcement procedures, which are heavily weighted in favour of governments. The Charter illustrates very clearly the limitations of a system based upon voluntary compliance, by contrast with a system (such as prevails in the European Community) in which objectives are secured by means, ultimately, of binding legislation.

The European Community's Social Charter (formally, the Charter on the Fundamental Social Rights of Workers) was adopted in December 1989 by the **European Council** at its meeting in Strasbourg, with the support of all member states except the United Kingdom. The Charter is backed up by a so-called 'Social Action Programme' of 47 proposals for legislation. The Social Chapter of the **Maastricht Treaty** – formally known as the Agreement on Social Policy or the Social Protocol – gave the Charter a legal basis and extended the scope of **qualified majority voting** (QMV) in the social field. The United Kingdom did not sign the 1989 Social Charter on the grounds that it was inconsistent with the three principles of the Community's involvement in the social field agreed at the European Council meeting in Madrid in June 1989: that the emphasis should be on job creation, that it should respect the doctrine of **subsidiarity**, and that it should reflect the diversity of national practice and traditions. The United Kingdom has, however, chosen to implement most of the proposals brought forward under the Social Action Programme and to submit an annual report on the state of social and employment rights, in common with other member states.

The Charter requires the **European Commission** to draw up an annual report on the application of the Charter. The scope of the Charter is very broad and includes living and working conditions, freedom of movement, social security, equal treatment for men and women, vocational training, health and safety, special measures for young people, the elderly, and the disabled, and the right to information, consultation and participation. The rights contained in the Charter have since been incorporated in the **Charter of Fundamental Rights**.

European Social Fund (ESF)

The oldest of the European Union's **structural funds**, the ESF was established under Article 146 (formerly 123) of the **Treaty of Rome**. This was done mainly at the instigation of Italy, the poorest country of **the Six**. Article 146, as revised by the **Maastricht Treaty**, states that the objective of the ESF is 'to render the employment of workers easier and to increase their geographical and occupational mobility within the Community, and to facilitate their adaptation to industrial changes and to changes in production systems, in particular through vocational training and retraining'. The ESF is administered by the **European Commission**, assisted by a committee of 'representatives of governments, trade unions and employers' organizations' (Article 147).

The ESF is concerned mainly with combating long-term unemployment, with special measures to assist people under the age of 25, and with helping workers adapt to technological change. As with the other funds, ESF assistance is directed more towards programmes than towards individual projects. Only organizations financially supported by a public authority may apply for ESF aid, which is, in nearly all cases, intended to complement aid from national sources (see **additionality**). Particular attention is paid to people with special difficulties, such as migrant workers, women and the disabled. Supplementing the projects brought forward by member states is the Union's own EQUAL programme, designed to promote transnational cooperation in the elimination of **discrimination** and inequalities in the labour market. In common with the other structural funds, the ESF was reviewed in 1999 as part of the *Agenda 2000* settlement.

The **Council of Europe** also operates a Social Fund (since November 1999 renamed the Council of Europe Development Bank).

European social model

The European social model, to which reference is often made in studies carried out by the European Union institutions on **employment** policy, was defined by the **European Commission** in a 1994 White Paper as a 'unique blend of economic well-being, social cohesiveness and high overall quality of life' (see **social policy**). President Chirac of France contributed a memorandum on the European social model to the Dublin meeting of the **European Council** in December 1996. Basically, the expression refers to the character of state involvement in the labour market and to welfare systems.

Although it is broadly true that among **the Six** (except Italy) there were marked similarities in their labour markets and welfare systems (based as they were on the 'Bismarckian' or 'Rhineland' model), there is no longer a single 'European social model' in the European Union. Most commentators distinguish the Rhineland model from the Anglo-Saxon model and from the Mediterranean model. Since 1995 there has been a Scandinavian model too. Some member states and many powerful trade union organizations are strongly opposed to the introduction of what they see as the more ruthless Anglo-American model of employment and welfare. More important than the *levels* of employment are the overall *patterns* of employment which the different models can be shown to deliver, in terms of the numbers of older men, young people, and women in employment, the pay differentials between groups, and the impact on business costs and competitiveness. There is a lucid and informative discussion of all these issues in Linda Hantrais, *Social Policy in the European Union* (Basingstoke, 1995).

European Space Agency (ESA)

Established in 1975, the ESA brought together the European Space Research Organization (ESRO) and the European Space Vehicle Launcher

Development Organization (ELDO). The ESA is not formally associated with the European Union. It has 15 member countries (Norway, Switzerland and all Union member states except Greece and Luxembourg) and its headquarters are in Paris. Canada is an associate. The ESA has a Research and Technical Centre in Noordwijk (The Netherlands), a Research Institute in Frascati (Italy), an Operations Centre in Darmstadt (Germany), and an Astronaut Centre in Cologne. In 1999 ESA's budget was €2.6 billion. Most of the ESA's work has been centred upon the launching from a site in French Guiana of satellites for communications, broadcasting, meteorology and space research, the underlying aim being to give Europe its own launching capability. The Ariane launcher was developed by the ESA, as was the Giotto space laboratory which studied Halley's Comet and the Hubble Space Telescope (jointly with NASA). Research continues into a staffed space laboratory (Spacelab), navigational and surveillance systems, the space shuttle and, in collaboration with the United States, a manned space station to which ESA has contributed a European Robotic Arm. The most ambitious current project is Galileo, a navigational system using some 30 satellites, due to be launched over the period 2004–8. Most of the funding for the ESA comes from participating states, although some revenue is earned from the launching of satellites on behalf of commercial interests. On 2 December 1999 the **Council of Ministers** of the European Union adopted a Resolution on developing a coherent European space strategy (*Official Journal*, C375, 24 December 1999). This was followed up on 16 November 2000 by the adoption, jointly with the Council of the ESA, of a common strategy for space (*Official Journal*, C371, 23 December 2000). The **European Commission** has drawn up an action plan for the period 2001–3 for a programme of Global Monitoring for Environment and Security.

European Trade Union Confederation (ETUC)
Founded as the European Secretariat within the International Confederation of Free Trade Unions in 1958, the ETUC dates in its present form from 1973. Its membership is made up of 74 national trades union confederations in 34 European countries, representing some 60 million trade unionists. The ETUC's main role is to seek to shape European legislation likely to affect the interests of trade unions and their members by lobbying the **European Commission**, the **European Parliament** and especially the **Economic and Social Committee**. A congress is held every four years.

European Training Foundation (ETF)
The ETF, which is based in Turin, is an autonomous European Union **agency** set up on 7 May 1990 under Regulation 1360/90 (*Official Journal*, L131, 23 May

1990). Operational since 1995, the ETF's task is to advise the **European Commission** on matters concerning vocational education and training in the countries of central and eastern Europe, the Mediterranean, and the former Soviet Union, and in Mongolia. Assisted by a National Observatory Network, it provides information, produces publications, and organizes meetings and visits, and is closely involved in the **Tempus** programme.

European Union

The phrase 'European Union' is not to be found in any of the original **Treaties**. However, the preamble to the **Treaty of Rome** opens with the words 'Determined to lay the foundations of an ever closer union among the peoples of Europe ...', a deliberate echo of the 'more perfect union' referred to in the Constitution of the United States. The commitment to a European Union was first formally made at the October 1972 Paris **summit**, at which the heads of government of the member states, the 'driving wheels of European construction', confirmed their intention of 'converting their entire relationship into a European Union before the end of this decade'. This was reaffirmed at the Copenhagen summit the following year (see also **European identity**). In fact, it was not until the 1991 **Maastricht Treaty**, the formal title of which is the Treaty on European Union, that a European Union was brought into existence.

'European Union' and similar phrases are to be found in many documents that mark the successive stages of the institutional development of the Union. Of the prewar proposals, the best known are the **Pan-Europa** of **Count Richard Coudenhove-Kalergi** and the plan for a European Federal Union put forward in 1929 by **Aristide Briand** in the **League of Nations**. The abortive draft Treaty establishing the **European Political Community** of 1953 described it as being 'founded upon a union of peoples and States'. The resolution adopted by the foreign ministers at the **Messina Conference** in 1955 referred to 'the setting up of a united Europe'. Even the 1962 **Fouchet Plan** (final version) spoke of 'a union of States and of European peoples, hereafter called "the European Union"'. The communiqué issued after the 1969 summit in The Hague referred to 'a United Europe capable of assuming its responsibilities in the world of tomorrow'.

Magniloquence apart, the first attempt to define what European Union might actually mean was made in the 1975 **Tindemans Report**. It identified the essential components of European Union as 'a united front to the outside world'; 'a common economic and monetary policy', backed by common policies for industry, agriculture, energy and research; and regional and social policies that would allow 'the solidarity of our peoples to be effective and adequate'. Above all, the European Union was to be founded upon 'institutions with the necessary powers to determine a common, coherent and all-inclusive political view, the efficiency needed for action, the legitimacy needed for democratic control'. Although little concrete action followed from the Tindemans Report, there was no dissent from its definition of European Union. Eight years later the member states reaffirmed the Paris summit commitment in the 1983 **Stuttgart Declaration** (formally known as the Solemn Declaration on European Union) in response to the proposals in the **Genscher–Colombo Plan**. The Declaration said that 'European Union is being achieved by deepening and broadening the scope of European activities so that they coherently cover … a growing proportion of Member States' mutual relations and of their external relations'. The member states undertook to review progress within five years, and to 'decide whether the progress achieved should be incorporated in a Treaty on European Union'.

The most ambitious scheme of the early 1980s was the **Draft Treaty establishing the European Union** (DTEU) adopted by the **European Parliament** in February 1984 (see also **constituent assembly**). Unlike the Maastricht Treaty, the DTEU proposed a uniform structure rather than one based on so-called **pillars**. The European Union, which would have its own **legal personality**, would take over the whole of the *acquis communautaire* and its institutions would assume the functions presently carried out by the institutions of the Community.

In the preamble to the 1986 **Single European Act** (SEA) the member states once again reaffirmed their commitment to European Union as expressed at the Paris summit. The SEA envisaged a union based upon the European Communities on the one hand and a strengthened, formalized system of **European Political Cooperation** on the other. The latter had its own, essentially intergovernmental, decision-making procedures (see **intergovernmentalism**). This model, employing what would later become known as separate pillars, was refined and developed in the European Union established five years later under the Maastricht Treaty.

The word 'union' has always posed difficulties for the United Kingdom. Historically, the word arouses associations with the 1707 Act of Union, which brought about the near-total integration of England and Scotland. In the view of **Roy Jenkins**, 'union' is thought of on the Continent as an overall direction, in the United Kingdom as a destination, which serves to explain the peculiarly British interest in defining exactly what 'union' would entail. Some of the difficulties may be evaded by the judicious use of 'unity' or 'unification' in certain contexts. The latter in particular may be used to characterize the 'ever closer union' referred to in the Treaty of Rome as a *process* rather than as an *end-state* (see also **United States of Europe**). In an essay called 'Towards European Union' contributed to the July/August 1947 edition of the *Partisan*

Review, George Orwell remarked that 'a Western European union is in itself a less improbable concatenation than the Soviet Union or the British Empire' (*Collected Essays, Journalism and Letters,* Vol. 4).

The report by the House of Lords Select Committee on the European Communities entitled *European Union* (23 July 1985) is a comprehensive study of the main issues raised by European Union and contains several of the basic texts. It also contains evidence from many expert witnesses (including that of Roy Jenkins noted opposite).

European Unit of Account

See **European Currency Unit**.

European University Institute (EUI)

Founded in 1976, the EUI is based in Fiesole near Florence, and offers postgraduate courses leading to a master's degree or a doctorate. There are four departments: history and civilization, economics, law, and political and social sciences. The EUI is also the repository of the historical archives of the **European Communities**. Although Article 9.2 of the **Treaty of Paris** specified that 'an institution of university status shall be established', the EUI is not a Union body and has its own legal personality independent of the **Treaties**. It is financed by direct contributions from member states. The President of the EUI heads a small administrative staff and a teaching staff largely composed of academics on three-year fellowships and Visiting Professors.

Europol

At the meeting of the **European Council** held in Luxembourg on 28–29 June 1991 it was decided on a proposal from the German government to establish a Community-wide organization, to be known as Europol, to facilitate cooperation between the police forces of member states. The decision was confirmed at a meeting of justice and home affairs ministers (the **Trevi Group**) in The Hague on 3 December 1991 and embodied in the **Maastricht Treaty** (Article 29). The Treaty provides for 'police cooperation for the purposes of preventing and combating terrorism, unlawful drug trafficking and other serious forms of international crime, including if necessary certain aspects of customs cooperation, in connection with the organization of a Union-wide system for exchanging information within a European Police Office (Europol)'. A Declaration on Police Cooperation was annexed to the Maastricht Treaty, instructing the Trevi Group and the **European Commission** to set up Europol 'at an early date'.

In the first phase Europol is planned as a system for the rapid and confidential exchange of information on issues such as drugs, suspected terrorists, arms shipments and asylum seekers. However, even this limited objective has met problems similar to those raised in the context of the **Schengen Agreement**, such as the individual's right to privacy, accountability for police action, different national laws (some of a constitutional nature) on such matters as extradition and public order and the role of the **Court of Justice**. All these issues were raised in the discussions between member states on the Europol Convention. Cooperation between police forces is made more difficult by the diversity of national police structures: the United Kingdom, for example, has 52 separate forces organized on a geographical basis, whereas the majority of other member states have at least one national force to supplement local forces. The first part of Europol to become operational was the Europol Drugs Unit in The Hague. The Europol Convention was not finally agreed until the Cannes meeting of the European Council in June 1995 (*Official Journal*, C316, 27 November 1995). The remit of Europol has been extended to cover illegal trade in nuclear materials and (from January 1999) terrorism. An annual report on Europol is forwarded to the **European Parliament**. The Convention came into force in October 1998, the definition of 'trafficking in human beings' having been extended to include child pornography.

Eurostat

Eurostat is the statistical office of the European Union. Based in Luxembourg, it is largely dependent on information supplied by member states, not all of it equally comprehensive and reliable and much of it posing problems of comparability. Eurostat publishes several series of statistics dealing with the economy, agriculture, trade, energy and employment. In most cases the tables incorporate comparisons between the Union's member states, other European countries, Japan and the United States. The annual *Eurostat Yearbook* is especially useful. See also **Intrastat**.

Excessive Deficit Procedure

One of the **convergence criteria** under the provisions on **Economic and Monetary Union** (EMU) added to the **Treaty of Rome** by the **Maastricht Treaty** is the curbing of excessive deficits in levels of planned or actual public expenditure in relation to revenue (Article 104). The reference values set out in a **protocol** annexed to the Treaty of Rome allow the excess of expenditure over revenue (i.e., government borrowing at national, regional and local level) to be no more than 3 per cent of gross domestic product (GDP) in any year, and allow total government debt to be no more than 60 per cent of GDP. Under Article 3 of the protocol member states are required to 'report their planned and actual deficits and the levels of their debt promptly and regularly to the **European Commission**, which in turn reports any cases of excessive deficit to the **Monetary Committee** and to the **Ecofin Council**. The Commission is allowed some latitude in the sense that countries in which the total public sector deficit, even if above 60 per cent, is obviously on a downward trend, may be said not to have an 'excessive' deficit. The member states with the worst overall deficits are Belgium, Greece and Italy.

A member state with a deficit found by the Ecofin Council to be excessive receives 'recommendations' from the Council. From the beginning of stage 3 of EMU these recommendations may, if persistently ignored, be followed up by other measures, such as a withdrawal of **European Investment Bank** lending facilities, the obligation to make 'a non-interest-bearing deposit of an appropriate size' with the Community until the deficit is corrected, or fines. Of the 15 member states, only Ireland and Luxembourg have not, at some time since the system came into operation, been found to have an excessive deficit. As part of the decision establishing stage 3 of EMU (see **convergence criteria**) in May 1998, outstanding Council decisions to the effect that excessive deficits existed in Austria, Belgium, France, Germany, Italy, Portugal, Spain, Sweden and the United Kingdom, were abrogated.

Exchange-Rate Mechanism (ERM)

Introduced as part of the **European Monetary System** (EMS) in 1979, the EMS was devised as a means of minimizing currency fluctuations. Each participating currency had a central exchange rate against the **ECU**, which in turn allowed a system of bilateral central rates to be calculated covering all the participating currencies. Each currency was allowed to fluctuate against the others by an agreed margin around these bilateral central rates: if it approached its top or bottom limit a 'divergence indicator' was triggered, and at this point the national central banks intervened on exchange markets to bring the two currencies back into line (see **European Monetary Cooperation Fund**). Other measures, such as adjustments to interest rates, could also be taken. If a currency could not be held within its agreed margins, a realignment could be negotiated in the **Monetary Committee**.

The ERM was the successor to a similar system for limiting currency fluctuations known as the **'snake in the tunnel'** (see also **Werner Report**). When the ERM first came into operation in March 1979, eight currencies took part in the system: the Belgian and Luxembourg francs, the French franc, the Danish krone, the Deutsche Mark, the Dutch guilder, the Italian lira and the Irish punt. The pound sterling did not take part, nor did the Greek drachma when Greece joined the Community in 1981. The Spanish peseta joined the ERM in June 1989, the pound sterling in October 1990, and the Portuguese escudo in April 1992. All currencies were allowed to fluctuate within a margin of 2.25 per cent on either side of their bilateral central rates (the 'narrow band'), except the peseta, the lira, the escudo and the pound sterling, which were allowed a 'broad band' of 6 per cent.

Currency speculation on an unprecedented scale on 16 September 1992 ('Black Wednesday') caused the pound sterling and the lira to leave the ERM and the peseta to be devalued by 5 per cent. This speculation was prompted at least in part by the possibility of a 'No' vote in the French referendum on the **Maastricht Treaty** four days later. In the recriminations that followed, Germany was blamed for maintaining high interest rates (see **German reunification**). On 2 August 1993 further large-scale speculation all but destroyed the ERM. The wide band was increased to 15 per cent and extended to all currencies (although the Germans and the Dutch agreed bilaterally to retain the narrow band between their currencies). The majority of currencies moved back to their pre-August 1993 alignments. The Austrian schilling joined the ERM in January 1995, the Finnish markka in October 1996 and the lira rejoined in November 1996. The Greek drachma joined in March 1998. The Swedish krona has not joined and the pound sterling has not rejoined.

General realignments within the ERM took place only infrequently. Between April 1986 and September 1992 there were no realignments involving more than three currencies, and only eight such realignments over the whole period from 1979. With the new, very broad bands of 15 per cent (see above), there was hardly any need for further realignments.

Before 1993 the ERM was widely credited with having achieved its primary goal of creating monetary stability among participating states, and in particular with having helped to shield their economies from the effects of the instability caused by the rise and fall of the dollar. The ERM removed the temptation to engage in competitive devaluations. It also contributed to economic convergence by serving to lessen interest-rate differentials over the period and in general acted as an external discipline of which member states have taken advantage in the fight against inflation.

The ERM is part of the *acquis communautaire*, so all states acceding to the Union are required to be prepared to join it (although not necessarily immediately). Observance of the 'normal fluctuation margins' within the ERM for at least two years is also one of the **convergence criteria** that must be met by a member state wishing to proceed to stage 3 of **Economic and Monetary Union** (EMU). Now that 12 countries have adopted the **euro**, a new **Stability and Growth Pact** and a new ERM ('ERM 2') have come into effect. ERM 2, set up under a Resolution adopted at the European Council meeting in Amsterdam (June 1997), is centred on the euro, with the currencies outside the euro area permitted to fluctuate within 15 per cent of their central rate against the euro.

External Frontiers Convention

The External Frontiers Convention, which remained unratified, dealt with the treatment of nationals of non-member states at the external frontiers of the European Union. It provided for the issuing of visas by member states to be based on an agreed list of the countries whose nationals required visas and for there to be mutual recognition of visas for 'short stay' visits of up to three months. It allowed member states to retain exclusive control over the admission of third-country nationals for stays longer than three months. It endorsed the principle of 'carriers' liability', under which airlines and other commercial transport operators could be fined if their passengers were found on arrival not to have a right of entry. Common procedures were laid down for the removal of illegal immigrants and overstayers. In common with the **Dublin Asylum Convention**, the External Frontiers Convention was based on the commitment in Article 7a (now 14) of the **Treaty of Rome** to create 'an area without internal frontiers in which the free movement of . . . persons . . . is ensured'.

In December 1993 the **European Commission** brought forward proposals in the form of a revised draft Convention under Article K3 of the **Maastricht Treaty** (now Article 62.2(b).i EC) and a Regulation containing a list of third countries whose nationals need a visa to enter the territory of the member states. Such a list was already provided for in the Convention (see above), but the Commission proposal was brought forward under Article 100 (c) EC as a separate measure with a view to speeding up the process of securing agreement among member states. Under Article 100 (c), added by the Maastricht Treaty but since repealed, decisions on visas could be taken by **qualified majority voting**. The visa list was adopted in September 1995, but was annulled by the **Court of Justice** in June 1997 (case C392/95) on the grounds that it should have been referred to the **European Parliament** in a **reconsultation**. However, its provisions remained in force. In May 1998 it was agreed to allow illegal immigrants to be fingerprinted (see **Eurodac**).

Work on all the matters covered by the two Conventions now proceeds within the framework laid down in the Maastricht Treaty for cooperation in the fields of **Justice and Home Affairs** (JHA; see also **free movement of persons**), but with the incorporation of the **Schengen** *acquis* into the European Union the External Frontiers Convention has been superseded.

Extradition

Within the European Union extradition is governed by a Convention (*Official Journal*, C 313, 23 October 1996) based in part on a 1957 Convention drawn up by the **Council of Europe** and on a Treaty on Extradition and Mutual

Assistance in Criminal Matters agreed among the **Benelux** countries in 1962. The Union's Convention sets out agreed definitions of extraditable offences and addresses the problems which arise from differences between member states' legal systems with respect to concepts such as conspiracy, 'political' offences and the various kinds of fiscal crime. The Convention also seeks to remove procedural obstacles to the handling of requests for extradition. Member states remain free not to extradite their own nationals. However, the Convention allows and encourages there to be a presumption of consent on the part of member states to whom applications for extradition are addressed. Since the Convention was adopted, member states have committed themselves in the **Charter of Fundamental Rights of the European Union** (Article 19.2) not to extradite anyone 'to a State in which there is a serious risk that he or she would be subjected to the death penalty, torture or other inhuman or degrading treatment or punishment'. Extradition is an important aspect of the area of freedom, security and justice.

The European Arrest Warrant (EAW), agreed by the Council of Justice Ministers on 11 December 2001 and due to be introduced on 1 January 2004, will supersede the current extradition procedures for offences carrying a custodial sentence of at least one year and for fugitives already sentenced to custody or detention for four months or more. For 32 serious offences – those carrying a sentence of at least three years – it will no longer be necessary to prove that the offence is recognized as such in the legal systems of both the country in which the EAW has been issued and the country in which the person charged with the offence has been apprehended ('double criminality').

F

Factortame case

The Factortame case (*R* v *Secretary of State for Transport, ex parte Factortame Ltd*, Case C213/89) arose when a number of companies, largely Spanish-controlled, sought a judicial review of certain provisions of the British Merchant Shipping Act 1988 which were alleged to be discriminatory in respect of the rules for registering fishing vessels as British. The system of quotas and total allowable catches under the **Common Fisheries Policy** made it attractive to seek British registration, and until the 1988 Act the rules for such registration were relatively lax (see **quota-hopping**). The companies, which also claimed that their rights under Treaty provisions on **freedom of establishment** were being infringed, sought interim relief (i.e., that the relevant provisions of the Act should be waived) while the case was being decided, initially in the British courts.

Such relief was granted, but both the Court of Appeal and the House of Lords took the view that the Divisional Court in which the action was first brought had no power to order a waiver from the provisions of the Act. The **Court of Justice** ruled that unless such a power existed the effectiveness of **EU law** would be impaired. The Factortame case served to underline the **primacy** of EU law and the importance attached by the Court to the removal of any impediment to an individual's power to assert rights arising from EU law. It is discussed in more detail in Weatherill and Beaumont, *EU Law* (3rd edn, Harmondsworth, 1999).

Faeroes, The

A small group of islands in the North Atlantic, the Faeroes have internal autonomy under Danish sovereignty. They have opted to remain outside the European Union and **EU law** does not apply in the Faeroes. However, the islands' trade is covered by free trade arrangements within the **European Economic Area** (EEA).

Failure to act

Article 232 of the **Treaty of Rome**, as amended by the **Maastricht Treaty**, states: 'Should the **European Parliament**, the **Council** or the [**European**] **Commission**, in infringement of this Treaty, fail to act, the Member States and the other institutions of the Community may bring an action before the **Court of Justice** to have the infringement established.' The institution concerned must first be 'called upon to act', and thereafter has two months within which to 'define its position'. If it does not, an action may be brought within a further two months. An institution that is found by the Court to have failed to act 'shall be required to take the necessary measures' (Article 233). It should be noted that the Court's power under Article 228 (as revised by the Maastricht Treaty) to impose a 'lump sum or penalty payment' on a member state found to be in default of its Treaty obligations does not extend to the Council as the collective embodiment of the member states. Any individual or organization possessing legal personality may complain to the Court 'that an institution of the Community has failed to address to that person any act other than a recommendation or an **opinion**'.

Only a few actions have ever been brought under Article 232. The best-known example was a case brought by the European Parliament in 1983 against the Council for the latter's failure to enact a **common transport policy** as required under Articles 3(e), 74 and 75 (now 3(f), 70 and 71) (Case 13/83). The Court ruling of 22 May 1985 found partially in the Parliament's favour, and even though progress since that date in the field of transport has been well short of spectacular the case was a moral victory for the Parliament and helped to bring pressure to bear upon the Council.

Falcone programme

The Falcone programme (1998–2002), set up under Joint Action 98/245 on 19 March 1998 (*Official Journal*, L99, 31 March 1998), is designed to allow those engaged in the fight against **organized crime** in the European Union to exchange information, undertake studies and compare initiatives across frontiers. Giovanni Falcone was an Italian judge who in the course of investigating the Mafia was murdered by them in May 1992 (Alexander Stille, *Excellent Cadavers*, 1995).

Federalism

See **Federation**.

Federation

Federation is a form of political organization characterized by a division of responsibility between a central authority and component parts (usually states, regions or provinces) enjoying autonomy in certain fields. The distribution of powers between the centre and the component parts in any federal structure will vary from case to case and may vary over time (see also **confederation**), and is normally embodied in a constitution. Federation was defined by A. V. Dicey in *The Law of the Constitution* (1885) as 'a political contrivance intended to reconcile national unity and power with the maintenance of states' rights'.

Within Europe there are several types of federation, and several examples of federal structures that proved too fragile to contain ethnic differences or other causes of tension, such as Yugoslavia and Czechoslovakia. Federation may be adapted to the needs of a previously unitary state in which the component parts are seeking greater autonomy, as in Belgium; and to those of countries or states choosing to become integrated to a greater or lesser extent within a larger political unit, such as **Benelux**.

Among the areas usually reserved to the central federal authority are defence, foreign trade, external representation and the negotiation of treaties, immigration, the rights and duties flowing from citizenship, and the management of the currency. The tax structure and the system for raising and allocating revenue will normally reflect the extent to which the component parts of the federation have spending responsibilities, such as those in the field of health, education, housing, public works and the administration of justice. Most federations have a central bank, a supreme court and a two-chamber parliament in which the upper chamber is composed of representatives of the states, regions or provinces of which the federation is composed. This is now known as 'Hamiltonian' federalism, effected by means of institutions: 'Proudhonian' federalism is based on free association motivated by common interests.

Federalist ideas were a powerful influence upon many of the pioneers of European integration, such as **Jean Monnet** and **Altiero Spinelli**, in the 1940s and early 1950s. The two world wars had done much to discredit **intergovernmentalism** and to call into question the nation-state as the basis for international relations. Federalist ideas, ambitions and assumptions are everywhere evident in the **Treaties** upon which the **European Communities** are based. Great importance is attached in the Treaties to supranational institutions of a federal type, and although the **European Commission** has not emerged as the real European government (with the **Council of Ministers** and the **European Parliament** as the upper and lower houses of a bicameral legislature) it is these institutions, together with the **Court of Justice**, that give the Community its distinctive quasi-federal structure. It was precisely the supranational and therefore federal character of the Community's main institutions that prompted the hostility of **Charles de Gaulle** and, later, **Margaret Thatcher**, both of whom interpreted the ambitions of

Commission presidents **Walter Hallstein** and **Jacques Delors** as a direct challenge to the integrity and authority of the nation-state and so to **sovereignty**. British reservations about 'federalism' were still sufficiently strong to secure the removal of the phrase 'of a federal type', to describe the European Union, from the final draft of the **Maastricht Treaty**. This was hailed, in the United Kingdom at least, as a triumph, in spite of the fact that the fundamentally federalist character of some of the Treaty's provisions (such as those empowering the Court of Justice to fine defaulting member states) not only remained intact but enjoyed vigorous British support. Another prominent feature of the Treaty, the doctrine of **subsidiarity**, is only meaningful in the context of a federal structure in which there is a balance of power between the Union institutions and national, regional or local authorities. For some time yet federation and federalism are likely to remain poorly understood. In some quarters they are thought to be synonymous with the 'European superstate', with 'rule from Brussels' and the decline of nationhood. In others, they are seen as safeguards against overweening central authority and the emergence of a Europe in which the hard-won rights of nations and communities to manage their own affairs are not only recognized but guaranteed.

FEOGA
See **European Agricultural Guidance and Guarantee Fund**.

Fiche d'impact
Appended to every important legislative proposal from the **European Commission** is a (usually rather cursory) assessment of its impact, known as the *fiche d'impact*. Depending on the nature of the proposal, the *fiche d'impact* will normally deal with its impact on employment or the environment and will draw attention to any special problems likely to arise for small and medium-sized enterprises (SMEs). The impact of the proposal on the Union's **Budget** is the subject of a separate assessment known as a *fiche financière* (see also **budgetary discipline**).

Finalités politiques
This phrase is sometimes used to denote the ultimate goals of the European Union, forming part of the *acquis communautaire* but not necessarily (yet) to be found in the **Treaties**. An objective set out in a **Resolution** of the **European Council**, for example, may be regarded as among the *finalités politiques* even before it has been embodied in the Treaties or given rise to legislation.

Financial control
See **Court of Auditors, discharge procedure, fraud**.

Financial framework

See **future financing**.

Financial services

The 1985 **Cockfield White Paper** identified the opening up of the financial services market (mainly banking, mortgage lending and insurance) as an essential element in the **Single Market** programme. Progress in this sector had been slow, with several member states justifying their own national regulations on (sometimes spurious) consumer protection grounds. Although in theory financial services were covered by general Treaty provisions on **competition policy, freedom of establishment** and **freedom to provide services**, in fact, as Article 61.2 (now 51) of the **Treaty of Rome** specified, liberalization was bound up with free movement of capital (see **capital movements**). Accordingly, it was not until the late 1980s that real progress was made, with Directives on credit institutions, funds, solvency ratios and the provision of financial services (the Second Banking Directive of 1989). Credit institutions may now establish branches freely in other member states and throughout the **European Economic Area** (EEA) while remaining subject to 'home country control', the conditions for which have been established on an agreed basis. To date, less progress has been made with opening up the insurance sector. This very complex field may be better understood with the aid of John A. Usher, *The Law of Money and Financial Services in the European Community* (Oxford, 1994).

Finland

Finland's proximity to the Soviet Union (in Tsarist times it was part of Russian territory as the Grand Duchy of Finland) meant that until recently the country's approach to all alliances with the countries of the West was extremely cautious. Although a member of the **Council of Europe** and an active partner in the **Nordic Council**, Finland did not join the United Nations until 1955 and was at first only an associate member of the **European Free Trade Association** (EFTA) (full member from 1986). As an EFTA state, Finland signed the free trade agreement with the Community that came into effect in January 1973 and later the agreement establishing the **European Economic Area** (EEA). Finland applied for full membership of the Community on 18 March 1992. The motives were largely political in the sense that it was a means of emerging from the long shadow cast by the former USSR. Like Sweden, Finland has a long-standing *de facto* commitment to **neutrality**. However, since the **Maastricht Treaty** does not establish a military alliance and allows member states to continue with individual defence arrangements, Finland considers its provisions to be not incompatible with neutrality.

The **Opinion** of the **European Commission** published later that year (*Bulletin of the European Communities*, supplement 6/92), noted that in a speech in Bruges (28 October 1992) President Koivisto accepted 'the *acquis communautaire*, the Maastricht Treaty and the *finalité politique* of the European Union'. The problems identified in the generally favourable Opinion included the need to make adjustments to the Finnish system of agricultural support and to the various state monopolies. Finnish industry and commerce were already adapting to the *acquis communautaire*, but certain anomalies remained in the fields of company taxation, direct taxation and social security. A peculiarity of the Finnish constitution is the autonomous status of the Swedish-speaking Åland Islands in the Gulf of Bothnia. This is of particular relevance to environmental legislation and to certain tax questions, for which the islands' Assembly has responsibility.

Negotiations with Finland were completed in March 1994, and resulted, *inter alia*, in a new Objective 6 category of region being created in relation to the **structural funds**. This allowed aid to be given in recognition of under-population and the peculiarly harsh conditions affecting agriculture in Finland and Sweden. The **European Parliament** gave its assent to Finnish **accession** in May 1994. An advisory referendum was held on 16 October 1994, membership of the Union gaining the support of 56.9 per cent of the vote; the Åland Islands also voted in favour in a separate referendum. This was confirmed in the Finnish Parliament on 18 November 1994, and Finland joined the Union on 1 January 1995. European elections were held in Finland on 20 October 1996.

The addition of Finnish to the list of official **languages** poses a particular problem since it is not related to any other language spoken in the Union.

Fisheries
See **Common Fisheries Policy**.

Flexibility
Sometimes referred to as 'differentiated integration', flexibility is an expression used to denote any set of arrangements within the European Union which represents a departure from the principle that all member states must move towards the same objectives at the same pace. Flexibility may apply to the *participants*, the *objectives*, the *pace*, or any combination of these. **Variable geometry**, the **opt-out**, and **two-speed Europe** are examples of flexibility, as is 'enhanced cooperation'. Calls for greater flexibility have been prompted by the frustration of certain member states within a system which obliges the convoy to move at the speed of the slowest ship.

The case for greater flexibility has been strengthened by the imminence of further **enlargement** and the accession of member states unable, however willing, to match the pace set by the leaders (the so-called '**hard core**'). On the other hand, there are concerns about the overall coherence and consistency of the Union, the equitable sharing of financial burdens, the homogeneity of **EU law**, fair competition, and the principle of non-discrimination between citizens of the Union.

The **Treaty of Amsterdam** attempted to reconcile these concerns in a new Article K15 (now 43) added to the **Maastricht Treaty** and a new Article 5(a) (now 11) added to the **Treaty of Rome**. These Articles allow member states 'which intend to establish closer cooperation between themselves ... to make use of the institutions, procedures and mechanisms' set out in the two Treaties on condition that the area of policy is not within the Community's exclusive competence, that the cooperation will not affect 'Community policies, actions or programmes', that it will neither affect **citizenship** of the Union nor entail discrimination among nationals of the member states, that it is 'within the limits of the powers conferred upon the Community by this Treaty', and that it does not affect trade or conditions of competition between member states (Article 11 EC).

Member states wishing to establish such cooperation must address a request to the **European Commission**. The Commission must then submit a formal proposal to the **Council of Ministers**, or give its reasons for not doing so. The Council may then, acting by **qualified majority** and having consulted the **European Parliament**, give its assent to the proposal, or refer the matter to the **European Council** for unanimous decision. Any member state may veto the taking of a vote to give the Council's assent. Once established, closer cooperation is 'subject to all the relevant provisions of this Treaty', and must remain open to other member states.

Some commentators have suggested that the terms of Article 11 are so strict as to make it impossible for 'closer cooperation' to take place. In particular, it is hard to see how member states could cooperate in an area covered by the Treaties without affecting 'Community policies, actions or programmes'. It has also been remarked that the Article says nothing about how any costs arising from enhanced cooperation will be met, nor does it specify a role for the **Court of Justice**.

Article 11 does not of course affect any present or future arrangements among member states (sometimes including non-member states) for collaboration on specific projects such as the **European Space Agency** which are outside the Union framework. The **Schengen Agreement** is an example of a 'flexible' collaboration which started outside the Treaties but which is gradually being incorporated into them.

The **Treaty of Nice** redrafts the Treaty provisions on closer cooperation, allowing only cooperation which is aimed at 'reinforcing' the process of integration and which involves a minimum of eight member states. Acts and decisions arising from closer cooperation are excluded from the *acquis communautaire*. Closer cooperation may not be extended to 'matters having military and defence implications'.

Food safety

European legislation on food safety was first enacted to enable food products to be traded freely within the European Community under the **Common Agricultural Policy** (CAP) and has always been an important component of **consumer policy**. The 1979 **Cassis de Dijon** case established the principle of mutual recognition of product standards, thereby reducing the need for detailed **harmonization**. In the 1980s the **Single Market** programme was accompanied by a strengthening of consumer protection measures in respect of matters such as permitted additives, labelling, and product specifications. By the 1990s public concern about food safety was mounting, partly as a result of the BSE and Foot and Mouth Disease outbreaks, partly in response to scientific developments such as irradiation, genetic modification, and the use of hormones. This in turn led to a new interest in traditional, 'organic' products. With advice from nine advisory committees and the Food and Veterinary Office in Dublin (which ensures that member states' authorities enforce European Community rules on food safety) the **European Commission** has sought to develop this area of policy with measures such as a 'biological agriculture' labelling scheme, another scheme to protect particular origin designations and traditional specialities, and – with the help of the new **European Food Safety Authority** – a more thorough monitoring of the whole process of food production 'from the farm to the fork'. A White Paper on food safety (COM(1999)719) was published on 12 January 2000.

The European Union is the world's biggest importer and the second most important food exporter. The Union cooperates in efforts to raise food standards worldwide and to facilitate trade in food products through the United Nations' 'Codex Alimentarius' and the **World Trade Organization** (WTO).

Fontainebleau Agreement

The Fontainebleau Agreement of June 1984 marked the conclusion of the long-standing dispute over the United Kingdom's contribution to the **Budget** of the European Community (see **British Budget problem**). At Fontainebleau the **European Council** agreed to grant the United Kingdom an **abatement**, calculated annually, on the element of the British contribution based on value-added tax (VAT) (see **own resources**). The system has remained in force and was renewed until 2006 at the Berlin meeting of the European Council in March 1999. The future of the abatement is touched on in the *Agenda 2000* study, published by the **European Commission** in July 1997. The Commission proposed not to re-examine the system until after the first **enlargement** because of the difficulty of forecasting the United Kingdom's relative prosperity over the period from 1999 to 2006.

Fortress Europe

'Fortress Europe' is a phrase used to embody the fears of the European Union's principal trading partners and supporters of free trade that the Union is becoming more protectionist. Such fears were prompted in the late 1980s by the moves to complete the 1992 **Single Market** programme, since it appeared that some member states were prepared to see the removal of barriers to trade within the Community only if it were accompanied by a strengthening of measures to control imports from non-member countries. It was thought that some member states would like to extend **Community preference** beyond agricultural trade to trade in manufactured goods and services. The lengthy dispute with the United States over agricultural export subsidies in the Uruguay Round (see **General Agreement on Tariffs and Trade** (GATT)) gave some substance to these fears, but on the whole, in spite of recession and high unemployment, the European Union has not resorted to protectionism.

'Fortress Europe' has a definite pejorative ring by virtue of its echo of Nazi Germany's *Festung Europa*, suggesting both impregnable defences and economic autarky.

Fouchet Plan

The Fouchet Plan of 1961–2 was a determined attempt by the French President, **Charles de Gaulle**, to alter the institutional balance of the European Community in favour of **intergovernmentalism** and in the process to establish a form of political cooperation that would secure Europe's independence from the Atlantic Alliance and the United States. Although unsuccessful, this initiative divided the advocates of closer European integration – with some, such as **Jean Monnet**, initially anxious to exploit de Gaulle's apparent preparedness to consolidate the political dimension of the Community – and provided a significant foretaste of the kind of intransigence which de Gaulle and his government were later to display on a number of European issues.

On 5 September 1960 de Gaulle unexpectedly stated at one of his regular press conferences in the Elysée Palace that 'ensuring regular cooperation in Western Europe is something which France considers desirable, possible and practicable in the political ... and defence fields'. To promote this, he advocated 'regular organized concertation by the governments responsible', based on a new intergovernmental structure, answerable to an assembly of national parliamentarians and enjoying public endorsement by means of a 'vast

European referendum'. The emphasis on strong ministerial or executive authority based on a direct mandate from the electorate – one of the most important features of Gaullism in France – was to be replicated at European level. Five months later, on 10 February 1961, the first-ever **summit** was hosted by de Gaulle in Paris. At this meeting he convinced the leaders of the five other member states to establish a special committee to consider possible amendments to the **Treaty of Rome** (although not formally constituted as an **Intergovernmental Conference** (IGC), this body served the same purpose). The intention was to add some form of political cooperation among the member states to the existing structure. The committee, chaired by Christian Fouchet, then a senior French diplomat and subsequently a minister under de Gaulle, met between March 1961 and April 1962. A second summit at Bad Godesberg in July 1961 reiterated political support for closer cooperation on foreign and security issues.

Instead of offering proposals likely to command consensus Fouchet attempted to redesign the Community's whole institutional structure, based on a stronger foreign policy component as a pretext for making the Community a looser, more intergovernmental organization.

The initial Fouchet proposals envisaged a 'union of states' to coexist with the existing Community in a number of new areas, most notably foreign policy, defence and culture. It would be governed by a political council of heads of government (or their foreign ministers) acting by **unanimity** and responsible to an assembly of national parliamentarians. The **European Commission** would be bypassed by a new Paris-based 'political commission' of national civil servants (similar in format to the body now known as COREPER). The first draft of the Fouchet Plan, tabled in November 1961, aroused little enthusiasm, especially from the **Benelux** countries, which regarded the Commission as a safeguard for the interests of small countries and were opposed to any diminution of its authority. Germany, under **Konrad Adenauer,** held back from criticizing the texts in the hope of reaching an accommodation. However, a second draft, tabled in January 1962, envisaged crucial additional changes that accentuated still further the intergovernmental character of the proposed 'union', with a new network of ministerial committees to parallel the original **Council of Ministers,** and the economic aspects of the existing Community being potentially subsumed within the 'union', so undermining the existing institutions and the supranational character of EU law. The second draft also foresaw European foreign and defence cooperation taking place outside the framework of the Atlantic Alliance. The five other member states indicated that they could not accept a revised European Community along anything like these lines. The negotiations were suspended on 17 April 1962 and never resumed.

At a press conference on 15 May 1962 de Gaulle launched a dramatic verbal assault on the Community institutions, directed in particular against Commission President **Walter Hallstein**. He satirized its functionaries as 'stateless people' and its technocratic jargon as a 'Volapük' (an artificial international language akin to Esperanto). He declared that it was the United States, not the people of the Community, who would act as 'federator' of Europe (see **Monnet method**), and that 'only the states are valid, legitimate and capable of achievement ... At present there is and can be no Europe other than a Europe of States – except of course a Europe of myths, fictions and pageants'. Exasperated by the growing bitterness and force of de Gaulle's attack on the Community, five pro-European ministers resigned from his government, including Maurice Schumann, a former foreign minister under the Fourth Republic, and Pierre Pflimlin, the penultimate Prime Minister of the Fourth Republic (in 1958) and subsequently a President of the **European Parliament** (1984–7). In addition, 296 French deputies signed a 'European Manifesto' protesting at the increasingly anti-European stance of the President.

The shock delivered to the Community by the Fouchet débâcle was severe. Although in Bad Godesberg they had expressed their intention to continue meeting regularly, the heads of government did not in fact reconvene for six years. A period of stagnation and crisis began, with de Gaulle announcing France's veto of the first British application to join the Community in January 1963, the Community becoming increasingly bogged down at French insistence in complex negotiations on the financing of the **Common Agricultural Policy** (CAP), France threatening to leave the Community in October 1964 unless agreement was reached on the CAP and, finally, in 1965 France boycotting the Council of Ministers in order to prevent the automatic introduction of **qualified majority voting** (QMV) planned for 1966 (the **empty chair crisis**). The consequent **Luxembourg Compromise**, which allowed unanimity to prevail wherever important national interests were at stake, frustrated Community decision-making for the next 20 years.

'Fouchet Plan' is still used as a term of abuse among supporters of European integration. When in 1985 **Jacques Delors** heard of a Franco-German proposal to create a secretary-general who would direct the Community's foreign policy, he intervened with President **François Mitterrand** to denounce the idea as redolent of the Fouchet Plan. The proposal was withdrawn (Charles Grant, *Delors: The House that Jacques Built*, 1994).

Four freedoms

The 'four freedoms' that underpin the **Single Market** are, in the order in which they are listed in Article 3.1(c) of the **Treaty of Rome**, the **free movement of goods**, the **free movement of persons**, **freedom to provide services** and free movement of capital (see **capital movements**).

France

Of all the member states of the European Union, France is unquestionably the one with the best claim to have shaped its political development. France has provided both the impulses and the hesitations: the country of **Jean Monnet** and of the **Schuman Plan**, it is also the country that destroyed the **European Defence Community** and later instigated the **empty chair crisis**. All the enthusiasm and all the reticence that have shaped the European Union as it exists today may be found in France.

Among the central facts in the outlook of any French person in the early 1950s was the knowledge that three times in as many generations France had been attacked by Germany. The Schuman Plan was born not solely from a desire to put relations between states on an entirely new footing but from the idea of containment. If Germany could be placed within a supranational framework that allowed it to recover its prosperity and self-respect and yet required it to act responsibly, then France would benefit. France (which until 1962 included Algeria) was confident of being able to influence the direction that the countries united within that framework would take. This had proved true in the **European Coal and Steel Community** (ECSC) and there was no reason why it should not continue to be true as **the Six** set themselves more ambitious goals within the **European Economic Community** (EEC).

Charles de Gaulle returned to power in 1958, the year in which the EEC came into operation. Whatever misgivings he had about its supranational character, he was sympathetic to its basic aim of containing Germany. But he saw immediately that the admission of the United Kingdom would destroy the nicely calculated balance of power that allowed France to retain political hegemony. Primarily for this reason, but also because he shared neither British sympathy with the Americans nor their attachment to free trade, he vetoed British accession twice, in 1963 and in 1967. He was well aware that the other member states favoured British accession, but, as was also the case with the 1962 **Fouchet Plan** and later the so-called **Luxembourg Compromise** of 1966, he was perfectly content to be in a minority of one. At the same time de Gaulle established good relations with **Konrad Adenauer** and, with the 1963 Elysée Treaty, laid the foundations for **Franco-German cooperation**.

The resignation of de Gaulle in 1969 led to a marked change in French attitudes towards European integration. President Georges Pompidou allowed the United Kingdom, Denmark and Ireland to join the Community (endorsed by a **referendum** in France in April 1972). His successor, **Valéry Giscard d'Estaing**, was and remains a convinced pro-European, yet in his proposal to strengthen the intergovernmental component in Community decision making by establishing a **European Council**, Giscard was giving expression to a traditionally French view of where ultimate power should lie.

It was Giscard too who in 1977 was strongly opposed to **Roy Jenkins**, as President of the **European Commission**, representing the Community as a whole at meetings of the **Group of Seven**.

Institutional questions aside, there are other areas of policy in which France has found itself in a minority. France has no record of enthusiasm for increasing the number of member states. This was understandable when Spanish accession was being negotiated, since Spain was thought to be a rival to French interests, especially in agriculture, but it is in fact part of a wider pattern of opposition to any diminution of French influence. In security issues France chose to remain outside the integrated military structure of the **North Atlantic Treaty Organization** (NATO) from 1966 until 1995 and is jealous of its status as a nuclear power. In spite of Franco-German cooperation, France was most unwilling to allow the number of German seats in the **European Parliament** to be increased to take account of reunification, and threatened to block a settlement until **Strasbourg** was finally chosen as the seat of the Parliament (see **seat of the institutions**). It was France which, by raising last-minute objections to the Uruguay Round of the **General Agreement on Tariffs and Trade** (GATT) negotiations, almost blocked the agreement. And it is France which continually pushes Union rules on **state aids** to the limit.

Until recently it could have been said that support for European integration extended to all political parties in France with the exception of old-guard Communists and the far right. However, the debate on the **Maastricht Treaty**, culminating in the extremely narrow 'Yes' vote in the referendum of September 1992, opened up clear divisions in the centre-right, where once again Gaullist ideas on the supremacy of the nation-state are in evidence. French Members of the European Parliament (MEPs) are scattered across more political groups than MEPs of any other nationality. However, since the 1980s France has drawn advantage from having, in **François Mitterrand**, **Jacques Delors** and Jacques Chirac, three of the most influential personalities in European politics. Whatever disagreements there may be between and within the parties on European issues, France is absolutely determined not to be outstripped by Germany. It was this determination that underpinned the so-called *franc fort* policy of matching the pace set by the Deutsche Mark, even at the price of high unemployment. Above all, France wishes to remain, with Germany, in the position of leadership in Europe established over five decades, and to which the country feels entitled.

Franco-British union

In June 1940 the imminent surrender of France to Germany prompted **Jean Monnet**, then working in London as Chairman of the Anglo-French Coordinating Committee, to propose that the British and French governments should make a declaration proclaiming the 'indissoluble union' of the two countries. This union would entail common citizenship, a common currency, a customs union and joint armed forces. The principle was approved by **Winston Churchill** and by the Cabinet, and the proposal was communicated by **Charles de Gaulle** to the French Cabinet, which had left Paris and was meeting in Bordeaux. By 18 June, however, it was clear that with the resignation of Paul Reynaud, the French Prime Minister, the French surrender was complete and that a declaration of union would not help to keep France in the war. The episode forms the first chapter of Monnet's *Memoirs* (English edn, 1978).

Franco-German cooperation

The cornerstone of postwar cooperation between France and Germany is the Treaty of the Elysée, signed by **Charles de Gaulle** and **Konrad Adenauer** on 22 January 1963. The 1950s had been marked by a gradual convergence of French and German interests. Both countries were founder members of the **European Communities**, both were members of the **North Atlantic Treaty Organization** (NATO) (France 1949, West Germany 1955) and, most importantly, they had resolved their long-standing territorial dispute over the **Saarland**. Even though at the time the Treaty was signed France and Germany were divided over the question of the United Kingdom's application to join the Community, the Treaty was a very explicit statement, enjoying cross-party support, of the two countries' determination to pursue their interests in common.

The Treaty provides a framework for cooperation in three main areas. First, it provides for regular Franco-German summits and for meetings every three months between the ministers for foreign affairs. These meetings have not only been a useful forum for the discussion of general foreign policy questions, they have also given rise to some of the most important initiatives in the field of European integration, such as direct elections to the **European Parliament** and the **European Monetary System** (EMS). They have also been supplemented by other forms of foreign affairs cooperation: for example, in May 1991 the French and German ambassadors accredited to the countries of central and eastern Europe met in Weimar to discuss political developments in the former Soviet bloc. The Franco-German summit in Nuremberg (9 December 1996) resulted in a joint letter to the President-in-office of the **European Council** and contributed towards the agreement at the Dublin meeting of the European Council on some of the institutional reforms set out in the **Treaty of Amsterdam** six months later.

The second and most controversial area of Franco-German cooperation set out in the Treaty is defence and security. For many years the Treaty provisions remained a dead letter. This was, perhaps, hardly surprising in the light of the confusion and acrimony that followed the failure to establish the **European**

Defence Community and the general willingness to rely on the Americans. Not until 1987 did French and German troops take part in joint manoeuvres. The same year, at a Franco-German summit in Karlsruhe, **François Mitterrand** and **Helmut Kohl** announced that a Franco-German Security Council would be set up: this was formalized the following year in a **protocol** signed in Bonn. The Bonn meeting also agreed on the joint development of a combat helicopter (Tiger) and a Franco-German brigade of 4,200 troops, operational since 1991. Four years later, at La Rochelle in May 1992, agreement was reached on a more ambitious Franco-German army corps (35,000 troops) with its headquarters in Strasbourg (see **Eurocorps**; see also **European Armaments Agency**).

The third area of Franco-German cooperation identified in the Treaty is education. At the first Franco-German summit in Bonn in July 1963, the two governments agreed on a 'Youth Bureau' with its headquarters at Bad Honnef, near Bonn. Since its creation this Bureau has overseen several million exchanges between French and German schoolchildren and many thousands of twinnings between schools. Several thousand French students study in German universities, and vice versa. The work of the Bureau is supplemented by initiatives in the field of language teaching and cultural cooperation (agreed at the Frankfurt summit of 1986).

The Bonn summit of January 1988 established not only a Security Council but also an Economic and Financial Council under a separate protocol to the Treaty. This protocol enjoins the Council every year 'to examine the broad outlines of the national budgets before their adoption by the governments and the vote in the national parliaments' and in general terms to coordinate French and German economic policies as closely as possible.

Franco-German cooperation is overseen within each government by inter-ministerial committees. In addition to the specific fields noted above cooperation between the two countries is extensive in other areas. Each is the other's most important trading partner, and each invests heavily in the other. The machinery for cooperation set out in the Elysée Treaty has underpinned the very good relations, political and personal, that have existed, regardless of party, between French and German leaders for more than three decades. And if some unresolved anxieties remain, Franco-German cooperation has not only brought benefits to the two countries concerned but also provided the Union as a whole with the stability that flows from a common sense of purpose between its two leading member states.

Francovich case

The Francovich case (*Francovich and others* v *Italy*, Cases C6/90 and C9/90) established the principle that the adoption of a Directive by the **Council of**

Ministers confers rights on individuals, even in the event of a member state having failed to transpose the Directive into national law. An individual who suffers damages as a consequence of such a failure may have a claim for compensation against the authorities of that state.

Mr Francovich was an employee of an Italian firm that went bankrupt. A 1980 Directive on the protection of employees in such cases of insolvency had not been given effect in Italian law. The **Court of Justice** ruled that Mr Francovich could claim appropriate compensation from the Italian state.

The Francovich case reinforced the general obligation laid upon member states by the **Treaty of Rome** to 'take all appropriate measures ... to ensure fulfilment of the obligations arising out of this Treaty or resulting from action taken by the institutions of the Community' (Article 10 EC) and is of great importance as an example of how **EU law** serves to extend individual rights. It is discussed more fully in Weatherill and Beaumont, *EU Law* (3rd edn, Harmondsworth, 1999). There is an exhaustive analysis of the implications of the case in Roberto Caranta, 'Governmental liability after *Francovich*', *Cambridge Law Journal*, Vol. 52, no. 2, July 1993.

Fraud

The **Maastricht Treaty** added a new Article 209(a) (now 280) to the **Treaty of Rome**. As amended by the **Treaty of Amsterdam**, this Article reads:

> Member States shall take the same measures to counter fraud affecting the financial interests of the Community as they take to counter fraud affecting their own financial interests ... [They] shall coordinate their action aimed at protecting the financial interests of the Community against fraud ... [and] shall organize, together with the Commission, close and regular cooperation between the competent authorities.

Fraud affects both the Union's income (i.e. **own resources**) and expenditure. Estimates of its extent differ widely; what seems certain is that reported fraud is only a small proportion of the whole. In 1998 'irregularities' (not all of them necessarily fraudulent) were found to affect some 5.8 per cent of the **Budget**. Of the 5,318 cases of suspected fraud investigated by the **European Commission**, 20 per cent were confirmed. Particularly serious was the loss to the Union's own resources of duties on cigarettes and alcohol.

In July 1994 a report by the House of Lords Select Committee on the European Communities (*Financial Control and Fraud in the Community*, July 1994) described such losses as a 'public scandal' and noted a 'worrying absence of indignation at the amount of fraud and mismanagement' and 'a lack of political will ... to take remedial action', in spite of the fact that the **European Council** has discussed fraud at three meetings (Edinburgh, December 1992; Copenhagen, June 1993; Essen, December 1994). Under the Maastricht Treaty the **Court of**

Auditors was given new status and can now, if necessary, bring actions in the **Court of Justice** against other Union institutions to protect its prerogatives, although not against member states. Under the **Treaty of Amsterdam** the Court's remit is extended to cover the whole Union, including the two **pillars**, and the Court is invited 'to report on any cases of irregularity'. The European Commission has put forward several proposals for dealing with fraud and established a new unit (known as UCLAF, *Unité coordinatrice pour la lutte anti-fraude*) reporting directly to the secretary-general. In April 1994 the British government proposed a **joint action** under the **Justice and Home Affairs** (JHA) provisions of the Maastricht Treaty for measures that would, *inter alia*, resolve some of the legal difficulties. Under this joint action, fraud would become a criminal, extraditable offence in all member states, attracting heavy penalties. An Advisory Committee for the Coordination of Fraud Prevention has been set up, composed of 50 experts from all member states, and a smaller group to expedite the recovery of misappropriated funds. The Commission has also set up a 'fraud hotline' in each member state, a telephone number that members of the public can ring free of charge to report suspected fraud. A Convention on the protection of the Communities' financial interests has been agreed, together with two supplementary **protocols** and an additional convention on making corruption at the official level a criminal offence (see also *Corpus Juris*).

Although under Article 274 EC the Commission is responsible for implementing the Budget of the Union 'having regard to the principles of sound financial management', in fact the disbursement of 80 per cent of Union funds is in the hands of member states. It is sometimes suspected that those states that are net beneficiaries of the Budget do not share the keen interest in fraud taken by those that are net contributors and that some national authorities, upon whom the responsibility for reporting fraud rests, prefer not to take action that reflects discredit on their own citizens, and that may result in repayments having to be made to the Budget. Few states support an extension of the power of the Commission or the Court of Auditors to undertake investigations on national territory.

As with most wrong-doing, the best deterrent is the likelihood of detection and the prospect of heavy penalties. Legislation and procedures with a bearing on the disbursement of funds should be made simpler, and easier to enforce, and so less vulnerable to fraud. Financial accountability should be a higher priority within the Commission. Their failure to deal with financial irregularities was a key factor in the resignation of the Santer Commission in March 1999. UCLAF (see above) was succeeded later that year by an independent body, OLAF (*Office pour la lutte anti-fraude*).

The best studies of fraud are the report by the House of Lords Select Committee noted above and an earlier report of February 1989, *Fraud against the Community*. Both contain testimony from expert witnesses and case-histories, which shed light not only on the kinds of fraud that are perpetrated but also on the relations between the institutions, national and European, concerned with the fight against fraud. The annual reports by the Court of Auditors are also useful; the report for 1993 is particularly critical of the Commission, especially in relation to the **European Agricultural Guidance and Guarantee Fund** (EAGGF). The Court has also published an excellent survey, *Sound Financial Management in the European Union Budget*, covering the period 1977 to 1997. The Commission publishes an annual report entitled *Fight against Fraud*.

Free movement of goods

Perhaps the most fundamental of the '**four freedoms**', the free movement of goods within a **customs union** lies at the heart of the **Treaty of Rome**. By this means **the Six** sought, in the words of the preamble to the Treaty, to lay 'the foundations of an ever closer union among the peoples of Europe' (see also **Beyen Plan**).

Article 3.1(c) refers to 'an **internal market** characterized by the abolition, as between Member States, of obstacles to the free movement of goods, persons, services and capital'. Article 14.2 defines the internal market as 'an area without internal frontiers in which the free movement of goods, persons, services and capital is ensured'. The preamble to the Treaty places the free movement of goods not only within a broader political context but marks it out as a European contribution to the development of closer, mutually advantageous trading relations worldwide.

Article 23.1 prohibits the imposition of 'customs duties on imports and exports and ... all charges having equivalent effect' between member states. Articles 28 and 29 prohibit quantitative restrictions (i.e., quotas) in similar terms, although in fact there were few such quotas on trade between the Six when the Treaty came into force (1958). The Treaty laid down a 12-year transitional period during which the removal of customs duties and quotas was to be effected, but in the event the removal was accomplished 18 months ahead of schedule. This allowed the **Common External Tariff** to be applied from 1 July 1968. Article 30 allows member states to prohibit or restrict imports 'on grounds of public morality, public policy or public security; the protection of health and life of humans, animals or plants; ... national treasures ...; or ... industrial and commercial property'.

The Treaty provisions left a number of instruments in the hands of national authorities wishing to favour or protect their domestic markets, of which the most important were tax measures (although Article 90 prohibits discriminatory taxation) and product specifications. These led to a number of cases in the

Court of Justice, many concerned with what the Treaty references to 'charges having equivalent effect' were intended to cover. Member states sought to justify their own national product specifications on (sometimes dubious) health and safety, consumer protection or environmental grounds. It was the attempt by the **European Commission** to lay down Europe-wide specifications that would enable goods to circulate freely which became known as the **harmonization** programme (see also **Articles 94 and 95**).

The Court, in its 1979 judgment in the case known as '**Cassis de Dijon**', laid down a new basis for ensuring the free movement of goods. Known as mutual recognition, it means essentially that goods in free and legal circulation in one member state cannot be excluded from others. Six years later, the 1985 **Cockfield White Paper** on the **Single Market** identified the remaining **nontariff barriers** to the free movement of goods, dividing them into technical barriers (differing product specifications), physical barriers (frontier controls, customs formalities) and fiscal barriers (see **tax harmonization**). Many of them were simply bureaucratic: the **Kangaroo Group** published a list of the 46 documents needed by the driver of a semi-articulated lorry travelling from West Germany to Italy via Austria. The White Paper pointed out that one of the main reasons why the removal of these barriers was such a slow process was the requirement under Article 100 (now 94) that agreement in the **Council of Ministers** must be unanimous. This led to the introduction in the **Single European Act** (SEA) the following year of a new Article 100a (now 95) allowing for the extension of **qualified majority voting** (QMV) to this area. Other measures were also taken, such as the introduction of the so-called Single Administrative Document to ease the crossing of internal frontiers, the abolition of road haulage quotas (see **common transport policy**), the simplification of transit procedures, and the removal of animal and plant health controls from the point of entry to offices inside member states. Frontier controls affecting the free movement of goods were finally removed on 1 January 1993.

Community law relating to the free movement of goods is reviewed in detail in Weatherill and Beaumont, *EU Law* (3rd edn, Harmondsworth, 1999).

Free movement of persons

Four Articles of the **Treaty of Rome** have a direct bearing on free movement. Article 3.1(c) refers to 'an **internal market** characterized by the abolition, as between Member States, of obstacles to the free movement of goods, persons, services and capital'. Article 18.1 says that 'every citizen of the Union shall have the right to move and reside freely within the territory of the Member States' (see **citizenship**). Article 39 lays down the principle of free movement for workers, 'subject to limitations justified on grounds of public policy, public security or public health', although employment in the public service is excluded. Article 43 extends the principle to the self-employed (see **discrimination on grounds of nationality**).

Because an open labour market was an essential component of an internal market, legislation to give effect to these Treaty requirements concentrated initially on 'workers'. The right of workers to move and reside freely within the member states with a view to taking up or seeking employment was laid down in a Regulation and a Directive (see **legal instruments**) of 1968. With the aid of rulings from the **Court of Justice**, the definition of 'worker' was gradually extended (see also **Van Duyn case**). By the mid-1980s it was obvious that the drive to complete the **Single Market** should include the removal of frontier controls between member states, and that the Treaty requirement for the free movement of 'persons' would have to be given legislative form. The so-called Palma Document, discussed at the Madrid meeting of the **European Council** in June 1989, identified the priorities for action. In 1990 the **Council of Ministers** adopted three linked Directives on the right of residence for students, retired people and nationals of member states not covered by other provisions. Basically, any citizen of the Union may now reside anywhere in the Union as long as he or she is covered by sickness insurance and is in receipt of welfare benefits or other income sufficient 'to avoid becoming a burden on the social assistance system of the host Member State' (Article 1 of Directive 90/364). The **European passport** is supposed to make it quicker and easier to recognize citizens of the Union at frontiers.

However, the commitment in the Treaty is to free movement for 'persons', not solely for citizens of the Union. Relaxation or removal of controls at internal frontiers was linked to a strengthening of controls at external borders, and hence common agreement on immigration, visas, the right of **asylum** and other matters with a bearing on the treatment of nationals of non-member countries. Discussion of these points soon revealed profound differences of attitude among member states. In 1985 those who were willing to make rapid progress signed the **Schengen Agreement**. Limited progress was also made in 1991 with the **External Frontiers Convention** and the **Dublin Asylum Convention**, but only the latter has been ratified by all member states (see also **area of freedom, security and justice**).

Frontier controls, internal and external, were initially dealt with under the **Justice and Home Affairs** (JHA) provisions of the **Maastricht Treaty**, which required them to be regarded 'as matters of common interest'. The exception to this was visa policy, which was covered in a new Article 100c (since repealed) added to the Treaty of Rome. The positioning of this Article placed it firmly within that portion of the Treaty dealing with the approximation of laws within the Single Market. This enjoined the Council, 'acting unanimously ... [to]

determine the third countries whose nationals must be in possession of a visa when crossing the external borders of the Member States' (now Article 62.2(b)i EEC). From 1 January 1996 such decisions could be taken by **qualified majority voting** (QMV). A list of third countries was drawn up in this connection and was agreed in September 1995: part of the argument was concerned with the need to extend visa controls to nationals of certain Commonwealth countries who did not require visas to enter the United Kingdom. The **Treaty of Amsterdam** amended Articles 73(i) to 73(q) (now 61 to 69) EEC in order to incorporate the **Schengen** *acquis* into the Treaty of Rome.

As one of the '**four freedoms**', free movement of persons is not only one of the most basic goals of the Treaty, it is also of great symbolic importance as part of a **People's Europe**. The right of free movement now exists throughout the whole **European Economic Area** (EEA; the five **Nordic Council** countries already operate a passport union for their own nationals). However, at least until police cooperation (see **Europol**) is stepped up, controls are likely to be maintained at least at some internal frontiers as part of the fight against terrorism, **organized crime** and drug-trafficking. Equally, as long as there is an obligation to offer proof of identity when passing from one member state to another it will be argued that free movement has not yet been achieved. Free movement of persons raises, and will continue to raise, important and sensitive issues, such as the use of identity cards and the treatment of persons resident in a member state who are not citizens of the Union. There are also substantial costs involved in some of the proposals: for example, the redesigning of most major airports (which are both internal and external frontiers) to allow citizens of the Union and nationals of non-member states to be treated separately, depending on whether they are travelling within the Union, travelling to or from a destination outside the Union, or are in transit.

A comprehensive survey of the arguments and issues raised by free movement of persons may be found in a report by the House of Lords Select Committee on the European Communities, *Visas and Control of External Borders of the Member States* (July 1994). See also Weatherill and Beaumont, *EU Law* (3rd edn, Harmondsworth, 1999).

Free trade area

A free trade area exists when two or more states (normally but not necessarily contiguous) agree to remove all restrictions on trade between them, but continue to make individual arrangements for their trade with countries not party to the free trade agreement. A **customs union** denotes not only free trade between participating states, but also a common set of arrangements with respect to trade with other countries. A common market is a customs union within which the free movement of goods, services, capital and labour is guaranteed (see **Single Market**). These broad distinctions serve to explain the difference between, for example, the **European Free Trade Association** (EFTA) and the **European Economic Community** (EEC). Under **World Trade Organization** (WTO) rules, a free trade area must cover at least 90 per cent of participating states' trade.

Freedom of establishment

Freedom of establishment – the right to practise a trade or profession – is guaranteed for the nationals of the member states throughout the European Union by Articles 43 to 48 of the **Treaty of Rome**, which cover both employed and self-employed persons. Article 45 excludes 'activities ... connected, even occasionally, with the exercise of official authority' (see **discrimination on grounds of nationality**). Freedom of establishment, which is an essential component of the wider issue of **free movement of persons** in the **Single Market**, is facilitated by the **mutual recognition of qualifications** (see also **freedom to provide services**).

The basic legislation on freedom of establishment was agreed in the form of a 'General Programme' in 1962. On the basis of this programme proposals were brought forward by the **European Commission** on particular sectors of economic activity, not including the professions, since progress first had to be made on the mutual recognition of qualifications. In the mid-1970s a number of judgments of the **Court of Justice** helped to accelerate the process of removing national restrictions on freedom of establishment: for example, doctors have been able to practise anywhere in the member states since 1976. With some exceptions, it is now the case that nationals of the member states are entitled to practise a trade or profession not only anywhere in the Union but throughout the **European Economic Area**. See Weatherill and Beaumont, *EU Law* (3rd edn, Harmondsworth, 1999).

Freedom to provide services

Freedom to provide services is different from **freedom of establishment** in that it is concerned with performance of services anywhere within the Union without the provider of the service having his or her place of business established in the country where the service is performed. The **Single Market** is defined in Article 3.1(c) of the **Treaty of Rome** as being 'characterized by the abolition, as between Member States, of obstacles to the free movement of goods, persons, services and capital'.

Article 49 requires member states to remove all restrictions on freedom to provide services with respect to citizens of the Union (see **citizenship**). The freedom may also be extended to nationals of non-member countries. Article 50 makes it clear that the Treaty provisions on services are supplementary to those relating to goods, persons and capital, and identifies four types of service in particular: industrial, commercial, professional and craft industries. Special considerations apply to transport, banking and insurance under Article 51.2 (see **common transport policy, financial services**). Member states are able to impose restrictions on public policy grounds and to exclude services involving the exercise of official authority.

A 'General Programme' adopted in 1962 identified the restrictions to be removed, such as those based on nationality, residence, qualifications and procedures for the cross-border transfer of funds to pay for the service. The General Programme was followed by legislation on particular professions, helped partly by rulings of the **Court of Justice**. However, it was not until the late 1980s, when substantial progress was finally made with the **mutual recognition of qualifications**, that freedom to provide services became more or less assured; it now applies throughout the **European Economic Area**. Much more detail on the application of **EU law** to the services sector may be found in Weatherill and Beaumont, *EU Law* (3rd edn, Harmondsworth, 1999).

Functionalism

Functionalism is one of several theories of integration (see also **federation, intergovernmentalism**). The term, which dates from the 1930s, denotes a form of integration between states that is based upon practical cooperation in well-defined areas with a minimum of institutional apparatus. By contrast with federalism, functionalism involves no institutional blueprint and is driven by economic, social and technical imperatives rather than by political forces. However, functionalists believe that as states acquire the habit of working together the number of areas in which they are willing to cooperate tends to be gradually extended (the concept of 'spillover'), a process that may lead eventually to demands for democratic control in these areas to be exercised by new supranational institutions. The term 'neofunctionalism' has been coined to denote the use of functionalist techniques to secure federalist objectives, of which the best example is the **European Coal and Steel Community** (ECSC; see also *engrenage*).

Applied to European integration, functionalism has always had an attraction for the British and the Scandinavians as being both more 'pragmatic' and less likely, at least in the short term, to raise sensitive issues of **sovereignty**. Attempts in the **Maastricht Treaty** and elsewhere to define more clearly the extent and nature of Community action – as opposed to action by national, regional, or local authorities – in the name of **subsidiarity** may be interpreted in functionalist terms as placing limits on the 'spillover'. The classic text on functionalism is David Mitrany, *A Working Peace System* (1943; new edition with additional material 1966).

Future financing

The first debate over the future financing of the European Union (i.e., the overall size and structure of the Union's income and expenditure) spanned the period from 1986 until the Edinburgh meeting of the **European Council** in December 1992. It centred upon two 'packages' of proposals, known as Delors I and Delors II after **Jacques Delors**, the President of the **European Commission**.

At the London meeting of the European Council in December 1986 Delors was invited to make a report on the finances of the Community. The accession of Portugal and Spain at the beginning of the year was placing new demands on the **structural funds**, and movements in world agricultural prices meant that once again expenditure under the **Common Agricultural Policy** (CAP) was threatening to run out of control. Delors's forecast was that the Community would run out of money in 1987, and the meeting invited him to make proposals to place the Community's finances on a firmer footing.

His package, entitled *Making a Success of the Single Act*, was drawn up two months later. By referring to the **Single European Act** (SEA) Delors hoped to get the member states to see his proposals in the context of the extra solidarity, or **cohesion**, that would be needed if the SEA were not simply to make the rich regions richer and the poor poorer. The SEA also envisaged more Community activity in areas such as **research** on a scale that would require extra resources in the **Budget**. In his proposals he suggested doubling the structural funds over five years, more spending on research, new measures to contain agricultural surpluses and a new system of agreeing the Budget based on a five-year framework covering the main items of expenditure (the 'financial perspective').

The reactions of the member states were mixed. The German government did not like the prospect of still higher net payments to the Budget arising from the increase in the structural funds, and the British government of **Margaret Thatcher** wanted tighter controls on CAP expenditure and stricter **budgetary discipline** overall. By the end of 1987 agreement had still not been reached, and a special meeting of the European Council in Brussels was called for February 1988.

In Brussels the European Council averted the crisis by agreeing on a doubling of the structural funds over six years, on a new **own resource** based on the gross national product (GNP) of member states, on a guideline limiting the growth of CAP expenditure, and a guarantee that by 1992 the Budget overall would represent no more than 1.2 per cent of Community gross domestic product (GDP; the 'own resources ceiling'). A further review of future financing was fixed for 1992.

Delors II, entitled *From the Single Act to Maastricht and Beyond: The Means to Match Our Ambitions*, was published in February 1992. The five-year (1992–7) financial perspective at the heart of the proposal indicated further substantial increases in the structural funds (now incorporating a **Cohesion Fund**) and in the very modest sum set aside for 'external actions', to allow the Community to respond to requests for financial assistance from central and eastern Europe. Overall, as a proportion of the Community's GNP, the Budget would rise from 1.2 to 1.37 per cent. In a revised financial perspective of November 1992 this was reduced to 1.32 per cent, and the system of own resources altered to the advantage of those countries with a GNP of less than 90 per cent of the Community average, with effect from 1995.

The Edinburgh meeting at which agreement was reached on the Delors II package took place against a background of severe public expenditure constraints in several member states, including most importantly Germany (as a result of **German reunification**). At the same time other member states and the Commission were seeking to develop new spending policies. In the event a seven-year (to 1999) financial perspective was drawn up, which allowed the own resources ceiling to remain fixed at 1.25 per cent of Community GNP until 1995, and thereafter to rise to 1.27 per cent by 1999. The own resources system was altered to lower the ceiling on contributions based on value-added tax (VAT), with other changes to benefit poorer countries by making the system less 'regressive' (i.e., weighing more heavily on poorer countries). The guideline for agricultural expenditure was reconfirmed, meaning that by 1999 CAP expenditure should be less than half the Budget. The structural funds were to be increased by about 60 per cent over the period, and spending on external actions by about 40 per cent (see **Edinburgh Growth Initiative**). The Commission was invited to make recommendations on a possible new own resource by 1999.

In sum, the Edinburgh agreement allowed for increases in the Budget less than half as large as those originally proposed in Delors II. It reconfirmed the agreement on the rebate for the United Kingdom (see **British Budget problem**). Overall, the six-year debate on future financing reflected the shifting balance between rich and poor member states brought about by the accession of Portugal and Spain, and, in particular, the concerns of poorer countries about the effects of the **Single Market** programme. It reflected too a number of external pressures, such as those from central and eastern Europe and, as far as CAP expenditure was concerned, from the United States and others in the context of the negotiations in the **General Agreement on Tariffs and Trade** (GATT).

The Commission's reflections on the financial perspective over the period from 2000 to 2006 were published in July 1997 as part of its *Agenda 2000* document. It concluded that it would be possible 'to face the challenges posed by the necessary reforms of some of the most important Community policies and those deriving from a first wave of accessions' (see **enlargement**) without raising the current own resources ceiling of 1.27 per cent of GNP. More detailed estimates, published in March 1998, assumed growth rates of 2.5 per cent annually in the fifteen current member states and 4 per cent in the applicant states. In March 1999 the European Council meeting in Berlin reached agreement on the *Agenda 2000* proposals. The agreement assumed that the first wave of enlargement from 2002 would add six new member states to the Union and allowed for the costs arising from enlargement (i.e. pre-accession aid and increased expenditure on agriculture and the structural funds) to rise to 18.6 per cent of the Budget by 2006. Resources set aside for enlargement would not be available to the 15 current member states, and *vice versa*.

G

General Affairs Council (GAC)

The GAC is a configuration of the **Council of Ministers** composed of member states' foreign ministers. In June 2002 it was renamed the General Affairs and External Relations Council. It is principally responsible not only for foreign affairs but also for general political questions. Although notionally all Councils are equal, the GAC is normally reckoned to be the 'senior' Council by virtue of the overall coordinating role it is supposed to play with respect to all Council business. The GAC also prepares meetings of the **European Council**. In recent years, with the rapid development of the Union's **Common Foreign and Security Policy** (CFSP) it has become more and more difficult to find time for coordination in meetings of the GAC. This and other problems affecting the Council's work were addressed in *An effective Council for an enlarged Union*, a set of 'guidelines for reform' adopted at the Helsinki meeting of the European Council in December 1999. Coordination is now expressly provided for on GAC agendas, the number of different configurations of the Council is strictly limited, and member states are encouraged to improve their own internal interdepartmental coordination. See Ricardo Gomez and John Peterson, 'The EU's impossibly busy foreign ministers', *European Foreign Affairs Review*, Vol. 6, no. 1, spring 2001.

General Agreement on Tariffs and Trade (GATT)

Based in Geneva, and since 1995 succeeded by the **World Trade Organization** (WTO), GATT was originally conceived as an independent agency of the United Nations, to be known as the International Trade Organization (ITO). The Agreement was negotiated in 1947 and came into effect with 23 signatories on 1 January 1948. However, difficulties arose with the ratification of the ITO Convention, and the project was abandoned. This left the Agreement as the only multilateral instrument for the orderly conduct of international trade, the lowering of tariffs, and the resolution of disputes. A small secretariat was established in Geneva. Signatory states of GATT were together responsible for about 90 per cent of world trade.

Successive 'rounds' of negotiations resulted in a general lowering of tariffs:

1947	Geneva	1959–62	Geneva ('Dillon')
1949	Annecy	1963–7	Geneva ('Kennedy')
1951	Torquay	1973–9	Geneva ('Tokyo')
1955–6	Geneva	1986–94	Geneva ('Uruguay')

Among the conclusions of the Uruguay Round was the decision to set up a World Trade Organization in place of GATT. Geneva was preferred to Bonn as the seat of the WTO. A new General Agreement was drawn up together with a separate agreement on trade in services (GATS). The WTO's remit now also extends to intellectual property.

Generalized System of Preferences (GSP)

The GSP scheme is a system of tariff preferences intended to benefit exports of manufactured goods and processed agricultural products from developing countries to the Union. It was introduced in 1971 in line with the recommendations of the United Nations Conference on Trade and Development (UNC-TAD) meeting in New Delhi in 1968, and has been revised or renewed many times since then. About 150 countries are covered by the GSP scheme, with special advantages being given to the least-developed developing countries (LDCs). However, since customs duties have been progressively reduced as a result of negotiations in the **General Agreement on Tariffs and Trade** (GATT), the benefits offered under the GSP scheme have become less attractive. Efforts to make them more attractive result in an erosion of the privileged position that the countries covered by the **Cotonou Agreement** expect to enjoy. The GSP scheme has also been criticized for failing adequately to discriminate between the highly competitive newly industrialized countries (NICs), mainly in South-East Asia, and the desperately poor countries in the developing world.

The current GSP scheme, drawn up within a 10-year guideline covering the period 1995–2004, seeks to address these criticisms. Exports from LDCs are exempt from all duties, although in some cases the country concerned has to agree to take measures in the fight against drugs. Other 'encouragement clauses' have been introduced in favour of social and environmental measures.

Genscher, Hans-Dietrich (b. 1927)

Hans-Dietrich Genscher was leader of the German Free Democrats (Liberal) Party from 1974 to 1985 and German Foreign Minister from 1974 until 1992. Genscher was a key figure in all Community foreign policy developments over this long period. He was, with Emilio Colombo, then the Italian Foreign

Minister, the architect of the so-called **Genscher–Colombo Plan** of 1981. Having been born in what later became the German Democratic Republic, Genscher took a close personal interest in **German reunification** and in establishing better relations with the countries of central and eastern Europe after the collapse of Communism.

Genscher–Colombo Plan

The Genscher–Colombo Plan was a bilateral initiative taken in November 1981 by **Hans-Dietrich Genscher** and Emilio Colombo, the German and Italian Foreign Ministers, in which they proposed the adoption of a 'draft European Act' to supplement the **Treaty of Rome**. The Plan envisaged a 'common foreign policy' and 'coordination of security policy' based on the further development of **European Political Cooperation**. The **European Council** would become the 'organ of political guidance', with its president-in-office reporting every six months to the **European Parliament**. The latter body would be consulted before the appointment of the president of the **European Commission** and before further **enlargement** of the Community.

According to the Plan, the structure of the **Council of Ministers** would be extended to include regular meetings of Ministers of Justice and Culture, and potentially of ministers in any other policy areas not covered by the **Treaties**. 'Decisive importance' was attached to following the Council voting procedures set down in the Treaties (see **Luxembourg Compromise**), with an obligation on any member state to explain in writing why it might be attempting to block a decision requiring only **qualified majority voting** (QMV). States would have the chance to defer a Council decision at two successive meetings. After that, by implication, a vote would be taken.

The reaction in the European Council to this proposal was somewhat ambiguous. France – which had yet to embark on the vigorously pro-European policy that would later characterize its new President, **François Mitterrand** – displayed little public enthusiasm either for the Bonn–Rome initiative, or for its clear exclusion from the exercise. The United Kingdom was fearful of the budgetary implications of an extension of Community activity into new areas and, with Denmark and Greece, concerned by any watering-down of the Luxembourg Compromise. The position in Bonn itself seemed uncertain as the commitment of Chancellor Helmut Schmidt to his Foreign Minister's proposals sometimes looked halfhearted.

In the event, the European Council, meeting in London on 26–7 November 1981, received the Genscher–Colombo text 'with satisfaction' and requested the foreign ministers to study it and report back in due course. During long negotiations in Brussels it was agreed to downgrade the document from a draft legislative text to a mere declaration without any binding effect. On this basis the Solemn Declaration on European Union was brought before the Stuttgart European Council 18 months later (see **Stuttgart Declaration**).

German reunification

The 1949 Constitution (*Grundgesetz*) of the Federal Republic of Germany (FRG) made provision for the eventual reunification of Germany without specifying in detail how it should be achieved. In the event, the FRG and the German Democratic Republic (GDR) agreed in 1990 that the individual *Länder* of the GDR (Brandenburg, Sachsen, Sachsen-Anhalt, Thüringen, Mecklenburg-Vorpommern and the city of East Berlin) would join the FRG under Article 23 of the Constitution, adding almost 17 million people to the population. However, this meant a *de facto* **enlargement** of the European Community of a kind not provided for in the **Treaty of Rome**. In April 1990 the **European Council** meeting in Dublin decided that the former GDR would be incorporated into the Community on reunification. The two Germanys consulted very closely with the Community institutions before reunification was finally and formally achieved under the Unification Treaty (*Einigungsvertrag*) on 3 October 1990.

Many of the most contentious issues were settled in the preparatory State Treaty (*Staatsvertrag*), which came into effect on 1 July 1990. In this Treaty the two Germanys agreed that **EU law** would apply in the former GDR with effect from reunification and that the GDR would progressively align its policies with Community practices and objectives. A **protocol** to the Treaty of Rome already allowed trade between the two Germanys to be regarded as 'internal trade' (i.e., not subject to the **Common External Tariff**) in line with the constitution of the FRG. Particular Articles of the State Treaty dealt with the application of the **Common Agricultural Policy** (CAP), monetary reform and, in general, the transition to a market economy.

On the Community side the reunification of Germany prompted a comprehensive review of the *acquis communautaire* and the identification of measures that would have to be modified to take account of the former GDR's special circumstances or applied only after a transitional period. A temporary committee of the **European Parliament** was set up for this purpose. An analysis was also made of the GDR's international obligations as set out in various treaties and agreements. In the institutional field the only major change consequent upon reunification was an increase in the number of German seats in the European Parliament. With effect from the date of reunification, 18 'observers' from the former GDR were added to the Parliament, with speaking rights in committees but without the right to vote. Initially, these observers were chosen by the GDR Parliament, the Volkskammer, but later by the Bundestag. In 1991 the Parliament voted by 241 votes to 62 (38 of whom were

French) formally to increase the number of German members from 81 to 99, with effect from the 1994 European elections. This decision was controversial in some member states, and it was not endorsed until the European Council meeting in Edinburgh in December 1992. German representation in other institutions was not increased, nor was the weighting attached to Germany's vote under the **qualified majority voting** (QMV) system.

The special status of Berlin, the presence of Russian troops in the GDR, the *de facto* incorporation of the former GDR into the **North Atlantic Treaty Organization** (NATO) and anxieties over a reunited Germany's eastern frontier with Poland gave rise to negotiations in July and August 1990 known as the 'Two plus Four' talks (i.e., the two Germanys plus France, the United Kingdom, the United States and the USSR). Agreement was reached on the ending of the Allies' special status in Germany, on a new German–Polish Treaty, on the granting of full sovereignty to a reunited Germany, including the right to join NATO, and on the withdrawal of Soviet forces from German soil. The last of the 550,000 Russians (350,000 soldiers plus civilian employees and families) left Germany in mid-1994, at a cost to the German taxpayer of about DM13 billion.

Although the GDR was economically the most advanced of the **COMECON** states, it was very backward indeed by comparison with the FRG. This has meant that Germany now has some of the richest and some of the poorest regions in the European Union. Levels of pollution in the GDR were particularly high, and the whole fabric of the country was in a poor state of repair. Dealing with these problems will demand huge resources for many years to come. However, the initial loss of population has been staunched and confidence is returning, helped in part by the decision to make Berlin once more the capital.

A very important unforeseen side-effect of German reunification was the breakdown of the **Exchange-Rate Mechanism** (ERM) of the **European Monetary System** (EMS) in September 1992. The German authorities were determined to maintain international confidence in the Deutsche Mark and kept interest rates high. This in turn required other governments to keep their own interest rates high, so that their currencies could remain within the permitted narrow band of fluctuation against the Deutsche Mark. By September 1992 the strain was too much, and sterling and the Italian lira left the ERM. Germany was widely criticized for pursuing an essentially domestic interest-rate policy, with little or no regard for the wider European responsibilities that flowed from the Deutsche Mark's position in the ERM.

Politically, reunification was a substantial triumph for **Helmut Kohl**. The uncertainty that it engendered meant that his calmness and fixity of purpose suddenly became very attractive to the German electorate, and his party did well in the first all-German elections of December 1990, the European elections of June

1994 and the national elections four months later. Reunification has strengthened Germany's position as the most influential member state of the Union.

For a detailed study of German reunification as it affected the Community see Jeffrey Anderson, *German Unification and the Union of Europe* (Cambridge, 1999).

Germany

Soon after the end of the Second World War it became clear in the light of the new threat from the East that the rehabilitation and reconstruction of Germany would have to be among the West's highest strategic priorities. The Federal Republic of Germany (FRG, or West Germany) was established in 1949 on the territory of the former American, British and French zones of occupation, with its capital in Bonn. Berlin remained divided into four sectors: from June 1948 until May 1949 the American, British and French sectors were blockaded by Soviet forces and supplied by the Berlin airlift. The first Chancellor of the FRG was **Konrad Adenauer**.

The FRG was admitted as a member of the **Council of Europe** in 1951 on the initiative of **Winston Churchill**. The previous year the **Schuman Plan** had been launched, and in 1951 **the Six** signed the **Treaty of Paris** establishing the **European Coal and Steel Community** (ECSC). The Treaty was unanimously supported in the West German Bundestag by the Christian Democrats, but opposed by the Social Democrats on the grounds that it formalized the division of Germany. Two years later the Social Democrats raised similar objections to the **European Defence Community** Treaty. One consequence of the internationalization of the coal and steel industries within the ECSC was the resolution of the **Saarland** dispute with France in 1955, which led to the incorporation of the territory into the FRG. The FRG joined the **North Atlantic Treaty Organization** (NATO) the same year: the Soviet Union responded by setting up the **Warsaw Pact** and by recognizing the sovereignty of the German Democratic Republic (GDR, or East Germany), thus completing the division of Germany.

The 1950s and 1960s were the decades of the 'German economic miracle'. The FRG actively supported the proposal to set up what became the **European Economic Community** (EEC) at the 1955 **Messina Conference**, although in the argument that then ensued it was France rather than the FRG which vigorously opposed the alternative of a wider free trade area (see **Maudling Committee**). The bargain upon which the EEC was founded was a wider market for German manufactured goods in exchange for guaranteed markets for French agricultural produce, and a politico-institutional framework in which neither country could dominate the other. Outside that framework **Franco-German cooperation** led to the signing of a Treaty of Friendship (the Elysée Treaty) in 1963.

Unlike France, the FRG was not opposed to British accession to the EEC. Nor did the FRG share French misgivings about the supranational character of the EEC's institutions (especially the **European Commission** under its German president **Walter Hallstein**), misgivings that led to the **empty chair crisis** of 1965. Within political circles the FRG's attitudes had little of the anti-American bias that characterized those of France until the resignation of **Charles de Gaulle** in 1969.

The election of Willy Brandt as Chancellor introduced the era of *Ostpolitik* – establishing better relations with the GDR within the framework of East–West détente. The policy was continued by his successor, Helmut Schmidt. However, this led to no slackening of interest in European integration: together with President **Valéry Giscard d'Estaing** of France, Schmidt played a key role in the establishment of the **European Monetary System** (EMS) in 1979.

Especially since **German reunification** Germany's economic ascendancy within the Union and the fact of its being by far the biggest net contributor to the **Budget of the European Union** have meant that no major development can take place without German support. Such support was initially only grudgingly given to the reform of the **Common Agricultural Policy** (CAP), primarily because a succession of Bavarian ministers of agriculture were devoted above all to the interests of German farmers. Another area in which, for constitutional reasons, Germany found it difficult until recently to give wholehearted support was defence and security policy. Under the 1949 Constitution German forces could not be deployed outside Germany, and all-party agreement could not be reached on changing this provision. The problem was resolved by a ruling of the Constitutional Court in June 1994: German forces may now be deployed outside Germany, but only in operations backed by the United Nations. Some German forces have been committed to the **Eurocorps** since 1989.

In parallel with German reunification German policy is now strongly oriented towards enlarging the Union by admitting the countries of central and eastern Europe. Another very high priority is the success of the **Economic and Monetary Union** (EMU) especially since the **European Central Bank** (ECB) is located in Frankfurt. As the 1994 'Lamers paper' (see '**hard core**') makes clear, the German government sees EMU as the 'cornerstone' of the European political union to which it is committed. In the institutional field Germany is a supporter of more powers for the **European Parliament**, in which it has had an increase in its share of seats since June 1994 (although it has not sought an increase in its weighting within the **qualified majority voting** (QMV) system in the **Council of Ministers**). Even if Helmut Kohl had not been re-elected in November 1994 for a fourth term as Chancellor, these German priorities, which have cross-party support, would have remained the same.

The passage of the **Maastricht Treaty** required Germany to make some adjustments to its relations with the Union. The Treaty gave rise to fears on the part of the *Länder* authorities that the Federal Government was ceding to the Union powers that, under the Constitution, belonged to the *Länder*. Furthermore, the Treaty was challenged in the Constitutional Court by anti-Maastricht campaigners led by a former *chef de cabinet* to Martin Bangemann, the German Commissioner responsible for industry policy (see **Karlsruhe judgment**). The Constitution (Article 23.1) specifically envisages German participation in the Union 'with a view to establishing a united Europe'. It requires any transfer of 'sovereign powers' to the Union to be approved by a two-thirds majority in both the Bundestag (the lower house of the German Parliament) and the Bundesrat (the upper house, composed of representatives of the *Länder*). When required, ministers from *Länder* governments may represent the FRG in the Council of Ministers (see **regionalism**).

'A united Germany in a united Europe' is the phrase most commonly used to summarize how Germany sees the future. The policy of high interest rates, which led to the break-up and near collapse of the **Exchange-Rate Mechanism** (ERM) in September 1992, led many to suppose that, of the two, a united Germany was the higher priority. Since then, Germany has been anxious to dispel the idea that it has lost interest in European integration. Germany is all too well aware of its responsibilities as the paymaster of the Union, its largest economy, its most successful exporter, and as the favoured European interlocutor of both the United States and Russia. European integration was attractive to Germany in the 1950s as an opportunity for a fresh start within a fair and equal partnership. A new generation of Germans now feels less need to expiate the guilt to which the Nazi era gave rise, but the European Union and 'the new Europe' remain attractive as a framework within which their formidable energies may be deployed in a common cause.

The most thoughtful as well as the most comprehensive politico-historical study of modern Germany is Timothy Garton Ash, *In Europe's Name* (1993). Noel Annan, *Changing Enemies* (1995) is an outstandingly interesting personal account of the emergence of modern Germany.

Gibraltar

Gibraltar has been under British sovereignty since the Treaty of Utrecht in 1713. The colony occupies a narrow peninsula on Spain's southern Mediterranean coast, and was once of great strategic importance. It is five kilometres long and a little over one kilometre wide, with a total area of six kilometres. Its population is estimated to be around 30,000.

The political status of the peninsula has long been the source of dispute between the United Kingdom and Spain. The first people to settle on the Rock were the Moors in 711. Gibraltar was under Spanish rule from 1462 until 1704, when it was captured by the British. Under the terms of the 1713 Treaty the Spanish have a first right of refusal – before the Gibraltarians themselves – in the event of British sovereignty being relinquished. The airport is an additional complication, since it is built on reclaimed land not forming part of the original territory and therefore, in the Spanish view, not covered by the Treaty.

On 10 September 1967, following a United Nations resolution on the decolonization of Gibraltar, a referendum was held to determine whether the Gibraltarians wished to retain their links with the United Kingdom. The result was an almost unanimous vote in favour of remaining British: out of a total electorate of 12,762 people, only 44 voted for Spain.

Although Gibraltar as a European territory for whose external relations the United Kingdom is responsible is covered by the **Treaty of Rome** (Article 299.4), not until 2004 will the Gibraltarians be represented in the **European Parliament**. The dispute over Gibraltar's status remains an irritant in Anglo-Spanish relations and has blocked the entry into force of the **External Frontiers Convention**. For a fuller treatment of the dispute, see D. S. Morris and R. H. Haigh, *Britain, Spain and Gibraltar 1945–90* (1992).

Gibraltar is self-governing in most domestic matters (the United Kingdom remains responsible for external affairs, defence and internal security), under a constitution that was introduced in 1969. Legislative power is vested in the House of Assembly, while executive authority is exercised by the governor, who is also commander-in-chief. The latter generally acts in concert with the Gibraltar Council.

Giscard d'Estaing, Valéry (b. 1926)

Valéry Giscard d'Estaing was elected to the Assemblée Nationale in 1956. By the 1960s he was leading his own party, the *Républicains Indépendants*, and serving under **Charles de Gaulle** as Finance Minister. He served President Georges Pompidou in the same capacity from 1969 until 1974, when he defeated **François Mitterrand** in the election for the presidency. As President, he was responsible for the initiative that transformed the system of irregular European Community '**summits**' into the **European Council**. He established good relations with Chancellor Helmut Schmidt of West Germany and throughout the 1970s Franco-German cooperation was the principal driving-force behind European integration. In particular, Giscard and Schmidt gave their strong personal support to **Economic and Monetary Union** (EMU) as relaunched by **Roy Jenkins** in 1977. In the same year Giscard first proposed the creation of an *espace judiciaire européen*.

Defeated by Mitterrand in the 1981 presidential election, Giscard partially withdrew from the European political scene. However, in 1989 he was elected to the **European Parliament**, where he became the leader of the Liberal Group (see **political groups**). At the end of 1991 he suddenly left the Liberals to join the Group of the European People's Party (Christian Democrats) and in 1993 left the Parliament altogether. In December 2001 he was appointed chairman of the Convention which is preparing the **intergovernmental conference** due to begin in 2004 (see **Laeken Declaration**).

A convinced European, Giscard nevertheless evinces a characteristically French distaste for the supranational character of the European Union's institutions, notably the **European Commission**. This accounts for the entertaining but not wholly sympathetic portrait of Giscard in Roy Jenkins's *European Diary* (1989) and in his *Portraits and Miniatures* (1993).

Greece

Greece was the first country to conclude an **Association Agreement** with the Community (Treaty of Athens, 1961). At the time this was to the Six an important and welcome token of international recognition. The Agreement made explicit reference to full membership at a later date. During the period of military dictatorship (1967–74) the Agreement was suspended, and the 10-year transition to a **customs union** with the Community was interrupted. A year after the restoration of democratic rule Greece applied for membership of the Community, by then composed of nine members.

The **Opinion** delivered by the **European Commission** was, in its original form, largely negative, on the grounds that neither Greece's economy nor its political and administrative system was yet ready for membership. This view was overturned by the **Council of Ministers**, who took the view that the overriding imperative was to consolidate Greek democracy. An **Accession** Treaty was signed in May 1979, and Greece became the tenth member of the Community in January 1981.

In October 1981 a Socialist government was elected on a platform openly critical of the accession terms negotiated by their political opponents. A **renegotiation** was demanded, similar to that which the 1974 Labour government in the United Kingdom had secured. The Greek government's demands were made more urgent by the fact that two more southern European countries, Portugal and Spain, were by then negotiating for admission. Eventually, a solution was found for Greece, partly within the new framework of **Integrated Mediterranean Programmes**, but the Socialist government, which remained in power until 1990, was, at best, ambivalent about Greek membership of the Community. This was especially evident in Greece's refusal to share in common foreign policy stances and actions (such as sanctions against Iran) agreed as part of **European Political Cooperation**.

Together with Portugal, Greece is the poorest of the member states, and has a rate of inflation some four times greater than the average. It benefits substantially from the **structural funds** and takes only an occasional interest in other areas of policy. As might be expected, Greece is an implacable opponent of Turkish entry into the Union and takes a lively interest in the problem of Cyprus. After a brief period out of office, the Socialists returned to power and continued their independent and idiosyncratic foreign policy (for example, by imposing an embargo on trade with the former Yugoslav republic of **Macedonia**, which was said to have designs on the Greek region of the same name). Relations with the European Union continue to be a divisive issue in Greek politics (the Communist Party has pro-European and anti-European wings; see **Communism**) and Greece remains among the least enthusiastic supporters of further moves towards closer integration. However, rather surprisingly, Greece chose to become one of the countries committed to the removal of internal frontier controls under the **Schengen Agreement**. The Greek drachma joined the **Exchange Rate Mechanism** (ERM) for the first time in March 1998. Although initially Greece was not judged eligible to take part in stage 3 of **Economic and Monetary Union** (EMU), it adopted the **euro** in 2002.

Greenland

Greenland is an island of over 2 million square kilometres – an area larger than France, Germany, Italy, Spain and the United Kingdom put together – with a population of only 50,000 people. Until 1953 Greenland was a Danish colony. After that date it became an integral part of Denmark itself. In January 1973, as part of Denmark, Greenland joined the European Community. In May 1979 Greenland was granted a substantial measure of home rule within Denmark, including the right to hold a referendum on whether to remain inside the Community. The vote was held in February 1982, with a majority in favour of withdrawal. A Treaty was accordingly signed in March 1984 'amending, with regard to Greenland, the Treaties establishing the European Communities', and Greenland's departure took effect in July 1986. Since then, it has been one of the **overseas countries and territories** (OCTs) of the Community. Unlike other OCTs, Greenland does not benefit from the **European Development Fund**, but instead receives an annual payment by way of compensation for access to its fishing grounds. Greenland also qualifies for assistance from the **structural funds**.

Grotius programme

The Grotius programme, established under Joint Action 96/636 on 28 October 1996 (*Official Journal*, L287, 8 November 1996), was designed to encourage 'legal practitioners' in the European Union to familiarize themselves with each other's legal and judicial systems and thereby 'to facilitate judicial cooperation between Member States'. The programme, originally due to end in December 2000, was extended for a further two years and adjusted to take account of the provisions in the **Treaty of Amsterdam** on judicial cooperation in criminal matters. Huig De Groot (1583–1645), Latinized as Grotius, was a Dutch jurist, diplomat and politician who is regarded as one of the pioneers of international law.

Group of Seven

The Western Economic Summits, better known as the Group of Seven or simply G-7 Summits, are regular meetings held since 1975 of the heads of government and finance ministers of the seven leading industrialized countries: the United States, Canada (since 1976), Japan, France, Germany, Italy and the United Kingdom. Since May 1977 the Group of Seven Summits have also been attended by the President of the **European Commission** on behalf of the European Union as a whole (an account by **Roy Jenkins** of how he overcame French opposition to this during his presidency may be found in his *European Diary*) and latterly also by the President of the Russian Federation (hence the name Group of Seven plus one). The President of the **European Central Bank** (ECB) attends meetings of the Group of Seven finance ministers.

The Group of Seven is to be distinguished from the Group of Twenty-four, the member countries of the **Organization for Economic Cooperation and Development** (OECD); and the Group of Ten, leading members of the International Monetary Fund: the Group of Seven plus Belgium, the Netherlands, Sweden and, since 1984, Switzerland, making, in fact, 11.

Gymnich meetings

Ministers representing the member states of the European Union sometimes meet informally with only very few officials and interpreters to have discussions in a relaxed atmosphere without the need to reach formal decisions. These meetings are known as 'Gymnich meetings' after Schloss Gymnich near Bonn, where the first of such meetings was held in April 1974 (see **Council of Ministers**).

Gypsies

Their numbers variously estimated at between 8 million and 10 million, Gypsies (or Roma, as they prefer to be called) have been in Europe since the fifteenth century. It is thought to have been the expansion of the Ottoman empire which pushed them westwards. In some countries in central and eastern Europe as much as 5 per cent of the population is said to be of Gypsy origin. In 1995 the Committee of Ministers of the **Council of Europe** set up a Special Group to address the problems arising from the denial in certain countries of Gypsies' civil rights. Attention is also being given to this in the framework of the **Stability Pact for South-Eastern Europe**.

H

Hallstein, Walter (1901–82)

Walter Hallstein was the first President of the **European Commission**. Pursuing an academic career until becoming an adviser to **Konrad Adenauer** in 1950, he led the German delegation in the discussions on the **Schuman Plan** and in 1951 became a minister in the Foreign Ministry, in which capacity he developed the 'Hallstein doctrine': the refusal to have diplomatic relations with countries that recognized East Germany as a state. Hallstein represented West Germany at the **Messina Conference** and was active in the negotiations that led to the signing of the **Treaties** establishing the **European Economic Community** (EEC) and the **European Atomic Energy Community** (Euratom).

In 1958 Hallstein became President of the Commission and remained in that office for nine years. He built up the Commission (then employing about 3,000 officials) into the embryonic European government he thought it should be. Under his presidency it was agreed that the Commission in Brussels would serve all three European Communities (see **Merger Treaty**). His vigorous defence of the Commission's authority and independence brought him into conflict with national politicians such as **Charles de Gaulle** who were wary of the pretensions of supranational institutions (de Gaulle was particularly irritated by Hallstein's insistence on the Commission accepting the credentials of ambassadors accredited to the Community). The most serious conflict between Hallstein and de Gaulle was that of 1965 (the so-called **empty chair crisis**), eventually resolved by the **Luxembourg Compromise** of 1966. Hallstein resigned the following year and retired from public life in 1972.

Although sometimes dismissed as a determined technocrat, Hallstein never had any doubts about the fundamentally political nature of what the Community was trying to achieve. He emphasized this in his book *United Europe: Challenge and Opportunity* (1962), which was based on lectures delivered at Tufts University, Massachusetts. He reminded his American audience that 'the Iron Curtain is nearer to Brussels than Washington, DC, is to Boston'. He said: 'The logic of economic integration not only leads on toward political unity by way of the fusion of interests; it also involves political action in itself.' Referring to the **Common Agricultural Policy** (CAP), member states' exchange-rate policies, and external trade issues, he added, 'Agreement on all these matters will require political courage certainly no less than that which was needed to sign the Community Treaties in the first place. And that courage was considerable, for the Treaties set in motion a process far more ambitious than the modest words "economic integration" would suggest.'

'Hard core'

A September 1994 paper entitled *Reflections on European Policy*, drawn up by Christian Democrats in the German Bundestag (and sometimes known as the 'Lamers paper' after one of its co-authors, Karl Lamers), drew attention to the existence of a 'hard core of [member states of the European Union] oriented to greater integration and closer cooperation' and called for it to be further strengthened in order 'to counteract the centrifugal forces generated by constant enlargement'. In the text that followed, it was made clear that the hard core was thought to be composed of Germany, France and the **Benelux** countries (i.e., the original **Six** with the exception of Italy).

Although the paper emphasized that the hard core 'must not be closed to other Member States ... [but] be open to every Member State willing and able to meet its requirements', the use of the phrase caused widespread offence to member states that felt excluded (see Preface). The idea of a hard core was denounced by opponents of a **two-speed Europe**, which is effectively what the explicit recognition of such a core would entail. The paper also made clear that among the most precise and demanding 'requirements' for membership of the hard core were the **convergence criteria** for the third stage of **Economic and Monetary Union** (EMU), described as 'the cornerstone of political union'.

In a special reference to the United Kingdom, the paper said that the existence of a hard core and the intensification of **Franco-German cooperation** did not imply 'the abandoning of hopes that Great Britain will assume its role in the heart of Europe and thus in its core'. Rather, they were taken to be 'the best means of exerting a positive influence on the clarification of Great Britain's relationship with Europe and on its willingness to participate in further steps towards integration'. In response to this John Major, in a speech in Leiden on 7 September 1994, endorsed the idea of a non-exclusive hard core as part of the **'flexibility'** he sought to encourage with respect to the pace and character of European integration.

In a speech to the Federal Trust in London on 17 November 1994 Lamers returned to the idea of a hard core, reiterating his 'firmly-held belief – a belief borne out by the entire course of European integration – that if a smaller group of countries presses ahead with particularly intensive and far-reaching economic and political integration, this group as core has a centripetal or magnetic effect on the other countries'.

Harmonization

The **free movement of goods** within the **common market** was one of the fundamental objectives of the **Treaty of Rome**. However, differences between national product standards meant that free circulation was difficult to achieve, and such standards allowed member states too much scope for introducing or maintaining barriers to trade on (sometimes spurious) scientific or health and safety grounds. With the removal of tariffs and quotas on trade between member states under Articles 9 and 34 (now 23, 28 and 29), product standards became the key instrument for protectionism. Throughout the 1960s and 1970s the **European Commission** sought to draw up common standards, a process usually known as harmonization but referred to in the Treaty as 'approximation'. Article 3.1(h) refers to the 'approximation of the laws of Member States to the extent required for the functioning of the common market' and the same expression is used in **Articles 94 and 95**, which together constitute the legal base for harmonization.

Although harmonization was supported in principle by industry and commerce, progress was extremely slow. Before the **Single European Act** (SEA), agreement had to be unanimous in the **Council of Ministers**, and the extraordinarily detailed draft legislation to which harmonization gave rise prompted not only ridicule but hostility. For this and for other reasons, and encouraged by the judgments of the **Court of Justice** in the **Cassis de Dijon case** of 1980 (Case 120/78), the Commission adopted the so-called 'new approach' based on mutual recognition (see Council Resolution of 7 May 1985, *Official Journal*, C136, 4 June 1985). It introduced the presumption that a product legally on sale in one member state may be sold in any other. The aim is now to set only minimum common standards on the basis of health and safety requirements, and to leave the technical details to be worked out by specialist bodies in consultation with manufacturers (see *Comité Européen de Normalisation*). Harmonization along these new lines is one of the essential foundations of the **Single Market** programme (see also **Cockfield White Paper**).

Heath, Edward (b. 1916)

Elected as a Conservative MP in 1950, Edward Heath made his maiden speech on the **Schuman Plan**. He was responsible as Lord Privy Seal for the negotiations that followed the United Kingdom's first attempt, in 1961, to join the European Community. The negotiations were brought to an abrupt conclusion by **Charles de Gaulle** in January 1963. Government documents suggest that Heath had been misled into thinking that the talks were going well, and that the ill-feeling caused by de Gaulle's veto was compounded by French accusations that the United Kingdom had signed 'secret agreements' with Washington (*The Times*, 1 January 1994).

In spite of this disappointment Heath continued to be involved with European issues as Secretary of State for Trade and Industry from 1963. After the Conservatives' 1964 election defeat he became the leader of the Conservative Party, which he led (rather unexpectedly) to victory in 1970. One of his government's first acts was to complete the negotiations that had followed the United Kingdom's second application for Community membership, made by the Labour government of Harold Wilson in 1967. Heath signed the **Treaty of Rome** on behalf of the United Kingdom in 1972. He was defeated in the elections held in February and October 1974, and in 1975 he lost the leadership of the Conservative Party to **Margaret Thatcher**.

Mrs Thatcher's policies towards Europe, especially after she became Prime Minister in 1979, provided Heath with many pretexts for criticizing the woman who had supplanted him. For this and for other reasons he became and remained a controversial figure within the Conservative Party. Nevertheless, his enthusiasm for Europe was genuine: in one of his best-remembered speeches, given in response to de Gaulle's 1963 veto, he declared 'We in Britain are not going to turn our backs on the mainland of Europe or on the countries of the Community. We are part of Europe by geography, tradition, history, culture and civilization. We shall continue to work with our friends in Europe for the true unity and strength of this continent.'

The phrase that gave Heath most trouble in the years preceding the **referendum of June 1975** was one he used in a speech to the British Chamber of Commerce in Paris on 5 May 1970. Speaking of the negotiations then in hand, he said that it would not be in the interests of the Community if it were to be enlarged without the 'full-hearted consent of the Parliaments and peoples of the new member countries'. The phrase was extensively used by opponents of British membership, Labour and Conservative, to strengthen the case for a referendum.

Heath has not written extensively on European questions, and for an understanding of his vision of Europe one must go back to his 1970 Godkin lectures delivered in the United States and published later that year as *Old World, New Horizons*. The fullest biography of Heath is by John Campbell (1994). His autobiography, *The Course of my Life*, was published in 1998.

Helsinki Final Act

Signed on 1 August 1975 by the 35 states that participated in the **Conference on Security and Cooperation in Europe** (CSCE) in Helsinki, the Final Act embodied the results of the Conference. Together with the **Charter of Paris** for a New Europe, signed on 21 November 1990, the Final Act is the legal basis for the **Organization for Security and Cooperation in Europe** (OSCE), which now encompasses 55 states (all European states plus the United States, Canada and the central Asian republics of the former USSR).

Hierarchy of acts

A translation of the French *hierarchie des actes*, this is the name given to a body of ideas relating to the reordering of the different types of European Union legislation, modelled on the French constitutional reforms of 1958. It is sometimes known as a 'hierarchy of norms'. At present, different types of **legal instrument** may be adopted under a variety of procedures, depending upon the legal base in the **Treaties** and in some cases upon the subject-matter. A 'hierarchy' would lay down different categories of legislation, ranging from the most important (e.g., Treaty amendments) to the most trivial, and specify the appropriate procedures. In so doing it would define the role of the various institutions, European and national, in the law-making process and establish a clear order of precedence. A 'Declaration on the hierarchy of Community acts' was annexed to the **Maastricht Treaty**, but the idea was not taken up in the **Treaty of Amsterdam**.

High Authority

One of the four institutions of the **European Coal and Steel Community** (ECSC), the High Authority was the forerunner of the **European Commission**. Its first president (1952–4) was **Jean Monnet**. Under the 1965 **Merger Treaty** the High Authority was merged with the Commission with effect from July 1967. Within its relatively narrow field, the powers of the High Authority were more extensive than those of the Commission. It was described as 'the first example of an independent supranational institution' (see **Schuman Plan**).

High Representative

In the mid-1990s it was proposed to give the European Union's **Common Foreign and Security Policy** (CFSP) a 'human face' by creating for the CFSP a secretary-general who would play a role similar to that of the secretary-general of the United Nations or of the **North Atlantic Treaty Organization** (NATO). Although this was discussed in the negotiations which led to the **Treaty of Amsterdam**, it was not included in the final text of the Treaty. Instead, for CFSP purposes, the secretary-general of the **Council of Ministers** has been given the title of 'High Representative', and the Council may in respect of particular issues appoint a 'special representative' (revised Article J8 (now 18) of the **Maastricht Treaty**). The **European Council** at its meeting in Cologne in June 1999 appointed Javier Solana, former secretary-general of NATO, as High Representative for the CFSP. In November 1999 Solana was also appointed secretary-general of the **Western European Union** (WEU).

Human rights

Among the first acts of the General Assembly of the United Nations was the adoption of the Universal Declaration of Human Rights (10 December 1948). This Declaration, although comprehensive, did not set out a means whereby respect for human rights could be enforced. When the **Council of Europe** was established the following year 'maintenance and further realisation of human rights and fundamental freedoms' were listed among its basic objectives. To this end a Convention for the Protection of Human Rights and Fundamental Freedoms was drawn up and signed in Rome on 4 November 1950. Less comprehensive than the Universal Declaration, the Convention was more ambitious in that it set up machinery for enforcement and required signatory states not only to accept certain duties of observance but also to recognize the fact of individuals having rights under international law. The Convention came into force on 3 September 1953.

Some states have incorporated the Convention into their domestic law. The Convention was never intended to supplant national measures for the protection of human rights, but to provide an additional guarantee at the international level. Exhaustion of national remedies is a precondition for bringing proceedings under the Convention.

The Convention has been amended several times since 1950 and several **protocols** have been added to it. It consists of 59 Articles. Among the rights guaranteed are: the right to life, liberty and security of person; the right to a fair trial, with the possibility of having the sentence reviewed by a higher tribunal; respect for privacy and family life; freedom of thought, conscience and religion; freedom of expression; freedom of the press; freedom of peaceful assembly and association; freedom from torture, inhuman or degrading treatment, slavery or forced labour; the prohibition of the death penalty; the right to leave or return to one's own country; and the elimination of discrimination in the enjoyment of rights and freedoms guaranteed under the Convention. As one authority has commented, 'some of these rights are crystal clear, others are very vague; some are unequivocal, others are heavily qualified' (C. A. Gearty, 'The European Court of Human Rights and the protection of civil liberties: an overview', *Cambridge Law Journal*, Vol. 52, no. 1, March 1993).

The European Court of Human Rights is based in Strasbourg. Judges are elected, half of them at a time in elections held every three years, for a renewable six-year term by the Parliamentary Assembly from lists of names, three for each vacancy, submitted by the signatory states. There are as many judges as there are members of the Council of Europe.

All applications are addressed directly to the Court, and sifted by a panel of three judges. They may be brought by persons, groups or private organizations or by one state against another. The complaint must show that all domestic legal remedies have been exhausted, and the complaint must be brought within six months of the final decision by the courts or authorities concerned. Cases accepted as admissible are normally heard by a chamber of seven judges. Once the facts have been established, provision exists for a 'friendly settlement' between the parties. If this is not accepted, the Court formally adjudicates. Exceptionally, cases may be brought before a Grand Chamber of 17 judges, either on appeal or by virtue of their importance. A judge from the state in which the case originated always sits in the Grand Chamber to ensure a proper understanding of that state's legal system. Responsibility for monitoring the enforcement of the Court's decision (decisions of the Grand Chamber are final) rests with the Committee of Ministers of the Council of Europe. All signatory states to the Convention are required to recognize the right of individual application to the Court and the Court's jurisdiction over all inter-state cases.

The Court receives about 5,000 complaints every year. Of these, about 3,500 are eliminated as clearly inadmissible. Of those that receive further investigation, about 10 per cent are declared admissible. Only one inter-state case has ever been referred to the Court: on methods used to interrogate terrorist suspects in Northern Ireland. The number of judgments delivered by the Court averaged only one a year during the Court's first 10 years, but the average is now more than 20. The procedure outlined above was introduced in November 1998 and was designed to speed up the Court's work. Under the old two-tier procedure it could take up to six years for a case to be decided.

The Council of Europe's human rights activities are increasing not only as a result of new accessions to the Council but also because the Convention itself has been supplemented by a **European Social Charter** (1965) and a European Convention for the Prevention of Torture and Inhuman or Degrading Treatment or Punishment (1989). New problems in the fields of biotechnology and the treatment of aliens are being addressed. Such activities (to which should be added the awarding of a Human Rights prize every two years) are the liveliest and most lasting of the Council of Europe's contributions to European integration (see Robert Blackburn and Jörg Polakiewicz, eds, *Fundamental Rights in Europe*, Oxford, 2001).

By contrast, the **Treaty of Rome** makes little mention of human rights. On 5 April 1977 the presidents of the **European Parliament** and the **European**

Commission and the president-in-office of the **Council of Ministers** signed a Joint Declaration on Fundamental Rights, in which reference was made to the European Convention. The Declaration binds the three institutions 'in the exercise of their powers and in pursuance of the aims of the European Communities' to respect the fundamental rights derived from the Convention and from the constitutions of member states. This Declaration, reiterated in the preamble to the 1986 **Single European Act** (SEA), became part of the *acquis communautaire* and so something that all states wishing to join the Union are obliged to accept. More recently, Article 6.2 of the **Maastricht Treaty** requires the European Union to respect the rights set out in the Convention and in the constitutions of member states as 'general principles of Community law'. The **Treaty of Amsterdam** introduces new provisions for the **suspension** of a member state found guilty of a 'serious and persistent' breach of human rights. At the meeting of the European Council in Nice (December 2000) a **Charter of Fundamental Rights** was adopted, and thereafter 'solemnly proclaimed' by the European Parliament, the Commission and the Council of Ministers.

Human rights considerations enter into all Commission **Opinions** on applications for membership, and have been used as an argument against Turkish membership. There is strong pressure from the European Parliament and elsewhere upon the Commission and the Council to insert human rights clauses into cooperation and **Association Agreements** with non-member countries. The **Cotonou Agreement** contains human rights provisions in accordance with the Parliament's wishes. A very wide range of cases of alleged abuses of human rights, both inside and outside the Union, are brought before the Parliament every month, and annual reports on human rights are drawn up. The Parliament has worked very closely through its Human Rights Unit with organizations such as Amnesty International and with internationally known human rights campaigners such as Andrei Sakharov (after whom the Parliament named its annual prize for Freedom of Thought). The Parliament's involvement in human rights has increased as a result of the formalization in the Maastricht Treaty of the right to present petitions to the Parliament and the establishment of an **Ombudsman**.

One widely canvassed option might have been for the Union itself to become a party to the Convention. Both the European Commission and the European Parliament were in favour of this, but the Council of Ministers sought the opinion of the **Court of Justice** and the Court ruled against it (Opinion 2/94). For human rights in the jurisprudence of the Court, see Philip Aston (ed.), *The EU and Human Rights* (Oxford, 1999) and Francis Jacobs, 'Human rights in the European Union: the role of the Court of Justice', *European Law Review*, Vol. 26, no. 4, August 2001. See also **minorities**.

Humanitarian Aid Office (HAO)

The HAO, formerly the **European Community Humanitarian Office** (ECHO), is a department of the **European Commission** responsible for the coordination of humanitarian aid (defined as aid given in response to specific emergencies, natural or man-made, rather than aid given as part of the Union's **development policy**: see also **EuropeAid Cooperation Office**). The legal base is Article 179 of the **Treaty of Rome** and Regulation 1257/96 of 20 June 1996 (*Official Journal*, L 163, 2 July 1996). Together with its member states, the Union is the world's largest donor of humanitarian aid, the cost of which is borne by the **Budget** and by the **European Development Fund**. The HAO also prepares feasibility studies, monitors aid programmes, organizes training for aid workers, and initiates pilot projects.

Hungary

Long regarded as the most liberal of the former **COMECON** states, Hungary played a key part in the revolution in eastern Europe by opening its border with Austria to refugees from East Germany in September 1989. Two years later, Hungary signed a **Europe Agreement** with the European Community which came into force in February 1994. On 31 March 1994 Hungary was the first former Communist state to apply for full membership of the European Union (see **enlargement**). Hungary was a founder member of the **Central European Initiative** and of the **Central European Free Trade Agreement** and is a member of the **Organization for Security and Cooperation in Europe** (OSCE), the **Council of Europe** and (since 1999) the **North Atlantic Treaty Organization** (NATO).

The **European Commission** published its **Opinion** on the Hungarian application in July 1997 (*Bulletin of the European Union*, supplement 6/97). It found that Hungary satisfied the **Copenhagen criteria** for membership, and noted that cooperation with Hungary under the Europe Agreement was working well. Over 70 per cent of Hungarian trade was already with the European Union. Accession negotiations with Hungary began in March 1998 in line with a decision of the **European Council** meeting in Luxembourg in December 1997. These negotiations were concluded in 2002. On 12 April 2003 the Hungarians voted by 83.76 per cent to 16.24 per cent to join the European Union (see **Treaty of Accession**).

I

Iceland

A Danish possession from 1380, Iceland became wholly independent in 1944. With a population of 265,000, the island has the lowest population density of any European country. About three-quarters of Iceland's export earnings are from fish products, for which the United Kingdom is by far the most important market. The Icelanders claim to have the oldest parliament in the world, the Althing.

In spite of its remoteness, Iceland has participated very extensively in European organizations as a member of the **Council of Europe**, the **North Atlantic Treaty Organization** (NATO), the **European Free Trade Association** (EFTA) and the **European Economic Area** (EEA), and as an associate member of the **Western European Union** (WEU). Iceland is also a member of the **Nordic Council**. Although there is some support in Iceland for membership of the European Union, no application is currently in prospect and none is likely to be forthcoming unless a means can be found of safeguarding the Icelandic fishing industry.

Immigration

See **area of freedom, security and justice, asylum, External Frontiers Convention**.

Implied competence

The **Treaties** establishing the **European Communities** give certain specific powers, or 'competences', to the Community institutions provided for in those Treaties. The doctrine of implied competence means that where Community institutions have the power to regulate a matter internally, they may also act externally. It was stated very clearly by the **Court of Justice** in an **Opinion**: 'The power to bind the Community vis-à-vis third countries ... flows by implication from the provisions of the Treaty creating the internal power and in so far as the participation of the Community in the international agreement is ... necessary for the attainment of one of the objectives of the Community' (Opinion 1/76). Furthermore, if the matter in question is the subject of formally established common rules, the Community's power to act externally becomes exclusive: individual member states may no longer act independently. Implied competence is of great importance in the field of external relations. See also ERTA case, occupied field.

Independent European Programme Group (IEPG)

The IEPG, formed in 1976, was a forum within which European members of the North Atlantic Treaty Organization (NATO) discussed and coordinated their research and development programmes and equipment requirements in the defence field. Such coordination was intended to act as a counterpoise to the United States' overwhelming dominance in this area and was later carried out within the Western European Union (WEU) framework in the Armaments Group.

Industry policy

Although the European Union's origins are rooted in industry (see European Coal and Steel Community) and although many of its policies have a direct bearing on industry (see especially competition policy, free movement of goods, public purchasing, Single Market, state aids), there is no industry policy as such. Article 157 of the Treaty of Rome, added by the Maastricht Treaty, defines the aim as being solely to 'ensure that the conditions necessary for the competitiveness of the Community's industry exist' by means of measures to promote adaptation to structural change, the creation of an economic environment favourable to initiative and cross-frontier cooperation, and the application to industry of technological developments. The European Commission may take 'any useful initiative'. The Council of Ministers may enact specific measures in support of action taken by member states, but only by unanimity. Industry may benefit from aid from the structural funds or from European Investment Bank (EIB) loans (see also Edinburgh Growth Initiative). Many research programmes are intended to bring benefits to industry. The first attempt at an industrial strategy dates from the Commission's 1990 study entitled *Industrial policy in an open and competitive environment*. Since then the Commission has drawn up an annual study entitled *Panorama of EU Industry*. Broadly speaking, Commission action has concentrated on the restructuring of older industries, such as steel, and on the attempt to place new industries on a Europe-wide footing to enable them to compete internationally (see defence industry, information society).

Although the Commission had extensive powers in relation to the steel industry under the 1951 **Treaty of Paris** (which was allowed to lapse in July 2002), the social and regional implications of restructuring (which meant reductions in capacity, shared equitably among national steel industries) were so sensitive that the Commission preferred to draw up an agreed plan and then allow the steel industry itself to work out the details and monitor its enforcement. The problem was made more complex by the fact that national steel industries (such as the British) that had already on their own initiative applied a restructuring programme involving massive job losses expected to have this taken into account when an overall plan involving further cuts was being drawn up. Added to this was the political pressure to open up the market to imports of steel products from central and eastern Europe. Ultimately, the Commission had to rely on its powers of persuasion, backed by threats to withdraw financial support or bring actions in the **Court of Justice**. Problems analogous to those in the steel industry also arose with respect to textiles, coal and shipbuilding.

The Commission's main efforts in regard to new industries are directed towards information technology and telecommunications (see **information society**). In the Commission's view the fragmentation of the market in Europe means that no producer can take advantage of the economies of scale in investment, research and product development that the Single Market should, in theory, provide. However, to overcome this fragmentation the Commission tends to become involved in the invidious (and often unwelcome) business of 'picking winners', even if only in terms of common technical specifications to which all manufacturers can work.

Underlying industry policy are fundamental national differences on the role of the state and, by extension, the role of the Union institutions. For example, French governments of whatever party have tended always to support the idea of a centrally planned industrial policy, whereas in several other countries (including, at least since 1979, the United Kingdom) the state's role is largely confined to creating and maintaining the economic circumstances in which industry can prosper. The minimalist requirements of Article 157 represent a kind of compromise between these two positions, coloured by the fact that even the enthusiasts for industrial planning are unwilling to see a substantial measure of responsibility transferred to Brussels.

Information society

Although the phrase 'information society' does not appear in the **Treaty of Rome**, there is an obvious need for the European Union to keep abreast of current developments in information and communications technology (ICT). Moreover, such developments have a bearing on existing areas of policy, such as **industry policy**, **competition policy** and **research**. Currently, the European Union represents 46 per cent of the global market for consumer ICT products, but supplies only 14 per cent of that market. The trade deficit in ICT products has increased tenfold in ten years.

In the 1980s the European Community set up the ESPRIT (European Strategic Programme for Research in Information Technologies) and RACE (advanced telecommunications) programmes and in 1987 the European Commission published a Green Paper on liberalising the market for telecommunications, but the first full scale study devoted to this topic was the so-called Bangemann report of 1994, named after Martin Bangemann, the member of the **European Commission** responsible for ICT. Entitled *Europe and the Global Information Society*, it made recommendations on how the Union could contribute to establishing the legal, technical and regulatory framework for new information technologies and how European industry could take full advantage of the rapidly expanding market for ICT products. The report was followed up later in the year by an action plan entitled *Europe's Way to the Information Society* (revised in 1996). A European IT Observatory has been set up to monitor developments.

Information technology is an important component of the fourth and fifth framework programmes for research. The fifth framework programme (1999–2002) set aside €3.6 billion (about £2.5 billion) for ICT research, concentrating on practical applications for the new technologies. The impact on private citizens was assessed in a 1996 Commission Green Paper *Living and Working in the Information Society: People First*. Among the conclusions of the Luxembourg meeting of the **European Council** in November 1997 (the 'Jobs Summit': see **employment**) was the decision to establish a European Technology Facility to provide venture capital to small and medium-sized enterprises (SMEs) in the high technology sector, many of them involved in ICT. The GSM standard for mobile telephones was developed in Europe, where there are now (2001) 260 million users: it has been adopted by 130 countries world-wide. In December 1999 the European Commission published *e-Europe – An information society for all* (COM(1999)687), which provided the basis for the e-Europe action plan adopted at the European Council meeting in Feira (June 2000). At its previous meeting in Lisbon (March 2000), the European Council committed itself to transforming the European Union into 'the most competitive and dynamic knowledge-based economy in the world'.

The World Wide Web was developed at the **European Organization for Nuclear Research** (CERN) by its inventor, Tim Berners-Lee.

Integrated Mediterranean Programmes (IMPs)

The IMPs were established in response to a 1981 memorandum from the newly elected Socialist government of Greece, which had joined the

Community at the beginning of that year. Basically, the memorandum expressed dissatisfaction with Greece's terms of **accession** and asserted that the country's special problems needed special help. A commitment to address Greece's complaints was given by the **European Council** in March 1984. The following year the European Council established the IMPs for seven years (1986–92) 'in favour of the southern regions of the present Community' (i.e., the whole of Greece, parts of southern France and most of southern Italy). The agreement was given special urgency by the fact of accession negotiations with Portugal and Spain having been largely completed, and the purpose of the IMPs was to enable the eligible regions 'to adjust under the best conditions possible to the new situation created by **enlargement**'. The IMPs were financed by a contribution from the **structural funds**, a special line in the **Budget** and a loan facility from the **European Investment Bank** (EIB). They were not renewed, but Greece, Ireland, Portugal and Spain now benefit from the **Cohesion Fund**.

Intergovernmental Conference (IGC)

IGCs are special committees of representatives of the governments of the member states convened to consider amendments to the **Treaties**. They meet at the request of the **Council of Ministers**, in accordance with Article 48 of the **Maastricht Treaty**. Their conclusions must be reached 'by common accord' (that is, unanimously) and must then be submitted to **national parliaments** (and, in some cases, electorates) for **ratification** on the basis of domestic constitutional requirements. Only member states' governments or the **European Commission** may present Treaty amendments.

Since the foundation of the Community there have been seven significant revisions of the Treaties: the 1965 **Merger Treaty**, the 1970 and 1975 Treaties on the budgetary powers of the **European Parliament**, the 1986 **Single European Act** (SEA), the 1992 Maastricht Treaty on European Union and the 1997 **Treaty of Amsterdam** (in force since May 1999), and the 2001 **Treaty of Nice** (not yet in force).

IGCs are, in effect, the constitutional conventions of the European Union. From being purely procedural mechanisms for presenting Treaty changes on which there is broad consensus among member states, they have emerged since 1985 as the key arenas in which competing visions of the structure and overall direction of the Union are articulated. The calling of an IGCs sets up a clear presumption in favour of reform, putting the opponents of change on the defensive. The convening of an IGC requires only a simple majority of the member states, and once negotiations are under way there are strong pressures on member states to compromise. So far no IGC has failed to agree a text.

Some advocates of closer European integration use IGCs as a means of moving towards federalism (see **federation**). For example, having failed in the Maastricht Treaty to secure as substantial a move towards political union as they wished, the immediate response of the German and **Benelux** governments was to obtain a commitment to convene another IGC in 1996 to review the Maastricht settlement. This was convened in Turin in March 1996. The result, the Treaty of Amsterdam, was signed in October 1997. In a **protocol**, it specified that 'at least one year before the membership of the European Union exceeds twenty', another IGC would be convened 'in order to carry out a comprehensive review of the ... composition and functioning of the institutions'. This IGC, convened in February 2000, had on its agenda the size of the European Commission, the reweighting of member states' votes in the Council (see **qualified majority voting** (QMV)) and the extension of QMV. Other issues included the individual responsibility of Commissioners, the allocation of seats in the European Parliament, and post-enlargement adjustments to the **Court of Justice**, the **Court of Auditors** and other institutions and bodies. The IGC presented a report to the December 2000 meeting of the **European Council** in Nice: the Treaty was formally signed on 26 February 2001. Most of these issues had been addressed in a report, *The institutional implications of enlargement*, drawn up at the request of **Romano Prodi** and published in October 1999 (the Dehaene Report). At Nice it was agreed to convene another IGC in 2004 (see **Laeken Declaration**).

As the IGC has developed as the constitution-making forum within the Union, so criticism has grown about the lack of **transparency**. Neither the Reflection Group which prepared the Treaty of Amsterdam IGC nor the similar body which prepared the Treaty of Nice IGC succeeded in dispelling the air of secrecy surrounding the IGC process. If the Union were simply an international organization like any other, it would be possible for governments to alter its founding Treaties at will behind closed doors. The fact that the Union has entered into the fabric of domestic political life makes this increasingly difficult.

Intergovernmentalism

Intergovernmentalism is both a theory of integration (see also **federation**, **functionalism**) and a term used to describe institutional arrangements and decision-making procedures that allow governments to cooperate in specific fields while retaining their **sovereignty**. The intergovernmental approach to European integration involves keeping supranational institutions to a minimum and is, accordingly, the opposite of federalism. The intergovernmental model is of a confederal Europe, sometimes known as a *Europe des patries*. The European Union of today has certain intergovernmental aspects, such as the so-called intergovernmental 'pillars' of the **Maastricht Treaty**. These represent an attempt on the part of governments to keep certain sensitive areas, such as immigration and security, firmly within the ambit of the **Council of Ministers** and out of the hands of the other Union institutions; i.e., not subject to the right of legislative initiative enjoyed by the **European Commission**, nor to the scrutiny of the **European Parliament**, nor to the arbitration in the event of a dispute that is the prerogative of the **Court of Justice**. Intergovernmentalism also allows governments to experiment with closer cooperation in a particular area of policy. They may allow the policy to become communitized (see **communitization**) at a later date.

Examples of international organizations that are essentially intergovernmental include the **European Free Trade Association** (EFTA), the **Organization for Economic Cooperation and Development** (OECD) and the **Council of Europe**. All three are equipped with central institutions and at least the nucleus of a permanent secretariat, but the real power rests with the governments of the countries that choose to participate, a power symbolized by the Committees of Ministers which take the final decisions.

Intergovernmentalism is attractive to defenders of both national and parliamentary sovereignty, although the extent to which individual **national parliaments** can in fact exercise control over governments acting in concert is very limited.

Interinstitutional agreements

Under Article 48 of the **Maastricht Treaty** major adjustments to the powers of and relations between the institutions of the European Union can formally be made only by Treaty amendment, requiring the unanimous consent of the member states and ratification by **national parliaments**. Minor adjustments are made under interinstitutional agreements, many of which are later embodied in Treaty amendments.

Internal market

This phrase is used to distinguish economic activity within the member states of the European Union from external trade. Under Article 3.1(c) of the **Treaty of Rome** the internal market must allow the free movement of goods, persons, services and capital, i.e., the **four freedoms**. See also **Single Market**.

Interpol

Interpol (the International Criminal Police Organization) grew out of the International Criminal Police Commission (ICPC) founded in Vienna in 1923. By the end of the 1930s 34 countries were members of the ICPC, but after the Anschluss in 1938, the organization fell into the hands of the Nazis and was effectively disbanded. When the ICPC was refounded in 1946, its statute prevented it from becoming involved in cases of a political, religious, racial or military character (Article 3). It has been known as Interpol since 1956.

Interpol is primarily an organization for the gathering and exchange of information and a forum in which matters of common interest (police training, counter-terrorism, technical progress in communications) can be discussed. Its headquarters and general secretariat are in Lyons, and are supplemented by National Central Bureaux within the police forces of each participating state. It is wholly dependent upon the voluntary cooperation of its member states, of which there are about 179. The member states of the Union and other European countries are the most active members of Interpol and provide most of its budget. Interpol provides one obvious model for **Europol**.

Intervention

Intervention is one of the key features of the price support mechanism under the **Common Agricultural Policy** (CAP). If a product cannot be sold at an agreed price for that marketing year, it 'goes into intervention': it is bought and stored for future disposal. The cost is borne by the **Budget**. The responsibility for managing intervention rests with national authorities, the Intervention Boards in the case of the United Kingdom. Since the early 1980s efforts to reform the CAP have sought to limit the volume for surplus produce qualifying for intervention with the aid of 'stabilizers', of which the best-known are **quotas**. Not all products are covered by the price support mechanism.

Intra-Community trade

By establishing a **customs union** under the **Treaty of Rome, the Six** sought to stimulate trade among themselves. Over the period 1958–68, during which restrictions on trade were being dismantled, trade among the member states grew by an annual average of 28.4 per cent, although this was an acceleration of a trend that in fact began in the early 1950s as part of a general postwar recovery.

The table overleaf shows the percentage of total imports and exports for each member state of the Union represented by trade with the other member states and the overall balance in such trade. In some cases these figures represent a substantial shift away from trade with non-member states. By 1993 52.5 per cent of British exports were to the other 11 member states, compared with 21.8 per cent in 1958. France, Portugal and Spain, three other countries with well-established trading links outside Europe, have experienced a similar shift towards trade with other member states.

Intra-Community trade (2000)

	Intra-EC trade as % of total trade	Balance on intra-EC trade (in billion €)
Austria	65.21	−8.9
BLEU[1]	72.83	18.8
Denmark	67.55	3.5
Finland	58.32	4.7
France	63.09	−17.4
Germany	55.71	42.0
Greece	53.82	−12.7
Ireland	62.53	18.6
Italy	55.61	−2.9
The Netherlands	63.35	77.7
Portugal	77.07	−11.3
Spain	68.05	−24.6
Sweden	59.70	2.1
United Kingdom	52.84	−7.8
EU-15	60.60	

[1]Belgo-Luxembourg Economic Union
Source: calculated from Eurostat

Intrastat

With the removal of frontier controls between member states under the **Single Market** programme, a new system, known as Intrastat, was devised to collect statistics on internal trade. Developed by the Statistical Office (see **Eurostat**) and operational from 1 January 1993, Intrastat involves collecting information directly from businesses and is closely linked to the system for assessing and collecting **value-added tax** (VAT). The administrative burden on small businesses has been eased by the application of a threshold, but in some member states problems of late or incomplete submissions are still being encountered. Under the Intrastat system, imports from other member states are known as 'arrivals' and exports to other member states are known as 'consignments'.

Ioannina Compromise

The Ioannina Compromise was an agreement reached by the foreign ministers of the European Union in Ioannina (northern Greece) in March 1994 on the reform of the **qualified majority voting** (QMV) system in the **Council of Ministers**. Although it was intended to be a temporary agreement pending a full-scale review of QMV in the Intergovernmental Conference (IGC) of 1996–7, it is likely to remain in force at least until the next round of **enlargement** since the IGC review was inconclusive. The agreement, which had to be adjusted to take account of Norway's decision not to join the Union, specifies that if 23 to 25 votes are cast against a proposal, the Council will do 'all in its power to reach, within a reasonable time ... a satisfactory solution'. Formally, a blocking minority remains 26 votes.

Ireland

In the 1960s Ireland applied to join **the Six** in the wake of the United Kingdom, but was blocked by the vetoes on the United Kingdom **accession** exercised by **Charles de Gaulle**. Ireland eventually joined the Community, with Denmark and the United Kingdom, on 1 January 1973, a May 1972 **referendum** having resulted in 83.1 per cent of the votes being cast in favour of membership. The great attractions of membership were wider markets and massive support for Irish agriculture, and participation in an institutional framework that, in most respects, placed Ireland on an equal footing with the United Kingdom. Six years later, the entry into force of the **Exchange-Rate Mechanism** (ERM) was the occasion for the breaking of the link between the Irish punt and the pound sterling.

Only two anxieties have interrupted Ireland's state of contentment with Community membership. The first arose in the mid-1980s, when the member states started to move slowly but decisively towards closer involvement in defence and security issues. This was incompatible with Irish neutrality, and led to a last-minute challenge to the **Single European Act** (SEA) in the Irish Supreme Court and a referendum in May 1987. Ireland has remained outside all military alliances. The second arose as a consequence of the strengthened commitment to the free movement of persons in the **Maastricht Treaty**. **Protocols** were added both to the Treaty and the **Treaty of Rome** saying that this commitment did not 'affect the application' of Article 40.3.3 of the Irish Constitution, under which abortion is prohibited. In February 1992 a 14-year-old girl who had been raped was prevented from leaving Ireland in order to have an abortion in England. This action was challenged in the Irish Supreme Court, partly on the grounds that **free movement of persons** was guaranteed under the Treaty. The following month the Court ruled that since the girl's life was in danger, she was free to travel. In spite of a supplementary declaration agreed by the member states on 1 May 1992, the absolute right of Irish citizens to travel in order 'to obtain ... services lawfully available in Member States' remained unclear. The Maastricht Treaty was approved by a majority of two to one in a referendum on 18 June 1992. On 22 May 1998 the Irish electorate also gave its approval to the **Treaty of Amsterdam** by a similar majority, but on 7 June 2001 they rejected the **Treaty of Nice**. This was reversed in a second referendum on 19 October 2002 with 62.9 per cent of the vote.

Islands

There are some 500 inhabited islands in the European Union, with a combined population of over 14 million people (islands are defined as a segment of a member state, not containing the capital of that state, with no physical link to the mainland). Only Austria, Belgium and Luxembourg have no islands as part of their national territory. The special problems of islands – many of which are in those parts of the Union furthest from the centre – were recognized in the **Treaty of Amsterdam** in an amendment to Article 130(a) (now 158) of the **Treaty of Rome** introducing a specific reference to islands and in a short Declaration on Island Regions. The Declaration refers to islands' 'structural handicaps ... the permanence of which impairs their economic development'. Such handicaps justify the taking of 'specific measures ... to integrate [the islands] into the internal market on fair conditions'.

Much of the research and most of the lobbying on islands come from the Islands Commission of the Conference of Peripheral Maritime Regions of Europe, which was founded in 1973 and has its headquarters in Rennes, Brittany. There is a very great deal of information on islands in a **European Commission** study, *Portrait of the Islands* (Luxembourg, 1994).

Isle of Man
See **Channel Islands**.

Isoglucose case

The so-called 'isoglucose' case, the subject of a **Court of Justice** ruling in 1980, was of great importance in confirming the essential role played by the **European Parliament** in the legislative process. In fact, the case (*SA Roquette Frères v Council*, Case 138/79) was one of several concerned with isoglucose, a form of sugar extracted from cereals. The events may be summarized as follows. On 7 March 1979 the **European Commission** submitted to the **Council of Ministers** a proposal for a revised Regulation on isoglucose. The Council, as it was obliged to do under Article 143.2 EEC (since repealed), sought the **Opinion** of the European Parliament and pointed out that, since the revised Regulation had to come into force on 1 July 1979, the Parliament would need to give its Opinion in April. In the event it was not until May that the Parliament considered the report drawn up by its Committee on Agriculture. The report was rejected and referred back to the Committee.

Because the first European elections were held in June 1979, the Parliament did not meet again in full session until 17 July 1979, by which time the Council had adopted the revised Regulation (25 June 1979) without any Opinion having been received. A firm affected by the production quota for isoglucose laid down by the Council therefore brought an action in the **Court of Justice** against the Council to have the revised Regulation declared void under Article 173 (now 230) EEC on the grounds that an essential procedural requirement had been infringed. In its judgment, the Court stated:

The consultation provided for [in the **Treaty of Rome**] is the means which allows the Parliament to play an actual part in the legislative process of the Community. Such power represents an essential factor in the institutional balance intended by the Treaty. Although limited, it reflects at Community level the fundamental democratic principle that the peoples should take part in the exercise of power through the intermediary of a representative assembly. Due consultation of the Parliament in the cases provided for by the Treaty therefore constitutes an essential formality, disregard of which means that the measure concerned is void.

The Court went on to say that the requirement of 'due consultation' cannot be satisfied 'by the Council's simply asking for [the Parliament's] opinion'.

Simple consultation of the type undertaken in the isoglucose case has largely been superseded by the **cooperation** and **co-decision procedures** introduced by the **Single European Act** (SEA) and extended by the **Maastricht Treaty** and the **Treaty of Amsterdam**. Nevertheless, the isoglucose judgment, given so soon after the first European elections, was of lasting importance in terms of the Parliament's prestige and self-confidence. Together with the other cases concerned with isoglucose, it is conveniently summarized and analysed in Bernard Rudden and Diarmuid Rossa Phelan, *Basic Community Cases* (2nd edn, Oxford, 1997); see also Weatherill and Beaumont, *EU Law* (3rd edn, Harmondsworth, 1999).

Italy

The poorest of **the Six**, Italy was attracted to membership of the European Community as a means of re-establishing stability, credibility and respectability after a quarter-century of Fascist rule. **Alcide de Gasperi**, Italy's most noted statesman of the postwar decade, was determined that his country should play its full part in both European integration and, as a founder member of the **North Atlantic Treaty Organization** (NATO), the Atlantic Alliance (see also **Count Carlo Sforza**)

There has always been a high level of support in Italy for European integration across all political parties and in every sector of society. This may be connected with a consistently low level of satisfaction with respect to the quality of national and local government in Italy and a corresponding readiness to see powers transferred to Brussels, and a pattern of personal and local loyalties in which the sense of nationhood does not loom very large. Italians are among the strongest supporters of federalism (see **Altiero Spinelli**): in 1984 the **European elections** in Italy were combined with a **referendum**, in which the Italian electorate enthusiastically endorsed the idea that the **European Parliament** should be a **constituent assembly** empowered to draw up a constitution for Europe.

Contrasting with this enthusiasm is a poor record with regard to the implementation and observance of Community law. In the great majority of cases this may be ascribed to the chaotic workings of Italian bureaucracy and to a somewhat freewheeling approach to law in general rather than to any deliberate act of defiance.

Italy has always been a strong supporter of the **structural funds** and a vigorous defender of the interests of Mediterranean agriculture, especially the wine and olive oil sectors. However, a lack of coherence and of strategic thinking in Italian governments and the inward-looking nature of Italian politics have resulted in there being few distinctively Italian policy stances and even fewer major Italian initiatives oriented towards Europe: with the partial exception of the 1981 **Genscher–Colombo Plan** there has been no such initiative at governmental level since the 1955 **Messina Conference**. Until the appointment of **Romano Prodi** there had been only one Italian President of the **European Commission** (Franco Maria Malfatti, 1970–72) and his presidency was short and undistinguished: Malfatti resigned nine months before the end of his term in order to return to Italian politics. Italy can claim, however, to have invented Eurocommunism (see **Communism**). Upheavals in 1994 brought to power a new party, Forza Italia, which initially at least promised to take a more robust approach to European integration. The Italian political scene has been enlivened by the rise of autonomist parties, such as the Lega Nord, who would very much prefer to deal with Brussels rather than with Rome.

J

Jenkins, Roy (1920–2003)

Roy Jenkins was elected as a Labour MP in 1948. He rose rapidly within the Labour Party and in 1965 he was made Home Secretary in the first government led by Harold Wilson. He was Chancellor of the Exchequer from 1967 until Wilson's defeat by **Edward Heath** in 1970. Jenkins was the leader of the 69 pro-European Labour MPs who defied the party whip in October 1971 when the United Kingdom's terms of **accession** to the European Community were finally agreed by the House of Commons (see **renegotiation**). He was also one of the leaders of the 'Britain in Europe' campaign in the **referendum of June 1975**. His outspoken support for Europe made him unpopular with many in the Labour Party and it came as no real surprise when he failed to secure the leadership after Wilson's resignation in 1976. The same year he was chosen to succeed François-Xavier Ortoli as President of the **European Commission**, and he remained in Brussels from 1977 until 1981, having resigned his House of Commons seat. Jenkins's presidency was marked by a steady growth in the Commission's standing and influence; against strong opposition from French President **Valéry Giscard d'Estaing**, Jenkins succeeded in ensuring that the president of the Commission attended the **Group of Seven** summits of the major industrialized nations, but his most enduring achievement was the relaunching of **Economic and Monetary Union** (EMU).

The author of many speeches and articles on European issues, Jenkins also published his *European Diary* (1989) covering his period in the Commission. Suavely written, this is uniquely fascinating as an insider's account of life at the top of the Community, with its extraordinary mixture of great issues and petty intrigue. Jenkins's character sketches of the politicians with whom he dealt are especially entertaining.

Joint action

The provisions in the **Maastricht Treaty** covering the new areas of Union competence, the **Common Foreign and Security Policy** (CFSP) and **Justice** and Home Affairs (JHA), do not allow for the use of the **legal instruments** specified in the **Treaty of Rome**. Instead, the **Council of Ministers** may adopt common positions and take joint actions (Articles 14, 15(a) and 31 TEU). In the case of the CFSP the Council of Ministers is empowered to 'recommend common strategies to the **European Council**' and implement them as joint actions or common positions (Article 13). In the case of JHA, any member state or the **European Commission** may propose a common action (Article 34), which the Council may adopt by **unanimity**. The use of a unanimity rule guaranteeing a right of **veto** underlines the essentially intergovernmental nature (see **intergovernmentalism**) of these areas of Union activity and was an important element in securing the acceptance of the Maastricht Treaty by member states. The **Treaty of Amsterdam** introduced a significant modification to the general rule of unanimity known as **constructive abstention** and in JHA substituted 'common action' for 'joint action'. Once a joint action has been agreed, the Council may decide to take follow-up decisions by **qualified majority voting** (QMV).

Joint European Torus (JET)

The JET project, based at Culham, Oxfordshire, is the most ambitious **research** venture so far undertaken by the countries of the European Union. Switzerland also participates. One of only four large-scale projects in the world in the field of nuclear fusion, JET employs some 300 scientists. The long-term aim is to develop nuclear fusion as a cleaner, safer, more efficient source of nuclear energy than nuclear fission.

Culham was chosen as the site for JET in October 1977, after a long dispute in which Germany pushed very hard for an alternative site at Garching, near Munich. The issue was eventually settled in the course of a bilateral meeting between Prime Minister James Callaghan and Chancellor Helmut Schmidt. The incident was used to illustrate the absurdity of a decision-making system in which such issues were decided at so high a level, having become embroiled with other unrelated issues, such as agricultural reform and the **British Budget problem**. It was alleged that Europe's lead in this particular area of research was set back at least two years as a result of the dispute.

Joint Research Centre (JRC)

Article 8 of the Treaty establishing the **European Atomic Energy Community** (Euratom) provided for the creation of a Joint Nuclear Research Centre. The centre, now officially known as the Joint Research Centre (JRC) since its work is no longer confined to nuclear research, is made up of eight separate institutes. Four of them are based at Ispra in northern Italy, the others at Geel in Belgium, Karlsruhe in Germany, Petten in the Netherlands, and Seville in Spain (the Institute for Prospective Technological Studies). The JRC is the responsibility of the Directorate-General for research in the **European Commission**. The various institutes carry out research in the fields of nuclear safety, remote sensing by satellite, materials research, the environment, information technology and systems engineering (see also **Joint European Torus**). Since 1 January 1995, the JRC has been required to compete for research contracts, including those put out to tender by the Commission itself. It has also been able to participate in 'research networks' with other public or private institutes situated in the member states (see also **research, Joint European Torus, European Space Agency, European Organization for Nuclear Research**).

Juste retour

The phrase '*juste retour*' became widely current in 1979–85, when the **British Budget problem** was a regular item on the agenda of the **Council of Ministers**. It means that in broad terms and over a period a member state should receive from the **Budget** of the Union a 'fair return' i.e., sums roughly equivalent to those made over as a contribution. Strictly applied, the principle would, of course, reduce still further the redistributive effect of the Budget between member states. A looser definition of *juste retour* takes account not only of member states' contributions but also their relative prosperity and the extent to which they draw benefit from other policies. The phrase *juste retour* is now seldom used, having come to symbolize a narrow profit-and-loss approach to membership of the Union (see also **contributions and receipts**).

As Prime Minister in the 1970s, Harold Wilson once mildly rebuked those critics who demanded a *juste retour* from the Budget by quoting Wordsworth:

> ...high Heaven rejects the lore
> Of nicely-calculated less or more.
> (*Ecclesiastical Sonnets*, no. 43)

Justice and Home Affairs (JHA)

In common with the other intergovernmental 'pillar' of the **Maastricht Treaty**, the **Common Foreign and Security Policy** (CFSP), cooperation in the fields of Justice and Home Affairs has grown out of a variety of *ad hoc* procedures, some more formal than others, on specific subjects. The scope and forms of cooperation are set out in Title VI of the Treaty, Articles 29 to 42. Articles 30 and 31 specify the subjects to be covered by JHA: operational cooperation, the collection, analysis, and exchange of information (especially on money-laundering), training and exchanges of personnel, forensic research, enforcement of decisions, extradition, and the adoption of minimum rules to define criminal acts and the penalties attached to organized crime, terrorism, and drug trafficking. Only member states and the **European Commission** have the **right of initiative**.

Article 34 obliges member states to 'inform and consult one another' in these areas and provides for action under five headings: the adoption of common positions, framework decisions, decisions, implementing measures, and conventions for adoption by member states. A coordinating committee of senior national officials assists the **Council of Ministers**, which can, in most areas, act only by unanimity. The Commission is 'fully associated' with JHA, but the involvement of the **European Parliament** is more ambiguous. Under Article 39 it must be kept informed and must be consulted on most aspects of JHA, upon which it may hold an annual debate. Additionally, Members of the European Parliament (MEPs) may put questions to the Council and make Recommendations.

As with the CFSP, operational costs arising from JHA action may be borne either by the **Budget** of the Union or directly by member states 'in accordance with the gross national product scale' (Article 41). Administrative expenditure is in all cases charged to the Budget.

Title VI contains what is commonly referred to as a *passerelle* (footbridge) clause, Article 42. This allows the Council, acting unanimously, to decide to transfer all matters concerned with police (but not judicial) cooperation to the **Treaty of Rome**. This would bring them within the scope of European Community (as opposed to intergovernmental) action, involving, *inter alia*, consultation of the European Parliament, the adoption of Regulations and Directives (see **legal instruments**), and the possibility of recourse to the **Court of Justice**. At present, the Court's jurisdiction is limited under Article 35 to giving **preliminary rulings** 'on the validity and interpretation of framework decisions and decisions, on the interpretation of conventions ... and on the validity and interpretation of the measures implementing them' and to reviewing the legality of framework decisions and decisions.

Under the **Treaty of Amsterdam**, the so-called 'Schengen *acquis*' (i.e., those aspects of JHA which are directly relevant to the **free movement of persons** across frontiers, including external border controls, **asylum** and immigration) is to be **communitized** within five years of the Treaty entering into force, i.e. by May 2004 (Articles 61 to 69 EC). Within the same period the Council is required to adopt, by unanimity and in consultation with the European Parliament, measures to remove internal border controls and to establish common procedures for external controls. Initially, the Council must act by unanimity, but after five years questions relating to external frontiers may by a unanimous decision of the Council become subject to the **co-decision procedure**. Other questions (except for those relating to visas, which will remain subject to the **consultation procedure**) may be transferred to co-decision by a unanimous decision of the Council. Annexed to the Treaty is a **protocol** on 'integrating the Schengen *acquis* into the framework of the European Union', and several other protocols setting out the special position of the United Kingdom and Ireland as non-signatories to the Schengen agreements, of Denmark as a country which has reserved its position on all questions relating to the free movement of persons except for those on visas, and of Iceland and Norway as countries linked to the Schengen process. See also **area of freedom, security and justice**.

With some exceptions, the JHA provisions of the Maastricht Treaty were a consolidation and a rationalization of various intergovernmental arrangements that had grown up over the previous 20 years (the most significant of which is described under **Trevi Group**). However, the prolonged debate in 1992–3 over the Treaty brought these arrangements into the open. On the one hand the sensitivity of the issues dealt with was said to justify their being kept in governments' hands; on the other, many parliamentarians and journalists concerned with civil liberties have argued that intergovernmental arrangements mean too much power in the hands of officials not subject to adequate democratic scrutiny either at the national or at the European level. Whether or not the arrangements in the Treaty of Amsterdam prove satisfactory in this respect remains to be seen.

It was, of course, inevitable that the creation of a European Union within which citizens of the Union (see **citizenship**) have the right to move and reside freely under Article 18.1 EC would make it necessary for member states to cooperate more closely on immigration, police matters and terrorism. The **Single Market** programme entailed the relaxation or removal of controls at internal frontiers and a shift of emphasis to the external frontiers. At the same time the member states are under greater pressure than ever before from immigration from the south and the east, and Germany in particular has been concerned to ensure that this pressure can be handled on a Union-wide basis. It is these three factors that have shaped JHA provisions as they now stand: whether or not the arrangements will work and how they will fit in with the more ambitious programme set out in the **Schengen Agreement** remain unclear.

K

Kaliningrad

Before the Second World War, the territory of Kaliningrad, then known as East Prussia, was part of the German Reich. It was separated from the rest of Germany by the so-called 'Polish corridor' which gave the Poles access to the Baltic, notably through the port of Danzig (Gdansk). In 1945 the northern portion of the territory was formally incorporated into the Soviet Union (the southern part was given to Poland), its main asset being the city and port of Königsberg (renamed Kaliningrad in 1946 after the Soviet politician Mikhail Kalinin). Its main importance was as a military base and as the headquarters of the Soviet Baltic Fleet. The end of the Cold War resulted in the withdrawal of large numbers of military personnel from the area.

With the **enlargement** of the European Union to include both Poland and Lithuania, Kaliningrad's neighbours, the prospect is that Kaliningrad with its 1,000,000 inhabitants will become a Russian exclave wholly surrounded by Union territory. Already Kaliningrad faces severe economic and social problems by virtue of its isolation, the widespread pollution, the lack of investment, and high crime rates; and the likelihood must be that it will fall still further behind its neighbours as they begin to draw benefit from incorporation into the European Union. All these and other problems are outlined in a Communication by the **European Commission**, *The EU and Kaliningrad* (COM (2001) 26, 17 January 2001).

The Communication suggests that special studies be made of the likely impact of enlargement on patterns of trade with Kaliningrad, of border crossings, of Kaliningrad's energy needs, of improvements to transport infrastructure in the whole region, and of fisheries. These will be discussed with the Russian authorities in the framework of the Partnership and Cooperation Agreement signed with Russia in 1994. Russia's suggestion that Kaliningrad be given a special status with respect to trade and economic development has not so far been worked out in detail, and its realization would in any case depend on Kaliningrad being given the necessary degree of autonomy. There is a great deal of information on Kaliningrad in James Baxendale, Stephen Dewar, and David Gowan (eds), *The EU and Kaliningrad* (2000).

Kangaroo Group

Subtitled 'the movement for free movement', the Kangaroo Group was founded in the first directly elected **European Parliament** by members (MEPs) of all parties led by British Conservative Basil de Ferranti (1930–88). One of the most successful single-issue pressure groups ever established at Community level, the Group has campaigned for the removal of **non-tariff barriers** to trade between member states. It played a very important part in providing the rationale and political impetus for the 1985 **Single Market** programme (see also **Cockfield White Paper**). The Group attempts to influence governments and businesses through conferences and publications of various kinds, including the newspaper *Kangaroo News*.

Karlsruhe judgment

The Karlsruhe judgment, delivered by the German Federal Constitutional Court in Karlsruhe on 12 October 1993, arose from an action brought by campaigners opposed to the **Maastricht Treaty**, led by Manfred Brunner, formerly *chef de cabinet* to Martin Bangemann, the senior German member of the **European Commission**. The action sought to challenge both the Treaty itself in terms of its compatibility with the Basic Law (*Grundgesetz*) of the Federal Republic and the amendments to the Basic Law that were consequent upon German ratification of the Treaty, in particular the new Article 23 on the transfer of powers to the European Union (in future, such transfers require a two-thirds majority in both the upper and lower chambers of the German Parliament). The Court rejected some of the specific complaints as inadmissible.

The judgment centred upon whether or not the provisions of the Treaty were consistent with Article 24 of the Basic Law, which permits 'sovereign powers' to be transferred to 'intergovernmental institutions', in the light of the fact that the Treaty sought to establish a Union that was more than merely intergovernmental. The Court ruled that since the **pillars** of the Union were essentially intergovernmental, it lacked certain attributes of statehood: the Treaty notwithstanding, it remained a *Staatenbund* (association of states) rather than a *Bundesstaat* (federal state). The second point of substance was whether the democratic guarantees in the Basic Law were compromised, particularly in the area of **Economic and Monetary Union** (EMU), by the transfer of powers from the national to the European level. The Court ruled that they were not, since the Treaty provisions allowed for adequate parliamentary supervision through the **European Parliament**.

The Karlsruhe judgment enabled Germany to ratify the Maastricht Treaty, the last member state to do so. Long extracts from the judgment are included in an article by Matthias Herdegen, 'Maastricht and the German Constitutional Court: constitutional restraints for an ever closer union', *Common Market Law Review*, Vol. 31, no. 2, April 1994.

Kohl, Helmut (b. 1930)

Helmut Kohl entered politics at the *Land* level in his home state of Rhineland-Palatinate. In 1973 he became leader of the Christian Democratic Union (CDU), and was their unsuccessful candidate for Chancellor in 1976. He became Chancellor six years later, when the Free Democrats (Liberal) Party switched coalition partners from the Socialists to the CDU, thus bringing about a change of government. He won four elections (1983, 1987, 1990 and 1994) as the leader of his party, losing finally, in 1998, to Gerhard Schroeder.

Kohl has always been a convinced pro-European in the tradition of **Konrad Adenauer**, and the size and strength of the German economy have enabled him to play a very influential role in Community affairs. He is also a staunch supporter of the Atlantic Alliance. He took a close personal interest, together with his Foreign Minister, **Hans-Dietrich Genscher**, in **German reunification**. The problems and uncertainties created by reunification gave rise to a political climate in which Kohl's virtues of dignity, sense of purpose and integrity were shown to particular advantage. He continued his predecessors' policy of maintaining good relations with the President of France (see **Franco-German cooperation**).

L

Laeken Declaration

Adopted at the **European Council** meeting in Laeken, Belgium (14 and 15 December 2001), the Laeken Declaration on the Future of the European Union posed, but did not seek to answer, a large number of questions with a bearing on the construction of 'a simpler Union, one that is stronger in the pursuit of its essential objectives and more definitely present in the world' (Presidency Conclusions, paragraph 3). The Declaration, provided for in the Declaration on the future of the Union agreed at the meeting of the European Council in Nice (December 2000; see **Treaty of Nice**), sets out the issues to be addressed in the **Intergovernmental Conference** (IGC) due to begin in 2003. To prepare this IGC the Laeken Declaration established a Convention chaired by **Valéry Giscard d'Estaing**, the composition of which is modelled on the Convention which prepared the **Charter of Fundamental Rights**, i.e. 15 representatives of the members of the European Council, 30 members of national parliaments, 16 members of the **European Parliament**, and two representatives of the **European Commission**. The applicant states (see **enlargement**) are also represented, making a total of 105 people. The Convention is supplemented by a Forum, a 'structured network of organizations' representing civil society. See Peter Ludlow, *The Laeken Council* (Brussels, 2002).

Languages

The rules governing the languages of the institutions of the Union are decided by the **Council of Ministers**, acting unanimously, under Article 217 of the **Treaty of Rome**. This was the legal base for Regulation 1 of 15 April 1958, which specified Dutch, French, German and Italian as 'the official languages and the working languages' in the institutions of **the Six** and gave them equal status. All official documents have to be available in all languages at meetings and full interpretation provided. With the accession of Denmark, Ireland and the United Kingdom in 1973 the number of working languages rose to six and the number of official languages to seven (although only a limited number of the documents, such as the **Treaties**, are available in Irish). Greek was added in 1981, Spanish and Portuguese in 1986, Finnish and Swedish in 1995. On 12 June 1995 the Council adopted a set of 'Conclusions' on 'Linguistic diversity and multilingualism in the European Union', in which it reaffirmed the importance of 'linguistic diversity [as] an essential aspect of the European dimension and identity and of the common cultural heritage'. It also underlined 'the equality of the official languages and working languages of the Union's institutions'.

Of the five main institutions of the European Union, only the **Court of Justice** is exempt from the requirement that all languages be accorded equal status. For each case before the Court, a procedural language or 'language of the case' is chosen, although full translation and interpretation are provided. In practice, English and French are the languages most widely used throughout the institutions for internal meetings and working-papers. The **Treaty of Amsterdam** amends the provisions on **citizenship** to give every citizen of the Union the right to use any of the official languages in writing to the institutions of the Union and to receive a reply in the same language.

The problem of language is slightly eased by a rigorous system of colourcoding applied to the different language versions of all official documents: pink for Danish, yellow for German, light blue for Greek, lilac for English, red for Spanish, dark blue for French, light green for Italian, orange for Dutch, dark green for Portuguese, royal blue for Finnish and pale yellow for Swedish.

Eleven languages give rise to no fewer than 110 language combinations: the formula is n^2-n, where n equals the number of languages in use. Each additional language adds a further $2(n-1)$ combinations: for example, a twelfth language would bring the total of combinations up to 132. Overall, approximately one-third of the officials working in the Union's institutions are employed in connection with interpretation and translation. The **European Commission** is one of the pioneers in the field of machine translation, using a system called Systran (originally developed in the United States for the rapid translation of transcripts of radio broadcasts from the Soviet Union). The Commission's translation service, which is based in Luxembourg, has an output of about 1 million pages a year. A new Translation Centre has been set up there to provide translations for the various new European Union bodies such as **Europol** and the **European Environment Agency**.

Interpreters work in teams of three per language at official meetings. For the more obscure combinations (Danish into Greek, for example) the interpretation is via a third language, a system known as 'relay'. A substantial number of interpreters are freelance and work for other international organizations. Their working conditions are strictly controlled, their discretion is absolute and their professional standards are very high indeed.

The **European Parliament** is the institution most seriously affected by the multiplicity of languages. In recent years, it has tried to cut down the number of languages used in meetings, particularly those held outside the member states. This can give rise to objections from Members (MEPs) representing minority languages, such as Danish, Greek or Portuguese, and who are sensitive to any suggestion that some languages are less important than others. A high proportion of the Parliament's budget is spent on language-related work: every amendment tabled in plenary session generates an average of 1,000 pieces of paper per language, and reports that attract more than 50 amendments are not uncommon.

Although some MEPs are good linguists, the interpretation inevitably has a deadening effect on debates. Repartee, interruptions, most forms of humour (especially irony), quotations, literary or historical allusions and vivid metaphors all tend to get lost. And mistakes can be made: interpreting *une grande déception* ('a big disappointment') as 'a great deception' can cause resentment as well as confusion. Other traps abound: a *pavillon de complaisance* is not something you might expect to find in a rococo pleasure-garden but, more prosaically, a flag of convenience used in merchant shipping.

Approximately 27 languages are spoken within the European Union, not counting those spoken by immigrants, with English by far the most widely taught second language, and German the most widely spoken first language. That only 11 should be used as working languages within the institutions is progress of a kind, but with **enlargement** the situation is certain to get worse. A referendum on membership of the Union in an applicant state would certainly be lost if the electorate were to be informed that their national language was not to be used in the Union institutions. Some have argued for a more rigid distinction to be made between 'official' and 'working' languages or for a distinction between 'public' and 'internal' working languages, with a view to reducing the latter to three or four, but this would not help the European Parliament: diplomats and international civil servants may be expected to work in languages other than their own, but not elected politicians, least of all when considering texts that will have the force of law in their home countries. The United Nations uses six languages: English, French, Spanish, Russian, Arabic and Chinese. Even in the **Common Foreign and Security Policy** (CFSP), where a good practical case could be made for reducing the number of languages used to a bare minimum, Declaration 29 annexed to the **Maastricht Treaty** requires the normal rules to apply. The Brussels-based European Bureau for Lesser Used Languages is a reliable source of useful information.

Latvia

In common with the other **Baltic states**, Latvia was annexed by the Soviet Union in 1940 and occupied by Germany from 1941 until 1944. Full independence was not regained until August 1991. Latvia has concluded a **Europe Agreement** with the European Union which came into force in February 1998 (a Free Trade Agreement came into effect in January 1995). Latvia's application for full membership of the European Union was made on 13 October 1995 (see **enlargement**).

The **Opinion** of the **European Commission**, published on 15 July 1997 (*Bulletin of the European Union*, supplement 18/97), noted that minorities account for almost 44 per cent of the population of Latvia, to such an extent that in seven of the eight largest towns Latvians themselves are in a minority. The acquisition of Latvian citizenship depends in part on a knowledge of the Latvian language and of the country's history, culture and institutions, and for a variety of reasons many of the Russian speakers who settled in Latvia when it was *de facto* part of the Soviet Union have neither Russian nor Latvian citizenship. These 'non-citizens' are affected by many forms of discrimination. Otherwise, in the Commission's view, Latvia satisfied the political requirements set out in the **Copenhagen criteria**.

Economically, Latvia has made great progress since its pre-1991 position of near-total dependence on the Soviet Union. However, the Opinion concluded that the economy was not yet strong enough to meet the competition which membership of the Union would entail, nor yet able to adapt to, apply and enforce the *acquis communautaire*. Nevertheless Latvia was included in the 'accession process' set out by the **European Council** at its meeting in Luxembourg in December 1997 (see also **European Conference**). Bilateral negotiations were concluded in 2002 and in April 2003 Latvia signed the **Treaty of Accession**.

Latvia is a member of the **Council of Europe** and of the **Organization for Security and Cooperation in Europe** (OSCE). See also **Nordic Council**.

League of Nations

The League of Nations was founded under a covenant of the Treaty of Versailles (1919) and came into existence on the date the Treaty came into effect (10 January 1920). The seat of the League was Geneva, Brussels having been rejected as too closely associated with the Great War. By the end of 1920 most European states had become members of the League, among them all the present member states of the European Union except Ireland (which joined as the Irish Free State in September 1923) and Germany (which joined in September 1926). In a speech to the National Assembly on 25 January 1925 French Prime Minister Edouard Herriot described the League as 'the first outline of the United States of Europe'. By October 1935 the League had 58 members world-wide, half of them European states. However, the United States Congress had refused to ratify the Treaty of Versailles in 1920, so the

United States was never a member of the League. Among League members were states as small as Panama and Honduras and as large as China and the USSR, but in terms of votes in the Council and the Assembly (see below) all were on an equal footing.

Under the terms of the Covenant members of the League committed themselves to 'the reduction of national armaments to the lowest point consistent with national safety' and to the exchange of 'full and frank information as to the scale of their armaments' (Article 8). The crucial Article 10 committed members of the League 'to respect and preserve as against external aggression the territorial integrity and existing political independence' of other members. Under Article 12 (as revised in 1924) members agreed to submit disputes to arbitration, judicial settlement or to an inquiry by the Council of the League and not to resort to war until at least three months after the adjudication was pronounced. A member that failed to respect this provision was 'deemed to have committed an act of war against all other Members of the League', which would then 'subject it to the severance of all trade or financial relations'; the nationals of the offending state would be denied contact with those of any other state, 'whether a Member of the League or not' (Article 16).

The permanent organs of the League were the Council, the Assembly, the Secretariat and the International Court of Justice at The Hague. Like the Security Council of the United Nations, the Council was composed of permanent and non-permanent members, the latter elected by the Assembly. At first, there were four permanent members: the British Empire, France, Italy and Japan; a fifth, Germany, was added in 1926, the German government having insisted on permanent membership of the Council as a condition of Germany's membership of the League. The number of non-permanent members grew from 4 in 1920 to 11 in 1936. The Council was empowered to deal 'with any matter within the sphere of action of the League or affecting the peace of the world' (Article 4.4) and in practice met three times a year. Each member of the Council had one representative and one vote. A member state not represented in the Council was entitled to send a delegate to Council meetings at which matters affecting that state were discussed, and the delegate was entitled to vote.

The Assembly was composed of three representatives and three substitutes appointed by the government of each member state. However, as in the Council, each member state had only one vote. Some representatives were parliamentarians, but many were not. The Assembly met in plenary session once a year in September in Geneva, but it was entitled to hold extraordinary sessions at other times and in other places. The Assembly's work was done in six (later seven) committees, to which each member had the right to appoint one representative: Legal Affairs, Disarmament, Budgetary Questions, and so on. More technical subjects, such as health and communications, were dealt with in committees of experts attached to the League, as were more recondite matters such as slavery, opium and European union (to consider the proposal for a European federation made in 1929 by **Aristide Briand**). The organs of the League were serviced by a small international secretariat headed by Sir Eric Drummond (Earl of Perth), later British Ambassador in Rome, and from 1933 by Joseph Avenol of France.

Although procedural matters could be settled by majority, substantive decisions of both the Council and the Assembly had to be unanimous (Article 5). Taken in conjunction with the absolute right of interested states to participate in Council deliberations (see above), this proved an insuperable obstacle to effective action. Although the League was responsible for several successful peacekeeping operations – such as the 1935 plebiscite in the **Saarland** – it failed totally to curb the aggressive policies of Hitler and Mussolini; indeed it was the failure to prevent Mussolini's invasion and annexation of Abyssinia (Ethiopia) that finally discredited the League and the ideals of interstate cooperation and collective security on which it was based. Both Germany and Italy were permanent members of the Council of the League until their withdrawal (1933 and 1937 respectively). With the outbreak of war in 1939 the League ceased to meet, but it was not formally dissolved until 1946, when it was succeeded by the United Nations.

The League was deliberately intended to mark a break with the 'old diplomacy', that is, with bilateral agreements (not all of them publicly acknowledged) between sovereign states, with the Great Powers playing the dominant role. Initially, it enjoyed widespread support, but, as Alfred Zimmern wrote in 1935,

Statesmen have been as profuse in professions of loyalty to the League as they have been timid and vacillating in their handling of concrete issues of policy. Indeed, the existence of the League, with its multifarious armoury of diplomatic implements, by increasing the means at their disposal, has afforded them new and up-to-date pretexts for procrastination or evasion. (*The League of Nations and the Rule of Law, 1918–1935*, 2nd edn, 1939.)

Few more recent studies of the League have found much to say in defence of the 'Geneva experiment', the importance of which today is as an idealistic model of international cooperation along intergovernmental lines (see **intergovernmentalism**) that was fatally compromised from the start by the frailty of the constraints it laid upon the **sovereignty** of the member states and by the absence of any effective means of enforcing its decisions. Many of the distinguishing features of the European Union – an independent **European**

Commission, a body of law taking precedence over national law, a directly elected **European Parliament** – can best be understood as springing from a determination on the part of **Jean Monnet** and others not to repeat the mistakes of the League (of which Monnet had been deputy secretary-general) and to move away from intergovernmental cooperation towards a system based upon supranational institutions.

Legal certainty

Legal certainty, although nowhere defined in the **Treaties**, is an important principle of **E U law** which has had some influence on cases before the **Court of Justice**. It requires Union law and the national law derived from Union law to be coherent, unambiguous, accessible and clear with respect to its scope, purpose, effect, and validity, and to be consistently applied. It is especially important in those areas of the law of immediate concern to business and commerce, since lack of certainty can inhibit investment decisions and lead to costly disputes. More generally, legal certainty has a direct bearing upon **simplification** and **transparency**. That the law should be 'certain' in the above sense may be regarded as a legitimate expectation on the part of the citizen.

Legal instruments

Article 249 of the **Treaty of Rome** lists five different types of legal instrument; the distinction between them is fundamental to an understanding of E U **law**.

A **Regulation** is of 'general application'. It is 'binding in its entirety and directly applicable in all Member States'. A **Directive** is 'binding, as to the result to be achieved, upon each Member State to which it is addressed', but leaves 'to the national authorities the choice of form and methods'. The expression 'framework Directive' is sometimes used to denote a Directive that identifies European Union objectives over a broad field and which in so doing prepares the way for legislative action on specific points. The essential difference between a Regulation and Directive is that whereas the latter must be transposed into national law (usually by a deadline) before entering into force, the former is directly applicable and therefore usually has **direct effect**.

A Decision is 'binding in its entirety upon those to whom it is addressed'. Recommendations and **Opinions** 'have no binding force': some authorities do not classify them as legal instruments. Article 254 requires Regulations, Decisions and Directives addressed to all member states to be published in the *Official Journal*. See also **Resolution, soft law**.

The choice of legal instrument in respect of particular actions is specified in the Treaty in some cases and in others left to the discretion of the **European Commission**, as the institution that has the **right of initiative**.

The description of legal instruments set out in Article 249 does not apply to measures undertaken in the fields of **Justice and Home Affairs** (JHA) and in the **Common Foreign and Security Policy** (CFSP). A **Declaration** annexed to the Treaty committed the 1996–7 **Intergovernmental Conference** (IGC) to reviewing all the different types of legal instrument with a view to establishing a **hierarchy of acts**, but in the event no such hierarchy was drawn up.

Legal personality

Article 281 of the **Treaty of Rome** says 'The [European] Community shall have legal personality'. Identical provisions may be found in the Treaties establishing the **European Coal and Steel Community** and the **European Atomic Energy Community**. This means that each of the Communities has rights and obligations under international law, including most notably those contained in international agreements. With respect to national law, Article 282 (and identical provisions in the other Treaties) confers upon the European Community 'the most extensive legal capacity accorded to legal persons' under the national laws of member states, including *inter alia* the right to acquire or dispose of property and to be a party to legal proceedings. Although the 1965 **Merger Treaty** gave the Communities common institutions, and although the **Maastricht Treaty** made them a component part of the European Union (see '**pillars**'), the Communities have retained their distinct legal personalities.

The European Union itself, by contrast, does not possess legal personality. The arguments for and against giving it legal personality were addressed in the 1996–7 **Intergovernmental Conference**. On the one hand, for the Union to possess legal personality would enable it to conclude international agreements and to deal on equal terms with other international bodies. It would not only make for greater legal clarity in such relations, it would also remove an apparent anomaly in the structure of the Union, whereby one of the 'pillars' possesses legal personality but not the others, nor the Union as a whole. On the other hand, to bestow legal personality upon the Union was seen by some member states as the first step towards merging the pillars into a single Community-driven entity: and this, anxious as they were to preserve the **intergovernmental** character of the pillars, they were not prepared to countenance. These latter arguments prevailed: the **Treaty of Amsterdam** does not change the legal status of the Union. However, over time it is clear that the Union, especially in the **Common Foreign and Security Policy** (CFSP) field, will act as though it possesses *de facto* legal personality, and sooner or later this will be reflected in an amendment to the Maastricht Treaty.

Much of the law relating to the legal personality of international organizations and their agencies has been established through the jurisprudence of the

International Court of Justice. See especially Bruno Simma (ed.), *The Charter of the United Nations: A Commentary* (Oxford, 1995), entries on Articles 104 and 105. The peculiar position of the European Union is very fully discussed in Astéris Pliakos, 'La nature juridique de l'Union Européenne', *Revue trimestrielle du Droit Européen*, 1993 (2). See also G. Federico Mancini 'Europe: the case for statehood' and J.H.H. Weiler 'Europe: the case against the case for statehood', *European Law Journal*, Vol. 4, no. 1, March 1998.

Legitimacy

When the legitimacy of the European Union is called into question, the debate normally centres not upon whether or not its institutions are duly constituted but upon whether they – and the decision-making system of which they are essential components – possess the necessary democratic credentials. These depend in turn not upon Treaty articles or constitutional provisions or the pronouncements of legal experts but upon such factors as accountability and **transparency**. To a greater or lesser degree all international bodies (and *a fortiori* all supranational bodies) must address this question of legitimacy, for without legitimacy there can be no authority, no public acceptance and therefore no effective action. If the question arises more frequently with respect to the institutions of the European Union, it is surely because their purview is so much wider and the impact of their decisions on people's lives and livelihoods so much more direct.

Our notions of legitimacy are formed largely within the context of national political systems and they cannot be transposed without modification to so complex a multinational entity as the European Union. The Union's claim to legitimacy rests upon the fact that it is based upon a compact freely entered into by six sovereign states and embodied in a Treaty (the 1957 **Treaty of Rome**). The nine states which have subsequently joined accepted the Treaty and the rest of the *acquis communautaire* of their own free will, as expressed through their **national parliaments** and in some cases by means of a **referendum**. All amendments to the Treaty of Rome and all post-1957 Treaties (not yet including the **Treaty of Nice**) have been approved by national parliaments (see **ratification**). Decision-making is entrusted to a **Council of Ministers** composed of ministers individually responsible to his or her national parliament, often acting jointly with a directly elected **European Parliament** (see **co-decision procedure**). Decisions are based largely upon proposals put forward by a **European Commission** composed of people appointed by agreement among national governments and endorsed by the European Parliament. All proposals are debated in public and together with all decisions are freely available. The principal differences between the Union system and that of all democratic states are the lack of a governing party (and therefore of an opposition), the substantial degree of political independence enjoyed by the Commission (see **right of initiative**), and the fact that only in some areas does the directly elected Parliament have the final say. But can these differences be said to rule out of court the Union's claim to legitimacy? Does not the fact that freely given consent underpins the Union edifice answer the charge that European integration entails the illegitimate usurpation by Union institutions of powers and prerogatives rightfully belonging to member states (see **sovereignty**)?

The comparison with national political systems brings out other peculiarities. Individually, members of the Council of Ministers are accountable to their national parliaments, but as a body the Council is accountable to no one. The Council cannot dissolve the Parliament and call an election, nor can the Parliament vote the Council out of office. The Parliament can however dismiss the Commission (see **censure motion**) and has a decisive say in the appointment of the President and the other Commissioners. However, Commissioners' authority depends not so much on endorsement by the Parliament as on the fact of having been chosen by agreement among sovereign governments and on the Commission having, in the words of Article 211 of the **Treaty of Rome**, 'its own power of decision'. It has been suggested that the President of the Commission should be directly elected, but would candidates of the right calibre come forward? What would the turnout be? And what would be the wider impact of this on the delicate balance between the institutions?

The treaty-based model of legitimacy tends to obscure the fact that the Treaties upon which the Union is founded are qualitatively different from those with which international law is mainly concerned. The Union Treaties set up institutions quite separate from those existing at national level which, in so far as they can be shown to be answerable to an elected parliament, draw their legitimacy directly from the people rather than through the member states.

Since 1979, when it was first directly elected, the European Parliament has been without question 'legitimate'. But with turnout, media coverage and public recognition in steady if slow decline, it may be asked whether the Parliament's standing is yet sufficient for it to be the legitimator of the whole system. The extension of the Parliament's powers under the co-decision procedure and the extension of co-decision itself into most areas of the Union's legislative activity may be held to legitimize Union decision-making at least in those areas, but what of those other areas, notably the so-called **pillars** and the management of the **euro**, in which the Parliament is much less involved? The extent to which the European public can feel any sense of identification with the Parliament – any sense of ownership, to use the current expression – is seriously curtailed by the fact that both the media and the political parties (often described as the transmission belts of political debate within a democratic system) remain orientated towards national politics.

Political scientists have spoken of a 'permissive consensus' – public acquiescence in the process of European integration, rather than positive support, founded largely upon lack of interest – and remarked how this consensus is under strain as the Union moves into sensitive areas as immigration, taxation and security policy. Broad public acceptance of the decisions and actions of the Union remains, however, essential, not least because the Union system of government is unique in having so few powers of coercion. Without legitimacy, such acceptance may sooner or later be withheld.

The shift from a treaty-based legitimacy to one centred upon the European Parliament is a theme which since the 1980s has run through the debate on the reform of the Union's institutions (see **Intergovernmental Conference, Constitution for Europe**). Thomas Banchoff and Mitchell P. Smith (eds), *Legitimacy and the European Union* (1999) is a useful and wide-ranging discussion of all these issues.

Leonardo

The Leonardo II programme for 2000–6 is concerned with vocational training as a contribution to the promotion of employment. It has an allocation of €1.15 billion (about £690 million) from the **Budget** over its seven-year span. Leonardo is open to participation from Cyprus, Malta and the countries of central and eastern Europe as well as from member states of the European Union.

Liberalism

In most member states of the European Union Liberal parties are descended from secular or dissenting parties with a strong base among the professional classes opposed to the influence of the Church, Conservatism and landed interests. Liberals were, broadly speaking, radical, progressive, republican, and often closely identified with agrarian reform. However, the introduction of universal suffrage and the rise of Socialist or Labour parties dislodged the Liberals from their traditional position. In some countries this pushed Liberals to the right, in others (including the United Kingdom) to the left. This fundamental difference is still discernible among the parties now linked in the European Liberal, Democrat and Reform Party (ELDR; see **transnational political parties**).

At no time since the Second World War have the Liberals and their allies in Western Europe overall come close to rivalling the Socialists or the Christian Democrats in terms of electoral support. However, in several countries they have not infrequently held the balance of power in coalitions, allowing Liberals to hold major offices of state, including the presidency of France, in the person of **Valéry Giscard d'Estaing**, from 1974 to 1981. Liberals have twice held the presidency of the **European Commission** (Jean Rey, 1967–70; Gaston Thorn, 1981–5). Other prominent Liberals include **Hans-Dietrich Genscher**, the German Foreign Minister from 1974 to 1992, Simone Veil, the first President of the directly elected **European Parliament** (1979–82) and Pat Cox, the Parliament's current President.

Liberals have a vigorous and long-standing tradition of support for European integration, having voted solidly in favour of the **Treaty of Paris** and, later, the **Treaty of Rome** in the 1950s. In the European Parliament the Liberals are the third largest of the **political groups** but are a long way behind the Socialist and European People's Party (Christian Democrats and Conservatives) Groups. Until 1999 the British Liberal Democrats, the largest Liberal party in Europe, were handicapped by the first-past-the-post electoral system: with 16.6 per cent of the vote nationally, they gained only two seats in June 1994, having had none at all since European elections were first held in 1979. The adoption of proportional representation in the United Kingdom allowed the Liberals to win 10 seats in the 1999 **European elections**.

In point of substance, the views of Liberals are, in most areas, indistinguishable from those of the Christian Democrats. There are, however, some differences of emphasis, Liberals tending to hold more progressive or libertarian views on moral issues and to be more outspoken in favour of free markets and free trade. On the great majority of institutional, foreign policy and security issues the Liberals vote with the Christian Democrats as committed federalists and supporters of the Atlantic Alliance.

The Liberals are not as well placed as their larger rivals to acquire new allies with **enlargement**. Even within the Union the Liberals are finding it increasingly difficult to establish and maintain a distinctive political profile and with it a secure share of the electoral middle ground. The German Liberals (the Free Democrats) disappeared from the European Parliament in June 1994, having failed to reach the 5 per cent national threshold. At the European level as well as at the national level, the Liberals' position between left and right is of little advantage to them as politics become less polarized. Their position serves also to draw attention to their own internal divisions, as they try to keep open the option of coalitions either to their right or to their left.

Liechtenstein
See **micro-states**.

LIFE
The European Union's LIFE programme for 2000–4 groups together several initiatives concerned with policies for the environment (see **environment**

policy), including the protection of natural habitats, the promotion of new technologies and the provision of training and information. Over this period LIFE has been allocated € 613 million from the **Budget**.

Linkage

'Linkage' denotes the practice, familiar in the European Union institutions and in all international bodies, of making agreement on one issue conditional upon the satisfactory resolution of another, there being no logical or material connection between the two. For example, the French government made their acceptance of additional seats for Germany and other member states in the **European Parliament** conditional upon an agreement to make Strasbourg the Parliament's official seat (see **seat of the institutions**). The scope for linkage is obviously greater when decisions can be taken only by **unanimity**, i.e., when individual member states have a right of **veto**. Linkage is an essential and an inescapable feature of the continuous, wide-ranging process of negotiation between member states and between institutions on which decisions in the European Union are based.

Lithuania

In common with the other **Baltic states**, Lithuania was annexed by the Soviet Union in 1940 and occupied by Germany from 1941 until 1944. The restoration of independence was declared in March 1989 but not recognized by the Soviet Union until September 1991. Lithuania has concluded a **Europe Agreement** with the European Union which came into force in February 1998 (a Free Trade Agreement came into effect in January 1995). Lithuania's application for full membership of the European Union was made on 8 December 1995 (see **enlargement**).

The **Opinion** of the **European Commission**, published on 15 July 1997 (*Bulletin of the European Union*, supplement 12/97), concluded with respect to the **Copenhagen criteria** that the Lithuanian economy was not yet in a position to meet the competition which membership of the Union would entail and that not enough progress had been made with adapting to the *acquis communautaire*. Moreover, the Commission was not convinced that the Lithuanian administration was sufficiently equipped to apply and administer the *acquis*. Nevertheless Lithuania was included in the '**accession** process' set out by the **European Council** in Luxembourg in December 1997 (see also **European Conference**). Bilateral negotiations were concluded in 2002. On 10–11 May 2003 the Lithuanian people voted by 91.07 per cent to 8.93 per cent to join the European Union (see **Treaty of Accession**).

Lithuania is a member of the **Council of Europe** and of the **Organization for Security and Cooperation in Europe** (OSCE). See also **Nordic Council**.

Lobbying

The fact that the decision-making procedures within the European institutions are little understood allied to the growing importance of the decisions taken (especially for industry and commerce) has provided fertile ground for Brussels-based lobbyists. Some, particularly trade associations, are well established, as are many single-issue lobbies in such fields as aid to the Third World, consumer protection, animal welfare and human rights. Many of the larger regions of the European Union, such as Catalonia, Scotland and the German *Länder*, as well as several states of the United States, have representative offices in Brussels besides those of the **national representations**. About 1000 interest groups are listed on line in CONECCS (Consultation, the European Community and Civil Society) dealing with matters as diverse as autism, railway engineering, natural gas, processed cheese, and polyurethane foam blocks.

Since 1985 there has been a spectacular growth in professional lobbying, firms who will for a fee monitor developments in a particular subject-area, suggest contacts, arrange meetings and generally assist in the putting of a case. As the European institutions are relatively open by comparison with most national bureaucracies, so far lobbyists of all kinds have had little difficulty in gaining access to them. However, the growth in professional lobbying has led to calls for it to be regulated. The **European Commission** has a list of several hundred bodies that it consults on technical aspects of legislation, with a bias towards bodies operating at European level, but neither the Commission nor the **European Parliament** has yet introduced a register of professional lobbyists.

A study edited by Sonia Maizey and Jeremy Richardson, *Lobbying in the European Community* (Oxford, 1993) and Justin Greenwood, *Representing Interests in the European Union* (Basingstoke, 1997) are good general surveys of how lobbies operate and of their impact on decisions. There is a list of lobbyists and pressure-groups in Alan Butt Philip and Oliver Gray (eds), *Directory of Pressure-Groups in the EU* (2nd edn, 1996) and some interesting case-studies in R. H. Pedler and M. P. C. M. Van Schendelen (eds), *Lobbying the European Union* (Aldershot, 1994). See also Euroconfidentiel, *Lobbying in the European Union* (Genval, 1998).

Lomé Convention

The Lomé Convention, signed in Lomé, the capital of Togo, in 1975 was a comprehensive trade-and-aid agreement between the member states of the European Union and 71 developing countries in Africa, the Caribbean and the Pacific (the **ACP states**). South Africa, although a signatory to the Convention, had its own trade agreement with the Union. The Convention was succeeded in June 2000 by the **Cotonou Agreement**, based in part on the analysis and recommendations in the *Green Paper on Relations between the European Union and the ACP Countries on the Eve of the 21st Century* published by the **European Commission** in November 1996.

Luns–Westerterp procedure

Originally, the **Treaty of Rome** required the **Council of Ministers** to consult the **European Parliament** only in respect of **Association Agreements** between the Community and non-member countries or international organizations. To strengthen this provision, a procedure was introduced informally in 1964 on the initiative of the Dutch Foreign Minister, Joseph Luns, whereby the Parliament became entitled to debate the matter before negotiations started, to be kept informed through the relevant committees of the progress of the negotiations, and to be told the substance of the outcome before the Association Treaty was formally signed. In 1973 this procedure, known as the Luns Procedure, was extended to trade agreements on the initiative of another Dutch minister, Tjerk Westerterp. Ten years later, in the **Stuttgart Declaration**, the **European Council** agreed to extend the Luns–Westerterp Procedure to 'all significant international agreements concluded by the Communities', upon which the Parliament now has the right to deliver a formal **Opinion**. These developments were incorporated into the Treaty as amendments to Articles 237 and 238 EEC by the 1986 **Single European Act** (SEA; see also **accession**). Since then, Article 237 has been repealed by the **Maastricht Treaty**, and the procedure for the admission of new member states is now set out in Article 49 TEU.

Luxembourg

See **Belgo-Luxembourg Economic Union**, **Benelux**.

Luxembourg Compromise

The Luxembourg Compromise was an informal arrangement, arrived at by **the Six** in January 1966, whereby decisions which the **Treaty of Rome** foresaw being taken by **majority voting** in the **Council of Ministers** could be postponed until unanimous agreement had been reached. Its effect was to create a national **veto** over all key decisions, and for over 20 years it acted as a constraint in many important areas of policy. Although the Luxembourg Compromise has never formally been abrogated, it only rarely has much bearing on Union decision-making. Majority voting now applies in all areas where it is provided for in the **Treaties**. A member state can veto a proposal only if **unanimity** is explicitly specified as the decision-making method.

The Luxembourg Compromise resolved an acute crisis in the Community's development, which had two linked but distinct components.

The first was the rejection by France in June 1965 of a series of key proposals: on the financing of the new **Common Agricultural Policy** (CAP), the introduction of **own resources** and the widening of the budgetary powers of the **European Parliament**. The second was the outright refusal by France to accept that, when the so-called 'third stage' of the transitional phase of the Community's development came into effect in January 1966, majority voting should automatically be introduced on a significant range of issues in the Council.

So long as these important problems remained unresolved, the President of France, **Charles de Gaulle**, instructed his ministers to boycott all Council meetings during the second half of 1965 – a period that conveniently coincided with his re-election to office at home (for the first time by universal suffrage) at the end of the year. The **empty chair crisis**, as it became known, effectively immobilized Community decision-making and delivered a severe blow to the prospect of closer European integration.

Although the 1965 crisis was prompted by the CAP and own resources proposals, it worsened spectacularly in September of that year when de Gaulle chose to broaden the issues at stake to include the planned shift to majority voting in the Council, and, as a subsidiary question, the growing independence of the **European Commission** under its German President, **Walter Hallstein**. The French President had long been hostile towards what he considered the dangerously federal implications of majority voting, having asserted at the time of the 1961–2 **Fouchet Plan** that 'there is no way that a foreign majority can constrain recalcitrant nations' in the Community.

As the autumn proceeded it became clear that no agreement between de Gaulle and the other member states was likely at least until the December presidential election in France was out of the way. In the event, that contest proved a catalyst for compromise. De Gaulle failed to win an outright victory on the first ballot against two pro-European opponents, **François Mitterrand** and Jean Lecanuet, and the government's resolve on European affairs began to weaken. The Prime Minister, Georges Pompidou, predicted just before the second ballot that France might resume negotiations with its partners soon after the election.

De Gaulle having been re-elected, two special Council meetings were held in Luxembourg in January 1966, without the Commission being present. At the first, on 17–18 January, the five other member states held firm against French demands on majority voting, but progress was made towards a settlement on CAP financing, and agreement reached that the introduction of own resources should be postponed until 1970 and with it greater budgetary powers for the European Parliament. At the second meeting, on 28–29 January, the Council agreed, by a set of non-binding conclusions entered in its Minutes, on a formula in respect of majority voting. This was the essence of what became known as the Luxembourg Compromise.

The Council conclusions stated that if one member state considered that 'a very important national interest' was at stake (often referred to as a 'vital' national interest), then the Council would endeavour to reach, within a reasonable period, solutions that could be adopted unanimously. The French delegation considered that when very important interests were at issue, discussion 'must be continued' until unanimous agreement was reached. However, this more maximalist formulation – which is the one most widely associated with the Compromise – was not accepted by the other member states, and to describe it as a 'compromise' is misleading. It was simply noted that there was a difference of opinion on what precisely would happen when a complete resolution of a dispute within the Council was not achieved.

In the event, the Luxembourg Compromise created a firm presumption within the Council in favour of unanimous voting remaining the norm after 1966, even where majority voting was explicitly provided for in the Treaty and no 'very important national interest' had been identified. Since any country could invoke the Compromise at any time, there was little point in pressing a proposal if strong objections were raised by one of the member states. Discussion that failed to elicit the necessary degree of compromise in the Council was simply stalled, sometimes to the point where the Commission would withdraw the proposal in despair.

In a limited number of areas – such as certain technical decisions on the CAP and the adoption of the Community's **Budget** – majority voting was used after 1966. It was necessary to the continued operation of the Community and suited the interests of France. The 1971 White Paper on British **accession** to the Community stated: 'All the countries concerned recognize that an attempt to impose a majority view in a case where one or more members considered their vital interests to be at stake would imperil the very fabric of the Community ... [In such cases] it is Community practice to proceed only by unanimity.'

From time to time attempts were made to encourage the Council to return to majority voting, but always without success.

Matters blocked on routine policy grounds by one member state continued simply not to get adopted. It was not necessary for the Luxembourg Compromise to be invoked formally – recourse was had to it perhaps only 10 times in the 15 years after 1966 – for decision-making on literally hundreds of Commission proposals over these years to be stillborn. This pervasive immobilism within the Council prevailed until the early 1980s, when for a variety of reasons the Compromise began to fall into disuse.

By the end of 1981 a new institutional reform agenda had started to emerge. The **Genscher–Colombo Plan** for a draft 'European Act' included proposals to limit the Luxembourg Compromise to genuine cases of 'vital' interest (Paragraph 8). This mood found a ready echo in the Commission and in the European Parliament. Guided by its specially formed Committee on Institutional Affairs (which began work in January 1982; see **Altiero Spinelli**), the Parliament became increasingly insistent on the need for the Council to follow strictly Treaty provisions on voting. It even launched a legal action in the **Court of Justice** against the Council for **failure to act** in respect of a **common transport policy**, for the establishment of which the Treaty of Rome had specified, in certain areas, recourse to majority voting. However, in the Parliament's 1984 **Draft Treaty establishing the European Union** (DTEU), the Luxembourg Compromise was to be maintained for a 10-year transitional period (Article 23.3).

In response to the Genscher–Colombo Plan, the **European Council** agreed a 'Solemn Declaration on European Union', in Stuttgart in June 1983, the so-called **Stuttgart Declaration**. On the question of voting, the document stated that the 'application of the decision-making procedures laid down in the Treaties is of vital importance' (Paragraph 2.2.2). It stopped short, however, of defining the limits of the Luxembourg Compromise – precisely because there was no agreement on what they were.

In the minutes of the Stuttgart meeting all governments entered statements about the Luxembourg Compromise, setting out their various interpretations. Belgium, Germany, Luxembourg, Italy and The Netherlands declared that 'the Presidency must have recourse to the vote where the Treaties allow for this'. France and Ireland declared that 'the President will have recourse to the vote where the Treaties allow for this, while accepting that the vote will be postponed if one or several Member States so request, in the name of defending a vital national interest of direct relevance to the subject under discussion, which they will confirm in writing'. Greece stated that 'discussion must continue until a unanimous decision has been reached where vital and essential national interests are at stake and written notification has been given to this effect'. The United Kingdom and Denmark entered a maximalist formulation redolent of the French position in 1966, insisting that 'when a Member State considers its very important interests are at stake, the discussion should continue until unanimous agreement is reached'.

The institutional reform debate of the early 1980s culminated at the European Council meeting in Milan in June 1985 with a decision by the heads of government to convene an **Intergovernmental Conference** (IGC), under Article 236 EEC, to draft amendments to the Treaty of Rome. Against spirited opposition from the United Kingdom, Denmark and Greece, the Italian presidency decided to push the issue to the vote, arguing that only a simple majority was necessary to convene an IGC. Opposing governments suggested that unanimity should apply because vital national interests might be at stake. The presidency replied that they could not be since the calling of an IGC was in itself a purely procedural decision. Only the outcome of the IGC could raise such questions, and there the right of veto was safeguarded because agreement to Treaty amendments would require the approval of all governments and ratification by **national parliaments**. This interpretation prevailed.

The subsequent **Single European Act** (SEA), agreed by the Luxembourg IGC of 1985 and signed in 1986, sanctioned a substantial extension of majority voting with a view to completing the **Single Market**. At the time the implications of this change for the Luxembourg Compromise were unclear. Most commentators and official sources held that although majority voting would now certainly become the norm in any area where it was formally provided for, the residual right to invoke the Compromise would remain in any case where a vital national interest was legitimately threatened. It was thought that the SEA would make no particular difference to whether the Compromise survived.

In practice, however, the importance of the Luxembourg Compromise was much dimished by the entry into force of the SEA in July 1987. The rules of procedure of the Council of Ministers were changed to enable a simple majority of member states to insist that a vote be taken whenever the Treaties so allowed. Since that date, there have been few attempts to use the Compromise.

Throughout its life the Luxembourg Compromise was never accepted by either the Commission or the **Court of Justice**. The Commission used its exclusion from the January 1966 Council meeting to argue that it had never been a party to the agreement. It subsequently denounced the Compromise on many occasions. The Court, for its part, has frequently ruled that Resolutions or Declarations of political will by the Council or the member states collectively cannot prevail against the rules contained in the Treaties. In 1988 the Court held that 'a mere practice on the part of the Council cannot derogate from the rules laid down in the Treaty' (*United Kingdom* v *Council*, Case 68/86). This view is now, it would appear, accepted in the Council itself, and neither in the negotiations resulting in the **Maastricht Treaty** nor in any other forum has any member state suggested reinvigorating the Luxembourg Compromise and giving it Treaty status. Moreover, the provisions on **constructive abstention** give member states an alternative to the veto, and 'closer cooperation' (see **flexibility**) allows member states willing to do so to move forward in areas which might otherwise be blocked by a veto.

M

Maastricht Treaty

Formally entitled the Treaty on European Union (TEU), the Maastricht Treaty was the outcome of two **Intergovernmental Conferences** (IGCs) and was agreed at a meeting of the **European Council** in Maastricht, the Netherlands, in December 1991. Formally signed in Maastricht on 7 February 1992, the Treaty entered into force in November 1993. Many of its main provisions were amended by the **Treaty of Amsterdam**, which substituted numbers for letters orginally used to denote the different Articles.

The two IGCs, one on **Economic and Monetary Union** (EMU) and one on European Political Union (EPU), were conducted in parallel. The EMU IGC was set in train by a decision of the European Council meeting in Madrid in June 1989, at which the **Delors Report** on EMU was discussed. The EPU IGC was based on an agreement reached a year later in Dublin, prompted by proposals on political union put forward by President **François Mitterrand**, Chancellor **Helmut Kohl** and the Belgian government the previous April. Both IGCs were to start in December 1990.

The EMU IGC, conducted by finance ministers, soon revealed disagreements about the pace of progress towards EMU and the institutions needed to manage it. A small minority of countries, the United Kingdom included, had deep reservations about the whole exercise. Germany too, obviously the most important participant in the discussions, had reservations of its own, based upon the German electorate's attachment to the Deutsche Mark and the suspicion that EMU would entail massive payments to the poorer or more profligate member states. The final compromise provided for an EMU in three stages (of which the first had already begun in 1990), set out in additions to the **Treaty of Rome** (Articles 109(a) to 109(m), now 112 to 124); the British and Danish governments secured '**opt-outs**' allowing them to take separate decisions on the transition to a single currency controlled by a **European Central Bank** (ECB).

The EPU IGC, conducted by foreign ministers, was responsible for the basic structure of the Treaty itself. The first part proclaims the establishment of the European Union (Article 1), sets out its aims (Article 2), and requires the Union to 'respect the national identities of its Member States' (Article 6.3). On British insistence, all references to **federalism** were removed. The second section contains amendments to the Treaty of Rome establishing the European Economic Community, henceforward to be called the European Community, and the third and fourth sections contain amendments to the **Treaty of Paris** and the **European Atomic Energy Community** Treaty. The fifth and sixth sections set up the so-called **pillars**, the **Common Foreign and Security Policy** (CFSP) and cooperation in the fields of **Justice and Home Affairs** (JHA). The seventh section contains general provisions, adapted from those formerly in the Treaty of Rome, on Treaty amendment (Article 48), the procedure for **enlargement** (Article 49) and **ratification** (Article 52). The Maastricht Treaty was concluded for an unlimited period (Article 53).

Annexed to the Treaty are 17 **protocols**, all but the last of which relate to matters covered in the Treaty of Rome. They include an agreement on the non-retroactive applicability of the Barber judgment (see **equal treatment**), the Statutes of the **European Central Bank** (ECB) and the **European Monetary Institute** (EMI), details of the **excessive deficit procedure**, the British and Danish **opt-outs** on EMU, the so-called Social Protocol (see **Social Chapter**), and a set of undertakings on cohesion (see **Cohesion Fund**) to benefit the poorer member states. Also annexed to the Treaty are 33 **Declarations**, of which the most important are those on the role of **national parliaments**, the **hierarchy of acts**, on police cooperation (see **Justice and Home Affairs**) and on the future role of **Western European Union** (WEU).

The amendments to the Treaty of Rome contained in the Maastricht Treaty, as well as laying down the stages for progress towards EMU, made provision for a new **co-decision procedure**, an extension of the **assent procedure**, new powers to allow the **European Parliament** a decisive say in the appointment of the president and members of the **European Commission**, and two new institutions, the **Committee of the Regions** and the **Ombudsman**. The **Court of Auditors** was given the full status of an institution and the **Court of Justice** the power to fine defaulting member states. The Treaty laid down the principle of **subsidiarity**, created **citizenship** of the Union and extended Community action in the fields of culture, education, vocational training, consumer protection, **trans-European networks** (TENs), industry policy, the environment and development policy.

The Maastricht Treaty ranged over a very wide field, but in spite of this evident attempt to satisfy all parties involved in the negotiations it was very nearly not ratified. It failed to secure the necessary five-sixths majority in the

Danish Parliament, and in the referendum that followed (2 June 1992) it was defeated by 50.7 to 49.3 per cent of the vote. The following month the other governments decided to press ahead with ratification, even though technically the Treaty could not enter into force without having been ratified in all 12 member states. A referendum in Ireland followed on 18 June 1992, the Treaty securing a 67 per cent majority. In July President Mitterrand announced that the Treaty would also be submitted to a referendum in France, even though there was no constitutional requirement to this effect. The referendum took place on 20 September, four days after the events of 'Black Wednesday' forced both the pound and the lira out of the **Exchange-Rate Mechanism** (ERM), and resulted in a tiny majority of only 51.05 per cent for the Treaty.

The Danish government was by now insisting on further opt-outs as the condition for holding a second referendum. These were specified in a paper of 30 October 1992 entitled *Denmark in Europe*. At the European Council meeting in Edinburgh in December Denmark was granted a permanent opt-out from stage 3 of EMU, and received the necessary clarifications on citizenship; Denmark's non-participation in 'decisions and actions of the Union which have defence implications' was formally recognized. A second Danish referendum was held on 18 May 1993, the Treaty securing a majority of 56.8 per cent.

It was in the United Kingdom that ratification posed the most serious problems. The result of the April 1992 general election gave John Major's Conservative government a much smaller majority, giving the Conservative MPs most hostile to European integration in general and the Treaty in particular much greater influence. The government promised that although the 'clause by clause, line by line' examination of the Maastricht Treaty Bill could be started, ratification would not be completed until the result of the second Danish referendum was known. The Labour Party, although not opposed to the Treaty, was fiercely critical of the opt-out from the Social Chapter, and understandably exulted in the government's discomfiture. The passage of the Bill through the House of Commons was slow and acrimonious. The final vote, on 24 July 1993, was won by a very narrow majority, achieved only by means of a threat to dissolve Parliament and call an election (see David Baker, Andrew Gamble, Steve Ludlow, 'The parliamentary siege of Maastricht', *Political Affairs*, Vol. 47, no. 1, January 1994).

In fact, the last member state to ratify the Treaty was Germany, where anti-Maastricht campaigners had succeeded in referring the Treaty to the German Constitutional Court in Karlsruhe. The legal arguments were not resolved until a ruling in favour of ratification on 12 October 1993, allowing the Treaty to enter into force the following month (see **Karlsruhe judgment**).

However well-intentioned, a treaty covering so many heterogeneous issues, some very sensitive, negotiated largely in secret, and for the most part unintelligible to the general public, could hardly be expected to win friends. The period during which it was ratified coincided with a low point in the Community's fortunes: impotence in Yugoslavia, monetary instability, and rows over the Uruguay Round of the **General Agreement on Tariffs and Trade** (GATT) all contributed to a general impression of a Community that had lost its way. Against this background, the Treaty's grander aspirations seemed absurd, and the detailed provisions trivial. At the same time, in spite of its assurances on subsidiarity, by moving into areas such as citizenship, police cooperation and a common currency the Treaty seemed to portend the much-feared 'European superstate'.

MacDougall Report

In 1974 the **European Commission** invited an expert group of seven economists to prepare a report on the role of public finance in European integration. Their report, generally known as the MacDougall Report after the group's chairman, Sir Donald MacDougall, then Chief Economic Adviser to the Confederation of British Industry, was published in April 1977.

It studied the role of public finance both in unitary states (France, Italy and the United Kingdom) and in federations (Australia, Canada, Switzerland, the United States, the Federal Republic of Germany), with particular emphasis on its redistributive effects, the allocation of responsibility for revenue-raising and the scope for counter-cyclical measures in the interests of sustainable long-term growth. It assumed that the Community wanted to move towards economic integration, and applied the lessons learnt from the study of public finance in the national context to developments in the Community.

The report identified three distinct stages beyond the *status quo*: pre-federal integration, federation with a small Community-level public sector, and federation with a large Community-level public sector. When the report was written, total spending by the Community institutions was about 0.7 per cent of the Community's gross domestic product (GDP). 'Pre-federal integration' meant raising the latter figure to between 2 and 2.5 per cent. A 'small' Community public sector was reckoned to be from 5 to 7 per cent, and a 'large' something approaching 25 per cent of GDP. On this calculation, the European Union is still well short even of the 'pre-federal' stage: in 2000, total Union expenditure was estimated at about 1.09 per cent of the Union's GDP.

The MacDougall Report was widely discussed, but, as the figures show, little concrete action flowed from it at the time, with the exception of the Commission's 1978 proposals on **own resources**. However, more recently, the growth in the **structural funds**, the **Cohesion Fund**, the extension of the Union's involvement in employment and training, and the emphasis on **convergence** are all in line with recommendations originally made in the report (see also **Padoa–Schioppa Report**).

Macedonia

The territory known since ancient times as Macedonia stretches from Albania in the west to the frontiers of European Turkey in the east. In 1913 at the end of the Second Balkan War Macedonia ceased to be part of the Ottoman Empire. However, no Macedonian state was created: half the territory was given to Greece and most of the other half to Serbia, with Bulgaria securing the remainder. Soon after the Second World War a Republic of Macedonia was created within **Yugoslavia**, and this became the focus for Macedonian nationalist aspirations as well as for Greek apprehensions about Macedonian encroachment (the Greeks do not recognize the Macedonians as a nation, regarding them as renegade Slav-speaking Greeks). The Former Yugoslav Republic of Macedonia (FYROM), as it is formally known, declared its independence from Yugoslavia in November 1992.

FYROM joined the **Council of Europe** in 1995. In 1996 it became eligible for European Union assistance under the **PHARE** programme. In March 2001 an agreement between FYROM and the Union was signed as part of the **Stabilization and Association Process** (the trade provisions came into effect in June 2001). Tetovo in FYROM has been chosen as the site of the South-East Europe University, one of the Union's most important projects in the region. See also **the Balkans**. J. Pettifer (ed.), *The New Macedonian Question* (Basingstoke, 1999) is a helpful study.

Maghreb

The Maghreb countries (*maghreb* is Arabic for 'western') are Algeria, Morocco and Tunisia, with each of which the Community has a **Cooperation Agreement** under Article 133 of the **Treaty of Rome** as part of its overall **Mediterranean policy** (see also **Mashreq**). These agreements, which entered into force on 1 November 1978, are administered by Cooperation Councils and provide for financial and technical assistance and political dialogue. Under the provisions governing the amount of aid to each country, such aid is in the form of both low-interest loans from the **European Investment Bank** (EIB) and grants from the **Budget**.

Majority voting

Within the **Council of Ministers** of the European Union, decisions may be taken either by unanimity or by majority voting, depending on which Treaty Article has been used as the legal base for the proposal in question. The vote of each member state is given a 'weighting', ranging from 10 in the case of the larger states to 2 in the case of the smallest (Luxembourg). Majority voting may be simple majority (i.e., 8 member states out of 15 voting in favour) or, more usually, **qualified majority voting** (QMV). Article 205.1 of the **Treaty of**

Rome lays down the general principle that 'the Council shall act by a majority of its members' (see also **veto**). See also **double majority, Treaty of Nice**.

Malta

Malta was taken from Napoleon by the British in 1800 and in 1814 became a British dependency. In 1956 a referendum showed a majority in favour of incorporation into the United Kingdom, but this was rejected as impractical. Instead, in 1964 the country gained its independence under the British crown and 10 years later declared itself a republic. Malta's constitution, with its commitment to **neutrality**, was last amended in 1987. The country remains a member of the Commonwealth, belongs to the United Nations and the **Council of Europe** and took part in the **Conference on Security and Cooperation in Europe** (CSCE).

Since 1970 Malta has had an **Association Agreement** with the Community, which was intended to lead in two five-year stages to Malta's becoming a part of the Community **customs union**. However, the Maltese Labour Party government that took office in 1971 was hostile to the idea of closer ties with the Community and the Association Agreement was effectively frozen at the conclusion of its first five-year stage. The pro-Community Nationalist Party took over the government in 1987, but instead of reactivating the Agreement decided to apply for full membership of the Community. The application was formally submitted on 16 July 1990. However, the Labour Party was returned to power in October 1996 and effectively withdrew the application. The application was renewed in September 1998.

The **Opinion** of the **European Commission** on the Maltese application identified three categories of problem: economic, institutional and political (*Bulletin of the European Communities*, supplement 4/93). Malta's economy is heavily protected, heavily subsidized and largely composed of very small firms. More than three-quarters of Maltese firms employed fewer than 5 people, and only 12 (out of 2,300 registered companies) more than 300. The public sector represented about 40 per cent of all employment. The structure of public revenue was such that about one-third of the government's total tax revenue was from customs and excise duties. The introduction of value-added tax (VAT), a *de facto* requirement of Community membership, proved difficult.

The most important industries in terms of output and employment were textiles, clothing and footwear; electrical and electronic equipment; and shipbuilding and ship-repairing, a relic of Malta's importance as a base for the Royal Navy. However, levels of productivity were below average, and few industries could have survived the exposure to competition and the removal of state subsidies that would have resulted from Community membership. Such removal of trade restrictions as there had been under the Association

Agreement had almost all been on the Community side, and very little progress had been made towards aligning Malta's customs tariffs and import levies with the Community's **Common External Tariff**.

On institutional questions, the Commission's **Opinion** noted that the fact of English being an official language in Malta might allow the Union to sidestep the problem of adding Maltese (of Semitic origin, and wholly unrelated to any other European language) to the list of official languages. More difficult was the fact of Malta having 'only a very few senior public officials with sufficient international experience to play a full part in the decision-making and operational processes of the Community institutions', most of whom would be kept fully occupied by the domestic reform process. Moreover, Malta has only about 15 embassies and consulates around the world. Against this background it would have been hard to imagine Malta assuming the responsibilities of the **presidency** of the Council.

The main political problem was that the political parties remained fundamentally divided over Maltese membership of the Union. During its previous term of office the Labour Party pursued a policy of developing closer relations with Libya and certain Communist countries, notably China. In so polarized a political society, it seems unlikely that the kind of cross-party consensus that would be needed to underpin the reform process (uncomfortable for many sectors of the economy) and make a success of Union membership could ever be forthcoming.

Maltese **neutrality** is at the heart of the argument between the parties. The Constitution declares that 'Malta is a neutral State actively pursuing peace ... by adhering to a policy of non-alignment and refusing to participate in any military alliance'. Nevertheless, in the memorandum addressed to the Community by the Maltese government on 11 September 1992 it was said to be 'in Malta's interest to subscribe to the European Union's common foreign and security policy, including the eventual framing of a common defence policy'. Whether or not this could be done without amending the Constitution, which requires a two-thirds majority in the House of Assembly, is not clear.

Malta is unquestionably a European state. Its history is bound up with European history, from St Paul's shipwreck to the Second World War. Among the most handsome buildings in Valletta are the eight *auberges* of the various *langues* of the Knights of St John, who took up residence in Malta on being expelled from Rhodes at the time of the Crusades: Aragon, Auvergne, Castile, England, France, Germany, Italy and Provence. Three-quarters of the country's foreign trade is with the Union. The country's institutions are based on European models and the population is staunchly Roman Catholic. Although poor, with a per capita gross national product (GNP) only 52 per cent of the Union average, Malta is so small that the impact of its accession on the **Budget** would be negligible. However, its very smallness raises in the most acute form those institutional questions common to all **micro-states** wishing to join the Union, to which no one has yet found satisfactory answers. Taken in conjunction, these facts account for the very guarded nature of the conclusion to the Commission's Opinion:

The Commission feels that it is important to send to the authorities and people of Malta a positive signal to encourage them to undertake vigorously the requisite reforms to transform Malta's economy into an open and competitive one ... Such a signal could be given by announcing that the Community is willing to open accession negotiations with Malta as soon as conditions allow.

A revised Opinion on Malta was published in February 1999. Negotiations with Malta were begun in 2000 and were concluded in 2002. On 8 March 2003 the Maltese people voted by 53.6 per cent to 46.4 per cent to join the European Union (see **Treaty of Accession**).

Management committee

Under the **Common Agricultural Policy** (CAP), since 1962 each commodity covered by the CAP has had its own management committee, composed of national civil servants, whose task is to assist the **European Commission** in the implementation of decisions taken by the **Council of Ministers**. Management committees have considerable power and this has given rise to concern over the extent to which they are sufficiently accountable (see **comitology**).

Mansholt Plan

The Mansholt Plan, named after Sicco Mansholt, then the vice-president, and later the President, of the **European Commission**, was the blueprint for the **Common Agricultural Policy** (CAP) adopted by the Community in 1972. Mansholt, who had been a Socialist minister of agriculture in the Netherlands from 1945 to 1958, produced the final version of his plan in 1968. He accepted that continental agriculture was badly in need of restructuring and that this would involve heavy job losses. The Plan allowed for generous compensation, to be paid for over the years by making agricultural production more cost-effective and so limiting the extent of price support through **intervention**. The Plan also laid emphasis on unified markets for each product, strict limits on national aids and a high degree of protection against imports. In spite of the balance it sought to strike between competing interests, the Plan was very controversial, and the CAP that eventually emerged was much less radical (see also **Stresa Conference**).

Marshall Plan

The Marshall Plan was the name given to the European Recovery Programme (ERP) under which the United States gave financial assistance totalling over $13 billion to promote the economic recovery of postwar Europe. Prompted by the realization that the countries of western Europe, even the United Kingdom and France, were too enfeebled by war to resist Communist encroachment, the United States government under President Harry Truman resolved to make available American aid and to invite the European countries to draw up an agreed estimate of 'the requirements of the situation'. The offer was made by Secretary of State George C. Marshall in a Graduation Day speech at Harvard on 5 June 1947. No country was to be excluded, the only condition being that the proposal for an economic recovery programme should be 'a joint one, agreed to by a number of, if not all, European nations'.

As a result of pressure from the Soviet Union, the countries of eastern and central Europe (even those which, like Czechoslovakia, had at first responded favourably to the American offer) declined to attend the conference in Paris in July 1947 at which the ERP was to be worked out in detail. At the conference the Europeans were told that the aim of the ERP was 'the speediest possible reactivation of the European economic machine and … its restoration to a self-supporting basis'. Two conditions of great importance for the process of European unification were laid down: that the European countries needed to start dismantling barriers to trade among themselves, and that a European organization must be set up to oversee the process of economic recovery. This latter condition led to the establishment of the Organization for European Economic Cooperation (OEEC) in 1948, which was transformed into the **Organization for Economic Cooperation and Development** (OECD) in 1961.

Reactions to the American proposals were mixed. Particularly among the parties of the Left, the Marshall Plan was interpreted as US economic imperialism on the very boldest scale. All kinds of forebodings, resentment and anxieties about **sovereignty** were expressed, solicitously encouraged by Stalin's USSR. General Marshall himself was accorded a prominent place in Soviet demonology. Among the European nations who had experienced German occupation there was deep concern at the importance that the Americans clearly attached to putting the German economy back on its feet. Nor was the Plan uncontroversial in the United States: the prodigious efforts of the Administration to secure the approval of Congress are recounted in detail in Charles L. Mee's *The Marshall Plan: the Launching of the Pax Americana* (New York, 1984). Indeed, had it not been for the conviction and farsightedness of a handful of key figures in the Truman Administration (Marshall himself, George F. Kennan, Dean Acheson and William Clayton) and of Europeans like **Paul-Henri Spaak**, Georges Bidault and Ernest Bevin it is doubtful whether the Plan would have come to fruition. An interesting perspective on the Plan may be gained from Sallie Pisani, *The CIA and the Marshall Plan* (Edinburgh, 1991).

Mashreq

The Mashreq countries (*mashreq* is Arabic for 'eastern') are Egypt, Jordan, Lebanon and Syria, with each of which the Community has a **Cooperation Agreement** under Article 133 of the **Treaty of Rome** as part of its overall **Mediterranean policy** (see also **Maghreb**). These agreements, which entered into force on 1 November 1978, are administered by Cooperation Councils and provide for financial and technical assistance and political dialogue. Under the provisions governing the amount of aid to each country, such aid is in the form of both low-interest loans from the **European Investment Bank** (EIB) and grants from the **Budget**.

Maudling Committee

By 1957 the British government had realized that **the Six** were in earnest in their desire to establish the **customs union** that was to be the basis of the **European Economic Community** (EEC; see also **Beyen Plan**, **Messina Conference**, **Spaak Committee**). Having failed to enlist American support in opposing the customs union idea, the government made a counter-proposal in the Organization for European Economic Cooperation (OEEC; see **Organization for Economic Cooperation and Development**): that a **free trade area** should be set up among all the European members of the OEEC, including the Six, but limited to trade in manufactured goods. In this way the British government hoped to avoid exclusion from continental markets while retaining Commonwealth preference for agricultural products. The OEEC appointed a committee under the chairmanship of Reginald Maudling, then President of the Board of Trade, to examine this proposal. Initially, it looked as though the West German government of **Konrad Adenauer** might support the British proposal, but by June 1958, with the return to power in France of **Charles de Gaulle**, it was clear that what the British called 'Plan G' was dead. Discussions in the OEEC were concluded later that year. The work of the Maudling Committee laid the foundations of the 1960 Stockholm Convention establishing the **European Free Trade Association** (EFTA). The whole episode is very fully described in Hugo Young, *This Blessed Plot* (1999).

MEDA programme

Development assistance to countries covered by the European Union's **Mediterranean policy** is granted under the MEDA programme. It is governed by Regulation 1488/96 of 23 July 1996 (*Official Journal*, L189, 30 July 1996) as revised by Regulation 2698/00 of 27 November 2000 (*Official Journal*, L311, 12 December 2000). Over the period 2000–6 the MEDA programme makes available €5.35 billion from the Union's **Budget**. Together with loans from the European Investment Bank development assistance to the region amounts to about €13 billion.

MEDIA Plus

The MEDIA Plus programme, with a budget of €350 million over the period 2001–5, is concerned with making Europe's audiovisual industry more competitive. It was first set up as the MEDIA programme in 1990 (*Official Journal*, L380, 31 December 1990). In its present form it is open to member states of the European Union, Cyprus, Iceland, Liechtenstein, Malta, Norway, Turkey, and the applicant states in central and eastern Europe (*Official Journal*, L336, 30 December 2000). The emphasis of the programme, in addition to improving competitiveness, is on encouraging technical advances, supporting linguistic and cultural diversity, and aiding production and distribution, especially through small and medium-sized enterprises (SMEs).

Mediterranean policy

Although for several decades the European Community had agreements of various types with the countries bordering the Mediterranean (see, for example, **Maghreb**, **Mashreq**), there was no comprehensive policy covering the area. At the meeting of the **European Council** in Corfu in June 1994 it was decided to draw up a proposal for such a policy, partly as a means of redressing the balance in the Union's trade and aid relations with its near neighbours, which had, since 1991, shifted decisively in favour of the countries of central and eastern Europe. It was also believed that financial assistance and more political contacts would help to stabilize the region and relieve migratory pressures on the Union's southern frontiers. About 5 million nationals of non-member Mediterranean states live in the Union, half of them Turks.

An ambitious proposal for a 'Euro-Mediterranean partnership' was announced by the **European Commission** on 18 October 1994. In the long term the aim is to establish by 2010 'the largest [industrial] free trade area in the world, covering the Union, the countries of Central and Eastern Europe ... and also all the Mediterranean third countries' (i.e., some 40 countries with a population of about 700 million people). The Mediterranean countries include the Maghreb and Mashreq states, Israel, Cyprus, Malta, Turkey, and the Palestinian territories (some 220 million people). In June 1995 the European Council meeting in Cannes agreed to provide development assistance to the region under the **MEDA programme** (operational since 1996). Among the specific measures proposed are scientific, technical and industrial cooperation and joint action on the environment, illegal immigration and the fight against drugs, as well as financial assistance from the **European Investment Bank** (EIB). Political stability in the region is being promoted as part of the **Common Foreign and Security Policy** (CFSP). Both France and Spain see the development of a Mediterranean policy as a means of preventing the Union's centre of gravity from shifting too far to the north and east with **enlargement** and the opening up of central and eastern Europe. The European Union and eleven Mediterranean countries (and the PLO) signed a 'Barcelona Declaration' on 28 November 1995. Euro-Mediterranean **Association Agreements** have been concluded or are now being negotiated with most of the signatories to the Declaration. These Agreements generally provide for the establishment of free trade over a 12-year period as well as human rights clauses and political dialogue. Human rights and democracy are promoted under the MEDA-Democracy programme. See V. Nieuhaus, 'Promoting development and stability through a Euro-Mediterranean free trade zone', *European Foreign Affairs Review*, Vol. 4, no. 4, Winter 1999.

Merger controls

The idea of a monopoly or of a merger possibly prejudicial to competition is meaningful only with respect to a particular geographical market. With the establishment of the **Single Market** national markets ceased to be the appropriate dimension within which to consider monopolies and mergers, the vetting of which is now an important part of **competition policy**. Since 1989 the **European Commission** has had sole authority to vet large-scale mergers, defined most recently in Regulation 1310/97 (*Official Journal* L180, 9 July 1997) as those involving concerns with a combined annual turnover of at least €2.5 billion, of which more than €100 million is generated in each of at least three member states. In each of these states, the turnover of at least two of the concerns must exceed €25 million. Overall, the Union-wide turnover of at least two of the concerns must exceed €100 million. However, if each of the concerns generates two-thirds of its Union-wide turnover in one member state, the proposed merger is vetted not by the Commission but by the relevant national authorities. The sensitivity of this issue may be inferred from the fact that it took the **Council of Ministers** 16 years to agree the original Regulation. Procedural rules on merger controls were first laid down in Regulation 4064/89 of 21 December 1989 (*Official Journal*, L395, 30 December 1989). The purpose of this Regulation was to simplify and speed up the process of securing approval for the merger, to clarify the responsibilities of the relevant authorities and to resolve the uncertainties arising from the differences in the law in the various jurisdictions.

As the Continental Can case (*Europemballage Corporation and Continental Can Co. Inc.* v *Commission*, Case 6/72) established in 1975, a merger or acquisition may constitute an 'abuse ... of a dominant position within the common market or in a substantial part of it', which is prohibited under Article 82 of the

Treaty of Rome. Such an 'abuse' may be proved even if the company cannot be shown actually to have exploited its market position to the detriment of competition. According to the most recent figures, over an 11-year period the Commission has refused to approve less than 1 per cent of mergers. In December 2001 the Commission published a Green Paper (COM(2001) 745/6) on possible changes to Regulation 4064/89.

Merger Treaty

The 1965 Merger Treaty, which entered into effect in July 1967, was the first amendment to the **Treaties** of Paris and Rome. The purpose was to create a common **Council of Ministers** and a common **European Commission** serving all three **European Communities**. This move was seen as an important step towards the complete integration of the three Communities, and had been advocated by the **Action Committee for a United States of Europe** throughout the early 1960s. Article 32 of the Merger Treaty referred in passing to a 'Treaty establishing a Single European Community', something that was never drawn up.

Formally speaking, the new 'Council of the European Communities' (Article 1) replaced the Special Council of Ministers of the **European Coal and Steel Community** (ECSC), and the Councils of the **European Economic Community** (EEC) and the **European Atomic Energy Community** (Euratom). Similarly the new 'Commission of the European Communities' replaced the High Authority of the ECSC and the Commissions of the EEC and Euratom (Article 9). It was not necessary to provide for the amalgamation of the **European Parliament**, the **Court of Justice** and the **Economic and Social Committee** in the Merger Treaty, since the 1957 'Convention on Certain Institutions Common to the European Communities' – signed in parallel to the **Treaty of Rome** and having the same legal status – had already stipulated that one body in each case would exercise the functions set out in the original Treaties. The Merger Treaty provided for a common **Budget** of the Communities to replace the three separate budgets (Article 20). It also created a 'single administration' composed of the officials of the three original Communities (Article 24). Its essential provisions having been incorporated into other Treaties, the Merger Treaty was repealed under Article 9.1 of the **Treaty of Amsterdam**.

The Merger Treaty had the effect of consolidating the Communities' activities in Brussels. Under pressure from the Luxembourg government, the member states signed a separate agreement on the 'provisional location' of the institutions that required the secretariat of the European Parliament to remain in Luxembourg together with the Court of Justice and the **European Investment Bank** (EIB). The Council of Ministers was required to meet in Luxembourg in April, June and October (see **seat of the institutions**).

Messina Conference

On 30 August 1954 the French National Assembly rejected the Treaty that would have established the **European Defence Community**. This meant that progress could not be made with the **European Political Community** either, so **the Six**, anxious to reaffirm their commitment to European integration and to extend its scope beyond the relatively narrow base of the **European Coal and Steel Community** (ECSC, with which, in December 1954, the United Kingdom had signed an **Association Agreement**), decided to explore what could be done to establish free trade among themselves within a **customs union**. In June 1955 the foreign ministers of the Six met in Messina to consider memoranda on closer economic integration drawn up by the **Benelux** countries (see **Beyen Plan**), Italy and West Germany. A compromise agreement was reached and an intergovernmental committee was set up under **Paul-Henri Spaak**. The committee presented its report to the foreign ministers in Venice in May 1956, and this was used as the basis for negotiating two new Treaties, one establishing a **European Economic Community** (EEC) and the other a **European Atomic Energy Community** (Euratom). These Treaties were signed 10 months later and were ratified in time for them to come into effect on 1 January 1958.

The significance of the Messina Conference is that at a low point in the history of European integration there was still enough energy and enthusiasm among the Six to allow two very complex and far-reaching Treaties to be negotiated in a remarkably short time. The United Kingdom was invited to participate in the Conference and in the Spaak Committee but sent only an Under-Secretary of State from the Board of Trade (who subsequently withdrew: the story is told in full in Michael Charlton's *The Price of Victory*, 1983).

Metrication

In 1979 the **Council of Ministers** sought to standardize units of measurement within the European Community on the basis of metric units laid down as the *Système International* (SI) in 1960. SI units were first introduced under a worldwide convention of 1875 on physical measurements. The Council's decision allowed other units to coexist with SI units until 1989 (later extended to 1999). Since then, international agreement has been reached on adjustments to the SI and a strong case has been made for a longer phasing-out period for other (mainly imperial) units. This would also allow the United States – the only major industrial power not using SI units – to modify its domestic legislation. For these reasons, the 1979 decision has again been revised, and the target date for the uniform and exclusive use of SI units within the European Union has been put forward to 2009.

Micro-states

'Micro-states' is a term used by political scientists and students of international relations to denote very small sovereign states. There are five such states in western Europe, ranging from Andorra, with a population of about 66,000, to Vatican City, with a population of 900. Several micro-states are wholly within the territory of a member state of the European Union, but none has sought to join the Union in its own right. The Union has established particular relations with each of them, and in all of them except Liechtenstein the **euro** is the currency. All except Monaco are members of the **Council of Europe**, all belong to the United Nations, and all participate in the **Organization for Security and Cooperation in Europe** (OSCE). None belongs to any defensive alliance.

Andorra

Until 14 May 1993, when the citizens of Andorra voted for a new republican constitution, the country was a 'co-principality' over which the Bishop of Urgell in Spain and the President of the French Republic (as heir to the rights and titles of the kings of France) exercised joint suzerainty. They remain the heads of state. The official language is Catalan. The accession of Spain to the European Community in 1986 resulted in Andorra becoming part of the Community's **customs union** with effect from July 1991, but special arrangements apply to agricultural products. The customs agreement is managed by a joint committee. Andorra remains fiscally independent but does not issue its own currency.

Liechtenstein

The principality of Liechtenstein has an area of 160 square kilometres and a population of about 33,000. Neutral in both world wars, it has had a customs union agreement with Switzerland since 1923 and the Swiss franc is used as the currency. As a member of the **European Free Trade Association** (EFTA), Liechtenstein took part in the negotiations for the creation of the **European Economic Area** (EEA) and its citizens confirmed their support for the EEA Agreement by referendum on 13 December 1992. However, a week earlier the Swiss had voted against EEA membership, and this necessitated certain adjustments to the Agreement. A second referendum was held on 9 April 1995, allowing Liechtenstein to join the EEA on 1 May 1995. This is a very radical step for Liechtenstein, since under the Agreement it is required not to discriminate against other EEA nationals in respect of the **free movement of persons**, capital and services, **freedom of establishment** and the ownership of land.

Monaco

The principality of Monaco has a population of about 32,000 but a very much smaller land area – less than 2 square kilometres. Ruled by the Grimaldi family since the Middle Ages, Monaco (which until 1860 included the communes of Menton and Roquebrune) has at various times been under the protection of France, Spain and the Kingdom of Sardinia. The present treaty with France dates from July 1918 and the present constitution from 1962.

Monaco has had a customs union with France since 1865. Certain senior posts (including that of Prime Minister) in the Monégasque civil service are reserved for French nationals. In response to French pressure, Monaco's fiscal system was reformed in the 1960s so that companies and individuals operating in France could no longer take advantage of Monaco's very favourable tax regime. Revenue from turnover taxes, including value-added tax (VAT), is shared with France on the basis of a complicated formula. Monaco cannot be said to have a foreign policy distinguishable from that of France, and Monégasque laws on foreigners' rights of sojourn and of residence have to be compatible with those of France.

Monaco's customs union with France is governed by a convention dating from May 1963. Since this date the principality has had *ipso facto* a customs union with the European Community.

San Marino

With a population of about 27,000 and an area of 61 square kilometres, the Republic of San Marino has existed as a separate entity (although not always wholly independent) since the early Middle Ages. In 1862 a treaty was concluded that placed San Marino under the protection of the newly founded Kingdom of Italy. Under the current treaty, dating from 1939 and amended in 1971, San Marino established a customs union with Italy and *ipso facto* with the European Community (EC).

In 1983 San Marino began negotiations with the EC on a customs union and cooperation agreement. The agreement was concluded in 1992, but because delays were expected in the ratification process an interim agreement was drawn up and entered into force in December 1992. The agreement, which is of indefinite duration, establishes free movement for most goods, industrial and agricultural, between San Marino and the EC, enjoins the EC to assist the San Marinese economy, provides for non-discrimination (but not the right of free movement) in respect of workers, and places relations between San Marino and the EC in the hands of a Cooperation Committee.

Vatican City

The territory of the Holy See, fixed by the Lateran Treaty of 11 February 1929, extends to the Vatican Palace, St Peter's, the Lateran Palaces and the Papal villa of Castel Gandolfo. The smallest political entity in the world, the Vatican City is outside Italian customs territory, and goods entering the City are wholly exempt from Italian customs duties and other taxes. By the same token the Vatican City is outside the scope of the European Community treaties, and no special arrangements govern relations between the European Union and the Vatican City, which are conducted through the papal nuncio accredited to the European Union in Brussels.

At different times international organizations have dealt with applications for membership from micro-states in different ways. The **League of Nations**, for example, opposed applications from San Marino and Liechtenstein mainly because of the problems that micro-states would pose within a decision-making system that allowed all members a veto and the same representation in the Assembly. Monaco's application was opposed on the grounds that Monégasque membership would in effect give France a second vote, although Andorra's application was opposed by France on the grounds that Andorra was not a sovereign state in international law. General misgivings were felt about the capacity of micro-states to meet the obligations set out in the Covenant of the League.

Since the end of the Second World War most international organizations have found ways to accommodate micro-states, many more of which came into being as a result of decolonization. The United Nations, for example, grew from 51 members in 1945 to 100 in 1960 and to 189 in 2002. As more micro-states were admitted, precedents were set and claims to sovereignty strengthened. Within Europe, both the Council of Europe and the OSCE have been willing to admit micro-states, and the states themselves have expressed great determination to assert their individual identity on the international scene.

Micro-states – and for these purposes Cyprus, Malta and Luxembourg must be included – continue to pose problems for the European Union. It is not merely that the range of obligations implicit in membership is much greater than is the case with other international organizations, but also the fact that the rights are so much more extensive: representation in the **Council of Ministers**, a **veto** in respect of many key decisions, a Commissioner, a judge in the **Court of Justice**, seats in the **European Parliament** and a turn at holding the **presidency**. The fact that a micro-state (Luxembourg) enjoys entrenched rights as one of the original **Six** makes the problem harder to resolve. Micro-states raise in the most acute form the conflict between **sovereignty** and effective collective action, between institutional efficiency and (in the words of the UN Charter) 'the equal rights ... of nations large and small'.

Minorities

Minorities are normally considered under three distinct headings: ethnic minorities, religious minorities and linguistic minorities. Some minorities, such as the Lapps (Saami) in the north of Finland, fall under all three headings, but most minorities in western Europe (not including immigrant communities) under only one.

The redrawing of political frontiers after the First World War took some account of ethnic frontiers. However, the correspondence between the two was far from exact. The Covenant of the **League of Nations** was the first international agreement of its kind to grant special rights to minorities. These rights were granted to individuals as members of minority groups, not to minority groups as a whole: it was feared that the latter would encourage secessionist trends. Hitler's claim to be protecting the rights of the German minority first in the Sudetenland and later in Poland underlined the extent to which the League's provisions were open to abuse.

After the Second World War more ambitious goals were set with respect to the protection of **human rights** generally. The 1948 Universal Declaration of Human Rights makes no specific mention of minority rights, since it was felt that if the rights in the Declaration pertaining to individuals were fully respected, further action in respect of minorities was unnecessary. This was not the view taken by the **Council of Europe** when drawing up the European Convention on Human Rights (ECHR). Article 14 of the ECHR prohibits, *inter alia*, any discrimination on the basis of 'membership of a national minority' with respect to the rights and liberties recognized by the ECHR. This provision, taken in conjunction with other Articles, lays an obligation on national authorities to create the conditions in which minorities can exercise to the full the rights and liberties laid down in the ECHR, i.e., to enact measures of positive discrimination in favour of minorities. This interpretation has given rise to three further Council of Europe agreements, the 1989 European Convention on the Protection of Minorities, the 1992 European Charter on Regional or Minority Languages, and the 1993 draft additional **protocol** to the ECHR. Minority rights issues were addressed at the Council of Europe's first-ever summit in Vienna in October 1993.

Neither the **Treaties** establishing the **European Communities** nor the **Maastricht Treaty** refer to minorities. The commitment of the Union's institutions to respect human rights generally is embodied in the tripartite declaration of 1977 (see **human rights**) and in the **Charter of Fundamental Rights**. The **citizenship** provisions of the **Treaty of Rome** apply equally to all nationals of the member states. Respect for the rights of minorities is one of the political criteria whereby applications for membership of the Union are judged (see **Copenhagen criteria**).

The rights of minorities have been studied and codified at length in the framework of the **Conference on Security and Cooperation in Europe** (CSCE). Initially, the provisions in the **Helsinki Final Act** of 1975 marked a return to the idea that machinery for the protection of individual rights would solve the problem of minorities, but in the Madrid and Vienna follow-up conferences, with strong backing from minority groups in central and eastern Europe, it was recognized that positive discrimination was needed. Furthermore, a monitoring mechanism was agreed, removing minority rights from the exclusive jurisdiction of national authorities. The **Organization for Security and Cooperation in Europe** (OSCE) has established a High Commissioner for National Minorities in The Hague.

The 1990 Copenhagen Conference on the human aspect of the CSCE took place at a time when the nations of central and eastern Europe were already beginning to reassert their identity. Partly for this reason, the document adopted at this conference was the most comprehensive statement to date on the rights of minorities. It obliged the signatory states to 'protect the ethnic, cultural, linguistic and religious identities of national minorities on their territory and ... create conditions suitable for encouraging the development of such identities'. The Copenhagen document was summarized in the relevant section of the 1990 **Charter of Paris.**

Minorities are protected under the constitutions of some member states of the European Union. In one case, Belgium, linguistic and cultural differences have resulted finally in the formation of a federal state under a new constitutional settlement, which also affords protection to the German-speaking minority in the east of the country. Denmark and Germany have reached bilateral agreement on the treatment of their linguistic minorities in the Schleswig-Holstein region. However, the treatment of minorities continues to cause tension between Austria and Italy in the South Tyrol, and, more seriously, in the Spanish Basque country and in Northern Ireland.

There is a summary of the minorities issue, with an account of work in the Council of Europe and the OSCE, in Hugh Miall (ed.), *Minority Rights in Europe* (1994).

Mitterrand, François (1916–96)

A deputy in the French parliament since 1946, by the 1950s François Mitterrand was already holding ministerial posts in successive Socialist administrations. In 1965 he stood unsuccessfully against **Charles de Gaulle** in an election for the presidency of France, attacking him not least for his idiosyncratic policies on European integration (see **empty chair crisis**). He became the leader of the Socialist Party in 1971, but three years later was defeated by **Valéry Giscard d'Estaing** in another attempt to secure the presidency. On his third attempt, in 1981, he was successful, and he was re-elected in 1988 for a second and final term.

Mitterrand's pro-European convictions were of long standing, and in spite of the electoral reverses suffered at various times by his own party he maintained them consistently. He benefited from his position as elder statesman at meetings of the **European Council**, deploying his long experience and political skills not only on behalf of French interests but also in the resolution of disputes; for example, it was under Mitterrand's presidency at Fontainebleau in 1984 that the **British Budget problem** was finally resolved (see also **Fontainebleau Agreement**).

Mitterrand's proposals on European Union, submitted jointly with **Helmut Kohl** to the Dublin meeting of the European Council in June 1990, led to the **Maastricht Treaty**. Later, on the domestic front, he made a rare error of judgement in holding a referendum in September 1992 on the Treaty to which approval was given by only a tiny majority. In common with his predecessors, Mitterrand attached great importance to **Franco-German cooperation** and lent his support to such proposals as the **Eurocorps**. On security issues generally, he was probably more of an Atlanticist by inclination than traditional French policy allowed him to be in fact.

Molitor Group

The Molitor Group, named after its German chairman, Bernhard Molitor, was a committee of national experts set up by the **European Commission** in 1994. An initiative of the German government, the Group was concerned with the legislative and administrative **simplification** of EU law and related national law, with a view to job creation, **competitiveness**, respect for **subsidiarity** and its impact on small and medium-sized enterprises (SMEs). The Group's report was presented at the Cannes meeting of the **European Council** in June 1995.

Monaco

See **micro-states**.

Monetary Committee

The Monetary Committee was established under the **Treaty of Rome** (Article 114) as an official-level advisory body to the **Council of Ministers** in the economic and financial field. It was consulted on all major legislative or non-legislative issues before the Council of Economics and Finance Ministers (**Ecofin Council**) and its president often attended the meetings of the Ecofin Council to present its **Opinions**. The Monetary Committee played an important role in the operation of the **European Monetary System** (EMS). It also coordinated the Union's positions in international financial institutions, most notably the International Monetary Fund.

The Monetary Committee provided an official-level negotiating forum to help determine parities whenever currencies realigned within the **Exchange-Rate Mechanism** (ERM) or new currencies joined.

During stage 2 of **Economic and Monetary Union** (EMU) the Monetary Committee assisted the Council in monitoring progress towards economic convergence by the member states, and gave advice on which countries met the various **convergence criteria**. The reports that it presented to the Council on this matter were separate from those drawn up by the Commission and the **European Monetary Institute** (EMI).

The Monetary Committee was replaced by a new **Economic and Financial Committee** at the beginning of stage 3 of EMU in January 1999.

Monnet, Jean (1888–1979)

Born in Cognac, Jean Monnet started his professional life as a salesman in his family's cognac business. During the First World War he worked in London in the field of economic cooperation among the Allies. In 1920 he was appointed deputy secretary-general of the newly established **League of Nations** and given an honorary knighthood by the British Government. He left the League in 1923 to return to his family business. For the next 15 years he was active in international finance before returning, this time in Washington, to planning economic cooperation between the United Kingdom, France and the United States. It was Monnet who, as France was in retreat before the German advance of June 1940, persuaded **Winston Churchill** to forward to Paul Reynaud, the French Prime Minister, a draft declaration proclaiming an 'indissoluble union' between France and the United Kingdom (see **Franco-British union**). He spent the remainder of the war in Washington as a British civil servant. After the war he was put in charge of the *Commissariat du Plan* responsible for the economic recovery of France. In 1950 he suggested to **Robert Schuman**, the French Foreign Minister, the idea of pooling French and German coal and steel production (see **Schuman Plan**). This led to the establishment of the **European Coal and Steel Community** (ECSC) with Monnet as the first president of the High Authority (the forerunner of the **European Commission**). However, his other great plan of this period, the **European Defence Community**, came to nothing, and in November 1954 he resigned from the High Authority to devote himself to freelance campaigning on behalf of European unification. At this time he created his **Action Committee for the United States of Europe**, with representatives of 20 political parties and 10 trade unions. The Committee was disbanded in 1975. Monnet died in 1979 and in November 1988 his body was transferred to the Panthéon.

Monnet's *Mémoires*, published in 1976, are an invaluable source-book for the history of European unification and the European Community in particular. Two principal ideas underpinned Monnet's tireless campaigning on behalf of Europe: that Europe would be built not on the basis of visions and generalities but on practical achievements (the *réalisations concrètes* of the speech setting out the Schuman Plan); and that common institutions, not intergovernmental cooperation, were the key to a durable European Community, since it is only through institutions, as repositories of experience and shared values, that human beings accumulate wisdom and transmit it to future generations.

Monnet was often in conflict with other political leaders in his own country, notably, of course, **Charles de Gaulle**, and was never a member of any political party. He appears to have had something of a technocrat's distaste for party politics and mistrust of politicians, especially of their inability to take a long-term view. He respected British pragmatism, and remained confident that the only way of convincing the United Kingdom to play a part in the unification of Europe was to create organizations that actually worked. There is a biography of Monnet by François Duchêne: *Jean Monnet: the First Statesman of Interdependence* (New York and London, 1994).

Monnet method

Sometimes known as the 'Community method', the Monnet method is a phrase used to denote the particular character of the system of law-making in which the institutions of the European Union have been engaged since the 1950s. The essence of the method is its use of supranational rather than intergovernmental institutions (see **intergovernmentalism**), most notably a **European Commission** enjoying a substantial degree of political autonomy. **Jean Monnet** believed that the method which bears his name would itself materially contribute to European integration by virtue of the phenomenon known as 'spillover' (see **functionalism**; see also *engrenage*). The enduring relevance of the Monnet method is an article of faith for orthodox pro-Europeans, who are deeply suspicious of procedures – such as those in the **pillars** first established under the **Maastricht Treaty** – which are essentially intergovernmental in character. The Monnet method has very many successes to its credit, of which perhaps the **Single Market** is the most striking, but it has been criticized for its lack of **transparency** and for the low priority given to effective democratic control (see **democratic deficit**, **legitimacy**).

In a declaration issued in 1962 as a rejoinder to **Charles de Gaulle**'s accusation that the United States was being used as the 'federator' of Europe, Monnet defined his method: 'It is quite new. It does not involve a central government, but it leads to decisions being taken on a Community basis in the

Council of Ministers, primarily because the solutions proposed by the independent European organization to common problems allows the obligation to seek unanimous agreement to be set aside. The Parliament and the Court of Justice underline the Community character of this set of arrangements. This method is the real "federator" of Europe'.

Monopolies

See **merger controls**.

Morocco

The Kingdom of Morocco, one of the **Maghreb** states, applied for membership of the Community in 1987 on the basis of its European orientation and its democratic credentials. Later that year, the **Council of Ministers** rejected the application on the grounds that Morocco was not a European state, the only occasion on which it has been found necessary to invoke the requirement under Article 237 of the **Treaty of Rome** (now Article 49 of the **Maastricht Treaty**) that only European states are eligible for membership.

Mostar

In the course of peace negotiations to end the conflict in the former Yugoslavia it was proposed and agreed that the town of Mostar should temporarily be placed under European Union administration. This was endorsed in the March 1994 Washington Agreement. On 16 May 1994 the **Council of Ministers** agreed to set up an administration in Mostar (EUAM) as a **joint action** under the **Common Foreign and Security Policy** (CFSP) with an initial budget of 32 million ECUs. On 5 July 1994 a Memorandum of Understanding was signed in Geneva to this effect by the **troika** (the foreign ministers of Germany, Greece and France), a representative of the **European Commission**, a representative of the President of the **Western European Union** (WEU), representatives of the government of Bosnia–Herzegovina, and the mayors of East and West Mostar. The administrator, Hans Koschnick, formerly Mayor of Bremen, took up his post on 23 July 1994 for a maximum two-year term.

This was the first, and so far the only, action of its kind in the history of the Union and a severe test of the Union's effectiveness in foreign affairs. An appropriate legal base was eventually found for the EUAM, which in turn allowed for resources to be drawn from the **Budget** of the European Union. On 12 December 1994 the Council adopted what was described as a 'Decision *sui generis*' which retroactively put the EUAM on a proper legal footing (*Official Journal*, L326, 17 December 1994). An Ombudsman was also appointed for the duration of the EUAM. The WEU provided a police force.

On the whole the EUAM was judged a success, in spite of the resignation of Mr Koschnick in February 1996. This was a protest against the fact that Croat politicians who had physically attacked him were allowed to take part in negotiations in Rome. He was succeeded by Sir Martin Garrod until the ending of the EUAM in July 1996. Sir Martin remained as 'Special Envoy' for the remainder of the year. The town was returned to the newly elected local administration on 1 January 1997.

In total, the EUAM cost 144 million ECUs, of which 127 million ECUs came from the Budget and the rest from member states. The fullest account of the EUAM is in a special report by the **Court of Auditors** (*Official Journal*, C287, 30 September 1996).

Mutual assistance in criminal matters

Mutual assistance in criminal matters between the authorities of the member states of the European Union is the subject of a Convention adopted under an Act of the **Council of Ministers** on 29 May 2000 (*Official Journal*, C197, 12 July 2000). The Convention builds on an earlier Convention adopted by the **Council of Europe** in 1959 (modified under a 1978 Protocol), a Convention agreed by the **Benelux** countries in 1962, and the 1990 Schengen Convention (see **Schengen Agreement**). The European Union Convention, which was drawn up as a consequence of the extension into criminal law of the Union's competence as redefined in the **Treaty of Amsterdam**, seeks to remove a wide range of procedural and other obstacles which impede cross-frontier law enforcement within the Union. In the words of the **European Council** meeting in Tampere (October 1999), 'criminals must find no ways of exploiting differences in the judicial systems of Member States. Judgments and decisions should be respected and enforced throughout the Union ... Better compatibility and more convergence between the legal systems of Member States must be achieved'. The Convention will come into effect 90 days after eight states have ratified it in those states and in other states once their ratification procedures are completed. See also **area of freedom, security and justice, Justice and Home Affairs**.

Mutual recognition of qualifications

The mutual recognition of qualifications is an essential aspect of **freedom of establishment**, and thereby part of the wider issue of **free movement of persons** within the Union and an important component of the **Single Market**. Initially, the **European Commission** sought to make progress by bringing forward draft Directives for each of the regulated professions. This proved very slow, primarily because not only the requirements but also the ways in which professions are regulated vary from one member state to another (in the United Kingdom, many professions are self-regulating). The notorious Architects' Directive was discussed for 15 years before it was adopted in 1985. This experience led the Commission, encouraged by rulings of the **Court of Justice**, to bring forward a proposal providing for the mutual recognition of all qualifications requiring at least three years of higher education and, where appropriate, the necessary professional training. This was agreed by the **Council of Ministers** in December 1988 and covers both employed and self-employed persons (Directive 89/48, *Official Journal*, L19, 24 January 1989). It was supplemented and amplified by a second Directive in 1992 (Directive 92/51, *Official Journal*, L209, 24 July 1992). Both now apply throughout the **European Economic Area** (EEA). Further information can be obtained from the NARIC (national academic recognition information centres) network.

N

National parliaments

National parliaments have always been involved in the process of European integration if only by virtue of the fact that members of the Parliamentary Assembly of the **Council of Europe**, of the **NATO Parliamentary Assembly**, and of the **Western European Union** (WEU) Assembly are drawn from national parliaments. Until 1979, when the first **European elections** were held, this was also true of the **European Parliament**, but now only a small minority of its Members (MEPs) are at the same time members of their national parliaments (see **dual mandate**). This has given rise to a sense of rivalry between MEPs and national parliamentarians, to overcome which various means have been devised, none of them wholly successful.

Dual membership aside, national parliaments are involved in European integration in other ways. First and most obviously, government ministers both in the **European Council** and the **Council of Ministers** of the European Union and in the Committee of Ministers of the Council of Europe remain responsible to national parliaments. This responsibility involves reporting back to the national parliament after meetings of ministers, answering questions and sometimes participating in a full debate. Second, the **Treaties** establishing the **European Communities** provide for the involvement of national parliaments in the ratification of agreements reached in certain areas (most notably, any new Treaties embodying changes to the existing Treaties, changes to the system of **own resources** and **accession** agreements with non-member states). Third, the most commonly used instrument of **EU law**, the Directive, requires implementing legislation to be put before and passed by national parliaments (see **legal instruments**).

All national parliaments of the member states of the European Union have committees specializing in European affairs. In two cases (Ireland and Spain) these are joint committees of the upper and lower house. In some cases (Belgium and Germany, for example) specific provision is made for the involvement of MEPs in the work of the committee. Such committees are brought together with a group of MEPs every six months in a body known as **COSAC** (*Conférence des Organes Spécialisées dans les Affaires Communautaires*) under the presidency of the parliament of whichever country is currently holding the **presidency** of the Council. This stems from an initiative of the French National Assembly in May 1989 at the Madrid Conference of Presidents of national parliaments and of the European Parliament. COSAC meetings afford an opportunity to discuss, with the help of a report from the presidency, current major topics of European integration; a communiqué or report is normally drawn up by consensus.

Presidents of national parliaments (the British House of Commons is represented by the Speaker) and of European parliamentary assemblies meet regularly in two different bodies: the 'large' or 'full' conference, embracing representatives of the parliaments of the members of the Council of Europe, of the European Parliament and of the WEU Assembly; and the 'small' conference, confined to the member states of the European Union and the European Parliament.

The European Parliament itself has regular formal contacts at parliamentary level through Joint Committees with the parliaments of those countries linked to the Union by **Association Agreements** and through interparliamentary delegations with the parliaments of other countries including those with **Europe Agreements**. These afford an opportunity for parliamentarians to discuss anything affecting political or economic relations between the Union and its principal trading partners.

The extent to which the national parliaments of the member states of the Union can or should control or influence the overall direction of policy is much debated. At the time when all important decisions in the Council were in effect subject to the national veto under the terms of the **Luxembourg Compromise** national parliaments could be said – by virtue of the control they exercised over individual members of the Council – to control (at least in a negative sense) what the Council decided. The extension of **qualified majority voting** (QMV) since the **Single European Act** (SEA) has reduced the importance of this kind of control, which was, in any case, never more than a very blunt instrument, with a corresponding increase in fears about the so-called **democratic deficit**. The effectiveness of national parliaments' **scrutiny** procedures for the examination of law emanating from the Union varies enormously. In some countries scrutiny is at best rudimentary; in others, very rigorous. Of the latter, the most instructive example is perhaps Denmark's 'Market Committee', which can vote formally in such a fashion as to bind the Danish minister negotiating in the Council, and on occasion make it necessary for him or her to telephone Copenhagen for further instructions. Even this, however, is an essentially negative power. At almost the opposite extreme are the comprehensive, thoughtful reports by the House of Lords Select Committee on the European Union, which are influential by virtue of their accuracy and fairmindedness, not by virtue of an implicit threat.

The psychology of relations between the European Parliament and national parliaments is affected by the electoral system. In those countries (the great majority) which have always used national or regional list systems for national and European elections, the ease with which parliamentarians can move from the European Parliament to the national parliament and vice versa is much greater, with the result that any sense of rivalry is less keenly felt. This, in turn, helps political parties, at a less formal level, to foster good (or at least constructive) relations between their national and European parliamentarians.

Those with misgivings – to put it no more strongly – about the European Union continue to attach importance to finding a more extensive and powerful European role for national parliaments as the embodiments of both national and popular **sovereignty**. At their most ambitious, their ideas have included establishing a 'European Senate', a **second chamber** perhaps drawn from members of national parliaments with substantial powers of veto and amendment over all Community legislation. Unsurprisingly, the European Parliament is not enthusiastic about this idea, and it was not endorsed by the 1996–7 **Intergovernmental Conference** (IGC) on institutional reform, not least because, with the establishment of the **Committee of the Regions**, a new layer of democratic control had only just been added.

Governments, among others, will nevertheless want to continue to press the claims of national parliaments for greater European involvement, or at least appear to do so. Of particular concern to national parliaments are the two additional 'pillars' of the **Maastricht Treaty**, the one relating to **Justice and Home Affairs** (JHA), the other to **Common Foreign and Security Policy** (CFSP) and the transition to the third stage of **Economic and Monetary Union** (EMU; see **Karlsruhe judgment**). In December 1993 it was announced that the Dutch Parliament was planning to use the Danish Market Committee model (see above) as a means of exercising control over the Dutch minister in JHA. The French government has given an undertaking that it will not let a matter be decided by a vote in the Council of Ministers until the French Parliament has had an opportunity to express its views. Members of national parliaments are involved in the Convention currently preparing the 2004 Intergovernmental Conference (see **Laeken Declaration**), which is modelled on the Convention which drafted the **Charter of Fundamental Rights**.

Two **Declarations** of relevance to national parliaments were appended to the Maastricht Treaty, the one enjoining the European Parliament and national parliaments to step up 'contacts ... and the exchange of information', the other inviting governments to 'ensure ... that national parliaments receive Commission proposals for legislation in good time' and supporting the idea of further **assizes**.

A **protocol** on the role of national parliaments was annexed to the **Treaty of Amsterdam**. It lays down a six-week minimum period for JHA proposals from the Commission (from the date of submission to the date of legislative action in the Council) to give national parliaments time to consider them. Otherwise, it adds little to the Maastricht Treaty declarations. For a recent general survey, see Philip Norton (ed.), *National Parliaments and European Union* (1996). For Westminster, see Philip Giddings and Gavin Drewry (eds), *Westminster and Europe* (Basingstoke, 1996).

National representations

Each member state of the European Union maintains an embassy in Brussels, the purpose of which is to manage the country's dealings with the various institutions of the Union, most especially its direct involvement in the legislative process through the **Council of Ministers**. These bodies exercise considerable influence in decision making, not only in Brussels but in national capitals. Their task is to represent and interpret the views of the member states within the Union institutions, while communicating back to national capitals accurate and complete information on developments in Brussels as the basis for domestic policy on European issues.

These embassies are officially known as permanent representations, and are more usually referred to as national representations. Only member states have representations to the Union; the embassies of other countries accredited to the Union are known as missions. The national representations to the Union are separate from the delegations to the **North Atlantic Treaty Organization** (NATO) or the embassies to Belgium also maintained by Union member states in Brussels. The British permanent representation is known as **UKREP**.

Each of the representations is headed by a permanent representative, or ambassador, who is normally a senior official of the country's foreign ministry. The ambassadors meet together regularly in *COREPER*, the powerful committee that prepares all Council meetings and operates as a central brokerage-point in the Union's legislative process. Ambassadors or their deputies sit beside ministers in meetings of the Council, and are second in importance only to heads of government and foreign ministers in their influence on European issues.

In addition to ambassadors and their deputies, national representations are composed of administrative-grade officials, drawn from both the country's foreign ministry and domestic government departments. The overall complement of the representation depends on the size of the country, its physical proximity to Belgium and whether or not it is currently (or soon will be) occupying the **presidency** of the Council. During the six-month presidency all representations are larger than at other times.

While ambassadors and their deputies normally devote most of their time to meetings of COREPER and the full Council and to high-level communication with their foreign ministries, the day-to-day work of the national representations on most policy issues is conducted at the less senior level of counsellors and first secretaries. These mid-rank civil servants attend all working groups of the Council, reporting the details of the discussions to their domestic departments, and then trying to convert the instructions they receive back from their national capital into a series of workable negotiating positions. Their task is to identify and hold the line on the issues that matter so that they can be resolved at a higher, more political level – namely in COREPER or the full Council – and to settle purely technical questions.

There is a fundamental conflict of interest at the heart of the role that national representations play. On the one hand national representations are guided by an operational imperative within the Council to discharge its business efficiently and to resolve differences. The culture of the Council, especially since the extension of **majority voting** by the **Single European Act** (**SEA**) and the diminishing importance of the **Luxembourg Compromise**, is biased towards splitting differences and doing deals.

On the other hand, national representations know that their very *raison d'être* is to defend and advance the particular position of the individual member states. Without the clear articulation of divergent national interests, the Council would lose its essentially intergovernmental character (see **intergovernmentalism**) and become little more than an adjunct to the **European Commission**. Member states guard that role in what they perceive as both their individual and collective interests, and are keen to ensure that decisions, so far as reasonably possible, should not offend particular national sensitivities, especially their own. Individual representations that fail to acknowledge this necessity would quickly lose the confidence of their national capitals and so forfeit the ability to speak authoritatively on behalf of their ministers.

NATO Parliamentary Assembly

Founded in July 1955 as the Conference of Members of Parliament from the member countries of the **North Atlantic Treaty Organization** (NATO), the Assembly became the North Atlantic Assembly in 1966. In 1990 it changed its name to the NATO Parliamentary Assembly. It is composed of 188 parliamentarians (ministers are not eligible) from the 19 NATO countries, appointed by **national parliaments**. Associate membership has been extended to parliamentarians from countries which belong to the **North Atlantic Cooperation Council** (NACC).

The role of the Assembly, which was not provided for in the 1949 Treaty of Washington and which remains independent of NATO, is to provide a parliamentary forum for the discussion of defence and security issues, to promote mutual understanding and to strengthen parliamentary links with the countries of central and eastern Europe. The Assembly meets in plenary session twice a year in different NATO or associated countries, its committees and subcommittees more frequently. Its opinions are expressed in the form of Recommendations and Resolutions. It has a small international secretariat at its headquarters in Brussels.

Netherlands, The
See **Benelux**.

Neutrality
A neutral state is one that adopts an attitude of impartiality between belligerents. The rights and duties of neutral states were laid down in 1907 in two conventions signed in The Hague. Briefly, a neutral state must neither assist nor hinder a belligerent; its territory (including its airspace and its territorial waters) is inviolable and must be defended; it must not allow recruiting activities on behalf of the belligerents on its territory, although it is under no obligation to prevent its nationals from volunteering to fight on one side or the other; it must not trade with a belligerent, although its nationals may do so as private individuals; and although the sick and wounded of a belligerent may transit the territory of a neutral state, any active members of a belligerent state's armed forces must be interned if they enter the territory of a neutral state (special provisions apply to warships undergoing essential maintenance, reprovisioning and so on in a neutral port). Some states are permanent neutrals in respect of all armed conflicts, other states declare themselves neutral in respect of particular conflicts (as Ireland did in the Second World War). Neutrality is to be distinguished from non-belligerency, which means favouring one side in a conflict without formally taking part in it.

Neutrality is an explicit provision of the constitutions of Switzerland (since 1815), Austria (since 1955) and Malta (since 1987). Other countries, such as Sweden and Finland, are effectively neutral by virtue of a long-standing policy. Neutrality poses a problem in the context of the **Maastricht Treaty**, which lays the foundations for collective action on the part of signatory states in the fields of foreign and security policy and which holds out the possibility of there being one day a 'common defence'. Clearly, neither common defence nor a collective action could be effective if a number of states chose not to take part on the grounds of their neutral status (see **constructive absten-tion**). With the ending of the Cold War, several countries – including those mentioned above – are redefining what 'neutrality' now means. See Sheila Harden (ed.), *Neutral States and the European Community* (1993).

Noël, Emile (1922–96)

Emile Noël began his career as a European civil servant in the **Council of Europe**, where he was involved in the drafting of the abortive **European Political Community** Treaty. From 1956 to 1958 he served in the office of the Prime Minister of France, whom he represented in the negotiations that led to the **European Economic Community** (EEC) and the **European Atomic Energy Community** (Euratom) in 1957. In 1958 he became secretary-general of the **European Commission** under its President, **Walter Hallstein**. Nine years later, with the entry into force of the **Merger Treaty**, he became secretary-general of the Commission serving all three Communities, a post he retained until his retirement in 1987. He was involved in the Commission's 1975 report on European Union and in the negotiations that led to the 1986 **Single European Act** (SEA). From 1987 until 1994 Noël was Principal of the **European University Institute**.

'Non-Europe'

A term made current by the 1988 **Cecchini Report** on the **Single Market**, 'non-Europe' means the fragmentation of the market in such areas as public procurement, telecommunications, building materials and product standards. The fragmentation, it was believed, could be costed ('the cost of non-Europe'), and to this end the Commission published a series of 13 sector-by-sector reports carried out by independent consultants. These reports provided the intellectual underpinning of the Single Market programme.

Non-paper

A non-paper is a discussion document on a matter of current controversy, put forward by a member state or an institution of the European Union but not embodying the formal position of that state or institution on the matter. Normally, the purpose of a non-paper is to test the reaction of other parties. Non-papers, circulated informally, may often serve, especially at the level of the **national representations**, to resolve issues that by virtue of their complexity or sensitivity cannot easily be settled in the more open and formal context of meetings of the **Council of Ministers** or the **European Council**.

Non-tariff barriers

A non-tariff barrier is an obstacle to trade arising not from the imposition of tariffs, levies or quantitative restrictions (quotas) but from different product specifications, discriminatory public purchasing policies, restrictive pricing or distribution agreements, patent or copyright difficulties, major discrepancies in the tax structure and so on (see Dennis Swann, *The Economics of Europe*, 9th edn, Harmondsworth, 2000). The establishment of the **customs union** in 1968 effectively removed tariffs, levies and quotas from **intra-Community trade**, and the need to remove non-tariff barriers was the prime purpose of the **Single Market** programme (1992). Non-tariff barriers afford many means of resorting to covert protectionism and their removal is also a priority for other bodies committed to free trade, such as the **Organization for Economic Cooperation and Development** (OECD) and the **World Trade Organization** (WTO).

Nordic Council

The five countries that participate in the Nordic Council – Denmark, Finland, Iceland, Norway and Sweden – have a long history of contact of various kinds: as colonies or possessions of each other, as unions brought about by conquest or intermarriage and as trading partners. Norway, a Danish possession until 1814, gained its independence from Sweden in 1905; Finland, formerly Swedish, was a Grand Duchy within the Russian Empire and became independent in 1917; Iceland secured dominion status under the Danish Crown in 1918 and independence in 1944. Denmark, Norway and Sweden established the Nordic Interparliamentary Union in 1907, and in 1919 the Norden Association, a private body, was set up to promote cultural contacts. In 1938 the Danish Foreign Minister proposed the creation of a Nordic Council but the idea was not taken up until after the Second World War. In the late 1940s unsuccessful attempts were made to establish both a Nordic Customs Union and a Nordic Defence Union; progress was made with a Passport Union (completed in 1958). In 1951, at the suggestion of the Danish Prime Minister, the Nordic Interparliamentary Union endorsed the idea of a Nordic Council, and by the end of 1952 the parliaments of Denmark, Iceland, Norway and Sweden had approved an agreement establishing the institutions of the Council and defining the scope of cooperation between the signatory states; because of Soviet hostility Finland did not join until 1955.

The Nordic Council consists of 87 parliamentary representatives: 20 chosen by each of the national parliaments of Denmark, Finland, Norway and Sweden, and 7 from Iceland. They are joined by an unspecified number of ministerial representatives, who have no voting rights. Special provision is made within the Danish delegation for representatives of the autonomous communities of **Greenland** and the **Faeroes** and within the Finnish delegation for the Åland Islands. The Council has six standing committees, but meets in plenary session only twice a year, the signatory states taking turns to host the meetings and act as president. Votes are taken by simple majority, but on measures affecting particular states only the representatives from those states may vote. Decisions, in the form of Recommendations, are communicated to the governments.

In 1962 the Nordic Council was given more formal status with the signing of a Treaty in Helsinki. The areas for cooperation were defined but not extended: juridical matters, cultural contacts, social security and communications (including passport union). With the revision of the Helsinki Treaty in 1971 came the establishment of a Nordic Council of Ministers, with a secretariat in Copenhagen, and a small permanent secretariat in Stockholm for the Nordic Council itself. The revised Treaty specified once again the areas in which the signatory states would cooperate: communications and transport, cultural matters, economic policy, juridical and social affairs; the protection of the environment was added three years later.

Since 1974 all five governments have had ministers specifically responsible for coordination through the Nordic Council of Ministers and who attend the meetings. Regular contact is maintained between government departments at official level in 14 specialist committees. The Nordic Council of Ministers oversees the work of the Nordic Investment Bank, the Nordic Fund for Technology and Industrial Development, the Nordic Cultural Fund and a number of joint development projects in the Third World. It provides the forum through which the five governments can coordinate their positions in other international bodies.

In recent years, the Nordic Council has established links with all the states bordering the Baltic Sea and has encouraged the **Baltic states** to set up their own machinery for cooperation. North of the Arctic Circle in the Barents Sea formal contacts have also been established at the regional level with Russia.

Although well established and with substantial achievements to its credit, the machinery of Nordic cooperation has proved inadequate in certain respects. Determined efforts to establish a Nordic Economic Union came to nothing: a customs union was achieved only within the **European Free Trade Association** (EFTA) in 1960; security coordination has been limited to discussion of a Nordic 'nuclear-free zone'; and the attempt to address the cultural, legal and technical challenges of satellite broadcasting failed almost entirely. Nordic cooperation is sometimes put forward as a model for wider European cooperation as an alternative to the more ambitious, supranational, legislation-based model followed by the European Community. Its limitations, however, are clear, in spite of the advantages the Nordic countries enjoy by virtue of a substantial degree of cultural, linguistic and economic homogeneity. The background to Nordic cooperation is well set out in Øystein Sørensen and Bo Stråth (eds), *The Cultural Construction of Norden* (Oslo, 1997).

North Atlantic Cooperation Council (NACC)

At a **summit** meeting of the **North Atlantic Treaty Organization** (NATO) in Rome in November 1991 agreement was reached on the establishment of the NACC. The purpose was to create a forum in which the member states of NATO could discuss and coordinate their positions on security issues with the countries of central and eastern Europe and the **Baltic states** without giving them immediate membership of NATO, in the light of NATO's changing role. By March 1996 the NACC had 40 members (16 NATO members, Albania, Bulgaria, the Czech Republic, Georgia, Hungary, Macedonia, Poland, Romania, Slovakia, Slovenia, the 3 Baltic states, and 11 CIS states). Full meetings of the NACC are normally held as an adjunct to the autumn meeting of NATO ministers (i.e., the North Atlantic Council). On 9 May 1994 the Council of Ministers of the **Western European Union** (WEU) agreed to extend 'Associate status' to six countries of central and eastern Europe and to the three Baltic states.

In 1997 the NACC was succeeded by a new Euro-Atlantic Partnership Council (EAPC) embracing both NACC activities and those covered by NATO's **Partnership for Peace** programme. The first meeting of the Council was in Sintra, Portugal, on 30 May 1997. EAPC membership includes all NACC and Partner states.

North Atlantic Treaty Organization (NATO)

On 17 March 1948 Belgium, France, Luxembourg, the Netherlands and the United Kingdom signed a 50-year agreement on economic, social and cultural collaboration and collective self-defence known as the **Brussels Treaty**. Three months later the beginning of the Berlin blockade marked a further deterioration in relations between the United States and the Soviet Union, and on 6 July 1948 talks began in Washington between the United States, Canada and the Brussels Treaty powers on a new collective security alliance to be known as the North Atlantic Treaty Organization (NATO) and covering the whole of the North Atlantic area. Formal negotiations began on 10 December 1948 and the draft Treaty was published three months later. Five more countries (Denmark, Iceland, Italy, Norway and Portugal) were invited to sign the Treaty, and – in spite of opposition from the Soviet Union, which claimed that the Treaty was contrary to the United Nations Charter – the signing ceremony took place on 4 April 1949. The Treaty entered into force on 24 August 1949. Greece and Turkey joined NATO in 1952, West Germany in 1955 and Spain in 1982 (confirmed by referendum on 12 March 1986). The headquarters of NATO and its various organs were initially in France, but with the withdrawal of France from NATO's integrated military structure in 1966 the headquarters were transferred to Brussels and the NATO Defence College was moved to Rome. The Spanish referendum on NATO membership of 1986 resulted in Spain also withdrawing from the integrated military structure.

The NATO Treaty contains only 14 articles. The commitment to collective security is in Article 5:

The Parties agree that an armed attack against one or more of them in Europe or North America shall be considered an attack against them all, and consequently they agree that, if such an armed attack occurs, each of them, in exercise of the right of individual or collective self-defence recognized by Article 51 of the Charter of the United Nations, will assist the Party or Parties so attacked by taking forthwith, individually, and in concert with the other Parties, such action as it deems necessary, including the use of armed force, to restore and maintain the security of the North Atlantic area.

On 2 October 2001 the North Atlantic Council decided that since the 11 September 2001 attack on the World Trade Center in New York was 'directed from abroad', it was covered by Article 5.

Article 6 defines the 'NATO area' as the territory of any of the signatory states in Europe or North America, the territory of Turkey and 'the islands under the jurisdiction [of any of the signatory states] in the North Atlantic area north of the Tropic of Cancer'. Russia has with great reluctance accepted that central and eastern European countries may join NATO as full members, and the Czech Republic, Hungary and Poland joined in 1999 (see below).

The principal civilian decision-making bodies are the North Atlantic Council (foreign ministers), the Defence Planning Committee (defence ministers) and the Nuclear Planning Group (defence ministers). All three bodies meet regularly at permanent representative (ambassador) level. The Military Committee, the highest military authority in the alliance, is composed for the most part of Chiefs of Staff. In addition, NATO has a staff of international civil servants headed by a secretary-general, and an international military staff (see also **Supreme Headquarters Allied Powers Europe**). A measure of democratic supervision is provided by the **NATO Parliamentary Assembly** which was founded in 1955 and meets in plenary session twice a year. It is composed of 188 members of **national parliaments** sitting in national delegations.

Various means were established within NATO to allow the European members to work together on specifically European security issues. The **Eurogroup**, never formally part of NATO, was an association of European defence ministers (except those of France and Iceland) holding regular meetings alongside full meetings of the alliance. Similarly, the **Independent European Programme Group** was a forum designed to promote all forms of cooperation among European NATO members in the field of the design, manufacture and supply of military equipment. The work of both groups has now been largely taken over by the **Western European Union** (WEU) as the body responsible for providing the organizational and operational nucleus for the European Union's growing involvement in security issues under the **Maastricht Treaty** (see **Common Foreign and Security Policy**).

The end of the Cold War prompted a reappraisal of NATO's role and structure, accompanied by cuts in national defence budgets. Since the NATO summit in Rome in November 1991 the organization has concentrated upon developing relations with the countries of central and eastern Europe, including the former Soviet Union (see **North Atlantic Cooperation Council, Partnership for Peace**), and defining for itself a broader peacekeeping and humanitarian role with the aid of an **Allied Command Europe Rapid Reaction Corps**. Legal difficulties remain, however, in the way of deploying NATO forces 'out of area' even in defence of NATO countries' extra-territorial interests.

The NATO summit of January 1994 confirmed that membership of the alliance remained open in principle to other European countries, and endorsed the concept of Combined Joint Task Forces (CJTF). The CJTFs would operate broadly within the NATO framework, but the possibility of involving forces from non-NATO countries would be left open. At a meeting in Prague (November 2002), it was decided to invite the Baltic States, Bulgaria, Romania, Slovakia and Slovenia (all of them CJTF participants) to join NATO.

The many recent changes to NATO's structure are very clearly set out in the 50th anniversary edition of the *NATO Handbook* (1998). See also Ted Galen Carpenter (ed.), *NATO Enters the 21st Century* (2001).

Norway

Norway was a founder member of the **North Atlantic Treaty Organization** (NATO), the **European Free Trade Association** (EFTA) and the **Council of Europe**. In 1962 and again in 1967 Norway applied for membership of the European Community and in response to the second application a draft Treaty of Accession was successfully negotiated. However, in September 1972 53.6 per cent of the voters opposed entry in a referendum.

In common with other EFTA states, Norway has had a free trade agreement with the Community since 1973 and in May 1992 became a signatory to the agreement establishing a **European Economic Area** (EEA). In spite of this high level of economic integration with the Community the Labour government of Mrs Gro Harlem Brundtland took the view – prompted by the fact that Austria, Sweden and Finland had already applied for membership – that once again Norway should seek to join the Community. The application was forwarded to the Council on 25 November 1992 and the generally favourable **Opinion** of the **European Commission** was given the following year (*Bulletin of the European Communities*, supplement 2/93). The Commission noted the extent to which Norway had already adapted to the *acquis communautaire* in several fields and the contribution that Norway could make by virtue of its healthy economic performance and record of achievement in environmental protection and Third World development. The Union is Norway's principal trading partner with energy exports assuming great importance. Norway, with one of the largest merchant fleets in the world, is particularly interested in the development of a maritime policy. Negotiations with Norway were completed in March 1994.

Membership of the Union proved to be still controversial in Norway, especially in rural areas. Emotionally, the people remain attached to independence (gained from Sweden in 1905) and to Nordic cooperation (Norway has always been active in the **Nordic Council**), and to many Norwegians most countries of the Union seem very remote. Church groups campaigned against the Union on the grounds that the breaking of the state monopoly on alcoholic drinks would lead to alcoholism and other social evils. Although the two main parties were officially in favour of membership, the Norwegian people rejected membership of the Union by 52.5 per cent to 47.5 per cent in a **referendum** held on 28 November 1994.

'Nouvelles Frontières' case

The 'Nouvelles Frontières' case (*Ministre Public* v *Asjes*, Cases 209–13/84) resulted from a challenge to the French Civil Aviation Code by a French travel agency, which queried the compatibility of the price-fixing arrangements in the Code with the **competition policy** provisions of the **Treaty of Rome**. In April 1986 the **Court of Justice** ruled that the competition provisions did apply and clarified the powers of the **European Commission** to enforce them. The case was an important step in the attempts to extend competition rules to air transport (see **common transport policy**).

O

'Occupied field'

An 'occupied field' is an area of policy in which the European Union is capable, under the **Treaties**, of taking legislative action. It may not have taken action, but the fact that it could may inhibit national authorities from acting independently, since **EU law** enjoys **primacy** over national law in member states.

An example of this occurred in relation to seat-belts in motor coaches. Two serious accidents in the United Kingdom involving coaches led to calls for all passenger-seats to be equipped with seat belts. This matter, in common with other technical specifications for coaches, is part of the broader issue of transport safety and as such is covered by Article 71.1(c) of the **Treaty of Rome**. It also relates to the **Single Market** requirement for common rules in respect of type-approval for motor vehicles, and is therefore also covered by **Article 95**. At the time of the accidents no action on seat-belts in coaches had been taken at Community level, but the **European Commission** was known to have considered the question and was quite clearly empowered under the Treaty to make a proposal. The British government therefore had to choose between taking unilateral action in advance of a Union-wide agreement, thereby running the risk of involving coach manufacturers and coach operators in two sets of costly changes, and awaiting such an agreement. Given the length of time it can take to reach agreement, one consequence of the 'occupied field' can be that years pass before any action is taken at all.

Odysseus programme

Based on the Sherlock programme (*Official Journal*, L287, 8 November 1996), the Odysseus programme was established by Joint Action 98/244 of 19 March 1998 (*Official Journal*, L99, 31 March 1998) to provide a framework for training, study and the exchange of information for officials of member states involved in questions of **asylum** and immigration.

Office for Harmonization in the Internal Market
See **Community trade mark**.

Official Journal

The *Official Journal of the European Communities*, normally referred to as the OJ, is published almost daily throughout most of the year in three distinct series and in all official **languages**. The 'L' (Legislation) series contains the texts of all legislative acts of the Communities, including **Decisions** taken by representatives of the governments of member states. The 'C' series (Communications) contains a wide range of other material (some of it only in the electronic or 'CE' series), including the texts of legislative proposals from the **European Commission, Opinions** thereon delivered by other institutions, lists of cases brought before the **Court of Justice**, key extracts from judgments of the Court, the daily value of the **euro** expressed in the currencies of the member states not belonging to the euro-zone, and appointments to Union bodies. The minutes of sittings of the **European Parliament** are also published in the 'C' series, the verbatim report of proceedings in an Annex. Since 1978 there has also been an OJ 'S' (supplement) series, concerned mainly with invitations to tender for public works contracts (see **public purchasing**) both within the **European Economic Area** and in countries eligible for aid from the **European Development Fund**. This is now only available electronically (Tenders Electronic Daily – TED) or by subscription on CD-ROM. Also available is a two-part monthly index to the OJ and an annual cumulative index. The OJ is published by the Office for Official Publications in Luxembourg and is available in the United Kingdom through the Stationery Office.

Publication of legislative acts in the OJ is an essential procedural requirement. Article 254 EC specifically provides for Regulations and Directives (see **legal instruments**) addressed to all member states to be published in the OJ and for them to enter into force 'on the date specified in them or ... on the twentieth day following their publication'. Care is taken to ensure that the date of publication of each issue of the OJ is, in fact, the date upon which the issue is actually available in all the official languages from the Office for Official Publications.

Ombudsman

The institution generally known as the Ombudsman is of Scandinavian origin (the first Ombudsman was appointed in Sweden in 1809). The Ombudsman acts as an intermediary between the citizen and the public authorities, local or national. Only a minority of European countries have an ombudsman, and the exact title is subject to many variations: in the United Kingdom, the

Ombudsman is known as the Parliamentary Commissioner for Administration, in France, simply as the *Médiateur*. The precise duties of the Ombudsman also vary, but broadly speaking they are directed towards the investigation of complaints brought by individuals against the authorities. The Ombudsman is required to be both impartial and independent of government.

The idea that there might be a European Community Ombudsman was first put forward in the 1970s, but it was not until the 1991 **Maastricht Treaty** that the matter was finally agreed. The Maastricht Treaty introduced a new Article 138(e) (now 195) into the **Treaty of Rome**, requiring the **European Parliament** to 'appoint an Ombudsman empowered to receive complaints from any citizen of the Union or any natural or legal person residing or having its registered office in a Member State concerning instances of maladministration in the activities of the Community institutions or bodies, with the exception of the **Court of Justice** and the Court of First Instance acting in their judicial role'. The use of the word 'maladministration' to describe the subject of the Ombudsman's investigations means that within the Community institutions the remit is similar to that of the Ombudsman in the United Kingdom. 'Maladministration' covers both incompetence (undue delay, failure to follow agreed procedures, etc.) and deliberate wrong-doing (see *Official Journal*, L113, 4 May 1994).

First elected in 1995, the Ombudsman may make investigations either on his own initiative or on the basis of complaints brought to his attention, either directly or through a Member of the European Parliament (MEP), except in relation to matters that are or have been the subject of legal proceedings. The Ombudsman has no powers of sanction. The results of his investigations are forwarded to the European Parliament and the institution concerned. His five-year term of office coincides with that of the European Parliament and he may be dismissed only by the Court of Justice at the request of the Parliament. He is required to submit to the Parliament an annual report 'on the outcome of his inquiries'.

A new Ombudsman, Nikiforos Diamondouros, took up his duties in April 2003. His office is in Strasbourg. In 2000 the Ombudsman received over 1,700 complaints, only a quarter of which proved admissible. Most of these alleged maladministration on the part of the **European Commission.**

Open method of coordination

First defined at the Lisbon meeting of the **European Council** in March 2000 (see Presidency conclusions, paragraphs 37 to 40), the open method of coordination is 'designed to help Member States to progressively develop their own policies'. It entails fixing guidelines, accompanied by timetables;

establishing indicators and benchmarks 'as a means of comparing best practice'; adjusting the guidelines so that they can be transposed to and applied at the national and regional level; and setting up systems for 'periodic monitoring, evaluation and peer review'. National, regional and local authorities as well as the social partners and civil society are consulted as part of the method, in line with the principle of **subsidiarity**. The open method of coordination is especially well adapted to policy-making in those areas in which responsibility is shared between the Union's institutions and those of member states. It is a particular feature of the **European Social Agenda** and is an important element in **European governance**.

Openness
See **transparency**.

Opinion
In the context of the European Union, 'Opinion' (the French word *avis* is sometimes used) has several distinct meanings:

1 The procedures in the **Treaty of Rome** for consulting the **European Parliament** empower it to give Opinions on the draft legislation referred to it. The Opinion is not only the resolution adopted in plenary session but also the suggested amendments to the draft in question. The expression *avis conforme* is used to denote one of that special category of Opinions given under the **assent procedure**: for example, on draft Treaties of **Accession** (see **enlargement**). The indispensability of the Parliament's Opinions in the Union's legislative process was established by the **isoglucose case**.

2 Within the Parliament, if a committee other than the one primarily responsible for preparing a report on a piece of draft legislation wants to contribute to the Parliament's consideration of the matter, it does this in the form of an Opinion.

3 Both the **Economic and Social Committee** and the **Committee of the Regions** are also entitled to give Opinions on draft legislation referred to them.

4 Under Article 249 EC Opinions are listed as one of the types of legislative act that may be delivered by the **Council of Ministers** or the **European Commission** (see **legal instruments**). However, unlike Regulations, Directives or Decisions, neither Recommendations nor Opinions are binding. See also **reasoned opinion**.

5 More importantly, under Article 49 of the **Maastricht Treaty** the Commission is required to give its Opinion before negotiations on accession can proceed with an applicant state (see **enlargement**).

6 In the **Court of Justice** the function of an **advocate-general** is to give an Opinion upon the basis of which the Court reaches its final judgment. Less commonly used is the procedure under Article 300.6 EC, which allows the Council, the Commission or a member state to seek the Opinion of the Court on the compatibility between the Treaty and an agreement that the Union proposes to conclude with a non-member state or an international organization. Such Opinions are binding (see **European Economic Area** for a recent example).

7 Under Article 248.4 EC the **Court of Auditors** may also deliver Opinions at the request of one of the other institutions.

8 The **European Central Bank** (ECB) may deliver Opinions (Article 110 EC), as may the **Economic and Financial Committee** (Article 114.2 EC).

9 Both the Coordinating Committee provided for in Article 36 TEU and the **Political and Security Committee** may deliver Opinions (see **Justice and Home Affairs, Common Foreign and Security Policy**).

Opt-out

A member state of the European Union that chooses not to participate in a Union activity covered by Treaty provisions is said to have an 'opt-out'. For example, Ireland and the United Kingdom have an opt-out from the arrangements on frontier controls which have been **communitized** by the **Treaty of Amsterdam**. An opt-out is formalized in a **protocol** to the Treaty in question. A Union characterized by member states opting out from particular activities would be one of **variable geometry** or **Europe à la carte**. See also **flexibility**.

Organization for Economic Cooperation and Development (OECD)

The OECD is a Paris-based intergovernmental organization (see **intergovernmentalism**) established to promote economic cooperation between industrialized states, to coordinate development assistance to the Third World and to provide a forum for the resolution of problems affecting world trade and economic growth. The OECD was founded as the Organization for European Economic Cooperation (OEEC) in 1948 to oversee the implementation of the European Recovery Programme established under the **Marshall Plan**. The founding members were Austria, Belgium, Denmark, France, Greece, Iceland, Ireland, Italy, Luxembourg, the Netherlands, Norway, Portugal, Sweden, Turkey, the United Kingdom, and the British, French and American zones of occupied Germany. The Federal Republic of Germany joined the OEEC in 1949, and the United States and Canada became associate members in 1950. Spain joined the OEEC in 1959. The OEEC had a small international secretariat but was intergovernmental in character: all important decisions were taken by a Council, which could act only by unanimity (abstentions not counted), each member state having one vote.

Among the first achievements of the OEEC was a European Payments Union, which allowed member states to settle their bilateral trading accounts on a multilateral basis through the **Bank for International Settlements** and was able to extend credit to economies in temporary difficulties. The OEEC was the forum in which **the Six** began the discussions that led to the **Messina Conference** and the **Treaty of Rome**. At the same time the United Kingdom sought to establish a **free trade area** among the OEEC states, but once the Six had established the more ambitious **European Economic Community** (EEC) the United Kingdom and its partners had to be content with a rival organization, the **European Free Trade Association** (EFTA), composed of Austria, Denmark, Norway, Portugal, Sweden, Switzerland and the United Kingdom (see **Maudling Committee**).

The EEC/EFTA division effectively split the OEEC. It was refounded and renamed with the United States and Canada as full members under the OECD Convention signed in Paris in December 1960. At the same time the scope of the organization was widened to include relations with developing countries, but its intergovernmental character remained unchanged. The OECD retains its importance in the field of international economic cooperation, and its reports on member countries' economic performance are authoritative and influential. Japan joined the OECD in 1964, Finland in 1969, Australia in 1971 and New Zealand in 1973. The OECD has also fostered the setting up of other organizations, such as the International Energy Agency and the **Group of Seven** (G7) leading industrialized economies. The OECD works very closely wherever necessary with the **European Commission**, for example, on development issues through the Development Assistance Committee. It was OECD member states (meeting as the Group of 24) that founded the **European Bank for Reconstruction and Development** in May 1990. The Czech Republic, Hungary, Korea, Mexico, Poland and Slovakia are now also members, bringing the total to 30 states.

The OECD Council, like its OEEC predecessor, can take decisions that are binding on member states and can make recommendations. The OECD can enter into agreements with non-member states and international organizations. However, unlike the European Union, the OECD has no supranational machinery for the resolution of disputes or the enforcement of decisions, nor do its workings create a body of law enjoying **primacy** over national law. It also lacks a parliamentary body responsible for general supervision of its activities.

There is an account of the political and economic background to the founding of OEEC in Alan Milward, *The Reconstruction of Western Europe 1945–1951* (1984). The OECD itself publishes many reports and studies.

Organization for European Economic Cooperation (OEEC)

The forerunner of the **Organization for Economic Cooperation and Development**.

Organization for Security and Cooperation in Europe (OSCE)

The OSCE, set up under the **Charter of Paris** of November 1990, is based on an earlier, looser organization which was responsible for the 1975 **Helsinki Final Act** and which is described under **Conference on Security and Cooperation in Europe** (CSCE). Membership of the OSCE includes virtually every European country, the central Asian republics once part of the USSR, the United States and Canada (55 states over a territory from Vancouver to Vladivostok).

Decision-making is the responsibility of a Senior Council, made up of foreign ministers, assisted by a Permanent Council which meets weekly at ambassador level and a Forum for Security Cooperation. The CSCE has its own secretariat, operating in Vienna since 1993, a Representative on Freedom of the Media, also based in Vienna, the Office for Democratic Institutions and Human Rights (formerly the Office for Free Elections) in Warsaw and a High Commissioner on National Minorities in The Hague. The CSCE also has its own Parliamentary Assembly, which met for the first time in Budapest in July 1992, and has its own secretariat in Copenhagen. Under a 1992 Convention the OSCE also has a Court of Conciliation and Arbitration in Geneva for the resolution of disputes between countries signatory to the Convention. The OSCE's budget for 2001 was €209.3 million, 84 per cent of which was spent on missions and field activities. These new institutions underline the shift that took place in Paris from securing new commitments in respect of human rights, open markets, democratic institutions and disarmament to ensuring that commitments already entered into are honoured.

The European Union is not represented as such in the OSCE. However, the Helsinki Final Act of 1975 was signed by Aldo Moro in his capacity as President-in-Office of the **Council of Ministers**, and the Paris Charter was signed by **Jacques Delors** as President of the **European Commission**. The position taken by the member states of the Union in the CSCE is now discussed as part of the **Common Foreign and Security Policy** (CFSP) and in meetings of the **European Council**.

All parties to the Charter of Paris are agreed on the need to make the conflict-prevention and dispute-settlement machinery more effective. The crisis in Yugoslavia underlined the weakness of machinery that is backed neither by military force nor by the threat of economic sanctions, and the difficulty of maintaining the credibility of an intergovernmental organization required to operate on the basis of consensus. An OSCE Charter on Security in Europe was agreed in November 1999. This allows conflicts which threaten to destabilize a whole region no longer to be considered the internal affair of a particular state (see also **Pact on Stability in Europe**).

Organized crime

At the meeting of the **European Council** in Dublin (13–14 December 1996) it was decided to set up a High Level Group on Organized Crime as an adjunct to the machinery for cooperation on **Justice and Home Affairs** (JHA) matters. The High Level Group submitted an action plan of 15 political guidelines and 30 specific recommendations to the Amsterdam meeting of the European Council six months later (16–17 June 1997). The European Council invited the **Council of Ministers** to 'take the necessary measures to implement the Plan'. The Plan sought to strike a balance between harmonizing the relevant national legal provisions and procedures, and intensifying cooperation between member states. The Plan also drew attention to the need to cooperate with neighbouring states, especially the applicant states (see **enlargement**). One of the main obstacles is that there is no agreed common definition of what constitutes 'organized crime': in some countries, proof of conspiracy is sufficient; in others, mere conspiracy is not in itself a crime and an alleged 'organization' has to do something (even if only open a bank account) before it can be shown to exist. The member states of the Union and the 11 applicant states adopted a pre-accession pact on organized crime in May 1998.

Other measures taken against organized crime include the Directive against money-laundering (June 1991), conventions on **extradition** between the member states (March 1995 and September 1996), on **Europol**, and **joint actions** on drugs (November and December 1996) and on trade in human beings and the sexual exploitation of children (February 1997). The **Falcone programme** (named after one of the Mafia's most prominent victims) provides money from the **Budget** for training officials engaged in law enforcement. The **Treaty of Amsterdam** reworded Article 2 of the **Maastricht Treaty** to make preventing and combating crime, 'organized or otherwise', one of the means whereby 'a high level of safety, within an **area of freedom, security and justice**' is to be achieved (see also *espace judiciaire européenne*). In December 1999 the Council's Multidisciplinary Working Group on Organized Crime published a report on *The Prevention and Control of Organized Crime* containing 36 recommendations.

A Draft Convention on **Mutual Assistance in Criminal Matters** between the member states of the European Union has been drawn up, building on a 1959 **Council of Europe** Convention, and preparations are in hand for a similar Convention providing for closer cooperation between customs authorities. The background to these developments and a full text of the Draft Convention may be found in a House of Lords report of February 1998, *Mutual Assistance in Criminal Matters*.

Overseas countries and territories (OCTs)

The OCT are the scattered remains, most of them very small islands, of the British, French and Dutch overseas possessions. Part IV of the **Treaty of Rome** sets out the legal framework for the association of the OCTs with the European Community, the purpose of which is 'to promote the economic and social development of the countries and territories and to establish close economic relations between them and the Community as a whole' (Article 182). **Greenland** is now also counted among the OCTs.

The OCTs may be listed in four groups:

1 *British* OCTs in the Caribbean: Anguilla, Bermuda, the British Virgin Islands, the Cayman Islands, Montserrat, the Turks and Caicos Islands; in the south Atlantic: the Falkland Islands, Saint Helena and its dependencies, South Georgia and the South Sandwich Islands; in the Pacific: Pitcairn; British Antarctic Territory; British Indian Ocean Territory.

2 *French* OCTs in the Pacific: French Polynesia, New Caledonia and its dependencies, Wallis and Futuna Islands; French Southern and Antarctic Territories. French OCTs also include the 'territorial collectivities' of Mayotte off the coast of Madagascar, and St Pierre and Miquelon (Newfoundland). The French overseas departments (Réunion, Guadeloupe, Guiana and Martinique) are an integral part of France and so of the European Union. They benefit from various forms of special assistance under Article 299.2, together with Madeira, the Azores, and the Canary Islands.

3 *Dutch* OCTs in the Caribbean: Aruba, the Netherlands Antilles.

4 *Danish* OCT Greenland.

Not only are the OCTs extremely diverse in respect of geography, resources, climate, population, population density and prosperity, but the provisions governing their status in relation to the European Union (and hence the applicability of **EU law**) also vary from one OCT to another, even among those historically associated with the same member state. In general terms EU law is applicable only to member states' European territory, not to their OCTs. However, member states apply to their trade with the OCTs the same treatment as they apply to each other, and the OCTs apply to every member state the treatment applied to the state with which they have special relations. Moreover, since citizens of the Danish, Dutch and French OCTs (and of the Falkland Islands among British OCTs) are nationals of the parent country, they are also citizens of the European Union (see **citizenship**).

Two problems in particular are of concern to the OCTs: **freedom of establishment** and **free movement of persons**. With respect to the first, Article 176 of Council Decision 86/223 (30 June 1986) enjoins the OCTs not to discriminate on the basis of nationality between Community firms or individuals wishing to invest or become established in an OCT. With respect to the second, Article 186 EC provides for freedom of movement between the OCTs and the member states to be the subject of a decision requiring unanimous agreement. No such decision has so far been reached, nor any measure been taken to clarify the legal situation in the member states of workers from an OCT, or in the OCTs of workers from a member state.

Underlying many of these legal and commercial issues is the broader question of whether or not the OCTs should enjoy a privileged relationship with the Union. At the very least, it would be illogical were their position to be less advantageous than that of **ACP states** countries, the great majority of which are former colonies that have opted for independence. Accordingly, the Union takes care to ensure that the periodic renegotiations of the principal trade-and-aid instruments do not result in the OCTs being left behind, and as far as possible the OCTs' interests are taken into account in decisions on the **Common Commercial Policy** and on the **European Development Fund** (EDF). In the course of the negotiations which led to the Cotonou Agreement it was decided that €175 million should be set aside for the OCTs over the period 2000–7. OCTs are also eligible for loans from the **European Investment Bank** (EIB).

Own resources

The revenue of the European Union, as defined by the **Council of Ministers** in Decisions of 21 April 1970 and 24 June 1988 (see below), is known as 'own resources' to distinguish it from the contributions made by member states to finance the **Budget** before the 1970 Decision, and to underline the fact that under the terms of this Decision certain revenues accrue to the Union as of right.

Article 201 (since revised; now 269) of the **Treaty of Rome** made provision for the contributions of member states to be replaced by a system of 'own resources'. The 1970 Decision established three sources of revenue: agricultural levies, customs duties and up to 1 per cent of national revenue from

value-added tax (VAT) applied to a uniform base. The Budget was to be financed from these sources of revenue with effect from 1 January 1975, but delays in the adoption and implementation of measures necessary to establish the uniform VAT base (the Sixth VAT Directive) meant that the new system was not introduced until the 1980 financial year. In a Council Decision of 7 May 1985 the VAT limit was raised from 1 per cent to 1.4 per cent. By 1987, however, it was clear that revenue was inadequate to finance existing policies and new policies laid down in the **Single European Act** (SEA) of 1986, not least because of the 'shrinkage' in the revenue drawn from customs duties and agricultural levies as a consequence of tariff cuts and of concessionary trade agreements. Accordingly, the **European Commission** submitted a set of proposals (the 'Delors package') that, *inter alia*, provided for a fourth 'own resource'. These proposals were discussed at meetings of the **European Council** in Brussels in June 1987 and February 1988. The new system of own resources was set out in Decision 88/376 (24 June 1988, *Official Journal*, L185, 15 July 1988), which came into force on 1 February 1989 with retroactive effect from 1 January 1988 (see **future financing**). A major British preoccupation in the negotiations leading up to the June 1988 Decision was, of course, the maintenance of the special arrangements for the United Kingdom contained in the **Fontainebleau Agreement**.

The Decision of 24 June 1988 set out four types of revenue. The percentages indicate the contribution which each source of revenue made to the 2001 Budget:

1 **Common External Tariff** (CET) duties and duties on products covered by the **European Coal and Steel Community** (ECSC) Treaty (13.3 per cent);
2 agricultural levies on trade with non-member countries, together with duties on sugar and isoglucose produced in the member states (2.1 per cent);
3 a portion (initially 1.4 per cent) of each member state's VAT revenue as applied to an assessment base 'determined in a uniform manner according to Community rules' (36.2 per cent);
4 a contribution from each member state related to its gross national product (GNP) at a rate determined annually in the light of the overall budgetary situation (46.7 per cent).

With respect to resources 1 and 2, member states were allowed to retain 10 per cent of the revenue to cover the costs of collection (this increased to 25 per cent in 2001). With respect to resource 3, the Decision specified that the uniform base for the assessment of VAT should not exceed 55 per cent of any member state's GNP. This safeguards the interests of poorer countries, since revenue from VAT, as a turnover tax, is not an accurate indicator of relative wealth. The limit is now 50 per cent for all member states.

For the first time, the Own Resources Decision provided for an overall limit on own resources, expressed as a percentage (1.27 per cent in 2000) of the Union's total GNP (see **budgetary discipline**). By introducing a fourth GNP-related resource the new system placed the Budget on a reasonably secure footing. But as the Union assumes new responsibilities – especially in eastern Europe – it is difficult to see how the question of new own resources can be left unresolved. Various proposals have been made, including one for a tax on hydrocarbons (which would, of course, tie in with the Union's policies for the environment), and at least in some quarters it has been suggested that eventually the Union should receive some of its revenue directly from the taxpayer. The 1977 **MacDougall Report** said that if the Budget were to have any substantial redistributive effect, it would need to rise to between 5 and 7 per cent of the gross domestic product (GDP). Since 1988 there have been two further own resources Decisions: Decision 94/728 of 31 October 1994 (*Official Journal*, L293, 12 November 1994) under which the VAT base was limited to 50 per cent for all member states from 1999; and Decision 00/597 of 29 September 2000 (*Official Journal*, L253, 7 October 2000) under which the maximum call-in rate for VAT was reduced to 0.75 per cent for 2002 and 2003 and to 0.5 per cent from 2004 and the contributions of Germany, Austria, The Netherlands and Sweden to the British rebate were reduced by 25 per cent.

The system of own resources sets the European Union apart from other international organizations and is an important symbol of its independence from member states. Because of its sensitivity, it is an area in which decisions at the level of the Council of Ministers must be unanimous and are subject to ratification by all **national parliaments**. It is also an area in which the **European Parliament** enjoys only a right of consultation (Article 269 EC), by contrast with its very much more extensive powers on the expenditure side of the Budget. There is much useful background material in Brigid Laffan, *The Finances of the European Union* (Basingstoke, 1997). The European Parliament's Directorate-General for Research publishes a very valuable short survey of possible new own resources in *The Own Resources of the European Union: Analysis and Possible Developments* (Luxembourg, 1997). See also **contributions and receipts**.

P

Pact on Stability in Europe

A proposal originating with French Prime Minister Edouard Balladur, the idea of a pact was endorsed at an inaugural conference held in Paris on 26–27 May 1994. It provides a new set of undertakings and a new framework within which signatory states (the list is broadly the same as the list of states which participated in the **Conference on Security and Cooperation in Europe** (CSCE)) can 'create a climate of confidence which will be favourable to the strengthening of democracy, to respect for human rights and to economic progress and peace, while at the same time respecting the identities of peoples' (paragraph 1.3 of the Paris document). Great emphasis is laid on neighbouring signatory states resolving disputes bilaterally and exploring new forms of cooperation. The Paris document set up two 'regional round tables', one for the **Baltic states** and the other for the countries of central and eastern Europe. The Pact was formally signed on 21 March 1995, thus establishing 'an area of lasting good-neighbourliness and cooperation in Europe'. It was not proposed to set up new institutions, but to entrust to the CSCE's successor, the **Organization for Security and Cooperation in Europe** (OSCE), responsibility for monitoring the implementation of the Pact and for putting in hand any follow-up activities.

Balladur made his proposal for a pact within the European Union framework, and so the initiative was one of the first **joint actions** taken under the **Common Foreign and Security Policy** (CFSP). The Union has offered its services as a 'moderator', if so desired, in the case of problems that prove difficult to resolve bilaterally. The Pact was welcomed by Russia as a continuation of work already undertaken in the CSCE context (see also **Charter of Paris, Partnership for Peace**).

Pan-Europa

One of several 'macro-nationalisms' (Pan-Slavism, Pan-Africanism, etc.), Pan-Europa is an idea most closely associated with the name of **Count**

Richard Coudenhove-Kalergi and is noteworthy as a forerunner of the idea of a United Europe (see **European Union**) in the interwar years. Under Coudenhove-Kalergi's scheme, the best prospect for world peace lay in the emergence of very large units encompassing, in most cases, many independent states or nations. The idea of Pan-Europa was linked to the widely held belief that, if it were to succeed, the **League of Nations** would have to be underpinned by strong regional groupings. There were to be five of these: the British Empire, Pan-Europa, Pan-America, China and Japan and the Soviet Union. Pan Europe was to be brought into being by a conference convened by Italy (on more or less friendly terms with all the great powers), Switzerland, Spain, The Netherlands, or a Scandinavian country (neutrals in the First World War). English would be the common language. This scheme clearly cut across several contemporary macro-nationalisms organized on straightforwardly ethnic lines (notably the Pan-Germanism developed under the Second Reich and taken to catastrophic extremes under the Third). Pan-Europa gave its name to Coudenhove-Kalergi's Pan-European Union and was the title of his best-known book (1923). The Pan-European Union is still in existence.

Partnership Agreement

Partnership Agreements were devised to suit the particular circumstances of the countries of the former Soviet Union. Like **Cooperation Agreements**, Partnership Agreements are drawn up under Articles 133 and 308 of the **Treaty of Rome**, but are more ambitious in respect of the provisions for political contacts at ministerial and parliamentary level, and are concluded for 10 years (with tacit prolongation) rather than 5. In fact, Partnership Agreements closely resemble **Europe Agreements**, the main difference being that they make no provision for eventual membership of the Union; however, in each case the preamble makes reference to the creation of a **free trade area**.

Partnership for Peace

The Partnership for Peace is an initiative of the **North Atlantic Treaty Organization** (NATO), intended, in the words of the document issued at the conclusion of the meeting of the North Atlantic Council that endorsed the initiative (10–11 January 1994), to 'forge new security relationships between the North Atlantic Alliance and its Partners for Peace'. Aimed principally at the countries of central and eastern Europe and the **Baltic states**, the Partnership for Peace framework document invites participating states to forward to NATO a document 'identifying the steps they will take to achieve the political goals of the Partnership and the military and other assets that might be used for Partnership activities ... Each subscribing state will develop with NATO an individual Partnership Programme.' Among the 'political goals' is 'ensuring democratic control for defence forces' in Partner states.

The Partnership for Peace initiative is a military complement to the **North Atlantic Cooperation Council** (NACC). It allows Partner states to establish liaison offices with NATO headquarters and with the 'Partnership Coordination Cell' at the **Supreme Headquarters Allied Powers Europe** (SHAPE), to participate (at their own expense) in planning and military exercises and in NATO peacekeeping, humanitarian, and search and rescue missions, and to share 'in a reciprocal exchange of information on defence planning and budgeting'. The NATO countries undertake to 'consult with any active participant in the Partnership if that Partner perceives a direct threat to its territorial integrity, political independence, or security' (paragraph 8).

This last undertaking falls some way short of the security guarantees enjoyed by full NATO members, but the Partnership for Peace initiative has been welcomed by the countries of central and eastern Europe. Most importantly, Russia indicated in May 1994 its willingness to enter into a partnership with NATO, on the basis of a programme that took account of Russia's status as a nuclear power (see also **Pact on Stability in Europe**). An enhanced Partnership for Peace programme was established in 1997 and now extends to 46 countries (19 NATO members and 27 partners) including Russia.

People's Europe

At various times and for various reasons, measures have been proposed to bring Europe, in the words of the 1975 **Tindemans Report**, 'close to the citizens'. The most ambitious proposals to date were those made by the Committee for a People's Europe, set up by the **European Council** meeting in Fontainebleau in June 1984 and sometimes known as the Adonnino Committee, after its Italian chairman. The Committee drew up two reports, the first submitted to the European Council meeting in Brussels in March 1985 and the second, longer report to the European Council meeting in Milan the following June ('A people's Europe', *Bulletin of the European Communities*, supplement 7/85).

Many of the Committee's proposals were enacted in the **Maastricht Treaty**, such as the provisions on **citizenship**, now incorporated in the **Treaty of Rome** (Articles 17 to 22), and the proposal for an **Ombudsman** (Article 195). Other proposals, such as those for a **European passport** and a **European flag**, were already well advanced by the time the Committee submitted its reports. A third category of proposals have been enacted in the context of the **Single Market** programme, including the easing of frontier controls (see **free movement of persons**), the **mutual recognition of qualifications** and the **freedom of establishment**.

Among the proposals not so far enacted are those for a **uniform electoral procedure** for European elections, the introduction of common postage stamps and the establishment of a Europe-wide lottery.

Outside the immediate context of the Committee, the phrase 'People's Europe' is used in connection with measures that have an immediate and beneficial effect on the lives of individuals (as opposed to those relevant primarily to states, public bodies and commercial enterprises) and that serve to promote a sense of **European identity**.

Permanent representations

See **national representations.**

Petersberg Declaration

The Petersberg Declaration was made on 19 June 1992 by the member states of the **Western European Union** (WEU) at a meeting in Petersberg, near Bonn. The Declaration marked an important stage in the post-Cold War review of WEU's role and activities. The Declaration identified three broad categories of WEU activity beyond those arising from the mutual defence commitment in the Brussels Treaty: humanitarian and rescue tasks; peacekeeping; and crisis management, including peacemaking. These, the so-called 'Petersberg Tasks', would, under the **Treaty of Amsterdam** (new Article 17 TEU), increasingly be carried out by WEU acting as the 'operational capability' of the European Union (see **Common Foreign and Security Policy**). The Petersberg Declaration also looked forward to the enlargement of WEU, and defined the rights and obligations of members, associate members, and observers.

PHARE

The PHARE programme (*Pologne, Hongrie, Assistance à la Réstructuration Economique*) was set up by a decision of the **Group of Seven** in July 1989 as the means whereby aid of all kinds from the industrialized world would be channelled to Poland and Hungary. It was agreed that PHARE would be administered by the **European Commission** and would come into operation in June 1990. PHARE was soon extended to Bulgaria, the former East Germany and the former Czechoslovakia, and now also covers Albania, Bosnia–Herzegovina, Macedonia, Romania, Slovenia and the Baltic states (see also TACIS). Aid from the European Union is given in the framework of the **Europe Agreements**.

The five areas upon which the PHARE programme concentrates are the restructuring and privatization of state-owned enterprises; aid to the private sector, especially small and medium-sized enterprises (SMEs); the services sector, especially tourism; the modernization of financial systems (tax, banking, insurance); and welfare systems (see also **European Training Foundation**). PHARE is also engaged in projects to consolidate democratic decision-making, by encouraging the growth of professional associations, trade unions and the media. PHARE works closely with other agencies active in this field (see **European Bank for Reconstruction and Development**) and with the Aid Coordination Authority in each beneficiary state. The Berlin European Council (March 1999) agreed to fix PHARE at €1.56 billion annually over the period 2000–6. In line with a recommendation in the Commission's *Agenda 2000* study, PHARE has been supplemented by two additional sources of assistance, ISPA (Instrument for Structural Policies for Pre-Accession) devoted to transport infrastructure and the environment and worth €1.04 billion a year and SAPARD (Special Assistance Programme for Agriculture and Rural Development) worth €520 million a year.

PHARE is an important element in the Union's **pre-accession strategy** with the countries of central and eastern Europe. At its meeting in Luxembourg in December 1997, the **European Council** decided that in future, PHARE assistance would concentrate on reinforcement of applicant states' administrative and judicial capacity (30 per cent) and their adaptation to the *acquis communautaire* (70 per cent).

Pillars

The expression 'pillars' springs from a metaphor commonly used to describe the structure of the European Union established by the **Maastricht Treaty**. The Union is said to resemble the pediment of a temple and to rest upon three pillars (Article 1 TEU): the **European Communities**, the **Common Foreign and Security Policy** (CFSP), and cooperation in the fields of **Justice and Home Affairs** (JHA). In some versions of this model the first pillar is composed solely of the European Community, formerly the European Economic Community. Essentially, the difference between the first pillar and the other two is that only the first makes use of the **legal instruments** and procedures set out in the **Treaty of Rome**. The CFSP and JHA pillars are dominated by the **European Council** and the **Council of Ministers**, with the **European Commission** and the **European Parliament** playing subordinate roles; the **Court of Justice** is largely absent. In other words, the CFSP and JHA pillars were to be essentially intergovernmental in character (see **intergovernmentalism**). See Eileen Denza, *The Intergovernmental Pillars of the European Union* (Oxford, 2002).

Pleven Plan

The Pleven Plan, named after the French Prime Minister René Pleven, was a proposal for a **European Defence Community** (EDC) among **the Six**. Put forward in the French National Assembly on 24 October 1950, it was approved by 343 votes to 225. The Plan was controversial principally because it provided for a rearmed Germany to contribute units to a defence force under a unified supranational command. The vote in the Assembly was in marked contrast to the vote against the EDC Treaty four years later. Pleven claimed that the inspiration for his Plan was drawn from **Winston Churchill**'s call in August 1950 for the creation of a **European Army**.

Poland

Poland, with a population of 38.6 million people, is the largest of the central and eastern European countries which have applied for membership of the European Union (see **enlargement**). A **Europe Agreement** was signed in the year in which the first free elections were held (1991) after the collapse of Communism. It entered into force on 1 February 1994 and the application for membership was presented two months later.

The **Opinion** drawn up by the **European Commission** and published in July 1997 (*Bulletin of the European Union*, supplement 7/97) said that Poland satisfied all three of the **Copenhagen criteria**. It noted impressive progress with the restructing of the Polish economy, although GDP per capita remains at only about 31 per cent of the Union average. Poland is a particularly active member of the **Central European Free Trade Agreement** and of the **Central European Initiative**, and belongs to both the **Council of Europe** and the **Organization for Security and Cooperation in Europe** (OSCE). Poland joined the **North Atlantic Treaty Organization** (NATO) in 1999.

The **European Council** meeting in Luxembourg in December 1997 agreed that negotiations with Poland should begin in 1998. They were concluded in 2002 and in April 2003 Poland signed the **Treaty of Accession**. On 7–8 June 2003 the Polish people endorsed Union membership by 77.45 per cent to 22.55 per cent.

Policy planning and early warning unit

A Declaration annexed to the **Treaty of Amsterdam** establishes a policy planning and early warning unit within the secretariat of the **Council of Ministers**. The role of the unit – now known simply as the policy unit – is to monitor and analyse developments in areas relevant to the **Common Foreign and Security Policy** (CFSP), to help identify the European Union's CFSP interests, to provide warning of situations likely to require some response under the CFSP, and to contribute to policy formation in the Council. The unit is composed of personnel drawn from the Council secretariat, the **European Commission**, the **Western European Union** (WEU), and from national bodies, and works under the **High Representative** for the CFSP, i.e., the secretary-general of the Council.

Political and Security Committee

The political directors of whom the committee is composed are very senior officials in the Foreign Offices of the member states of the European Union who in 1970 were entrusted with the system of foreign policy coordination known as **European Political Cooperation**. Meeting approximately once a month under the chairmanship of whichever country held the **presidency** of the **Council of Ministers**, the political directors discussed foreign policy issues and prepared meetings of the **General Affairs Council**.

Under the **Common Foreign and Security Policy** (CFSP) provisions of the **Maastricht Treaty** as revised by the **Treaty of Amsterdam** the system of political directors was maintained. Article 25 TEU refers to 'a Political Committee' whose task is to 'monitor the international situation' in areas covered by the CFSP, 'contribute to the definition of policies ... [and] monitor the implementation of agreed policies' (see also **COREU**). Since March 2000 the Political Committee has been superseded by the Political and Security Committee 'composed of national representatives of senior/ambassadorial level.'

Political groups

Members of the **European Parliament** (MEPs) sit neither in national delegations nor in alphabetical order but in groups formed on the basis of party political affiliation. The existence of such groups dates back to the very beginnings of the Parliament, since they were also a feature of the Common Assembly of the **European Coal and Steel Community** (ECSC). MEPs have sat in the political groups to which they belong since March 1958 and this practice sets the Parliament apart from all other international parliamentary bodies. Political groups also exist in the Parliamentary Assembly of the **Council of Europe** and in the **Committee of the Regions**.

For the formation of a political group, Rule 29 of the Parliament's rules of procedure requires a minimum number of members: 23 members if from two states, 18 members if from three states, or 14 if from four or more states. A group must contain members from more than one state. Once formed, a group is required to deposit its name, the signatures of its members and the names of its officers with the president of the Parliament. Once formally recognized, the group is automatically entitled to its own funds from the Parliament's budget and to employ a secretariat composed of people recruited by the group but paid by the Parliament (technically known as *agents temporaires*). The size of the funds and the number of people in the secretariat are related primarily to the size of the group and are recalculated after every European election. A very critical report by the **Court of Auditors** on the funding of political groups was published in 2000 (*Official*

Journal, C181, 28 June 2000). Each group is also entitled to a proportionate share of the various posts in the Parliament (vice-presidencies, committee and delegation officers, etc.) and, within each committee, of the **rapporteurs** appointed to prepare the reports on matters coming before the committee. This apportionment is done in accordance with a mathematical formula known as the **d'Hondt system**. Speaking time in plenary session debates is shared out among the groups in proportion to the number of members, and a member called to speak on behalf of his or her group will normally be among the first speakers in a particular debate.

This summary of the advantages enjoyed by political groups explains why, in a Parliament of 626 MEPs, in which about 100 political parties are represented, only very few MEPs are genuine independents (known as '*non-inscrits*' or non-attached MEPs). However, even they have their own budget, their own secretariat and their own share of speaking time.

Over the years the size and composition of the various political groups have been constantly changing (see **European elections**). Groups have been formed only to disappear, or to reappear under a different name. MEPs have switched from one group to another. MEPs elected under proportional representation on a single list have joined different groups on taking their seats in the Parliament. And some groups are in the process of becoming **transnational political parties**.

In the Common Assembly of the ECSC only the three established political 'families' of continental Europe – Socialists, Christian Democrats and Liberals – were represented as political groups. The period of the indirectly elected Parliament of **the Six** (1958–72) saw the emergence of a European Democratic Union (Gaullist) Group composed exclusively of French MEPs who had left the Liberal Group: the rules were changed to allow this to happen.

With the first enlargement of 1973 an Anglo-Danish European Conservative Group and a Franco-Italian Communist Group were formed, bringing the total number of groups to 6 in a Parliament of 198. With direct elections in 1979 and the increase in the number of MEPs to 410, the opportunity could have been taken to increase substantially the number of members (originally 17 but reduced in 1965 to 14) necessary to form a group, but a vigorous rearguard action by MEPs from very small political parties prevented this. The period since 1979 saw the establishment of some groups whose members had only the very loosest political affinity and even of groups that specifically disclaim any such affinity. A group of this type, the so-called 'Technical Group of Independent Members', was formed by the Italian Radicals and the French National Front in 1999, but after losing an action in the **Court of First Instance** the Group was disbanded (Cases T222, T327 and T329/99, judgment of 2 October 2001). Of the groups formed during this period the Greens still survive, but the others have radically changed. In 1989 the Communist Group finally abandoned the long struggle to keep its Stalinist and Eurocommunist elements together and split into two groups, one known as the Group for the European Unitarian Left (most of whom joined the Party of European Socialists Group in January 1993) and the other, confusingly, as Left Unity. In May 1992 MEPs belonging to the Conservative Group (officially the European Democratic Group since 1979) joined the Group of the European People's Party (Christian Democrats) as allied members.

The particular position of political group leaders should be noted. All are elected by their colleagues in the group, but their powers of patronage – and so, ultimately, their ability to enforce discipline – are shared with the leaders of the national sections of which the group is composed. Their patronage is also limited by the absence of a coherent career structure within the Parliament, by the need to take nationality as well as ability into account and by the operation of the d'Hondt system. The leaders of the national sections – but not necessarily the group leaders – can play a decisive role in deciding the order of the names when parties draw up their lists, regional or national, for European elections.

The present composition of the Parliament is as follows (April 2003):

Group of the European People's Party/European Democrats (EPP/ED Group, 232 members). MEPs from all the Christian Democratic parties in the member states, together with MEPs from New Democracy (Greece), the Partido Popular (Spain), the Social Democrats (Portugal), Forza Italia (Italy), the RPR (France), and the Danish, Swedish, and Finnish Conservatives and Moderates. The British Conservative MEPs sit as allied members of the EPP Group.

Group of the Party of European Socialists (PES Group, 175 members). MEPs from all the Socialist, Social Democratic and Labour parties in the member states.

European Liberal, Democratic and Reformist Group (ELDR Group, 53 members). MEPs from all the Liberal parties in the member states (except the German Free Democrats, who failed to reach the 5 per cent threshold in the June 1999 European elections).

Group of the United European Left/Nordic Green Left (GUE Group, 49 members). Communist MEPs from Italy, Greece and France and MEPs from various left-wing parties in Scandinavia.

Groups of the Greens/European Free Alliance (45 members). MEPs from various ecology and regionalist parties.

Europe of the Nations (EN Group, 23 members). Composed largely of French and Italian anti-Maastricht MEPs, together with Fianna Fail MEPs from Ireland.

Group for a Europe of Democracies and Diversities (18 members). Danish anti-Maastricht MEPs, French defenders of rural traditions, United Kingdom Independence Party MEPs.

Independents (31 members). Austrian Freedom Party and French National Front MEPs, Italian Radicals and Dr Ian Paisley from Northern Ireland.

This summary of the present composition of the political groups in the European Parliament illustrates the fact that the Parliament has developed into a two-party system in which the two big groups command almost two-thirds of the votes. This trend is likely to be confirmed as more parties become represented in the Parliament with **enlargement,** since the great majority of parties in the applicant states already have close links with either the Socialists or the Christian Democrats. Until 1999 the relative strength of the ELDR Group was significantly diminished, and the overall balance between left and right seriously affected, by the use of the first-past-the-post electoral system in the United Kingdom. Under this system, the Liberal Democrats – the largest Liberal Party in Europe – failed to win any seats in European elections until June 1994, while the wild swings to which the system was prone resulted in Conservative MEPs dropping from 60 (1979) to 18 (1994) and Labour MEPs increasing from 17 (1979) to 62 (1994). The existence of two very large groups and the extent of the collusion between them have made it easier for the Parliament to organize its business and to muster the votes necessary for it to play its part in the **cooperation, co-decision** and **assent procedures.** The leaders of the political groups, together with the president, act as business managers (the 'usual channels' in a Westminster-type system) and are involved, through the Conference of Presidents, in all decisions affecting the day-to-day running of the Parliament: its budget, senior staff appointments, the composition of its committees, and so on. Although the interests of the small groups are to a certain extent protected by the widespread use of the d'Hondt system, the two big groups can, if they reach an agreement, dominate every aspect of the Parliament's workings, including most obviously the election of its president. More generally, it is open to question whether or not the representativeness and, therefore, the credibility and authority of the Parliament in the eyes of the European electorate are best served by the emergence of a two-party system based upon a 'left versus right' model of doubtful relevance to many of the issues laid before the Parliament.

Political groups also exist in the Parliamentary Assembly of the **Council of Europe,** although its members and substitutes appointed by **national parliaments** in the 44 member states sit in alphabetical order. Under Rule 41 of the Assembly's rules of procedure at least 15 members or substitutes of at least 3 nationalities are needed to form a group (a requirement more exacting than the equivalent provision in the rules of the European Parliament). At present (May 2002) there are five political groups:

Socialist Group (201 members). Socialists from nearly all the member states.
Group of the European People's Party (153 members). Christian Democrats from most of the member states and representatives of the True Path Party from Turkey.
Liberal, Democratic and Reformers Group (90 members). Liberals and Republicans from most of the member states and Irish Fianna Fail members.
European Democratic Group (86 members). Conservatives from the United Kingdom, Denmark, Sweden and Norway, French Gaullists, members of the Turkish Motherland Party, Progressives from Iceland, and other representatives from Hungary, the Czech Republic, Poland, Finland and Italy.
Group of the Unified European Left (40 members). Left-wing Socialists and Communists mainly from Russia and Romania, the remainder from seven other countries.

There are 33 independent members and vacancies in several delegations.

The Committee of the Regions contains four political groups, although its members sit in alphabetical order. They are the Socialists, the European People's Party (Christian Democrats and Conservatives), the Liberals, and the European Alliance composed of members of smaller parties.

Pompidou Group

Set up in 1971 on the initiative of French President Georges Pompidou, the Pompidou Group is concerned with cooperation between national authorities in the fight against drugs. Initially composed of representatives of **the Six** and the United Kingdom, the Group now involves 34 European countries. It has met within the framework of the **Council of Europe** since 1980.

Portugal

A founder member of both the **European Free Trade Association** (EFTA) and the **North Atlantic Treaty Organization** (NATO), Portugal was initially barred from membership of the European Community because of the non-democratic nature of the Portuguese government under the premierships of Antonio Salazar (1932–68) and Marcelo Caetano (1968–74). The Armed Forces Movement seized power in April 1974 and democracy was finally re-established in 1976. By then, Portugal, together with other EFTA states, was benefiting from special trading arrangements with the Community, but for political reasons – mainly bound up with the consolidation of democracy and the personal commitment of the Prime Minister, Mario Soares – an application for full membership was made on 28 March 1977. A favourable **Opinion** from the **European Commission** was published the following year, and Portugal joined the Community on 1 January 1986. Like Spain, Portugal was attracted to membership of the Community as a means of modernizing its economy and society and of re-emerging on the European stage. Community membership stood for prosperity, stability and self-respect.

Portugal remains, with Greece, the poorest of the member states, and has taken a keen interest in the **structural funds**. Portugal also has substantial fishing and agricultural interests, and, since many Portuguese work in other member states (especially France, Belgium and Luxembourg), the Portuguese government has done its best to facilitate **free movement of persons**. On the whole, the Portuguese negotiating style is to allow larger, more vociferous southern European states like Spain and Italy take the lead and then to insist upon Portugal's share of the proceeds. The only opposition to European integration in Portugal is from the Communist Party.

Positive and negative integration

These terms were first used by the British political scientist John Pinder in an article in *The World Today* (January 1968) to describe two broad categories of integration between member states. In a later work Pinder summarized the distinction as follows: 'The removal of barriers to free trade needs to be accompanied by the integration of policies beyond trade liberalization ... with the removal of barriers termed negative integration and the making of common policies beyond that termed positive integration' (*European Community: The Building of a Union* (1991)). Whether or not it is accepted that they must accompany one another (for example, the removal of barriers to trade under the **Single Market** programme needs to be complemented by a 'social Europe'), the distinction between these two basic types of integration remains useful.

Pre-accession strategy

The **European Council** meeting in Essen (December 1994) defined a pre-accession strategy with the countries of central and eastern Europe which had or were negotiating **Europe Agreements** with the European Union, some of which had already applied for full membership (see **enlargement**). The strategy was to be based on the Europe Agreements, the **structured dialogue**, and the PHARE programme. At its meeting in Luxembourg in December 1997, the European Council decided to develop the strategy by establishing pre-accession partnerships with each of the applicants. Applicant states may already, on a case-by-case basis, participate in and contribute towards certain programmes, for example, in the fields of education, training and research.

Precautionary principle

The precautionary principle is referred to, but not defined, in Article 174.2 of the **Treaty of Rome**: 'Community policy on the environment shall aim at a high level of protection, taking into account the diversity of situations in the various regions of the Community. It shall be based on the precautionary principle'. A Communication by the **European Commission** of February 2000 (COM(2000)1) set out how the Commission intended to apply the principle, with a view to establishing a 'common understanding' of what the principle entails. A Resolution on the precautionary principle was agreed at the meeting of the **European Council** in Nice (December 2000).

The principle is already a feature of much international law on the environment. Basically, it allows preventative action to be taken as a precautionary measure. A clear indication of its meaning was given in the Ministerial Declaration of the Second International Conference on the Protection of the North Sea (1987): 'In order to protect the North Sea ... a precautionary approach is necessary which may require action ... even before a causal link has been established by absolutely clear scientific evidence'. The so-called Rio Declaration of 1992 includes the precautionary principle among the rights and obligations of signatory states: 'The precautionary approach should be widely applied...Lack of full scientific certainty shall not be used as a reason for postponing cost-effective measures to prevent environmental degradation' (Principle 15).

Although the origin of the principle is in the field of environmental policy, it is clearly capable of being applied more widely in such sensitive areas as food safety, the transport of dangerous goods, consumer protection and public health.

Precursors

The idea of European union may be traced back through several centuries. Of the most frequently cited proposals, the first was motivated by the need to offer more effective resistance to the Turks. The other proposals were prompted by the desirability of avoiding war and, to a lesser extent, of promoting commerce.

In 1463, Antoine Marini, a Frenchman in the service of George, King of Bohemia, drew up his *Traité d'alliance et confédération entre le Roy Louis XI, Georges Roy de Bohême et la Seigneurie de Venise, pour résister au Turc*. This alliance was to be overseen by an assembly voting by simple majority (meeting for the first five years in Basel, Switzerland, then in a French city, then in an Italian city), and a Court of Justice for the settlement of disputes. It would be equipped with its own army. Its budget would be drawn largely from the dues paid to the Church. For this and for other reasons, the plan met with strong opposition from the Pope and was not adopted.

More fully worked out and more influential was the 'Grand Design' of the Duc de Sully (1560–1641), who in his *Mémoires* (1638 and 1662) attributed it to Henri IV. Under this proposal the eleven monarchies (five elective, six hereditary) and four republics which made up Europe from the Atlantic to the Balkans and the border with Russia, would come together in a *Conseil de l'Europe* composed of six provincial councils (in Danzig, Nuremberg, Vienna, Bologna, Constance, and one other city), and a 40-member *Conseil Général* meeting in a different city every year. The larger states would send four representatives; the smaller, two. The *Conseil Général* would be responsible principally for the peaceful settlement of disputes but it would also have a role in promoting trade, notably through the removal of customs barriers.

At about the same time, the Moravian scholar Amos Comenius (1592–1670) proposed in his *Panegersia* (1645, published 1666) a transnational peace plan based on mergers between national bodies. Learned societies would amalgamate to form a 'Council of Light', ecclesiastical courts would form a Europe-wide 'Consistory', and national tribunals a 'Court of Justice'.

Peace was also the main preoccupation of the English Quaker William Penn (1644–1718), whose *Essay towards the Present and Future Peace of Europe* was written in 1692–4. He envisaged a 'General Diet', meeting either every year, or every two or three years as necessary, composed of the representatives of sovereigns with a mandate to resolve, by secret ballot, disputes upon which ambassadors were not able to reach agreement. A state which did not accept the Diet's decisions would be compelled to do so (and pay an appropriate indemnity) by the other states acting in concert.

Similar to Penn's proposal was the *Projet de Paix perpétuelle* (1712) of the Abbé de Saint-Pierre (1658–1743). Based upon a system of *arbitrage perpétuel*, peace would be secured by a '*Union Européenne … une Société, une Union permanente & perpétuelle entre les Souverains*' represented by 24 deputies meeting as a Congress or Senate in a free city. In addition, the Congress would be responsible for ensuring that the laws governing trade were '*égales & réciproques pour toutes les nations, & fondées sur l'équité*'. The Congress would oversee all bilateral treaties between European sovereigns, which would be valid only if endorsed by at least three-quarters of the deputies. The Abbé's project was widely discussed in its day, attracting both commendation from Rousseau and ridicule from Voltaire.

Most of these proposals were directed towards linking the separate political authorities (the sovereigns or sovereign republics) within a finely drawn framework of supranational institutions. From this political union would flow the benefits in which the authors of the proposals were chiefly interested: peace and free trade. The same consequences might follow from a different kind of political union, as was proposed by many theorists, now largely forgotten, during that brief period when Napoleon held sway over a substantial part of western Europe. The first proposal marking a decisive break with this tradition by virtue of the fact that economic integration was to be the principal *engine* of unity rather than the *consequence* was by the French political economist Saint-Simon (1760–1825), who published his *De la réorganisation de la Société européenne* in 1814. He envisaged a *parlement européen*, to which would be elected, for every million electors capable of reading and writing (60 million people was his estimate), a businessman, a scholar, an administrator and a magistrate, making a total of 240 deputies. This Parliament, with its own extraterritorial capital, would have the power to raise taxes and the responsibility for directing large-scale public works, drawing up a moral code, and guaranteeing liberty of conscience and of worship.

Many other writers, including Goethe, Burke, Kant and Hugo (see **United States of Europe**), have touched on the idea of European Union. The fullest anthology is Denis de Rougemont, *Vingt-huit siècles d'Europe*, included in Vol. III, no. 1, of his *Oeuvres complètes* (Paris, 1994). See also **Europa**, **Aristide Briand**, **Count Richard Coudenhove-Kalergi**.

Preliminary ruling

Article 234 of the **Treaty of Rome** allows national courts and tribunals to refer to the **Court of Justice** requests for rulings on points of **EU law**. Such references are mandatory in the case of courts against whose judgments there is no possibility of appeal in national law (in the United Kingdom, this definition would include the House of Lords). The national court must propose precisely which point of EU law should be the subject of the Court's ruling, and it must be a point directly relevant to the outcome of the case. The Court is careful in its preliminary rulings to address only the points specifically raised, which are normally on the substance or the applicability of EU law, and to deal only with the facts of the case as established by the national court. Under Article 107 of the 1992 Agreement establishing the **European Economic Area** (EEA), the right to seek a preliminary ruling is extended to the courts of **European Free Trade Association** (EFTA) states. The procedure is set out in Protocol 34 of the Agreement.

Presidency

The presidency of the **Council of Ministers** and the **European Council** rotates among the member states of the European Union every six months. The president of any individual Council – whether of Agriculture or Finance or Industry Ministers – will be styled president-in-office of that Council, but as the senior national representative in the Council of Ministers, it is always the foreign minister of the member state concerned who is president-in-office of the Council of Ministers as a whole. The head of government of the same member state is termed president-in-office of the European Council. The member state holding the presidency occupies two seats in the Council, one as president, one as a national delegation. The positions adopted in these two guises need not be identical.

Until January 1993 the presidency was held by the member states in alphabetical order, each state's position in the order being determined by the country's name in the language of that country. This had one disadvantage: it tended always to be the same states holding the 'shorter' presidency in the second half of the year, which coincides with the summer and Christmas holiday periods. Agreement was reached to reverse each annual pair of presidencies, so that Danmark would precede Belgique, Ellas (Greece) would precede Deutschland, and so on. This cycle came to an end in 1998 and a different cycle has been laid down which provides for each **troika** of presidencies to include one large member state (see below). The cost to a member state of occupying the presidency has been estimated at about €75 million. A meeting of the European Council can cost the host country between €10 million and €30 million (*European Voice*, 25 January 2001).

The presidency is responsible for managing the business of the Council during its six-month term. It convenes meetings, establishes the agenda, drafts compromise texts from the chair, and calls votes where **majority voting** applies. The presidency represents the Council and the member states in dealings with third countries and speaks for the Council before the **European Parliament**, the **Economic and Social Committee** and other bodies. It replies on behalf of the Council to oral and written questions posed in the European Parliament, and both presents its prospectus to the Parliament at the beginning of each term and reports back to it at the end of each term. Although the foreign minister normally speaks for the presidency in the Parliament, heads of government have taken to delivering the six-monthly report-back in person. A decision of principle was taken by the heads of government in June 1981 to institute this process, and it fell to **Margaret Thatcher** to inaugurate it at the end of the British presidency in December 1981. The new practice was confirmed in the **Stuttgart Declaration** of June 1983 and has been consistently followed since then.

Each presidency usually tries to secure agreement on as many issues as possible on the Council agenda. During the passage of the **Single Market** programme (1985–92) it became common to assess presidencies very largely on the basis of their legislative output. This pressure to deliver results, facilitated by the extension of majority voting under the 1986 **Single European Act** (SEA), has combined with the growing importance of the European Council to revitalize the Council of Ministers as a decision-taking body. In particular, successive presidencies try to ensure that meetings of the European Council reach agreement on major issues.

The presidency has acquired increasing public prominence as a result of the growing importance of the Union's role in world affairs. Speaking for the Union in multilateral fora such as the United Nations General Assembly and in meetings with third countries, the president-in-office can easily gain a world prominence that his or her own national activities might rarely merit. This kind of exposure is likely to increase as progress is made with the **Common Foreign and Security Policy** (CFSP) introduced under the **Maastricht Treaty**.

At a meeting in Brussels (October 2002) the European Council decided to allow new member states (see **enlargement**) to hold the presidency from 2007. Until then the presidency will be held in the following order:

2003	Greece	2005	Luxembourg
	Italy		United Kingdom
2004	Ireland	2006	Austria
	The Netherlands		Finland

Presidency conclusions

The responsibility for drawing up a record of the conclusions reached at meetings of the **European Council** rests with the member state holding the **presidency**. The Conclusions embody points of agreement, statements of the European Union's position on current events, reviews of progress, the setting of targets and deadlines, and indications of future legislative action. Strictly speaking, these have no legal force, so when some more formal expression of the European Council's position is required it is published as a **Declaration** or as a **Resolution**. Each set of Presidency Conclusions has annexed to it a full list of the documents submitted to the meeting.

Primacy

The primacy (sometimes known as supremacy) of **EU law** over national law was established by the judgment of the **Court of Justice** in the *Costa* v *ENEL* case (Case 6/64). The Court ruled that:

The law stemming from the Treaty ... [cannot] be overridden by domestic legal provisions ... The transfer by the States from their domestic legal systems to the Community legal system of the rights and obligations arising under the Treaty carries with it a permanent limitation of their sovereign rights against which a subsequent unilateral act incompatible with the concept of the Community cannot prevail.

The primacy of EU law over constitutional law was established in the Internationale Handelsgesellschaft case (Case 11/70). Together with **direct**

effect, primacy is one of the fundamental principles of EU law (see Karen J. Alter, *Establishing the Supremacy of European Union Law* (Oxford, 2001); see also **occupied field**). A parallel may be found in Article 27 of the 1969 Vienna Convention on the Law of International Treaties: 'A party may not invoke the provisions of its internal law as justification for its failure to perform a treaty.'

Prodi, Romano (b. 1939)

An academic economist, Prodi first held ministerial office in Italy as Minister for Industry in 1978. From 1982 until 1989, and again in 1993–4 he was chairman of *Istituto per le Ricostruzione Industriale* (IRI), the holding company for state-controlled industries. In 1995 he founded a coalition of centre-left political parties, *l'Olivo*, and the following year became Prime Minister. He left office in 1998. At the Berlin meeting of the **European Council** in March 1999 he was named President-designate of the **European Commission** to succeed **Jacques Santer**, who together with other Commissioners had resigned two weeks before. Prodi was confirmed as President by the **European Parliament** in September 1999.

Proportionality

Like **subsidiarity**, proportionality is a principle devised with a view to restraining what is thought to be the excessive enthusiasm of the **European Commission** for detailed regulation. Proportionality requires the legislative means to be no more than the strict minimum required to achieve a particular end. In fact, there is plenty of evidence (particularly in the United Kingdom) to suggest that overzealous enforcement on the part of local or national authorities is the main cause of excessively detailed legislation, coupled with the willingness of national civil servants to add extra requirements to European Directives when they are passed into national law (a practice sometimes referred to as 'gold-plating'). The **Treaty of Rome**, as revised by the **Maastricht Treaty**, refers to proportionality in Article 5 (the subsidiarity Article), which says: 'Any action by the Community shall not go beyond what is necessary to achieve the objectives of this Treaty.' In fact, the **Court of Justice** had already established proportionality as a general principle of EU law (see Weatherill and Beaumont, *EU Law*, 3rd edn, Harmondsworth, 1999). A **protocol** annexed to the **Treaty of Amsterdam** deals with 'the application of the principles of subsidiarity and proportionality' but does not extend them. Articles 6 and 7 of the protocol say 'the form of Community action shall be as simple as possible, consistent with satisfactory achievement of the objective of the measure and the need for effective enforcement ... [and] leave as much scope for national decision as possible'. See E. Ellis (ed.), *The Principle of Proportionality in the Laws of Europe* (Oxford, 1999).

Protocol

Most Treaties have annexed to them protocols and **Declarations**. A protocol has legal force, and usually embodies detailed provision on matters touched on in the Treaty to which it is attached. For example, the Statute of the **Court of Justice** is annexed as a protocol to the **Treaty of Rome**. An **opt-out** from a Treaty undertaking is formalized in a protocol, thus providing scope for **variable geometry** or **Europe à la carte**. A Declaration has no legal force, but is intended to have political force, and may touch on matters not otherwise dealt with: for example, a Declaration on animal welfare was annexed to the **Maastricht Treaty** at the behest of the British government.

Public health

Article 3.1(p) of the **Treaty of Rome**, as amended by the **Maastricht Treaty**, refers to 'a high level of health protection', but makes it clear that Union action in this field is complementary to that of member states. Under Article 152 EEC, the Union is empowered to 'contribute towards ensuring a high level of human health protection by encouraging cooperation between the Member States and, if necessary, lending support to their action'. The **Treaty of Amsterdam** redrafts this Article without affecting its basic import. Some degree of coordination between national authorities responsible for public health is necessary in relation to the free movement of persons and goods: **Article 95** EC repeats the requirement that a high level of protection must be the basis for legislation arising from such coordination.

The framework for action in the public health field was set out in a **Council of Ministers** Resolution of 2 June 1994. The highest priority is to be given to cancer research, drug dependence, AIDS and other communicable diseases, the collection of comparable data on health issues, and measures in respect of health promotion, education and training. The Council also emphasized the need for closer coordination between Union institutions, national authorities and the relevant international organizations. The **European Commission** published a *Communication on the Health Strategy of the European Community* (COM(2000) 285) in May 2000. An action programme covering the period 2001–6 was adopted in 2002.

Public purchasing

The annual value of contracts placed in the public service sector in the European Union has been estimated at about 14 per cent of the Union's GDP (€1,000 billion), a sum roughly equivalent to half the German economy. For this reason the opening up of public purchasing has long been a Community objective, with a direct bearing on both **competition policy** and the **Single Market**. Before the Community took action, it is estimated that barely 2 per cent of contracts went to non-national suppliers. Public purchasing is also being liberalized internationally, notably under the Government Procurement Agreement negotiated in the **World Trade Organization** (WTO).

Two Directives of 1971 and 1977 established the ground-rules for public purchasing. The distinction was drawn between public supply (or procurement) and public works. Public supply and public works contracts above a certain value had to be advertised in the *Official Journal* and tendering procedures were harmonized. However, certain key sectors (telecommunications, energy, transport, water, military equipment) were excluded.

A review of public purchasing in 1984 revealed that public authorities were still finding ways of favouring local suppliers: for example, by subdividing contracts so that they fell below the threshold requiring them to be advertised in the *Official Journal*, or by inserting skilfully drafted special requirements into the specifications, or by abusing 'fast track' procedures for awarding contracts. Accordingly, as part of the Single Market programme, the Directives were revised and the so-called 'excluded sectors' (see above) were brought within the scope of the system. This was an important step, since these sectors represent some 80 per cent of all contracts, the percentage of high technology contracts being even higher. The public purchasing system now applies not only within the Union, but to the **European Economic Area** (EEA) and to very many countries associated with the Union (such as those covered by **Europe Agreements** and by the **Cotonou Agreement**). It is governed by three Directives, Directive 92/50 of 18 June 1992 (*Official Journal*, L209, 24 July 1992) on public services, and Directives 93/36 and 93/37 of 14 June 1993 (*Official Journal*, L199, 9 August 1993) on public supply and public works. The threshold values are €200,000 for supplies and services, €5 million for public works, and €400,000 in the formerly excluded services sectors (with a higher threshold of €600,000 for telecommunications). However, at a time of high unemployment the system remains very vulnerable to domestic political pressures, and although every year there are over 140,000 invitations to tender in the *Official Journal* (compared with 19,000 in 1988), the **European Commission** is still not satisfied that it is working properly. In November 1996 the Commission published a Green Paper, *Public Purchasing in the European Union: Exploring the Way Forward* (COM(96) 583) and in May 2000 made proposals to simplify and modernize the legislation on which the system is based. See Christopher Bovis, *EC Procurement Law* (1997).

Q

Qualified majority voting (QMV)

The most widely used method of voting in the **Council of Ministers**, QMV entails giving the vote of each member state a 'weighting', which very broadly reflects its population. These weightings are specified in the **Treaty of Rome** (Article 205), as is the total number of assenting votes (the threshold) necessary for a measure to be adopted under QMV. At present, the weightings are as follows (but see also **Treaty of Accession**):

France	10	Austria	4
Germany	10	Sweden	4
Italy	10	Denmark	3
United Kingdom	10	Finland	3
Spain	8	Ireland	3
Belgium	5	Luxembourg	2
Greece	5		
The Netherlands	5	Total	87
Portugal	5		

The total number of votes necessary for a measure to be adopted on a proposal from the **European Commission** is 62 (an abstention is equivalent to a vote against). A very small number of Treaty Articles allow the Council to take a decision by QMV without a Commission proposal: in such cases the 62 votes must be cast by at least 10 member states. This is sometimes known as 'reinforced' QMV and is widely used in the **Common Foreign and Security Policy** (CFSP) where the Commission has no exclusive **right of initiative**.

QMV applies to the first stage – the Council's 'common position' – of any measure brought forward under the **co-decision procedure** (Article 251) or the **cooperation procedure** (Article 252) and may apply at various stages thereafter. It also applies to most stages of the **Budget** procedure.

The subject areas covered by QMV, already numerous in the Treaty of Rome, were greatly extended by the 1986 **Single European Act** (SEA) and again by the 1991 **Maastricht Treaty**. The SEA extended QMV mainly into areas connected with the **Single Market** programme, including many previously subject to **unanimity**. The Maastricht Treaty did not substitute QMV for unanimity in any area, but provided for QMV in most of the areas that were either wholly new (such as **trans-European networks** (TENs), education and **public health**) or subject to more extensive provisions (such as the environment and economic and monetary policy). In relation to the **excessive deficit procedure** (Article 104), QMV operates on the basis of a two-thirds majority of votes weighted in the normal way, not counting the votes of the member state allegedly guilty of the deficit.

Additionally, the Maastricht Treaty allows QMV to be used in both the CFSP (see above) and in the field of **Justice and Home Affairs** (JHA). In both cases the Council must, as a general rule, act by unanimity, but may enact implementing measures in an area already the subject of a **joint action** or **common position** by QMV (Articles 23 and 34 TEU). See also **constructive abstention**.

The QMV system arose as a direct consequence of the enormous disparity between the original **Six** in terms of the size of their populations. Then as now, Luxembourg was much the smallest country, with barely a third of a million inhabitants, while at the other end of the scale France, Italy and West Germany each had a population of over 50 million. Giving each member state one vote was clearly not an option, but the smaller states needed some safeguards against the larger. Accordingly, a system of weightings was devised, and so framed as to favour the smaller states:

France	4	Belgium	2
Italy	4	The Netherlands	2
West Germany	4	Luxembourg	1

For a measure to be adopted, 12 assenting votes were necessary, cast by 4 member states in the absence of a Commission proposal.

QMV was introduced gradually. Initially (1958–65), most votes were taken by unanimity. The prospect of changing to QMV was one of the causes of the **empty chair crisis**, which led ultimately to the **Luxembourg Compromise**.

The system needs to be adjusted for each **enlargement**. The first enlargement (Denmark, Ireland, the United Kingdom) in 1973 resulted in the following weightings:

France	10	The Netherlands	5
Italy	10	Denmark	3
United Kingdom	10	Ireland	3
West Germany	10	Luxembourg	2
Belgium	5		

Assent required 41 votes, cast by at least 6 member states in the absence of a Commission proposal. In 1981 Greece was given a weighting of 5, and 45 became the minimum for assent. With the **accession** of Portugal and Spain in 1986 the minimum was raised to 54 out of 76 votes.

Certain features of QMV have remained constant. The system continues to favour small states (Belgium, for example, has a population roughly one-eighth the size of Germany's, yet a weighting under QMV of 5 compared with Germany's 10). A blocking minority has remained more or less constant at approximately a third of available votes (35.3 per cent until 1973; 31 per cent 1973–80; 30.2 per cent 1981–5; 30.3 per cent 1986–94; 29.9 per cent since 1995). The position of large states has become weaker: before 1973, the three large states could, theoretically, force through a Commission proposal opposed by the others; since 1973, the large states have not had enough votes to do this, and even with the addition of Spain from 1986 the large states, which represent almost 80 per cent of the Union's total population, need at least two allies to secure the enactment of a measure by QMV.

Various factors have drawn attention to the anomalies in QMV and prompted a debate on possible adjustments to it. First, in 1987 the SEA introduced an extension of QMV in association with the Single Market programme. This was accompanied by the greatly diminished role of the right of veto embodied in the Luxembourg Compromise. Second, the reunification of Germany increased the discrepancy between the largest member state and the smallest (although the German government has been careful at no time to suggest an addition to Germany's QMV weighting). Third, the emergence of North versus South rivalry in budgetary and agricultural issues has created alliances that transcend the differences between large states and small, which QMV was designed to resolve. And fourth, the prospect of membership being extended to four small, prosperous, northern countries prompted a reconsideration of the balance between large countries and small, especially in the light of the fact that two very small countries, Malta and Cyprus, had also submitted applications for membership.

In the final stages of the enlargement negotiations with Austria, Finland, Norway and Sweden, it was the British government that was most concerned about adjustments to QMV. The argument centred not upon the weightings to be given to the new members (Austria 4, Sweden 4, Finland 3, Norway 3) but on the size of the blocking minority. The Greek **presidency** proposed an increase in the threshold from 54 votes out of 76 to 64 votes out of the new total of 90 (this assumed that all four countries would join the Union at the same time). Although this proposal kept the percentage of votes necessary to block an agreement more or less the same, it meant that the blocking minority was 27 votes rather than 23. This represented, in the British government's view, a further weakening of the position of larger states such as the United Kingdom, and made the system still less 'democratic' in terms of the correlation between population and voting strength. It would mean, for example, that a combination of countries such as Germany, the Netherlands and the United Kingdom, representing 154 million people, would be less able to defend their interests than a group of small states representing about 45 million people. Put another way, it would mean that a combination representing over 40 per cent of the Union's population could be outvoted. It would also mean that the larger states, which at present represent 86.5 per cent of the population but have only 63 per cent of the votes, would see their position still further weakened to 53 per cent of the votes and 80 per cent of the population.

The dispute was settled at a meeting of foreign ministers in Ioannina, northern Greece, at the end of March 1994. The foreign ministers agreed that the whole system of QMV (i.e., not just the weightings but the threshold too) would be examined in the course of the **Intergovernmental Conference** (IGC) in 1996, and that the qualified majority would be fixed at 64 out of 90 votes. The British objection was met by a commitment binding the Council to do 'all in its power to reach, within a reasonable time ... a satisfactory solution' were a proposal to be confronted by a blocking minority commanding 23 to 26 votes. This compromise, which, like the presidency proposal, was posited on the assumption that all four applicant states would accede to the Union at the same time, was to remain in force until the Treaty provisions on QMV were formally amended in line with the decision of the IGC. The applicant states expressed their agreement with this arrangement. With effect from 1 January 1995, the qualified majority was changed to 62 votes and the blocking minority became 23 to 25 votes to take account of Norway's decision not to join the Union. This remains the position: the 1996–7 IGC, which resulted in the **Treaty of Amsterdam**, did not reform the system. The only outcome was a protocol which linked QMV reform to the question of how many Commissioners there should be in an enlarged Union and which committed the Union to a further IGC, to be convened 'at least one year before the membership of the European Union exceeds twenty' (this IGC was convened in February 2000 and resulted in the **Treaty of Nice**, under which QMV was extended and the system of weightings revised). A Declaration extended the **Ioannina compromise** until the next enlargement. A separate Declaration, by Belgium, France and Italy, called for a 'significant extension' of QMV.

The argument over QMV in an enlarged European Union has reopened some of the most fundamental questions of democracy, efficiency, member states' rights and the protection of minority interests. The **European**

Parliament views the dispute and the compromise that resolved it as an unwelcome reassertion of national interests in contradistinction to those of the Union. However, it is clear that had the matter not been raised in the enlargement negotiations in 1993–4 it would most certainly have been raised in the context of the second round of enlargement later in the decade – by which time precedents thought to be prejudicial to the interests of larger states would have been set.

The dispute illustrated a number of characteristic national attitudes. Neither France nor Germany took much part in it, probably by virtue of that lively sense of their own indispensability in the integration process that allows them to be less dependent on procedural means of safeguarding their interests. Italy, as a large Mediterranean state, could appreciate both the British and the Spanish arguments, but eventually sided with the majority. The smaller states, understandably, were perfectly content with a system that serves them well.

In fact, QMV is part of a broader strategy in accordance with which smaller states are overrepresented in the institutions of the Union. Each German Member of the European Parliament (MEP) represents over 800,000 people: each Luxembourg MEP 66,667. The average is about 590,000 people for each MEP, but the figures for all the smaller states are well below that.

Had the Six adopted the model of Congress embodied in the United States Constitution – equal representation for all states, regardless of population, in the upper house (the Council) and population-related representation in the lower (the European Parliament) – QMV would, of course, never have existed, but it is highly unlikely that such a system could ever have worked. In the twenty-second of the Federalist Papers (14 December 1787), James Madison reviewed the arguments for and against allowing states of unequal size equal representation:

Sophistry may reply, that sovereigns are equal, and that a majority of votes of the States will be a majority of federated America. But this kind of logical legerdemain will never counteract the plain suggestions of justice and common-sense. It may happen that this majority of States is a small minority of the people of America: and two-thirds of the people of America could not long be persuaded, upon the credit of artificial distinction and syllogistic subtleties, to submit their interests to the management and disposal of one third. The larger States would after a while revolt from the idea of receiving the law from the smaller.

(See also paper no. 62 on 'a compound republic, partaking both of the national and federal character ... founded on a mixture of the principles of proportional and equal representation'.)

Another comparison is to be found in the **League of Nations**, which allowed each member state, regardless of size, one vote in the Council and one vote in the Assembly, and like its successor, the United Nations, favoured certain large states only by granting them permanent membership of the Council. This solution was clearly inapplicable to an integration process that sought to move beyond an intergovernmental model.

The most radical reform of QMV would have been to substitute it for a '**double majority**', meaning a majority of member states (four-fifths, for example) representing a similar majority of the Union's population: weightings could have been abandoned. It was suggested that such a majority could be introduced for measures currently requiring unanimity, such as a change to the Treaties. However, the Treaty of Nice rejected the introduction of a double majority, admitting it only as a population-based check upon the validity of an agreement reached by QMV in the normal way. The idea of a double majority, which allows for many different permutations, had a precedent in Article 28 of the **Treaty of Paris** establishing the **European Coal and Steel Community** (ECSC). This Article allowed the ECSC Council to adopt a measure by 'an absolute majority of the representatives of the Member States, including the votes of the representatives of two Member States which each produce one ninth of the total coal and steel output of the Community'. Similarly, when the 15 finance ministers are acting as the Board of Governors of the **European Investment Bank** (EIB), they use QMV with the additional refinement that the 54 assenting votes must be cast by countries representing 50 per cent of the Bank's subscribed capital (Article 10 of the Statute of the European Investment Bank). For each member state's vote to be weighted not solely in accordance with population but also with economic performance or economic weight would be the most radical reform of all.

Specialists in QMV should read Madeleine O. Hosli, 'Coalitions and power: effects of qualified majority voting in the Council of the European Union', *Journal of Common Market Studies*, Vol. 34, no. 2, June 1996 (see especially the 'Shapley–Shubik power index').

Quota

Under the **Common Agricultural Policy** (CAP) quotas were introduced into the dairy sector in 1984 as 'stabilizers' to limit the quantity of milk qualifying for **intervention** under the price-support system. This was as a consequence of the failure of an earlier scheme, the co-responsibility levy, to bring spending on the dairy sector under control. Sometimes known as maximum guaranteed quantities (MGQs), quotas have since been extended to other products, in spite of the many legal, technical and administrative problems involved. Quotas are applied at the level of individual holdings, within a framework of production quotas for each member state.

In trade policy generally, quotas are a form of quantitative restriction, and are prohibited as far as trade between member states is concerned under Article 28 of the **Treaty of Rome**.

Quota-hopping

Quotas and total allowable catches (TACs) for particular species of fish were introduced under the **Common Fisheries Policy** (CFP) as a way of apportioning fish stocks in the North Sea among the member states of the European Union. Latterly, they became important as conservation measures. Quota-hopping arises when a 'foreign' vessel secures a listing on another member state's shipping register and thereby becomes entitled to fish against that state's quota.

The best-known cases of quota-hopping have arisen from Spanish-owned vessels fishing, perfectly legally, under the British flag and against the British quota (see **Factortame case**), having taken advantage of the relative ease with which a listing can be secured on the United Kingdom's shipping register, and having obtained a licence to fish by purchasing the vessel to which the licence is attached from its British owner. However, too strict a set of rules for registration and for licensing run the risk of being in conflict with the **Treaty of Rome** provisions which outlaw **discrimination on grounds of nationality** and which define fisheries products as subject to common market rules under Article 32.

The **Court of Justice** has ruled that the underlying purpose of quotas may be held to justify measures 'designed to ensure that there is a real economic link between the vessel and the Member State whose flag it is flying', in order to enable 'the populations dependent on fisheries and related industries' in that state to benefit from the system of quotas (letter from the President of the **European Commission** to the Prime Minister of the United Kingdom, 17 June 1997). This would allow, for example, the imposition of measures requiring a certain proportion of the catch to be landed in the flag state, or a certain proportion of the crew to be resident in the flag state. On this basis a series of compromises common to all member states can be reached which satisfy all parties and bring the ill-feeling caused by quota-hopping to an end.

R

Racism and xenophobia

In Strasbourg on 11 June 1986 the presidents of the **European Parliament** and of the **European Commission** and the president-in-office of the **Council of Ministers** signed a 'Joint Declaration against Racism and Xenophobia'. This Declaration, which was largely an initiative of the European Commission, condemned 'all forms of intolerance, hostility and use of force ... on the grounds of racial, religious, cultural, social or national differences' and committed the three institutions 'to protect the individuality and dignity of every member of society and to reject any form of segregation of foreigners'. The Declaration, like the Joint Declaration on Fundamental Rights of 1977 (see **human rights**) and the 2000 **Charter of Fundamental Rights**, has no legal force but is part of the *acquis communautaire*. Earlier in the same year (16 January 1986) the European Parliament had adopted a comprehensive report by an all-party Committee of Inquiry into 'the rise of racism and fascism in Europe'.

A series of incidents involving racially motivated violence, prompted in part by an increase in the number of immigrants from central and eastern Europe, led the **European Council** at a meeting in Corfu in June 1994 to set up a Consultative Commission of 'eminent personalities' to advise the institutions of the Union on action against racism. The Commission's report was discussed at the Cannes and Florence meetings of the European Council in June 1995 and June 1996. The following year it was agreed to establish a European Monitoring Centre on Racism and Xenophobia in Vienna under Regulation 1035/97 of 2 June 1997 (*Official Journal*, L151, 10 June 1997) which publishes an annual report. The **Treaty of Amsterdam** made 'combating racism and xenophobia' one of the aims of member states' cooperation in **Justice and Home Affairs** (Article 29 TEU).

The background is well set out in Geoffrey Harris, *The Dark Side of Europe* (2nd edn, Edinburgh, 1993) and in Roger Eatwell, 'The Fascist and racist revival in western Europe', *Political Quarterly*, Vol. 65, no. 3, July–September 1994.

Railways

The development of the railway network in Europe affords one of the earliest examples of cross-frontier cooperation between public and private bodies. Prompted by practical needs rather than by a broader political vision, it has both successes and failures to its credit.

At an early stage of the great period of railway building (1830–80) the track gauge was standardized for nearly all main lines at 4 feet 8½ inches (1.435 metres). The only exceptions to this were on the periphery of Europe: in Ireland, Northern Ireland, Russia and other parts of the former Russian Empire (including Finland), Portugal and Spain, all of which used a broader gauge (although in the case of Spain the new high-speed line from Madrid to Seville, the AVE, is built to standard gauge). The load-gauge (the height and width of the rolling-stock) is also standardized to what is known as the Berne Gauge, except in the United Kingdom. This is why special rolling-stock has to be used for the **Channel Tunnel**, British bridges and tunnels being built to smaller dimensions. However, there was no agreement on left-hand versus right-hand running, and to this day, although right-hand running is the general rule, left-hand running is retained on many lines (such as those in Belgium and the northern region of France) originally built under British influence as well as on those in the British Isles.

More seriously, when electrification was introduced, although the over-head catenary system became universal (except on Southern Region in England, once again posing problems for the Channel Tunnel) there was no agreement on the type of current or the voltage. This still hampers through running on many international lines.

The railway companies have a long history of cooperation at the administrative level, with respect to such matters as tickets and timetables. In the last century the railways were one of the most powerful influences in favour of the adoption of standard time zones. Cross-frontier cooperation was further developed with the extension of sleeping-car and boat–train services and, later, of long-distance freight. However, patterns of ownership and of state involvement varied widely, as did levels and types of subsidy, and these were to pose a problem later in the framework of the **common transport policy** provided for in the **Treaty of Rome**.

After several decades of declining market shares for both passengers and freight, railways are now entering a period of expansion. Helped in part by their relatively modest impact on the environment and their economic use of energy, railways are in a better position to compete in particular sectors, such as bulk freight and suburban passenger services in large conurbations. At present, emphasis is on the development of high-speed services, but the two main competing systems, the French TGV and the German ICE, are incompatible. Unless such differences can be resolved, the longer-term position of high-speed railways within the **trans-European networks** (TENs) may be compromised. A system of non-stop, long-distance international 'freightways', introduced in January 1998, is intended to make the railways more attractive for the transport of goods and to improve peripheral regions' access to the principal markets.

Railway companies in over 84 countries cooperate internationally through the International Union of Railways (founded in 1922), in which their votes are weighted in accordance with the number of kilometres operated. Railways within the European Union plus Norway, Switzerland and several applicant states work together in the Community of European Railways, which, through its headquarters in Brussels, is the main point of contact between the railways and the institutions of the Union. The **European Commission**'s proposals for the European rail network of the future may be found in the *Official Journal*, C220, 8 April 1994. In February 2001 three Directives, known collectively as the 'infrastructure package', were adopted by the Council of Ministers (Directives 01/12, 01/13, and 01/14, *Official Journal*, L75, 15 March 2001). The Commission put forward some ideas for a second package in *Towards an Integrated European Railway Area* (COM(2002)18) in January 2002, the emphasis being on safety, improved interoperability of systems and equipment, more open access to the market for rail freight, and the possible creation of a European Railway Agency.

Rapid reaction mechanism (RRM)

Established under Regulation 381/01 of 26 February 2001 (*Official Journal*, L57, 27 February 2001) and drawing on agreements reached at the **European Council** meeting in Helsinki (December 1999), the RRM is intended to make the Union's response to non-military emergencies 'rapid, efficient and flexible'. By contrast with humanitarian aid, the principal aim of which is to alleviate human suffering, aid given by means of the RRM is aimed in particular at actual or threatened breakdowns of civil order. In 2002 the RRM had a budget of €25 million. It is not to be confused with the **Allied Command Europe Rapid Reaction Corps**.

Rapporteur

A feature of many continental parliamentary systems, a rapporteur is the member of a committee who is responsible for drawing up a report on a matter referred to that committee or examined by that committee acting on its own initiative. Once the report is adopted in the committee, the rapporteur will be responsible for presenting the report on the committee's behalf to the full parliament and for advising members on the amendments tabled to it. The job of being a rapporteur is obviously attractive when the subject of the report is important or politically sensitive, and rapporteurships are normally allocated among members by agreement among the political parties or groups represented in the committee. Although there is scope for the rapporteur to inject his or her personal bias into the report, the need to represent the views of the committee as a whole and to gain the support of a majority both in committee and in the full parliament imposes a constraint. The system of rapporteurs is used in the **European Parliament** and in most other international parliamentary assemblies.

Ratification

In international law ratification is the confirmation of an international agreement. Originally, this entailed formal approval by the sovereign of an agreement entered into on his or her behalf by an agent; in those rare instances of agreements concluded between sovereigns on the basis of direct negotiations (such as the 'Holy Alliance' of 1815 between Russia, Prussia and Austria) ratification was not necessary. Although in some countries, including the United Kingdom, ratification remains a prerogative of the head of state, the term is now most frequently used to denote parliamentary approval of an international agreement.

Most major agreements contain a ratification clause. This may specify that the agreement will not enter into force until all signatories have ratified it, or allow for entry into force as soon as a certain number of signatories have ratified. All the major treaties and agreements on which the European Union is based are of the former type, and the same provisions apply to any amendments to them. The **Treaty of Rome** (Article 313), for example, says: 'This Treaty shall be ratified by the High Contracting Parties in accordance with their respective constitutional requirements ... This Treaty shall enter into force on the first day of the month following the deposit of the instrument of ratification by the last signatory state to take this step.'

The *de facto* 'constitutional requirements' of most member states involve parliamentary approval. In some cases approval is by popular **referendum** (whether or not 'advisory' in character). For example, had approval of the **Maastricht Treaty** secured a five-sixths majority in the Danish parliament, the narrowly lost Danish referendum of June 1992 would not have been necessary. The French referendum of September 1992 was a political option, not a constitutional requirement. The Irish referendum of June 1992 was based on a constitutional requirement: in Ireland, as in several other countries, an agreement involving a change to the constitution must be put to a referendum.

In proposals to amend the **Treaties**, use is sometimes made of a ratification formula that allows the new draft to enter into force as soon as some of the contracting parties have ratified. This is an attempt to force or at least encourage the laggards to move with the majority and is usually denounced as an attempt to create a **two-speed Europe** (see **Draft Treaty establishing the European Union**).

The role of the **European Parliament** in the approval of treaties and international agreements is set out under **assent procedure**. It has no formal role in approving amendments to the Maastricht Treaty or the other Treaties upon which the European Union is founded.

Reasoned opinion

The **European Commission** has the power to bring actions in the **Court of Justice** against member states under Article 226 of the **Treaty of Rome**. The first stage is a 'letter of formal notice' to the member state in question. The second is a 'reasoned opinion', in which the Commission sets out in full its appreciation of the circumstances of the case and the grounds for the legal action. At either of these stages the matter may be settled before it reaches the Court. Only as a last resort, and only in a minority of cases, does the Commission bring an action in the Court.

Reconsultation

If a legislative proposal is amended in a way substantially at variance with the **European Parliament**'s amendments after the Parliament has delivered its formal **Opinion**, or if the facts of the matter with which the proposal is concerned substantially change, then the Parliament may require the **Council of Ministers** to reconsult it. This right dates back to an **interinstitutional agreement** between the Parliament, the Council and the **European Commission** in 1973 and has been recognized by the **Court of Justice** (Cases C65/90 and C388/92).

Referendum

In many member states of the European Union any change to the constitution must be put to the people in a referendum. Accordingly, a change to the **Treaties** with a bearing on the constitution can be ratified only by means of a referendum. As well as being a constitutional requirement, a referendum may also be a political option, held to resolve an issue that has proved intractable or for some other reason. Some referendum results are constitutionally binding, others (in theory) only advisory. The following table sets out some notable referendum results:

Country	Issue	Date	Result %	
			Yes	No
France	EC enlargement	21 April 1972	67.7	32.3
Ireland	EC membership	10 May 1972	83.0	17.0
Norway	EC membership	25 September 1972	46.5	53.5
Denmark	EC membership	3 October 1972	63.3	36.7
United Kingdom	Staying in EC	5 June 1975	67.2	32.8
Greenland	Staying in EC	23 February 1982	48.0	52.0
Denmark	Single European Act	27 February 1986	56.2	43.8
Ireland	Single European Act	26 May 1987	70.0	30.0
Denmark	Maastricht Treaty	2 June 1992	49.3	50.7
Ireland	Maastricht Treaty	18 June 1992	67.0	33.0
France	Maastricht Treaty	20 September 1992	51.0	49.0
Denmark	Maastricht Treaty	18 May 1993	56.8	43.2
Austria	EU membership	19 June 1994	66.4	33.6
Finland	EU membership	16 October 1994	56.9	43.1
Sweden	EU membership	13 November 1994	52.2	46.9
Norway	EU membership	28 November 1994	47.5	52.5
Ireland	Treaty of Amsterdam	22 May 1998	61.7	38.3
Denmark	Treaty of Amsterdam	28 May 1998	55.1	44.9
Ireland	Treaty of Nice	7 June 2001	46.1	53.9
Ireland	Treaty of Nice	19 October 2002	62.9	37.1

Referendum of June 1975

Until it became part of Labour's policy of **renegotiation**, no political party in the United Kingdom had been in favour of a referendum on British membership of the Community. On 10 December 1969 a back-bench motion calling for a referendum was defeated in the House of Commons, having been opposed by leading members of all parties whether or not they were in favour of membership of the Community.

The Referendum Bill was passed by the House of Commons on 10 April 1975. Since the issue crossed the normal divisions between the parties, the campaign was fought by all-party organizations: 'Britain in Europe' in favour of the Community and the 'National Referendum Campaign' against it. Each organization prepared a booklet that was widely circulated with the aid of public funds. In addition the government circulated its own booklet, *Britain's New Deal in Europe*, in which it summarized the results of the renegotiation and committed itself to abide by the decision of the electorate. A Referendum Information Unit was set up in the Cabinet Office to prepare factual briefing.

In the referendum, which was held on 5 June 1975, 64.5 per cent of the electorate voted. In response to the proposition 'Do you think that the United Kingdom should stay in the European Community (the Common Market)?'

17,378,581 votes (67.2 per cent) were cast in favour and 8,470,073 (32.8 per cent) against. Results were counted on a county basis (except in Northern Ireland) and all counties of the United Kingdom except the Shetlands and the Western Isles pronounced themselves in favour of continued membership.

Published accounts revealed gross disparities between the two sides' expenditure. Each was given £125,000 from public funds. 'Britain in Europe' claimed to have spent £1,481,583 on the campaign, their opponents less than one-tenth of that sum (£131,354).

It cannot be said that the June 1975 referendum, the only national plebiscite of its kind in British history, resolved the question of Community membership once and for all. It did not even resolve the differences within the Labour Party, which by 1983 was once again formally opposed to membership. These two facts have been used as arguments against the more recent calls for referenda on other issues, such as the **Maastricht Treaty**, although the main arguments remain the extent to which a referendum is a negation of that parliamentary sovereignty that many opponents of the Community are passionately concerned to defend and the difficulty of requiring yes or no answers to complex questions.

Reflection Group

The **European Council** meeting in Corfu on 24–25 June 1994 set up a Reflection Group over the period June–December 1995 to prepare the 1996 **Intergovernmental Conference** (IGC). Composed mainly of representatives of the foreign ministers, the Group met under a Spanish chairman, and involved two members of the **European Parliament**. It was specifically mandated to solicit the views of other institutions on progress towards **European Union** and possible amendments to the **Maastricht Treaty**. The Group had its first meeting in Messina on 2 June 1995 and presented its report to the European Council meeting in Madrid in December 1995. The IGC was convened in Turin in March 1996. The outcome of the IGC, the **Treaty of Amsterdam**, was signed on 2 October 1997. A similar group prepared the IGC which resulted in the **Treaty of Nice**, but the IGC due to be convened in 2003 is being prepared by a Convention (see **Laeken Declaration**).

Regionalism

The idea that European integration along supranational lines would provide an overarching framework for the re-emergence of the regions of Europe can be traced back at least as far as the immediate postwar years. Several bodies providing for direct cooperation between regions were founded in the 1950s (see below). Some, but not all, regions have an ethnic or linguistic dimension (Flanders, the Val d'Aosta, Catalonia) and considerations of national unity, notably in France, the United Kingdom and Franco's Spain, led many countries to resist the emergence of powerful regional entities within their borders (see also **minorities**). The original **Treaty of Rome** made no explicit provision for regional representation in decision-making. However, under the **Maastricht Treaty** Article 146 EC was amended to allow for representatives of regional governments occasionally to take the place of national ministers in the **Council of Ministers** and a **Committee of the Regions** was set up.

The position of subnational levels of government varies widely within the member states. Some states, such as Portugal and France, are unitary states, while others, such as Germany and Belgium, have an explicitly federal structure. Both Spain and Italy have regions with a special constitutional status, as does the United Kingdom in respect of Scotland. Supporters of devolution have been quick to point out that the **subsidiarity** principle may be applied to the division of responsibility between national and regional government as well as to that between member states and the institutions of the Union. Some, but not all, of the responsibilities that regional governments exercise or are seeking have a European dimension in the sense that they are covered by the **Treaties**. One of the reasons why the Maastricht Treaty was challenged in the German Constitutional Court (see **Karlsruhe judgment**) was that among many of the *Länder* it was felt that the federal government was ceding to the Union powers that under the Constitution belonged wholly or partly to them.

A quite different type of regional activity has emerged in areas possessing a common economic interest. For example, in the Franco–German–Swiss region between the Vosges, the Black Forest and the Jura and centred upon the international Basle–Mulhouse–Freiburg airport a number of bodies have been set up for regular consultations on issues affecting the area. This and many similar regions are members of the Association of European Border Regions founded in 1971. An association of a similar type is the Conference of Peripheral Maritime Regions in Europe, set up in 1973 with its headquarters in Rennes. The Conference aims to represent the common interest of coastal regions from the Western Isles to the Aegean and from the Baltic to the Azores in fishing, tourism, the environment and the coastal economy.

The **Council of Europe** has a long-standing involvement in regional government. Initially through the Standing Conference of Local and Regional Authorities of Europe and since January 1994 through the Congress, the Council seeks to engage local and regional authorities in all aspects of its work. The composition of the Congress replicates that of the Council's Parliamentary Assembly. However, unlike the Committee of the Regions, the Congress is bicameral, with one chamber for regional authorities and a second for local authorities. A standing committee allows the Congress's work to be continued between the annual sessions.

A quite separate body, the Council of European Municipalities (CEM) and Regions, was founded in 1951. It seeks to enlist the support of its membership of some 100,000 local and regional authorities in 20 countries for a 'united and democratic Europe', and in recent years has been engaged in re-establishing effective local government in central and eastern Europe. The CEM, which has its headquarters in Paris, is responsible for the 'town-twinning' programme (involving bizarre conjunctions such as that between Mainz, Valencia, Zagreb, Dijon and Watford) and helps local authorities with applications for aid from the European Union's **structural funds**.

A third body, the Assembly of European Regions (AER), was founded as the Council of European Regions in 1985. It has its headquarters in Strasbourg and a representative office in Brussels. The main aim of the AER is 'to promote regionalism and federalism in Europe' and 'to reinforce regional representation within the European institutions'. Like the CEM, the AER is extending its membership to central and eastern Europe.

Charlie Jeffery (ed.), *The Regional Dimension of the European Union* (1997) is a helpful survey of this subject.

Regional policy

See **Committee of the Regions, European Regional Development Fund, regionalism, structural funds**.

Regulation

A Regulation, under Article 249 of the **Treaty of Rome**, is of 'general application'. It is 'binding in its entirety and directly applicable in all Member States'. Much of the day-to-day management of the Common Agricultural Policy (CAP), for example, is carried out by means of Regulations, which the **European Commission** can adopt using powers delegated to it by the **Council of Ministers**. For the difference between a Regulation and a **Directive**, see **legal instruments**. See also **EU law**.

Renegotiation

In June 1971 the Conservative government of **Edward Heath** completed the negotiations on British entry into the European Community. The conclusions were set out in a White Paper and laid before the House of Commons. The Labour Party was seriously split on the issue, and the best formula the Labour leader, Harold Wilson, could devise was for the Party to remain in favour of the principle of membership but to oppose the so-called 'Tory terms'. Accordingly, on 28 October 1971 a majority of Labour MPs voted against British membership. In April 1972 the Labour Party came out in favour of a referendum on the issue and in July 1972 Labour's strategy of 'renegotiation' was set out in *Labour's Programme for Britain*. The United Kingdom joined the Community on 1 January 1973.

By a narrow margin, the Labour Party won the February 1974 election. The manifesto contained a commitment to 'renegotiate' the United Kingdom's terms of entry and to submit the results to the British people in order to allow the renegotiated terms to be endorsed 'through a General Election or a Consultative Referendum'. In January 1975 Harold Wilson confirmed that a referendum would be held.

The renegotiation centred on the United Kingdom's contributions to the Community **Budget**, reform of the **Common Agricultural Policy** (CAP), control over capital movements, the possible extension of value-added tax (VAT), **Economic and Monetary Union** (EMU), development policy and the powers of Parliament to decide on regional and fiscal policies. The renegotiation was completed at the Dublin meeting of the **European Council** on 10–11 March 1975. A week later the Cabinet voted by 16 votes to 7 in favour of recommending a 'Yes' vote in the referendum. This was endorsed by a majority of 226 in the House of Commons on 9 April 1975.

The 'renegotiation' exercise was a disastrous start to the United Kingdom's membership of the Community. It remains the only example of a member state having renegotiated its terms of entry and held a referendum *after* accession; and although the result (see **referendum of June 1975**) was a triumph for those in favour of membership, the uncertainty it engendered meant that for two and a half years, British business was slow to concentrate its energies on Europe. Little of substance was achieved in the negotiations, and nothing that could not have been, in Mr Whitelaw's words, 'obtained in the course of the Community's normal development and without the whole business of renegotiation under threat of withdrawal' (*Hansard*, 7 April 1975). Nor in the event did the renegotiation resolve the divisions within the Labour Party. A special conference on 26 April 1975 condemned the renegotiated terms, and by 1983 the Party was once again formally opposed to British membership of the Community. Moreover, by 1977 it was clear that the 'corrective mechanism' agreed in Dublin to prevent the United Kingdom's net contribution to the Community Budget from becoming disproportionately large was not working (see **British Budget problem**). Worst of all, the renegotiation exercise confirmed other member states' fears about the halfhearted and self-interested nature of British commitment to the Community, symbolized by the fact that from January 1973 until July 1975 the Labour Party sent no representatives to the **European Parliament**.

Research

Initially, various legal bases for research policy in the European Community were to be found in all three of the founding **Treaties**. A Resolution adopted by the **Council of Ministers** on 14 January 1974 was the first attempt to introduce a coherent overall strategy, based primarily on the coordination of national policies and the identification of projects of Community interest. This provided the basis for provisions introduced into the **Treaty of Rome** by the **Single European Act** (SEA) and further amended by the **Maastricht Treaty**.

Article 163 EC defines the objective of research policy as 'strengthening the scientific and technological bases of Community industry and encouraging it to become more competitive at international level'. Under Article 164 four activities were specified: promoting cooperation with and between undertakings, research centres and universities (see **Joint Research Centre**); promoting cooperation with non-member countries and international organizations; dissemination of research findings; and improving the training and mobility of researchers in the member states. Article 165 empowers the member states and the Community to coordinate their research activities. Articles 166 to 170 provide for research to be undertaken within a multiannual framework programme, drawn up by the Council of Ministers and the **European Parliament** under the **co-decision procedure**. However, specific programmes for each sector are subject only to consultation with the Parliament and the **Economic and Social Committee**.

European Union activity in research and technology is set out in a series of multi-annual framework programmes. The first, with a budget of €3.25 billion, began in 1984. The current programme, the fifth (1999–2002), has a budget of €14.96 billion. Its principal themes are 'unlocking the resources of the living world and the ecosystem'; 'creating a user-friendly information society'; 'promoting competitive and sustainable growth'; and 'energy, the environment, and sustainable development'. A budget of €17.5 billion has been proposed for the sixth framework programme (2003–6). The European Commission made proposals for the future in *Towards a European Research Area* (COM(2000)6) published in January 2000.

The sums available from the **Budget** are small by comparison with overall research expenditure, representing some 4 per cent of publicly funded research in the member states (2 per cent of public and private expenditure on research). Unlike the **structural funds**, resources in the Budget for research are not subject to national quotas: project sponsors apply direct to the Commission. As a general rule, only projects at the 'pre-competitive' stage are eligible for financial assistance (i.e., projects sufficiently far advanced to be close to competing in the open market are not normally supported) and all projects must involve cooperation between partners from at least two member states.

Public expenditure on research in the member states is low by comparison with that in Japan or the United States, measured as a percentage of gross domestic product (GDP). If private expenditure is taken into account, research expenditure represents 1.8 per cent of GDP in the member states, by comparison with 2.8 per cent in the United States and almost 3 per cent in Japan. The European Union's annual deficit in high-technology products is about €20 billion. See also **COST, EUREKA, European Organization for Nuclear Research, European Space Agency, information society, Joint European Torus.**

Resolution

A Resolution by the **Council of Ministers** or the **European Council** is a type of decision not recognized in the original **Treaties**. It is used to embody a firm political consensus, yet in a strict sense has no legal force. For example, the original 1978 agreement in the European Council establishing the **European Monetary System** (EMS) was in the form of a Resolution, as was the 1981 decision by member states' representatives on the **European passport**.

Resolutions are also used by the **European Parliament** to express its views and form part of the Parliament's **Opinions**. The expression 'legislative resolution' denotes Opinions given under the **consultation, cooperation, co-decision** and **assent procedures** to distinguish them from Resolutions delivered on the Parliament's own initiative.

Right of initiative

The expression 'right of initiative' denotes one of the essential prerogatives of the **European Commission**, its responsibility for drafting proposals for legislation under the **Treaties**. Although the object, character and timing of the draft legislation may spring from a decision of the **European Council**, the **Council of Ministers** or the **European Parliament**, the draft itself is the work of the Commission and it remains the Commission's proposal throughout the legislative process in the sense that the Commission may withdraw or modify it at any time. In fact, it is estimated that 90 per cent of these proposals owe their origin to organizations other than the Commission, including member states, trade associations and pressure groups. The right of initiative is the most jealously guarded token of the Commission's independence.

Article 211 of the **Treaty of Rome** empowers the Commission to 'participate in the shaping of measures taken by the Council and by the European Parliament in the manner provided for in this Treaty'. Before formally submitting a draft proposal, the Commission will take soundings among interested parties and may issue a consultation document (for which the English expressions Green Paper or White Paper are often used). The proposal will also figure in the **annual work programme**, and the Parliament's comments at this stage may well be reflected in the final draft. Increasingly, the Commission has to give careful thought not only to the detail of the draft but also to its legal base in the Treaties, since this will dictate the voting procedures used at the various stages of the legislative process and may materially affect its chance of being adopted. All but the simplest proposals are discussed collectively by the Commissioners at one of their weekly meetings. Once adopted by the Commission, draft proposals are published in the *Official Journal*.

The right of initiative enjoyed by the Commission applies also to the **Budget** and to the negotiation of external agreements. In the former case the Commission forwards to the Council and to the European Parliament a preliminary draft budget based on its own expenditure estimates and on those drawn up by other institutions. In the latter case the Commission submits to the Council 'recommendations' (Article 300.1), which form the basis of the Commission's negotiating mandate.

In recent years several proposals have sought either to remove the Commission's right of initiative or to allow the right to be shared with other institutions and with member states. The **Maastricht Treaty** came close to granting the European Parliament a right of initiative in Article 138(b) (now 192) EC, under which it may, 'acting by a majority of its Members, request the Commission to submit any appropriate proposal on matters on which it considers that a Community act is required for the purpose of implementing this Treaty'. In the **Common Foreign and Security Policy** (CFSP) provisions of the Maastricht Treaty the Commission and member states may 'submit proposals' to the Council (Article 22.1 TEU). A similar provision (Article 34.2 TEU) applies to **Justice and Home Affairs** (JHA). Under the **Treaty of Amsterdam**, the Commission will (after a five-year transitional period) enjoy a full right of initiative in respect of those JHA matters which have been **communitized** by the Treaty.

In a wider sense the Commission has a power of initiative outside the legislative process. Spectacular examples of this include the 1977 speech by **Roy Jenkins**, as President of the Commission, in which he relaunched the idea of **Economic and Monetary Union** (EMU); the **Cockfield White Paper** of 1985; and the 1987 proposals on the **future financing** of the Community put forward by **Jacques Delors**.

The right of initiative is one of the features of the Commission's powers that distinguish it from other international bureaucracies. It affords a direct link with the idea espoused by **Jean Monnet** and others that the Commission should be an embryonic European government (see **High Authority**), and this in turn has made the right of initiative an obvious target for opponents of **federalism**. Nevertheless, it is hard to see how the European Union could work on any basis other than that of draft legislation being brought forward and steered through the legislative process by a body that is independent of member states; and the more member states there are, the more essential such an independent body will be.

Romania

Romania's **Europe Agreement** with the European Community entered into force in February 1995, barely five years after the overthrow of the Ceausescu dictatorship in December 1989. Four months later, in June 1995, Romania presented an application for full membership of the Union. The **Opinion** of the **European Commission**, published in July 1997 (*Bulletin of the European Union*, supplement 8/97), concluded that Romania satisfied none of the **Copenhagen criteria** and recommended that accession negotiations with Romania should not be opened until 'sufficient progress' had been made.

Romania is the second largest (after Poland) of the central and eastern European countries which have applied for membership of the Union and (after Bulgaria) the second poorest. Its economy remains dominated by what the Commission describes as 'state-owned, loss-making monopolies and value-subtracting enterprises'. Per capita GDP is only about 27 per cent of the Union average. Agriculture is still of great importance in the Romanian economy, representing some 14.8 per cent of GDP of gross value added.

Among Romania's population of 22.45 million people are substantial Hungarian (7.8 per cent) and Roma or gypsy (about 6 per cent) minorities. The Hungarian minority, mainly in Transylvania (gained in 1919, lost in 1940, and recovered in 1947), is now treated more favourably than in the Communist era, under an agreement with Hungary signed in September 1996. Discrimination against the Roma minority is believed to be still widespread.

At their meeting in Luxembourg in December 1997 the **European Council** decided that bilateral negotiations with Romania should not begin in 1998 but Romania should be included in the '**accession** process' (see also **European Conference**). Two years later in Helsinki it was decided that bilateral negotiations should begin with Romania in 2000. However, Romania is not one of the countries due to join the Union in 2004: the target date is 2007.

Romania is a member of the **Council of Europe**, the **Organization for Security and Cooperation in Europe** (OSCE) and the **Central European Initiative**.

S

Saarland

The economic importance of the Saarland, one of the smallest of the German *Länder*, resides in the richness of its coalfields, which lie along the frontier of Lorraine in north-eastern France and upon which the steelworks of that region largely depend. For this reason the French government insisted at the end of the First World War that the coalmines be given to France as compensation for the loss of those in northern France and that the territory be governed for 15 years by an international commission under the auspices of the **League of Nations**. Under this arrangement a plebiscite was to be held: in 1935 the local population – who had retained their German nationality – voted in favour of the Saarland being restored to Germany.

At the end of the Second World War the Saarland lay within the French zone of occupied Germany. A customs barrier was created in 1947 between the Saarland and the rest of the zone, and with the support of 83 per cent of the population a statute of independence was drawn up. In 1950 the Saarland became an associate member of the **Council of Europe**. More importantly, as a territory economically integrated into France, the Saarland became part of the **European Coal and Steel Community** (ECSC) in 1951 (Saarbrücken, the capital of the Saarland, was proposed by **Robert Schuman** as the **seat of the institutions** of the ECSC, but this was opposed by the German government). By this time, support for the reintegration of the Saarland was growing in the newly established Federal Republic of Germany. In 1955 the people of the Saarland rejected a French proposal to give the territory a special autonomous status (see **Western European Union**). Negotiations then began for the reincorporation of the Saarland into West Germany, a process that was completed in July 1959.

The dispute over the Saarland, one of the longest-running territorial disputes in European history, was an irritant in Franco-German relations throughout the formative years of the European Community. The absence of a formal peace treaty concluding the Second World War and establishing postwar frontiers meant that France and West Germany were obliged to resolve the matter on a bilateral basis. The amicable settlement finally reached was an important token of **Franco-German cooperation**, made possible by the fact that the original cause of the dispute – the coalfields – had been effectively internationalized by the establishment of the ECSC.

San Marino

See **micro-states**.

Santer, Jacques (b. 1937)

Jacques Santer was Prime Minister of Luxembourg from 1984 until January 1995, when he succeeded **Jacques Delors** as President of the **European Commission**. Together with his 19 colleagues in the Commission Santer resigned in March 1999. He was elected as a Member of the **European Parliament** in June 1999.

At the Corfu meeting of the **European Council** in June 1994 John Major, the Prime Minister of the United Kingdom, blocked the candidacy of Jean-Luc Dehaene, the Prime Minister of Belgium, to succeed Delors, in spite of his having the support of a clear majority of the other governments. Since the **Treaty of Rome** (Article 214.2) requires the governments to act 'by common accord' in choosing their nominee, Major's veto resulted in no decision being taken.

Jacques Santer, like Dehaene and Lubbers a Christian Democrat from a **Benelux** country, emerged as a compromise choice. However, primarily because of the behind-the-scenes wrangling among the member states between the Corfu meeting and the special meeting of the European Council in Brussels (15 July 1994), the **European Parliament**, using its new power under the **Maastricht Treaty** to approve the appointment, very nearly failed to endorse Jacques Santer at its July 1994 session (Santer was approved by 260 votes to 238, with 23 abstentions). Santer's speech to the Parliament on that occasion confirmed what had been widely suspected at the time of the European Council meeting in Corfu: that his attachment to what he referred to as 'the Community model' of European integration was no different from Dehaene's.

Schengen *acquis*

The Schengen *acquis* is what has been achieved so far in the areas of policy covered by the **Schengen Agreement**. Annexed to the **Treaty of Amsterdam** is a **protocol** 'integrating the Schengen *acquis* into the framework of the European Union'. Both the United Kingdom and Ireland have **opt-outs** (and Denmark a partial opt-out) from this provision. For further details, see **Justice and Home Affairs**. Acceptance of the Schengen *acquis* is, under Article 8 of the protocol, a condition of applicant countries' admission into the Union. A collection of key texts, *The Schengen Acquis Integrated into the European Union*, was published by the **Council of Ministers** in May 1999.

Schengen Agreement

Schengen is a village in Luxembourg, where on 14 June 1985 the three **Benelux** countries, France and the Federal Republic of Germany signed an agreement 'on the gradual abolition of controls at the common frontiers'. The 33 articles of the Agreement are divided into short-term measures (abolition of systematic checks, easing of formalities, approximation of visa regulations, closer cooperation between border police, etc.) and long-term measures (strengthening the external frontiers, harmonization of value-added tax (VAT), excise duties, duty-free allowances, etc.). The Agreement was followed by a 'Convention on the application of the Agreement', signed in Schengen on 19 June 1990. The Convention, composed of 142 Articles, sets out in detail exactly how the Agreement should be applied, how disputes should be resolved, and a series of provisions on complex and sensitive questions, such as extradition, the transmission of personal data, control of drugs and firearms, and asylum. The Schengen Agreement and the Convention were widely regarded as models of how frontier controls could be eased or abolished as part of creating the **Single Market** (they do not apply to the **overseas countries and territories** (OCTs) of France and The Netherlands). At the same time they were criticized for their essentially intergovernmental character (the Community institutions were not involved in the negotiations) and by upholders of civil liberties for the fact that so many questions with a direct bearing on the rights of the individual had been agreed between governments without any parliamentary approval or consultation. In particular, the Schengen Information System (computerized personal data freely exchanged between participating states) was held to be in conflict with national legislation on data protection. After many delays, the Schengen Convention entered into force in March 1995 in the original five signatory states, together with Portugal and Spain. Austria, Greece and Italy began to apply the Convention from the end of 1997. Denmark, Finland and Sweden have also joined the Schengen group: the three countries are already linked to Iceland and Norway in a passport union (see **Nordic Council**). There is a good study of the difficulties in Alexis Pauly (ed.), *Schengen en panne* (Maastricht, 1994). See also **area of freedom, security and justice, free movement of persons, Justice and Home Affairs, Schengen** *acquis*.

Schuman, Robert (1886–1963)

Although he was born in Luxembourg, Robert Schuman made his political career in France. A member of the *Mouvement Républicain Populaire* (MRP), the closest French equivalent to Christian Democracy, he rose to be Prime Minister (1947–8) and Foreign Minister (1948–53). His claim to be regarded as one of the founding fathers of the European Union rests upon the **Schuman Plan**. The anniversary of the day upon which Schuman announced his proposal for the pooling of French and German coal and steel production, 9 May 1950, is still celebrated within the Union institutions as a holiday. According to **Jean Monnet**, the originator of Schuman's proposals, Schuman 'didn't really understand the treaty which bore his name' (i.e., the **Treaty of Paris** of 1951), a remark recorded by **Roy Jenkins** after a conversation with Monnet on 20 February 1978 (Jenkins, *European Diary*, 1989). Schuman's name is also given to medals awarded annually by the Schuman Foundation to persons who have given distinguished service to the cause of European unity. In his speech announcing the Schuman Plan, Schuman said 'Europe will not be built at a stroke, nor constructed in accordance with some overall plan: it will be built upon concrete achievements [*réalisations concrètes*] which first create a *de facto* solidarity.'

Schuman Plan

On 9 May 1950 **Robert Schuman**, the French Foreign Minister, proposed that French and German coal and steel production should be 'pooled' and placed under a common supranational authority. This proposal was the basis for the first of the three **European Communities**, the **European Coal and Steel Community** (ECSC), and was largely the work of **Jean Monnet**. The Plan, which remains among the most powerful symbols of Franco-German postwar reconciliation, was based at least in part on the experience gained from the International Authority for the Ruhr (set up in 1949 and composed of Representatives from the **Benelux** countries, France, West Germany, the United Kingdom and the United States).

Three months later Schuman presented his proposal to the Consultative Assembly of the **Council of Europe**. Referring to what became the High Authority of the ECSC (the forerunner of the **European Commission**) he said: 'The signatories of the treaty will, with certain guarantees, submit to the authority that they will have set up ... The Authority ... will be the first example of an independent supranational institution.' Among the contributors to the debate was Harold Macmillan MP. He said: 'To the great majority of Europeans, by far the most significant aspect of M. Schuman's initiative is the political. It is not, in its essentials, a purely economic or industrial conception; it is a grand design for a new Europe; it is not just a piece of convenient machinery; it is a revolutionary, almost mystical, conception.' It was precisely the supranational element in the Schuman Plan that led both the Labour government in 1950 and the Conservative government that came into office the following year to reject the idea of participation. As Macmillan put it, 'We will not hand over to any supranational Authority the right to close down our pits or our steelworks ... No government could do it; no party could stand for it' (see also **Konrad Adenauer, Winston Churchill**). For the background to the Schuman Plan, see John Gillingham, *Coal, Steel and the Rebirth of Europe, 1945–1955* (Cambridge, 1991).

Scrutiny

'Scrutiny' is the word used to denote the various procedures whereby **national parliaments** monitor and seek to influence legislation emanating from the European Union. In the United Kingdom, for example, the procedure is centred upon the 'scrutiny reserve', under which no British minister in the **Council of Ministers** may give his or her agreement to any legislative proposal until the House of Commons Select Committee on European Legislation (the 'Scrutiny Committee') has completed its examination of the proposal or until the House, on the recommendation of the Committee, has come to a resolution on the matter (Resolution of the House of 24 October 1990).

Seat of the institutions

The long-running dispute over where the main European institutions should be located, one of the most arid and unedifying in the Union's history, was resolved at the Edinburgh meeting of the **European Council** in December 1992 (*Official Journal*, C341, 23 December 1992). The **Council of Ministers** now has its 'seat' in **Brussels**, but continues to hold its April, June and October meetings in Luxembourg. The **European Commission** has its seat in Brussels, certain departments remaining in Luxembourg. The **Economic and Social Committee** is also located in Brussels, together with the **Committee of the Regions**. Luxembourg is the seat of the **Court of Justice**, the **Court of First Instance**, the **Court of Auditors** and the **European Investment Bank** (EIB). A **protocol** to this effect is annexed to the **Treaty of Amsterdam**.

The decision on the seat of the **European Parliament** was more complicated and more controversial. Its seat was designated as **Strasbourg**, 'where the twelve periods of monthly plenary sessions ... shall be held ... Additional plenary sessions shall be held in Brussels. The Committees of the European Parliament shall meet in Brussels. The General Secretariat of the European Parliament and its departments shall remain in Luxembourg' (Article 1a). Initially, the Parliament viewed the Edinburgh decision as inconsistent with the provisions of the Treaties, but it has now accepted the judgment of the Court of Justice (1 October 1997, Case C 345/95) which upheld the decision. The Parliament has extensive new premises in Brussels for the committee meetings and 'additional plenary sessions' specified in the decision.

The dispute over the seat of the institutions has legal, linguistic and political dimensions. Article 77 of the 1951 **European Coal and Steel Community** (ECSC) Treaty says: 'The seat of the institutions of the Community shall be determined by common accord of the Governments of the Member States.' Identical provisions are to be found in Article 289 of the **Treaty of Rome** and Article 189 of the Treaty establishing the **European Atomic Energy Community** (Euratom). Two points should be noted. First, the fact that the word 'seat' is in the singular implies, but does not conclusively prove, that the intention was to have all the institutions – Council, Commission, Parliament, Court – in one place. Second, the expression 'by common accord of the Governments of the Member States' means that a decision on the seat must be taken by the governments meeting *as governments*, not as the Council or the European Council, and that it must be unanimous.

The High Authority of the ECSC was located in Luxembourg on a provisional basis. Both the Council and the Court were also established there, but Luxembourg could not offer facilities for the Common Assembly (the forerunner of the European Parliament). Accordingly, the Assembly borrowed the building in Strasbourg used by the Consultative Assembly of the **Council of Europe** for its plenary sessions, although its staff were based in Luxembourg. Six years later the **European Economic Community** (EEC) and Euratom were established. Until the 1965 **Merger Treaty** the three Communities had separate Councils of Ministers and separate Commissions (that of the ECSC continuing to be known as the High Authority), but from 1958 the Court of Justice and the European Assembly (as the ECSC Common Assembly was now called) served all three Communities. The EEC Commission and the Euratom Commission were based in Brussels. The three Councils met in Brussels. The committees of the European Assembly were by now meeting in Brussels, but the staff of the Assembly remained in Luxembourg and plenary sessions continued to be held in Strasbourg.

This situation, based on a series of 'provisional' decisions, was brought to a head by the Merger Treaty. Under this Treaty the institutions of the three Communities were to be merged; and the Luxembourgers, fearing that they would lose everything to Brussels, insisted that Luxembourg retain a share of the institutions. Strasbourg too wanted to keep the plenary sessions of the Assembly. The result was the 'Decision … on the provisional location of certain institutions and departments of the Communities' annexed to the Merger Treaty (8 April 1965). In this Decision the governments decided that 'Luxembourg, Brussels and Strasbourg shall remain the provisional places of work of the institutions of the Communities' (Article 1). In April, June and October the Council would meet in Luxembourg (Article 2). The Court would remain in Luxembourg (Article 3), as would the staff of the European Parliament, as the Assembly was now called (Article 4). The EIB would be based in Luxembourg (Article 5), as would certain Commission departments (Article 4). No specific mention was made of the committees and plenary sessions of the European Parliament.

The effect of this Decision, which was 'without prejudice' to the eventual application of those Treaty Articles empowering the governments to take a final decision on the seat of the institutions, was to confirm the *status quo* and to strengthen the position of Luxembourg. It also introduced a new juridical concept: instead of 'seat' the Decision spoke of 'places of work'. From 1967 the Parliament began of its own volition to hold some of its monthly part-sessions in Luxembourg; this practice continued throughout the 1970s against the opposition of the French.

The position of Luxembourg was seriously weakened in 1979 by the fact that there was nowhere in Luxembourg for the new 434-member directly elected Parliament to meet. Members of the European Parliament (MEPs) accordingly got used to the idea of holding part-sessions exclusively in Strasbourg; and on 7 July 1981, not long after a newly built chamber became available to the Parliament in Luxembourg, they voted to hold all part-sessions in Strasbourg and all committee meetings in Brussels. Luxembourg challenged the legality of this decision in the Court of Justice, since at the Maastricht meeting of the European Council in March 1981 the governments had confirmed the *status quo* as set out in the 1965 Decision. The Court, however, ruled that the Parliament's decision was legal, since it had the right under the Treaties 'to adopt appropriate measures to ensure the due functioning and conduct of its proceedings' and that since the Parliament had held part-sessions in Luxembourg since 1967 of its own volition, it was free to abandon the practice at any time (Case 230/81, 10 February 1983). The governments' right under the Treaties to determine the seat of the institutions was confirmed, the Court merely observing that it was a duty as well as a right. The Court's decision also allowed the Parliament to transfer small numbers of staff to Brussels in the interests of 'due functioning', but the great majority were obliged to remain in Luxembourg.

Many attempts were made to resolve the question of the seat. As early as June 1958 the European Parliament – the institution most seriously affected by the absence of a single seat – voted in favour of a 'European district' in which all the institutions would be located. In the first vote on the choice of city Strasbourg emerged, by one vote, as the favourite over Brussels, followed by Nice, Milan, Luxembourg, Paris, Stresa, Turin, Monza and Oise. In the second and final vote Brussels was nine votes ahead of Strasbourg, followed by Milan, Nice and Luxembourg. Subsequent votes in the Parliament on where its working place should be have consistently given Brussels a lead over Strasbourg, but Strasbourg is still strongly supported by the French, some German MEPs and a substantial proportion of MEPs from southern Europe.

The Parliament is affected in five ways. First, certain basic facilities (such as the main library and the general secretariat) remain in Luxembourg, where few MEPs ever go. Second, the Parliament is physically remote from the two institutions, the Commission and the Council, over which it is supposed to exercise a measure of democratic control. Third, the dispersal of its activities over two cities means that the Parliament has to organize its work on the basis of a monthly cycle, which is both inefficient and exhausting. It is also expensive: the cost to the Parliament of not being in one place has been estimated to be at least 10 per cent of its annual budget. Fourth, the willingness of the media to cover the proceedings of the Parliament is greatly reduced by the cost and inconvenience of having to send correspondents to Strasbourg. And finally, the Parliament is denied the symbolic advantage of a building clearly associated in the public mind with the idea of democratic control exercised at European level.

Since 1979, the Parliament has made only halfhearted attempts to resolve the question of its place of work. In 1982 a special part-session was held for the first time in Brussels, but it was devoted to one issue (unemployment) and was not a typical part-session in respect of the practical requirements (staff, printing facilities, electronic voting, etc.). On 24 October 1985 the Parliament adopted a resolution by 132 votes to 113, with 13 abstentions, calling for the construction of a new 600-seat building, that would enable part-sessions to be held in Brussels. This was promptly challenged in the Court of Justice by the French and Luxembourg governments, and the Court eventually ruled against the Parliament. In January 1989 the Parliament adopted by 222 votes to 176, with 4 abstentions, a report that called for the transfer of staff from Luxembourg to reflect Parliament's operational needs and reasserted the right to hold occasional part-sessions outside Strasbourg. Even this very modest proposal, in a report that specifically confirmed the historic and political importance of Strasbourg, was carried by a surprisingly small majority and was challenged, once again, by both the Luxembourg and the French governments. The president of the Parliament made no mention of the seat issue in his address to the Edinburgh meeting of the European Council. The Parliament could not challenge the Edinburgh decision in the Court of Justice because it has no power to bring actions against the governments *acting as governments* (and not as the Council).

The French government has never been anything other than nakedly opportunistic in any matter affecting the future of Strasbourg. In 1991 it threatened to block all decisions on the siting of new institutions (such as the **European Environment Agency**) unless the governments finally declared Strasbourg to be the seat of the European Parliament. This was opposed by the Belgians and the Luxembourgers. It was **German reunification** that gave the French government the weapon it needed to secure the decision it wanted. The French, both in the government and in the Assemblée Nationale, made it clear that they would block the agreement giving Germany (and certain other member states) extra seats in the Parliament from June 1994 unless Strasbourg was made the seat of the Parliament and the Parliament's authorities bound themselves to lease the new premises being built in Strasbourg for the 12 plenary sessions specified in the Edinburgh decision. In March 1994 the Parliament agreed to the French demand, but in adopting its calendar of meetings for 1996 provided for only 11 plenary sessions in Strasbourg. The French government challenged this decision in the Court of Justice and won its case (Case C345/95).

Whatever arguments there may be in favour of not having all the main institutions of the European Union in one place, there can be no argument in favour of having the Parliament's activities spread over two locations while its secretariat remains in a third. However, by the time the Edinburgh decision was taken the *status quo* had been in effect for so long that a substantial physical and commercial infrastructure had built up around the Parliament in Brussels, Luxembourg and Strasbourg, involving several massive new buildings and annual rents in all three cities. The extent of this infrastructure and its commercial importance to the cities involved made the issue of the seat more difficult to resolve.

The Belgian government was never willing to press as hard as some MEPs wished to have the Parliament located in Brussels. Many of the Flemish-speaking majority in Belgium view the presence of international institutions as strengthening the hand of the Francophones, and many Bruxellois regard the European institutions as responsible for high prices, ugly buildings and urban congestion. This ambivalence on the part of the Belgian government further enhanced the position of Strasbourg.

The Edinburgh decision was sufficiently satisfactory to the French to enable the member states meeting as the European Council in Brussels in October 1993 to take decisions on the location of other bodies (*Official Journal*, C323, 30 November 1993). Of these, the most important were the **European Monetary Institute** and the **European Central Bank** (Frankfurt), **Europol** and the Europol Drugs Unit (The Hague) and the **European Environment Agency** (Copenhagen). Other new bodies were to be located in London (the **European Medicines Evaluation Agency**), Turin, Lisbon, Ireland and Spain. In a declaration annexed to the decision, it was agreed to move the **European Centre for the Development of Vocational Training** from Berlin to Thessaloniki.

It is now highly unlikely that there will ever be a major change in the location of the institutions. No member state and no institution except the Parliament has an interest in raising the issue. The Edinburgh decision contained a commitment to give priority in the siting of new bodies to member states other than Belgium, France and Luxembourg, thus giving every one an interest in maintaining the *status quo*. The various schemes put forward in the past for a European capital territory (along the lines of Canberra, Washington, DC, or Brasilia) will never be revived. For the Parliament, the implications are profound, since it is condemned for the foreseeable future to the expensive, inefficient and discreditable monthly cycle of activity summed up in the phrase 'a travelling circus'. The possibility that this is precisely what the governments of the member states had in mind cannot be wholly ruled out. **Jean Monnet** relates in his *Memoirs* how, with only weeks to go before the

ECSC was due to come into operation in 1952, Luxembourg was put forward as the compromise choice between the competing claims of Liège, Turin and The Hague. 'That night,' Monnet wrote, 'gave us the final proof ... that a Europe of sovereign States was incapable, despite its leaders' good-will, of reaching the sensible decisions that were needed for the common good.'

Second Chamber

Although provided for in the abortive Treaty of 1952–3 establishing a **European Political Community**, a second chamber or 'Senate' was not a feature of the institutional structure set out in the **Treaty of Rome**. Instead, democratic oversight was entrusted to a single-chamber Assembly (now the **European Parliament**), its members initially appointed by and from member states' national parliaments but directly elected from 1979. However, since the debate on Treaty revision began in earnest in the mid-1980s, various proposals have been made to move to a two-chamber system. This, it is suggested, might help to solve the problems associated with the alleged remoteness of the European Parliament, raise the level of public confidence in the Union's decision-making by enhancing its **legitimacy**, bridge what is thought to be a widening gap between politics at European level and politics in the member states, and reduce the **democratic deficit**.

The idea has some distinguished supporters: to name only the most eminent, the German President (Johannes Rau), the German Chancellor (Gerhard Schroeder), the German Foreign Minister (Joschka Fischer), two French Presidents (François Mitterrand and Jacques Chirac), the British Prime Minister (Tony Blair), and a former vice-president of the **European Commission** (Lord Brittan). But there is no agreement on how the second chamber should be composed. There are basically three possibilities: the **Council of Ministers** should be transformed into a **Chamber of States**; the members of the second chamber should be directly elected; or they should be nominated (chosen or elected) by national parliaments or regional assemblies. Nor is there agreement on what the second chamber's remit should be, although a majority of those who support the idea see it as helping to enforce **subsidiarity** and strengthening democratic control over the extra-Community **pillars**, notably the **Common Foreign and Security Policy** (CFSP).

The main argument against a second chamber of any kind is that it would make what the public already believes to be too complex a system still more complex, thereby increasing – rather than diminishing – public dissatisfaction. Inevitably, a second chamber would either duplicate the work of the European Parliament (and the **Committee of the Regions**) or have such powers as to enable it to overrule the Parliament. Depending on its powers and prestige, a second chamber might or might not attract politicians of sufficient stature, energy and expertise to make a real contribution to Union decision-making.

All these arguments are fully and fairly set out in a report by the House of Lords Select Committee on the European Union, *A Second Parliamentary Chamber for Europe: an Unreal Solution to some Real Problems* (November 2000).

Security and defence

See **Common European Security and Defence Policy** (CESDP).

Services of general interest

This expression is used in the European Union to denote services of benefit to the general public. They may be commercial (energy, telecommunications), non-commercial (education, social security) or obligations of the state (law enforcement). Such services are recognized in Article 86.2 of the **Treaty of Rome**, which specifies that commercial services 'of general economic interest' should be subject to Community rules on **competition policy** 'in so far as the application of such rules does not obstruct the performance ... of the particular tasks assigned to them'. However, the French government has on various occasions (most recently in the 1996–7 **Intergovernmental Conference**) pressed for all such services to be given a wider range of exemptions from competition rules, complemented perhaps by a public service charter. These ideas were not reflected in the **Treaty of Amsterdam**, although Article 16 EC now accords services of general economic interest a place in the 'shared values' of the European Union and a role in 'promoting social and territorial cohesion'. A statement annexed to the **Presidency Conclusions** of the European Council meeting in Nice (December 2000) describes services of general economic interest as playing an 'irreplaceable part in ensuring the overall competitiveness of the European economy'. The European Commission submitted a report (COM(2001)598) on services of general interest to the European Council meeting in Laeken in December 2001: the report refers to and supplements two earlier treatments of the subject published in 1996 and 2000.

Set-aside

Introduced in 1988 as a means of limiting overproduction under the **Common Agricultural Policy** (CAP), 'set-aside' allows farmers to be paid compensation for taking at least one-fifth of their land out of production for at least five years. To qualify for compensation, 'set-aside' land must be kept in environmentally sound condition.

Sforza, Count Carlo (1872–1952)

Sforza had the unusual distinction of being Foreign Minister of Italy both before (1920–1) and after (1947–51) the Fascist period. His *Makers of Modern Europe* (1930) and *Europe and Europeans* (1936), written during his years of exile, were influential contributions to the pro-European cause before the

Second World War. In the latter he wrote 'There is in Europe but one big obstacle – the tendency of those groups who continue to consider criminal any cession, however trifling, of a parcel of our different national sovereignties on behalf of some idea or organization vaster and more complex than our present states'. Sforza was a well-known figure both in the United States, where he delivered a series of lectures published as *The Totalitarian War and After* (Chicago, 1941), and in France. Together with **Alcide de Gasperi**, Sforza did much to restore Italy's international reputation in the late 1940s and his pro-European, pro-American stance helped to set the pattern for Italy's post-war foreign policy. He was closely involved in Italy's participation in the **Marshall Plan**. As Foreign Minister he signed the Statute of the **Council of Europe**, the Treaty of Washington (see **North Atlantic Treaty Organization** (NATO)), and the **Treaty of Paris** on behalf of his country.

Simplification

In the context of the European Union, simplification refers to the efforts currently being made in the name of **transparency** to simplify legislation. These were prompted primarily by the need to impose order and intelligibility on the mass of legislation required to complete the **Single Market**: a specific programme, Simplification of Legislation in the Internal Market (SLIM), is now in hand.

Simplification normally entails consolidation of legislation. This may be 'vertical' (the original instrument and subsequent amendments are brought together into one text) or 'horizontal' (instruments all with a bearing on one issue are combined into one text). In both cases legislation which is no longer relevant may be repealed.

Simplification is also being extended to the **Treaties**. The **Treaty of Amsterdam** (TA) recast and renumbered the **Maastricht Treaty** and the **Treaty of Rome** and repealed all irrelevant Articles (Article 12 TA). Declaration 41, annexed to the Treaty of Amsterdam, asks for this work to continue 'as speedily as possible with the aim of drafting a consolidation of all the relevant Treaties'.

Single Currency

See **euro, Economic and Monetary Union**.

Single European Act (SEA)

The 1986 SEA, which came into force in July 1987, was the first substantial revision of the **Treaties**. The first part of the SEA contained a small number of common provisions, of which the most important gave the first formal Treaty recognition to the **European Council** (Article 2 SEA). The second part set out additions and amendments to the Treaties. The third part was a new, separate Treaty text formalizing the procedures known as **European Political Cooperation** (EPC). The document was called the *single* European Act (*Acte Unique*) to underline the fact that it was to be regarded as a coherent whole, an agreement among member states that might fall to pieces if picked apart when submitted for **ratification**.

The SEA was the member states' response to the demands for institutional reform that emerged in the early 1980s. Of these, the most important were the 1981 **Genscher–Colombo** proposals, which resulted in the **Stuttgart Declaration**, pressure from the **European Parliament** (see **Draft Treaty establishing the European Union**) and the realization in the **European Commission** and elsewhere that the prospect of further **enlargement** to include Portugal and Spain made institutional reform necessary and urgent. By 1985 it was clear too that if the ambitious legislative programme set out in the **Cockfield White Paper** for the completion of the **Single Market** were to be accomplished, decision-making procedures would have to be accelerated.

The Milan meeting of the European Council in June 1985, which endorsed the Cockfield White Paper, also considered the final report of the **Dooge Committee**, which had been set up the previous year. Among the Committee's recommendations was that an **Intergovernmental Conference** (IGC) should be convened to consider amendments to the Treaties. Against British, Danish and Greek opposition, this was agreed.

The first meeting of the IGC took place the following September. At the Luxembourg meeting of the European Council in December political agreement was reached on all but a few points: these were left to be resolved by the General Affairs Council later in the month. By January 1986 the draft, now known as the Single European Act, was ready for signature. In all but two countries this gave rise to no difficulty. The Italian government made its acceptance conditional upon the European Parliament's approval, and the Danish parliament voted to reject the SEA on the grounds that it gave too many new powers to the European Parliament. The member states were not prepared to reopen the negotiations, so 9 of the 12 (i.e, all except Denmark, Greece and Italy) signed the SEA in Luxembourg in February 1986. In a referendum on 27 February the Danish people voted in favour of the SEA, and the following day a second and final signing ceremony took place in The Hague. However, the SEA was not ratified in all the member states in time for it to enter into force by the target date of January 1987. The last member state to ratify was Ireland, where a referendum was held on 26 May 1987 because of a High Court ruling that the SEA entailed a change to the Irish constitution. The SEA came into force five weeks later.

The main changes to the Treaties introduced by the SEA were the extension of **qualified majority voting** (QMV); the **cooperation procedure**; the **assent procedure**; the **Court of First Instance**; the 31 December

1992 deadline for the completion of the Single Market; and new Treaty Articles on **cohesion**, research and technology, and **environment policy**. Many of these changes have since been modified, superseded or supplemented by the **Maastricht Treaty** and the **Treaty of Amsterdam**, as has the third section on European political cooperation (see **Common Foreign and Security Policy**).

The SEA fell far short of the European Parliament's hopes and was widely regarded as being only of technical interest as an exercise in tidying up the Treaties. In fact, the provisions on QMV and the cooperation procedure proved to be of great importance, far beyond anything that could have been achieved on the basis of the 'gentlemen's agreement' that the British government originally favoured as an alternative to changing the Treaties.

The most comprehensive collection of texts on the IGC and the SEA is *Towards European Union II*, edited by Marina Gazzo and published by Agence Europe in Brussels (1986).

Single European sky

In November 2000 a High Level Group of national experts in civil and military aspects of airspace management submitted at the request of the **European Commission** a report on the 'single European sky'. In October 2001 the Commission put forward proposals to rationalize airspace management with a view to improving safety, relieving congestion and ensuring the interoperability of equipment. The aim is to create a 'single European sky' in the upper airspace by the end of 2004. Both Norway and Switzerland were associated with the report of the High Level Group. See also **Eurocontrol**.

Single Market

Sometimes known as the 'internal market' to distinguish it from the European Community's external trade, the Single Market is the totality of economic activity within the member states, with particular emphasis on **intra-Community trade**. The phrase used in the Treaties is 'common market', meaning a unitary market governed by a single set of rules. Article 2 of the **Treaty of Rome**, before it was amended by the **Maastricht Treaty**, said:

The Community shall have as its task, by establishing a common market and progressively approximating the economic policies of the Member States, to promote throughout the Community a harmonious development of economic activities, a continuous and balanced expansion, an increase in stability, an accelerated raising of the standard of living and closer relations between the States belonging to it.

The Article is quoted at length to demonstrate how high the expectations were of the benefits that would flow from the achievement of this, the most basic of the Community's objectives.

In the years immediately after the Second World War the idea that the economic recovery of Western Europe would be accelerated if countries refrained from re-erecting barriers against each other's goods found many supporters. It was fundamental to American policy and to the thinking behind the **Marshall Plan**. Paul Hoffman, the head of the American Economic Cooperation Administration, which supervised the disbursement of Marshall Aid, called for the creation of a 'single large market' in western Europe in a speech in Paris on 31 October 1949. In this respect, the newly founded **Organization for European Economic Cooperation** was a disappointment to the Americans and others who hoped that it might lead to the creation of federal institutions capable of reorganizing the economy and the commerce of western Europe on a continental scale.

Against this background the decision, announced in the **Schuman Plan** of 9 May 1950, to create a single market for coal and steel seems relatively modest. But by the end of the decade **the Six** had agreed to form a **customs union** and to embark upon a programme for 'the approximation of the laws of Member States to the extent required for the proper functioning of the common market' (Article 3.1(h) EC; see **harmonization**).

The customs union was completed by 1 July 1968, but the Single Market had to wait rather longer. According to the account in Nicholas Colchester and David Buchan, *Europe Relaunched* (1990), several tributaries flowed into the stream that became the 1992 programme. First was the impact of the 1979 '**Cassis de Dijon**' judgment by the **Court of Justice**. Second was the **Kangaroo Group** in the European Parliament and the report they commissioned, *Towards European Economic Recovery in the 1980s* (known as the Albert–Ball Report). Third was the feeling among leading European industrialists that the fragmentation of the Community market was hampering the ability of European firms to compete internationally. And fourth were the two leading figures in the drive to complete the Single Market, **Jacques Delors** and Lord Cockfield. Delors, who in 1984 was appointed as the next President of the **European Commission** believed that the Community was badly in need of a bold, imaginative idea upon which to focus its energies. The idea that seemed to command most support in national capitals was the completion of the Single Market. The following year the **Cockfield White Paper** started the process by identifying the legislative measures that would need to be taken. The deadline of 1992 was chosen as the lifespan of two Commissions.

In parallel with the moves towards completing the Single Market were the negotiations that led to the **Single European Act** (SEA). It was generally recognized that the ambitious legislative programme set out in the Cockfield White Paper could not be completed unless decision making was speeded up by the use of **qualified majority voting** (QMV) in the **Council of Ministers**. Accordingly, a new **Article 95** was added to the **Treaty of Rome** to allow

Single Market measures to be agreed not by **unanimity** (as under the original **Article 94**) but by qualified majority, the only exceptions being 'fiscal provisions, ... the free movement of persons [and] the rights and interests of employed persons' (Article 95.2 EC). Another new Article gave the 31 December 1992 deadline formal status, and defined the internal market as 'an area without internal frontiers in which the free movement of goods, persons, services and capital is ensured in accordance with the provisions of this Treaty' (Article 14 EC). The SEA came into force on 1 July 1987.

The publicity surrounding the Single Market programme aroused great interest among businessmen. Governments of member states mounted 'awareness' programmes to ensure that their own businessmen were prepared for the more intense competition likely to flow from it. The date '1992' achieved an extraordinarily high level of recognition even among the general public and, as *Eurobarometer* showed, those who thought it would be 'a good thing' outnumbered those who thought the opposite by three to one. Perhaps most beneficial of all, successive presidencies of the Council competed with each other to see how many items of Single Market legislation could be agreed within each six-month period.

By December 1992 some 260 out of the original list of 282 legislative measures had been agreed, although a number of these had not yet been transposed into national law and many had not yet entered into force. Nevertheless, the Single Market was firmly in place, and on 31 December 1992 members of the Kangaroo Group hired a cross-Channel ferry to celebrate the ease with which goods could now be carried across frontiers.

Goods

In 1988 the introduction of the Single Administrative Document (SAD) simplified frontier formalities for goods in transit from one member state to another. Formalities were removed altogether from 1 January 1993.

Tax

Differing rates of **value-added tax** (VAT) were responsible for many of the delays at frontiers. New procedures agreed in the Council in 1991 allowed tax controls to be removed from the frontiers, and tax matters are now dealt with at points within member states. **Tax harmonization** measures agreed in 1992 introduced a minimum standard rate of VAT of 15 per cent, with exceptions for certain essentials. According to experts, tax differences have an impact on cross-border shopping only if they exceed 6 per cent, so standard rates can be fixed at up to 21 per cent. The 1992 agreement was renewed in December 1996. The member states are also committed to making VAT payable in the country of origin rather than (as now) in the country in which the goods are finally sold.

Duty-free goods

The logic behind **duty-free goods** disappears once consumers are free to buy goods anywhere in the Union wherever they are cheapest and bring them home without paying additional duty. However, under pressure from airports and others it was agreed that tax-free sales would be maintained even for intra-Union travellers until 1999.

Tax-paid goods

From 1 January 1993 there was a substantial rise in the quantities of alcoholic drinks and tobacco products for personal use that travellers could freely convey across the Union's internal frontiers, as long as both tax and duty had been paid in the country of purchase.

Barriers to trade

Although the principle of mutual recognition established in the 'Cassis de Dijon' case removed many of the obstacles to trade caused by different product standards, some harmonization remains necessary in the fields of public health, product safety and consumer protection. Purely technical harmonization is left to the relevant industries to sort out themselves, along broad guidelines laid down by public authorities, and in many cases no longer involves legislation.

Since 1 January 1994, most Single Market legislation has applied throughout the **European Economic Area**. See M. Egan, *Constructing a European Market* (Oxford, 2001).

Six, The

'The Six' refers to the six countries – Belgium, France, Italy, Luxembourg, the Netherlands and West Germany – that formed the **European Coal and Steel Community** (ECSC) in 1951 under the **Treaty of Paris** and went on to form the **European Economic Community** (EEC) and the **European Atomic Energy Community** (Euratom) under two Treaties signed in Rome in 1957. With the accession of Denmark, Ireland and the United Kingdom, the Six became the Nine in 1973, the Ten in 1981 with the accession of Greece, the Twelve in 1986 with the accession of Portugal and Spain, and the Fifteen in 1995 with the accession of Austria, Finland and Sweden. In the pre-1973 literature on the European Community 'the Six' is often used to distinguish the member states of the Community from 'the Seven', the members of the **European Free Trade Association** (EFTA).

Slovakia

With the election of Václav Havel, a leading member of the Charter 77 reform movement, as President in December 1989, Czechoslovakia was re-established as a free and independent country. However, less than three years later, the Czech and Slovak parliaments passed a resolution in October 1992 creating two separate countries with effect from 1 January 1993 (they remain linked in a **customs union**). The **Europe Agreement** between Czechoslovakia and the European Union, signed in December 1991, had to be renegotiated. The Agreement with Slovakia came into effect on 1 February 1995.

Slovakia applied for membership of the European Union on 27 June 1995. The **Opinion** of the European Commission, published on 15 July 1997 (*Bulletin of the European Union*, supplement 9/97), concluded that Slovakia did not satisfy the political requirements laid down in the **Copenhagen criteria**. The Opinion noted the Slovak government's failure to 'respect the powers devolved by the Constitution to other bodies' and described the use made of the police and the secret services as 'worrying'. Shortcomings were found in the treatment of the Hungarian and Roma (Gypsy) minorities. In addition, the Opinion noted the need for further structural reforms in the Slovak economy and a greater willingness to enforce the *acquis communautaire* (most especially with respect to the environment and employment law). Foreign direct investment was very low. Nevertheless, Slovakia was included in the 'accession process' set out by the **European Council** at its meeting in Luxembourg in December 1997 (see also **European Conference**). Bilateral negotiations were concluded in 2002. On 16–17 May 2003 the Slovak people voted by 92.46 per cent to 6.20 per cent to join the European Union (see **Treaty of Accession**).

Slovakia is a member of the **Council of Europe**, the **Organization for Security and Cooperation in Europe** (OSCE), the **Central European Initiative** (CEI) and the **Central European Free Trade Agreement** (CEFTA).

Slovenia

With a population of just under 2 million people (9 per cent of the total), Slovenia, the most northerly part of the former Yugoslavia, was also the most prosperous, generating some 16 per cent of the country's GDP and 27 per cent of its foreign trade (1990). Slovenia became an independent state in June 1991. The population is almost exclusively Roman Catholic. A Cooperation Agreement with the European Community was signed in September 1993, and a **Europe Agreement** on 10 June 1996. An application for membership of the European Union was made on the same day. In its **Opinion**, published on 15 July 1997 (*Bulletin of the European Union*, supplement 15/97), the **European Commission** found that Slovenia satisfied all the **Copenhagen criteria** and recommended that negotiations for full membership should begin with Slovenia in 1998. This was endorsed at the **European Council** meeting in Luxembourg in December 1997.

The only shadow which has fallen over relations between Slovenia and the Union stems from a dispute dating back to the end of the war. In 1947 the Yugoslav Communists forcibly incorporated Istria, which had been part of Italy since 1919, into the new People's Republic, and some 350,000 ethnic Italians fled to Italy. Their claims for compensation and a 'right to return' were not met, and the Italian government blocked the conclusion of the Europe Agreement for two years. On 23 March 2003 membership of the Union was endorsed in a referendum with 89.61 per cent of the votes.

'Snake in the tunnel'

The 'snake in the tunnel' was the popular name for a 1972 agreement to allow the currencies of member states only a narrow margin of fluctuation against the dollar (1.125 per cent on either side) and so against each other (see **Werner Report**). Developed from an earlier, simpler 'snake', the 'snake in the tunnel' was a form of **Exchange-Rate Mechanism** (ERM), but by 1976 it had been abandoned by all participants except West Germany and the **Benelux** countries. The 'snake' was the fluctuating line created as currencies rose and fell, the 'tunnel' was the 1.125 per cent limit above and below the dollar.

Soames affair

On 4 February 1969, President **Charles de Gaulle** invited Sir Christopher Soames, the British Ambassador to France, to a private meeting at which he outlined his concerns about the integrationist direction in which **the Six** seemed to be moving. He indicated that France might after all prefer to be part of a **free trade area** including the United Kingdom, Ireland and Scandinavia, to be run largely by the four big countries, France, Italy, the United Kingdom and West Germany. What he was looking for was an indication that this might be acceptable to the British, whose application to join the Six he had twice vetoed (in 1963 and 1967).

These revelations posed a problem for the British government, which did not want to be a party to a French plot against the Community. Accordingly, the West German government was informed, together with the United States and the other members of the **Western European Union** (WEU). Inevitably, the story found its way into the French newspapers. The French government reacted by accusing the British of betraying diplomatic confidences. Two months later de Gaulle resigned, and in December the French veto on the British application was formally lifted by the new President, Georges Pompidou.

Social Chapter

Not to be confused with the **European Social Charter**, the Social Chapter, as its name implies, was originally intended to form part of that section of the

Maastricht Treaty containing additions to the Treaty of Rome (which already contained a Title or 'chapter' on social policy). At the Maastricht meeting of the European Council in December 1991 John Major, the Prime Minister of the United Kingdom, refused to accept amendments to the Social Chapter, with the result that they were taken out of the draft Treaty and signed by the other 11 member states as an Agreement in a separate Social Protocol (the so-called 'British opt-out'). Decision-making in the Council of Ministers was adjusted to take account of the non-participation of the United Kingdom.

Article 1 of the Agreement committed the 11 member states to 'the promotion of employment, improved living and working conditions, proper social protection, dialogue between management and labour, the development of human resources with a view to lasting high employment and the combating of exclusion'. It required account to be taken 'of the diverse forms of national practices … and the need to maintain the competitiveness of the Community economy'. Exceptionally, Article 2.4 of the Agreement allowed management and labour (that is, the social partners) to be responsible, 'at their joint request', for measures to implement Directives adopted under the Agreement.

In September 1994 the British opt-out was exercised for the first time in relation to draft Directives on works councils and parental leave brought forward under normal Treaty Articles. The exercise of the opt-out meant that the proposals were withdrawn and resubmitted under the Social Protocol. In this form, they were adopted.

All of the countries that joined the European Union in 1995 accepted the Social Protocol. The British Labour government signed the Protocol in June 1997, having secured agreement on its implementation over a period of two years. The Treaty of Amsterdam puts the substance of the Social Protocol back into the Treaty of Rome (Articles 136 to 145: see social policy).

Social dumping

'Social dumping' occurs when one member state, by virtue of less restrictive labour laws or lower labour costs, succeeds in attracting or retaining job-creating investment in competition with other member states. The state thereby 'exports' unemployment to other states. The accusation of 'social dumping' is frequently made when a multinational company cuts production and jobs in one country and moves them to another within the Union, as happened in February 1993 when Hoover switched production from Dijon in France to Cambuslang near Glasgow. The United Kingdom's opt-out from the Social Chapter was widely believed in other member states to confer an advantage on British industry and commerce by opening up opportunities for 'social dumping' (see social policy).

Social partners

By origin a French expression (*partenaires sociaux*), 'social partners' denotes what in English are better known as 'the two sides of industry', i.e., employers and employees. Within the European Union the **Economic and Social Committee** (ESC) is the institutional expression of the corporatism implicit in the idea of 'social partners'.

Social policy

'Social policy' is the expression normally used to denote labour law, the promotion of **employment**, working conditions and certain aspects of vocational training. Within the European Union it is governed by Articles 136 to 145 (formerly 117 to 127) of the **Treaty of Rome**. In its original form, Article 136 said only that member states agreed 'upon the need to promote improved working conditions and an improved standard of living for workers' and that they 'believed' that this would be brought about by the functioning of the common market and by legislative action. The role of the **European Commission** was to promote 'close cooperation between Member States in the social field' with respect to employment, labour law and working conditions, vocational training, social security, health and safety at work, and the rights of employees. The Commission, having consulted the **Economic and Social Committee** (ESC), was empowered to deliver **Opinions** in this field, to make studies and to arrange consultations. Article 118(b) (now 139) EEC required the Commission to 'endeavour to develop the dialogue between management and labour at European level' (see **social partners**). Other Articles dealt with **equal treatment** of men and women and the **European Social Fund** (see also **education policy, European Centre for the Development of Vocational Training, European Foundation for the Improvement of Living and Working Conditions**). All these measures were intended to secure what Article 2 EC describes as 'a high level of employment and of social protection ... the raising of the standard of living and quality of life, and economic and social cohesion and solidarity among Member States'.

This apparently straightforward legal base in the Treaty was made more complicated by the so-called 'British **opt-out**' from the **Social Chapter** over the period 1993–7, foreshadowed by the earlier refusal to sign the 1989 Social Charter (see **European Social Charter**). The Commission was obliged to bring forward legislative proposals in the normal way on the basis of the Treaty, and in the event of objections from the United Kingdom, resubmit them under the Social Chapter (officially, the 'Agreement on Social Policy' or Social Protocol).

Disputes have arisen over the legal base for social policy legislation: for example, in November 1996 the British government lost an action in the **Court of Justice** seeking to challenge the legal base upon which in November 1993 the **Council of Ministers** had adopted a Directive on working time. This had been proposed as a health and safety measure under Article 118(a) (now 137) EC, which allowed it to be adopted by **qualified majority voting** (QMV). The British government argued that the substance of the measure had little or no connection with health and safety, and that either **Article 94** or **Article 308** – both of which require unanimous agreement – should have been chosen as the legal base (Case C84/94).

The ending of the British opt-out in 1997 allowed the whole of the Social Protocol to be reincorporated, under the **Treaty of Amsterdam**, into the Treaty of Rome as Articles 136 to 143. Article 136 lists the objectives: 'the promotion of employment, improved living and working conditions ... proper social protection, dialogue between management and labour, the development of human resources with a view to lasting high employment and the combating of exclusion'. Legislative and other measures must 'take account of the diverse forms of national practices ... and the need to maintain the competitiveness of the Community economy'. **Co-decision** with QMV in the Council is the general rule, but in respect of social security, rights at the workplace, the employment of nationals of non-member states, and financial contributions to job creation schemes, the Council must act unanimously in consultation with the **European Parliament** (see also **Employment and Labour Market Committee**).

Social policy is one of the few areas of Union activity in which there are political as well as national differences of real substance permeating the debate. It has moved a long way from its modest beginnings as a means of ensuring that European-wide labour standards contributed to equal conditions of competition (see **social dumping**), and although the accusation of 'social engineering' is still sometimes heard, there is now widespread acceptance of the idea that something that is called a Community must have a social dimension. See also **European Social Agenda**, **European social model**. The legal background to social policy is very clearly set out in Noreen Burrows and Jane Mair, *European Social Law* (Chichester, 1996).

Social Protection Committee

The Social Protection Committee is a new European Union body established by the **Treaty of Nice** under Article 144 of the **Treaty of Rome**. Possessing advisory status, its task is 'to promote cooperation between Member States and with the [**European Commission** on social protection policies'. Each member state and the Commission will have two representatives on the Committee. The Committee may tender advice either on its own initiative or at the request of the Commission or the **Council of Ministers**.

Socialism

Socialist and Social Democratic parties are the largest political family in Europe, although the Group of the Party of European Socialists (PES; see transnational political parties) is now only the second largest of the **political groups** in the **European Parliament**. Among the newly emergent parties in central and eastern Europe, there are many that call themselves Socialist or Social Democrat, although several are largely made up of former Communists.

Historically, by comparison with Christian Democrats or Liberals, the Socialists have been less committed to European integration. In Italy and West Germany the Socialists voted against the **Treaty of Paris** when it was laid before **national parliaments** for their approval; in Belgium they abstained. French and Italian Socialists abstained when the **Treaty of Rome** was put to the vote, and in West Germany the Socialists expressed strong reservations. By far the most prominent Socialist pro-Europeans of the early years were the Belgian **Paul-Henri Spaak** and the Dutchman Sicco Mansholt (see **Mansholt Plan**). Well into the 1980s the British Labour Party, among the largest Socialist parties in Europe, was formally opposed to membership of the Community (the Party boycotted the European Parliament for the first two and a half years of British membership).

In recent years the Socialists, although not opposed in principle to the **Single Market** programme, have none the less demanded a price for their support in the form of measures in the social and employment field. For example, in the European Parliament the PES Group effectively blocked measures to open up the insurance market until progress was made with the 1989 **European Social Charter**. The Socialists have also tended to be more critical than other groups of the **Common Agricultural Policy** (CAP) and have been very active on environmental and consumer protection issues and in relation to the rights of minorities.

In spite of some reverses in national elections the Socialists seem certain to remain the most influential political force in Europe. **Enlargement** will bring into the Union many Socialist parties already closely involved with the PES. By comparison with most other parties, the Socialists have a longer and livelier tradition of cross-frontier cooperation between parties, not least because the notion that class interests cut across those of the nation still informs much Socialist thinking.

There is a very extensive literature on Socialism, although much of the research is based on individual Socialist parties in particular countries. For Socialists' attitudes to European integration, see Kevin Featherstone, *Socialist Parties and European Integration: a Comparative History* (Manchester, 1988).

Socrates

The Socrates programme of 1995–9 replaced the earlier ERASMUS (European Community Action Scheme for the Mobility of University Students) and Lingua programmes in the field of student and teacher exchanges, language teaching and other activities concerned with the European dimension in education (see **education policy**). With a budget of

€ 1.85 billion (approximately £1.17 billion) over the period 2000–6 Socrates II covers the whole of the **European Economic Area** (EEA). ERASMUS remains a constituent element in the Socrates II programme with 51 per cent of the budget, together with the Comenius programme (school exchanges, language teaching), and the Grundtvig programme (further education).

Soft law

'Soft law' is an expression used to denote agreements and decisions which possess no formal legal force. Already an established feature of much international decision-making (for example, in relation to the environment), soft law in the European Union includes codes of conduct, guidelines, **Recommendations** and **Opinions** (see **legal instruments**), **Declarations, Resolutions, interinstitutional agreements**, and the like. Some of these may possess considerable political or suasive force and may on occasion be referred to in actions before the **Court of Justice**. The current trend is to make more use of soft law rather than **Directives** and **Regulations** (see **European governance, open method of coordination**) and with **enlargement** this trend is likely to be confirmed. Decisions reached by organizations with no power to make law (for example, the **Council of Europe** or the United Nations) can all be classified as soft law: they are effective only in so far as states choose to abide by them.

Solemn Declaration on European Union

See **Stuttgart Declaration**.

Sovereignty

If sovereignty in relation to states is defined as an exclusive and comprehensive right of independent action, then it must follow that the member states of the European Union remain sovereign only in the sense that they could secede from the Union if they so wished. First under the **Treaty of Paris** and later under the **Treaty of Rome**, the signatory states committed themselves to creating, in the words of the preamble to the Treaty of Rome, an 'ever closer union among the peoples of Europe', and established independent supranational institutions enjoying their own exclusive jurisdiction. These institutions were endowed by Treaty with a capacity for making laws possessing both **primacy** and **direct effect** in the signatory states. The Treaty of Rome (unlike the Treaty of Paris) was concluded for an indefinite period.

It is sometimes said that in signing the **Treaties** the member states 'pooled' or 'merged' their sovereignty in the sense that they thereby committed themselves to exercising their sovereignty in common in certain specified areas. This idea is not consistent with the definition of sovereignty given above, under which the joint exercise of sovereignty is a contradiction in terms. It is more helpful to regard member states as having delegated their powers within certain well defined limits to the institutions of what is now the European Union, albeit for an indefinite period. Such a delegation has occurred with respect to both internal and external actions. Member states have also chosen in those areas in which the European Union acts on an intergovernmental basis to exercise their powers in cooperation with one another (see **intergovernmentalism**).

In many contexts the word 'sovereignty' refers in fact to what is more accurately described as 'parliamentary sovereignty'. This may be defined as the exclusive and comprehensive right of a **national parliament** to make laws within the national constitutional framework. However, there now exists a Union-wide constitutional framework (see **EU law**) and as a consequence of this, national parliaments have lost their exclusive right to make laws that are binding upon their citizens. Until the **European Parliament** was directly elected in 1979, it could have been said that national parliaments had 'pooled' their sovereignty by appointing the Members of the European Parliament (MEPs), but now that direct elections have given the MEPs their own democratic **legitimacy** such authority as the Parliament enjoys is no longer dependent on the pooling of national parliamentary sovereignty.

That membership of the European Community or *a fortiori* of the European Union entails 'loss of sovereignty' is among the most basic of all the arguments deployed by anti-Europeans, especially in the context of **federalism**. It is usually countered by the assertion that the only sovereignty that counts is the ability of a state to defend or promote its own interests, and that to this end there may be some marginal sacrifice of the trappings of sovereignty in order to retain the substance.

Most treaties curtail the freedom of action of the signatory states in certain specific areas. To take only the most obvious example, the Washington Treaty establishing the **North Atlantic Treaty Organization** (NATO) obliges the signatory states to come to the aid of any NATO member threatened by aggression, and if necessary to go to war. All treaties embodying obligations entail a loss of sovereignty; however, in international law a capacity freely to enter into obligations laid down by treaty is part of the definition of a sovereign state. What makes the Treaty of Rome and its successor Treaties qualitatively different from other treaties is the fact that the supranational institutions they create are able to draw up and adopt laws that are binding upon the signatory states. Moreover, the range of subjects goes well beyond those external actions with which most international treaties are concerned.

There is an extensive theoretical literature on sovereignty. Both provocative and accessible is Noel Malcolm, *Sense on Sovereignty* (1991), which is also useful for its references to other treatments of the subject. Still well worth reading is Stanley Hoffmann, 'Reflections on the Nation-State in Europe today', *Journal of Common Market Studies*, Vol. 21, nos 1 and 2 (1982), reprinted in *The European Sisyphus* (Boulder, Co, 1995).

Spaak, Paul-Henri (1899–1972)

Paul-Henri Spaak was a prominent figure in Belgian politics before the Second World War, holding ministerial office (including that of Foreign Minister) in various Socialist administrations. During the war he was a member of the Belgian government-in-exile in London. Much of his postwar career was in international or European politics. He was the first president of the General Assembly of the United Nations in 1946 and of the Consultative Assembly of the **Council of Europe** (1949–51, a post he resigned in protest against the United Kingdom's rejection of the **Schuman Plan**). A leading figure in negotiations among **the Six**, he chaired the committee (see **Spaak Committee**) set up after the **Messina Conference** to do the detailed preparatory work for the **European Economic Community**. From 1957 until 1961, he was secretary-general of the **North Atlantic Treaty Organization** (NATO), before returning to Belgian politics as Foreign Minister.

Spaak was among the best-known advocates of European integration. At the same time, he was a strong Atlanticist and a keen supporter of British membership of the Community.

Spaak Committee

One of the decisions of the 1955 **Messina Conference** was to set up 'a Committee of government delegates' chaired by **Paul-Henri Spaak** to make proposals for closer economic integration among **the Six** (see also **Beyen Plan**). The Spaak Committee met for the first time in September 1955 and again in February 1956. Its final report was presented to the foreign ministers of the Six in Venice in May 1956.

The report, which was the basis for the two Treaties establishing the **European Economic Community** (EEC) and the **European Atomic Energy Community** (Euratom), was in three parts: the common market, nuclear energy, and the priority sectors requiring urgent action (including non-nuclear energy, transport and telecommunications). The foreign ministers accepted the report after only a brief discussion, the single proviso being that the **overseas countries and territories** (OCTs) of the signatory states should be included in any new economic unit (a concession to France). The report dealt only cursorily with institutional questions, proposing an institutional model broadly similar to that already established for the **European Coal and Steel Community** (ECSC): a Council of national ministers, an independent Commission, a Parliament and a Court of Justice.

The United Kingdom government had sent an observer to the Messina Conference but, although invited, took no part in the work of the Spaak Committee. Officially, its position was that the **customs union** towards which the Six were obviously moving was incompatible with the United Kingdom's preferential trading arrangements with the Commonwealth. However, against the background of the Suez Crisis and the abortive Hungarian uprising, the Six were determined to move ahead as rapidly as possible. Ten months after the Venice meeting the EEC and Euratom Treaties were signed in Rome (see also **Pierre Uri**).

The Spaak Committee is often referred to as a turning-point in the prehistory of European Union. Its success was in part attributed to the fact that it was composed not of officials but of people who by virtue of their experience and seniority enjoyed the confidence of the leaders of the various governments. For this reason the 1984 **Dooge Committee** was deliberately modelled on the Spaak Committee.

Spain

Spain originally applied to join **the Six** in 1962, but the application was blocked on the grounds that the regime of General Francisco Franco was undemocratic. After Franco's death in 1975, Spain applied again (28 July 1977), three months after Portugal. A favourable Commission **Opinion** was published the following year and Spain joined the Community on 1 January 1986.

Like Portugal, Spain was attracted to Community membership as a means of re-entering the European political and economic mainstream after more than a generation of near-total isolation. However, unlike Portugal, Spain was a formidable commercial, industrial and agricultural rival to the Community's member states, especially France and Italy. **Accession** negotiations were long and difficult, not least because adaptation to Community disciplines required Spain to dismantle much of the protectionist, corporatist apparatus that was part of the Francoist legacy. Community membership was particularly attractive to many of the larger Spanish regions, such as the Basque provinces and Catalonia, as providing an alternative institutional framework to the one offered by the Spanish state. The **structural funds**, for example, from which Spain has drawn substantial benefits, were interesting to the regions as a pretext for direct contacts with Brussels: and in the **Maastricht Treaty** negotiations Spain was a strong supporter of the proposal for a **Committee of the Regions**. In the same negotiations Spain put forward the proposals on **citizenship**.

Internationally, Spanish accession resulted in a reorientation of the Community's trade and development policies towards Latin America, although perhaps not on the scale that the Spanish would have liked. **Gibraltar** remains an irritant in relations with the United Kingdom. Spain has an enormous fishing fleet and the **Common Fisheries Policy** has always been a high Spanish priority.

Latent anti-American feeling led to a divisive referendum in 1986 on Spain's continued membership of the **North Atlantic Treaty Organization** (NATO), which the country had joined in 1982. More recently, Spain has decided to commit forces to the **Eurocorps**.

There is no significant opposition to European integration in Spain. Europe remains identified with liberty, modernization, prosperity and the energetic pursuit of Spanish interests.

Spinelli, Altiero (1907–86)

Born in Rome, Altiero Spinelli was a lifelong advocate of **federalism**. A journalist and a vigorous opponent of fascism, he was arrested in 1927 and spent 10 years in prison and a further 6 in 'confinement'. During the Second World War he was interned on the island of Ventotene in the Gulf of Gaeta along with some 800 others hostile to Mussolini's regime.

In June 1941 Spinelli and a small group of federalists completed a 'manifesto', the final version of which was written on cigarette papers and concealed in the false bottom of a tin box. It was circulated clandestinely within the Resistance and adopted as the programme of the *Movimento Federalista Europeo*, which Spinelli founded in August 1943. It has been published both in Italian and in translation many times since.

The manifesto began with a critique of the totalitarian state, which had developed from the 'ideology of national independence' and 'the seeds of capitalist imperialism'. However, the defeat of Germany would merely allow the British and the Americans to restore the nation-states in their old form, in a pattern consistent with their economic and geopolitical interests. This must be resisted at all costs: federalists must seize the opportunity presented by the turmoil and uncertainty that would accompany the end of the war to establish a 'European Federation ... a free and united Europe'. Chief among the tasks of such a federation must be social reconstruction, ending the pre-eminence of the Catholic Church, and the abandonment of corporatism. In short, the federalists should prepare a set of new institutions as the moulds into which the 'incandescent lava' of popular feeling could be allowed to pour, there to cool and settle.

After the war Spinelli resumed his career as a journalist. He was the founder of the *Istituto per Affari Internazionali* in 1967 and in 1970 became a member of the **European Commission**, with responsibility for industrial policy. He resigned towards the end of 1976 in order to stand for election to the Camera dei Deputati, where he served on the Foreign Affairs Committee and became chairman of his parliamentary group. At the same time he was nominated as a Member of the **European Parliament** (MEP).

In 1979 he was elected to the European Parliament as an Independent of the Left (*Indipendente di Sinistra*) in the first direct elections, and joined the Communist Group. Although a man of the Left (he joined the Italian Communist Party in 1924 but resigned in 1937), Spinelli was too independent to fit at all easily into any particular party. A powerful rather than subtle orator, his ability to persuade people rested upon his force of personality and the tenacity with which he pursued an argument.

Until his death in 1986, Spinelli campaigned vigorously for wide-ranging reforms to the Community institutions. He did this first through a series of informal meetings known as the **Crocodile Club** (after the Strasbourg restaurant in which the Group was founded in July 1980) and from January 1981 in the newly established Committee on Institutional Affairs. The European Parliament's **Draft Treaty establishing the European Union** (DTEU), which was adopted in February 1984, was the principal monument to the final period of Spinelli's life.

In his autobiography, *Come ho tentato di diventare saggio* (How I Sought To Become Wise), Spinelli outlined the intellectual basis of his passionate attachment to federalism and to European unity. Ironically, in the light of the very cool reception his ideas received in the United Kingdom, he always claimed that his principal source of inspiration were the federalist ideas of British and American theorists such as Lothian and Madison. Although his DTEU did not in the end command widespread support outside the Parliament, there were many who argued (among them **Jacques Delors**) that without it the **Single European Act** (SEA) could never have been brought into being. John Pinder (ed.), *Altiero Spinelli and the British Federalists* (1998) is a collection of writings by Spinelli (including the Ventotene Manifesto), Sir William Beveridge and Lionel Robbins.

Stabilization and Association Process (SAP)

The SAP is the name given to the European Union's relations with the Western Balkans (Albania, Bosnia–Herzegovina, Croatia, the Former Yugoslav Republic of Macedonia (FYROM) and the Federal Republic of Yugoslavia). It was set in train by the **European Commission** in May 1999 and endorsed in June 2000 by the **European Council** meeting in Feira. At this meeting the SAP countries were offered the prospect of Union membership in the longer term in line with the **Copenhagen criteria**. In November 2000 a European Union–SAP countries meeting was held in Zagreb to define the SAP in more detail and in particular to work out a programme of assistance. Each of the five countries is to have a Stabilization and Association Agreement with the Union (the first, with FYROM, was signed in July 2001). These agreements entail the gradual implementation of free trade and the progressive assumption by the SAP countries of Union standards in areas such as human rights, the rule of law, the protection of the environment, and competition policy. Aid to SAP countries is given under the **CARDS programme**. The Zagreb meeting encouraged the SAP countries to establish closer cooperation among themselves in areas such as trade and regional planning and in response to threats such as illegal immigration and organized crime. See also **European Agency for Reconstruction**, **Stability Pact for South-Eastern Europe.**

Stability and Growth Pact

Not to be confused with the **Pact on Stability in Europe** or the **Stability Pact for South-Eastern Europe,** the Stability and Growth Pact was adopted by the **European Council** at its meeting in Amsterdam (16–17 June 1997). The Pact builds on and strengthens the **convergence criteria** used to assess which countries qualified for stage 3 of **Economic and Monetary Union** (EMU), with a view to ensuring that all member states, whether or not they participate in stage 3, contribute towards the overall climate of stability and financial prudence upon which the success of EMU depends.

Preparatory discussions on the Pact took place at European Council meetings in Madrid (December 1995), Florence (June 1996) and Dublin (December 1996), at which the main elements in the Pact were identified. In the accompanying statement agreed in Amsterdam, the European Council underlined 'the importance of safeguarding sound government finances as a means to strengthen the conditions for price stability and for strong sustainable growth conducive to employment creation. It is also necessary to ensure that national budgetary policies support stability-oriented monetary policies.'

The Pact, which is in twelve parts addressed to the member states, the European Commission and the Council of Ministers, enjoins all parties to engage in the prompt and vigorous implementation of the **excessive deficit procedure**. Although the Pact as such has no legal force, it is backed up by two Council Regulations. Essentially, the effect of these is to tighten up the surveillance procedure and to minimize the degree of discretion which the relevant authorities enjoy under Articles 103 and 104 of the **Treaty of Rome** in the event of a member state's economy moving away from its agreed targets. At the meeting of the European Council on 2 May 1998 at which the choice of countries participating in stage 3 of EMU was made, the heads of government adopted the 'Waigel Declaration' (named after Theo Waigel, the German Finance Minister) which confirms and strengthens the pact. See A. Brumila, M. Buti, and D. Franco (eds), *The Stability and Growth Pact* (Basingstoke, 2001).

Stability Pact for South-Eastern Europe

The Stability Pact was drawn up at a meeting in Cologne of member states' representatives, international agencies and other interested organizations on 10 June 1999 (it had been discussed by the **European Council** at its meeting in Cologne earlier in the month). The Pact governs relations between the countries of former Yugoslavia (except Slovenia, which already has a **Europe Agreement** with the Union), Albania and the European Union and is intended, in the words of the European Council 'to enhance peace, stability and prosperity in, and cooperation between, countries in the region'.

Initially, the Federal Republic of Yugoslavia was excluded from the Pact pending a resolution of the Kosovo crisis. The Pact is supplemented by 'Stabilization and Association Agreements' between the European Union and individual countries in the region, described by the European Council as ' a new kind of contractual relationship … with a prospect of European Union membership' (see **Stabilization and Association Process**). The first of these agreements, with the Former Yugoslav Republic of Macedonia, was signed in April 2001. Aid to the countries covered by the Stability Pact (amounting to €4.65 billion over the period 2000–6) is managed with the help of the **European Agency for Reconstruction** in Thessaloniki. In overall charge is a Special Coordinator for the Stability Pact appointed by the Union.

The Stability Pact is the Union's principal contribution to the wider South-East Europe Cooperation Process (SEECP) involving Greece, the Former Yugoslav Republic of Macedonia, the Federal Republic of Yugoslavia, Albania, Bosnia–Herzegovina, Bulgaria, Turkey and Romania (with Croatia as an observer). An Action Plan for Regional Economic Cooperation was adopted by the SEECP countries at a meeting in Skopje in February 2001.

State aids

State aids – financial assistance from public funds to commercial enterprises, public or private – that distort conditions of competition within the Union are subject to strict rules laid down in Articles 87 to 89 of the **Treaty of Rome** as part of **competition policy**. Such aids must in all circumstances be notified to the **European Commission**, which can block them or, in the case of state aids already granted, insist upon repayment. To be approved, state aids must be of a specified amount and time-limited, and in the case of an enterprise in difficulties may be given only in conjunction with a restructuring programme. They may also be approved if it can be shown that they are consistent with broader regional policy aims, likely to create new investment, given in response to emergency needs, linked to 'an important project of common European interest' or designed to 'remedy a serious disturbance in the economy of a Member State'. The **Court of Justice** is the ultimate arbiter of the lawfulness of state aids.

Decisions on state aids can be controversial. The long list in the Treaty of circumstances in which state aids may be granted provides plenty of scope for ingenious economic arguments driven by essentially political motives. Under the **European Economic Area** (EEA) Treaty the rules on state aids now apply throughout the EEA. They are contained in Regulation 659/99 of 22 March 1999 (*Official Journal*, L83, 27 March 1999). The European Commission publishes a regular 'scoreboard' of state aids (see COM(2001) 782 of 20 December 2001) which currently amount to about 1 per cent of the Union's GDP. The

European Council at its meeting in Stockholm (March 2000) called upon the member states to 'demonstrate a downward trend in State aid by ... 2003'. Of the 1982 instances of state aids referred to the Commission over the period 1998–2000 only 7 per cent were refused. There is a clear and helpful treatment of state aids in Dennis Swann, *The Economics of Europe* (9th edition, Harmondsworth, 2000).

Strasbourg

The capital of Alsace, Strasbourg is an ancient cathedral city of about 500,000 inhabitants on the French side of the Rhine. In common with the rest of Alsace, Strasbourg has changed hands several times between France and Germany over the centuries and its inhabitants speak both French and a German dialect known as *Elsässisch*. For this reason the city has been regarded as a symbol of Franco-German reconciliation since the Second World War.

In 1949, on a proposal from the British Foreign Secretary Ernest Bevin, Strasbourg was chosen as the seat of the **Council of Europe**. A Palais de l'Europe was built, which by 1952 was serving not only as the headquarters of the Council of Europe but also as the place in which meetings of the Common Assembly of the **European Coal and Steel Community** (ECSC) were held (see **seat of the institutions**). Since 1958 the **European Parliament**, the successor to the Common Assembly, has held most of its monthly part-sessions in Strasbourg. A larger Palais was built in 1977 to accommodate the directly elected European Parliament, but by the late 1990s this too had been outgrown and a third, even larger Palais was opened in July 1999.

Strasbourg's status as the self-styled 'parliamentary capital of Europe' was for many years under threat from moves to concentrate the main institutions of the European Union in **Brussels**. Although the Council of Europe, the European Court of Human Rights and, since 1991, the **Eurocorps** would in any case have remained in Strasbourg, the city was determined to retain the part-sessions of the European Parliament. This position has always been defended with peculiar tenacity by French governments of whatever political complexion, to the point of Strasbourg's status being non-negotiable. By showing themselves prepared to block other decisions on the siting of newly created European institutions, the French finally secured agreement at the Edinburgh meeting of the European Council in December 1992 that Strasbourg should be the 'seat' of the European Parliament and that its normal monthly part-sessions should continue to be held there. Since this decision did not curb the desire of many Members of the European Parliament (MEPs) to move to Brussels, the French National Assembly, backed by the French government, took the further step in 1994 of blocking the agreement to increase the number of MEPs in time for the June 1994 European elections until 'precise and written' assurances were given on the holding of 12 part-sessions a year in

Strasbourg and the lease on the new premises was signed. A **protocol** annexed to the **Treaty of Amsterdam** confirms the Edinburgh decision.

Although the behaviour of the French on the subject of Strasbourg may be thought unreasonable, they are not alone in their attachment to the city as a symbol of Franco-German reconciliation. Many Germans feel the same way: as Chancellor Helmut Schmidt once replied when asked whether he favoured Brussels or Strasbourg, 'My head is in Brussels but my heart is in Strasbourg.'

Stresa Conference

In July 1958, soon after the **Treaty of Rome** came into force, Sicco Mansholt (see **Mansholt Plan**), the Dutch vice-president of the **European Commission** responsible for the **Common Agricultural Policy** (CAP), convened a conference of Commission officials, national experts and representatives of farmers' organizations to decide how to accomplish the objectives of the CAP as set out in Article 39 (now 33) EEC. The conference was held at Stresa on Lake Maggiore. Perhaps its most far-reaching decision was to support agriculture through a system of guaranteed prices rather than direct income aids (see **intervention**).

Structural funds

The term 'structural funds' is used to denote the **European Social Fund** (ESF), the **European Regional Development Fund** (ERDF), the 'guidance' section of the **European Agricultural Guidance and Guarantee Fund** (EAGGF) and the **Cohesion Fund**. They are the principal means whereby aid is directed towards the less-developed regions of the European Union. In total, the structural funds amounted to about € 27.5 billion in 2000, and represent almost one-third of the Union's **Budget**. When the first reform of the structural funds came into effect in 1989 five basic objectives were identified:

Objective 1 assisting underdeveloped regions;
Objective 2 assisting regions affected by the decline of traditional industries;
Objective 3 combating long-term unemployment (defined as more than 12 months) and the integration of young people (under-25s) into the labour market;
Objective 4 helping workers adapt to technological change;
Objective 5 (a) structural reform of agriculture and (b) helping rural areas.

Of these, Objective 1 was by far the most important, absorbing some 66 per cent of total funds. The **enlargement** negotiations with Austria, Finland, Norway and Sweden resulted in the creation of an Objective 6 category, designed primarily to allow assistance to be given to the Arctic regions. Overall, some 51 per cent of the Union's population lived in areas covered by Objectives 1, 2, 5b and 6. The aim of the **European**

Commission was to reduce this to 40 per cent, which meant that, with **enlargement**, many regions would lose their eligibility for assistance from the structural funds.

Detailed proposals for reform were made as part of the Commission's *Agenda 2000* programme which was adopted by the **European Council** in Berlin in March 1999. The criteria for eligibility were modified and the seven 'Objectives' reduced to three:

Objective 1   assisting underdeveloped regions, i.e. those with a per capita GDP less than 75 per cent of the Union average;

Objective 2   helping areas facing structural difficulties;

Objective 3   education, training and employment in areas not covered by Objective 1.

Relief in the form of transitional arrangements was to be made available to regions which lost assisted area status.

Maps must be drawn, and periodically redrawn, to define which areas qualify for assistance. This is done by the Commission in consultation with member states. Objective 1 regions cover approximately 22 per cent of the Union's total population including the whole of Greece, Ireland (except Dublin), Portugal (except Lisbon), most of Spain, the French overseas territories, southern Italy, Sardinia, Sicily, all the former East Germany (except Berlin), and parts of Finland, Sweden and the United Kingdom. In all cases financial assistance from the structural funds, which is always given in the form of grants, is intended to complement assistance given at the national level (see **additionality**). In certain cases assistance may also be given in the form of loans from the **European Investment Bank** (EIB). Total annual receipts from the structural funds (including the **Cohesion Fund**: see below) should not exceed 4 per cent of a country's GDP. Six per cent of structural fund aid is reserved for initiatives devised and administered directly by the Commission, such as Interreg III (for cross-border projects), Leader + (for rural areas), and URBAN (for inner cities).

The accession of Greece in 1981 and of Portugal and Spain in 1986 posed a challenge to the commitment in the preamble to the **Treaty of Rome** to 'reduce the differences existing between the various regions and the backwardness of the less-favoured regions'. It was also argued that the programme for the completion of the **Single Market** would increase still further the advantages enjoyed by the core regions over those on the periphery. **Integrated Mediterranean Programmes** (IMPs) were set up to give special help to Greece and the Mediterranean regions of France and Italy, and between 1987 and 1993 the structural funds were doubled in size. At the Edinburgh meeting of the **European Council** in December 1992 it was agreed to double the funds again over the period 1994–9 (see **Edinburgh Growth Initiative**). The **Maastricht Treaty** set out the role of the structural funds in amendments to the Treaty of Rome (Articles 130(a) to 130(e), now 158 to 162) under the title 'Economic and social cohesion' and required a Cohesion Fund to be set up before 31 December 1993. The Berlin agreement (see above) fixed the structural funds at €213 billion (about £133 billion) over the period 2000–6, of which 69.7 per cent has been allocated to Objective 1. Each member state has a quota of structural fund receipts.

Although they have grown substantially since their inception, the structural funds amount to just over a third of 1 per cent of the member states' combined GDP. As the **MacDougall Report** demonstrated in 1977, this is well short of the sums required for a significant redistributive effect. In some countries, notably Italy, Spain and the United Kingdom, the structural funds have had an impact on particular regions. It has been estimated that by 1999, 600,000 jobs in Objective 1 regions had been the direct result of assistance from the structural funds.

Structured dialogue

Structured dialogue (or structured relations) between the European Union and the countries with which the Union has **Europe Agreements** is an important element in the **pre-accession strategy**. Foreshadowed in the decision of the **European Council** meeting in Copenhagen (June 1993) to give these countries regular access to the deliberations of the institutions of the Union, the structured dialogue was reviewed and developed at the European Council meeting in Essen (December 1994) on the basis of a report from the **Council of Ministers**. Essentially, the structured dialogue involves an element of privileged regular access to meetings of the European Council and the Council of Ministers and the right to make formal submissions on all matters of wider European interest, such as those discussed in **Intergovernmental Conferences**. The structured dialogue also extends to the **Common Foreign and Security Policy** (CFSP) and **Justice and Home Affairs** (JHA) pillars of the European Union. See also **enlargement**, **European Conference, Laeken Declaration**.

Stuttgart Declaration

The Stuttgart Declaration, formally known as the Solemn Declaration on European Union, was a wide-ranging statement concerning the institutions and policies of the European Community issued by the **European Council** meeting in Stuttgart on 17–19 June 1983. It represented the first serious attempt by the European Council to address the question of institutional reform and to push forward the 1972 objective of converting the Community into some form of **European Union**. In terms deliberately reminiscent of the 1972 Paris **summit**, the heads of government restated their determination to 'transform the whole complex of relations between their states into a European Union', envisaging for the first time the future adoption of a Treaty on European Union. It also attempted to codify the evolving role of the European Council in decision-making, and suggested that the position of the **European Parliament** should be significantly enhanced and the scope of Community activity further broadened.

The Stuttgart Declaration was the governments' response to the **Genscher–Colombo Plan**, the text of which it echoed in a number of respects. It stressed the importance of developing **European Political Cooperation** and of common action in respect of 'the political and economic aspects of security', although it fell short of proposing a 'common foreign policy'. It explained the European Council's role in promoting closer integration, declaring that henceforth the European Council would be able to act 'in its capacity as the Council [of Ministers]' in any area of Community responsibility (which was, in fact, legally invalid, since action still required the latter's separate and subsequent endorsement). It confirmed that the president-in-office of the European Council would report to the European Parliament at least once every six months.

The Stuttgart Declaration did not attempt to subvert the **Luxembourg Compromise,** but it did assert that 'the application of the decision-making procedures laid down in the Treaties is of vital importance in order to improve the EC's capacity to act' (Paragraph 2.2.2). The Declaration did not endorse the proposal in the Genscher–Colombo Plan to establish new Councils for policy areas not provided for in the **Treaties**.

The Declaration was generous in its acknowledgement of the growing role of the European Parliament. It took up the proposal in the Genscher–Colombo Plan to engage in non-binding consultation with the Parliament before the president of the **European Commission** was appointed and before new member states were admitted to the Community. Consultation was extended to include all 'significant' international agreements (see **assent procedure**).

The Declaration sought to extend Community activity across a broad range of pressing issues in order to counteract the effects of recession. It spoke of an 'overall economic strategy' to combat unemployment and inflation, and to promote convergence among national economies. It proposed a strengthening of the **European Monetary System** (EMS), including the development of a European Monetary Fund. It identified the 'completion of the internal market' – one of the first official statements to use this phrase – and the 'development of an industrial strategy' as key Community objectives. It asserted that European Union was being achieved 'by deepening and broadening the scope of European activities so that they coherently cover … a growing proportion of Member States' mutual relations', a process it evidently welcomed.

The fact that the Stuttgart Declaration was a statement of political will, not a Treaty, rendered its conclusions ultimately unenforceable. However, the striking fact is that many of them were given legal force three years later in the **Single European Act** (SEA). The two exercises were linked by the commitment at the end of the Declaration to decide within five years on 'whether the progress achieved [in the interim] should be incorporated in a Treaty on European Union'.

The Stuttgart Declaration was widely criticized in the European Parliament and elsewhere for the non-binding nature of its commitments (the Parliament's much more ambitious **Draft Treaty establishing the European Union** (DTEU) was adopted the following year). The Declaration did, however, mark a decisive shift in favour of closer integration. It was under a French **presidency** that the Versailles European Council set up both the **Dooge Committee** and the Adonnino Committee on a **People's Europe** in June 1984.

Subsidiarity

Subsidiarity is the principle that decisions should be taken at the lowest level consistent with effective action within a political system. Held to be a guiding principle of federalism (see **federation**), it has also been widely invoked in recent years as a means of limiting the European Union's competence. The **Maastricht Treaty** introduced a subsidiarity clause into the **Treaty of Rome**: 'In areas which do not fall within its exclusive competence, the Community shall take action, in accordance with the principle of subsidiarity, only if and in so far as the objectives of the proposed action cannot be sufficiently achieved by the Member States and can therefore, by reason of the scale or effects of the proposed action, be better achieved by the Community' (Article 5; see also **proportionality**). Annexed to the **Treaty of Amsterdam** is a protocol on the application of the principles of subsidiarity and proportionality. Although the principle now enjoys Treaty status, most commentators are uncertain about its long-term significance in the integration process. In particular, many lawyers doubt that the principle is 'justiciable', that is, sufficiently precise in point of substance and intent to be capable of being enforced.

The principle of subsidiarity finds a parallel in the Tenth Amendment to the United States Constitution and in Article 30 of the German Constitution, both of which reserve to the states or *Länder* powers not specifically allocated to the federal government. The principle is also to be found in Pope Pius XI's encyclical '*Quadragesimo Anno*' of 1931, in which it was invoked as a means of maintaining the authority of the Church against the ever-encroaching power of the State.

In the context of European integration, the first reference to subsidiarity in an official document was in the **European Commission**'s submission to the **Tindemans Report** on European Union in June 1975. Paragraph 12 states: 'No more than the existing Communities have done so, European Union is not to give birth to a centralizing superstate. Consequently, and in accordance with the *principe de subsidiarité*, the Union will be given responsibility only for those matters which the Member States are no longer capable of dealing with efficiently.' The Commission's motive for invoking subsidiarity was to reassure those who feared that conversion of the Community into a European Union would substantially erode the powers of national governments and parliaments.

Subsidiarity was revived in February 1984 when the **European Parliament** adopted its ambitious and highly integrationist **Draft Treaty establishing the European Union** (DTEU). Like the Commission in 1975, the Parliament sought to invoke subsidiarity as a means of forestalling concern within national political circles that closer European integration must necessarily involve an open-ended transfer of powers to centralized bodies at European level. The Parliament's text sought to entrench subsidiarity as a central principle of further unification by writing it into the Draft Treaty – the proposed successor document to the Treaty of Rome – in two ways: first, by a general reference in the preamble, and second, in a more specific Article defining the relationship between the new Union and the member states in areas where they shared competence.

In the preamble, Parliament's aim was 'to entrust common institutions ... only with those powers required to complete successfully the tasks they may carry out more satisfactorily than the states acting independently'. The more detailed formula later in the text asserted that 'the Union shall only act to carry out those tasks which may be undertaken more effectively in common than by the Member States acting separately, in particular those whose execution requires action by the Union because their dimensions or effects extend beyond national frontiers' (Article 12(2)).

This was taken up in the 1986 **Single European Act** (SEA) which inserted a new Article into the Treaty of Rome: 'The Community shall take action relating to the environment to the extent to which [objectives] can be attained better at the Community level than at the level of individual Member States' (Article 130(r).4, since repealed).

Although not yet of general application, the principle of subsidiarity was invoked from the mid-1980s by national governments intent upon keeping the Commission in check. In 1989 the British government cited subsidiarity as one of the reasons for not signing the Social Charter (see **European Social Charter**). By the time the Maastricht Treaty was finally agreed in December 1991, subsidiarity had also become important to the German government, which was seeking to address the problems of **German reunification** while maintaining its strongly pro-integration stance in European affairs. Defeats in *Länder* elections had resulted in a loss of control of the Bundesrat (composed of representatives of the *Länder*) and the government turned to the subsidiarity principle as a means of affirming its attachment both to the rights of the *Länder* and to strong European institutions. The Maastricht Treaty itself described the new European Union as one 'in which decisions are taken ... as closely as possible to the citizen' (Article 1). A fuller definition of subsidiarity was drawn up at the Birmingham meeting of the **European Council** in October 1992: 'Decisions must be taken as closely as possible to the citizen. Greater unity can be achieved without excessive centralization. It is for each Member State to decide how its powers should be exercised domestically ... Action at the Community level should happen only when proper and necessary.' At the Brussels meeting of the European Council in December 1993 the Commission was required to produce an annual report on the application of the subsidiarity principle.

As the wording of Article 5 EC makes clear, subsidiarity applies only to areas that do not fall within the 'exclusive competence' of the Community. This means that however effective the subsidiarity principle may prove to be as a way of preventing the Union institutions from moving into new areas, it is of only very limited use to those who would like to see the institutions returning powers to national or local authorities in areas already covered by the **Treaties**. The wording gives no guidance with regard to how an assessment could be made of whether an objective might be 'better achieved by the Community', and it is this reliance on essentially subjective judgments that is at the root of the legal difficulties posed by the subsidiarity clause.

The long-term importance of subsidiarity will depend on how and if the **Court of Justice** chooses to interpret and apply the principle. The Court may either find the subsidiarity clause to be too general to use in specific rulings, or choose to interpret its ambiguous provisions in a consistently pro-integrationist direction, so defeating the purpose for which it was intended. Some experts fear that it will introduce a new legal principle that cuts across the whole basis of existing jurisprudence in an unpredictable and confusing way, further politicizing the Court and prejudicing its authority. The **Council of Ministers** has denied that subsidiarity has any bearing on the allocation of powers within member states. Moreover, the European Council has stated that the subsidiarity principle does not have **direct effect** (see Joint Answer to Written Questions by Mr Arbeloa Muru, *Official Journal*, C102, 11 April 1994).

Subsidiarity already has a literature of its own, much of it in learned periodicals. See especially *Subsidiarity: the challenge of change* (proceedings of the Jacques Delors colloquium at the European Institute of Public

Administration, Maastricht, 1991); Akos Toth, 'Is subsidiarity justiciable?', *European Law Review*, Vol. 19, no. 3, June 1994; John Peterson, 'Subsidiarity: a definition to suit any vision', *Political Affairs*, Vol. 47, no. 1, January 1994.

Summer time

Summer time begins and ends on the same day (the last Sunday in March and the last Sunday in October) throughout the **European Economic Area** (EEA). The **Council of Ministers** agreed when adopting the Ninth Directive on summer time in January 2001 (Directive 00/44, *Official Journal*, L31, 2 February 2001) that the **European Commission** should publish, every five years, a table confirming the exact dates for the succeeding five years. It is not proposed to make the EEA a single time zone. The sun rises in the most easterly part of Finland or Greece some two and a half hours earlier than in the west of Ireland.

Summit

Meetings of heads of government are often referred to as summits. The first summit involving heads of government of the member states of the European Community (then **the Six**) was held in February 1961 (see **Fouchet Plan**). Formalized since 1975, such summits are now known as meetings of the **European Council**.

Supremacy

See **primacy**.

Supreme Headquarters Allied Powers Europe (SHAPE)

In December 1950 a Supreme Allied Commander Europe (SACEUR) was appointed within the framework of the **North Atlantic Treaty Organization** (NATO). SACEUR's headquarters, known as Supreme Headquarters Allied Powers Europe (SHAPE), were set up the following year in Rocquencourt, near Paris. In 1967, when France withdrew from NATO's integrated military command structure, SHAPE was moved to its present site outside Mons, Belgium. Over 1,000 officers and 2,000 other service personnel (plus 1,500 civilians) make up the SHAPE staff, including the national military representatives accredited to SACEUR. Under the **Partnership for Peace** initiative, Partner states are entitled to establish liaison offices at SHAPE. See **Allied Command Europe**.

Suspension

The **Treaty of Amsterdam** introduced a new provision into the **Maastricht Treaty**, under which a member state found guilty of a 'serious and persistent breach' of the 'principles of liberty, democracy, respect for human rights and fundamental freedoms, and the rule of law' (i.e., the principles in Article 6 TEU, as amended by the Treaty of Amsterdam) may be liable to forfeit 'certain of the rights deriving from the application of this Treaty ... including the voting rights ... in the **Council of Ministers**' (Article 7 TEU). Responsibility for determining such a breach rests with the Council of Ministers, meeting at the level of heads of state or government, and acting by unanimity or a proposal from at least one-third of the member states or from the **European Commission** and with the **assent** of the **European Parliament**. The decision with respect to which rights the offending state shall forfeit may be taken by **qualified majority voting** (QMV) as may any subsequent decisions to vary or revoke this decision. The member state accused of a breach has the right to be heard, but at no stage in the proceedings is its vote taken into account. The new Article 7 makes it clear that the offending member state's 'obligations ... under this Treaty continue to be binding on that state'. Parallel provisions in the **Treaty of Rome** and in the Treaties establishing the **European Coal and Steel Community** and the **European Atomic Energy Community** ensure that a member state's suspension applies to all three Communities.

This provision must be seen as part of the European Union's attempt to strengthen its commitment to fundamental rights (see **human rights**). It is also a safeguard against the possibility, perhaps less remote after the next round of **enlargement** than it is now, that a member state might cease to conform to an acceptable pattern of democratic behaviour complemented by respect for individual rights. Some might have preferred a simpler mechanism for exclusion rather than suspension, but because of the intricate pattern of legal, political, contractual and financial obligations between the Union and public and private bodies and individuals which flow from membership, there are real difficulties in the way of expelling a member state. Partly as a consequence of the arguments prompted by the sanctions imposed on Austria in 2000, Article 7 TEU was revised in the **Treaty of Nice**.

Sweden

Although Sweden, a neutral country in both World Wars, has consistently followed a policy of not joining military alliances, it was nevertheless a founder member of the **Organization for Economic Cooperation and Development** (OECD), the **Council of Europe** and the **European Free Trade Association** (EFTA). Sweden has also played a very active role in the **Nordic Council**. Like Austria, Sweden sought at an early stage to establish closer economic ties with the Community, but the negotiations of the 1960s and 1970s resulted only in the free trade arrangement extended to all EFTA countries with effect from January 1973 and, later, in Sweden's membership of the **European Economic Area** (EEA). The question of full membership of the Community remained an issue in Swedish politics and eventually an application for membership was deposited by the Socialist Government of Ingvar Carlsson on 1 July 1991. On the conclusion of the **Maastricht Treaty** in December 1991 Carlsson's successor, the Conservative Carl Bildt, reaffirmed his government's commitment to the aims of the European Union established by the Treaty, including its provisions for a **Common Foreign and Security Policy** (CFSP): this was particularly significant in the light of Sweden's long-standing unilateral commitment to **neutrality**. In 1991 the decision was taken to link the Swedish krona to the **ECU** (the krona has never been in the **Exchange-Rate Mechanism** (ERM)).

In point of performance the economy of Sweden – one of the most prosperous countries in the world – posed few problems. However, as the Commission's generally favourable **Opinion** pointed out, the structure of the economy, and notably the numerous state monopolies, cartels and the absence of competition generally, required some adjustment in order to conform with the **Treaty of Rome** (*Bulletin of the European Communities*, supplement 5/92). Much of this adjustment was being undertaken in the context of the EEA Treaty, and Sweden already applied most of the **Single Market** legislation. Unlike Austria's, Sweden's commitment to neutrality was not enshrined in the constitution, but was none the less well established over a long period. The decline in East–West tension prompted a debate within Sweden on what 'neutrality' now meant in practice, with the result that it was held to be compatible with the European Union's aspirations towards a common security policy and with the concrete actions arising from it.

The negotiations with Sweden were completed in March 1994. Two months later the **European Parliament** gave its assent to membership. The public debate that preceded the **referendum** of 13 November 1994 (in which membership was supported by 52.2 per cent of the vote) centred upon the future of Swedish agriculture and the impact on the 'Swedish model' of society. The Union has benefited from Sweden's prosperity, stability and high standards in such areas as education, the environment and respect for women's rights. Sweden has also brought into the Union a strong tradition of openness (see **transparency**) in public affairs. Equally, Sweden may hope to gain from exposure to more vigorous competition and the challenge of having to play a role on a wider political stage. Sweden became the fifteenth member of the European Union on 1 January 1995. In the September 1995 European elections, 11 of Sweden's 22 MEPs were elected from anti-European parties. In 1997 the Swedish parliament voted decisively against Sweden's participation in stage 3 of **Economic and Monetary Union** (EMU).

Switzerland

Switzerland's well-established policy of not joining the international organizations to which most other Western countries belong began to change in the 1990s. Switzerland became a member of the International Monetary Fund and the World Bank in 1992, but in the same year membership of the **European Economic Area** (EEA) was rejected in a **referendum**. Although a member of the **Council of Europe** since 1963 and a founder member of the **European Free Trade Association** (EFTA), Switzerland remained only an observer member of the United Nations, until voting for full membership in a March 2002 referendum. In June 1992 the Swiss government applied for membership of the Union; the rejection of the EEA Agreement resulted in the application being left in abeyance. In common with other EFTA states, Switzerland already had free trade arrangements for manufactured goods with the European Community, but the establishment of the **Single Market** and the relaxation of East–West tension led to a reappraisal of Swiss interests and of the country's long tradition of **neutrality**.

Intra-Community commercial traffic through Switzerland has long been governed by a series of transit agreements. In February 1994 the Swiss voted in a referendum effectively to ban all commercial road traffic through their country with effect from 2004. This decision is being followed up in a number of very ambitious projects involving new railway tunnels through the Alps (notably the St Gotthard route) and the further development of combined road–rail transport.

Switzerland is a confederation, with four official languages, in which a very strong sense of local identity co-exists with an equally strong sense of national identity. For this reason Switzerland has occasionally been held up as a model of how a united Europe could work. In fact, the Swiss nation was built up gradually over some 700 years on the basis of a very particular combination of geographic, political, religious and historical circumstances. The country is governed at the federal, cantonal and communal level, at each of which recourse may be had to a referendum under constitutional provisions introduced in 1874 as a means of limiting the power of central government. Among the most prosperous countries in the world, Switzerland could easily meet the economic obligations of membership of the Union. What is less certain is whether the Swiss, with their lively attachment to direct democracy, neutrality and separate identity, are yet prepared to adapt to a system in which supranational institutions play a pre-eminent role and which would require them to open both their frontiers and their economy to other Europeans. See Cédric Dupont and Pascal Sciarini, 'Switzerland and the European integration process: engagement without marriage', *West European Politics*, Vol. 24, no. 2, April 2001.

T

TACIS

The TACIS programme (Technical Assistance to the Commonwealth of Independent States, CIS) dates from a December 1990 decision by the **European Council** meeting in Rome. Its main objective is to help the so-called Newly Independent States (NIS; the 10 members of the CIS plus Azerbaijan and Georgia) make the transition to a market economy and a democratic society. TACIS, which is administered by the **European Commission**, became operational in 1991. Assistance of the type given by TACIS has been extended to Mongolia (see also **PHARE**).

Five priority sectors were identified in 1991: training (see also **European Training Foundation**), energy (including, most importantly, nuclear safety), transport, support for industrial and commercial enterprises, food production and distribution. TACIS aid is given in the form of grants, on the basis of indicative programmes drawn up in consultation with the beneficiary states. Together, the TACIS and PHARE programmes amount to about a third of the sums allocated to 'external actions' in the **Budget**.

Tax harmonization

Tax harmonization has always been subsidiary to other Treaty objectives, never an area of Community action in its own right, and is almost wholly limited to indirect taxation. Articles 90 to 92 of the **Treaty of Rome** require member states not to apply discriminatory taxes in order to favour domestically produced goods. Article 93 empowers the **Council of Ministers** to 'adopt provisions for the harmonization of legislation concerning turnover taxes, excise duties and other forms of indirect taxation to the extent that such harmonization is necessary to ensure the establishment and the functioning of the internal market'. Tax measures may also be taken under **Articles 94 and 95**. An indication of the sensitivity of the subject is the fact that, as an exception to what is now the general rule where **Single Market** measures are concerned, **unanimity** is required for all Council measures on tax (see also **value-added tax**). Some proposals on direct taxation of companies were first put forward as long ago as 1960. However, on 1 December 1997 the **Ecofin Council** reached agreement on a 'Code of Conduct' to end 'harmful fiscal competition' between member states with respect to rates of company taxation. This code, which came into force on 1 January 1998, prefigures the setting of minimum rates by 1 January 2003.

The 1985 **Cockfield White Paper** identified the fiscal barriers to trade within the Single Market. Among these were different rates and systems of excise duties. Minimum rates of duty for alcohol, tobacco, cigarettes and mineral oil were agreed in 1992. However, as part of the removal of frontier controls, the point at which goods are taxed has been moved from the country of destination to the country of origin: this means that whatever differences there may be in national tax systems and tax rates, adjustments to the amounts of tax paid no longer have to be made at borders between member states.

Areas in which proposals are currently under consideration are taxation and employment, company tax, and taxation and the environment. See a report by the House of Lords Select Committee on the European Communities, *Taxes in the EU: Can Co-ordination and Competition Co-exist?* (July 1999).The background to tax harmonization is set out very clearly in Dennis Swann, *The Economics of Europe* (9th edn, Harmondsworth, 2000).

Tempus

The Tempus (trans-European mobility scheme for university studies) programme was established in 1990 (*Official Journal*, L131, 25 May 1990) and has been renewed for the period 2000–6 (*Official Journal*, L120, 8 May 1999). Tempus, which is linked to the **PHARE** and **TACIS** programmes of assistance to the countries of central and eastern Europe, the former Soviet Union and Mongolia, is an aid programme for the restructuring of education and training in recipient countries. Albania, Bosnia–Herzegovina, Croatia and Macedonia now also participate in the programme. The budget for Tempus is drawn from the resources made available for PHARE and TACIS. Tempus is open to all Group of Twenty-four countries (G-24, the member states of the **Organization for Economic Cooperation and Development** (OECD)); however, G-24 states outside the Union which are not covered by PHARE or TACIS must pay the costs of their participation in Tempus. Tempus is managed by the **European Commission** with assistance from the **European Training Foundation**.

Thatcher, Margaret (b. 1925)

Margaret Thatcher defeated **Edward Heath** in the contest for the leadership of the Conservative Party (then in opposition) in February 1975. Four years later, in May 1979, the Conservative Party was returned to power under her leadership and the following month, the Conservatives won 60 out of the 78 seats in Great Britain in the first **European elections**.

In the **referendum of June 1975** Mrs Thatcher campaigned conscientiously but not especially enthusiastically in favour of the United Kingdom remaining a member of the Community. Her first quarrel with the Community began in November 1979 over the level of the British net contribution to the Budget (see **British Budget problem**). The dilatory manner in which this problem was addressed (it remained unresolved until the **Fontainebleau Agreement** of June 1984) did little to inspire confidence and respect on Mrs Thatcher's part for the institutions and procedures of the Community. She was frustrated too in her efforts to reform the **Common Agricultural Policy** (CAP). However, in the **Single Market** programme, launched the year after the Fontainebleau settlement, Mrs Thatcher found a Community objective to which she could give whole-hearted support. In 1986 she endorsed the **Single European Act** (SEA), primarily as a means of speeding up decision-making on Single Market legislation. She was later to argue that at the time she was not made fully aware of the implications of the SEA for the balance of power between the Community institutions and, in particular, for member states' rights of veto (see **qualified majority voting**).

Mrs Thatcher's view of how European integration should move forward was broadly similar to that of **Charles de Gaulle**: she shared his hostility to the supranational character of the **European Commission** and the **European Parliament** and his belief in the pre-eminence of the nation-states. The fullest expression of her views was in the **Bruges speech** of September 1988.

In June 1989 Mrs Thatcher was eventually persuaded to agree at the Madrid meeting of the **European Council** to the United Kingdom's participation in the first stage of **Economic and Monetary Union** (EMU). Both her Chancellor of the Exchequer, Nigel Lawson, and her Foreign Secretary, Sir Geoffrey Howe, had threatened to resign if she continued to block progress towards EMU. At the Strasbourg meeting of the European Council in December 1989 she refused to sign the Social Charter (see **European Social Charter**).

By 1990 Mrs Thatcher's increasingly strident opposition to the European Community was giving rise to concern among Conservative MPs and among her Cabinet colleagues. In November 1990 Sir Geoffrey Howe's resignation from the Cabinet prompted a leadership election from which Mrs Thatcher withdrew after the first ballot, having failed to secure the necessary majority for an outright win over Michael Heseltine.

Mrs Thatcher's adversarial style of politics was particularly ill-adapted to the conventions and procedures of a consensus-oriented decision-making system. In her autobiography *The Downing Street Years* (1993) she expressed no regrets with respect to her robust stance on European issues. She blamed the Conservatives' very poor results in the 1989 European elections on the unwillingness of candidates to follow her lead. She justified her defence of nation-states by describing them as 'functioning democracies' and as 'intractable political realities which it would be folly to seek to override or suppress in favour of a wider but as yet theoretical European nationhood'.

Three Wise Men

The **European Council** meeting in Brussels in December 1978 decided to appoint three 'eminent persons' to report on ways of making the Community institutions more effective and on progress towards **European Union**. They were required to work within the provisions and procedures of the **Treaties** and in the light of the probable **enlargement** of the Community from 9 to 12 members. The 'Three Wise Men', as they were called, were Barend Biesheuvel, a former Prime Minister of the Netherlands; Edmund Dell, who had just resigned as Secretary of State for Trade in the Labour government in the United Kingdom; and Robert Marjolin, a French economist and former vice-president of the **European Commission**. Their *Report on European Institutions*, published in October 1979, contained both general reflections, most of them well founded, on the overall health of the institutions and many practical proposals on how procedures could be improved. The Report was studied in detail by the foreign ministers and featured briefly on the agenda of European Council meetings in Dublin (November 1979) and Luxembourg (April and December 1980), but very few of its recommendations were put into effect.

Tindemans Report

Published in 1975, the Tindemans Report, drawn up at the request of the **European Council** by Leo Tindemans, then Prime Minister of Belgium, was a wide-ranging study of **European Union** and of the steps that might be taken to achieve a more integrated Europe closer to the citizen (see **People's Europe**). The contribution by the **European Commission** to the Tindemans Report was noteworthy for having contained the first official reference to **subsidiarity** in the Community context (see also **two-speed Europe**).

Trade

See **Common Commercial Policy, Intra-Community trade**.

Trans-European networks (TENS)

Article 154 of the **Treaty of Rome** provides for 'the establishment and development of trans-European networks in the areas of transport, telecommunications and energy infrastructures'. The second part of the Article refers to 'the interaction and interoperability of national networks' and to 'the need to link island, landlocked and peripheral regions with the central regions of the Community'. This and the two following Articles 155 and 156 were added to the Treaty of Rome by the **Maastricht Treaty**. At its meeting in Essen (December 1994), the **European Council** decided on a priority list of 14 transport TENs and a further 10 TENs in the energy sector.

TENs are intended to complement the **Single Market** by allowing transport, telecommunications and energy grids (electricity supplies, oil and gas pipelines) to be planned on a Union-wide basis, sometimes with a contribution from the **Budget**. Funds were allocated to TENs as part of the **Edinburgh Growth Initiative** (see also **cohesion**). TENs are also intended to help the Union's regional policy by enabling outlying regions to be more efficiently linked with the centre. Detailed planning remains the responsibility of member states; the **European Commission** is entitled to 'take any useful initiative', such as the identification of transport bottlenecks and the provision of technical assistance. The guidelines for TENs, decided under the **co-decision procedure**, are intended to identify 'projects of common interest'.

Among the TENs being built in the energy field are links between the electricity grids of Greece and Italy, and between those of Ireland and the United Kingdom. In the transport field the high-speed rail network (incorporating the **Channel Tunnel**) between London, Paris, Brussels, Cologne and Amsterdam is among the most ambitious of the TENs. Other TENs in this field include improvements to the railway–ferry connections between Great Britain and Ireland and to the 'Nordic triangle' of rail connections between Copenhagen, Oslo and Stockholm. In the telecommunications field progress is being made with new digital exchanges, cross-border electronic clearing systems for banks and credit card operations, data transmission and mobile telephone networks.

Some TENs link the Union with countries outside its borders. Examples include natural gas pipelines between Algeria and Italy, and between Algeria and Spain. In the planning of future TENs much emphasis is being laid on developing better links between the Union and the countries of central and eastern Europe.

Transitional period

The phrase 'transitional period' normally refers to the period of grace during which a new member state may be allowed progressively to introduce and apply Union rules, the immediate adoption of which would cause difficulties. Agreement as to the length of any transitional periods and their field of application is reached in the course of the **enlargement** negotiations and laid down in the Act of **Accession**.

'Transitional period' has a secondary meaning with reference to the history of the Community. Article 8 of the original **Treaty of Rome** required **the Six** to establish the **Common Market** 'during a transitional period of twelve years, ... divided into three stages of four years each'. Article 14 specified in detail the stages by which tariffs, customs duties and quantitative restrictions on trade between the Six were to be removed, starting on 1 January 1958. In the event, the process was completed ahead of schedule, on 1 July 1968. The Treaty commitment to more **majority voting** at the beginning of the third stage of the transitional period on 1 January 1966 was one of the causes of the **empty chair crisis**.

Transnational political parties

The establishment over the past 50 years of parliamentary institutions operating at European level has encouraged the growth of transnational party federations. Further impetus was given by the first **European elections** to the **European Parliament** in 1979, and five of the party federations have been transformed into political parties. This development was recognized in the **Maastricht Treaty** in an additional Article 138(a) (now 191) inserted into the **Treaty of Rome**: 'Political parties at European level are important as a factor for integration within the Union. They contribute to forming a European awareness and to expressing the political will of the citizens of the Union'. The Treaty of Nice added a second paragraph to Article 191 enjoining the Council of Ministers, by **qualified majority voting** (QMV), to lay down 'regulations governing political parties at European level' (the so-called 'statute'). Preliminary work on such a statute revealed disagreement between the member states on how to verify the democratic nature of parties seeking recognition, the threshold which would qualify a party to be regarded as 'European' (the Council has suggested 5 per cent of the vote at European, national, or regional level in at least three member states), and the rules regarding the acceptance of donations or sponsorship. It is hoped that the possibility of reaching agreement by QMV once the Treaty of Nice enters into force will allow these differences to be overcome. The Court of Auditors has been critical of the lack of transparency in relations (especially financial relations) between **political groups** in the Parliament and the transnational parties.

Party of European Socialists (PES)

A confederation of Socialist parties in the European Community was formed in 1974 within the Socialist International. This replaced the Liaison Bureau among the Socialist parties of **the Six**, which had been in operation since 1957. The confederation became the PES in November 1992. It has a total of 20 member parties and a further 21 associates and observers. MEPs belonging to

PES member parties make up the PES Group in the European Parliament, the second largest of the **political groups**. The leader of the PES Group is an ex-officio member of the PES Party Leaders' Conference. Socialist members of the **European Commission**, the President of the European Parliament (when a Socialist), and the leaders of the PES Group in the Parliamentary Assembly of the **Council of Europe** and in the parliamentary assembly of the **Organization for Security and Cooperation in Europe** all have consultative status in the presidency of the PES, which meets 'not less than three times a year'. Socialist party leaders, in and out of government, meet under PES auspices before every meeting of the **European Council** to coordinate their positions, together with Socialist members of the Commission.

The Congress is the 'supreme organ' of the PES. Held every two years and at least six months before every round of European elections, the Congress elects the officers of the PES, passes resolutions on the activities of the PES and of the PES Group in the European Parliament, and adopts the PES manifesto for European elections. A Council meets in the years when there is no Congress.

Article 7.3 of the PES Statutes adopted in Berlin in May 2001 says that 'political decisions shall in principle be taken on the basis of consensus'. However, decisions that may be taken by majority in the **Council of Ministers** may be taken by **qualified majority voting** (QMV) in the PES. Decisions on administrative and organizational matters may be taken by simple majority in the presidency of the PES.

European People's Party (EPP)

Forty-two Christian Democrat (CD; see **Christian Democracy**) and allied parties are linked as full members (23) or associates (19) in the EPP, founded in 1976, with its headquarters and a small secretariat in Brussels. Another 5 parties have observer status. Within the Parliament, the MEPs belonging to EPP member parties, together with a number of allies (of which the most numerous are British Conservative MEPs), form the Group of the European People's Party, the largest of the political groups in the Parliament. The EPP is the only transnational political party to make provision for individual membership (Article 6 of the Statutes adopted in 1990).

A Congress of EPP member parties is held every two years. Most decisions require an absolute majority of those present and entitled to vote. Day-to-day decisions are in the hands of the president and vice-presidents (the 'presidency'), the EPP Council (the presidency, the party leaders and secretaries-general of EPP parties, and EPP Commissioners), and the 'political bureau'. The EPP also has a number of sections: a women's section, a trade union section, a young people's section, etc. It is funded (on a modest scale) mainly by subscriptions from member parties and from the EPP Group in the European Parliament. The EPP maintains close and regular contacts with members of the European Commission. More importantly, it is the forum in which leaders of Christian Democrat and allied parties, in and out of government, meet before meetings of the European Council.

European Liberal, Democrat and Reform Party (ELDRP)

A federation of European Liberal parties was formed in 1976 as part of the Liberals' preparations for direct elections to the European Parliament. The ELDRP was founded in December 1993. Its aims are similar to those of the PES and EPP: preparation of a common programme, mutual assistance and support, and discussion of problems of common interest. At present it has 28 members and 10 'affiliates'. MEPs from ELDR member parties form the ELDR Group, the third largest political group in the European Parliament.

A Congress is held annually. Most decisions are taken (by majority) in the Council, composed of representatives of member parties, members directly elected by the congress, Liberal members of the European Commission, the leader of the ELDR Group in the European Parliament, and a representative of the Liberals' European youth movement. The Party is funded by member parties and by the ELDR Group. Its very small secretariat is based in Brussels.

European Federation of Green Parties (EFGP)

In March 1984 the Green parties of Europe established a coordinating body at a conference in Liège, Belgium. This developed into the EFGP under a set of statutes and a statement of 'guiding principles' adopted at a conference in Masala, Finland, in June 1993 (revised March 1998 and October 1999). The EFGP has 32 member and 5 observer parties from all over Europe. Its headquarters are in Brussels.

According to its statutes, the EFGP is founded upon 'the common wish to establish a European House built on ecological, democratic, social and pacifist principles'. The statement of guiding principles is binding upon member parties at the European level, but at the national and regional level the parties 'maintain their name, identity and autonomy'. The EFGP is represented in the European Parliament by the Greens/European Free Alliance (see **political groups**). The organs of the EFGP are a Congress (meeting every three years), a governing council and an administrative committee. Representation of member parties in these bodies is based upon complicated formulae involving numbers of members and votes obtained in national and European elections. Most decisions are taken by a two-thirds majority.

The guiding principles commit the Green parties to 'ecodevelopment', equity and social justice, 'planetary solidarity', women's rights, an increased role for the United Nations, a Europe of the Regions, an end to nuclear energy, disarmament and 'a pan-European security system' based upon the **Organization for Security and Cooperation in Europe** (OSCE).

European Free Alliance (EFA)

Also known as the Democratic Party of the Peoples of Europe, the EFA was founded in 1981. In 1994 it was transformed into a transnational party, made up of 23 'nationalist, regionalist and autonomist' parties in the European Union and two observers. Its principal decision-making body is a General Meeting, which takes place once a year. Day-to-day management is in the hands of a Bureau. It is represented in the European Parliament by the Greens/EFA Group.

If the test of a genuinely transnational political party is a single leader, common policies, provision for individual membership, a common system for the adoption of candidates and a unified budget, none of the parties listed above would qualify. Even the most ambitious of them are in fact little more than fora for the exchange of ideas, for the drawing up of common programmes for European elections and for various kinds of mutual support of a practical nature.

The transnational party manifestos for European elections have not so far proved to be of more than marginal interest except to political scientists and, occasionally, to journalists. In all cases such manifestos are necessarily pitched at a level of generality that obscures substantial points of difference between the parties, and are expressed in language so abstract as to be almost unreadably bland. Most national parties continue to produce their own manifestos, so that at this stage all the transnational manifestos can provide is an overarching framework.

There are immense problems in the way of the transnational parties developing any further. First, their constitutional and legal status is uncertain. This, in turn, affects their financial status with respect, for example, to their liability for value-added tax (VAT) in different member states, and inhibits their cross-frontier political activities in other ways. The fact that such parties are now recognized in the Treaty is the first step towards giving them an official status at the European constitutional level. Second, the transnational parties are almost wholly dependent for staff and income on their member parties and the political groups in the European Parliament, and all are kept on very tight budgets. Third, until such time as party political activity at the European level becomes more important than that at the national level, with Union-wide issues separating the parties and Union-wide media in which such issues can be debated, the natural focus for politicians' energies and the electorate's attention is national politics. There is very little evidence that party political interests and alliances are at all important in the European Council and the Council of Ministers. The transnational parties can offer no independent career structure to the aspiring politician, since nearly all key posts are held either *ex officio* or by virtue of behind-the-scenes agreements between national parties. Fourth, progress towards a **uniform electoral procedure** for European elections has been very slow; were such a procedure to be adopted, it would open up new opportunities for parties to cooperate and compete freely across frontiers. Fifth, political parties as they exist at national level have many diverse origins – political, social, ethnic and historical – and, by and large, the transnational parties represent an attempt to transpose the established political 'families' to the European level. Whether such a transposition can be achieved as an act of will, or whether it should happen naturally if at all, are the central questions facing transnational parties.

Transparency

A term frequently encountered in recent years in discussion within or about the European Union and its institutions, 'transparency' relates not only to the clarity of the decision-making procedures used therein but also to the extent to which the public has access to them. 'Openness' is sometimes used instead of 'transparency'.

In common with other bureaucracies the institutions of the European Union have frequently been criticized as remote, secretive and subject to all kinds of hidden influences. The need for greater transparency was a theme that ran through the negotiations that led to the 1991 **Maastricht Treaty**. At the Maastricht meeting of the **European Council** in December 1991 a Declaration was adopted on the right of access to information. 'Transparency of the decision-making process,' it said, 'strengthens the democratic nature of the institutions and the public's confidence in the administration,' and the **European Commission** was invited to submit proposals. The following year allegations about the secretiveness of the Brussels bureaucracy played a part in delivering the Danish 'no' vote to the Maastricht Treaty in the June 1992 **referendum**, and the European Council meeting in Birmingham returned to the theme of transparency, in conjunction with its declaration on **subsidiarity**, in October 1992.

Well before the Commission published its proposals in a Communication entitled *Public Access to the Institutions' Documents* (May 1993) it had already taken steps to reform its own practices. These reforms included more extensive use of Green Papers to promote discussion on legislative proposals, earlier publication of its **annual work programme** and better public distribution of key documents. The Commission put forward some general guidelines and hinted very strongly that these should also be followed by the **Council of Ministers** and the **European Parliament** and by the member states. It thus laid the foundations for a tripartite Council–Commission–Parliament 'declaration on democracy, transparency and subsidiarity' agreed in Luxembourg on 25 October 1993. In this **Declaration** the institutions reaffirmed 'their attachment to the implementation of transparency', and each set out the steps it proposed to take or was already taking towards this end. The most important of these was a new Article 255 in the **Treaty of Rome**, added by the **Treaty of Amsterdam**, granting a general right of access for all citizens of the Union and 'any natural or legal person residing or having its registered office in a Member State' to European Parliament, Commission, and Council of Ministers documents. The Council was to lay down rules governing the exercise of this right within two years of the Treaty of Amsterdam entering into force (see also **simplification**). The Treaty of Amsterdam amended Article 1 of the Maastricht Treaty by referring to the European Union as one 'in which decisions are taken as openly as possible and as closely as possible to the citizen'.

Transparency affects the different institutions in different ways. As far as the European Parliament's formal business is concerned, either in committee or in plenary session, transparency is not a problem, since most meetings are open to the public (although the way individual Members vote in committee is hardly ever recorded and is recorded in plenary session only upon request). Indeed, the Parliament goes to great lengths – not very successfully – to interest the electorate in its affairs. Transparency is of more concern to the Parliament as a guarantee that *other* institutions should be under an obligation to provide information to the Parliament in its capacity as the guardian of the public interest.

The problem for the Commission is rather different. The Commission receives a very great deal of information and documentation from public authorities, interest groups, international bodies, governments of non-member states, companies and individuals, some of it furnished on a confidential basis. This confidentiality may impose a constraint on the Commission when it is pressed for information or when invited to say how and why it reached a particular conclusion. For this reason the Commission had difficulty in giving a general undertaking to divulge information in its possession; it has, however, undertaken to consult more widely and more systematically before finalizing its legislative proposals, to make documents available more promptly, and to improve its contacts with the general public (see **European governance**).

The Council of Ministers is the least transparent of the institutions and likely to remain so. The reasons are clear: ministers in the Council are engaged in a process designed to reach consensus if at all possible, for the attainment of which a willingness to compromise is an absolute precondition. Compromise may well entail the surrendering of a position previously taken up, and this is something more easily done in private. Once compromise is reached, the surrender can be justified to press and public on the basis of some greater benefit obtained in exchange. Among Council papers are also 'interpretative statements' on legal texts. If these were made public, they could give rise to confusion, since only the **Court of Justice** has the formal power to make such interpretations, and so infringe the principle of **legal certainty**.

Attempts to open up the proceedings of the Council have been made for many years. The Council, it was pointed out, was the only legislative body in the western world to legislate in secret. Its rules of procedure were not published in the *Official Journal* until July 1979. Information about Council proceedings was available only in the form of leaks or anodyne press releases, and answers given in response to Members of the European Parliament (MEPs) were bland or evasive, or both. However, an important distinction was established between the 'deliberative' (i.e., negotiating) function of the Council and the 'legislative' function (both may, of course, be combined in a single Council meeting). The former would remain confidential, but the latter would be fully minuted and the minutes would be published. Most important of all, votes would be recorded. This distinction has been maintained in a new draft of Article 151 EC, introduced by the Treaty of Amsterdam, which requires the Council to allow 'greater access' to documents used in its legislative capacity and to make public the results of votes, any explanations of vote, and any statements in the Council minutes. Under the tripartite declaration of October 1993 the Council has undertaken to open some of its meetings to the public on a regular basis, publish records of voting, publish its **common positions**, and improve the provision of information to the press and public.

At a Council meeting on 6–7 December 1993 the Council and the Commission agreed on a 'Code of conduct concerning public access to Council and Commission documents'. The Code laid down the general principle that 'the public will have the widest possible access' to such documents, but applications for access to documents not originating with either institution would be referred to the original authors. General exceptions allowing applications to be refused included the protection of the public interest, the individual right of privacy, commercial and industrial secrecy, and the Union's financial interests. Most importantly, either Council or Commission could 'refuse access in order to protect the institution's interest in the confidentiality of its proceedings'. At the same meeting the Council amended, by simple majority, its own Rules of Procedure in order to meet its obligations under the tripartite declaration of October 1993 (see above). Henceforth, votes in the

Council were to be made public 'systematically ... whenever the Council acts as legislator' unless by simple majority it decided otherwise. Other votes might be published if it was so decided, by simple majority, at the request of a member state. However, when the Council was acting under the procedures laid down in Titles V and VI of the Maastricht Treaty (the **Common Foreign and Security Policy** or cooperation in the fields of **Justice and Home Affairs**) a decision to publish the voting record must be unanimous. If the record were made public, explanations of vote would automatically be made public too. The Dutch and Danish foreign ministers voted against these new procedures on the grounds that they did not go far enough; the Greek foreign minister opposed them because they went too far. Further refinements were made by the Council at a meeting on 20 December 1993 (see Council Decision 93/731, published in the *Information Handbook of the Council of the European Union*).

There is a wealth of information on all these matters in a Council publication of February 2000, *Basic Texts on Transparency Concerning the Activities of the Council of the European Union*.

Of all the problems associated with transparency, among the most sensitive are those associated with the **Ombudsman** and with the European Parliament's **Committees of Inquiry**. Clearly, if the Ombudsman is successfully to investigate allegations of 'maladministration' on the part of the Union institutions, he or she must have very extensive access to institutions' files. Member states are, however, reluctant to allow the Ombudsman free access to documents that they may have communicated to Union institutions. A compromise was reached at the same meeting that agreed the October 1993 tripartite declaration the Ombudsman has access to all files held by Union institutions except on 'duly substantiated grounds of secrecy'. Access to material 'originating in a Member State' and classified as secret is given only with the permission of that member state; access to non-secret material may be given if the relevant member state is so informed. Member states are laid under a general obligation to provide, through their **national representations**, any information that may help to clarify instances of maladministration by Union institutions or bodies unless such information is secret. The Ombudsman and his staff are, in turn, laid under an obligation not to divulge any information secured in the performance of their duties. A similar compromise has been reached with respect to the European Parliament's Committees of Inquiry.

See Deirdre M. Curtin, 'Citizen's' fundamental right of access to EU information', *Common Market Law Review*, Vol. 37, no. 1, February 2000.

Transport
See **common transport policy**.

Treaties

The European Union is based upon and governed in accordance with a number of Treaties between the member states. These Treaties are the most fundamental part of the *acquis communautaire* and in every case have been the subject of (sometimes prolonged) negotiations leading to unanimous agreement among governments and **ratification** by **national parliaments** and, in some cases, by **referendum** too. The Treaties not only serve as the Union's constitution but are also prescriptive in that several of them set objectives for the future, usually accompanied by a deadline and sometimes by a precise timetable. Most of the Treaties contain provisions for their own amendment (see **Intergovernmental Conference**) and, with one exception, were concluded for an unlimited period. In common with the rest of the *acquis communautaire*, the Treaties must be accepted in their entirety by states wishing to join the Union.

The table below lists the main Treaties and Acts in chronological order, together with the date of entry into force and a brief summary, where relevant, of how each relates to the others. The first three Treaties, establishing three legally distinct Communities (see **legal personality**), are sometimes referred to as the 'founding Treaties'. Most are the subject of separate entries.

Treaty	In force	Summary
European Coal and Steel Community (ECSC) Treaty (Treaty of Paris, 1951)	1952	Concluded for 50 years among **the Six** on the basis of the **Schuman Plan**: allowed to lapse in July 2002
European Economic Community (EEC) Treaty (Treaty of Rome, 1957)	1958	Concluded on the model of the ECSC Treaty but with a much broader range of objectives; the most important of the Treaties
European Atomic Energy Community (EAEC or Euratom) Treaty (also signed in Rome, 1957)	1958	A sector-specific Treaty of limited application
Treaty establishing a Single Council and a Single Commission of the European Communities (Merger Treaty, 1965)	July 1967	Amended the ECSC, EEC and Euratom Treaties to create a Council and a Commission serving all three Communities. Repealed by the Treaty of Amsterdam
Treaty amending certain Budgetary Provisions of the Treaties establishing the European Communities (and of the Merger Treaty) (Treaty of Luxembourg, 1970)	1971	Laid down a new procedure for settling the **Budget** and introduced the system of '**own resources**'

Treaty	In force	Summary
Treaty amending certain Financial Provisions of the Treaties establishing the European Communities (and of the Merger Treaty) (1975)	1978	Refined the budgetary procedure to give the **European Parliament** more power and set up the **Court of Auditors**
Act concerning the election of the representatives of the European Parliament by direct universal suffrage (European Elections Act, 1976)	1978	The basis for the first (1979) and subsequent **European elections**
Single European Act (1986)	July 1987	Amended and expanded the EEC Treaty (most importantly, by extending the scope of **qualified majority voting**) and laid down new procedures for foreign policy cooperation
Treaty on European Union (Maastricht Treaty, 1992)	November 1993	Established the European Union; amended and expanded the EC Treaty; created the **co-decision procedure**; created '**pillars**' of **Common Foreign and Security Policy** (CFSP) and **Justice and Home Affairs** (JHA)
Treaty of Amsterdam (1997)	May 1999	Amended the Maastricht Treaty and the EC Treaty; extended co-decision; added new provisions on **social policy**; incorporated the **Schengen acquis** into EC Treaty; created '**constructive abstention**'; strengthened **transparency**
Treaty of Nice (2001)	February 2003	Amended the Maastricht Treaty and the EC Treaty; modified provisions on **suspension** and **flexibility**. Protocol on the enlargement of the European Union repealed in **Treaty of Accession**

Treaty of Accession

The Treaty of Accession, signed in Athens on 16 April 2003 by the fifteen member states and ten of the thirteen applicant states (all but Bulgaria, Romania and Turkey: see **enlargement**), provides for the new members to join the Union, subject to **ratification** by all signatories, on 1 May 2004. In the accompanying Act of Accession the new members accept the *acquis communautaire*, the **Schengen** *acquis* and **Economic and Monetary Union** (EMU), although all of them have a **derogation** from the adoption of the **euro**. New post-enlargement allocations of seats in the **European Parliament**, the **Committee of the Regions** (CoR) and the **Economic and Social Committee** (ESC) and weightings for **qualified majority voting** (QMV) in the **Council of Ministers** are set out in Articles 11 and 12 (see table). Each new member may nominate a judge in the **Court of Justice** (Article 13). The composition of all other Union institutions (see especially **European Commission**) is adjusted, and provision made for the number of new members falling short of the expected ten. The 'Protocol on the enlargement of the European Union' annexed to the **Treaty of Nice** is repealed. Articles 29 to 35 and Annex XV set out the financial arrangements. The number of official and working **languages** is raised to 20. Most of these changes were agreed at a meeting of the **European Council** in Brussels in October 2002 (see also **presidency**).

Institutional adjustments for enlargement

	Seats in EP	QMV weighting	Seats in CoR/ESC
Austria	18	10	12
Belgium	24	12	12
Cyprus	6	4	6
Czech Rep.	24	12	12
Denmark	14	7	9
Estonia	6	4	7
Finland	14	7	9
France	78	29	24
Germany	99	29	24
Greece	24	12	12
Hungary	24	12	12
Ireland	13	7	9
Italy	78	29	24
Latvia	9	4	7
Lithuania	13	7	9
Luxembourg	6	4	6
Malta	5	3	5
Netherlands	27	13	12
Poland	54	27	21
Portugal	24	12	12
Slovakia	14	7	9
Slovenia	7	4	7
Spain	54	27	21
Sweden	19	10	12
United Kingdom	78	29	24
Totals	732	321	317

Under the new QMV system (which comes into effect in November 2004: from accession until 31 October 2004 an interim system is in force) a measure must be supported by 232 votes cast by a majority of member states (Commission proposal) or by two-thirds of them in all other cases. Any member state may request verification that the measure is supported by states containing 62 per cent of the Union's total population which, if all ten new members join, will rise to about 450 million people.

Treaty of Amsterdam

The Treaty of Amsterdam, the outcome of the third large-scale revision of the **Treaties** upon which the European Union is founded (see also **Single European Act, Maastricht Treaty**), was agreed at the Amsterdam meeting of the **European Council** on 16–17 June 1997 and formally signed on 2 October 1997. After **ratification** by the member states it came into force on 1 May 1999.

The negotiations which led to the Treaty of Amsterdam were set in train by the commitment in the **Maastricht Treaty** (Article N2 TEU, since repealed) that an **Intergovernmental Conference** (IGC) would be convened in 1996. The original object of this IGC was to review the new decision-making procedures introduced by the Maastricht Treaty (see especially **co-decision procedure**); to consider adding new Treaty provisions on civil protection, energy and tourism and establishing a **hierarchy of acts**; and to examine the system of **qualified majority voting** (QMV) in the light of the fact that further **enlargement** of the Union was likely within the next decade. By the time the IGC was formally convened in Turin on 26 March 1996 two further items had been added to its agenda: a review of the role of the **Western European Union** (WEU); and a review of the procedure for adopting the **Budget** arising from an **interinstitutional agreement** of October 1993.

The European Council meeting in Corfu (24–25 June 1994) set up a 'Reflection Group' composed of foreign ministers' representatives, a representative of the **European Commission**, and two Members of the **European Parliament**. The Reflection Group began its work in June 1995. Its mandate was to solicit the views of other European institutions on possible Treaty amendments, to identify areas of difficulty, and to lay the foundations for agreement. The existence of a Reflection Group was intended to make the process of Treaty revision more open and so more intelligible.

The Reflection Group's report was presented to the European Council meeting in Madrid (14–15 December 1995) which welcomed it as a 'sound basis' for the IGC. In the words of the European Council's conclusions, the IGC's role was 'to examine the improvements which will have to be made to the Treaties to bring the Union into line with today's realities and tomorrow's requirements'. The European Parliament was to be 'closely associated' with the IGC, and the countries which had concluded **Europe Agreements** with the Union, together with Malta, Cyprus, and the countries of the **European Economic Area** (EEA), would be regularly briefed on its proceedings and given an opportunity to contribute their views.

The Treaty of Amsterdam (TA) falls into four parts. The first, by far the longest, contains amendments to the Treaties and to the 1976 **European Elections Act** (Articles 1 to 5 TA). The second (Articles 6 to 11 TA) simplifies the Treaties by pruning them of all provisions which are no longer relevant, rewriting the Articles as necessary (and substituting numbers for the capital letters used in the Maastricht Treaty), and repealing both the 1957 Convention on Certain Institutions Common to the European Communities and the 1965 **Merger Treaty**. The third part contains 13 **protocols** and the fourth, 50 **Declarations**. Details of the changes set out in the Treaty of Amsterdam will be found under the appropriate headings in this book.

With respect to the issues which the IGC was invited to address (see above), the Treaty of Amsterdam must be judged to have been only partially successful. It simplified the co-decision procedure, which became the normal mode of adopting legislation. It failed to address the system of QMV (linked to the question of the number of Commissioners, this was specifically referred to a future IGC in Protocol 11). It made no progress on the hierarchy of acts. It incorporated the **Common Foreign and Security Policy** (CFSP) into the main body of the Treaty on European Union without making any substantial change to the procedures (see also **High Representative**). It made only one very minor change to the Treaty provisions on the Budget, and did not address the question of **compulsory expenditure**. On the other hand, the Treaty of Amsterdam introduced reforms which went some way towards equipping the Union institutions to adapt to further enlargement. The number of Members of the European Parliament (MEPs) was capped at 700 (increased to 732 by the **Treaty of Nice**). The position of the president of the Commission was strengthened by giving him or her more say in the appointment of other Commissioners and in the allocation of portfolios. National parliaments were encouraged to take a closer interest in Union affairs (see also **COSAC**). A new provision on **suspension** was introduced as a sanction against 'serious and persistent breaches' of respect for human rights and the rule of law. It provided for the transfer, five years after the Treaty entered into force, of actions governing the **free movement of persons** from the **Justice and Home Affairs** (JHA) 'pillar' into normal European Community business. It added a new chapter on employment. It laid down new ground-rules on **flexibility** in a wider, more heterogeneous Union.

In addition, the progress made in simplifying and consolidating the Treaties (to the continuation of which the member states committed themselves in a Declaration) is an important step towards a clearer, more intelligible constitution for the Union (see **simplification**).

Treaty of Nice

The foundations of the Treaty of Nice, signed on 26 February 2001, were laid in the **Treaty of Amsterdam**, which annexed a '**Protocol** on the institutions with the prospect of enlargement of the European Union' to the Treaty on European Union (TEU; the **Maastricht Treaty**) and the Treaties establishing the **European Communities**. The Protocol implicitly acknowledged that certain reforms essential to the success of enlargement had not been included in the Treaty of Amsterdam and that another **Intergovernmental Conference** (IGC) under Article 48 TEU would have to be convened 'at least one year before the membership of the European Union exceeds twenty' (Protocol, Article 2). However, because the institutional reforms had a direct bearing on the negotiations with the applicant states, the **European Council** meeting in Cologne in June 1999 decided to convene an IGC in 2000.

The agenda for IGC 2000 was settled in Cologne and at the European Council meeting in Helsinki in December 1999. The main items were the so-called 'Amsterdam left-overs': the size and composition of the **European Commission**; reform of the **qualified majority voting** (QMV) system in the **Council of Ministers**; and the possible extension of QMV. The Helsinki European Council also agreed that the IGC itself would be the responsibility of member states' foreign ministers, and that preparatory work would be undertaken by a group composed of representatives of member states' governments and two Members of the **European Parliament**. The involvement of the Parliament was to be further assured by regular contacts with the President of the Parliament. The Commission was to be involved at both the preparatory and the political level (the President-designate, **Romano Prodi**, had already received a report from a small group of independent experts, *The Institutional Implications of Enlargement*, published on 18 October 1999). IGC 2000 was formally opened on 14 February 2000.

In addition to addressing the issues left unresolved in Amsterdam, IGC 2000 was given the task of drawing up other amendments to the Treaties made necessary by enlargement or by the need to ensure the smooth implementation of the Treaty of Amsterdam (which entered into force in May 1999). For this reason, the text of the Treaty agreed at Nice contains a large number of amendments on many different aspects of the Union's institutions and procedures. The Treaty falls into three parts: amendments to the Maastricht Treaty; amendments to the **Treaty of Rome** (EC; the Treaty establishing the European Community); and seven annexes.

Of the amendments to the Maastricht Treaty, three stand out. Article 7 TEU (see **suspension**) is modified to allow 'a clear risk' of a breach of **human rights** by a member state to become grounds for action on the part of the other member states, acting by a majority of four-fifths with the assent of the European Parliament. Articles 29 and 31 TEU are amended to give recognition to and define the role of **Eurojust**, described in a Declaration annexed to the Treaty as 'a unit composed of national prosecutors and magistrates ... detached from each Member State'. Finally, the provisions on 'enhanced cooperation' (see **flexibility**) in Article 11 EC are thoroughly overhauled, extended to the **Common Foreign and Security Policy** (CFSP) and to **Justice and Home Affairs** (JHA), and incorporated into the Maastricht Treaty.

The amendments to the Treaty of Rome are characterized by a wide-ranging substitution of QMV for unanimity in Council decision-making and an extension of the **co-decision procedure** as set out in Article 251 EC. Most of these modifications apply to relatively minor matters: anti-discrimination measures (Article 13), financial assistance to member states (Article 100), measures to enhance the Union's international competitiveness (Article 157), and appointments to the **Court of Auditors** (Article 247), for example. In more sensitive areas the introduction of QMV or co-decision is postponed: until May 2004 for decisions on refugees and **asylum** (Article 67), and until January 2007 for decisions on the **structural funds** (Article 161) and on financial regulations (Article 279). In other areas to which co-decision is extended, some aspects are specifically excepted: for example, passports and social security questions are not included in the application of co-decision to the **free movement of persons** provisions of Article 18.

QMV is extended to the nomination of the President-designate of the Commission, subject to the assent of the European Parliament (Article 214). QMV is also to be used for the nomination of other members of the Commission 'by common accord' with the President-designate, the whole Commission being then submitted to the Parliament for its assent. Formal appointment then follows, again by QMV. Under Article 217 the position of the President is strengthened, notably by virtue of the provision that 'a Member of the Commission shall resign if the President so requests'.

Among other changes introduced by the Treaty are increases in the maximum size of the European Parliament (732 rather than 700 members, Article 189), limits on the size of the **Economic and Social Committee** and the **Committee of the Regions** (350 members each, Articles 258 and 263), greater recognition of **transnational political parties** (Article 191) and the creation of a **Social Protection Committee** (Article 144). The *Official Journal* becomes the *Official Journal of the European Union* (Article 254). The statute of the **Court of Justice** is revised and set out in a Protocol to be annexed to the Treaties. A Declaration calls for one European Council meeting in each **presidency** to be held in **Brussels** with effect from 2002 and for Brussels to be the sole venue as soon as the number of member states reaches 18.

The main treaty reforms were set out in a 'Protocol on the enlargement of the European Union' which repealed the similarly entitled Protocol agreed in Amsterdam. However, the Nice Protocol and the Declaration which followed it have been repealed and largely superseded by the **Treaty of Accession** which the ten new member states signed in Athens in April 2003.

Future developments are addressed in a 'Declaration on the future of the

Union', which calls for greater debate about the future of the European Union, and commits the Swedish and Belgian presidencies to encouraging 'wide-ranging discussions with all interested parties', including the applicant states. Four topics in particular have already been identified: the division of competences between European and national authorities, 'reflecting the principle of **subsidiarity**'; the status of the **Charter of Fundamental Rights**; the simplification of the Treaties; and the role of **national parliaments**. The Declaration acknowledges 'the need to improve and to monitor the democratic legitimacy and **transparency** of the Union and its institutions, to bring them closer to the citizens of the Member States'. All these issues will be addressed in an IGC to be convened in 2003 (see **Laeken Declaration**).

It was not to be expected that IGC 2000 would deliver convincing, clearcut answers to all the problems it was invited to address. In the trade-off between what is acceptable to the 15 member states and what is intelligible to the public, acceptability wins every time, however complex the compromise. Noone can really predict what the pressures on the Union's institutions and procedures arising from enlargement are likely to be, and therefore no one can say what Treaty changes are needed to withstand them. More than ever, the Union is entering a period of trial and error with respect to its internal organization. The Treaty of Nice must be regarded as a further chapter in the story which began with the **Single European Act** and continued with the Treaties of Maastricht and Amsterdam. It will be seen in retrospect as an important chapter, in which the member states at last addressed what an engineer might call the load-bearing parts of the Treaties: how the Council takes decisions; the balance of power between large and small states; and the relations between the Union's institutions and national governments. See Alan Dashwood, 'The constitution of the European Union after Nice: lawmaking procedures', *European Law Review*, Vol. 26, no. 3, June 2001.

Treaty of Paris

Signed in April 1951, the Treaty of Paris established the **European Coal and Steel Community** (ECSC) among **the Six**. The ECSC, which owed its origins to the 1950 **Schuman Plan**, was the model for the other **European Communities**. Concluded for 50 years, it was allowed to lapse in July 2002.

Treaty of Rome

Signed by **the Six** in March 1957, the Treaty of Rome established the **European Economic Community** (EEC). The Treaty establishing the **European Atomic Energy Community** (EAEC or Euratom) was signed at the same time. The main features of the Treaty of Rome are described in separate entries: the institutions and procedures laid down in the Treaty were modelled largely on the **European Coal and Steel Community** (ECSC). See also **Beyen Plan, Treaties, Messina Conference, Spaak Committee.**

Treaty on European Union

See **Maastricht Treaty.**

Trevi Group

At the **European Council** meeting in Rome in December 1975 it was agreed on the basis of a British proposal that 'Community Ministers for the Interior (or Ministers with similar responsibilities) should meet to discuss matters coming within their competence, in particular with regard to law and order'. The following year, in the wake of several cases of terrorism and hostage-taking, it was decided to invite ministers of justice to participate in this work. The first meeting of what became known as the Trevi Group was held in Luxembourg on 29 June 1976. The origin of the name 'Trevi' is disputed. It may have been a pun on the name of Mr Fonteijn, the Director-General in the Dutch Ministry of Justice, who was one of the initiators of the Group, or a reference to the Trevi Fountain in Rome, where the decision to establish the Group was first taken. 'Trevi' was subsequently turned into an acronym for '*terrorisme, radicalisme, extrémisme, et violence internationale*'. From 1993 the work of the Trevi Group was incorporated into the **Justice and Home Affairs** (JHA) provisions of the **Maastricht Treaty** (Articles 29 to 45).

The Trevi Group was an informal body for cooperation in the field of law and order. Most of its concerns were outside the scope of the Treaty, and the **European Commission** was not associated with the work of the Group.

Ministers were not obliged to answer questions about their Trevi activities from Members of the **European Parliament** (MEPs). However, ministers remained accountable to their **national parliaments**; and once in every **presidency**, the minister currently chairing meetings of the Trevi Group reported to the European Parliament's Committee on Civil Liberties and Internal Affairs.

Troika

'Troika' is a Russian word meaning a sledge drawn by three horses. It was first introduced into politics in the early 1960s, when the Soviet Union suggested that the Secretary-General of the United Nations should be replaced by a troika composed of representatives of the Eastern bloc, the Western alliance and the non-aligned states. In the European Union it means a three-member group composed of the current president of the **Council of Ministers** together with his or her immediate predecessor and successor. Such groups are most commonly used in foreign affairs to ensure a measure of continuity from one **presidency** to another, and were first introduced in 1977 as an operational necessity in the field of **European Political Cooperation**. The **Euro-**

pean Council meeting in Brussels in December 1993 agreed to introduce from 1996 a rotation system for the presidency of the Council which would ensure that in every troika there is a minister from one of the large member states.

Turkey

Turkey first concluded an **Association Agreement** with the Community in 1963, the second country to do so. The Agreement was 'frozen' during periods of military rule in Turkey, but it provided for Turkey eventually to become part of a **customs union** with the member states. In March 1995 the Association Council agreed to establish a customs union (not including agricultural goods) with effect from January 1996.

On 14 April 1987 the Turkish government applied for full membership of the Community. The **Opinion** of the **European Commission**, delivered in December 1989, was unfavourable. The Commission took the view that 'any decision to open negotiations ... must be based on a strong conviction that a positive conclusion is possible, indeed probable, within a reasonable period'. In the case of Turkey there was no such conviction, the difficulties being compounded by the country's high birth-rate and relative poverty: the Turkish population reached almost 65 million in 2000, while its per capita gross domestic product (GDP) is less than half that of Greece, the poorest of the member states. The Commission also expressed doubts about whether the country's **human rights** record was consistent with Community standards, and whether membership might have 'negative effects' on the Greek–Turkish dispute over Cyprus. The conclusion was that 'it would not be useful to open accession negotiations with Turkey'. Instead, the Commission proposed an intensification of relations with Turkey within the Association Agreement. These conclusions were broadly endorsed by the member states.

By the mid-1990s the applications for membership from the countries of central and eastern Europe (see **enlargement**) had led to renewed pressure from the Turkish government to begin membership negotiations. On 29 April 1997, the European Union confirmed at a meeting of the Association Council that Turkey was eligible for membership of the Union. On 15 July 1997, the Commission presented a 'Communication ... on the further development of relations with Turkey' to coincide with the publication of its Opinions on the applications for membership from the countries of central and eastern Europe. The Communication described the customs union as 'working satisfactorily' and 'a sound basis for the further development of relations', although it reiterated the Union's concern over democratization and human rights, relations between Greece and Turkey, and the need for a 'just and lasting settlement in Cyprus'. The Commission proposed consolidating the customs union, liberalizing trade in services, promoting structural reforms in Turkish agriculture, and a number of other measures to strengthen Turkey's ties with the Union. At the **European Council** meeting in Luxembourg on 12–13 December 1997 it was agreed to invite Turkey to the '**European Conference**' of member states and applicant states held for the first time in London in March 1998. The Turkish government declined the invitation. The difficulty of reestablishing good relations with Turkey was made greater by Greece's refusal to consent to the payment of financial assistance owed to Turkey since the entry into force of the customs union. Turkey was finally accepted as an applicant state at the Helsinki European Council in December 1999. In Copenhagen (December 2002) Turkey was assured that if by December 2004 the country met the **Copenhagen criteria** a firm date would be fixed for the start of accession negotiations.

Turkey, by virtue of its membership of the **Council of Europe** and the **North Atlantic Treaty Organization** (NATO), has always been considered a European state, even though 96 per cent of it is geographically in Asia. Turkey also took part in the **Conference on Security and Cooperation in Europe** (CSCE). See also **Black Sea Economic Cooperation**.

Two-speed Europe

Sometimes known as a 'two-tier Europe', the idea of a two-speed Europe (*Europe à deux vitesses*) was first set out in the **Tindemans Report** of 1975. This report sought to recognize the fact that not all member states were willing and able to proceed towards integration at the same pace, and that some means should be found of allowing the more enthusiastic to make progress without being held back by the others. Which countries proceeded at which speed would vary from case to case, and those opting for the slower speed would do so on the basis of reasons recognized as valid by the **Council of Ministers** on a proposal from the **European Commission**. The Report also enjoined those countries proceeding at the faster pace to lend as much assistance as possible to the others.

Like much else in the Report, the idea of a two-speed Europe did not find favour with the governments of the member states, especially those which feared that they would find themselves on most issues in the second rank. A two-speed Europe would, it was argued, have damaging consequences for the uniform application of the *acquis communautaire*, for Community solidarity (especially in external relations) and for the Community **Budget**. It would also call into question the rights of member states to an equal share in decision-making. However, although formally rejected, something very close to a two-speed Europe was given *de facto* recognition in 1979 with the setting up of the **Exchange-Rate Mechanism** (ERM) of the **European Monetary System** (EMS); and with a larger and more heterogeneous Union in prospect as a consequence of **enlargement**, the idea is by no means dead (see also **concentric circles, flexibility, 'hard core'**).

U

UKREP

UKREP is the acronym for the United Kingdom Permanent Representation to the European Union. Each of the member states maintains a **national representation** or 'embassy' in Brussels to manage its dealings with the various Union institutions, most especially its direct involvement in the legislative process in the **Council of Ministers**. UKREP is one of the largest of the representations and is sometimes considered the most professional. All officials dealing with institutional and foreign policy issues normally come from the Foreign and Commonwealth Office (FCO), including the permanent representative or ambassador. The deputy permanent representative and most of the officials dealing with technical matters – such as transport, environment or energy – are seconded from Whitehall departments. It is usual for the officials dealing with financial and agricultural matters to be on loan from the Treasury and the Ministry of Agriculture. All officials, regardless of their department of origin, are responsible, through UKREP, to the FCO in London.

UKREP officials spend a large amount of time in meetings of **COREPER** and working groups within the Council structure. Every meeting is reported back to London together with news of the **European Commission** initiatives, events in the **European Parliament** and other political developments of potential significance. These reports are circulated in Whitehall and form the basis of the government's collective intelligence on European affairs. UKREP also monitors the position of British officials in the Brussels institutions.

Unanimity

Decisions in the **Council of Ministers** of the European Union may be taken either by unanimity or on the basis of **majority voting**. Only in respect of the former do individual member states enjoy a right of **veto** under the **Treaties** (see **Luxembourg Compromise**). Decisions taken 'by common accord' by representatives of member states' governments acting *as governments* and not as the Council (for example, the appointment of members of the **European Commission**) also require unanimity. See also **constructive abstention**.

Uniform electoral procedure

The idea that the **European Parliament** should be elected on the basis of a uniform electoral procedure (UEP) used throughout the member states is to be found in the 1951 **Treaty of Paris** establishing the **European Coal and Steel Community** (ECSC). It was repeated in the **Treaty of Rome**: Article 138.3 (original version) said: 'The European Parliament shall draw up proposals for elections by direct universal suffrage in accordance with a uniform procedure in all Member States.' It was repeated again in Article 7 of the 1976 European Elections Act (see below), but in spite of several efforts to establish such a procedure **European elections** are still held on the basis of different national systems and arrangements for these elections remain in the hands of national authorities. The drawing up of proposals for a UEP is the one area in which the European Parliament, not the **European Commission**, specifically enjoys the **right of initiative**. There is no deadline by which a UEP must be in place. The **Treaty of Amsterdam** made a small but very significant change to these provisions. As an alternative to a uniform procedure, the Parliament was empowered to propose a procedure 'in accordance with principles common to all Member States' (Article 190 EC). This sidesteps the difficulties which lie, as history shows (see below), in the way of a UEP; the Parliament adopted a procedure based on common principles in July 1998, although the Council of Ministers has not acted upon it.

The difficulties were threefold: procedural, political and legal. The Treaty required proposals from the European Parliament, unanimity in the Council, an absolute majority in the Parliament for the Council's conclusions, and ratification in the member states. Each of these four stages was problematic, and taken together they constituted a process that could not be accomplished within one of the Parliament's five-year mandates. The Treaty did not allow for a UEP to be established in stages.

The political difficulty sprang from the word 'uniform'. It was not enough for all member states to use PR, it had to be the *same* form. Member states such as France and Spain are as attached to the national list system of PR as Belgium and Italy are to the regional list. Experience showed that to secure the necessary majority in the Parliament, a proposal had to be so hedged about with compromises, qualifications and special cases as to be no longer consistent with what the Treaty clearly meant by uniformity. Electoral systems in the member states are founded upon historical and political processes and assumptions that cannot easily be gainsaid. Inevitably, every political party, every government and every individual MEP approached UEP in terms of party political advantage, and the notional Treaty commitment to uniformity was simply not strong enough to overcome this.

The legal difficulties sprang from the word 'procedure'. An electoral procedure is not just a voting system or a formula for translating votes into seats. Its scope is much wider: it embraces, for example, the question of the voting age, the right to stand for election, the electoral threshold, disqualifications, the rules governing independent candidates, and so on. Many of these are sensitive issues in their own right. The Parliament had implicitly acknowledged this by dealing with such matters in its own proposals and it was confirmed in the Court of Justice's judgment of 1985 in the case of *Les Verts* v *the European Parliament* (Case 294/83). The Court ruled, in effect, that all provisions governed by law with a bearing on the equality of candidates' chances were covered by the notion of a 'procedure'. The Council was of the view that the Parliament's June 1992 report (see above) contained only 'general principles' and that 'much more specific provisions' would be required (Answer to Written Question by Mr Vertemati, *Official Journal*, C333, 8 December 1993).

Another problem with UEP was that it raised the question of the number of seats allocated to each member state in the European Parliament. Under the present arrangements the smaller member states are over-represented in terms of electors per seat, and the changes agreed at the Edinburgh **European Council** in December 1992 made only a modest difference. This highly political question, made more complex by **enlargement** and the decision in the Treaty of Amsterdam to limit the Parliament to 700 members (raised in the **Treaty of Nice** to 732), could never be settled at anything other than European Council level.

If progress is ever to be made towards a genuinely uniform electoral procedure, it can only be on the basis of an agreement between the institutions to proceed in stages. The least contentious questions (such as the voting age) would be addressed in the first stage and only at the end of this process would the most difficult issues (such as the system whereby votes are translated into seats) be raised. Meanwhile, there is nothing to prevent member states from agreeing outside the Treaty framework on a procedure that happens to suit them and enacting it individually but in concert. No member state and very few political parties show any interest in moving towards a UEP, not least because changes agreed at European level would have an impact on national electoral law. Whether the present diversity of procedures seriously affects the standing of the European Parliament in the eyes of the electorate is an open question.

Union of Industrial and Employers' Confederations of Europe (UNICE)

UNICE was founded in 1958 as the Union of Industries of the European Community. Composed of 39 organizations in 31 countries, UNICE is the principal European-level lobbying organization for industry and commerce, and is an important channel of communication between the European institutions (notably the **European Parliament**, the **European Commission**, and especially the **Economic and Social Committee**) and business interests.

United Kingdom

To the disappointment of **the Six**, the United Kingdom chose not to take part in the negotiations in 1950 that followed the **Schuman Plan** and led a year later to the establishment of the **European Coal and Steel Community** (ECSC). Similarly, five years later the British government sent only a middle-ranking official from the Board of Trade as an observer to the 1955 **Messina Conference** at which the outline of the **European Economic Community** (EEC) was first discussed. In both cases the main obstacle was the supranational character of the institutions upon which the Communities were to be founded and the conviction, shared by **Winston Churchill** and others, that the country's destiny lay with a wider English-speaking fraternity of nations centred upon the countries of the British Empire. By contrast, the United Kingdom played an active part in all the other European organizations – the **Council of Europe**, the Brussels Treaty Organization (from 1954 known as the **Western European Union**), the Organization for European Economic Cooperation (see **Organization for Economic Cooperation and Development**) and the **European Free Trade Association** (EFTA) – established in the postwar period.

In 1961 the Conservative government of Harold Macmillan decided, with cross-party support, to make an application to join the European Community. This was prompted by the realization that the Six had established a working arrangement that was bringing benefits in terms of stability, prosperity and global influence from which the United Kingdom did not wish to be excluded. At the same time it was becoming clear that the Commonwealth was in the longer term no longer an adequate basis for British political and economic interests. As for the 'special relationship' with the **United States of America**, the Americans had long been in favour of a United Europe that included the United Kingdom.

Macmillan's application and the Labour Government's application of 1967 were both effectively vetoed by **Charles de Gaulle**, primarily because he (with some justice) took the United Kingdom's traditionally pro-American, pro-free-trade stance to be inconsistent with French interests. Moreover, he realized that the United Kingdom would certainly compete with France for the political leadership of the Community, although, ironically, de Gaulle's essentially intergovernmental model of the Community, as typified in the **Fouchet Plan**, could certainly have won British support. Even though British membership of the Community was strongly and consistently supported by the other member states, it was not until de Gaulle was succeeded as President of France in 1969 by Georges Pompidou that the French veto was lifted and negotiations with the United Kingdom, Denmark, Ireland and Norway were begun in earnest.

In 1971 the Conservative government of **Edward Heath** brought the negotiations to a successful conclusion. Later that year the House of Commons approved the European Communities Act. However, by this time elements in the Labour Party were opposed to membership in principle and the Party as a whole was officially opposed to the so-called 'Tory terms'. In 1974, the year after British **accession**, the Labour Party won the February and October elections with a commitment to 'renegotiate' the terms, and the following year the **referendum of June 1975** was held, endorsing British membership of the Community by a majority of two to one. The whole episode had nevertheless been a disastrous start to the United Kingdom's relations with its new partners, and in particular allowed the British commitment to the underlying purposes of the Community to be called into question.

Soon after the Conservative government of **Margaret Thatcher** came to power in 1979 another source of tension arose in the form of the **British Budget problem**, which remained unresolved until 1984. It was hardly to be expected that a prime minister who scorned consensus and was committed to a reduction in the role of the state and a raising of national self-confidence would resist the temptation to be outspokenly critical of 'Brussels'. Not until the 1986 **Single European Act** (SEA) could it be said that the British had contributed positively to the Community's development, with the **Single Market** programme and the extension of **European Political Cooperation** (unless one counts the **European Regional Development Fund**, operational from 1975, and the inclusion of many Commonwealth countries in the first **Lomé Convention**, also dating from 1975). Since 1986 the British have been among the most enthusiastic supporters of **enlargement**, tempered only by a reticence with regard to the institutional reforms that, in the view of many, must accompany it (see **wider versus deeper, qualified majority voting**).

Among other areas upon which United Kingdom policy has concentrated are reform of the **Common Agricultural Policy** (CAP), **budgetary discipline** and **competition policy**. The United Kingdom has always supported the rigorous and equal enforcement of **EU law**, although the preoccupation with **sovereignty** has so far prevented this support from being expressed in terms of wanting inspectorates responsible to the Union rather than to member states individually.

The acrimonious debate in the House of Commons on the **Maastricht Treaty** brought out two key themes that featured very prominently in the British approach to the 1996–7 **Intergovernmental Conference** (IGC). One was the continuing importance of **subsidiarity** in the division of responsibility between the institutions of the Union and those of member states. The other was a preference for intergovernmental procedures (as typified in the additional '**pillars**' introduced by the Maastricht Treaty).

Perhaps in no area is a certain British ambivalence towards the Union more consistently evident than in relation to the powers of the **European Parliament**. Before the United Kingdom joined the Community in 1973, one of the arguments most commonly heard in favour of the United Kingdom's membership was that the United Kingdom's long and unbroken tradition of parliamentary democracy would serve to make Community decision-making more democratic; or, as the argument is now expressed, that the **democratic deficit** would be reduced. In fact, from January 1973 to July 1975 the Labour Party refused to take up its entitlement of seats in the European Parliament; and the first **European elections** were held a year after the original 1978 target date because of difficulties in getting the necessary legislation through the House of Commons. The United Kingdom has had easily the lowest average turnout in the four European elections held so far. British support for additional powers for the European Parliament has been extremely grudging, and in no member state is there a keener sense of rivalry between the **national parliament** and the European Parliament.

Neither defeated nor occupied in the course of the Second World War, the United Kingdom did not share the desire of the Six to place political and economic relations between western European states on a radically new footing. Nor had confidence in British institutions been shaken to the extent of the United Kingdom being prepared to countenance new supranational institutions that cut across traditional notions of sovereignty. To this extent, in the crucial postwar years the United Kingdom was set apart from those impulses that led to the foundation of the Community. The afterglow of victory cast quite a different light on what seemed the obvious way forward to **Jean Monnet** and others.

The European Union is the only major organization to which the United Kingdom belongs of which it is not a founder member. A great deal of British energy has gone into reforming policies that, had the United Kingdom joined with the Six, could have been shaped from the beginning in a fashion more consistent with British interests and preferences. Few of the arguments have been won as quickly and as convincingly as the United Kingdom would have wished. The British Budget problem in particular soured relations with other member states across the whole field. More importantly, it reduced public support for British membership to dangerously low levels, which in turn limited the scope for political initiatives designed to restore the country's European credentials and capture the imagination of the electorate.

The decision-making system within the European Union is oriented towards consensus, whereas the British political system is essentially adversarial. The British system delivers winners and losers, majorities and minorities, and governments accustomed to being able to carry out their legislative programmes with a minimum of compromise. This affects the way political issues are reported and understood, and, as far as European issues are concerned, it serves to distort the nature of the negotiating process in Brussels. A British minister putting a case to his or her colleagues in the Council of Ministers is said to have 'clashed' with them; making any concession in the course of negotiation is 'giving way'; a final decision not on all points consistent with the original British position is a 'defeat'; and a discussion that breaks up without a decision is a 'row'. The use of such language, day after day, can only confirm in the public mind the impression that the Union is either incapable of taking action or acts regularly in a fashion hostile to British interests. Added to this is the willingness of the Opposition to draw attention to any aspect of a decision reached in Brussels that can be laid as a 'failure' at the government's door.

When in 1930 **Aristide Briand** presented his plan for a European Federal Union to the **League of Nations**, the Foreign Office advised that the government's attitude 'should be one of caution, though cordial caution' (internal memorandum, quoted in James Joll (ed.), *Britain and Europe*, 1950). The memorandum went on to speak of the need for 'a discriminating sympathy for all such re-organization of Europe as is not in unjustified contravention of British rights and interests'. More than two generations later the caution still outweighs the cordiality, and the sympathy is as discriminating as ever.

United Nations (UN)

Since the 1960s and the beginnings of **European Political Cooperation** (see **Common Foreign and Security Policy**) the member states of the Community have sought, on the whole successfully, to act as one within the UN. This is done on the basis of regular coordination at official level and among foreign ministers and is symbolized by the fact that the president-in-office of the Council (see **presidency**) addresses the UN General Assembly every year on behalf of the Union.

The European Community (not the European Union: see **legal personality**) has observer status in the UN General Assembly and in the Economic and Social Council, but the only UN organ in which it participates as a full member is the Food and Agriculture Organization.

Two member states, France and the United Kingdom, are permanent members of the UN Security Council, together with China, Russia and the United States. It has been suggested that membership should be extended to the Union as a whole, with France and the United Kingdom ceasing to be members in their own right. This view is not held by either the French or the British government, not least because it would lead to the 'European' voice in the Security Council being reduced by half. Meanwhile, under Article 19.2 of the **Maastricht Treaty**, France and the United Kingdom are responsible for keeping the other member states 'fully informed' and ensuring 'the defence of the positions and the interests of the Union' in the Security Council.

United States of America

The United States of America has always been broadly sympathetic to the idea of European unification. It was the **Marshall Plan** in the immediate postwar period that led to the founding of the Organization for European Economic Cooperation (see **Organization for Economic Cooperation and Development** (OECD)). One of the first public utterances in favour of western Europe becoming a 'single large market' was made by an American in 1949 (see **Single Market**). The American perception that in the Cold War the front line was on the Rhine led to the formation of the **North Atlantic Treaty Organization** (NATO) under a treaty signed in Washington in 1949, and in January 1994 President Bill Clinton confirmed that 100,000 American troops would remain stationed in Europe for the foreseeable future. In the debate between **the Six** and the supporters (including the United Kingdom) of a **free trade area** (see **Maudling Plan**), American support was decisively on the side of the Six. Every two years a meeting takes place between the president of the United States, the president-in-office of the **European Council** and the president of the **European Commission**. The Transatlantic Declaration of November 1990 and the New Transatlantic Agenda of December 1995 laid down a framework for regular consultations between the European Union's foreign ministers and the US Secretary of State, and between the Commission and the US government. The background to postwar American attitudes may be found in John Lamberton Harper, *American Visions of Europe* (Cambridge, 1994).

The idea of a **United States of Europe** has been a source of inspiration to advocates of European unity from Victor Hugo to **Winston Churchill** (see **Zürich speech**), and the United States Constitution served as an indirect model for several key phrases and concepts in the **Treaties**. From the very beginning, American officials and scholars, brought up on the history of their own constitution, showed an informed understanding of the problems of integration. Two of the earliest and best studies of the nascent European Community are by Americans (see Ernst B. Haas, *The Uniting of Europe*, 1958, and Leon L. Lindberg, *The Political Dynamics of European Economic Integration*, 1963).

On most issues Americans and Europeans have cooperated regularly and successfully in international institutions. Disagreements have arisen with respect to trade issues, such as **Airbus**, agriculture (especially export subsidies), and the extra-territorial application of some United States legislation. However, these commercial differences, although occasionally dramatic, are relatively minor by comparison with the extent of overall cooperation. In May 1998 the United States and the European Union agreed on a new Transatlantic Economic Partnership (TEP) to promote and facilitate trade. The United States agreed to waive for Union member states the extra-terrestrial application of its legislation on trade with Cuba, Libya and Iran.

More serious have been disagreements over security policy. At least from the early 1980s the argument that the Europeans were wealthy enough to assume a larger share of the overall burden of security within the Atlantic Alliance steadily gained ground among American politicians and the American public. On the European side, there were those who argued that if the Europeans did more, the Americans would seize the opportunity of doing less, and that this was a risk Europe could not take. Equally, there were others who argued that *unless* the Europeans did more, the Americans, under pressure to cut defence spending, would lose patience.

It was Henry Kissinger who wrote in 1969 that 'American policy has been extremely ambivalent: it has urged European unity while recoiling before its probable consequences'. The end of the Cold War has resulted in this ambivalence becoming less marked. Nevertheless the experience of the Gulf Crisis and Yugoslavia has underlined how far the European Union has to go before becoming the self-reliant, stable, prosperous and dependable partner that the United States would like it to be.

United States of Europe

Although the best-known use of this phrase is a passage in **Winston Churchill**'s 1946 **Zürich speech**, the origin of the idea of a United States of Europe is much earlier. In 1849 Victor Hugo told a conference in Paris:

There will come a day when all of you, France, Russia, Italy, Britain, Germany, all you nations of this continent, without losing your distinctive qualities or your glorious individuality, will merge closely into a higher unity and will form the fraternity of Europe, just as Normandy, Brittany, Burgundy, Lorraine, Alsace, all our provinces, have merged to become France ... Two huge groups will be seen, the United States of America and the United States of Europe, holding out their hands to one another across the ocean … (quoted in Denis de Rougemont, *The Meaning of Europe*, English edn, 1965).

In fact, the period that followed this speech was marked by the apogee of nationalism and national rivalries in Europe and by the channelling of Europe's energies into the acquisition of colonies overseas. The idea of a United States of Europe continued to be put forward as a way of resolving these rivalries; for example, the anthropologist J. G. Frazer in an essay of 1906 entitled 'Pax Occidentis: A League of the West' called for

a federation … among the European powers [which] beginning as a League of Peace and Defence between two or three states … might in time expand into a federation of the whole of Europe: the United States of Europe might stand beside the United States of America as friendly rivals in the promotion of civilization and peace (*The Gorgon's Head and other literary pieces*, 1927).

The idea of a United States of Europe retains a certain resonance but the phrase is now seldom used. This stems partly from the realization that the **European Union** created by the **Maastricht Treaty** is *sui generis* and partly from the desire to avoid misleading parallels between two quite different processes of integration: the one between relatively small, newly founded states enjoying a high degree of cultural and political homogeneity, the other between much larger, more complex and long-established entities, each with its own distinctive history and traditions. The first citation in the *Oxford English Dictionary* for 'United States of Europe' dates from 1869. See also **Pan-Europa**.

Uri, Pierre (1911–92)

The French economist Pierre Uri was the most important colleague of **Jean Monnet**. Having helped to draft the **Schuman Plan**, he went on to draft the **European Coal and Steel Community** (ECSC) Treaty of 1951. Five years later he was invited to draft the two Treaties establishing the **European Economic Community** (EEC) and the **European Atomic Energy Community** (EAEC or Euratom) on the basis of the recommendations of the **Spaak Committee**, in whose work he had been involved. In the 1960s and 1970s he wrote a large number of books and, as a Socialist, became a close associate of **François Mitterrand**, although he never held any government office. According to his obituary in *The Independent* (24 July 1992), Uri was 'a man without a trace of self-doubt and … an admired if formidable academic and negotiating figure' (see also *The Times* of 24 July 1992). In his *Memoirs* (English edn, 1978) Jean Monnet wrote of Uri's 'exceptional ability to think out new and rigorous solutions to the most complex problems … [He] gets to the heart of them, where everything is simple; but this can only be done after going through the maze of details in which very intelligent people seem almost to enjoy losing their way'.

V

Value-added tax

In 1967 **the Six** agreed two Directives that required all member states to adopt a system of value-added tax (VAT), and since that date VAT has been a *de facto* requirement of membership of the European Community. VAT-based revenue is an important part of the Union's **own resources** (36.2 per cent in 2001): each member state pays a contribution to the **Budget** of up to 1.4 per cent, not of VAT actually collected, but of the VAT that would have been collected had VAT been applied at common rates to an agreed range of goods and services. In fact, initially, rates differed widely, as did the 'base' to which VAT was applied across the member states. Because these differences affected patterns of trade (and therefore competition) and made fiscal controls necessary at the Community's internal frontiers, the Commission's 1985 White Paper on the completion of the **Single Market** proposed an approximation of VAT rates. This was followed up in a 1987 proposal for a 'standard' rate and a 'reduced' rate, each represented by a band of a few percentage points. Little progress having been made, a second proposal was made in 1989 for a minimum 'standard' rate of 15 per cent. At a meeting of the **Ecofin Council** on 19 October 1992 agreement was reached on this proposal (renewed in December 1996: at the same meeting the Council agreed informally a maximum rate of 25 per cent). Member states may also apply 'reduced' rates to a specific list of goods and services, and existing zero-rates (a particular feature of the British system) may be maintained but not extended. At present, standard rates vary from the 15 per cent minimum in Germany and Luxembourg to 25 per cent in Denmark and Sweden.

A common system of VAT on second-hand goods and works of art is in force under the so-called Seventh VAT Directive. Sales between private individuals are exempt. VAT is levied at the standard rate on the seller's margin for professional sales on the origin principle (see **tax harmonization**). Special rules apply to works of art. To be classified as 'second-hand' a car must have been in use for six months and clocked up at least 6,000 kilometres.

It is clear that a single market can exist without VAT rates and the VAT base being exactly the same throughout that market. Economists differ on the degree of variation that may be permitted without significantly distorting competition. VAT approximation is sensitive not only because very large amounts of revenue are at stake at a time when member states are trying to reduce their budget deficits, but also because the right to fix tax rates is, in many people's view, an essential component of national and parliamentary **sovereignty**. Since the removal of fiscal frontiers between member states on the completion of the Single Market, VAT returns are now the basis of statistics on trade within the Union (see **Intrastat**).

Van Duyn case

The van Duyn case (*Yvonne van Duyn* v *Home Office*, Case 41/74) concerned a Dutch Scientologist who in 1973 was refused entry into the United Kingdom to take up employment at the Hubbard College of Scientology in East Grinstead. The British authorities justified their refusal on the grounds that it was 'undesirable' to admit persons intending to work for a cult they regarded as 'socially harmful'. In this they relied upon the 'public policy' exceptions to the right of **free movements of persons** set out in Article 48 (now 39) of the **Treaty of Rome** (although there was no prohibition on British nationals working for the College of Scientology). Miss van Duyn argued that these exceptions, which had been defined more fully in a 1964 Directive, could be applied only in relation to her personal conduct. The case was referred to the **Court of Justice**.

In its ruling the following year the Court held that Article 48 conferred a right of free movement directly on individuals (see **direct effect**) without any need for implementing measures at the national level, a right that must be upheld by national courts.

Variable geometry

This phrase denotes a model of European integration in which member states decide whether or not to participate in a particular activity, although there will normally be a number of 'core activities' in which all states take part (see **concentric circles**). If it were always the same states that chose not to take part in new activities, then this could lead to a **two-speed Europe**. For this reason, with a few notable exceptions (such as the introduction of the **euro**), the European Union has chosen to venture into new areas of activity only if all member states are willing to become involved. The legal, political, proce-dural and budgetary complexities of a Union in which member states are active only in areas of direct benefit to them are obvious. Nevertheless, with the prospect of a larger, more heterogeneous Union the 'variable geometry' model is sure to find some supporters on the grounds that it offers greater flexibility and corresponds more closely to political reality. See also **Europe à la carte, flexibility, hard core.**

Vatican City

See **micro-states.**

Vedel Report

In March 1972 a working-party of independent experts chaired by the French political scientist Professor Georges Vedel published a report requested by the **European Commission**, which was intended to take account of the new system of **own resources** and the new arrangements for the Community **Budget** laid down in the 1970 Treaty of Luxembourg. In fact, the report dealt at some length with the legislative powers of the **European Parliament**, and recommended that these be increased by granting it a right of co-decision, a right of consultation and a suspensory veto and by extending co-decision to cover more or less the whole field of Community legislation (see **co-decision procedure**). The report also recommended that the Parliament should be involved in the appointment of the president of the Commission. In the event, only the recommendations on the Parliament's budgetary powers were followed up, and formed the basis of the new procedures adopted in 1975. The recommendations on co-decision and on involving the Parliament in the appointment of the president of the Commission were taken up 19 years later in the **Maastricht Treaty**.

Veto

The mechanism known as the 'veto' allows any member state, however small, to block a decision, both in the **Council of Ministers** and when representatives of the member states are meeting outside the Council framework (see below). Formally, the right of veto exists in all Treaty articles that require the Council to take decisions by **unanimity**. The number of such articles has declined over the years (see especially **Single European Act**), but many key areas – such as **own resources, free movement of persons**, amendments to the **Treaties**, and the **accession** of new member states – are still included. Unanimity in the Council is also required at various stages of the **cooperation** and **co-decision procedures**. In some areas the Treaty provides for decisions to be taken by representatives of the governments of member states acting 'by common accord', and this too allows for a right of veto: examples include appointments to the **European Commission** and decisions on the **seat of the institutions**.

The Council is under a general obligation to act by unanimity in respect of the **Common Foreign and Security Policy** (CFSP) and **Justice and Home Affairs** (JHA) provisions of the **Maastricht Treaty**, but may decide upon measures to implement **joint actions** or **common positions** by **qualified majority voting** (QMV). See also **constructive abstention**.

Outside the Treaty, a right of veto was for many years frequently invoked by virtue of the so-called **Luxembourg Compromise** of 1966. Briefly, this allowed any member state that considered a 'very important' national interest to be at stake to insist in the Council that discussion be continued until a satisfactory consensus was found, even in matters that could under the Treaty be decided by QMV. The veto was, in fact, rarely used under this procedure, since normally the mere threat of invoking the Luxembourg Compromise was enough.

The veto is seen by some as an essential safeguard against coercion; on the other, as a bar to collective action and a means by which a minority can frustrate the will of the majority. On the whole, the compromise laid down in the Treaties (a right of veto in certain key areas, decisions by majority, simple or qualified, in all other fields) has worked well. Clearly, the European Community could not have worked on the same basis as the **League of Nations**, in which every state, however small, had a right of veto over all but procedural decisions. Nor could the Community have adopted a two-tier system like that of the **United Nations**, with the larger member states enjoying a right of veto by virtue of permanent membership of the Security Council. By comparison with those in other international decision-making systems, the rights of veto enjoyed by individual member states in the European Union are very limited, and with the **enlargement** of the Union this trend seems bound to continue. In this perspective, the **opt-out** (and the **variable geometry** to which it gives rise) may replace the veto as member states' weapon of last resort.

Visegrad states

The 'Visegrad states' are the Czech Republic, Hungary, Poland and Slovakia. In February 1991 in Visegrad (Hungary), the leaders of Hungary, Poland and what was then Czechoslovakia met to discuss their approach to European integration. Since 1989 the three countries had been cooperating within the **Warsaw Pact**. They confirmed their wish for 'total integration into the European political, economic, security and legislative order' and agreed to cooperate in their progressive achievement of such integration. As a first step, all four countries have concluded **Europe Agreements** with the European Union and have joined the **Council of Europe**. For most purposes, Bulgaria and Romania are now included with the Visegrad states. See also **Central European Initiative** (CEI), **Central European Free Trade Agreement** (CEFTA).

W

Warsaw Pact

On 7 May 1955 the USSR formally annulled the wartime alliances concluded with the United Kingdom (1942) and France (1944). A week later in Warsaw, the USSR, Albania, Bulgaria, Czechoslovakia, Hungary, Poland and Romania signed a mutual defence treaty. The treaty required signatory states to assist each other in the case of 'armed aggression in Europe' (Article 4) and provided for 'a joint command of their armed forces' (Article 5). East Germany became a member in 1956, and Albania withdrew in 1968. East Germany withdrew on being reunited with West Germany in 1990 (see **German reunification**), one year before the Pact was formally dissolved. The Warsaw Pact enabled the USSR to station forces in the states of the Eastern Bloc on a 'friendly' basis (as many as 20 Soviet divisions were based in East Germany). The USSR provided about three-quarters of the Warsaw Pact forces, as well as successive commanders-in-chief. The Warsaw Pact – signed in the same month in which the Western Allies recognized the independence of West Germany and admitted it to the **North Atlantic Treaty Organization** (NATO) – marked the end of Soviet ambitions to 'neutralize' Germany and a new hardening of attitudes in the Cold War.

Werner Report

The Werner Report of 1970 was an early blueprint for the achievement of **Economic and Monetary Union** (EMU). It inspired a number of important initiatives, including the 1971 European currency management system known as the '**snake**' and a commitment by heads of government in 1972 to move to a single currency by 1980. The EMU process embarked upon was, however, unexpectedly disrupted by the successive effects of dollar instability in 1971 and the worldwide recession begun by the first oil crisis of 1973–4. By the mid-1970s there was little to show for this ambitious project.

In December 1969 the heads of government, meeting in The Hague, decided that EMU should be a long-term Community objective and to move from the third stage of the 'transitional' phase of the Community's development (which had begun in 1966; see **transitional period**) to the final phase, starting in 1973. Work was put in hand within the **Ecofin Council** on devising transitional arrangements on the road to full EMU. Differences of opinion emerged, however, about the best way forward.

In March 1970 the Council established a special study group under Pierre Werner, the Prime Minister and Finance Minister of Luxembourg.

The Werner Report proposed a three-stage move to full EMU, lasting from 1971 to 1980. The first stage would be directed at getting the economic underpinnings right and preparing the ground for any institutional development. The second stage would consolidate the economic and institutional progress of the first, leading in the third stage to the irrevocable fixing of exchange rates and finally the adoption of a single currency. The single currency was deemed to be desirable, but not strictly necessary, to the project. During the first two stages, the domestic economic policies of member states would be increasingly closely coordinated at European level to promote convergence. In parallel, there would be a progressive narrowing of currency fluctuation bands, starting as soon as possible.

In March 1971 the Ecofin Council agreed a lengthy resolution on attaining EMU 'during the coming decade.' The member states committed themselves 'from the beginning of the first stage and on an experimental basis' to intervene to ensure that their currencies fluctuated against each other by less than the existing fluctuation margin allowed by the IMF against the US dollar: a 1.2 per cent band within a 1.5 per cent one.

The new exchange-rate arrangement – which was dubbed the 'snake' because the currencies of the Six were now tied to one another, rather than simply to the dollar, but on a flexible basis – was soon rendered unworkable by the instability of the dollar (which became a freely floating currency in August 1971) and the collapse of the Bretton Woods system of cross-rate parties.

In the course of 1972 efforts were made to salvage the project. The snake was relaunched in April as the so-called 'snake in the tunnel': currencies were allowed to fluctuate within a 2.25 per cent band against the dollar, as opposed to the 4.5 per cent band laid down by the International Monetary Fund. Within a year the currencies of four countries (the United Kingdom, Ireland, Denmark and Italy) had withdrawn from the system. Nevertheless, the meeting of heads of government in Paris in October 1972 – in which the United Kingdom took part for the first time – strongly reaffirmed the Community's EMU objective, formally committing member states to its full realization by

1980. In the interim 'fixed but adjustable parities' would be pursued. Already, however, the credibility of the whole exercise had been fatally prejudiced. When the Commission duly proposed in April 1973 that the Community move to the second stage of EMU on schedule in 1974, there was no agreement in the Ecofin Council. Work on the Werner project was left in abeyance, and the 1980 EMU objective was quickly forgotten.

Western European Union (WEU)

After the rejection by the French Assemblée Nationale of plans for a **European Defence Community** in August 1954, Anthony Eden, then Foreign Secretary, convened a meeting of the **Brussels Treaty** powers (the United Kingdom, France and the **Benelux** countries) together with West Germany, Italy, Canada and the United States to discuss ways of strengthening collective defence and extending cooperation into other areas. A ministerial conference was held in Paris in October 1954, and agreement was reached on modifications to the Brussels Treaty. Italy and West Germany were to be invited to become signatories to the Treaty. West Germany was allowed to rearm and was admitted to the **North Atlantic Treaty Organization** (NATO), and the last vestiges of the Allied occupation were to be removed from the Federal Republic. A condition of German rearmament was a prohibition on the possession of atomic, biological and chemical weapons. The United Kingdom agreed to maintain a certain level of forces on mainland Europe. With the ratification of these modifications, the WEU was established on 6 May 1955, with its headquarters in London. The original Brussels Treaty was concluded for an initial period of 50 years, after which member states were free to withdraw. Some authorities, however, calculate this period from the modified Brussels Treaty of 1954. Article 5 of the Brussels Treaty reads 'if any of the High Contracting Parties should be the object of an armed attack in Europe, the other High Contracting Parties will ... afford the Party so attacked all the military and other aid and assistance in their power'. Article 9 requires the WEU Council to submit an annual report to the WEU Assembly (see below).

The seven original members of the WEU were later joined by Portugal, Spain and Greece. Denmark and Ireland are observer members, together with (since 1995) Austria, Finland and Sweden. Associate status has been extended to the other European members of NATO (Iceland, Norway, Turkey, the Czech Republic, Hungary and Poland). Seven central and eastern European countries are 'associate partners'.

The WEU got off to an inauspicious start. Its proposals to resolve the question of the **Saarland** were rejected by referendum in 1955. Its new powers, under the modified Brussels Treaty, for cooperation in the field of social and cultural affairs were transferred to the **Council of Europe** in 1960. The WEU's importance in the 1960s stemmed primarily from the fact that it was the only European organization in which **the Six** and the United Kingdom – whose application to join the Six had been blocked by **Charles de Gaulle** – were able to meet regularly. However, in October 1984 a WEU Council meeting in Rome decided to reactivate the WEU as a forum for the discussion of specifically European security questions. This was followed up three years later in The Hague with the adoption of the 'Platform on European Security Interests', which contained the commitment to develop a 'more cohesive European defence identity'. In 1990 the military response on the part of west European countries to the Gulf crisis was coordinated through the WEU. At the **European Council** meeting in Maastricht in December 1991 the member states of the WEU agreed to transfer the headquarters of the WEU from London to Brussels. In their '**Petersberg Declaration**' of June 1992 the WEU Foreign Ministers widened the organization's remit to include peace-keeping, humanitarian and rescue tasks. Further progress was made at a WEU Council meeting in Lisbon in May 1995.

In the words of the decision reached in The Hague, the WEU is being transformed into the 'defence component of the European Union'. This decision was annexed to the **Maastricht Treaty** in a Declaration. The Treaty describes the WEU as 'an integral part of the development of the Union', and invites it 'to elaborate and implement decisions and actions of the Union which have defence implications' (Article 17; see **Common European Security and Defence Policy** (CESDP)). The Declaration set out the 'gradual process' by which the role of the WEU and its relations with the European Union and the Atlantic Alliance are to be strengthened. As part of a general tidying-up of European security structures, the WEU's Western European Armaments Group (WEAG: see **European Armaments Agency**) has assumed responsibility for most of the work formerly done by the **Eurogroup** and the **Independent European Programme Group**. With effect from 1998, the presidency of the WEU Council (member states' foreign and defence ministers) was aligned as far as possible with the **presidency** of the European Union. The WEU Assembly, which is composed of 364 parliamentarians (and an equal number of substitutes) drawn from the 28 participating states' representatives in the Parliamentary Assembly of the Council of Europe, meets twice a year in Paris. Only parliamentarians from the 10 full members have full voting rights in the Assembly, which styles itself 'the interim European Security and Defence Assembly'.

The position of the WEU was further clarified in the **Treaty of Amsterdam**. In the revised text of Article 17 (TEU), the WEU is described as supporting the Union 'in framing the defence aspects of the common foreign and security policy'. The Union commits itself to fostering 'closer institutional relations with the WEU with a view to the possibility of the integration of the WEU into the Union, should the Council so decide'. When the Union 'avails itself of the WEU to elaborate and implement decisions of the Union', all member states, whether or not they belong to the WEU, are entitled 'to participate fully and on an equal footing in planning and decision-taking in the WEU'. These new provisions are complemented and amplified by a Declaration adopted by the WEU Council on 22 July 1997 and annexed to the Maastricht Treaty. Relations between the Union and the WEU were further strengthened in November 1999 by the appointment of Javier Solana, the Union's **High Representative** for the CFSP, as secretary-general of the WEU. The WEU Council, meeting in Marseilles in November 2000, declared itself satisfied that the European Union was able to assume the obligations set out in the modified Brussels Treaty (see above), especially those contained in Articles 5 and 9 (see above). In July 2001 Brussels formally became the head-quarters of the WEU (including the WEAG) and in January 2002 the European Union took over responsibility for the WEU's Satellite Centre in Torrejon, Spain, and for the WEU's Institute for Security Studies in Paris.

The operational capability of the WEU is drawn from the growing number of 'forces answerable to WEU'. These now include the **Eurocorps**, the Belgian–German–Dutch–British Multinational Division, the British–Dutch amphibious force, EUROFOR and EUROMARFOR, the Italian amphibious force, and the German–Dutch HQ 1st Corps.

Anne Deighton (ed.), *Western European Union 1954–1997: Defence, Security, Integration* (Reading and Oxford, 1997) is the best recent treatment of the WEU.

Wider versus deeper

An argument that arises frequently in the context of the **enlargement** of the European Union, 'wider versus deeper' is concerned with two contrary propositions. On the one hand there are those who believe that enlarging the Union is a political imperative and that 'deepening' it – that is, extending the range of the Union's activities and strengthening the Union's institutions – would make enlargement more difficult, given the obligation laid upon all new member states to accept the *acquis communautaire*. On the other hand there are those who emphasize the fact that enlargement will make the Union more heterogeneous and institutionally more unwieldy, and that if progress towards the 'ever closer union' called for in the **Treaty of Rome** is to be maintained, deepening must accompany, or even precede, widening.

Much can be read between these lines. The prospect of enlargement and its alleged consequences are used to strengthen the case, on the one hand, for slowing down the integration process and, on the other, for speeding it up. A third position, held by those governments that support the fundamentally intergovernmental character of much of the **Maastricht Treaty**, points to **intergovernmentalism** as the key to the problem: it allows for further 'pillars' to be added within a Union structure, yet in a way more likely to be palatable to new member states concerned about possible loss of **sovereignty** and more flexible in terms of the degree of active involvement.

The proposals of the **European Commission**, entitled 'Europe and the challenge of enlargement' (*Bulletin of the European Communities*, supplement 3/92), were submitted to the Lisbon meeting of the **European Council** in June 1992, and were unequivocal. The Commission concluded that 'the accession of new members will increase the [European Union's] diversity and heterogeneity. But widening must not be at the expense of deepening. Enlargement must not be a dilution of the Community's achievements.' The European Council itself concluded that 'if the challenges of a European Union composed of a larger number of Member States are to be met successfully, parallel progress is needed as regards the internal development of the Union'.

World Trade Organization (WTO)

Based in Geneva, the WTO is the successor of the **General Agreement on Tariffs and Trade** (GATT). It has 144 members and 31 countries with observer status (including Russia). The WTO was an initiative of the European Community (backed by Canada and Japan) in the Uruguay Round of GATT negotiations, formally concluded in April 1994. A new round of trade talks was launched in Doha (Qatar) in November 2001. The deadline for their completion is 1 January 2005. The European Community has been a member of the WTO in its own right since 1995.

The WTO Agreement enjoins signatory states to reduce tariffs and not to engage in unilateral action likely to damage trade. It defines certain basic terms (such as 'dumping') used in international trade. It prohibits quantitative restrictions. It makes provision for retaliatory action and for the resolution of disputes, and is based upon non-discrimination (i.e., trading privileges granted to one state must be extended to all), although this does not apply to agriculture, to textiles (which are governed until 2005 by a separate Agreement), to 'regional trading arrangements' (see **customs union**) or, since 1971, to trading privileges granted to developing countries (see **Generalized System of Preferences**).

All member states of the European Union belong to the WTO, several of them as founder-members of GATT. Under Article 113 of the **Treaty of Rome** the **European Commission** represents the member states in international trade negotiations, and did so in GATT since the Kennedy Round. The Commission operates on the basis of a mandate laid down by the **Council of Ministers** and in consultation with the **Article 113 Committee**. Under Article 229 EC the Commission is responsible for maintaining 'appropriate relations' with the WTO.

Y

Yaoundé Convention

The Yaoundé Convention was a trade and aid agreement between **the Six** and the 18-member Associated African States and Madagascar (AASM), signed in Yaoundé, Cameroon, in 1963. Most of the AASM states were former French or Belgian colonies. The Convention entered into force in June 1964, was renegotiated in 1969, and was superseded by the **Lomé Convention** of 1975.

Youth

Established in 1988, Youth is a European Union action programme that allows financial assistance to be given from the **Budget** for a wide range of projects relevant to young people, especially in the fields of education, **equal treatment** and **citizenship** (*Official Journal*, C210, 22 July 1999). The applicant states (see **enlargement**), Iceland, Liechtenstein, Norway, and Switzerland may also participate. Over the period 2000–6 the programme has been allocated €520 million.

Yugoslavia

The Kingdom of Serbs, Croats and Slovenes – as Yugoslavia was originally called – was created after the First World War out of the Kingdom of Serbia (with Montenegro) and territories formerly part of the Austro-Hungarian Empire, some of them Catholic (Slovenia, Croatia), others largely Orthodox or Muslim. Serbs made up almost half the population. The name Yugoslavia, adopted in order to play down ethnic divisions, dates from 1929. However, ethnic and other tensions characterized the political history of Yugoslavia throughout the 1920s and 1930s (the King was assassinated in 1934), many of them prompted by Croat and Macedonian separatist aspirations. The Second World War resulted in invasion and occupation and the creation in Croatia of a puppet state sympathetic to Germany. From 1945 until the break-up of the country which began with the secession of Slovenia in July 1990 Yugoslavia was under Communist rule, although Marshal Tito and his successors succeeded in maintaining a substantial degree of independence from Moscow. Each constituent part of the old Yugoslavia – Bosnia–Herzegovina, Croatia, Macedonia, Slovenia and the Federal Republic of Yugoslavia – has its own entry in this book: see also the **Balkans**, **CARDS programme**, **Stability Pact for South-Eastern Europe**, **Stabilization and Association Process**. The classic description of Yugoslavia between the wars in all its complexity is Rebecca West, *Black Lamb, Grey Falcon* (1942). There is a lively account of Balkan politics in John Gunther, *Inside Europe* (1936).

Yugoslavia, Federal Republic of (FRY)

Established in April 1992, FRY is composed of the Republic of Serbia, with the Vojvodina in the north and Kosovo in the south, and the Republic of Montenegro in the south-west (providing FRY's only access to the sea). Montenegro is currently seeking independence.

The Serbs were the most numerous element when the Kingdom of the Serbs, Croats and Slovenes was first created in 1918 (see **Yugoslavia**). Their long-standing desire for absolute dominance of the region continued after the collapse of Communism to lead them to resist the demands for independence first made by Slovenia and subsequently by Croatia, Bosnia–Herzegovina and Macedonia. It also resulted in violently repressive policies against the Albanians of Kosovo. The intransigence and non-democratic nature of the regime in Belgrade led to the imposition of sanctions and diplomatic isolation. In June 2000 the **European Council** meeting in Feira sought to encourage the pro-democracy forces in FRY by affirming that 'a democratic, cooperative FRY living in peace with its neighbours' would be 'a welcome member of the European family of democratic nations'. Sanctions were brought to an end in October 2000. By the beginning of the following year the European Union's **CARDS programme** had been extended to FRY and a preferential trade agreement drawn up. See also **Stabilization and Association Process**, the **Balkans**.

Z

Zürich speech

In March 1946 **Winston Churchill** made his famous 'Iron Curtain' speech in Fulton, Missouri, in which he drew attention to the threat posed by the USSR to world peace. Four months later, at a meeting of foreign ministers in Paris, relations between the United States and the USSR took a decisive turn for the worse, and it became clear that the idea of a lasting peace underwritten by the Great Powers was not likely to be realized. Churchill therefore returned to a theme that he had touched on in a speech to both houses of the Belgian Parliament on 16 November 1945, the idea of a '**United States of Europe**, which will unify this Continent in a manner never known since the fall of the Roman Empire'.

Churchill's prime concern was to set out what Europe could do to contain the Soviet threat. In a speech in Zürich on 19 September 1946 he painted a characteristically broad and vivid picture of postwar devastation in Europe: 'Over wide areas a vast quivering mass of tormented, hungry, care-worn and bewildered human beings gape at the ruins of their cities and homes, and scan the dark horizons for the approach of some new peril, tyranny or terror'. But, he said, there was a 'sovereign remedy ... to re-create the European family, or as much of it as we can, and provide it with a structure under which it can dwell in peace, in safety, and in freedom. We must build a kind of United States of Europe'.

Churchill went on to make it clear that the United States of Europe would be a regional organization within the United Nations that 'could give a sense of enlarged patriotism and common citizenship to the distracted peoples of this turbulent and mighty continent'. From this passage and from others in the same speech it is evident that Churchill did not see the United Kingdom as part of the United States of Europe but as its 'friend and sponsor': the primary British obligation was to another 'natural grouping', the Commonwealth.

Then followed the passage that, as Churchill was well aware, was the most striking of the whole speech:

I am now going to say something that will astonish you. The first step in the re-creation of the European family must be a partnership between France and Germany. In this way only can France recover the moral leadership of Europe. There can be no revival of Europe without a spiritually great France and a spiritually great Germany. The structure of the United States of Europe, if well and truly built, will be such as to make the material strength of a single state less important. Small nations will count as much as large ones and gain their honour by their contribution to the common cause.

(Robert Rhodes James ed., *Winston S. Churchill: His complete speeches, 1897–1963*, Vol. VII)

The speech concluded with a practical suggestion: 'The first step is to form a **Council of Europe**. If at first all the states of Europe are not willing or able to join the Union, we must nevertheless proceed to assemble and combine those who will and those who can.'

The impact of this speech was enormous. The fact that a statesman of Churchill's standing had taken up the European cause gave it fresh impetus, and made Churchill the obvious choice as the man to preside over the **Congress of Europe** two years later. At the same time, the speech gave a misleading impression of the extent to which the United Kingdom or, more especially, the Conservative Party (of which Churchill, although no longer Prime Minister, was then still leader) was prepared to become involved in European integration.

European Union Documentation

Since this book was first published, documents (including legislation) have become much more readily available from the institutions and agencies of the European Union. To help readers take advantage of this I have sought to provide full references for all important EU documents. A very brief note on how documents may be obtained will be found below. To go into more detail would probably be misleading, since the system whereby documents are made available is changing all the time.

The main database for European Union documentation is CELEX. This is divided into several sectors:

- Treaties, including Treaties of Accession;
- agreements with non-member countries and international organizations;
- legislation, including Regulations, Directives, Decisions, the Budget, Resolutions, Declarations, EU institutions' rules of procedure, and decisions taken in the Common Foreign and Security Policy (CFSP) and Justice and Home Affairs (JHA) fields;
- documents with a bearing on actual or proposed legislation, including Commission Green and White Papers, European Parliament Resolutions, Common Positions of the Council of Ministers, reports of the Court of Auditors, Opinions of the Committee of the Regions and the Economic and Social Committee;
- material from the Court of Justice and the Court of First Instance;
- measures taken by the member states to implement EU legislation;
- oral and written questions from Members of the European Parliament;
- documents relevant to EU-EFTA relations and to the European Economic Area.

A small charge is payable for using CELEX's search engine. However, since 2001 access to CELEX and to other relevant databases has been free of charge via EUR-Lex, which is now the single portal for all access to EU documentation and which has its own search engine. This is entirely adequate for most purposes.

All EU documents have a number, sometimes known as a 'natural' number to distinguish it from the numbers used in the CELEX and EUR-Lex databases. The year of issue is always a component element in the number and is normally expressed as two digits. However, the problems posed by the year 2000 resulted in a change of practice, and years are now often expressed in full. Most search engines require the full four-digit year. In the case of Regulations the year follows the series number, but Directives are the other way round. Finding a piece of legislation is a great deal easier if the number is known, because searching by keyword – in the title or in the text – is much more laborious. Since all legislation is published in the *Official Journal*, I have given references to the relevant issue of the *Official Journal* for most legislation specifically mentioned in this book.

Formal proposals for legislation have a COM number in which the year of issue, given in full, appears in the brackets before the series number. These proposals appear both in paper form and also (without the explanatory memorandum) in the electronic version of the *Official Journal*. Consultation documents, White and Green Papers, and other Communications from the Commission also bear COM numbers. Most, but not all, are accessible electronically, but only very few are published in the *Official Journal*.

Two services, Prelex, operated by the secretariat-general of the Commission, and the European Parliament's Legislative Observatory (OEIL), allow the progress of an item of draft legislation to be monitored as it makes its way through the legislative process. Judgments of the Court of Justice and of the Court of First Instance (CFI) have their own numbering systems. They appear in summary form in the *Official Journal*. The full versions are most easily found in *European Court Reports* or on the Court of Justice's own website (CURIA) under the appropriate case number (made up of a series number followed by the year, expressed as two digits, in which the case was brought). Since the CFI was established, cases before the Court have been denominated with a 'C', those before the CFI with a 'T'. There is also a thematic index.

General browsing is best done via the website of the appropriate institution or agency, all of which are reachable through the Europa website (for list, see p. 574). Each directorate-general in the Commission has its own site, and on each site will be found 'Legislation in force' in that subject-area and pointers to further information.

Bibliography

There is a vast and steadily expanding literature on the subject of European integration, and even a list of those books and articles currently available in English would be well beyond the scope of this *Companion*. However, the radical changes brought about by the Single European Act, the collapse of the Soviet Union, the Treaties of Maastricht, Amsterdam, and Nice, the launch of the euro and the prospect of further enlargement have meant that many works are neither sufficiently up-to-date to be useful nor old enough to be historically interesting.

Some of the more specialized bibliographical references are to be found in the entries that form the main part of this book. In the bibliography that follows, which is limited, with few exceptions, to works in English, I have listed a broad selection of books both old and new, most of which contain bibliographies of their own. For reasons of space, I have had to omit all references to periodicals (the main ones are listed in Section 10). With very few exceptions, I have also omitted references to biographies and autobiographies of postwar politicians (such as Harold Macmillan, Konrad Adenauer or Georges Pompidou), even though many of these contain information or insights with a bearing on European integration, and to books aimed primarily at specific professional groups (such as businessmen or lawyers wanting to know more about the Single Market).

The most up-to-date bibliography of material in English on the European Communities is by John Paxton in the International Organizations series of 'selective, critical, annotated bibliographies' (Clio Press, Oxford, 1992). This work, with 682 entries, contains only a small selection of references to periodical literature. Also very helpful is Eva Evans, *A Selective Bibliography of Books on European Integration 1990–1994* (1995). Some idea of the quantity of pre-1977 material may be gained from Karl Kujath's *Bibliographie zur Europäischen Integration* (in German, French and English: Bonn, 1977), which runs to 732 pages.

A comprehensive range of materials may be found in the Commission's library in Brussels or in the European Parliament's main library in Luxembourg (there is a subsidiary collection in Brussels): both grant access to *bona fide* researchers, but neither lends material nor supplies documentation. The historical archives of the European Communities are kept at the European University Institute at Fiesole, near Florence. The Commission publishes a useful *Guide to the Archives of Member States' Foreign Ministries and European Union Institutions* (2nd edn, 1996).

Most of the major European organizations put out regular publications, either free or on subscription. The titles of these publications may be obtained either from the organization direct or from the appropriate entry in, for example, the *Yearbook of International Organizations*. Many of these organizations also have libraries open to the public or a press and information service. For European Union documentation, see above.

Except where stated otherwise, the place of publication for all books listed below is London.

1 General reference

Boudant, Joel, and Gounelle, Max, *Les grandes dates de l'Europe communautaire* (Paris, 1989).
A comprehensive and well-arranged chronology, the fullest of its kind.

Blair, Alasdair, *The Longman Companion to the European Union since 1945* (Harlow, 1999).
Useful and reliable for facts, but short on analysis.

Brandstetter, Gerfried, *Chronologisches Lexicon der Europäischen Integration* (Vienna, 1996).
Not as full as Boudant and Gounelle (see above) but very useful for the period 1988 to 1995.

Cook, Chris, and Paxton, John, *European Political Facts, 1900–1996* (4th edn, Basingstoke, 1998).
The standard reference book in English, although the emphasis is on the European states rather than on European integration (in relation to which there are many striking inaccuracies).

Cook, Chris, and Stevenson, John, *The Longman Handbook of Modern European History 1763–1997* (3rd edn, Harlow, 1998).
Concise, reliable reference book.

Drost, Harry, *What's What and Who's Who in Europe* (1995).
Uniquely comprehensive 'fact book' on current affairs.

The Economist Pocket Europe (5th edn, 2002).
   The most accessible one-volume collection of facts about the European
   states and international institutions, plus basic statistics.

Europe: A Thematic Atlas (1992).
   Published by *The Economist*, the atlas is a clear and comprehensive, if in
   places idiosyncratic, presentation of a wide range of data.

Fernandez-Armesto, Felipe (ed.), *The Peoples of Europe* (2nd edn, 1997).
   Very useful socio-ethnographic handbook to all the national groupings in
   Europe, large and small.

Leonard, Dick, *The Economist Guide to the European Union* (7th edn, 2002).
   The best general handbook.

Ramsay, Anne, *Eurojargon* (1997).
   The fullest guide to the acronyms and argot of the Brussels institutions.

The Times Guide to the European Parliament (1979, 1984, 1989 and 1994
   edns).
   Short biographies and photographs of all MEPs, with useful data on the
   results, the issues, the campaigns, etc., in all the member states. (Series
   now discontinued.)

Urwin, Derek, *Dictionary of European History and Politics since 1945*
   (Harlow, 1996).
   Concise, comprehensive and authoritative.

Vanthoor, Wim, *A Chronological History of the European Union 1946-1998*
   (Cheltenham, 1999).
   The most up-to-date of the chronologies.

Young, John W., *The Longman Companion to Cold War and Detente 1941–91*
   (1993).
   Very useful factual guide to the politico-military background to European
   unification.

2 History

Armstrong, David, Lloyd, Lorna, and Redmond, John, *From Versailles to
   Maastricht* (Basingstoke, 1996).
   The Union in the context of international governance.

Barker, Sir Ernest, Clark, Sir George, and Vaucher, P. (eds), *The European
   Inheritance* (3 vols, Oxford, 1954).
   A survey by an international team of scholars, from the Bronze Age to 1950.

Beloff, Max, *The United States and the Unity of Europe* (1963).
Classic study, now partially superseded by Duignan and Gann (see below).

Bossuat, Gérard, *Les fondateurs de l'Europe unie* (Paris, 2001).
Contains a wealth of detail not easily found elsewhere on the early history of European integration.

Brugmans, Hendrik (ed.), *Europe: Dream, Adventure, Reality* (Brussels, n.d.).
A valuable collection of essays, many of them by pioneers of integration, prepared for the 30th anniversary of the Treaty of Rome.

Bussière, Eric, Dumoulin, Michel, and Trausch, Gilbert, *Europa* (Antwerp, 2001).
Handsome gift book with a worthwhile text and valuable iconography.

Davies, Norman, *Europe* (Oxford, 1996).
Lucid and comprehensive history.

Dell, Edmund, *The Schuman Plan and the British Abdication of Leadership in Europe* (Oxford, 1995).
First-class analysis of a very revealing turn of events.

Delouche, Frédéric (ed.), *Illustrated History of Europe* (1993).
Wide-ranging, well-balanced narrative by an international team.

Duignan, Peter, and Gann, L. H., *The United States and the New Europe, 1945–1993* (Oxford, 1994).
The fullest and most recent account of US-Europe relations.

Duroselle, Jean-Baptiste, *Europe: A History of its Peoples* (trs. Richard Mayne, 1990).
A succinct history of Europe from a 'European' point of view.

European Movement, *The European Movement and the Council of Europe* (n.d.).
Of great interest for its account of the 1948 Congress of Europe in The Hague.

Fursdon, Edward, *The European Defence Community: A History* (1980).
A very clear background to European states' postwar collaboration in the defence field; the standard work in English.

Haas, Ernst B., *The Uniting of Europe: Political, Social and Economic Forces, 1950–1957* (Stanford, 1958).
Pioneering and sympathetic study by an American scholar.

Hay, Denys, *Europe: the Emergence of an Idea* (rev. edn, Edinburgh, 1968).
A pioneering study, still the only one of its kind in English.

Hogan, Michael, *The Marshall Plan: America, Britain, and the Reconstruction of Western Europe, 1947–1952* (Cambridge, 1987).
Not as readable as Mee (see below), but more detailed.

Joll, James, *Europe since 1870* (3rd edn, Harmondsworth, 1983).
Reliable and well-written concise history.

Laqueur, Walter, *Europe in Our Time* (Harmondsworth, 1993).
A handy supplement to tell (see above) covering the postwar period.

Laughland, John, *The Tainted Source: the Undemocratic Origins of the European Idea* (1997).
Highly original but not wholly convincing.

Lindberg, Leon L., *The Political Dynamics of European Economic Integration* (Stanford, 1963).
Perceptive study within a conceptual framework still widely used; particularly strong on the customs union versus free trade area debate.

Lipgens, Walter, *A History of European Integration, Vol. 1, 1945–1947* (only volume published: Oxford, 1982).
Very detailed; the standard work (only volume published).

Lipgens, Walter (ed.), *Documents on the History of European Integration* (Berlin/New York): Vol. 1, *Continental Plans for European Union, 1939–1945* (1985); Vol. 2, *Plans for European Union in Great Britain and in Exile, 1939–1945* (1986); Vol. 3, *The Struggle for European Union by Political Parties and Pressure Groups in Western European Countries, 1945–1950* (1988).
Voluminous and authoritative collection of documents, with commentary; the only work of its kind.

Long, D., and Wilson, P., *Thinkers of the Twenty Years' Crisis: Inter-war Idealism Reassessed* (Oxford, 1995).
Valuable for the intellectual background to European integration.

Mayne, Richard, *The Community of Europe* (1962); *The Recovery of Europe* (1970); *Postwar: The Dawn of Today's Europe* (1983).
Although these three books overlap, they are all worth reading as lucid, well-informed accounts of European integration written from the inside.

Mayne, Richard, and Pinder, John, *Federal Union: The Pioneers* (1990).
The only comprehensive study of the contribution made by British federalists to European integration, but too partisan for the non-specialist.

Mee, Charles L., *The Marshall Plan: The Launching of the Pax Americana* (New York, 1984).
Stronger on the politics than the economics, but a readable account of a decisive episode (see also Hogan).

Milward, Alan, *The Reconstruction of Western Europe 1945–1951* (1984).
The most authoritative account in English of the early years of European integration.

Milward, Alan, *The European Rescue of the Nation-State* (2nd edn, 2000).
Very detailed and independent-minded study of the birth of the European institutions; the basic thesis is implicit in the title.

Murray, Philomena, and Rich, Paul (eds), *Visions of European Unity* (Oxford, 1996).
Full of valuable insights.

Rietbergen, Peter, *Europe: A Cultural History* (1998).
A surprisingly successful and coherent history of European creativity.

Scott, George, *The Rise and Fall of the League of Nations* (1973).
Clearly written non-specialist study of the League, offering some instructive parallels with postwar European institutions.

Shore, Chris, *Building Europe* (2000).
An account of the 'cultural politics' of integration, yielding many insights.

Stirk, P. M. R. (ed.), *European Unity in Context: The Interwar Period* (1989).
Very useful collection of essays.

Stirk, P. M. R., *A History of European Integration since 1914* (1996).
Original and persuasive with an unusually wide range of sources.

Temperley, A. C., *The Whispering Gallery of Europe* (1938).
An inside account of the League of Nations by the man who acted as military adviser to successive British delegations.

Urwin, Derek, *A Political History of Western Europe since 1945* (5th edn, Harlow, 1997).
Serviceable and reliable history.

Weigall, David, and Stirk, Peter (eds), *The Origins and Development of European Integration* (1999).
Digs deeper and more widely than most comparable studies, to good effect.

Western European Union, *Ten Years of Seven-Power Europe* (Paris, 1964).
Concentrates on security issues, but contains a very good essay by Peter

Kirk MP, the first Conservative leader in the European Parliament, on 'The British Question-mark to Europe'.

White, Theodore H., *Fire in the Ashes: Europe in Mid-Century* (1954).
Stimulating survey of postwar Europe by a distinguished American historian.

Winand, Pascaline, *Eisenhower, Kennedy, and the United States of Europe* (Basingstoke, 1993).
Essential to an understanding of US influence in the early years.

Young, John W., *Britain, France and the Unity of Europe 1945–51* (Leicester, 1984).
Standard history of Franco-British relations in the immediate postwar years: particularly valuable for its account of the origins of the Council of Europe and the British reaction to the Schuman Plan.

3 The United Kingdom and Europe

Baker, David, and Seawright, David (eds), *Britain for and against Europe* (Oxford, 1998).
Excellent collection of essays.

Black, Jeremy, *Convergence or Divergence? Britain and the Continent* (1994).
Comprehensive survey of relations between the United Kingdom and the Continent since the time of the Romans.

Bullen, Roger, and Pelly, M. E. (eds), *Documents on British Policy Overseas*, Series 11, Vol. 1 (1986).
Documents from official archives on the Schuman Plan and the Council of Europe, 1950–52, with introduction, detailed chronology and explanatory notes.

Charlton, Michael, *The Price of Victory* (1983).
Uniquely interesting and valuable account of the United Kingdom's attitude to European integration, much of it based on interviews with the politicians and civil servants directly involved.

Denman, Roy, *Missed Chances* (1995).
Polemical, first-hand account of the United Kingdom's mishandling of its European opportunities.

Forster, Anthony, *Euroscepticism in Contemporary British Politics* (2002).
Astute study of an enduring phenomenon.

George, Stephen, *Britain and European Integration since 1945* (2nd edn, Oxford, 1994).

Similar in scope to Young (see below), and reaches broadly the same conclusions.

George, Stephen, *An Awkward Partner: Britain in the EC* (3rd edn, Oxford, 1998).
Balanced general survey.

Gowla, David, and Turner, Arthur (eds), *Britain and European Integration 1945–1998* (2000).
A useful 'documentary history'.

Joll, James (ed.), *Britain and Europe: Pitt to Churchill, 1793–1940* (1950).
Selected texts with a commentary.

Kaiser, Wolfram, *Using Europe, Abusing the Europeans* (Basingstoke, 1996).
Vigorous account of the early years (1945–63) of the United Kingdom's relations with Europe.

Kitzinger, Uwe, *Diplomacy and Persuasion: How Britain joined the Common Market* (1973).
The standard history.

Lindsay, Kenneth, *European Assemblies* (1960).
Indispensable for the early history.

Lord, Christopher, *Absent at the Creation: Britain and the Formation of the European Community, 1950–52* (Aldershot, 1996).
Concise but thorough and well-balanced (see also Dell in section 2).

Ludlow, Piers, *Dealing with Britain* (Cambridge, 1997).
Authoritative politico-diplomatic account of the United Kingdom's relations with the European Community.

Mather, Janet, *The European Union and British Democracy* (Basingstoke, 2000).
The impact of the EU process and institutions on British political life.

Nutting, Anthony, *Europe Will Not Wait* (1960).
Widely read in its day, a plea by a former minister of the Foreign and Commonwealth Office, who resigned over Suez, for Britain to get more involved in European integration.

O'Neill, Sir Con, *Britain's Entry into the European Community* (2000).
An authoritative account, drawn up in 1972, of the negotiations by the head of the negotiating team, never before published.

Passerini, Luisa, *Europe in Love, Love in Europe* (1999).
Idiosyncratic study of Europe's place in the British imagination between the World Wars.

Radice, Giles, *Offshore* (1992).
Penetrating politico-psychological study by a pro-European Labour MP.

Seton-Watson, R. W., *Britain in Europe 1789–1914* (Cambridge, 1937); *Britain and the Dictators* (Cambridge, 1938).
The historical background to British attitudes to Europe, diplomatic and political.

Skidelsky, Robert, 'Britain and Europe' in *Interests and Obsessions* (1993).
Thoughtful and suggestive essay.

Wilkes, George (ed.), *Britain's Failure to Enter the European Community 1961–63* (1997).
Revealing study of the first application.

Young, Hugo, *This Blessed Plot* (1999).
A thoroughly humane, well-written and widely researched study of ambivalence.

Young, John W., *Britain and European Unity, 1945–1992* (1993).
Useful study of the European argument in the United Kingdom, from Clement Attlee to John Major.

4 The Institutions of the European Union

Abeles, Marc, *La vie quotidienne au Parlement Européen* (Paris, 1992).
Lively 'anthropological' study of the Parliament and its inhabitants, their rituals, social organization and belief-systems.

Archer, Clive, *The European Union: Structure and Process* (3rd edn, 2000).
A good general handbook.

Bulmer, Simon, and Wessels, Wolfgang, *The European Council* (1987).
No longer up-to-date, but useful as background.

Cini, Michelle, *The European Commission: Leadership, Organization and Culture in the EU Administration* (Manchester, 1996).
Among the best recent studies of the Commission.

de La Guerivière, Jean, *Voyage à l'intérieur de l'Eurocratie* (new edn, Paris, 1993).
Entomological study of the Eurocrat.

Edwards, Geoffrey, and Pijpers, Alfred (eds), *The Politics of European Treaty Reform* (1997).
Detailed study of the 1996–7 Intergovernmental Conference which resulted in the Treaty of Amsterdam.

Edwards, Geoffrey, and Spence, David (eds), *The European Commission* (2nd edn, 1997).
The fullest and clearest description of the Commission in English.

Hayes-Renshaw, Fiona, and Wallace, Helen, *The Council of Ministers* (Basingstoke, 1997).
Thorough and up-to-date.

Hix, Simon, *The Political System of the European Union* (Basingstoke, 1999).
Clear, well-informed analysis.

Hooghe, Liesbet, *The European Commission and the Integration of Europe* (Cambridge, 2001).
Wide ranging description and analysis of the Commission's central role.

Jacobs, Francis, Corbett, Richard, and Shackleton, Michael, *The European Parliament* (4th edn, 2000).
Authoritative and comprehensive study by a team of insiders.

King, Preston, and Bosco, Andrea (eds), *A Constitution for Europe* (1991).
Study by a team of federalists, with much recondite historical information.

Kreppel, Amie, *The European Parliament and Supranational Party System* (Cambridge, 2002)
Microscopically detailed analysis of voting patterns.

Laursen, Finn, and Vanhoonecker, Sophie (eds), *The Intergovernmental Conference on Political Union* (The Hague, 1992).
The institutional and political background to the Maastricht Treaty; for specialists only.

Lodge, Juliet, and Herman, Valentine, *Direct Elections to the European Parliament* (1992).

Lodge, Juliet (ed.), *Direct Elections to the European Parliament 1984* (1986).
The first of these books sets out the political and legislative background to the first (1979) European elections, the second is a survey of the 1984 European elections campaign throughout the member states.

Marquand, David, *Parliament for Europe* (1979).
A suggestive and stimulating study, written at the time of the first European elections.

Middlemas, Keith, *Orchestrating Europe* (1995).
Based on 'elite oral history', a stimulating but not always accurate study of 'informal politics'.

Nugent, Neill (ed.), *At the Heart of the Union* (Basingstoke, 1996).
Specialist study of the Commission.

Page, Edward C., *People who Run Europe* (Oxford, 1997).
Wide-ranging and lucid analysis of the institutional undergrowth.

Rometsch, Dieter, and Wessels, Wolfgang (eds), *The European Union and the Member States: Towards Institutional Fusion?* (Manchester, 1996).
Solid collection of essays, some more visionary than others.

Spierenburg, Dirk, and Poidevin, Raymond, *The History of the High Authority of the European Coal and Steel Community* (1994).
Comprehensive and specialized; the standard work.

Stevens, Anne, with Stevens, Handley, *Brussels Bureaucrats?* (Basingstoke, 2001).
Revealing and on the whole sympathetic.

Usher, John A., *EC Institutions and Legislation* (Harlow, 1998).
An admirably clear and compact handbook.

Van Schendelen, M.P.C. (ed.), *EU Committees as Influential Policy-Makers* (Aldershot, 1998).
Clear and informative behind-the-scenes study.

Wallace, H. and W. (eds), *Policy-Making in the European Union* (4th edn, Oxford, 2000).
Thoroughly revised edition of a classic study.

Wallace, Helen, and Young, Alasdair (eds), *Participation and Policy-making in the European Union* (Oxford, 1997).
Vivid description of industry's role in the political process.

Westlake, Martin, *Britain's Emerging Euro-Elite? The British in the European Parliament, 1979–1992* (Aldershot, 1994).
The impact of British MEPs in the Parliament since the first European elections.

Westlake, Martin, *The Commission and the Parliament* (1994).
Careful, slightly clinical study of the Commission – Parliament relationship, with many incidental insights.

Westlake, Martin, *The Council of the European Union* (rev. edn, 1999).
One of the few up-to-date studies of the Council.

5 Law

Arnull, Anthony, *The European Union and its Court of Justice* (Oxford, 1999).
A conspicuously clear and helpful account.

Church, Clive H., and Phinnemore, David, *The Penguin Guide to the European Treaties* (2002)
Full texts of the Treaties, with useful commentary.

Craig, Paul, and de Burca, Grainne, *EU Law* (3rd edn, Oxford, 2003).
Comprehensive, well-organized general handbook.

Curtin, Deirdre, and Heukels, Ton (eds), *Institutional Dynamics of European Integration* (Vol. II of *Essays in Honour of Henry G. Schermers*) (Dordrecht, 1994).
Outstanding collection of essays on almost every aspect of Community law.

Duff, Andrew (ed.), *The Treaty of Amsterdam* (1997).
Text with politico-legal commentary.

Green, Nicholas, Hartley, Trevor C., and Usher, John A., *The Legal Foundations of the Single European Market* (Oxford, 1992).
The best work in its field.

Hartley, Trevor C., *The Foundations of European Community Law* (5th edn, Oxford, 2003).
Excellent general background.

Janis, Mark, Kay, Richard, and Bradley, Anthony, *European Human Rights Law* (Oxford, 1995).
Clear and comprehensive handbook.

Lasok, K. P. E., *Law and Institutions of the European Union* (7th edn, 2002).
A standard work, many times revised.

Lenaerts, Koen, and Van Nuffel, Piet, *Constitutional Law of the European Union* (1999).

Lenaerts, Koen, and Arts, Dirk, *Procedural Law of the European Union* (1999).
Two outstanding additions to the range of material on Community law.

Loubay, Julian, and Biondi, Andrea (eds), *Remedies for Breach of EC Law* (Chichester, 1997).
Useful for specialists.

Macleod, I., Hendry, I., and Hyett, S., *The External Relations of the European Communities* (Oxford, 1996).
Comprehensive, authoritative, well-organized legal commentary.

Markesinis, Basil (ed.), *The Gradual Convergence* (Oxford, 1994).
How the different legal systems in Europe are learning from each other.

Mathijsen, P. S. R. F., *A Guide to European Union Law* (7th edn, 1999).
Solid general introduction.

Monar, Jörg, Neuwahl, Nanette, O'Keefe, David and Robinson, William (eds), *Butterworth's Expert Guide to the European Union* (1996).
Useful for quick reference and accessible to non-lawyers.

Oppenheimer, Andrew (ed.), *The Relationship Between European Community Law and National Law: The Cases* (Cambridge, 1994).
Clear account of a key aspect of Community law.

Paterson, Gerald, *The European Patent System* (2001).
Authoritative account of an increasingly important area of law in the European Union.

Rasmussen, Hjalte, *European Court of Justice* (Copenhagen, 1998).
An entertainingly pungent critique of the Court.

Rudden, Bernard, and Phelan, Diarmuid Rossa, *Basic Community Cases* (2nd edn, Oxford, 1997).
A selection of the key cases that bring out fundamental principles of Community law.

Rudden, Bernard, and Wyatt, Derrick, *Basic Community Laws* (7th edn, Oxford, 1999).
Key passages from the Treaties, with commentary.

Schiemann, Sir Konrad, 'Europe – our common legal principles', *Yearbook of European Law 1999–2000* (Oxford).
Outstandingly interesting and helpful essay.

Toth, A. G., *Encyclopaedic Dictionary of European Community Law* (Oxford, 2002, only available in USA).
Comprehensive and authoritative.

Tridimas, Takis, *The General Principles of EC Law* (Oxford, 1999).
Authoritative theoretical survey.

Weatherill, Stephen, *Cases and Materials on EC Law* (5th edn, 2000).
Assembles for each main area of activity the relevant Treaty passages plus key legislation and Court of Justice rulings: an extremely useful book.

Weatherill, Stephen, and Beaumont, Paul, *EU Law* (3rd edn, Harmondsworth, 1999).
Clear, comprehensive and accessible handbook.

Weiler, J. H. H., *The Constitution of Europe* (Cambridge, 1999).
Lively and provocative essays by a distinguished American lawyer.

Wyatt, Derrick, and Dashwood, Alan, *European Union Law* (4th edn, 2000).
Latest edition of a standard work: more emphasis on legal concepts than Lasok (see above).

6 Economics and the Single Market

Colchester, Nicholas, and Buchan, David, *Europe Relaunched: Truths and Illusions on the Way to 1992* [published in the US as *Europower*] (1990).
Lively and well-informed account of the personal and political background to the Single Market programme.

Eichengreen, Barry, *European Monetary Unification: Theory, Practice, and Analysis* (Cambridge, MA, 1997).
Clear, well-written, thoughtful and authoritative.

El-Agraa, Ali M., *The European Union: History, Institutions, Economics and Policies* (5th edn, 1998).
Well-established standard textbook.

Ludlow, Peter, *The Making of the European Monetary System* (1982).
The standard work in English.

Padoa-Schioppa, Tommaso, *Efficiency, Stability, and Equity* (Oxford, 1987).
The Commission's study of the effects of the Single Market programme.

Padoa-Schioppa, Tommaso, *The Road to Monetary Union in Europe: The Emperor, the Kings, and the Genies* (Oxford, 1994).
Narrative and analytical account of EMU: accessible and well-informed.

Swann, Dennis, *The Economics of Europe* (9th edn, Harmondsworth, 2000).
The standard textbook, many times revised.

Tsoukalis, Loukas, *The New European Economy Revisited* (Oxford, 1997).
Lively but authoritative study, especially good on trade policy.

7 Politics and political parties

Bell, David, S., and Lord, Christopher (eds), *Transnational Parties in the European Union* (Aldershot, 1998).
Well informed general survey: not quite up-to-date.

Bomberg, Elizabeth, *Green Parties and Politics in the European Union* (1998).
Sympathetic and up-to-date account of Green parties and their problems.

Butler, David, and Jowett, Paul, *Party Strategies in Britain* (1985).
Appraises the campaign and the results in the 1984 European elections.

Butler, David, and Marquand, David, *European Elections and British Politics* (1981).
Examines the 1979 European elections as a phenomenon in British politics.

Butler, David, and Westlake, Martin, *British Politics and European Elections 1994* (Basingstoke, 1995).
The fullest account of the 1994 campaign.

Day, Alan J., *Directory of European Union Political Parties* (2000).
Essential reference work.

de Winter, Lieven, and Türsan, Huri, *Regionalist Parties in Western Europe* (1998).
Useful specialist survey.

Featherstone, Kevin, *Socialist Parties and European Integration* (Manchester, 1988).
Especially useful for the historical background to Socialist attitudes.

Fogarty, Michael P., *Christian Democracy in Western Europe, 1820–1953* (1957).
Pioneering study. Essential as background.

Hix, Simon, and Lord, Christopher, *Political Parties in the European Union* (Basingstoke, 1997).
Outstandingly interesting and lucid survey.

Irving, R. E. M., *The Christian Democratic Parties of Western Europe* (1979).
Out of date, but useful as background reading.

Jansen, Thomas, *The European People's Party* (Basingstoke, 1998).
Authoritative account of the EPP by its first secretary-general.

Kalyvas, Stathis N., *The Rise of Christian Democracy in Europe* (Cornell, 1996).
See especially Chapter 4 on 'the puzzle of nonformation' in France.

Kirchner, Emil J. (ed.), *Liberal Parties in Western Europe* (Cambridge, 1988).
Still useful as background.

Ladrech, Robert, and Marlière, Philippe (eds), *Social Democratic Parties in the European Union* (Basingstoke, 1999).
Comprehensive survey of the largest political family.

Lamberts, Emiel (ed.), *Christian Democracy in the European Union* (Leuven, 1997).
Valuable survey, especially for Thomas Jansen's article on 'the dilemma for Christian Democracy'.

Lodge, Juliet (ed.), *The 1999 Elections to the European Parliament* (Basingstoke, 2001).
Sound and thorough, but not especially revealing.

Reif, Karlheinz, *Ten European Elections* (1985).
Underlines the separateness of national campaigns in the 1984 European elections.

8 Memoirs and biographies

Acheson, Dean, *Present at the Creation* (New York, 1969).
A privileged account of the period 1941–52, as seen from the State Department, including the Marshall Plan, the Schuman Plan, and the birth of NATO.

Bond, Martyn (ed.), *Eminent Europeans* (1997).
Biographical studies, most of them excellent, of key figures in the history of European integration.

Brinkley, Douglas, and Hackett, Clifford (eds), *Jean Monnet: The Path to European Unity* (New York, 1991).
Essays on Monnet, many by people who knew him personally.

Duchêne, François, *Jean Monnet: The First Statesman of Interdependence* (New York and London, 1994).
A very full and readable biography, by one of Monnet's associates.

Grant, Charles, *Delors: The House that Jacques Built* (1994).
Excellent biography of Jacques Delors, with much incidental detail on the workings of the Commission.

Jenkins, Roy, *European Diary, 1977–1981* (1989).
Lively and informative account of the author's presidency of the Commission.

Loth, W., Wallace, W., and Wessels, W. (eds), *Walter Hallstein: The Forgotten European?* (Basingstoke, 1998).
Important study of a key figure.

Marjolin, Robert, *Architect of European Unity: Memoirs 1911–1986* (1989).
The author, a distinguished economist, was a member of the Commission from 1958 to 1967 and later one of the 'Three Wise Men'.

Monnet, Jean, *Memoirs* (trs. Richard Mayne, 1978).
Essential reading, especially valuable for his account of the Schuman Plan and the Treaty of Paris.

Ross, George, *Jacques Delors and European Integration* (Cambridge, 1995).
Close-up study by an American political scientist, based on extensive contacts with the Delors *cabinet*.

Spaak, Paul-Henri, *The Continuing Battle* (1971).
Autobiography by the Belgian statesman, a key figure in European integration during the postwar period.

Spender, Stephen, *European Witness* (1946).
Illuminating account of a visit to occupied Germany in 1945, to report back on what remained of German intellectual life.

9 General studies

Arter, David, *The Politics of European Integration* (1994).
Ingenious and original account of the external and internal forces that shaped the integration process.

Beetham, David, and Lord, Christopher, *Legitimacy and the European Union* (Harlow, 1998)
Short but penetrating and helpful study of a controversial topic.

Beloff, Max, *Europe and the Europeans* (1957).
Ambitious report from a Council of Europe study group.

Blokker, Niels M., and Schermers, Henry G. (eds), *Proliferation of International Organizations* (The Hague, 2001).
Excellent articles on the Maastricht Treaty.

Bretherton, Charlotte, and Vogler, John, *The European Union as a Global Actor* (1999).
Useful study of EU foreign policy.

Browning, Alison, *L'Europe et les intellectuels* (Paris, 1984).
Intelligent interviews with leading European intellectuals.

Brugmans, Henri, *L'idée européenne* (Bruges, 1965).
Historical analysis of the 'European idea' since 1918.

Budge, Ian, and Newton, Kenneth, et al., *The Politics of the New Europe* (Harlow, 1997).
Excellent collection of essays, not confined to the European Union.

Burgess, Michael, *Federalism and European Union: The Building of Europe 1950–2000* (2000).
How federalist ideas have influenced European integration since 1950.

Burgess, Michael (ed.), *Federalism and Federation in Western Europe* (1986).
Collection of essays on the federalist contribution to European integration and on federal systems in Europe.

Butler, Michael, *Europe: More than a Continent* (1986).
General survey by the former British Permanent Representative in Brussels, with a lucid account of the British Budget dispute.

Cole, G. D. H., and Cole, Margaret, *The Intelligent Man's Review of Europe Today* (1933).
Pioneering prewar survey.

Cole, John, and Cole, Francis, *The Geography of the European Community* (2nd edn, 1997).
Integration from a geographical point of view, with many revealing insights into regional policy, transport, energy, etc.

Curry, George (ed.), *Tomorrows in Europe* (Columbia, South Carolina, 1973).
Three excellent studies, originally delivered as lectures: by Hugh Seton-Watson on nationalism in central Europe, by Roy Jenkins on EC–US relations, and by Robert Rhodes James on Churchill.

Dahrendorf, Ralf, *Reflections on the Revolution in Europe* (1990).
Consciously modelled on Burke, a stimulating essay on the collapse of Soviet hegemony in eastern Europe.

de Giustino, David, *A Reader in european Integration* (1996).
Useful source-book, containing many well-chosen original texts.

de Rougemont, Denis, *28 siècles d'Europe* (1961, rep. Brussels, 1990).
The 'European idea' from its origins to modem times.

de Rougemont, Denis, *The Meaning of Europe* (trs. Alan Braley, 1965).
Wide-ranging, ruminative essay by a once-influential Swiss writer.

Delors, Jacques, *Our Europe* (trs. Brian Pearce, 1992; originally published as *La France par l'Europe*, Paris, 1988).
Authoritative but slightly bland: Charles Grant's biography (see Section 8) is more revealing.

Ducci, Roberto, and Olivi, Bino, *Europa incompiuta* (Padua, 1973).
Pioneering and valuable collection of historic documents in their original languages.

Duursma, Jorri, *Self-determination, Statehood and International Relations of Micro-States* (doctoral thesis, University of Leyden, 1994).
A comprehensive and interesting survey of how micro-states (Andorra, Liechtenstein, Monaco, San Marino and the Vatican City) survive and prosper.

Eatwell, Roger (ed.), *European Political Cultures: Conflict or Convergence?* (1997).
Original and informative study of an underexplored topic.

George, Stephen, *Politics and Policy in the European Union* (3rd edn, Oxford, 1996).
Solid, clear, well-written survey.

Ginsberg, Roy H., *Foreign Policy Actions of the European Community* (Boulder, CO, 1989).
Thoroughgoing analysis of the EC's performance in foreign affairs, with complete list of 'foreign policy actions' 1958–85.

Gowan, Peter, and Anderson, Perry (eds), *The Question of Europe* (1997).
Acute and well-argued collection of essays by a distinguished team.

Greenwood, Justin, *Representing Interests in the European Union* (Basingstoke, 1997).
Valuable and up-to-date account of lobbying in the widest sense.

Gunther, John, *Inside Europe* (rev. illustrated edn, November 1938); *Inside Europe Today* (1961).
These two books by John Gunther, the best-known American journalist of his day, are lively, well-informed, occasionally cynical reviews of the state of Europe, with many entertaining biographical sketches.

Hallstein, Walter, *United Europe: Challenge and Opportunity* (1962).
Originally delivered as lectures in the US, these are forceful and well-argued reflections by the first President of the Commission.

Hallstein, Walter, *Europe in the Making* (1972).
An English translation of Hallstein's *Der Unvollendete Bundesstaat* (1969), this is more wide-ranging and more polemical than *United Europe*.

Harryvan, A. G., and van der Harst, J. (eds), *Documents on European Union* (Basingstoke, 1997).
Comprehensive collection of original texts.

Hayward, Jack (ed.), *The Crisis of Representation in Europe* (1995).
Essays on most aspects of democracy in Europe.

Hesse, Joachim Jens, and Wright, Vincent (eds), *Federalizing Europe?* (Oxford, 1996).
Valuable study of federal systems at the national and the European level.

Hinsley, F. H., *Sovereignty* (2nd edn, Cambridge, 1986).
Short, authoritative study from the viewpoint of international relations.

Hix, Simon, *The Political System in the European Union* (Basingstoke, 1999).
Solid, clear, and accessible handbook.

Hodges, Michael (ed.), *European Integration* (Harmondsworth, 1972).
Pioneering collection of academic texts.

Hoffman, Stanley, *The European Sisyphus* (Boulder, CO, 1995).
Thoughtful essays 1964–94 by a distinguished American scholar.

Holland, Martin, *European Integration* (1994).
Good chapters on the United States of Europe and the enlargement of the Union.

Judt, Tony, *Europe: A Grand Illusion?* (Harmondsworth, 1997).
Outstandingly original essay, constructively pessimistic in tone.

Kramer, Jane, *Unsettling Europe* (New York, 1980); *Europeans* (New York, 1988).
Two extremely well-written and sympathetic accounts of the lives of ordinary Europeans, by a *New Yorker* journalist.

Leonardi, Robert, *Convergence, Cohesion and Integration in the European Union* (Basingstoke, 1995).
Well-ordered and well-informed synthesis.

McKay, D., *Rush to Union: Understanding the European Federal Bargain* (Oxford, 1996).
Valuable introduction to some fundamental questions.

Mikkeli, Heikki, *Europe as an Idea and an Identity* (Basingstoke, 1998).
Thoughtful and original treatment of an elusive topic.

Milward, Alan, et al., *The Frontiers of National Sovereignty* (1993).
Case histories by an international team of the postwar tension between interdependence and integration in Europe.

Nelsen, Brent F., and Stubb, Alexander C. G. (eds), *The European Union* (1994).

Classic texts by politicians (Schuman, Thatcher, Delors, et al.) and political scientists with commentary.

Niedermayer, Oskar, and Sinnott, Richard (eds), *Public Opinion and Internationalized Governance* (Oxford, 1995).
Astute and helpful survey of an underexplored topic.

Nikolaidis, Kalypso, and Howse, Robert (eds), *The Federal Vision* (Oxford, 2001).
Panorama of federalism in Europe and the US.

Nugent, Neil, *The Government and Politics of the European Union* (5th edn, Basingstoke, 2003).
Clear, solid guide to how the institutions work.

Oakeshott, Michael, *The Social and Political Doctrines of Contemporary Europe* (1939).
Key texts, with interlinking essays.

O'Neill, Michael, *The Politics of European Integration: A Reader* (1996).
Good selection of academic texts.

Pagden, Anthony (ed.), *The Idea of Europe* (Cambridge, 2002).
Good collection of essays on Europe through the ages.

Phillipson, Robert, *English-only Europe?* (2003)
Comprehensive and intelligent study of the language issue.

Pinder, John, *The Building of the European Union* (3rd edn, Oxford, 1998).
Lucid, non-specialist account of European integration past and present.

Richardson, Jeremy (ed.), *European Union: Power and Policy-Making* (1996).
Good collection of essays (see especially Mark Franklin, 'European elections and the European voter').

Roberts, Geoffrey K., and Hogwood, Patricia, *European Politics Today* (Manchester, 1997).
Good general handbook.

Rosemond, Ben, *Theories of European Integration* (Basingstoke, 2000).
A lucid and helpful analysis.

Salmon, Trevor C., and Nicoll, William, *Building European Union* (Manchester, 1997).
Good general introduction, using original texts with interlinking commentary.

Shonfield, Andrew, *Europe: Journey to an Unknown Destination* (Harmondsworth, 1973).
The Reith lectures, in the year of the UK's accession to the EC.

Siedentop, Larry, *Democracy in Europe* (Harmondsworth, 2000).
The development of the EU institutions in the wider historical and political context: a thoughtful and original book.

Smith, Anthony D., *National Identity* (Harmondsworth, 1991).
Very informative and clearly written account of how national identity is shaped and expressed.

Stauridis, Stelios, Mossialos, Elias, Morgan, Roger, and Machin, Howard (eds), *New Challenges to the European Union: Policies and Policy-Making* (Aldershot, 1997).
Disparate but useful collection of essays.

Taylor, Paul, *The European Union in the 1990s* (Oxford, 1996).
See especially 'National identity and participation in the European Union'.

Thomas, Hugh, *Europe: the Radical Challenge* (1973); *Ever Closer Union* (1991).
Two stimulating essays by a distinguished historian 'in private practice' and unconventional European.

Tugendhat, Christopher, *Making Sense of Europe* (Harmondsworth, 1986).
Thoughtful analysis by long-serving British Commissioner, with entertaining brief survey of national attitudes.

10 Periodicals

The best-known periodicals on European integration are:

Common Market Law Review
European Foreign Affairs Review
European Union Politics
Journal of Common Market Studies
Journal of European Public Policy
West European Politics

However, other periodicals concerned with law, politics and current affairs (such as *The World Today* and *Government and Opposition*) also quite frequently include articles or book reviews on various aspects of European integration.

Europe, published six days a week throughout the year by Agence Europe in Brussels, covers every single development in European institutions and

European politics and carries full texts of key documents. Widely read by professionals, it is available only on subscription. Less comprehensive but still useful is the weekly *European Voice*. More specialized publications cover developments in agriculture, energy, the environment, the Third World, etc.

Synoptic Index

The following broad subject-headings are intended to help the reader find the main entries relevant to particular aspects of European Union. All member states of the European Union, all member states of the European Economic Area and all applicant states including Malta, Switzerland and Turkey are the subject of separate entries. Belgium, Luxembourg and The Netherlands are to be found under Benelux. Andorra, Liechtenstein, Monaco, San Marino and the Vatican City may be found under micro-states.

Economic integration and the Single Market

History

Institutions and organizations

Committee of the Regions
Council of Europe
Council of Ministers
Court of Auditors
Court of Justice
Economic and Social Committee
European Atomic Energy
  Community
European Coal and Steel
  Community

European Commission
European Council
European Economic Community
European Parliament
National representations
Ombudsman
Organization for Economic
  Cooperation and Development
Presidency
Western European Union

Law

Acquis communautaire
Area of freedom, security and
  justice
Court of Justice
Direct effect
Directive
EU law
Implied competence

Legal instruments
Opinion
Primacy
Proportionality
Right of initiative
Sovereignty
Subsidiarity

Institutional questions

Chamber of States
Concentric circles
Confederation
Constitution for Europe
Europe *à la carte*
European Union
Federation
Flexibility

Hard core
Intergovernmentalism
Pillars
Positive and negative integration
Two-speed Europe
Variable geometry
Wider versus deeper

Political aspects

Christian Democracy
Communism
Conservatism
European elections
Liberalism

National parliaments
Political groups
Socialism
Transnational political parties

Procedures

Assent procedure
Co-decision procedure
Common position
Conciliation
Constructive abstention
Cooperation procedure

Joint action
Opt-out
Qualified Majority Voting
Rapporteur
Scrutiny
Veto

Security and defence

Brussels Treaty
Common Foreign and Security Policy
Common European Security
   and Defence Policy
Conference on Security and
   Cooperation in Europe

Dunkirk Treaty
European Army
European Defence Community
North Atlantic Treaty Organization
Partnership for Peace
Western European Union

Treaties and agreements

Brussels Treaty
Charter of Fundamental Rights
Cotonou Agreement
Europe Agreements
European Economic Area
European Free Trade Association
Maastricht Treaty
Merger Treaty

Protocol
Ratification
Schengen Agreement
Single European Act
Treaty of Amsterdam
Treaty of Nice
Treaty of Paris
Treaty of Rome

Website Addresses

The main public website for the European Commission and for the other institutions of the European Union, known as Europa, is at:

http://www.europa.eu.int

Europa is linked to individual sites for the main institutions, notably:

Council of Ministers:	http://www.ue.eu.int
Court of Auditors:	http://www.www.eca.eu.int
Court of Justice:	http://curia.eu.int
European Central Bank	http://www.ecb.int
European Ombudsman	http://www.euro-ombudsman.eu.int
European Parliament:	http: //www.europarl.eu.int

Four specialized website addresses may also be of use to readers of this book:

Statistical office (Eurostat):	http: //www.europa. eu.int/comm/eurostat
Legislation (CELEX database):	http://www.europa.eu.int/celex
Legislation (EUR-Lex database):	http://www.europa.eu.int/eur-lex
Information and contacts:	http://www.europa.eu.int/geninfo

The Europe Direct website can be found at:

http://europa.eu.int/citizens

Non-EU organizations may be reached as follows:

Council of Europe:	http://www.coe.fr
North Atlantic Treaty Organization:	http://www.nato.int
Organization for Economic Cooperation and Development:	http://www.oecd.org
Organization for Security and Cooperation in Europe:	http://www.osce.org
World Trade Organization:	http://www.wto.org